Life Histories of
North American Wood Warblers

Life Histories of
North American Wood Warblers

by

Arthur Cleveland Bent

in two parts

Part 2

Dover Publications, Inc.

New York

Published in the United Kingdom by Constable
and Company, Limited, 10 Orange Street, London
W. C. 2.

This Dover edition, first published in 1963, is an
unabridged and unaltered republication of the work
first published in 1953 by the United States Government Printing Office, as Smithsonian Institution
United States National Museum *Bulletin 203*.

Standard Book Number: 486-21154-1

Manufactured in the United States of America

Dover Publications, Inc.
180 Varick Street
New York 14, N. Y.

ADVERTISEMENT

The scientific publications of the National Museum include two series, known, respectively, as *Proceedings* and *Bulletins*.

The *Proceedings* series, begun in 1878, is intended primarily as a medium for the publication of original papers, based on the collections of the National Museum, that set forth newly acquired facts in biology, anthropology, and geology, with descriptions of new forms and revisions of limited groups. Copies of each paper, in pamphlet form, are distributed as published to libraries and scientific organizations and to specialists and others interested in the different subjects. The dates at which these separate papers are published are recorded in the table of contents of each of the volumes.

The series of *Bulletins*, the first of which was issued in 1875, contains separate publications comprising monographs of large zoological groups and other general systematic treatises (occasionally in several volumes), faunal works, reports of expeditions, catalogs of type specimens, special collections, and other material of similar nature. The majority of the volumes are octavo in size, but a quarto size has been adopted in a few instances in which the larger page was regarded as indispensable. In the *Bulletin* series appear volumes under the heading *Contributions from the United States National Herbarium*, in octavo form, published by the National Museum since 1902, which contain papers relating to the botanical collections of the Museum.

The present work forms No. 203 of the *Bulletin* series.

REMINGTON KELLOGG,
Director, United States National Museum.

CONTENTS

Part 2

LIFE HISTORIES OF NORTH AMERICAN WOOD WARBLERS

ORDER PASSERIFORMES

BY

ARTHUR CLEVELAND BENT
Taunton, Massachusetts

DENDROICA PENSYLVANICA (Linnaeus)

CHESTNUT-SIDED WARBLER

PLATES, 45, 46

HABITS

Many changes have taken place in the distribution and relative abundance of many birds in different parts of our land since the settlement of the country, owing to the changes wrought in the landscape by man. The beautiful little chestnut-sided warbler is one of the species that has benefited, flourished, and increased with the spread of civilization. It seems strange that such a common, well-marked, and familiar species, as we now know it to be over so much of northeastern North America, should have been largely unknown by the early writers on American birds.   Edward H. Forbush (1929) tells the story very well as follows:

Audubon met with it but once; Wilson saw little of it; Nuttall, who considered it rare, evidently knew little about it, and saw very few. Since his time, however, its numbers have increased until it has become one of the commonest of eastern warblers. Its increase was favored by the destruction of the primeval forest and the continued cutting away of subsequent growths, and later by the increase of neglected fields and pastures with their growths of bushes and brambles, for it is not a frequenter of deep woods, nor yet of well-kept gardens, orchards or farmyards, but prefers neglected or cut-over lands, with a profusion of thickets and briers. So we may find it usually away from houses, in low roadside and brookside thickets, or in sproutlands rather recently cut over. As the coppice grows up the bird retires to other quarters or to the edges of the woods.

According to William Brewster (1906), the chestnut-sided warbler began to appear in the Cambridge region in about 1830 or 1831, when Nuttall began to find it, but he writes: "Dr. Samuel Cabot told me a year or two before his death that when he was at Harvard College (1832–1836) the Chestnut-sided Warbler was certainly very rare in eastern Massachusetts, and that for some years later it was not common although it gradually but steadily increased in numbers after 1835." A similar increase in numbers has been noted in other places. Dr. Chapman (1907) says: "In my own experience, covering the past twenty-five years, at Englewood, N. J., I have seen this Warbler become established as an increasingly common summer resident." And A. Radclyffe Dugmore (1902) writes, in reference to the same general region: "In the summer of 1897, the first year that I did any systematic bird work in this locality, these birds were so little in evidence that I did not observe a single specimen." During the next two years a few pairs were discovered in suitable clearings, but "in 1900 the Warblers were comparatively common, every clearing containing several pairs, and last summer they were still more abundant, four pairs occupying a clearing of only a few acres, while in the large clearing there were more than could be counted with accuracy; probably not less than seven or eight pairs."

The breeding range of the chestnut-sided warbler is now known to extend from central Saskatchewan and Newfoundland on the north throughout southern Canada and the northern half of the United States east of the great plains; but it is much commoner in the States than in Canada, and its breeding range extends farther south in the Alleghenies, to northern Georgia. Writing of the birds of the central Allegheny Mountains, Prof. Maurice Brooks (1940) calls it "one of the most abundant warblers in mountainous cut-over areas. It is a characteristic bird of the 'chestnut sprout' association, and reaches the edges of the spruce forests. In northern West Virginia it breeds down to 1200 feet, and it occurs up to 4800 feet where the habitat is suitable. Mountain laurel thickets offer a favorite nesting place, and dead chestnut trees are often used as singing places." Referring to northeastern Georgia, Thomas D. Burleigh (1927a) writes: "I have noted a few singing males as low as 3500 feet, but it is only above an elevation of 4000 feet that these birds occur in any numbers. Within a few hundred yards of the top of Brasstown Bald the south slope is covered with small stunted oaks that are few enough in number to encourage a thick undergrowth of laurel and huckleberry bushes. In this limited area the Chestnut-sided Warblers are actually plentiful, and are among the few birds that can be found breeding there."

Spring.—According to Dr. Chapman (1907), "the Chestnut-sided Warbler passes through eastern Mexico and the Gulf States from northwestern Florida to eastern Texas. It is casual in southern Florida and the Bahamas."

M. A. Frazar (1881) saw "quite a number" migrating across the Gulf of Mexico, when his ship was about 30 miles south of the Mississippi delta. In the great wave of migrating warblers and other small birds that I saw on the islands in Galveston Bay, Texas, on May 4, 1923, chestnut-sided warblers were much in evidence, as they generally are in all of these transient hosts; here they were buffeted about by a northerly gale and were seeking shelter behind every little eminence or clump of bushes, to rest before struggling again against the wind.

The spring migration along the eastern route seems to be mainly along the Allegheny Mountains, or near them. E. S. Dingle tells me that he has but one record for coastal or southern South Carolina, April 24, 1929; and Arthur T. Wayne (1910) does not include it in the birds of that State.

According to Dr. Chapman's (1907) data, nearly a month (25 days, to be exact) elapses between the average dates of arrival at Atlanta, Ga., and arrival at Scotch Lake, New Brunswick. And on the interior route it seems to take just a month for the birds to travel from southern Texas to Aweme, Manitoba.

Nesting.—My local experience with the nesting of the chestnut-sided warbler dates back to the old "ministerial road" in Rehoboth, Mass., a typical locality in which to find the nests of this warbler. This narrow, neglected, country road skirted the border of the village cemetery, with an open field on the other side, while between the stone wall that bordered the field and the road was a long narrow strip of very small trees and underbrush, mainly hazel bushes. Along the quarter-mile stretch of this road we could always count on finding several pairs of this warbler nesting in the hazel bushes, generally at heights of 2 or 3 feet in the thickets of small bushes; one nest was as low as 14 and one only 18 inches above the ground. We found numerous nests elsewhere along the edges of country roads, in old neglected pastures, in sproutlands, and about the borders of woodlands, where there was suitable shrubbery. Fully 90 percent of the nests were in hazels, but occasional ones were found in huckleberry bushes, blackberry tangles, hardhacks, or small saplings.

Most of the nests are flimsy affairs and loosely built, the walls so thin that daylight shows through them in one or more places; but some are fairly compactly woven. Four nests before me vary considerably in size and construction. The smallest and most compact measures about 2¼ by 2½ inches in outside diameter, is about 2 inches high externally, and the inner cavity is about 1¾ wide and 1¾ inches deep. The largest nest measures 3½ by 4 inches in outside diameter, but has about the same height and inside dimensions as the smallest nest and differs from the others in having the whole upper part, or nest proper, made entirely of the finest grasses and extremely fine reddish brown fibers built on a foundation of the usual materials. The other nests are intermediate in size and shape, and are made of both coarse and fine strips of inner bark from cedars or grapevines, weed stems shredded finely, fine grasses, other plant fibers, and some little pieces of plant down; they are lined with very fine grasses, and sometimes also with a little horsehair or cowhair.

I saw two nests in the woods near Asquam Lake, N. H., where the black-throated blue warblers were breeding (a location described under that species) ; one of these was built in a mountain laurel bush after the manner of the black-throated blue, and the other was in a crotch in a bunch of maple sprouts in an open clearing. The nests found by Mr. Burleigh (1927a) in northeastern Georgia were all "within two feet of the ground, two being in laurels and one in a huckleberry bush." Some observers have referred to the nests of the chestnut-sided warbler as being firmly, compactly, or strongly built, but my experience usually agrees with that of Mr. Burleigh, who says: "The nests were alike in construction, and distinct enough not to be confused with those of any other species found here, being loosely and somewhat shabbily built." Nests have been reported by others as located in hazel, huckleberry, raspberry, blackberry, blueberry, barberry, viburnum, spirea, rhododendron, and azalea bushes, and in saplings of oak, maple, birch, beech, and hornbeam. Probably many others might be added to the list.

Mr. Forbush (1929) gives the following account of nest-building, as observed by F. H. Mosher:

The female did all the actual work. She laid straws and plant fibers in a fork of an arrow-wood bush, then went to a tent caterpillar colony and tearing off some of the web bound the forking branches about with it, thus tying them together and forming a deep cup-like framework for the habitation; she also bound the foundation firmly in place with more of the same web, then brought dried grasses or straws and placed them around to form the sides of the nest and bound them to the branches with more caterpillars' webs. Having finished the sides, she put in a lining of soft grasses, fine rootlets and plant fibers. This nest when completed at the end of five days was much less bulky than the usual nest of the Yellow Warbler, and much firmer, with walls not more than one-fourth as thick.

Eggs.—Four eggs seem to form the usual set for the chestnut-sided warbler, but this sometimes consists of only three, or more rarely five. The eggs are ovate, sometimes tending toward elongate ovate, and they have only a slight lustre. The ground color may be white, creamy white, or very pale greenish white. They are speckled, spotted, and blotched with "auburn," "bay," "Brussels brown," "raw umber," "chestnut-brown," "cinnamon-brown," "mummy brown," or "Mars brown," with undertones of "dark brownish drab," "pale brownish drab," or "light purplish drab." The color and amount of the markings vary considerably, ranging from eggs that are delicately spotted, or speckled only with drab colors, to those boldly blotched with browns that form a solid ring around the large end, completely covering the undertones. On some the spots are scattered over the entire surface, but generally they are concentrated and tend to form a wreath. A few eggs have the spots confined to a tight, narrow ring, leaving the rest of the surface almost immaculate. The measurements of 50 eggs average 16.7 by 12.4 millimeters; the eggs showing the four extremes measure 18.0 by 12.5, 17.3 by 13.2, and 15.2 by 11.7 millimeters (Harris).

Young.—The period of incubation for the chestnut-sided warbler seems to be between 12 and 13 days; Frank L. Burns (1915b) says 10 to 11 days, but this seems in error. Only the female incubates. The young remain in the nest 10 to 12 days. Cordelia J. Stanwood MS. says in her notes: "The young come from the eggs blind and limp, covered with short, fine, sparse down and scarcely larger than bumblebees. About the close of the second day, or the beginning of the third day, they commence to open their eyes and the feather spaces begin to show as dark, swollen tracts. Near the end of the sixth day, not far from the beginning of the seventh, the quill stage ends, and the tips of the feathers show beyond the quill casings. By the eighth day the young are pretty well feathered out, and can leave the nest successfully, but, if undisturbed, they usually remain in the nest until the tenth or the eleventh day. While in the nest the young preen, stretch, yawn, beg for food, and utter various calls. Both the parent birds feed the little ones and cleanse the young of parasites and other vermin, although I have noticed in many cases that the female bird generally seems to be the one that burows under the nestlings and cleanses them and the nest lining of annoying pests. * * * All these warblers that I have watched caring for the young in the early stages of nest life begin by feeding the little ones by regurgitation. At the same time an occasional moth or caterpillar that is crushed and mixed with digestive juices is fed directly. At first smaller and softer insects are doled out; later, larger and tougher moths, caterpillars, crane-flies, and the like are fed to them." Her notes show that the young were fed at frequent intervals, often only one minute apart; sometimes the intervals between feedings were from 5 to 8 minutes, and occasionally as much as 12 minutes.

The parent birds become quite excited when a nest with young is approached, and are sometimes quite bold in their defense of their young; A. D. Du Bois tells me of one that flew at his face, coming within two feet of it as he followed the escaping young; and both parents kept near him, chirping and fluttering.

Plumages.—Dr. Dwight (1900) describes the juvenal plumage, in which the sexes are alike, as "above, dark raw umber-brown, obscurely streaked on the back with dull black. Wings and tail dull black, chiefly edged with ashy or plumbeous gray; the secondaries, and tertiaries with olive-yellow, the coverts with buff forming two wing bands yellow-tinged. Below, pale umber-brown, grayer on the throat and sides of head, the abdomen and crissum dull white."

The first winter plumage, in which the sexes begin to differentiate, is acquired by a partial postnuptial molt, beginning late in June and involving the contour plumage and the wing coverts, but not the rest of the wings or the tail. Dr. Dwight (1900) describes the young male in this plumage as "above, bright olive-yellow concealing black spots on the back and rump, the upper tail coverts black, tipped with cinereous gray and olive-yellow. The wing coverts black, edged with olive-yellow, two broad wing bands canary-yellow mixed with white. Below, grayish white, pearl-gray on sides of head, throat, breast and flanks, a trace of chestnut striping the flanks terminating in a lemon-yellow spot. Conspicuous white orbital ring." The young female is similar, but the white below is duller, the sides are grayer, and the chestnut stripes are lacking.

The first nuptial plumage is acquired by a partial prenuptial molt in late winter or early spring, that involves most of the contour plumage and the wing coverts, but not the rest of the wings or the tail. Young and old birds are now indistinguishable, except for the browner wings and tail of the young bird. The colors of the female are duller and less intense than those of the male in this and in subsequent plumages.

Subsequent molts consist of a complete postnuptial molt in July and August, and a partial prenuptial molt as in the young bird. Adult females in the fall have some chestnut on the sides, but not so much as the males.

Food.—The chestnut-sided warbler is almost wholly insectivorous, though it has been known to eat a few seeds or berries when hard-pressed for food. Its foraging range is between the ground and the tops of small trees, or in the lower branches of some of the larger trees; but mainly it gleans through the foliage of shrubbery or low plants, seldom seeking its food on the ground.

The insects mentioned under the food of the young are all doubtless eaten regularly by the adults; when securing tent caterpillar webs in nest building, it probably does not object to eating a few of the smaller caterpillars but the large, hairy ones may be refused. Spiders are eaten to some extent. No very comprehensive study of the food seems to have been made, but Forbush (1907) makes this general statement: "The food of the Chestnut-sided Warbler is such that the bird must be exceedingly useful in woodland and shrubbery, and in orchard and shade trees as well, whenever it frequents them. It is probable that at times it destroys considerable numbers of parasitic hymenoptera, as it is rather expert as a flycatcher; but it is very destructive to many injurious beetles and caterpillars, being one of the most active consumers of leaf-eating insects. Small borers or bark beetles, plant bugs and plant lice, leaf hoppers, ants, and aphids are eaten."

Professor Aughey (1878) reports that a stomach examined in Nebraska contained 17 locusts and 21 other insects. F. H. King (1883), reporting for Wisconsin, mentions one eating a small grasshopper and canker worms that were feeding on oaks, hazel, hickory, plum, cherry, apple, pear, and currant. Du Bois tells me of one he watched gleaning its food in an elm tree: "In order to secure insects from the under side of an elm leaf, he hovered like a hummingbird at a flower, and thus picked the food from the leaf while poised in the air." Forbush (Chapman, 1907) writes:

A Chestnut-sided Warbler was seen to capture and eat, in fourteen minutes, twenty-two gipsy caterpillars, that were positively identified, and other insects that could not be seen plainly were taken during that time. * * * A Chestnut-sided Warbler took twenty-eight browntail caterpillars in about twelve minutes. When we consider that the short hairs on the posterior parts of this caterpillar are barbed like the quills of a porcupine and will penetrate the human skin, causing excessive irritation and painful eruptions, we may well wonder if the little bird lived to repeat this performance. But many small birds eat these caterpillars at a time when probably the noxious hairs have not fully developed, and others seem to have learned to divest the larger caterpillars of their hairs by beating and shaking their prey and thus loosening the hairs, which are shed as the porcupine sheds its quills. The insect is then eaten with impunity and even fed to the young birds.

Audubon (1841) tells us that five chestnut-sided warblers, taken during a light fall of snow in May, had eaten nothing but grass seed and spiders.

Behavior.—The chestnut-sided warbler is one of the prettiest of the wood warblers, some regarding it as quite the prettiest. It is certainly one of the most attractive, as it flits about in the roadside shrubbery near us, with its tail elevated, its wings drooping, and its pure white breast swelling as if with pride in its beauty. It is a sprightly, active little bird and far from timid, allowing a near approach as it busily gleans among the foliage or darts out to seize some flying insect. On its nest, which is usually well screened among the leaves, it will sit quietly, confident of its concealing coloration, until we can almost touch it; then suddenly it is gone, out of sight under the bushes; but it soon appears again, nervously flitting about in the taller bushes or trees to scold at our intrusion.

The following note on the behavior of the parent birds at the nest is contributed by Dr. Alexander F. Skutch: "Following the parents as they carried food, I found a nest of the chestnut-sided warbler situated 3 feet above the ground in the midst of a clump of *Cornus racemosa* on a scrubby hillside near Ithaca, N. Y. It contained two half-grown cowbird nestlings, which squealed a little as I took them in hand, and drove the poor, misguided foster-parents to frenzied efforts to entice me from the nest. The male warbler fluttered from twig to twig in front of me, vibrating his wings and spreading his tail; while his mate descended to the ground beneath the dogwood clump, where she crouched on the dead leaves with vibrating wings and spread tail, moving forward slowly and lamely, after the usual manner of distressed parents. I squatted down in the midst of the bushes the better to see her; and the male, becoming uncommonly bold and loudly chirping his protests, displayed so close before me that every most delicate marking of his plumage was visible: The golden crown, the white sides of the head, the rich chestnut bands along the flanks and sides, and every streak of black and white and gray on the wings and back and tail. I might have reached forward and touched him, had he only remained still. On the following day, the performance was repeated for my benefit."

Voice.—Aretas A. Saunders contributes the following full account of the songs of this warbler: "The chestnut-sided warbler is one that has two different songs, which show seasonal differences, so that they may be referred to as territory and nesting songs. The territory song is the first to be heard, during migration and upon the first arrival on the nesting grounds, while the nesting song is not commonly heard until nesting is established. During the nesting period both songs are to be heard. In common with other species that have two songs, the territory song is fairly definite in form but the nesting song is exceedingly variable. Both have the same quality; they are quite loud, of musical quality, but rather chatterlike and not especially sweet, nor are they so pleasing as those of other musical warblers of this genus.

"The territory song consists of 4 to 9 notes on a medium pitch, usually rhythmic and of even length, followed by a louder, high-pitched, strongly accented note, and then by a lower terminal note. This is the song commonly translated as *very, very, pleased to meetcha.* In all but 3 of 30 records of this song the beginning notes are 4, 5, or 6 in number. In 20 records the first notes are single notes, and in the other 10 they are 2-note phrases. This song is always rather short, varying from 1⅖ to 1⅘ seconds.

"The nesting song is so variable that it is difficult to say about it much that is definite. Some notes, near the end of the song, are usually high-pitched and strongly accented, but there are numerous exceptions to this. Of 41 records, 19 are composed wholly or mainly of slurred notes, while 21 are single notes or 2-note phrases in a loud, rapid chatter. In the slurred songs the notes are run together. In some records the notes are continuous throughout, without a pause. In the non-slurred songs the notes are distinctly separate. The nesting song is somewhat longer than the territory song, varying from 1⅗ to 2⅘ seconds.

"The pitch of both songs is about the same, varying from E''' to A'''', a range of two and a half tones more than an octave but about an octave lower than that of such species as the blackpoll and the Blackburnian. The song is to be heard from the arrival of the bird in migration till the midle of July. The average date of the last song in Allegany State Park, in 14 years of observation, is July 17. The earliest is July 12, 1931, and the latest July 24, 1927."

Albert R. Brand (1938) gives the approximate mean number of vibrations per second in the song of the chestnut-sided warbler as 5,125, with the highest having 8,775 and the lowest 3,100 vibrations per second. This compares with a mean of 8,900 for the black-poll warbler and 8,600 for the grasshopper sparrow, or an average of 4,000 for passerine songs in general. Francis H. Allen tells me he once found one "with a song consisting of a hurried repetition of a single note as *wit-wit-wit-wit-wit-wit-wit-wit.* Sometimes this was followed by the characteristic warble of the weaker song, and only with this addition was the song recognizable as that of the chestnut-sided warbler. The call note of the species is a thick *chip* with an *L* in it." Miss Stanwood (MS.) writes the song as "*wee-wee-wee-wee-chi-tee-wee.*"

It seems to me that the rhythm of the ordinary song can be well expressed in human words, or catch phrases; for instance, to Sidney E. Ingraham (1938) it sounded like: "*I wish, I wish, I wish to see Miss Beecher!* except that we should normally need three or four seconds to say it, whereas Miss Beecher's lively little friend takes scarcely more than one second. The song is much more like an emphatic sentence made up of words than it is like a phrase of abstract music. The rhythm, of course, is very familiar, actually that of iambic blank verse, rising with force and intention to a climax. Harmonious intervals are lacking, but there are complex inflections ending with the characteristic, explosive little slur up and down." Other catch phrases seem to call the song to mind quite vividly, are *very, very glad to meet you* (Hoffmann, 1904), or Ralph B. Simpson's (Todd, 1940) *dis-dis-dis-dismiss-you*, both with a strong accent on the penultimate syllable. This is, of course, the easiest song to recognize, and the only one the amateur is likely to have firmly fixed in his mind.

Field marks.—The chestnut-sided warbler is one of the easiest of the family to recognize, as both sexes are much alike, the colors of the female being only a little more restricted and duller. The yellow crown, two yellowish wing bars, chestnut sides, and pure white breast, together with the black and white head pattern, are all conspicuous field marks for the adults. The young bird in fall plumage lacks the bright yellow crown and most of the chestnut sides, the upper parts being bright greenish yellow and the under parts grayish white, but it has the wing-bars and a white eye ring.

Enemies.—This warbler is well known to be one of the commonest victims of the cowbird, and Dr. Friedmann (1929) records two cases in which the egg of the imposter had been buried in the bottom of the nest.

Harold S. Peters (1936) mentions one louse and one mite as external parasites on this species.

Winter.—The following notes are contributed by Dr. Alexander F. Skutch: "While the black and white warbler spreads in winter over a vast area and appears to be nowhere really common, the chestnut-sided warbler does exactly the reverse, crowds in winter into an area far smaller than its breeding range, and becomes there, during half the year, one of the most abundant of birds. Known in northern Central America only as a rarely recorded bird of passage, this warbler winters in great numbers in Costa Rica and Panamá. In these countries, it appears to be equally well represented in the lowlands of both the Caribbean and Pacific sides, and continues to be abundant upward to an elevation of about 4,000 feet, above which it rapidly decreases in numbers. There appear to be no definite mid-winter records for altitudes above 5,000 feet, although as a transient it is sometimes found considerably higher.

"In the lofty lowland forests of Costa Rica and Panamá the chestnut-sided warbler is, during the period of its sojourn, the one abundant member of the family, whether migratory or resident. It is by no means restricted to the forest but is found wherever trees grow fairly close together, as in coffee plantations with their planted shade trees or along tree-bordered rivers flowing through the cultivated lands. It habitually forages among the crowns of the trees, usually well above the ground. Solitary in disposition, it does not form true flocks; but because of its great abundance several are at times seen in neighboring trees. By early March, the males, which at the time of their arrival are hardly to be distinguished from the females, are clad in their attractive nuptial dress. On April 5, 1937, among the forests of southern Costa Rica, I found a male so attired who repeated over and over a subdued version of his song—an unusual event, for these warblers seldom sing while in Central America.

"The chestnut-sided warbler has not been known to arrive in Central America before the second half of September, a late date for warblers. By the beginning of October, it becomes numerous; before the end of April, it has vanished.

"Early dates of fall arrival in Central America are: Guatemala—Chimoxan, September 27 (Griscom). Honduras—Tela, October 1, 1930. Costa Rica—San José, September 25 (Underwood), and September 28 (Cherrie); El Hogar, September 27 (Carriker); Basin of El General, September 15, 1936, and October 3, 1942.

"Late dates of spring departure from Central America are: Panamá—Barro Colorado Island, Canal Zone, April 6, 1935. Costa Rica—Basin of El General, April 15, 1936, April 21, 1937, April 25, 1939, April 20, 1940, April 12, 1942, and April 17, 1943; San José, April 24 (Cherrie); Pejivalle, April 28, 1941. Guatemala—Motagua Valley, near Los Amates, April 24, 1932."

DISTRIBUTION

Range.—Eastern North America to Panamá.

Breeding range.—The chestnut-sided warbler breeds **north** to central Saskatchewan (Emma Lake and Hudson Bay Junction); southern Manitoba (Duck Mountain, Lake St. Martin, and Hillside Beach); central Ontario (Kenora, Chapleau, and Lake Abitibi); and southern Quebec (Blue Sea Lake, Quebec, and Gaspé). **East** to southeastern Quebec (Gaspé); Nova Scotia (Antigonish, Halifax, and Yarmouth); and the coast of New England south to Martha's Vineyard. **South** to southern Massachusetts (Martha's Vineyard); southern Connecticut (Saybrook, New Haven, and Bridgeport); northern New Jersey (Elizabeth and Morristown); southeastern Pennsylvania (Berwyn); northern Maryland (Reisterstown); south through the mountains of Virginia, West Virginia, North Carolina, South Carolina (Caesars Head and Highlow Gap); to central northern Georgia (Brasstown

Bald [first breeding record for the State, 1925], Mount Oglethorpe, and Burnt Mountain) ; southwestern Kentucky (Log Mountain and Black Mountain) ; central and northwestern Ohio (Columbus and Toledo) ; northern Illinois (Chicago and Lacon) ; and central Iowa, rarely (Coralville, Grinnell, and Des Moines). West to central Iowa (Des Moines) ; central to western Minnesota (Minneapolis, Brainerd, Walker, and White Earth) ; central northern North Dakota (Turtle Mountains) ; southwestern Manitoba (Carberry) ; and south-central Saskatchewan (Valeport, Wingard, and Emma Lake).

There is a single record for Alberta of a specimen taken at Red Deer, probably only casual.

Winter range.—The winter home of the chestnut-sided warbler is in Central America from southern Nicaragua (Río Escondido) throughout Costa Rica and western Panamá (Barro Colorado, Canal Zone, and Chitré).

Migration.—Late dates of spring departure from the winter home are: Panama—Barro Colorado, Canal Zone, April 6. Costa Rica— El General, April 25. British Honduras—Cayo District, April 27. Tamaulipas—Cañón Cavelleros, May 16.

Early dates of spring arrival are: Alabama—Anniston, April 16. Georgia—Macon, April 16. South Carolina—Columbia, April 10. North Carolina—Raleigh, April 19. Virginia—Naruna, April 17. West Virginia—Bluefield, April 26. District of Columbia—Washington, April 19. Pennsylvania—Berwyn, April 23. New York— Geneva, April 22. Massachusetts—Taunton, April 25. Vermont— Burlington, May 1. Maine—North Livermore, May 1. Nova Scotia—Halifax, May 4. New Brunswick—Scotch Lake, May 9. Quebec—East Sherbrooke, May 5. Louisiana—New Orleans, March 21. Mississippi—Gulfport, April 14. Arkansas—Delight, April 12. Tennessee—Athens, April 10. Kentucky—Bowling Green, April 26. Indiana—Richmond, April 22. Ohio—Cincinnati, April 25. Michigan—Ann Arbor, April 20. Ontario—Guelph, May 4. Missouri— St. Louis, April 27. Iowa—Iowa City, April 30. Wisconsin—Madison, April 30. Minnesota—Waseca, April 30. Texas—Corpus Christi, March 24. Nebraska—Stapleton, April 25. South Dakota— Lake Poinsett, May 12. North Dakota—Harrisburg, May 15. Manitoba—Margaret, May 14. Saskatchewan—Regina, May 15.

Late dates of the spring departure of transients are: Alabama— Long Island, May 15. Georgia—Atlanta, May 23. South Carolina— Spartanburg, May 18. North Carolina—Greensboro, May 19. Virginia— Charlottesville, May 23. District of Columbia—Washington,

June 2. Louisiana—Thibodaux, May 3. Mississippi—Corinth, May 16. Arkansas—Winslow, May 20. Tennessee—Chattanooga, May 20. Kentucky—Lexington, May 15. Iowa—Sioux City, June 4. Texas—Amarillo, May 25. Oklahoma— Kenton, May 21. Kansas—Topeka, May 20. Nebraska—Omaha, May 28. North Dakota—Cando, June 1.

Late dates of fall departure are: Manitoba—Aweme, September 22. North Dakota—Wilton, September 24 (bird banded). South Dakota—Yankton, September 23. Kansas—Osawatomie, October 12. Minnesota—Minneapolis, September 15. Wisconsin—Oshkosh, October 10. Iowa—Davenport, October 2. Ontario—Kingston, September 29. Michigan—Ann Arbor, October 11. Ohio—Oberlin, October 12. Illinois—Lake Forest, October 4. Kentucky—Bowling Green, October 20. Tennessee—Memphis, October 21. Mississippi—Ariel, October 19. Quebec—Quebec, August 28. New Brunswick—Saint John, September 10. Maine—Phillips, September 17. New Hampshire—Hanover, September 19. New York—Rhinebeck, October 8. Pennsylvania—Berwyn, October 15. District of Columbia—Washington, October 14. West Virginia—Bluefield, October 5. North Carolina—Highlands, October 18. South Carolina—Clemson College, October 26. Georgia—Round Oak, October 27. Alabama—Birmingham, October 18.

Banding.—Like most warblers, few of the chestnut-sided have been banded. One return is of some interest. It was banded as an adult at Holderness, N. H., on June 25, 1926, and was retrapped at the same station on July 3, 1927.

Casual records.—In 1887 a specimen was collected near Nanortalik, Greenland, four have been taken in western Cuba, in 1940 and 1941, and one was collected at Cheyenne, Wyo., on May 23, 1889. In Colorado a specimen was taken at Barr Lake, May 16, 1933; one was reported near Denver on May 31, 1935; and another at Boulder, April 29, 1942. In California, one was reported at Sherwood, Mendocino County, September 21, 1908, and another was caught in a banding trap, September 24, 1946, at Manor, Marin County. There is one record for New Providence, Bahamas, without date.

Egg dates.—Massachusetts: 86 records, May 22 to July 2; 64 records, May 30 to June 9, indicating the height of the season.

New York: 27 records, May 30 to July 5; 14 records, June 1 to 9.

Pennsylvania: 18 records, May 27 to June 17; 10 records, May 31 to June 7 (Harris).

DENDROICA CASTANEA (Wilson)

BAY-BREASTED WARBLER

PLATE 47

HABITS

Bartram's "Little Chocolate-breasted Titmouse" was given the above name by Wilson (1832), based on a specimen taken in eastern Pennsylvania. Both he and Audubon considered it a rare species and had little to say about it. This is not strange, for they probably never saw it on its breeding grounds and probably overlooked it on its rather rapid migrations, or perhaps confused it with others in the host of migrants. To see the bay-breasted warbler to advantage one must visit the coniferous forests of northern New England and southern Canada east of the Great Plains; here it is often an abundant bird, and in some places it is the commonest of the warblers.

In Maine, according to Ora W. Knight (1908), "the species is rare and local, even in migration, and as a summer resident is chiefly confined to the deeper wilder sections of the State within the Canadian fauna. * * * The few pair that remain to nest in southern Penobscot County are to be found in the low, rather swampy maple and birch growth, mixed with firs and spruces. * * * In northern Maine I have met with the species in the rather swampy evergreen or mixed growth about the ponds and lakes and judge these localities are their favorite haunts."

Of its range in New Hampshire, Dr. Glover M. Allen (1903) writes: "In the White Mountains and northward it is a fairly common summer resident mainly of the upper Canadian zone. The range of this species in summer overlaps that of the Black-poll Warbler for about 1,000 feet, and extends below it to nearly an equal amount. Thus one finds breeding birds at an altitude of from 1,800 feet in rich, damp coniferous woods on southern exposures, up to about 4,000 feet among the small balsam timber."

Spring.—How the bay-breasted warbler reaches the coast of Texas from its winter home in Colombia and Panamá seems to be unknown. Alexander F. Skutch tells me that it is perhaps only an accidental transient in Central America north of the Isthmus of Panamá. It seems to be unknown in Mexico, but George G. Williams (1945) lists it among the warblers that occur regularly and frequently along the coast of Texas each spring. I saw it in the wave of migrating birds that I observed on an island in Galveston Bay on May 4, 1923. In order to avoid Mexico, it may fly partially across the Gulf of Mexico, or perhaps it may fly only along the coastline. It has also been ob-

served flying directly across the Gulf from Yucatán to the Gulf States.
Dr. Chapman (1907) says:

On the way to its summer home, the bird shuns Mexico, the West Indies,
and the United States south of Virginia, east of the Allegheny Mountains; the
great bulk passes north through the Mississippi Valley, west to eastern Texas
(Corpus Christi, Port Bolivar), Missouri (Freistart), and Iowa (Grinnell);
casual or accidental in South Dakota (May 1888), Montana (Big Sandy, May
24, 1903), and Alberta (Medicine Hat). * * * Although close observation
will reveal the presence of Bay-breasts during both the spring and fall migrations, they are generally to be classed among the rarer Warblers the mere sight
of which is stimulating. Occasionally, however, the weather so affects their
migration that they come *en masse* and for a brief period are actually abundant.

William Brewster (1906), referring to the Cambridge region of
Massachusetts, writes: "During the spring flight northward, which
passes late in May, they usually occur singly and in dense woods,
especially such as consist largely of white pines, hemlocks or other
coniferous trees. A remarkable exception to this rule happened in
1872. On May 26 of this year several birds were seen in the heart
of Cambridge, and on the following morning I found upwards of
forty, most of them females, feeding in the tops of some large oaks."
This is about as far east as the bay-breasted warbler usually comes
in Massachusetts; it is an exceedingly rare bird in the southeastern
corner of the state; I can count on the fingers of one hand all that
I have ever seen there. Most of the birds probably pass up the Connecticut Valley, or farther westward.

Nesting.—It was while I was visiting with Mr. and Mrs. Richard
B. Harding at their summer camp on the shore of Lake Asquam,
N. H., that I saw my first and only nest of the bay-breasted warbler.
The nest was placed on a horizontal branch of a white pine standing on
the edge of a clearing in heavy mixed woods, within 20 yards of a
cottage, and it was about 30 feet above the ground. On June 5, 1930,
the nest was not quite finished. On June 8, Mr. Harding climbed
the tree and found that the nest contained two eggs, but on the six-
teenth the nest was empty, and was taken. Mrs. Harding described
it in a letter to me as being made largely of coarse, dried grass stalks,
with a few hemlock twigs and a piece of string—a loosely built structure, with straws and twigs protruding from it on all sides. The
inner wall of the nest was made of dried grasses and pine needles,
with a thin lining of fine, black rootlets and horsehairs.

Miss Cordelia J. Stanwood has sent me some extensive notes on the
home life of this warbler, in which she describes the building of the
nest as follows: "First a few culms of hay were placed in the fork
of several twigs on a flat limb; next fine spruce twigs were anchored
to the various points of attachment, and the nest shaped of these. The

lining consisted of a very few runners of cinquefoil, a very few pine leaves, and much horsehair and human hair."

Philipp and Bowdish (1917) during two seasons in New Brunswick found nine nests of the bay-breasted warbler. Of the six nests found in 1915, all "were in small spruces, two of them being well out on horizontal limbs, the others close to the trunk, at heights varying from four to ten feet. None were very well concealed and some of them were remarkably open, but they blended so well with their surroundings that they were exceedingly difficult to discern. All of the nests of this species that we found resemble large structures of the Magnolia Warbler, being rather loosely constructed, of fine spruce of similar twigs, exteriorly, a little dead grass and some insect webs entering into the composition, and fine, black rootlets being commonly used as a lining." Two of the nests found in 1916 were higher up; one was "fifteen feet from ground, supported by two horizontal branches, against the main stem of a small balsam, near its top, in a clump of same, in partial clearing in spruce forest." The other was "twenty feet up against the trunk of a spruce tree at the edge of a clearing. This latter nest was in a very thick portion of the foliage and absolutely invisible from the ground, being found only by flushing the bird." F. H. Kennard mentions in his notes several nests, found in New Hampshire, that were from 25 to 40 feet up, "in the lower, outreaching branches of tall spruces." William Brewster (1938) mentions one that was 50 feet up.

A nest before me, taken by Richard C. Harlow in New Brunswick, was placed 12 feet up and 10 feet out toward the end of a long horizontal limb of a small, slender spruce in a high, dry spruce forest. It is very well and compactly made, mainly of fine spruce twigs firmly woven into a solid and fairly smooth rim, with only a few fine grasses woven in. It is neatly and smoothly lined with a thick bed of the finest black rootlets. The nest was so placed that another limb was only two inches directly above it.

The measurements of several recorded nests vary from 2 to 2¾ inches in outside depth, from 1¼ to 1½ in inside depth, from 4 by 3½ to 5⅔ in outside diameter, and from 2¹⁄₁₀ to 2½ inches in inside diameter, according to Mendall (1937).

Eggs.—The bay-breasted warbler lays large sets of eggs, from 4 to 7, but 5 is by far the commonest number, though sets of 6 are not very rare. The eggs vary in shape from ovate to elongate ovate and they are slightly glossy. The ground color is white, creamy white, pale bluish white or pale greenish white. They are handsomely speckled, spotted and blotched with "auburn," "bay," "raw umber," "argus brown," "chestnut," "chestnut-brown," "Mars brown," or "snuff brown," with underlying spots of "light Quaker drab," "light

mouse gray," "deep brownish drab," "vinaceous drab," or "light purplish drab." There is a wide variation in the manner of markings,
some being spotted with the reddish browns, others with shades of
"Brussels brown" or "snuff brown." Then too, eggs may have two or
three shades of brown mixed with the undertones of drab; or they may
be marked only with tones of a single shade of brown and drab. Generally they are boldly spotted, sometimes with a few scrawls of black;
while the coloring is concentrated at the large end, there is less tendency
to form a distinct wreath than in many other warbler eggs. The
measurements of 50 eggs average 17.7 by 12.9 millimeters; the eggs
showing the four extremes measure **19.0** by 13.4, 18.0 by **13.5, 16.4** by
13.3, and 17.5 by **12.3** millimeters (Harris).

Young.—Howard L. Mendall (1937) gives the following summary
of his study of the home life of the bay-breasted warbler:

The period of incubation was observed to be slightly over twelve days, and the
eggs hatched at intervals, with more than two days between the hatching of the
first and the fifth egg. Two young left the nest at eleven days of age. Incubation and brooding apparently are carried out solely by the female, which is, at
least part of the time, fed on the nest by the male. During the observation
periods from June 28 to July 3 (when there were five young in the nest), the
female averaged 26.4 feedings per hour, while the male fed on the average of 13
times an hour. However, under certain conditions and for short periods of time,
the male performed a much greater proportion of the nesting duties. Both adults
and one of the young were still together in the vicinity of the nest eight days
after the home had been forsaken.

He observed that, during a heavy thundershower, the female stood
over the young and sheltered them with her wings spread over the
sides of the nest; on a hot, sunny day she protected them from the
heat of the sun in a similar manner. Two of the young were killed
by a red squirrel and the last one disappeared before leaving the nest.
Only the first two to leave the nest survived.

Miss Stanwood's notes contain the following account of the activities
of the young a day or two before leaving the nest: "One little bird after
another pushed his way to the top of the bird heap, pecked at the oil
gland situated on the rump, wet his beak with oil, then dragged one
wing up slowly and oiled one feather at a time, pulling the feather
firmly through his beak from the root to the tip. Thus he made his
feathers waterproof and beautiful; thus, also, he removed those
annoying quill casings. After moistening his beak with oil the bird
rests; after preening a wing the bird rests again; then he moistens his
beak once more, rests, then preens the other wing and rests. The bird
may have been fed a number of times while this process is going on.
After feeding once more, and after the parent has again carried away
the excreta, he is thoroughly rested and his toilet is in perfect condition. He is now ready to let another little warbler press to the top
of the nest in his place."

Plumages.—Miss Stanwood (MS.) refers to the natal down as brown. Dr. Chapman (1907) describes the nestling in juvenal plumage as "above grayish olive, the head sometimes paler, nearly buffy, back heavily spotted with wedge-shaped black marks; below whitish thickly spotted with *rounded* black marks; median wing-coverts broadly tipped with white or buffy white on both webs, the greater coverts, on only the outer web."

A partial postjuvenal molt, involving the contour plumage and the wing coverts but not the rest of the wings or the tail, occurs in July and August and produces the first winter plumage. Dr. Dwight (1900) describes the young male in this plumage as "above, yellowish olive-green, with dusky streaks on the crown, a few concealed black spots on the back, the upper tail coverts cinereous gray. Wing coverts edged with olive-green and two broad wing bands white tinged with yellow. Below, cream-color washed with straw-yellow on the throat and with a very little chestnut on the flanks." It resembles the young blackpoll, but is "a yellower olive above, a buffier yellow below and a wash of chestnut on the flanks, with less definite streaking above and none below." The female is distinguishable from the male in the first winter plumage, "which is a clearer green without the crown streaks of the male, the black spots on the back duller and usually even a trace of chestnut is lacking on the flanks."

The first nuptial plumage is acquired before the birds come north by a partial prenuptial molt "which involves most of the body plumage and wing coverts but not the rest of the wings nor the tail. The deep chestnut crown, paler throat and lateral stripes, black sides of the head and forehead, olive-gray back streaked with black, the rich buff patches on the sides of the neck and the black wing coverts, plumbeous-edged and white-tipped, are all assumed." Adults and young are now practically indistinguishable, except for the worn and duller wings and tail in the young bird. The female has the same color pattern as the male but the colors are much duller and there is less chestnut.

Adults have a complete postnuptial molt, mainly in July. Dr. Dwight (1900) describes the plumage of the winter male as "similar to first winter dress, but the crown, nape and back distinctly streaked with black, creamier tints below and the flanks striped distinctly with chestnut, the wings and tail blacker and the edgings grayer rather than greener as in the young bird; a few chestnut feathers sometimes appear on the throat and crown." The adult female in winter is similar to the first winter female, "but whiter below, with a wash of chestnut on the flanks and with crown streaks and the dorsal spots better defined, resembling closely the male first winter dress, although usually rather duller."

The prenuptial molt of adults is similar to that of young birds.

Food.—Like other wood warblers, the bay-breasted is almost wholly insectivorous, indulging occasionally, perhaps, in a little wild fruit. No intensive study of its food seems to have been made.   Edward H. Forbush (1929) says that "it takes locusts, caterpillars, ants, beetles and leaf-hoppers." Miss Stanwood (MS.) saw moths and other insects and their larvae fed to the young.

Behavior.—At the nest studied by Mr. Mendall (1937)—

The adult birds showed a remarkable degree of adaptability in the face of the four changes in location to which the nest was subjected. In fact, for a species of the woodlands, the Bay-breasted Warbler appears to be exceedingly tame and unsuspicious in the presence of man. * * * She was reluctant to leave the nest, even when I had climbed within three feet of her, and it was not until the branches had been pulled to one side that she departed. Injury-feigning was very much in evidence. The bird dropped to a lower limb of the tree and almost literally crawled through the foliage in front of me. The left wing was extended and drooped, the tail was twisted to the left and the feathers spread. The bird uttered no sound, but continued to move through the branches for about fifty seconds after which she flew around me, several times coming very close to my head, and scolded violently. This protest brought the male to the scene and he joined his mate in uttering notes of alarm, though with less vigor.

Voice.—Aretas A. Saunders contributes the following study: "The song of the bay-breasted warbler is much like that of the blackpoll in high pitch and quality, and in having little or no change in pitch throughout. The time, however, is not even and regular; short and long notes are alternated or irregularly mixed. There is no definite increase in loudness.

"I have only 18 records of this song, as the bird is uncommon and seems to sing less frequently on migration than the other species. Six of these songs show no change in pitch, while the others change but slightly, half a tone to a tone. The pitch in the different songs varies from B'''' to E''''', a range of only two and a half tones. A larger number of records would probably show a greater range than this.

"All but one of my records are from migrating birds in Connecticut. One record from the breeding grounds in the Adirondacks is remarkably different, particularly in the matter of time. The records from migrating birds vary from ⅗ second to 2 seconds, but the record from the breeding grounds is 4⅗ seconds. This record is also remarkable in its rhythm, containing groups of three notes each that, in their time arrangement, suggest the 'peabody' notes of the song of the white-throated sparrow. The song, which is all on one pitch, might be written *Teee teelelee te te teee teee teelelee teelelee teelelee tee*. With only this one record of the summer song, I cannot determine whether it is typical of the breeding songs of this species or is unusual."

Gerald H. Thayer wrote to Dr. Chapman (1907) :

In a grouping based on songs, the Bay-breast should stand in a quintette with the Blackburnian, the Black-poll the Black and White and the Cape May. These five heard singing together in the same trees, as I have heard them on the Hudson River, make 'confusion worse than death' for any bird-student but the most adept. But with patience and a good ear one can learn to differentiate them surely. All five are thin-voiced, "sibilant," singers; but each has its own slight, prevailing peculiarity of tone, in addition to the differences, varied but never wholly violated, of phrasing and accentuation. The Bay-breast's singing, in the spring at least, is the most liquid and inarticulate of the lot, and sometimes the loudest. It varies greatly, from the bases of at least two and probably three clearly distinct main songs. In one of these, the six or more barely-separated lisping notes are all alike in volume, accentuation, tone, and speed. They are slightly louder than the Black-poll notes, and not quite so smooth in tone. Another song begins in about the same way, but ends with three or four clearly-separated louder notes, which have a more nearly full-voiced ring. A third, uncommon, song, which I have all but surely traced to the Bay-breast, is louder throughout, and otherwise very different. It begins with about ten penetrating notes, in close-knit couplets like those of the Black and White's shorter song, and of much the same tone, but louder; and it ends, abruptly, with a single, lower-toned, much richer note, like a fragment of Oven-bird song.

Philipp and Bowdish (1917) say : "The song is of a character quite similar to that of the Blackburnian Warbler, but slightly stronger and louder. It is delivered for long periods, with considerable frequency, and at all times of day, though less frequently toward the middle of the day. It appears that the female sings from the nest, in answer to the male, and the song is markedly weaker, being scarcely distinguishable from that of the Blackburnian Warbler. The approach of an intruder is apt to cause the female to become silent."

Field marks.—The adults of both sexes are unmistakable, with their conspicuous chestnut markings on crown, breast, and sides, black cheeks and a buffy spot on the side of the neck, in spring plumage, the females being duller in colors and with less chestnut. Fall birds might easily be mistaken for blackpolls, which they closely resemble, but adults usually have some trace of chestnut wash on the sides, less streaking above, and none below. Young birds have no trace of chestnut on the sides. The under tail coverts of the bay breasted warbler are cream-color, while those of the blackpoll are pure white.

Fall.—Bay-breasted warblers are often very common on the fall migration, sometimes really abundant. That they are sometimes commoner than we realize is a result of the difficulty of distinguishing them from the blackpolls as the two are migrating through the treetops together. As a rule, however, the bay-breasted warblers are earlier migrants, passing through New England during the last half of August and the first week of September, then in company with the blackpolls for the next two weeks, after which very few of them may be seen. In my experience, the blackpolls far outnumber them in New England, being by far our commonest warbler in the fall. The fall migration route of the bay-breasted warbler is apparently a reversal of the route followed in the spring, southward west of the Alleghenies and west of or across the Gulf of Mexico to Panamá and Colombia.

DISTRIBUTION

Range.—Southern Canada to northwestern South America.

Breeding range.—The bay-breasted warbler breeds north to northeastern British Columbia (Lower Liard Crossing); northern Alberta (Athabaska Lake near Chipwyan); casually north to southwestern Mackenzie (Wrigley); central Saskatchewan (Flotten Lake); central Manitoba (Berens Island, Lake Winnipeg, and possibly Oxford House); central Ontario (Gorman Creek, Patricia district; Lac Seul, Lake Nipigon, and Moose Factory); and southern Quebec (Mistassini Post, Piasti, and Natashquan); casual north to Hamilton Inlet, Labrador. East to southeastern Quebec (Natashquan); west-central Newfoundland (Grand Lake); and Nova Scotia (Baddeck, Pictou, and Halifax). South to Nova Scotia (Halifax); southern Maine (Ellsworth and Thomaston); central and southwestern New Hampshire (Tamworth, Webster, and Mount Monadnock); northern New York (Adirondack Mountains); southern Ontario (Southmag and French River); northern Michigan, rarely (Sugar Island, St. Mary's River, and Isle Royale); northern Minnesota (Clear Lake and Itasca Park; possibly Elk River); southwestern Ontario (Off Lake, Rainy River district); southern Manitoba (Indian Bay, Lake of the Woods, and Aweme); central Saskatchewan (Flotten Lake); central Alberta (Glenevis, Faust, and Sturgeon Lake); and central eastern British Columbia (Charlie Lake). West to northeastern British Columbia (Charlie Lake and Lower Liard Crossing; possibly Indian Point Lake and Tatana Lake).

Winter range.—In winter the bay-breasted warbler is found north to central Panamá (Canal Zone); the coastal region of Colombia (Santa Marta region); and Venezuela (Rancho Grande and Tortuga Island). South to northern Venezuela (Tortuga Island, Mérida, and La Uraca); and west central Colombia (Valvidia). West to western Colombia (Valvidia and Río Frío); and eastern Panamá (Cana and Canal Zone).

Migration.—Late dates of departure from the winter home are: Colombia—Malena, March 10. Panamá—Toro Point, April 27.

Early dates of spring arrival are: Mexico—Gómez Farías, Tamaulipas, April 2. Florida—Pensacola, April 23. Alabama—Sand Mountain, April 20. Georgia—Roswell, April 21. North Carolina—

Piney Creek, April 24. Virginia—Lynchburg, May 3. West Virginia—Wheeling, May 2. District of Columbia—Washington, May 2. Pennsylvania—Philadelphia, May 2. New York—Ithaca, May 1. Massachusetts—Amherst, May 7. Vermont—St. Johnsbury, May 5. Maine—Lewiston, May 10. Quebec—Montreal, May 18. New Brunswick—Scotch Lake, May 10. Nova Scotia—Yarmouth, May 21. Louisiana—Thibodaux, April 12. Mississippi—Deer Island, April 19. Arkansas—Monticello, April 24. Tennessee—Greenbrier, April 10 (specimen). Kentucky—Bowling Green, April 29. Indiana—Bloomington, April 29. Ohio—Oberlin, April 28. Michigan—Ann Arbor, May 3. Missouri—St. Louis, May 1. Iowa—Giard, May 7. Wisconsin—Madison, May 3. Minnesota—St. Paul, May 4. Texas—Olmito, April 23. Kansas—Topeka, May 8. Nebraska—Greeley, May 3. South Dakota—Yankton, May 10. North Dakota—Fargo, May 9. Manitoba—Margaret, May 13. Saskatchewan—Indian Head, May 10.

Late dates of spring departure of transients are: Florida—Pensacola, May 13. Alabama—Long Island, May 22. Georgia—Athens, May 13. South Carolina—Clemson (College), May 16. North Carolina—Asheville, May 19. Virginia—Charlottesville, May 28. West Virginia—Morgantown, May 22. District of Columbia—Washington, June 5. Pennsylvania—Laanna, June 7. New York—Brooklyn, June 3. Massachusetts—Northampton, June 9. Louisiana—New Iberia, May 15. Mississippi—May 16. Arkansas—Rogers, May 27. Tennessee—Nashville, May 24. Kentucky—Danville, May 19· Illinois—Chicago, June 5. Indiana—Notre Dame, June 4. Michigan—Ann Arbor, June 6. Ohio—Toledo, June 5. Missouri—St. Louis, June 2. Iowa—Sioux City, June 4. Wisconsin—Berlin, June 3. Texas—Laguna Vista, May 15. Oklahoma—Kenton, June 4. Nebraska—Hastings, May 25.

Early dates of fall arrival are: Minnesota—Minneapolis, August 21. Wisconsin—New London, August 15. Michigan—McMillan, August 6. Ohio—Toledo, August 6. Indiana—Dune Park, August 20. Illinois—Glen Ellyn, August 13. Kentucky—Bardstown, September 15. Tennessee—Roan Mountain, September 23. Mississippi—Bay St. Louis, September 23. Massachusetts—Harvard, September 5. New York—Rhinebeck, August 11. Pennsylvania—Pittsburgh, August 20. District of Columbia—Washington, August 17. West Virginia—Bluefield, August 29. Virginia—Lexington, September 19. North Carolina—Mount Mitchell, September 12. Georgia—Young Harris, September 29. Alabama—Birmingham, September 13.—Florida—Pensacola, October 1. Panamá—Cocoplum, October 24. Colombia—Novita, September 20.

Late dates of fall departure are: Manitoba—Aweme, September 26. Minnesota—St. Paul, September 29. Wisconsin—Racine, October 8.

Iowa—Lamont, October 2. Michigan—Detroit, October 19. Ontario—Point Pelee, October 15. Ohio—Youngstown, October 21. Indiana—Indianapolis, October 20. Illinois—Olney, October 20. Kentucky—Danville, October 20. Tennessee—Memphis, October 28. Mississippi—Saucier, October 24. Louisiana—New Orleans, October 11. New Brunswick—Grand Manan, September 16. Quebec—Montreal, October 12. Maine—Avon, September 17. Vermont—Wells River, October 13. Massachusetts—Taunton, October 8. New York—Geneva, October 12. Pennsylvania—Jeffersonville, October 20. District of Columbia—Washington, November 6. Virginia—Lawrenceville, October 12. North Carolina—Asheville, October 19. South Carolina—Mount Pleasant, October 18. Georgia—Athens, November 15. Alabama—Birmingham, October 25. Florida—Pensacola, October 27.

Casual records.—A bay-breasted warbler was collected at Big Sandy, Mont., on May 24, 1903; and one was carefully observed in a bird bath at Fort Morgan, Colo., on May 19, 1933. A juvenile was shot at Narssaq, near Godthaab, Greenland, on October 15, 1898. A specimen has been taken in Bermuda.

Egg dates.—Maine: 8 records, June 3 to 16; 5 records, June 10 to 15.

New Hampshire: 9 records, June 12 to 28; 5 records, June 13 to 18.

New Brunswick: 52 records, June 5 to July 2; 30 records, June 17 to 25, indicating the height of the season (Harris).

DENDROICA STRIATA (Forster)

BLACK-POLLED WARBLER

CONTRIBUTED BY ALFRED OTTO GROSS

PLATE 48

HABITS

The common or vernacular name black-polled warbler owes its origin to the conspicuous and distinctive black crown of the adult male. The beginner, when first learning to differentiate the warblers, is likely to compare the blackpoll with the black and white warbler, since these two birds have the same color combination and lack the bright colors of many of the other species of warblers. In the autumn, however, it is hard for him to believe that the little greenish birds are the same black and white warblers he saw in spring.

The black-polled warbler is a very successful species in its competition with others. Although it encounters many hazards on its very long migration, and countless numbers meet death at this time,

it has nevertheless been able to maintain a large and growing population. Anyone who has experienced seeing the great migration waves
that arrive late in the season will agree that it is one of our most
abundant warblers. One reason for this is the extensive breeding
range in the seclusion of the northern coniferous forests stretching
across the entire continent from Alaska to the Labrador coast. To be
sure, the unusual numbers in eastern United States during the migration are due in part to the fact that the black-polled warblers, breeding in the extensive region to the north, pass in an ever narrowing
migration route to their exit at the Florida Peninsula. In spring a
reverse condition exists in which the birds spread out as they go north
to occupy the great fan-shaped area.

Spring.—This warbler arrives late in the season, at a time when the
majority of the trees are in blossom or well leaved out, and since
it often frequents the taller tree tops it is sometimes difficult to see,
but the frequent songs give evidence of its presence. The blackpoll
is deliberate in its movements and usually unsuspicious and approachable. Often during the height of the migration I have seen them
along fences and stone walls and even in open fields and pastures
searching for food and going about their business apparently unaware
of my presence. At times they appear in my garden and backyard,
in fact they seem to be in evidence everywhere I go. Then at night,
if I am stationed in a quiet place, I hear their characteristic high-
pitched calls as, high in the air, they journey on their way.

Migration.—The blackpolls migrate chiefly at night, and since they
are readily attracted by bright lights during their flight, we often
find concentrations of them in the parks of our larger cities, where
they are reported as being seen under the electric lights at night.
When daylight comes they naturally seek out places such as parks
and public gardens where trees and shrubs provide temporary resting
and feeding places. In Central Park, New York City, for example,
G. E. Hix (1905) states that the black-polled warbler outnumbers all
others put together.

The black-polled warbler winters in northern South America.
Birds in migrating to North America may follow a route along the
coast of Central America and Mexico, as does the cliff swallow, or
they may fly directly over the Caribbean via Cuba and the intervening
islands to Florida, the route invariably chosen by the blackpoll. It
reaches the Florida coast about April 20, and as it is one of the latest
to migrate it seldom reaches the Gulf States before the last week of
April. It proceeds leisurely and may be seen long after the majority
of other warblers have passed on their way to their nesting grounds.
On this part of its migration it travels at a rate not exceeding 30 to
35 miles a day and does not reach southern New England and the

northern tier of Central States until about May 15. The individuals that cross the upper Mississippi Valley through Minnesota and the Dakotas then greatly accelerate their pace to about 200 miles per day so that a week later they have reached the central part of the Mackenzie Valley and by May 30 they arrive at the far distant breeding grounds in northwestern Alaska. This long distance is covered in about the same time that the slower-moving eastern contingent arrives in southern Quebec and Newfoundland. About 25 to 30 days are required to travel the distance of 1,000 miles from Florida to Minnesota, whereas the final lap of 2,500 miles is accomplished in less than two weeks. This remarkable change in speed can be correlated with the fact that the advance of spring in the northern interior is much more rapid than it is in the Mississippi Valley and Gulf coast. In the northland spring comes with a rush, and during the height of migration the temperature of the Mackenzie Valley is about the same as it is in Minnesota.

The black-polled warbler breeds principally in Canada and none farther south than southern New Brunswick, the mountains of the northeastern states and in the Rocky Mountains. This means that no blackpoll migrates a distance of less than 2,500 miles, while those individuals that winter in Brazil and nest in northwestern Alaska must travel more than 5,000 miles to reach their nesting grounds. These are straight-line distances, and do not take into account the deviations in the course or the random flights in search for food.

The migration route of the blackpoll from Alaska has been evolved over a long period of time. It is apparent that this bird extended its range from the eastern part of North America to northwestern Alaska. Instead of using the Pacific flyway it retraces its journey across the mountains and moves southeastward over the ancestral route to leave the United States for South America through a funnellike exit by way of Florida. In Arkansas, Louisiana, and the southern part of the Mississippi flyway it is a comparatively rare bird.

In autumn the blackpoll begins leaving its outpost in Alaska in August and, as in spring, it moves more rapidly over the northern section of its journey. After it reaches the States early in September its speed is less pronounced. These warblers are among the last to leave; they may be seen in the United States throughout September and October, and the last individuals do not leave Florida until November.

The distribution of this warbler is not uniform over the entire area included in the migration, and the details of its course taken in spring may vary from that followed in autumn. T. D. Burleigh (1934), in a study of the distribution and abundance of the black-polled and bay-breasted warblers in the southeastern States during the spring and fall migrations, notes that at Athens, Ga., and in the Piedmont region in general the blackpoll is an abundant spring migrant but in the fall is exceedingly scarce. Likewise at Asheville in the mountains of North Carolina, it is an abundant spring migrant and completely absent in autumn. On the coast it is common only in fall. Mr. Burleigh states: "It apparently, in the west to east migration in the fall from its breeding grounds in the far northwest, is moved by some impulse to reach the coast as soon as possible, and as a result it is at best merely a straggler over much of the area it occupies in the spring migration."

Swales and Taverner (1907) have noted that the black-polled warbler, though one of the most abundant fall migrants in southeastern Michigan, is conspicuously absent in the region of Detroit, Wayne County, in spring. No explanation is offered to account for this peculiar situation in that section of its migration journey.

The fall migration of the blackpolls as it occurs in the White Mountains of New Hampshire is of interest. These birds breed commonly in the upper Canadian Zone mainly above 3,000 feet on southern exposures and down to 2,000 feet on the northern slopes. During September they swarm in migration over the low country of the southern part of the State and beyond, but in the valley bottoms among the mountains they are rare. Here they migrate mainly at the upper levels and along the mountain tops. The tendency to migrate at the higher elevations along mountain ranges has been observed in other sections of the migration course. On September 15, 1900, Glover M. Allen (1903) observed a great flight of black-polled and myrtle warblers starting at 4:30 a. m. and continuing for 2 hours in the White Mountains. Several hundred birds passed, of which three-fourths were blackpolls. These warblers came flying in from the south, high in the air, making straight for Carter notch, a great rift in the mountain with a valley opening out toward the north and another to the south. "It seemed," Dr. Allen writes, "as if the black-poll warblers from all of the forests immediately to the south were moving north in a concerted manner to pass through the notch and off beyond. Possibly they were heading for the Ammonoosuc Valley to continue thence down the Connecticut; this would be a natural course, and one cannot suppose that their northward flight at this season could have been more than some such local movement."

Norman Criddle (1922) has taken migration records of the blackpoll over a period of 21 years at Aweme, Manitoba, Canada, where he finds the average date of appearance in spring to be May 14, with his earliest date on May 9, 1902. In autumn the average date of last birds seen was September 9, and the latest record was one observed on September 15, 1912.

The observations and dates of the spring and fall migration made by M. B. Trautman (1940) at Buckeye Lake, Ohio, are typical of the midwestern section of the migration route. He writes as follows:

The black-poll warbler was among the last of the warblers to make its appearance in spring. The latest date for spring arrivals was May 15. In the average year a few could be seen daily after May 15, and by May 18 the species was common. At the peak of migration, between May 18 and 27, 10 to 40 birds could be observed daily. The species then generally disappeared suddenly, for by May 29 all except a few stragglers had departed.

The first southbound transients were seen between August 31 and September 14, and the species was always rare until September 15. An increase became apparent by September 17, and from then until October 10 it could be regularly recorded. The peak of migration came between September 25 and October 10, and then 10 to 150 individuals could be daily observed. A sharp decrease in numbers took place between October 10 and 15, and by October 23 the species was usually absent. * * *

The black-poll and bay-breasted warblers were close associates during migrations. Both were late spring and fall transients, both chiefly inhabited trees, and their maximum numbers during migrations were almost equal.

In Maine and Massachusetts the main migration wave of blackpolls comes late in May, but a few forerunners can be expected during the second week of the month and a few exceptionally early records have been made during the first week. It is the only one of the transient warblers that remains until June, and in some years a few belated stragglers linger after the second week in southern Maine. It nests in the northern part of the state.

In autumn the blackpolls arrive in force in September, with some forerunners appearing late in August. They are with us through September and much of October; in Massachusetts dates of last appearances have been reported for November, and one was seen as late as December 17, 1939, at Plum Island, Mass., by Richard Stackpole (1939) and others.

Nesting.—The blackpoll is a bird of the northern spruce forests; in fact, the spruce seems to be an essential requirement for its nesting site. At Kent Island, Bay of Fundy, New Brunswick, I have seen 9 nests, all in small white spruces and all located within the narrow range of 2 to 7 feet from the ground and built snugly against the trunks of the trees. The somewhat bulky structures were well supported in each case by one or two horizontal branches. Most of these New Brunswick nests were well concealed from view by canopies of overhanging branches. A typical nest had an outside diameter of 4½ inches and was 3 inches in depth. The internal dimensions of the cup were 2 inches wide and 1½ inches deep. The foundation was made of small twigs and sprays of spruce, pieces of bark, dried grasses, and weeds mixed with bits of moss, lichens, and wool. The interior of the structure consisted of plant fibers and fine rootlets, some hair, and a liberal lining of white gull feathers. The lining of feathers is characteristic, being as essential to the nest structure as the spruce tree is for a nesting site. The kind of feathers used, of course, depends on the kind that are available; on Grand Manan Island, New Brunswick, it is commonly goose feathers, in the Magdalen Islands in the Gulf of St. Lawrence, duck feathers; in Labrador, duck or ptarmigan feathers; and at Lost River in the White Mountains I have seen nests lined with grouse feathers and odd feathers of song birds. The myrtle warbler also uses feathers in lining its nest, which is more compactly built than the blackpoll's and is generally placed on a horizontal limb away from the trunk of the tree.

J. P. Norris (1890a) describes 17 sets of eggs of the blackpoll and gives the location of 15 nests collected on Grand Manan Island as follows: "They were all found in spruce trees, one of them was found only a foot from the ground; another was eighteen inches; a third two feet up; a fourth three and a half feet; two more were each four feet high; five were five feet up; two were seven feet from the ground; another was eight feet and still another was ten feet high." William Brewster (1882a) describes a nest containing three eggs which he found in the Magdalen Islands on June 23, 1882:

The nest was built in a low, thick spruce, which stood on the edge of a swamp, near a brook. It was placed on a horizontal branch at a height of about three feet, and was well concealed by the clusters of densely-imbricated needles above. * * * The main body of the structure is composed of Usnea moss, weedstalks, and dry grasses, closely matted and protected outwardly by coarser stalks and a few dead spruce twigs. The lining is of slender, black moss-stems (which curiously resemble horse hair) cow's-hair and a few feathers. The whole affair is remarkably solid and bulky for a Warbler's nest.

R. M. Anderson (1909) cites an exception to the rule that the blackpoll nests in trees saying of a nest he found June 24, 1908, on Moose Island near Fort Resolution, Great Slave Lake:

I stepped across a small dead spruce lying on the ground, and a small plainly colored bird darted from the mass of tall dead grass which surrounded the trunk of a fallen tree. The bird disappeared in the underbrush at once without uttering a sound. Concealing myself, I watched about twenty minutes and the bird stealthily approached the nest hopping from bush to bush, occasionally uttering a sharp, nervous *tsip* like the alarm note of the Junco. The bird proved to be a female Blackpoll Warbler. The nest was placed directly on the ground in the middle of a clump of dead grasses, immediately underneath a small, fallen spruce, the trunk of which was lying about ten inches above the ground. The nest was composed of dead grasses, mixed with cottony substances and a little moss, lined with finer grasses, and a few feathers including one tail feather of a fox sparrow. The four eggs were advanced in incubation.

R. MacFarlane (1891) found several nests of the blackpoll on the ground along Anderson River of northwestern Mackenzie well above the Arctic Circle. In the Mackenzie Delta region bordering the Arctic Ocean the blackpoll is found in dense alder thickets in gullies and ravines; nesting some distance beyond the tree limit. A. R. Porsild (1943) found a nest in an alder thicket near the water's edge on the south end of Richards Island, off the Delta, on August 16, 1934. The nest contained many feathers and was lined with the down of *Epilobium* and willow.

At Kent Island, New Brunswick, the blackpolls usually arrive during the last week of May, and they may be heard singing or be seen feeding among the thick spruce growth which covers a large portion of the 2-mile-long island. Courtship and nest building is a slow deliberate proceedure and nests with eggs are not to be found before the second or third week of June.

The major part of nest building was performed by the female, in one instance under observation; the male was in full song during this time, and while he may have assisted in gathering nesting material I never saw him do any construction work at the nest. The nest contained one egg on June 16, 1932, but it was not until June 22 that the fifth and final egg of the set was laid. Two nests found by Ernest Joy, warden at Kent Island, contained one egg each on June 11, 1943. Each set of five eggs was complete on June 15, indicating that in these two cases an egg was laid each day until the sets were completed.

The female sits very closely when incubating; by moving cautiously I have approached within a few feet of the bird before she fluttered away. At the New Hampshire Nature Camp, Lost River, N. H., in the White Mountains, a blackpoll built a nest in a small spruce tree standing alongside a trail used frequently each day by numerous students. The incubating female paid no attention to passing persons unless they stopped to examine the nest more closely. When thus forced to leave the nest, she slipped off into the dense growth of spruces but emerged soon to utter sharp alarm notes. These calls invariably brought the male to the scene, and together they would protest the intrusion. The male guards his territory zealously and is ever ready to challenge a bird of his own kind or any stranger that appears in the vicinity. In addition to his singing and duties as guardian I have seen him bring food to the female at the nest. One of the best ways to locate a nest containing eggs is to follow a male carrying some larvae or insect to his mate. A nest of course can be quite easily located in this manner after it contains young, by watching either parent.

Dr. Herman R. Sweet made a study of nesting black-polled warblers at Kent Island during the summer of 1933. His arrival at the island was too late to observe their behavior during courtship, nest building, or incubation, save for 2 hours spent in the blind erected within 4 feet of the nest, on June 29, the day before the eggs hatched.   During the 2 hours the female incubated the eggs for a total of 92 minutes, in five periods.   The shortest time spent incubating was 11 minutes, and the longest 25 minutes, the average being 18.5 minutes. I have noted that other incubating warblers often exhibit considerable restlessness toward the end of incubation and at this time leave the nest more frequently and for longer periods of time.   Presumably the same may have been true of the blackpoll observed by Dr. Sweet.

When not on the nest the female could be heard flying about in the nearby trees searching for food, but she made not the least sound when approaching the nest.   She invariably came to the nest from a lower level and after reaching the base of the reclining spruce in which it was located hopped up to the nest.   While incubating she often dozed with her eyes shut, but upon hearing the least sound she suddenly became alert.

Eggs.—Complete sets of black-polled warbler eggs vary from three to five, but four or five are more usual.   The eggs have a white or light creamy buff or sometimes a pale greenish ground color, with brown and umber specks scattered over the whole surface and numerous spots and blotches of reddish brown and subdued shades of lilac and lavender concentrated at the larger end, sometimes forming a wreath.

The weights and measurements of a set of eggs found on Kent Island, June 28, 1932, were taken by Dr. Sweet as follows: 1.7 by 1.4 cm., 1.8 gm.; 1.9 by 1.35 cm., 1.8 gm.; 1.85 by 1.7 cm., 1.7 gm.; 1.85 by 1.9 cm., 1.9 gm.   The average of 77 eggs collected by J. P. Norris (1890a) is .72 by .54 inch.   Of this series the eggs showing the four extremes measure .79 by .54, 73 by **.55**, **.68** by .49, and **.69** by **.47** inch. The average of 15 eggs collected by P. B. Philipp (1925) is .70 by .55 inch; the largest measures .74 by .56, and the smallest .66 by .54 inch. A set of eggs collected by N. S. Goss (1891) on June 19, 1880, at Grand Manan, New Brunswick, were unusually large, with the following measurements: .77 by .55, .78 by .56, .78 by .56, and .79 by .56 inch.

The measurements of 50 eggs average 17.9 by 13.4 millimeters, the eggs showing the four extremes measure **21.8** by 13.7, 18.3 by **14.7,** and **16.3** by **12.7** millimeters (Harris).

Young.—The incubation period of the blackpoll is at least 11 days, but the exact time was not determined because it was not possible to ascertain the exact date when incubation started.   Apparently it may start before the set of eggs is completed, for in one instance 2 days elapsed between the hatching of the first and last of five eggs.

After the young appear the adults exhibit even less fear of a human observer.   At Lost River, N. H., on June 30, 1932, I stood in full view, within 5 feet of a nest to take pictures of the adults feeding the young. The female was not in the least disturbed by my presence, but the male at times displayed some reluctance in coming directly to the nest. Both male and female feed the young, but often the male would present his mate at the nest with a larva, which she would accept and in turn feed it to the young. At first small green larvae and aphids were fed to the young but by the time they were 6 days old spiders and large adult insects also were delivered. The nest was always kept clean; the fecal sacs were eaten or carried away as soon as they appeared. As is true of many other passerine birds, the adults after feeding a youngster may stimulate it with a gentle stroke of their beak, causing the fecal sac to appear.

The following observations are from the unpublished notes of Dr. Herman Sweet on black-polled warblers nesting at Kent Island. On June 30, 1933, three of the eggs hatched, one in the morning at 9:40 a. m. the other two at 7:45 p. m. A fourth egg, which was cracked, failed to hatch and was removed by the following morning. One of the three young died and was removed by Dr. Sweet on the second day. At the time of hatching, the natal plumage consists of delicate tufts of grayish down located on the head, humeral, crural, alar, and caudal tracts.

The first young to hatch opened its mouth widely for food as soon as it was free from the egg although the adults were not present to stimulate such behavior. After this occurred, both the female and male arrived at the nest but neither had food for the young. The male left the nest at once and the female left later, to return in 5 minutes without food. After brooding the lone young for 11 minutes she left again and returned in 5 minutes with a green larva. The larva was minced in her bill and fed to the young just 43 minutes after it had left the shell. The female brooded 5 minutes then left in search of more food. This procedure was repeated six times during the period of observation 9:40 to 11:08. The female brooded 63 minutes or 71.4 percent of the time. The longest single period was 21 minutes and the shortest 5 minutes. Of the six times she left the nest she returned with food four times. During observations made between 2 and 3 p. m. the female did not make any feedings, although she left the nest occasionally. One of the remaining eggs was pipped at this time.

At 7:45 p. m. two more eggs had hatched and the shells had been removed. At 7:59 the male appeared at the nest; the female sat on the rim while he fed the young a minced green caterpillar. He left in 25 seconds and the female again brooded. At 8:12 the male was back again with more larvae. This time the female paid no attention to his presence. The male then uttered a soft twittering sound, whereupon she hopped up on one side of the nest and he fed at least one young. At 8 : 45 p. m. a flashlight was turned on the nest. She raised up her breast, inspected her young and then settled down for the night.

On July 2, when 2 days old, the young had developed noticeably, with feather papillae showing on ventral tracts. On the following day feather papillae also appeared on the caudal, alar, crural, and humeral tracts, and tail. None had yet appeared on the head and femoral regions. On July 4, at 4 days, sheathed feathers appeared on all tracts except the head. When the male came to the nest to feed the young, if they did not open their mouths he uttered a *tweet* to which they all responded. The young twittered weakly when fed. On July 5 their eyes were open and the feathers on the caudal and ventral tracts were beginning to unsheath at their tips.

As the young grew larger and acquired their juvenal plumage at 8 or 9 days, they frequently stood on the edge of the nest when alone and went through gymnastic exercises by flapping their wings, thus gaining strength in preparation for the time of their first flight. They also frequently preened their rapidly growing feathers to assist in removing the sheaths.

At 10 days, the young exhibited distinct signs of fear. The following day the nest was empty. (By the eleventh day, in another nest under observation, two of four young had left the nest.) The adults continued to feed the young in the vicinity of this nesting site for several days, after which the entire family disappeared from the scene.

Plumages.—Jonathan Dwight, Jr. (1900), has described the plumages and molts of the blackpoll as follows:

[Juvenal plumage] above, including sides of the head, olive-gray obscurely streaked or mottled with dull black. Wings and tail, clove-brown edged with dull olive-green, whitish on the tail, tertiaries and wing bands. Two rectrices with white terminal spots on the inner webs. Below, dingy white mottled with dull black. Bill and feet pinkish buff, the former becoming dusky, the latter sepia.

First winter plumage acquired by a partial postjuvenal molt in July and August in eastern Canada, which involves the body plumage and the wing coverts, but not the rest of the wings and the tail.

Similar to previous plumage but unspotted. Above, including sides of head, olive-green, olive-gray on tail coverts, rather obscurely streaked, chiefly on the back, with black. The wing coverts clove-brown edged with olive-green and tipped with white, yellow tinged. Below, very pale canary-yellow, white on abdomen and crissum with a few obscure grayish streaks on the throat and sides. A narrow and obscure superciliary line and orbital ring pale canary yellow, the lores whitish, a faint dusky transocular stripe. One or two black crown feathers are occasionally assumed.

Resembles *D. castanea* and *D. vigorsii* but distinguishable from either of them by the streaked back and duller colors.

First nuptial plumage acquired by a partial prenuptial molt which involves most of the body plumage, the wing coverts and tertiaries, but not the rest of the wings nor the tail. Young and old become indistinguishable. The black cap and black and white plumage are assumed, at first evidently, somewhat veiled by whitish edgings.

Adult winter plumage acquired by a complete postnuptial moult in July. Similar to first winter dress but whiter below, the streaking often distinctly black and extending to the chin, which is spotted here and there; above the crown is decidedly streaked or marked with stray black feathers; the wings and tail are blacker and the edgings are darker and grayer especially on the tertiaries. The slight sprinkling of black feathers is like that found in *Dolichonyx orizivorus* and some other species in the autumn.

[Female] * * * plumages and moults correspond to those of the male, from which it is first distinguishable in first winter plumage, but not in every case. Females are then a little greener above and yellower below including the crissum, the streaks on the side extremely faint. The first nuptial plumage acquired by moult is a little paler than the first winter, the head, back and sides with distinct black streaks; resembles the male in first winter dress but more decidedly streaked. The adult winter plumage is practically indistinguishable from the first winter but rather paler and with the wing edgings darker. The adult nuptial plumage much resembles the male in adult winter dress and is merely tinged with yellow and streaked on crown, back, sides of chin, and sides with black. The black cap and broad streaking of the male are never acquired.

The fall or winter plumage of the blackpoll is so similar to the first winter plumage of the bay-breasted warbler that even the most experienced field observers find them extremely difficult to differentiate during the fall migration. This confusion has often lead to errors in field identification, so that reports of the relative abundance and distribution of these two species during the fall migration are sometimes confusing.

The upper parts of the blackpoll are duller and more streaked, the wings are edged with a yellow-green in place of gray-green; the underparts are yellowish instead of buffy. These differences are not constant, and some individuals of the bay-breasted warbler can be distinguished only by the trace of chestnut on the flanks and under tail coverts. Perhaps the best field mark is the color of the legs, which in the blackpoll is light, approaching a yellowish, while in the bay-breasted warbler it is dark brown and in some instances almost black. It is true these warblers are more deliberate in their movements, offering better opportunities for detailed observation, but even so, positive identifications are often impossible in the field.

Concerning the postjuvenal molt and the acquiring of the fall or winter plumage E. A. Preble (1908) writes of blackpoll warblers observed and collected in the Mackenzie region of northwest Canada.

The blackpoll occurs in summer throughout the region north to the very edge of the wooded country. It arrives on its breeding ground late in May, and some individuals are on their way south again in late July, molting as they travel, into the olivaceous plumage common to old and young in autumn. * * * Birds of the year taken July 19, 23, and 29 are in the spotted juvenal plumage, but with the yellowish-green of the fall plumage [first winter] appearing on the back, throat, chest, and sides; the change was about half completed in most of the specimens. An adult taken July 26 also is molting, the yellowish-green forming a patch on each side of the breast. Took specimens in the transition from the breeding to the autumnal plumage near Lake St. Croix, August 14, when the species was abundant.

An immature female blackpoll that I collected on the mainland west of Nain, Labrador, on August 12, 1934, represents a transitional state between the juvenal and first winter plumage, with feathers of each plumage about equally represented. Another specimen, a male taken near the same place on August 18, 1937, has its winter plumage practically completed. At Lost River, in the White Mountains of New Hampshire, I have seen young in various stages of transition from the juvenal to the first winter plumage during the last week of July.

Alexander Wetmore (1936), who has made counts of the number of contour feathers of passeriform and related birds, found that a male blackpoll weighing 17.6 grams, taken October 15, 1933, had 1,583 contour feathers with a total weight of 1.2 grams.

S. P. Baldwin and S. C. Kendeigh (1938) have made the following weighings of black-polled warblers: 1 adult taken in May, 12.4 gm.; 3 males taken in September average 11.4 gm.; 1 female taken in September, 12.8 gm.; 3 immature birds taken in September average 11.5 gm.; and 4 in October average 13.9 gm.

Albinistic plumages of the black-polled warbler apparently are not rare. J. Harris Reed (1888) describes the plumage of a male taken May 12, 1888, at Upper Chichester, Delaware County, Pa., as follows:

The entire crown, with the exception of three or four small black feathers over the eyes, is pure white, the edges of the feathers tipped with cream color which is more decided fringing the neck. The upper tail-coverts and rump are pure white, extending high up on the back and passing irregularly through the interscapulars and joining the white on back of neck and crown; rather silky across the rump. The interscapulars form an irregular bar across the shoulders. The scapulars and tertiaries are sparsely spotted with white, most prominent on the right side. The sides of breast are streaked as usual, although of a rusty color, rather obsolete as they approach the chin which is pure white. The throat and breast are ochroleucous. Otherwise the plumage is natural. * * * The white feathers are immaculate from the quills out, none being edged or spotted with the natural colors.

Charles H. Townsend (1883) states that a black-polled warbler in the Academy of Natural Sciences of Philadelphia has the entire plumage suffused with white, and William Dutcher (1888) found a perfect albino blackpoll killed by striking Fire Island light on September 23, 1887. Other cases of pure and partial albinism have been reported, indicating that this abnormality may be expected.

Food.—Anyone who has observed the blackpolls during migration and especially in their nesting haunts in the coniferous forests is well aware of their insect-feeding habits. Not only do they glean the leaves and twigs of insects and their larvae, but frequently they dart out from the concealment of the foliage to capture some passing flying insect with a sharp snap of the bill, after the manner of the flycatcher. At Kent Island, New Brunswick, I have frequently seen them on the terminal branches of the spruce trees feeding upon the spruce gall lice and other insects which infest these trees. All the food that I have seen eaten by the adults or delivered to their young during the nesting season consisted wholly of insects and spiders.

The blackpoll, like many other species of insect-eating birds, may at times neglect its usual food to take extraordinary numbers of those species which, for any reason become superabundant for a time, thus this bird serves well in doing its part to extirpate serious local infestations of insects. E. H. Forbush (1907) cites a case in which warblers completely eliminated an infestation of plant lice as follows:

I have had several opportunities, within the last fifteen years, to watch the checking of insect uprisings by birds. One morning in the fall of 1904 I noticed in some poplar trees near the shore of the Musketaquid a small flock of myrtle and black-poll warblers, busily feeding on a swarm of plant lice. There were not more than fifteen birds. The insects were mainly imagoes, and some of them were flying. The birds were pursuing these through the air, but were also seeking those that remained on the trunks and branches. I watched these birds for some time, noted their activity, and then passed on, but returned and observed their movements quite closely all day. Toward night some of the insects had scattered to neighboring trees, and a few of the birds were pursuing them there; but most of the latter remained at or about the place where the aphids swarm was first seen, they were still there at sundown. The swarm decreased rapidly all day, until just before sunset it was difficult to find even a few specimens of the insect. The birds remained until it was nearly dark, for they were still finding a few insects on the higher branches. The next morning at sunrise I went to the trees to look for more specimens. The birds, however, were before me, I was unable to find a single aphis on the trees.

S. A. Forbes (1883) made an investigation of the food eaten by birds found in a 45-acre apple orchard, in Illinois, heavily infested with cankerworms. Of the birds collected and their stomach contents examined, four blackpolls had eaten cankerworms to the extent of 67 percent of their stomach contents. In addition there were boring bettles (*Psenocerus*), 15 percent; other Coleoptera (beetles), 4 percent; ants, 4 percent; gnats 4 percent; traces of Hemiptera and mites; and some undetermined seeds. Samuel Aughey (1878) studied the food of Nebraska birds during the great invasion of Rocky Mountain migratory locusts on the western prairies and plains during the period 1873–1876. The blackpoll was prominent among the birds which preyed upon the locusts. Of four blackpoll stomachs examined, each contained an average of 30 locusts and 12 other insects; no seeds, grains, or other food was found. Sylvester D. Judd (1902) made a special study of the birds on a Maryland farm. On May 13–15, 1900, he observed blackpolls feeding on mayflies at the top of a cedar tree so heavily infested that it was gray with these insects. On May 17 he also found these warblers doing their part in suppressing an infestation on pine trees by sawflies (*Pteronus*). The stomachs of 11 specimens collected on the farm revealed that they had also eaten freely of ants, weevils, wasps, and bees. The blackpoll warbler has been known to feed ravenously on winged termites at times when these insects appear in immense swarms. There are numerous reports that in the far north these birds devour hundreds of troublesome mosquitoes.

In fall the blackpoll eats a few seeds and berries, such as the pokeberry (*Phytolacca americana*), but they are mainly insectivorous at all seasons. When passing through Florida in autumn they devour large numbers of spiders and their eggs, plant lice, and scale insects found on the citrus and native plants. It is obvious that the blackpoll is useful as an insect-eating bird and that they often play an important role in suppressing insect infestations.

Voice.—Late in May in New England after the host of warblers have arrived and many of them have passed on their way, we may expect to hear the unpretentious, high-pitched, insectlike but characteristic song of the black-polled warbler. It is in full song when it arrives and continues to sing throughout its stay, one of the most frequently heard warbler songs at that season. Its song is not musical, but the ebb and flow of its rapidly uttered series of high-pitched, accented syllables is most agreeable. It sings on the average only two or three times a minute, and seldom more than four times a minute, but in any favorable woodland there are sure to be several individuals singing, so that the song is always in evidence. Although these birds may be well hidden by the foliage, the song always assures one of their presence, but it is not always easy to trace to its source, as it has certain deceiving ventriloquial qualities.

Aretas A. Saunders (1941) gives his analysis of the black-polled warbler's song as follows: "The song of this bird is weak, high-pitched, and much like those of the Bay-breast and Black and White in quality. The commoner form of song is a series of notes all on the same pitch and in even time, but growing louder in the middle and softer again to the end. The number of notes varies from six to eighteen, and the notes are sometimes slow and measured and at other times quite rapid. In a less common form the notes are so rapid as to be uncountable, and the song becomes a trill, swelling in loudness in the middle."

Ralph Hoffmann (1904) in describing the song writes: "It is a high thin *tsit tsit tsit tsit tsit*, of a penetrating quality, delivered with a crescendo and diminuendo; the last notes are by some birds run rapidly together with almost a sputtering effect."

Rev. J. H. Langille (1884) states: "That song, though one of the most slender and wiry in all our forests, is as distinguishable as the hum of the Cicada or the shrilling of the Katydid. *Tree-tree-tree-tree-tree-tree-tree-tree*, rapidly uttered, the monotonous notes of equal length, beginning very softly, gradually increasing to the middle of the strain, and then as gradually diminishing, thus forming a fine musical swell. * * * There is a peculiar soft and tinkling sweetness in this melody, suggestive of the quiet mysteries of the forest, and sedative as an anodyne to the nerves."

On their nesting grounds in the White Mountains of New Hampshire and at Kent Island, Bay of Fundy, New Brunswick, I have heard the full song of the blackpoll throughout the nesting season but rarely after the young left the nest. I have seen them perched in full view at the very top of a spruce or fir tree pouring forth their simple but earnest song. They have a call note, a high-pitched lisp which resembles *zeet*, and when suddenly surprised or alarmed they utter a strong chirp.

The blackpoll is usually silent in autumn, but at times it has been heard in full song late in the season, after having acquired its winter plumage. During the fall migration the diurnal note *tsit* is the commonest heard.

Though the blackpoll does not excel as a songster, its song has one characteristic which makes it stand out in marked contrast to all others. Albert Brand (1938), who determined the vibration frequencies of 59 passerine birds, found that the song of the blackpoll has the highest pitch of all the bird songs he studied. Its average frequency was 8,900, midway between C sharp 8 and D 8, or over an octave above the highest tone on the piano. The blackpoll also produced the highest avian frequency studied, 10,225, a quarter tone under E 8. The lowest frequency recorded in various songs of the blackpoll was 8,050. By comparison, the mean frequency in songs of the northern pine warbler is 4,150, the highest 5,125, and the lowest only 3,300. Indeed the song of the blackpoll is of such a high frequency that it is well beyond the range of hearing of many persons. I must admit, in recent years, I have observed the blackpoll singing and could see by its posture and the movements of its beak and throat that it was singing, but I was unable to hear the song.

Enemies.—The blackpoll is subject to the usual enemies of other woodland birds, but all these apparently exact an insignificant toll when compared to the hazards experienced during migration. In crossing the wide expanses of the Caribbean Sea from the winter quarters in South America, some of them take refuge on passing boats during bad weather, but the vast majority after battling adverse winds and storms reach the Florida and Gulf coast in a weakened or exhausted condition.   C. J. Maynard (1896), who landed April 27, 1884, on a small key in the Bahamas, found great numbers of black-polls, some of which he found dead apparently due to exhaustion. W. E. D. Scott (1890) in writing of the spring migration at Tarpon Springs in 1888 states:

It is so rare that one finds any birds dying or dead from other than accidental causes, generally connected in some way with innovations caused by the settle-ment of a country, as telegraph wires, light-houses, and the like, that it seems worth while to give the following details of an epidemic.   It was apparently confined, as far as I am aware, to the representatives of this species alone, and only to those individuals which visited the Anclote Keys and Hog Island.   These keys are four in number, and are four miles from the main land, in the Gulf, and extend in a north and south line for about twenty-five miles.   I found in late April and early May many *D[endroica] striata* dead, and others apparently ill unto death on these islands.   *   *   *   I picked up dead on April 29, 1888, in a short walk on South Anclote Key, upwards of twenty-five.

Scott presents no evidence of disease or cause of the so-called epidemic, and I am inclined to believe these birds were members of a late migra-tory wave that had met with adverse conditions and died of exhaustion.

The habit of migrating at night is indirectly a cause of great mor-tality when waves of these birds encounter lighthouses and lighted towers.   Often very serious conditions prevail during cloudy or foggy nights when the birds, losing their bearings and attracted by the bright light, descend from their high-level flight and are dashed to death on striking some part of an illuminated tower.   William Dutcher (1888) writes that of the 595 birds killed by striking the Fire Island Light on Long Island on September 23, 1887, no less than 356 were blackpoll warblers.

W. E. Saunders (1930) has reported great destruction at the Long Point Lighthouse, Ontario, on Lake Erie, during September 1929.   On September 7 there were 31, on September 9, 6 and on September 24–29, 199 blackpolls that met their death by flying into the light. Similar conditions prevail along the Maine coast where during cloudy and stormy nights many warblers, including a large percentage of blackpolls, are killed.

High towers such as the Washington Monument also exact a heavy toll on night-flying birds.   Robert Overing (1938) reports that in the course of an hour and a half, 10 :30 p. m. to midnight of September 12, 1937, 576 individual birds, chiefly warblers and including the black-poll, were dashed to their death.   At this time the humidity ranged from 65 to 75 percent, and a mist enveloped the top of the shaft. These and numerous other instances indicate that lighthouses and towers are a great menace to a night-migrating bird such as the black-poll.   Probably more individuals meet violent death in this manner than by any other way.

I have not been able to find any record of a case of parasitism of the blackpoll by the cowbird. This, however, is to be expected as the ranges of the two birds do not greatly overlap. The cowbird is of no importance in its relation to the life of this warbler.

DISTRIBUTION

Range.—North America and northern South America.

Breeding range.—The black-polled warbler breeds **north** to northern Alaska (Kobuk River and Fort Yukon); northern Yukon (La Pierre House); northern Mackenzie (Richards Island, Fort Anderson, Black-water River, and Hanbury River); northern Manitoba (Lac du Brochet and Churchill); northern Quebec (Bush Lake, Fort Chimo, and Indian House Lake); and northern Labrador (Nain). **East to** the coast of Labrador (Nain, Cape Aillik, and Cartwright) and New-foundland (Fogo Island, Trinity, and St. John's). **South** to southern Newfoundland (St. John's and St. Pierre); Nova Scotia (Baddeck, Halifax, and Yarmouth); southern Maine (Calais, Waterville, and Auburn); southern New Hampshire (Tamworth and Peterborough); northwestern Massachusetts (Mount Greylock); northern New York (Mount Marcy and Leyden, rarely Slide Mountain in the Catskills); northern Ontario (Trout Lake); central Manitoba (Oxford House); central Saskatchewan (Cumberland House and Flotten Lake); central Alberta (Flat Lake, Stony Plain, and Hythe); and central and northwestern British Columbia (Summit Lake, Tatana Lake, and Atlin); southern Yukon (Carcross) and southern Alaska (Chitina Maraine, Lake Clark, and Nushagak). **West** to western Alaska (Nushagak, Bethel, St. Michael, Nome, and Kobuk River).

Winter range.—The blackpoll winters in northern South America **east** to eastern Cayenne (Oyapock River). **South** to southern Cayenne (Oyapock River); western British Guiana (Roraima); southern Venezuela (Casiquiare); northwestern Brazil (Marabitanas); and north-central Ecuador (Sara-yacu). **West** to north-central Ecuador (Sara-yacu and Archidona) and western Columbia (La Morelia, Río Frío, and the Santa Marta region).

Migration.—Late date of spring departure from the winter home is; Ecuador—Río Suno, April 10. Early dates of spring arrival are; Cuba—Habana, April 24. Bahamas—Cay Lobos, April 15. Florida—Sombrero Key, April 14. Alabama—Barachias, April 22. Georgia—Milledgeville, April 11. South Carolina—Aiken, April 20. North Carolina—Raleigh, April 16, Virginia—Lynchburg, April 18. West Virginia—Wheeling, April 31. District of Columbia—Washington, April 21. Pennsylvania—Jeffersonville, May 4. New York—Brooklyn, May 1. Massachusetts—Quincy, May 7. New Hampshire—East Westmoreland, May 2. Maine—Portland, May 7. Nova Scottia—

Halifax, May 15. New Brunswick—Fredericton, May 18. Newfoundland—Tompkins, May 17. Quebec—Montreal, May 18. Labrador—Cartwright, May 27. Louisiana—Grande Isle, April 20. Mississippi—Oxford, April 23. Arkansas—Winslow, April 22. Tennessee—Chattanooga, April 19. Kentucky—Russellville, April 25. Indiana—Bloomington, April 28. Ohio—Cleveland, April 29. Michigan—Battle Creek, April 28. Missouri—Independence, April 27. Iowa—Marshalltown, May 3. Wisconsin—Milwaukee, May 1. Minnesota—Red Wing, May 5. Kansas—Wichita, May 2. Nebraska—Red Cloud, May 1. South Dakota—Sioux Falls, May 3. North Dakota—Grafton, May 4. Manitoba—Aweme, May 6; Churchill, June 6. Saskatchewan—Regina, May 8. Mackenzie—Providence, May 16. Colorado—Boulder, May 6. Wyoming—Cheyenne, May 8. Montana—Great Falls, May 12. Alberta—McMurray, May 8. British Columbia—Tetama Lake, May 22. Alaska—Bethel, May 20.

Late dates of the spring departure of transients are: Haiti—Gonave Island, May 15. Cuba—Habana, May 16. Bahamas—Andros Island, May 23. Florida—Daytona Beach, June 1. Alabama—Long Island, May 22. Georgia—Savannah, June 3. North Carolina—Raleigh, June 3. Virginia—Norfolk, June 7. District of Columbia—Washington, June 16. Pennsylvania—Haverford, June 10. New York—Far Rockaway, June 18. Massachusetts—Harvard, June 17. Louisiana—Grande Isle, June 4. Mississippi—Deer Island, May 29. Tennessee—Nashville, June 2. Illinois—Chicago, June 9. Ohio—Cleveland, June 10. Michigan—Sault Ste. Marie, June 5. Ontario—Ottawa, June 12. Missouri—St. Louis, June 6. Iowa—Grinnell, June 10. Wisconsin—Madison, June 13. Minnesota—St. Paul, June 9. Oklahoma—Copan, June 5. South Dakota—Faulkton, June 10. North Dakota—Argusville, June 10. Manitoba—Aweme, June 24. Saskatchewan, Indian Head, June 9. Colorado—El Paso County, June 1. Wyoming—Laramie, May 26. Montana—Great Falls, June 8.

Early dates of fall arrival are: Manitoba—Aweme, August 18. South Dakota—Yankton, August 8. Kansas—Lawrence, September 18. Ontario—Rainy River, August 5. Minnesota—Lanesboro, August 27. Wisconsin—Herbster, August 10. Iowa—Wall Lake, August 28. Missouri—Montier, August 29. Michigan—Detroit, August 20. Illinois—Glen Ellyn, August 23. Ohio—Toledo, August 14. Kentucky—Danville, August 31. Tennessee—Nashville, September 8. Louisiana—New Orleans, September 21. Vermont—Burlington, August 24. Massachusetts—Boston, September 1. New York—Rochester, August 28. Pennsylvania—Berwyn, August 20. District of Columbia—Washington, August 17. Virginia—Charlottesville, August 20. North Carolina—Chapel Hills, September 16. Georgia—Augusta, September 23. Alabama—Birmingham, September 7. Florida—Fort

Myers, September 25. Bahamas—Watling Island, September 28. Dominican Republic—San Juan, September 27. Puerto Rico—Cartagena Lagoon, September 24. Barbados—October 20. Colombia—Santa Marta region, September 29.

Late dates of fall departure are: Alaska—Fort Yukon, September 18. Yukon—Macmillan Pass, September 7. British Columbia—Atlin, August 27. Mackenzie—Leith Point, Great Bear Lake, August 29. Alberta—Edmonton, September 25. Montana—Great Falls, October 3. Saskatchewan—South end of Last Mountain Lake, September 3. Manitoba—Churchill, September 6; Shoal Lake, September 26. North Dakota—Fargo, October 23 (bird banded). Nebraska—Hastings, October 16. Kansas—Lawrence, October 23. Oklahoma—Norman, November 8. Wisconsin—New London, November 4. Iowa—Davenport, October 4. Missouri—La Grange, October 13. Ontario—Ottawa, October 11. Michigan—Grand Rapids, October 29. Ohio—Youngstown, October 21. Illinois—Murphysboro, October 20. Tennessee—Nashville, October 23. Quebec—Fort Chimo, August 23; Montreal, October 6. Newfoundland—Cape Anguille, October 3. Maine—Bath, October 7. Vermont—Wells River, October 17. Massachusetts—Harvard, November 24. New York—Orient, November 20. Pennsylvania—Doyleston, November 7. Virginia—Lexington, October 28. North Carolina—Raleigh, November 6. South Carolina—Mount Pleasant, November 14. Georgia—Athens, November 1. Florida—Clewiston, November 24. Bahamas—Watling Island, November 9. Puerto Rico—Cartagena Lagoon, November 26.

Casual records.—The blackpoll has occurred several times in Greenland. In 1853, one was shot near Godthaab; a juvenile was collected in Isua Lichtenfelsfjord on October 14, 1911, and two more were taken there late in the same month; on October 15, 1911, another juvenile was shot near the Isua copper mine in the Ivigtut District; and on September 18, 1919, a juvenile was shot near Narssarmiut in the Sukkertoppen District. Several occurrences in Bermuda have been recorded: one was seen March 12 to 15, 1901; six were seen October 12, 1929; and one was seen October 21, 1929. On June 17, 1858, an adult male was collected at Collico near Valdivia, Chile. It has been surmised that this may have been an escaped cage bird.

Destruction.—Lighthouses and high buildings have, at times, taken heavy toll of the black-polled warbler and this species is nearly always on the list of those striking. At Sombrero Key, Fla., they have been reported to strike the lighthouse from April 14 to May 20 and from September 25 to November 16. The highest number striking in spring was on May 19, 1887, when 60 birds struck the light, of which half were killed. The fall migration takes a heavier toll, for on the night of October 14, 1887, 160 blackpolls struck, of which 95 were killed, and during the four nights October 14 to 17, 124 birds were killed out of 322 that struck the light. Blackpolls have been reported as seen about the light at Montauk Point, N. Y., from September 29 to October 27, but no figures are available as to the number killed. At Fire Island Light on the night of September 23, 1887, of the 595 birds that were killed, 356 were blackpolls. In the fall of 1920 many were killed around the light at Long Point, Ontario. From September 7 to 29, 236 were killed; 199 of them between September 24 and 29. More lately, on the night of September 10, 1948, four blackpolls were killed by flying against the Empire State Building in New York City.

Egg dates.—Alaska: 3 records, June 10 to 21.

New Brunswick: 38 records, June 10 to July 3; 23 records, June 12 to 20, indicating the height of the season.

New Hampshire: 11 records, June 16 to July 16; 7 records, June 20 to 28.

Quebec: 16 records, June 19 to July 4; 9 records, June 23 to 27 (Harris).

DENDROICA PINUS PINUS (Wilson)

NORTHERN PINE WARBLER

HABITS

Both Wilson and Audubon, referring to its habitat and behavior, called this bird the pine-creeping warbler, a most appropriate name; but each gave it a different scientific name. Audubon's name, *vigorsii*, which stood for many years as the specific name, has given way to *pinus*.

Except on its migrations and some of its summer wanderings, this warbler is essentially a bird of the more open pine woods. In eastern Massachusetts we have always associated the pine warbler with the pitch pines (*Pinus rigida*), with their undergrowth of scrub oak, that cover many miles of sandy barrens on Cape Cod and adjacent regions; where it is a quite characteristic and very common breeding bird. We seldom see it in the denser forests of white pines (*Pinus strobus*) that are the characteristic summer home of the black-throated green warbler. Farther north it is sometimes found breeding in them, but as a general rule it shuns them. Farther west it finds a congenial home in the jack-pine barrens. Elsewhere it frequents Norway pines, red pines, short-leaved pines, scrub pines, and other pines of similar growth. N. S. Goss (1891) writes: "This species, as its name indicates, prefers the pine trees, and usually makes its summer home in the coniferous growths. I have, however, on several occasions met with them during the early summer months in the heavily timbered bottom lands, far away from evergreen trees, and during migration and the winter months they seem to be as much at home in the deciduous trees as among the pines, often visiting the orchards and lowland thickets." Frederick V. Hebard tells me that in the Southern States it shows a decided preference for the longer-leafed pines.

Spring.—The pine warbler is one of the few North American wood warblers whose winter ranges include much of their breeding range; hence its migrations are not much in evidence, except in the northern part of its summer home. West of the Mississippi Valley and in the Great Plains region, where pine woods are scarce or absent, it occurs only as a migrant on its way to the northern pine forests. In the southeastern States it is present at all seasons, and it is an abundant migrant east of the Alleghenies, northward to New England and southern Canada. It begins to migrate from the northern boundary of its winter range during the last week in March or earlier and passes through New England mainly in April. In Massachusetts we regard it as about the earliest of our warblers, usually appearing in advance of the yellow palm or the myrtle warbler; we can always expect it early in April and occasionally before the end of March. As soon as the warm spring sun brings out the fragrance of the pine needles, and the first pink blossoms of the trailing arbutus are peeking out from under their winter covering, we may breathe the delightful odors of the pine barrens, listen to the simple trills of the pine warblers among the treetops, and look for the first of the hermit thrushes in the scrub oaks.

Nesting.—My experience with the nesting of the northern pine warbler is limited to the finding of a few nests in southeastern Massachusetts. These nests have always been in pitch pines in the dry, sandy pine barrens of Plymouth and Barnstable Counties; I have heard the birds singing in isolated groves of these pines elsewhere but have never happened to find a nest there. The nests I have seen have been placed on horizontal branches at heights varying from 10 to 25 feet above ground, for the trees are seldom very tall; a favorite site seems to be on a branch overhanging a road or path. They were usually well concealed in a cluster of pine needles, but were sometimes in plain sight from the road. The nests are well made and compact; and are usually warmly lined with small feathers, as the birds are early nesters; one especially pretty nest was beautifully lined with bluebird feathers.

Forbush (1929) describes the nests as made "of weed-stems, barkstrips, pine needles, pine twigs, caterpillars' or spiders' webs or similar material; lined with pine needles, fern-down, hair, bristles, or feathers." Nuttall (1832) found a nest of this warbler near Mount Auburn in eastern Massachusetts that was about 40 feet from the ground in a Virginia juniper, or red cedar; "it was firmly fixed in the upright twigs of a close branch. The nest was thin, but very neat; the principal material was the wiry old stems of the slender knot-weed (*Polygonum tenue*), circularly interlaced, and connected externally with rough linty fibres of some species of *Asclepias*, and blended with caterpillars' webs."

In the Carolinas, where the northern pine warbler breeds abundantly, the nests are always built in pines at heights varying from 8 to 80 feet above the ground, but more commonly between 30 and 50 feet up. Arthur T. Wayne (1910) has found nests in South Carolina as high as 135 feet in the tallest pines. The nest may be saddled on a horizontal limb, concealed in the needles at the end of the branch, or hidden in a bunch of cones near the top.

Eggs.—The pine warbler lays from 3 to 5 eggs in a set, but usually 4. These are ovate or short-ovate and are practically lusterless. The ground color is white, grayish white, or greenish white, and is speckled, spotted, or blotched with a wide variety of browns, such as "bay," "chestnut," "auburn," "argus brown," "Brussels brown," "Prout's brown," "liver brown," or "chestnut-brown," with undertones of "light brownish drab," "brownish drab," or "vinaceous-drab." The spottings are usually concentrated at the large end, where a loose wreath may be formed by numerous brown specklings, or a solid band of bold blotches or cloudings may be produced. In some cases the drab markings are the more numerous, with a few scattered spots of the darker browns or with a few scrawls of black. Occasionally, on eggs that are spotted with "Brussels brown" or "Prout's brown," the undertones may be a "buffy citrine," instead of the usual drabs. The measurements of 50 eggs average 18.1 by 13.5 millimeters; the eggs showing the four extremes measure **20.0** by 14.0, 19.1 by **14.2**, and **16.5** by **12.6** millimeters (Harris).

Young.—The period of incubation does not seem to be definitely known. Several observers have noted that the male shares with the female the duties of incubation. Both parents are industrious and devoted in the care and feeding of the young. In a nest watched by Dr. T. S. Roberts (1936), "they brought spiders and insects of various kinds, including large green larvae, caterpillars, and flies, many so small they could scarcely be seen even at close range. The supply was gathered almost entirely from among the foliage and cones of the jack-pines near by, and the birds could often be seen dragging the larvae from between the scales of the latter. The larger insects were killed and mashed by pounding them on a large limb before they were brought to the young. The parents came and went rapidly, often once or twice a minute. They sometimes fed the same bird several times in succession."

Plumages.—Dr. Dwight (1900) calls the natal down sepia-brown, and describes the juvenal plumage as "above, drab, shading to hair-brown. Wings and tail deep olive-brown the secondaries and rectrices with greenish gray edgings, the tertiaries and wing coverts edged with drab; two dull white wing bands. Below, olive-gray washed with drab on the throat and sides and indistinctly mottled with deeper gray. Orbital ring white." A partial postjuvenal molt, involving the contour plumage and the wing coverts, but not the rest of the wings or the tail, begins late in July in the north, and produces for first winter birds an entirely different plumage, in which the sexes are first distinguishable. Of the young male, Dr. Dwight says: "Above bright olive-green veiled with drab-gray edgings, the upper tail coverts grayer. Wing coverts black, edged with greenish olive-gray; two white wing bands. Below, including superciliary stripe and orbital ring bright lemon-yellow, fading to dull white on abdomen and crissum, veiled with whitish edgings, the flanks washed with drab-gray, a few concealed dusky streaks on the sides of the breast. Lores and postocular spot dusky." The first winter plumage of the female "is much browner than that of the male, being olive-brown above and pale wood brown below with scarcely a tinge of yellow."

The first nuptial plumage is "acquired by wear which is excessive, birds becoming greener above and greener yellow below by loss of the edgings, the breast streaks being also exposed." The first nuptial plumage of the female is grayer than in the fall, easily distinguishable from that of the male. Old and young birds are now practically alike, except for the duller juvenal wings and tail.

A complete postnuptial molt in July and August produces the adult winter plumages of the two sexes, much like those of the first winter, but yellower, with more streaking and less veiling, in the male and also yellower in the female, the latter resembling the first winter male. Nuptial plumages are acquired by wear, as in young birds.

Food.—A. H. Howell (1932) reports that the examination of seven stomachs of pine warblers, some of which might have been of the Florida subspecies, all taken in Florida, "showed the food to consist largely of insects and spiders, with small quantities of vegetable debris. The insects taken included grasshoppers, grouse locusts, moths and their larvae, beetles, ants and other Hymenoptera, bugs, flies, and scale insects." It has been known to eat the cotton boll weevil, aphids, and the eggs and larvae of other insects. As it obtains most of its food on the pine trees, it is evidently very useful in ridding these trees of the various insect pests that injure them, seeking them in the crevices in the bark of trunks and branches and, in the clusters of needles and under the scales of cones.

It is an expert fly-catcher, but in winter, when insects are not so easily obtained, and probably at other times to some extent, it feeds largely on vegetable food, mainly the seeds of the various pines, but also on wild fruits and berries, such as those of dogwood, wild grapes,

ivy, bayberry, Virginia creeper, and sumac. It is often seen feeding
on the ground probably on grass and weed seeds. Its food habits
seem to be wholly beneficial.

Behavior.—The pine warbler is normally quite deliberate in its
movements, as it creeps in a leisurely manner over the trunks and
larger branches of the pines, searching for insect eggs or larvae in
the crevices in the bark. It clings to or climbs over the trunks as
easily as a brown creeper, and explores the bases of the needle clusters
or hangs from them in the manner of a titmouse. It is quite lively at
times, as it flies from the top of one tree to another, sometimes for a
long distance, or as it darts out into the air after a passing insect.
It frequently feeds on the ground, picking up seeds, grubs or insects;
Ridgway (1889) says that "when on the ground it progresses by a
graceful gliding walk, much after the manner of the Red-poll Warbler (*D. palmarum*)." If disturbed while feeding on the ground, it
flies up and clings to the trunk of the nearest tree; but it is usually
rather tame and approachable. On its breeding grounds it is almost
constantly in song, flying about from tree to tree, and where it is
common, the voices of several may be heard in various directions.
R. E. Stewart (1943) writes:

In late August and September, following the breeding season, these birds show
a drastic change in habits and frequently occur in small flocks around the headquarters buildings. Here they generally may be found associating with Bluebirds (*Sialia sialis*) and Chipping Sparrows (*Spizella passerina*), feeding on the
ground as well as in the bushes and trees of the orchards and landscaped areas.
While watching these mixed flocks it was noticed that the Pine Warblers were
extremely quarrelsome, frequently fighting among themselves, as well as giving
chase to Bluebirds, Chipping Sparrows and, on one occasion, a Vesper Sparrow
(*Pooecetes gramineus*).

Voice.—Aretas A. Saunders contributes the following study: "The
song of the pine warbler is a short trill or series of rapid notes. It is
not loud but is quite musical and pleasing in quality. The notes are
rarely all on one pitch but vary up or down a half tone. The number
of notes, in those songs in which the separate notes are distinct, varies
from 8 to 27, averaging 13. A few songs are made up of a single
trill, that is, the separate notes so rapid that they cannot be counted.

"Of my 17 records of this song, only 2 are all on one pitch, the remainder showing variation. This slight variation in pitch is one of
the characters of this song that distinguishes it from chipping sparrows, juncos, or other species that sing a simple trill. The pitch in
my records varies from A''' to E'''', a range of three and a half
tones. Single songs rarely vary more than a tone and a half. Songs
vary in length from 1 to 2⅗ seconds.

"I have noted no difference that is definite between the songs of
migrating birds and of those on breeding grounds. I have no definite

data on the song period, but in the New Jersey pine barrens birds are still in song in the middle of July."

In New England, pine warblers sing more or less all summer and up to the middle of September or a little later. Francis H. Allen, who has heard one singing while feeding on the ground, tells me: "The ordinary song is, of course, a simple, sweet, liquid trill, but not infrequently I hear a song consisting of two trills, the second pitched lower than the first. On April 18, 1932, at Pembroke, Mass., I heard from a pine warbler a number of times a slow *wip wip wip wip wip*, etc., followed sometimes by the rapid trill of the ordinary song. And on April 17, 1935, at Westwood, Mass., I found several singing in white pine woods with a good deal of variety in rapidity and pitch, and sometimes a downward inflection at the end of the trill. I have noticed on two or three occasions that when the bird sings the bill is opened and closed with each note of the trill and the bird quivers all over, fluttering the wings very noticeably.

"I have heard from a young bird in August a confused, lisping song, warblerlike but not at all like the regular song of the species. From young birds in September I have heard a chatter, while they were being fed, that ended in a heavy note; I recorded it as *tip tip tip tip sip*. The call-note resembles that of the black-poll warbler but, as I have heard it, seems somewhat more prolonged and fainter. Another is a sharp, high *chip* or *tip*, lighter and clean-cut."

Albert R. Brand (1938) records the number of vibrations per second in the song of the northern pine warbler as varying from 5,125 to 3,300, with an approximate mean of 4,150. The latter is the lowest figure for any of the Dendroicae.

Enemies.—The pine warbler seems to be a rare victim of the cowbird; I have been able to find only seven records in the literature.

Harold S. Peters (1936) lists only one tick, *Haemaphysalis leporispalustris* Packard, as an external parasite on this warbler.

Field marks.—The adult male has a bright greenish-yellow breast, greenish-olive upper parts, two whitish wing bands, and white patches at the ends of the two outer tail feathers. The female is duller throughout, with less yellow on the breast. Both sexes are duller and more brownish in the fall. Young birds are very plainly colored, with no bright colors, and are decidedly brown above, but the dull whitish wing bands and white markings in the tail are good field marks.

Winter.—As the pine warbler spends the winter in approximately the southern third of its breeding range, it becomes exceedingly abundant in the southern States at that season. A few hardy individuals occasionally remain in winter as far north as Massachusetts, but the great majority join the resident birds from Virginia and southern

Illinois southward to Florida and the Gulf States. Dr. Chapman (1907) writes: "The pine barrens of Florida have no more characteristic bird than this abundant Warbler. Even on frosty mornings one may hear its trilled monotone rising distinctly above the accompaniment of Palm Warbler *chips*, Bluebird whistles, and Nuthatch chatter. By February 1 they are singing in numbers and to one who is much in the pines, their voice becomes as much an audible expression of the mood of the trees as the sighing of the wind through their branches."

N. S. Goss (1891) says that in Kansas during the winter months, "they seem to be as much at home in the deciduous trees as among the pines, often visiting the orchards and lowland thickets. I found a few wintering in the cypress swamps in eastern Arkansas, also in Florida, where they are quite common, and usually in small flocks."

Referring to the sandhills of North Carolina, Milton P. Skinner (1928) writes: "During the winter these warblers are found in little groups of from two to six individuals. Sometimes a single bird is seen, but when that is the case it is almost always with other birds such as Myrtle Warblers, Juncos, Hermit Thrushes, Bluebirds or White-throated Sparrows. * * * On January 15, 1927, several were seen foraging amid the fallen leaves and pine straw at the edge of a scrub oak forest. Here they tore old oak leaves apart and devoured the eggs and young of gall insects."

DISTRIBUTION

Range.—Southern Canada, the eastern United States and the Bahamas.

Breeding range.—The pine warbler breeds **north** to central Alberta (Athabaska and Flat Lake; possibly Lac la Biche) ; central Saskatchewan (Wingard) ; southern Manitoba (Aweme and Winnipeg); southern Ontario (Rainy River, upper Michipicoten River, Algonquin Park, and Ottawa) ; and southern Quebec (Inlet P. O., Montreal, and Chambley) ; it has also occurred but without evidence of breeding in southeastern Quebec (Esquimaux Bay) ; Prince Edward Island; and New Brunswick (Grand Manan and Fredericton). **East** to southeastern Quebec (Chambley) ; central southern Maine (Bangor and Bucksport) ; and the Atlantic coast south to southern Florida (Miami and Homestead) ; also the Bahamas. **South** to southern Florida (Homestead and Long Pine Key) ; the Gulf coast of Florida, Alabama, and Mississippi to southern Louisiana (Madisonville and Bayou Bara) ; and southeastern Texas (Sour Lake and Conroe). **West** to eastern Texas (Conroe, Waskam, and Texarkana) ; southeastern Oklahoma (Broken Bow and Wilburton) ; eastern Kansas (Hesston and Bendena) ; northeastern Illinois (Riverside) ; southwestern Wisconsin

(North Freedom); north and central Minnesota (Mille Lacs, Gull Lake, and Itaska Park); southern Saskatchewan (Indian Head); and central Alberta (Castor and Athabaska).

Winter range.—The pine warbler winters **north** to northwestern and central Arkansas (Rogers and Hot Springs); central Mississippi (Deemer); north-central Alabama (Birmingham); north-central Georgia (Atlanta); northern South Carolina (Chester); central North Carolina (Charlotte and Raleigh); and southeastern Virginia (Lawrenceville). It has occurred casually in winter north to Memphis and Knoxville, Tenn.; Summersville, W. Va.; Geneva, N. Y.; Morristown, N. J.; and Framingham, Mass. **East** to southeastern Virginia (Lawrenceville); eastern North Carolina (Roanoke Island and Lake Mattamuskeet); the coast of South Carolina (Charleston); Georgia (Savannah); and Florida (St. Augustine, Miami, and Homestead). **South** to southern Florida (Homestead); the Gulf coast of Florida (St. Marks and Whitfield); Mississippi (Biloxi); Louisiana (New Orleans and Chenier au Tigre); and Texas (Houston and Cameron County); and there is a single record for northeastern Mexico (Matamoras).

The range as outlined includes the entire species, of which two races are recognized on the continent of North America. The northern pine warbler (*D. p. pinus*) occupies all of the range except the southern part of the peninsula of Florida where, from Volusia, Lake, and Citrus Counties southward, it is replaced by the resident Florida pine warbler (*D. p. florida*). Other races occur in the Bahamas.

Migration.—Early dates of spring arrival are: Alabama—Shelby, March 18. Virginia—Lynchburg, February 25. District of Columbia—Washington, March 5. Pennsylvania—Swarthmore, March 15. New York—Orient, March 23. Massachusetts—Boston, March 28. New Hampshire—Concord, April 3. Maine—Lewiston, March 30. Quebec—Montreal, May 6. Tennessee—Athens, February 22. Kentucky—Berea, March 29. Missouri—St. Louis, April 11. Illinois—Riverside, April 7. Indiana—Indianapolis, April 17. Ohio—Columbus, March 29. Michigan—Grand Rapids, April 16. Ontario—Toronto, April 13. Iowa—Sabula, April 17. Wisconsin—Reedsburg, April 19. Minnesota—St. Paul, April 17. Manitoba—Aweme, April 17.

Late dates of fall departure are: Manitoba—Aweme, September 25. North Dakota—Fargo, September 18 (bird banded). Minnesota—Hutchinson, October 15. Wisconsin—Trout Lake, October 11. Iowa—Lamont, October 1. Missouri—St. Louis, October 24. Ontario—Ottawa, October 10. Michigan—Ann Arbor, October 25. Ohio—Toledo, October 22. Indiana—Washington, October 27. Illinois—Olney, October 23. Kentucky—Versailles, October 20. Quebec—Montreal, October 18. Maine—Portland, October 17. Vermont—Wells River, October 6. Massachusetts—Martha's Vineyard, November 23. New York—New York, October 29. Pennsylvania—Philadelphia, November 6. Delaware—Dover, November 28. District of Columbia—Washington, October 31. Virginia—Charlottesville, October 22.

Banding.—At Thomasville, Ga., among several wintering pine warblers trapped in January and February 1924, was one that had been banded there the previous year. Several pine warblers banded in Massachusetts have yielded data on longevity: A pine warbler banded at North Eastham on Cape Cod on August 4, 1931, was retrapped at the same station, April 16, 1934; another banded September 1, 1934, was retrapped at the same station on May 27, 1939; another banded at this station on September 7, 1934, was killed by an auto on June 20, 1939, nearby. A pine warbler banded at East Wareham, Mass., on April 16, 1926, was retrapped at the same station on March 29, 1929, and April 9, 1932, being at least six years and nine months old when last seen.

Casual records.—A juvenile was shot at Godthaab, Greenland, on October 1, 1899. There are several records of the occurrence of the pine warbler in Bermuda, usually in small flocks. They were found in the islands September 27, 1849; October 5, 1850; October 15, 1850; March 16, 1875; and October 4, 1930. On October 16, 1930, one came aboard a ship about 100 miles off Cape Hatteras.

Egg dates.—Florida: 23 records, April 8 to May 26; 13 records, April 11 to 27.

Massachusetts: 18 records, May 22 to June 28; 10 records, May 23 to 31.

New Jersey: 23 records, May 9 to June 21; 13 records, May 13 to 30, indicating the height of the season.

North Carolina: 9 records, April 4 to May 1; 5 records, April 14 to 23.

DENDROICA PINUS FLORIDA (Maynard)

FLORIDA PINE WARBLER

PLATE 49

HABITS

C. J. Maynard (1906) described this subspecies as the resident form of southern Florida, from Volusia, Lake, and Citrus Counties to Homestead and Long Pine Key in the southern Everglades. It has a longer bill and the upper parts are slightly more yellowish. It is evenly distributed in the extensive pine forests throughout its range. Arthur H. Howell (1932) says that—

nesting begins late in March or early in April. Nicholson observed two nests in process of construction at Orlando, March 12, 1911, one 30 feet up in a cypress tree, the other 40 feet up in a pine. In the same locality, on April 18, he found a nest containing 4 eggs, 30 feet up in a pine, and 10 feet from the trunk at the end of a branch. The nests are usually near the tips of slender limbs and well concealed in clumps of leaves or bunches of cones. They are deeply cupped, constructed of grass and plant down, with a few pine needles, and neatly lined with thistle down. * * * Examination in the Biological Survey of the stomachs of 7 specimens taken in Florida showed the food to consist largely of insects and spiders, with small quantities of vegetable debris The insects taken included grasshoppers, grouse locusts, moths and their larvae, beetles, ants and other Hymenoptera, bugs, flies, and scale insects.

The eggs of the Florida pine warbler are similar to those of the northern bird. The measurements of 12 eggs average 18.0 to 13.6 millimeters; the eggs showing the four extremes measure 19.0 by 13.1, 18.2 by 14.2, and 16.9 by 13.1 millimeters (Harris).

DENDROICA KIRTLANDII (Baird)

KIRTLAND'S WARBLER

PLATES 50–52

CONTRIBUTED BY JOSSELYN VAN TYNE

HABITS

Kirtland's warbler was not described until 1852; yet the earliest scientific specimen was collected by Dr. Samuel Cabot, Jr., aboard ship near Abaca Island of the Bahamas in the second week of October 1841. Cabot, however, was on his way with John L. Stephens to Yucatán, and he became so preoccupied with his studies of the spectacular tropical birds of a country then entirely untouched by ornithologists that the little Bahaman warbler skin, brought back to Boston and deposited in his collection, remained unnoticed for more than 20 years (Baird, 1865).

On May 13, 1851, Charles Pease at Cleveland collected a male of the still unnamed warbler and gave the specimen to his father-in-law, Jared P. Kirtland, the well-known naturalist. A few days later, Spencer F. Baird, returning to Washington from a scientific meeting in Cincinnati, stopped a day in Cleveland with his friend Kirtland and was given the specimen to take back to the Smithsonian Institution (see Dall, 1915, p. 264). The next year (1852) Baird published his description of the new warbler, naming it *Sylvicola kirtlandii* in honor of Dr. Kirtland, "a gentleman to whom, more than [to] any one living, we are indebted for a knowledge of the Natural History of the Mississippi Valley."

In the following 27 years, five more specimens, four in Ohio and one in southern Michigan, were taken, all during spring migration. Then on January 9, 1879, Charles B. Cory, collecting a specimen on Andros Island of the Bahamas, discovered the winter home of the species. The location of the breeding ground, although many guesses were made about it, remained unknown until 1903, when E. H. Frothingham, of the University of Michigan Museum, and T. G. Gale went trout fishing in Crawford and Oscoda Counties in north-central Michigan. There, on the jack-pine plains, they found numbers of an unfamiliar warbler in full song. They preserved one collected by Gale, and when they returned to Ann Arbor, Norman A. Wood identified it as the still little-known Kirtland's warbler. Wood immediately went north to investigate; on July 8 he found a nest with two young and one egg and on July 9 a nest with five well-grown young (Wood, 1904).

Kirtland's warbler proved to be restricted to the fairly dense stands of young jack-pines (*Pinus banksiana*) that spring up after forest fires. The exact environmental requirements have not been definitely determined; they include a stand of small trees, predominantly jack-pines (though a considerable number of small oaks and other deciduous trees may be scattered among them) and a fairly thick ground cover—usually made up of blueberry (*Vaccinium myrtilloides*), aromatic wintergreen (*Gaultheria procumbens*), bearberry (*Arctostaphylos uva-ursi*), sheep laurel (*Kalmia angustifolia*), sweet fern (*Comptonia peregrina*), or various combinations of these. The warblers first appear in this cover 9 to 13 years after a fire, when the new pines may be barely 5 feet high. The nesting warblers usually occur in very loose colonies varying from a few pairs to hundreds, but isolated pairs have sometimes been found. As the pines grow, they increasingly shade out the ground cover; after 6 to 12 (rarely 15) years, when the pines have become 12 to 18 feet high, the habitat is no longer used by the warblers. A thick, even stand of pines becomes unattractive to Kirtlands sooner than a thin or uneven stand.

Courtship.—Up to the present, apparently, nothing about the courtship of Kirtland's warbler has been published. Verne Dockham, who has watched and recorded the arrival of Kirtlands in Oscoda County for 11 years, believes that the warblers are paired when they arrive on the breeding ground. At least, he reports, he always finds a female with each "first-arrival" male.

On June 8, 1945 (a very late season), northeast of Red Oak, Oscoda County, I watched a pair on their territory all day. The female spent much of her time on or near the ground, apparently searching for a nest site. (Actual construction of the nest began early in the morning, June 10.) The pair kept close together most of the time, with the female—who searched all parts of the chosen area, even the very edge—usually in the lead. The male made a few long flights from one side to the other of the territory, which was roughly circular, measuring 195 yards from north to south and 212 yards from east to west. A number of times (always in the immediate vicinity of the female) the male performed what seemed to be a courtship or display flight. This began at a height of 6 or 8 feet and was made with rapidly beating wings. It was a slow, slightly descending flight, usually carrying the bird directly over the female.

The male sang steadily except on the infrequent occasions when he participated, briefly, in the search along the ground for a nest site. Several times he drove from his territory the males of three adjoining areas. Once this led to a melée of three birds—the intruding male and both birds of the pair I was following—but the action was so fast that I could not tell whether the female took any active part.

Nesting.—The nests are usually very well concealed in the ground cover, often completely arched over by vegetation, with entrance from one side only. They are almost always placed within a few feet (commonly within a few inches) of a jack-pine; occasionally, though still among pines, they are in quite open situations. They are always built directly on the ground and are usually made of dead grass and other such fibrous vegetable materials. Sometimes they are lined simply with finer grasses, but commonly with red sporophyte stalks from moss or with white deer hair. They measure 40 to 45 millimeters inside depth and 48 to 55 millimeters inside diameter.

The nest is constructed entirely by the female, but the male is always nearby and seems to follow the work closely. As Axtell (1938) observed, the approach of a female with nest material is "invariably heralded by a resumption of song on the part of the male." Between June 10 and 13, 1945, near Red Oak, Harold Mayfield and I watched the entire building of a nest. The female (who had searched the whole territory most of the day on June 8) began investigating the site a half hour after sunrise. An hour later she brought what was quite surely the first piece of nest material. Except for short periods devoted to feeding, she worked hard through the remainder of the day, obtaining most of the material at certain favored spots 50 to 70 feet from the site. She made 131 trips that day and 59 on the following, thus completing the main structure of the nest. On the third day she made 7 trips, and on the fourth day 6 trips, for the lining (a total of 203 trips with nest material). The first warbler egg was laid on the fifth day (June 14) about an hour after sunrise.

Unless normal routine is disturbed by a cowbird, the eggs are laid in the early part of the morning and on successive days. Incubation, performed by the female alone, begins with the laying of the third egg. The male brings food for the female at intervals, and she commonly leaves the nest at his approach, meeting him in a nearby pine and fluttering her wings like a young bird. As incubation progresses, the male sometimes comes to the nest to feed his mate. When flushed from the nest, the female usually flutters along the ground in an "injury feigning" display. Incubation routine seems to consist of 10- to 15-minute periods of absence from the nest, alternating with periods of an hour or more on the nest (extremes: absent, 4 to 23 minutes; on the nest, 48 to 112 minutes).

Eggs.—There are usually four or five eggs in a set. Most nests reported with 3-egg sets probably contain incomplete clutches or have been raided by cowbirds; many such nests contain one to three cowbird eggs. The eggs of Kirtland's warbler are ovate to short ovate and are rather variable in color and pattern. They are creamy white or slightly pinkish white, speckled and blotched with "fawn color" and "wood brown." Occasionally the markings are rather uniformly distributed over the whole surface, but usually there is a concentration of markings in a wreath or cap about the larger end. In spite of this great range in markings, cowbird eggs can be distinguished from them by their larger size, more bluish ground color, and the fact that the two ends are marked alike. The eggs of Kirtland's warbler usually measure about 18.5 by 14 millimeters; extremes recorded are: **19.25** by 14.75; **18.0** by 14.75; 18.5 by **15.0**; 18.5 by **14.0** millimeters

Young.—The incubation period is reported by Verne Dockham as 14 days and by L. H. Walkinshaw as 14 to 15 days. My extreme dates for young on the nest are June 9 (1944) and July 17 (1930), but most dates of hatching come between June 11 and June 20. Hatching ordinarily occurs in the early part of the day. The female carries away the eggshells. During the first day or two, the female may stay on the nest much of the time and give to the young the food that the male brings; later both parents feed the young directly. Frequently a male is observed that makes more trips to the nest than the female does. When disturbed at a nest with young, both parents give quite elaborate "injury feigning" displays. The young normally remain in the nest 12 to 13 days. Only one brood is raised, but a second nest is built if the eggs or small young in a first nest are destroyed.

Plumages.—The natal down is "hair brown." The juvenal plumage was described by N. A. Wood (1904) as follows:

Above dark slate color, lighter on the head, each feather tipped with light sepia brown; those of the mantle broadly edged with whitish spots; those of the back, with buffy white; wings and tail dark, slightly edged with light brown; * * * lesser and middle coverts * * * like the back; * * * greater coverts broadly edged with buffy brown, making distinct bars; lores, sepia brown; sides of head otherwise similar in color to the upper parts, but rather paler, fading gradually into pale buffy brown on the chin and throat, this gradually changing to light brown on chest, sides and flank; each feather of the chest and sides with a dark center, widening at the tip, giving a distinct striped effect; abdomen, pale buffy, tinged with yellow.

Early in July the young begin to molt into the first winter plumage, which is apparently similar in the two sexes and is much like the winter plumage of the adult female, except that the young's breast is heavily speckled. This molt does not affect the flight feathers, but the body plumage is completely changed. Wayne (1904) reports collecting an immature male in South Carolina with molt not yet entirely completed on October 29. The prenuptial molt takes place "late in February, and the new plumage is assumed by March 10" Maynard (1896). However, Bonhote (1903) described a male taken March 25 on Little Abaco, Bahamas, as "undergoing a thorough moult of the head and throat." The prenuptial molt involves most of the body plumage but is less complete in first-year birds than in adults. First-year males in May and June show a mottled appearance above, with fresh bluish feathers on the crown and sides of the head and old grayish feathers on the nape and back. Males in their first breeding season are usually distinguishable, even in the field, by the paler yellow of the under parts and the presence of a speckled band (sometimes very faint) across the breast. The type specimen is a first-year male, and Baird (1852), with remarkable acumen, noted that it was "not quite matured." Maynard (1896) described this distinctive first breeding plumage of Kirtland's warbler, but his description has been completely ignored, and the statement is generally made that *Dendroica chrysoparia* (golden-cheeked warbler) is the only *Dendroica* requiring two years to reach the adult plumage. Adults have a complete postnuptial molt (which may begin as early as July 4).

Food.—Kirtland's warblers feed mainly in the small jack-pines among which they nest, but they also hunt insects in the little oak trees among the pines, usually remaining 3 to 8 feet up, and often flying out from a tree to catch an insect on the wing. Sometimes they feed on the ground (especially in the dense pine thickets where the ground is nearly bare) and sometimes in the tops of tall jack-pines, fully 50 feet from the ground. However, one seen near the tops of tall pines is usually a singing male and is perhaps not there primarily in search of food.

N. A. Wood (1904) reported that the food of the Kirtland on its nesting grounds "seemed to be span-worms, living upon jack pines, and a small light-colored span-worm moth." He "saw the warblers capture these moths during flight," and he shot a male Kirtland that had a deer fly in its mouth. Leopold (1924) wrote: "The food consists largely of centipedes, worms, and caterpillars. However, the birds also eat deer [flies] and horse flies, grasshoppers, crickets, white and dusky millers, with relish. . . . The birds also eat or drink the white pitchlike fluid which exudes from the branches of the pine."

My own observations indicate that the Kirtland's food consists of several kinds of Lepidoptera (adults and larvae), tabanid flies, winged ant-lions, small Orthoptera, and other insects. The young are first fed principally on little green and little reddish caterpillars, but after a few days, moths, adult ant-lions, and other winged insects are brought to them. Feces are usually eaten (by both parents) in the first days, later carried away.

Food is apparently very easy to get in the Michigan jack-pine country. In fact, we can probably say that, within the breeding area of this warbler, food supply is never a critical factor. Parents feeding young will often do much of their hunting within 30 or 40 feet of the nest. It is even common to see a warbler leave the nest after feeding, pick up some insects within a yard or two of the nest, and turn back immediately to feed the young again.

Kirtland's warblers have apparently never been seen drinking water, and they refuse water offered to them experimentally near the nest. However, as Leopold noted, they sometimes take drops of liquid pitch from the surface of jack-pines, and I have seen one eagerly pick up and eat drops of black automobile lubricant it found on a twig near its nest.

Behavior.— C. J. Maynard (1896) reported that Kirtland's warbler is a shy bird while in its winter range in the Bahamas, but all observers comment on its tameness in the Michigan nesting area. However, there is great individual variation. Some nesting pairs are much tamer than others, and it is common to find one member of a pair definitely tamer than its mate. Leopold (1924) found the males of two pairs much tamer than the females, and one male actually ate from his hand. L. H. Walkinshaw found a very tame female at a nest, with eggs, near Red Oak on June 21, 1932. As he lay on the ground near the nest, the bird hopped around on him and even allowed herself to be caught in his hand and banded. Her mate would not come near. Southeast of Mio in June 1944, I had similar experience with a female warbler. The bird frequently alighted on me as I inspected the nest, and if I found her on the nest when I wanted to examine the young, I usually had to push her off with my finger. She not only hopped about on the nesting-area map, which I once laid on the ground near by, but she even hopped into my open box of bird bands, picked up a string of bright yellow celluloid bands and flew up into a tree with them.

A very noticeable characteristic of Kirtland's warbler is its habit of "wagging" its tail (actually, the tail is jerked downward and then—

more slowly—returns). The mannerism is more pronounced when the warblers are disturbed or excited, but it is quite conspicuous at all times.

Although they nest in a very dry habitat, often miles from any surface water, they nevertheless take water-baths. One June 21, 1944, an hour after sunrise, I watched a male about 6 feet up in a small oak among the pines take repeated baths by splashing among the heavily dew-laden leaves—singing in the intervals between baths. (The temperature was 47° F.) He finally flew over to a jack-pine and began to shake himself and preen his feathers—still singing at regular intervals.

On June 15, 1943, about 3 hours after sunrise, I watched a female sun bathe. Perching about 5 feet above the ground on the southeast side of a small jack-pine, she tilted her body sidewise, fluffed her feathers, and thus basked in the sun for a minute or two.

Voice.—Song is an important factor in this warbler's life and also in our efforts to study the species. The males sing so loudly and so persistently that they are easily found even in the thick cover they usually frequent. Fortunately, Axtell (1938) has published a good account of the song and of the warbler's habits while singing. He writes:

Even at * * * the nest-building season, there were frequent periods * * * when no sound was heard for several minutes from * * * the six or more males. If any one individual was observed constantly for some time, it was noted that there were frequent intervals of silence * * * even in the early morning. * * * After a period of silence lasting from half a minute to an hour or more, a bird might sing two or three repetitions of its song or might remain vocal for more than half an hour. During the singing period the song, itself less than two seconds in length, was commonly repeated with considerable regularity at intervals of from eight to twelve seconds. But here, also, some irregularities might frequently be injected. * * *

At this season, each male did a great deal of his singing while patrolling his territory, sometimes alone, at other times accompanied by his mate. Her presence or absence on these tours did not seem to determine whether or not he sang. I observed one singing from a stick within a foot of the ground and another nearly fifty feet up in the tip-top of one of the tallest trees in his territory. The greater part of the singing was done from the branches of the dense growth of ten-foot-high jackpines, perhaps several songs from one branch and only one song from the next, while the bird fed between. One individual interspersed preening with rather evenly timed singing while perched nonchalantly almost within arm's reach of me. Any dead tree, rising above the level of the pine-tops, seemed often to influence a bird to perch and sing from one of its higher branches, sometimes for several minutes, whether the tree were near his nest or in the farther reaches of his territory. On a later trip through the same part of his domain, the bird might choose to do his singing from a different dead tree nearby, or might ignore such high perches in that vicinity until a later round.

It is remarkable how persistently the males will sing in spite of all sorts of unfavorable factors. On a clear day at the height of the season they may begin singing as much as 40 minutes before sunrise, and they may sing until sunset. They will sing in spite of temperatures as low as 25° F., and even a pouring rain may not stop them. They sing wherever they are—in the trees, on the wing during a flight from one tree to another (though their mouths may be full of insects they are taking to the young), on the ground (though this is rare), and even on a perch within a foot of their nest and young. When singing most steadily, they commonly repeat the song about seven times a minute. Early in the morning I have counted, during such singing, 237 to 250 songs per hour.

None of the various syllabifications that have been used to describe the song is very satisfactory. Perhaps this is not remarkable, for (as shown by the sound-film record made by the Cornell party) there may be more than 100 up or down slurs in one second, and pitch changes of several tones in less than one-hundredth of a second. Axtell (1938) very rightly compared the song with that of the northern waterthrush (*Seiurus noveboracensis*) and the house wren (*Troglodytes aëdon*), saying that they "are the most likely sources of confusion" in the identification of Kirtland's warblers by song. "The Water-thrush's song starts high and descends; the Kirtland's starts low, goes higher, and may end either high or low. As compared with the wren, the warbler's song is shorter, of fewer notes, and has a more definite beginning and ending." "The *loudness* of the song is one of its most outstanding characteristics. In the bird's desolate jack-pine haunts it may be heard from a quarter to a half mile. Its liquid, bubbling quality, and its lively, emphatic manner of delivery seem to be invariable features." Axtell adds that the Kirtland has the lowest-pitched song of any of the eastern Dendroicas.

I have sometimes noticed a Kirtland change his style of song, but only rarely after the early part of the season. Most individuals have quite characteristic songs, and after spending a few days in a given area of the nesting range, one can recognize by his song the owner of every territory within earshot.

A strange characteristic of Kirtland's warbler is its habit of singing incomplete songs. Occasionally a song will be broken off abruptly at any point and for no apparent reason. Sometimes an incomplete song is followed almost immediately by a complete one.

Rarely I have found a male that has an extremely aberrant song—quite unrecognizable as that of a Kirtland. Two males that I noted in Oscoda County (June 16, 1941, and June 6, 1944) had songs that were harsh, completely unmusical "rattles," reminding me somewhat of a cowbird. Another male (noted June 1, 1945) gave a simple trill very like that of the field sparrow (*Spizella pusilla*) except that it suddenly increased in speed toward the middle and dropped slightly in pitch near the end.

Kirtland's warblers usually scold very little unless the provocation is great. They use a note for scolding described by Axtell (1938) as varying from *tsyip* to *tshyook*, and like the "common scolding note of the Oven-bird" (*Seiurus aurocapillus*). Adults use a low *churk* to arouse the nestlings at feeding time. On the Kirtland's wintering grounds in the Bahamas, Maynard (1896) heard only a "harsh chirp."

Unlike many warblers, this species continues to sing throughout the incubation period and even while raising the young. However, most individuals have stopped entirely, or almost entirely, by mid July; late records are July 24, 1939 (Verne Dockham, Oscoda County), and August 1, 1932 (Leonard Wing, Crawford County).

Field marks.—Kirtland's warbler is a large, rather slow-moving warbler, described by Peterson (1939) as "gray above and yellow below, with some large sparse spotting on the breast and sides. * * * The bird *wags* its tail much like a Palm Warbler; no other *gray-backed* Warbler has this habit." (As previously noted, the "wagging" is an up-and-down motion.) After their first winter, the two sexes are easily distinguished even in the field; males, especially if fully adult, are more blue above than females, and the black in front of their eye and about the base of their bill (absent in females) always gives the appearance of a dark mask. Kirtland's warblers are usually discovered by hearing the song, and a study of Axtell's excellent description (1938) should enable an observer with previous experience of bird song to recognize a Kirtland readily.

In fall, even the adult plumage is very brown above, and all plumage markings are less distinct; few people are able to identify a fall-plumaged Kirtland in the field.

Enemies.—There have been oddly contradictory statements about the adverse factors in the life of Kirtland's warbler. In his first paper on the species, N. A. Wood (1904) mentioned the fires that sweep the jack-pine plains, and in a later paper he (1926) stated that "fire is without doubt the greatest menace to the Kirtland warbler colonies, since it destroys the habitat as well as the nests of the birds." It is, of course, quite true that a fire, if it occurs in their breeding area before mid July, will destroy the nests in its path. However, since this warbler nests exclusively in the dense stands of jack-pine that spring up after a fire, one can truly say that fires are the Kirtland's greatest need. Not only do fires in the older jack-pine stands result in suitable nesting conditions, but fires that occur in areas largely covered with red and white pine (never inhabited by the Kirtland's) promote the spread of jack-pine. Completely successful fire prevention can actually extirpate Kirtland's warbler from a given region—as happened recently in Alpena and Kalkaska Counties.

Leopold (1924, p. 57) was probably correct in considering the cowbird the most important enemy of Kirtland's warbler. As indicated, a very large number of Kirtland nests are parasitized by the cowbird; frequently the competition is too great, and the warbler young do not survive. However, there seems to be no reason to share Leopold's fear that the cowbird "may soon" exterminate this warbler. It is probable that the major changes that have been observed in the number of Kirtland's are the result of changes in the amount of suitable habitat in Michigan or in the Bahamas.

I have seen a female cowbird spend hours apparently watching a female Kirtland building a nest. The nest was entirely unguarded when the warbler was not actually working on it, and as soon as the main structure was finished—even before the lining was added—a cowbird (presumably the one that had been watching the nest-building) came early in the morning and laid in it. After watching many hours at recently completed, or nearly completed, Kirtland nests, I would judge that cowbirds laying in a Kirtland's nest during this early part of the cycle, which is the period most favorable for the cowbirds' chances of producing young, run very little risk of detection and attack. But after the warbler has begun incubation, the nest is rarely left unguarded, and the female warbler will attack violently and drive away any cowbird she finds in the vicinity.

The only predator I have actually observed to kill a Kirtland's warbler is the sharp-shinned hawk (*Accipiter striatus velox*), although the conditions were not natural in that instance, for the warbler was in a trammel net. However, this hawk, as well as Cooper's hawk (*Accipiter cooperi*) and, more frequently, the marsh hawk (*Circus cyaneus hudsonius*), occur regularly in the habitat of Kirtland's warbler, and they undoubtedly take an occasional warbler. Crows (*Corvus brachyrhynchos*) and blue jays (*Cyanocitta cristata*), common in jack-pine areas, presumably rob the nests of this warbler as well as of other birds. Red foxes (*Vulpes fulva*), red squirrels (*Sciurus hudsonicus*), spermophiles (*Citellus tridecemlineatus*), and masked shrews (*Sorex cinereus*) are potential mammal enemies that occur regularly in the warbler habitat. I have some reason to attribute a few cases of nest destruction to red squirrels or to spermophiles. Nesting female Kirtland's, under observation from a blind, have shown great excitement at the approach of a shrew, and have attacked it and driven it away.

Ants seem to be a serious enemy of the nestlings. The parents, especially the female, pay much attention to guarding the young against ants and can be seen frequently picking the ants from the nestlings' bodies. If parent birds are kept away from a nest for more than a few minutes when the temperature is fairly high and the ants active, the biting ants cause the young to squirm and jump about violently. Ants collected from a Kirtland's nest near Clear Lake, Montmorency County, June 27, 1935, were identified by Frederick M. Gaige as *Crematogaster lineolata*. Kirtland's warblers seem to be very free of external parasites. It is rare to find even Mallophaga on them.

Fall.—Soon after the postnuptial molt begins, the males cease to sing, and this, as well as the inactivity of both adults and young during the molt, makes them extremely difficult to find. Few observers have ever seen a Kirtland's warbler later than July. Verne Dockham believes that after July they largely leave the jack-pine habitat; he has several times seen them in August, always near the ground, in the adjoining hardwood. The only known Michigan specimens taken later than September 1 are several in the Max M. Peet collection found in jack-pine near Luzerne September 5 to 9, 1916, and one male found September 28, 1919, in jack-pine seven miles south of Houghton Lake village. Kirtland's warbler has never been recorded in Michigan in the fall south of the jack-pine plains.

Winter.—Charles B. Cory (1879), who discovered the winter home of Kirtland's warbler when he collected a female on Andros Island in the Bahamas on January 9, 1879, reported that its actions resembled those of the myrtle warbler and that it seemed to prefer the thick brush. Its stomach contained insects. However, most of our knowledge of the winter habits of this species is derived from C. J. Maynard's account (1896) of his experience with it in the Bahamas in 1884:

Kirtland's Warblers are shy birds of solitary habits, for never in any case did I find two together. They inhabit the low scrub, preferring that which is only three or four feet high, but retire at night to roost in the higher, more dense shrubbery near the spots which they frequent during the day. Those taken were, with one or two exceptions, found in an exceedingly limited area, within a mile or two of the city, and always in old fields grown up to low shrubbery. I have never heard Kirtland's Warbler sing, the only note that they uttered was a harsh chirp, with which they greeted me when alarmed at my approach. When one was not secured at first sight, it generally retreated into the bushes and silently disappeared. The thick and tangled character of the scrub rendered any quiet or swift pursuit impossible, thus a retreating bird was never seen again that day, and a number seen escaped in this way.

As with many shy birds, however, these warblers presented strange exceptions to the usual rule; twice at least as I was making my way through the thickets in search of the Greater Yellow-throat, I was confronted by a Kirtland's Warbler. In both instances the birds appeared from out of the thicket within a yard of my path, remained a few seconds then darted off into the scrub.

The earliest autumn record for the Bahamas seems to be November 13 (1891, Eleuthera) ; and the latest spring record, April 25 (1887, New Providence).

Twomey (1936) has made the interesting point that the temperature and rainfall conditions in the Bahamas during the period December through April are very similar to those in the Kirtland's range in Michigan during the breeding season.

DISTRIBUTION

Breeding range.—Kirtland's warbler breeds in Michigan **north** to Montmorency County (Clear Lake), **east** to Alpena County (southwest of Alpena) and Iosco County (west of Oscoda), **south** to Ogemaw County (west of Rose City) and Clare County (northwest of Harrison), and **west** to Wexford County (north of Manton) and Kalkaska County (northeast of Kalkaska).

Winter range.—The winter range is restricted to the Bahamas. The species has been recorded from: Abaco, Little Abaco, Berry, Eleuthera, New Providence, Athol, Andros, Watling, Green Cay, and Caicos Islands.

Migration.—Early dates of spring arrival are: Florida—West Jupiter, April 27. Georgia—Cumberland Island, April 12. South Carolina—St. Helena Island, April 27. Missouri—St. Louis, May 8. Ohio—Avondale, May 4; Columbus, May 8; Cleveland, May 13. Illinois—Glen Ellyn, May 7. Indiana—Wabash, May 4. Ontario—Toronto, May 16. Minnesota—Minneapolis, May 13. Michigan—Ann Arbor, May 6; Oscoda County, May 8.

Fall dates are: Ontario—Point Pelee, October 2. Ohio—Holland, September 22; Columbus, September 11. Virginia—Fort Myer, September 25. South Carolina—Chester, October 11; Mount Pleasant, October 29; Charleston County, October 4.

Egg dates.—Michigan: 40 records, May 28 to June 30 (July 17 in the case of a second nesting after the destruction of the first set of eggs).

DENDROICA DISCOLOR DISCOLOR (Vieillot)

NORTHERN PRAIRIE WARBLER

PLATES 53, 54

HABITS

The common name of this bird is a decided misnomer, as it is not to be found on the real prairies of the Middle West. Perhaps it was given the name because it has been found on the so-called prairies or flat, grassy lands among scattered trees in the southern States in winter. Wilson and Audubon both used the name, but neither of them knew the bird very well, and their accounts of its nesting habits are decidedly erroneous.

The prairie warbler is one of the birds that has benefited by settlement of the country, for the clearing away of the forests has provided suitable habitats for it in brushy clearings and open sprout lands. Consequently, it has greatly extended its range and increased in abundance until now it is a very common bird in certain favored localities. Its range is quite extensive in the eastern United States, but its distribution is very spotted and its numbers seem to vary considerably from year to year. Dr. F. A. E. Starr wrote to me a long time ago that the prairie warbler had "of late years" extended its range into Ontario; he first met with it in 1916. It seems to have been very erratic in its appearance since then, for Dr. Paul Harrington, of Toronto, writes to me: "At Wasaga Beach (Simcoe County), bordering Georgian Bay, the prairie warbler was a common bird in 1914–15. In 1919 the birds were becoming rarer, and in 1924 only two males were observed and only one deserted nest found. In 1937 the birds were again fairly common, although in nothing like their former abundance. The birds have decreased yearly since then, and in 1941 only one singing male was heard. The birds occupied only a narrow strip covered with ground juniper, bordering the shore line. These birds have never been observed in other apparently suitable habitats further inland."

I have noted a decided increase in the numbers of prairie warblers in southeastern Massachusetts during the past 40 years. In the region where I formerly hunted, we were lucky if we could find one or two nests in a season; but in 1944 we could find as many as a dozen in a day, if we searched thoroughly. And, driving along the old country roads anywhere, if we happen to pass a brushy hillside, or an old clearing that has grown up to sprout land, we are almost sure to be greeted by the thin crescendo notes of this warbler, a most distinctive and easily recognized song.

Brewster (1906) gives this attractive sketch of the haunts of this warbler near Cambridge, Mass.:

Many and delightful were the days I used to spend looking for nests of the Prairie Warbler in the hill pastures of Arlington and Belmont. These breezy uplands are attractive at any season, but most so in early June when the barberry bushes blossom. This is the time when our Prairie Warblers have full sets of fresh eggs. A search for their nests among the handsome, dome-shaped barberry bushes, covered with young foliage of the tenderest green, and with graceful, pendant clusters of golden yellow flowers that fill the air with fragrance and attract myriads of droning bees, is a fascinating and memorable experience, whatever be its material results.

Dr. Coues (1888) describes a well-populated locality near Washington, D. C., as follows: "The locality is along the Potomac River, on the Virginia side, about seven miles from the city, among some small hills from which all the large trees have been cut away, and which are now grown up to a thick scrub of hickory, dogwood, and laurel (*Kalmia latifolia*), with here and there a few young pines and cedars. Here we found breeding within a small area an astonishing number of the birds, perhaps more than fifty pairs."

On the pine barrens of Cape Cod, Mass., where the prevailing trees are pitch pines (*Pinus rigida*), more or less widely scattered, the prairie warbler finds a congenial summer home in the undergrowth of scrub oaks. Similar haunts are frequented on the pine barrens of New Jersey and farther west and south, where the shortleaf pine (*Pinus echinata*) is the characteristic tree. In such places the pine warblers live mainly in the pines and the prairie warblers in the underbrush, both birds being usually found wherever such conditions prevail, each in its own sphere.

Spring.—Dr. Chapman (1907) writes of the spring migration: "From its winter home in the West Indies and Florida, the Prairie Warbler begins to move northward early in March, though the full tide of migration does not start until the last of the month.

"The latest records of striking the southern lighthouses are in the first half of May and the earliest spring date is March 7. Thus the period of spring migration in the southern United States extends through more than nine weeks."

Territory.—We have sometimes found as many as a dozen pairs of prairie warblers nesting within a limited area, but we have never seen any such concentration as that mentioned by Coues. Forbush (1929), however, says: "Although it breeds occasionally in colonies, the nests are widely scattered, and each male seems to patrol a certain small territory to which he lays claim, and where he is always ready to give battle to any rival who encroaches on his section; but if danger in the shape of some enemy threatens the family of any one of them, the entire colony soon joins in protesting the invasion or threatening the invader."

Nesting.—In our egg-collecting days of long ago, we used to find plenty of nests of the chestnut-sided warbler in the fringe of low hazel bushes that lined the old country roads in Rehoboth, Mass. What few nests of the prairie warblers we found were in the more extensive sprout lands or on the brushy hillsides, well back from the roads. But in 1944 we were surprised to find that the prairie warblers had almost entirely replaced the chestnut-sided and were nesting in the hazel thickets along the road sides. The nests were artfully concealed in the densest parts of the foliage, about 2 or 3 feet about the ground, and could be seen only by parting the bushes. Other nests were found where woods had been cut off or burned over and a low growth of deciduous saplings had sprung up, mixed with tangles of blackberries and sweet fern. One nest was only 20 inches from the ground, well-hidden in a thick clump of sweet fern; others were in oak, poplar, wild apple, or cherry, or maple saplings, seldom over 3 or 4 feet above the ground, and often plainly visible. On the pine barrens of Cape Cod we find the nests in the leafy tops of the scrub oaks, and at similar heights among the pines.

Of the nests found by Dr. Coues (1888) near Washington, D. C., one was about 2½ feet up in a triple prong of a low laurel bush; another was 5 feet from the ground in a blackberry bramble, "made almost entirely of dandelion down, closely felted, and further secured with a few straws, and is stuccoed over outside with small dry leaves. The inside is copiously lined with red cowhair, making a marked color contrast with the other materials." A third was placed in a very young pine, about 1½ feet from the ground and against the main stem. Another was in an unusual situation, in a mass of grapevine twigs, about three feet from the ground.

Harold H. Bailey (1913) says that, in Virginia, "the earliness or lateness of the season has much to do with the location of their nests. Late springs, when the foliage is retarded and little shelter or protection is given the nest, it is invariably placed in a clump of holly scrub, or wax myrtle, whose foliage remains green throughout the entire winter. Sometimes I have found them in a small sapling cedar, placed near the trunk and ten feet from the ground, other times equally as high or higher, on a horizontal limb of a tree on the edge of a clearing."

T. E. McMullen has sent me the data for 14 nests found in New Jersey, 11 of which were in hollies in large woods. Richard C. Harlow tells me that on the coast of Virginia the prairie warbler nests commonly at heights of 10 or 15 feet in pines; he found one occupied nest 25 feet up and 10 feet out near the end of a horizontal pine limb. In North Carolina, according to Pearson and the Brimleys (1919), this warbler "seams to prefer sweet-gum saplings as nesting trees near Raleigh, nine out of seventeen nests examined by C. S. Brimley having been thus situated. Two were in elms, two in huckleberries, and one each was found in pine, sumac, black haw and *Ilex decidua*." All the Ontario nests referred to in notes from Dr. Starr and Dr. Harrington were in clumps of low junipers, 1 to 3 feet above the ground.

Edward R. Ford writes to me: "One of the few localities in the Chicago region in which it nests does not seem to be well selected. On the sunny, wind-swept shore dunes of Lake Michigan, in Porter

County, Ind., the sandcherry (*Prunus pumila*) forms a sparse cover on slope and crest. Two or three feet up in this slight vegetation, whose smooth stems afford only a precarious fastening for the nests, several have been found. The writer noted one which had slipped from its place and spilled the four eggs unbroken on the sand."

A typical nest before me, collected in Taunton, Mass., was well concealed, only 20 inches above the ground, in a cluster of branches and twigs in a dense clump of sweetfern, close beside a woodland path in a burnt-over woodlot growing up to sprout land. It is well and compactly made of very fine grayish plant fibers, a little very fine grass, some fine shreds of soft inner bark and a quantity of buff-colored down from cinnamon ferns, as well as some other soft, gray, downy substances, all firmly bound with spiders' silk. It is lined with soft, gray and white hairs and a few small white feathers. Externally it measures 3 by 2¾ inches in diameter, and about 3¼ in height; the inner diameter averages about 2 inches, and the cup is nearly 2 inches deep.

Eggs.—Three to five eggs, usually four, constitute the full set for the prairie warbler. The eggs vary in shape from ovate to short ovate, with occasionally a tendency toward elongate-ovate. They are only slightly lustrous. The ground color is usually white, some-times creamy white or slightly greenish white. They are spotted or speckled with "chestnut," "auburn," or "russet," with underlying marks of "brownish drab." Some eggs are marked only with the brown shades; others have the drab undertones predominating. Some eggs are spotted with "Mars brown" and "mummy brown," with un-dermarkings of "deep mouse gray," but this type of marking is not as common as the reddish-brown shades. Usually a distinct wreath is formed at the large end where the spots are concentrated. The meas-urements of 50 eggs average 15.9 by 12.3 millimeters; the eggs showing the four extremes measure **17.6** by 13.2, 15.9 by **13.8, 14.7** by 11.7, and 16.3 by **11.2** millimeters (Harris).

Young.—The period of incubation is probably about 14 days, and the young remain in the nest about 10 days (Burns, 1915b and 1921). It would seem as if the incubation period might be somewhat shorter and the nest life a little longer, but accurate data appear to be lacking. The female probably does all the incubating and brooding, but both parents feed the young and take good care of them. The nest life does not seem to have been carefully studied.

Plumages.—Dr. Dwight (1900) describes the juvenal plumage, in which the sexes are alike, as "above, dull olive-green, browner on the pileum. Wings and tail clove-brown edged with dull olive-green; two wing bands buff. Below, dull brownish white, pale straw-color on the abdomen. Sides of head drab; eyelids white."

The postjuvenal molt, involving the contour feathers and the wing coverts, but not the rest of the wings or the tail, begins about the middle of July. He describes the young male in first winter plumage as "above, grayish olive-green, an area of concealed chestnut on the back. Wing coverts black, edged with olive-green; two wing bands white. Below, pale canary-yellow, streaked on the sides of the throat and breast with dull black veiled by yellowish edgings. Malar stripe and transocular streak grayish black; orbital ring, suborbital region and obscure superciliary stripe white, yellow tinged; auriculars mouse-gray." The female "is browner above and paler below with fainter streaking; the auriculars and transocular streak being grayer, the chestnut on the back a mere trace; the wings and tail are duller."

The first nuptial plumage is acquired by a partial prenuptial molt, "which involves chiefly the crown, sides of head, chin and throat but not the rest of the body plumage the wings nor the tail, as shown by specimens taken in Jamaica, W. I., November 27th, December 30th, January 3d, 13th, 19th, 24th and 31st. * * * The black auriculars and transocular stripe and the yellow feathers of the superciliary stripe, the chin and throat are assumed, wear bringing the chestnut of the back into prominence. Young and old become practically indistinguishable." The female is similar, but the yellow is paler, the streaking less extensive and the chestnut fainter.

Adults have a complete postnuptial molt in July and a partial prenuptial molt, as in the young birds. Winter adults are like the first winter birds, but the colors are richer and deeper.

Food.—No very comprehensive study of the food of the prairie warbler seems to have been made. However, the stomachs of 15 prairie warblers collected in Puerto Rico by Dr. Wetmore (1916) were found to contain 100 percent animal matter in percentages as follows: Hemiptera, 43.78; Coleoptera, 16.00; Hymenoptera, 3.82; Diptera, 0.35; spiders, 19.59; and miscellaneous, 3.76. Mr. Forbush (1929) says that it takes quantities of plant-lice and some grasshoppers and locusts.

Behavior.—The prairie warbler is a lively little bird, very active in pursuit of its insect prey, and quite demonstrative in the defense of its nest, flitting about in the vicinity of the intruder and sometimes becoming quite bold or inquisitive. It is not particularly shy. Francis H. Allen (MS.) says that it "has a habit of twitching its tail nervously from side to side, as it hops and flits among the bushes. I have seen it catching flies on the wing and, also, taking insects from the tops of low bushes by hovering before them with blurred wings like a hummingbird." The tail-wagging of the prairie warbler is not so pronounced or so persistent as with the palm warbler, with longer intervals between these motions. Although it is essentially a bird of the underbrush and low growths, where it obtains most of its food, it often selects a singing perch near the top of a fair-sized tree.

Voice.—Aretas A. Saunders has sent me the following careful study of the song of this warbler: "The song of the prairie warbler is the most distinctive one I know in the genus *Dendroica.* It consists of a series of notes rising gradually higher in pitch to the end of the song. They are separated and distinct from each other and not run together in a trill or linked in 2-note phrases. The quality is sibillant, but pleasingly musical and of medium loudness.

"Songs vary considerably in details. The change in pitch between the lowest and the highest notes of the song varies all the way from one to five and a half tones, averaging two and a half tones. While the first note of the song is the lowest in pitch, it is not always true that each succeeding note is a little higher, but often the first few notes are all on the lowest pitch. There may be anywhere from 1 to 6 notes on this lowest pitch before the rise in pitch begins. My 35 records show that 2, 3, or 4 notes on the low pitch are more frequent than only 1. The number of notes per song varies from 5 to 13, averaging 9. When 5 or 6 notes, at the beginning, are all on the same pitch, more than half of the song is over before a rise in pitch begins. In all but 4 of my records the last note stands alone as the very highest, but in 2 records there are 2 highest notes at the end, and in 1 there are 4. Only a single record has the next to the last note the highest, and in that record the last note drops to a pitch lower than the note at the beginning.

"The pitch varies from A''' to G sharp'''', half a tone less than an octave. The upward grading of pitch is usually in half-tone steps, but is sometimes less regular, and in 10 of my records are quarter tones, that could not be played on a piano or any graded instrument.

"In a majority of records the notes are all of equal length, but in 9 records the first 3 to 6 notes are longer and slow, and the last notes shorter and about twice as fast. Songs vary greatly in the rapidity of the notes. The length of songs varies from $1\frac{2}{5}$ to $2\frac{3}{5}$ seconds. The longest song, in time, contains only 9 notes, whereas the largest number of notes, 13, took $2\frac{1}{5}$ seconds.

"The period of song lasts from the arrival of the bird in migration to the middle of July. In only four seasons have I had opportunity to hear this song in July. These show an average date of July 17 for the last song, extreme dates being July 14 and July 24. Rarely the bird revives its song in early September. In most years it is apparently entirely silent at this season."

Francis H. Allen writes to me: "I found one singing in the same pasture with a field sparrow and singing a song that puzzled me until I got a view of the singer. Comparing the songs of the two birds, I found that the opening four notes, all on the same pitch, were almost precisely alike except that the warbler's were simple, *tee, tee, tee, tee*, while the sparrow's were slightly dissyllabic, *t'wee, t'wee, t'wee, t'wee*. The pitch, tone, and quality were the same. The rest of the warbler's song went up the chromatic scale characteristically, while the sparrow's ended with a descending trill. The two birds kept near together and sang antiphonally, or apparently so. This seemed like a clear case of imitation on the part of the prairie warbler." More likely this was one of the variations in the warbler's songs, as described by Mr. Saunders, rather than an imitation.

Field marks.—The prairie warbler should be easily recognized, as it is distinctively marked, with its bright-yellow under parts, more or less streaked with black on the sides, two yellowish wing bands, and largely white outer tail feathers. The chestnut marks on the back are not always very conspicuous. Females and winter birds are not much different, merely duller in colors. The song is easily recognized.

Enemies.—The northern prairie warbler is a common victim of the cowbird. Dr. Friedmann (1929) had 10 records from its limited range, in the eastern States. Harold H. Bailey (1925) says that the nest is often abandoned after the cowbird's egg is laid in it, but that "often this warbler has been known to construct a false bottom over the Cow-bird egg, and any of her own that were in the nest, as well, and start laying again." Harold S. Peters (1936) lists as external parasites of the northern prairie warbler a louse, *Ricinus pallens* (Kellogg), and a tick, *Haemaphysalis leporis-palustris* Packard.

Fall.—In Massachusetts, the southward migration begins early. As soon as the young are fully grown the family parties wander about in the brushy pastures during July, and after molting some of them start south before the end of that month. The migration is well under way during August, very few remaining in September. In the more southern States, the migration continues from the middle of August until the first week in November. It has been recorded in northern Florida as early as July 27, and has struck the light on Sombrero Key as early as August 1 and as late as November 4, indicating a much-prolonged migration season.

Winter.—A few northern prairie warblers may winter in the southern half of Florida, but probably most of the wintering birds in Florida are of the southern race. The main winter home of the northern birds is in the Bahamas and the West Indies. C. J. Maynard (1896) writes: "The Prairie Warblers were very abundant in the dense thickets on the island of Key West during the autumn and early winter of 1870. They frequented the drier portions of the Key but did not sing." Those that he reported in the mangroves along the coast of the mainland were probably Florida prairie warblers, which are known to frequent such localities. The following remark perhaps refers to both forms: "The Prairie Warbler is by far the most abundant of all the genus on the Bahamas, even as far south as Inaugua, throughout the winter, remaining as late as the last week in April. They are found everywhere, in pine woods, scrublands, fields, and even among the mangroves of the little outlying keys. I found them also abundant about Kingston, Jamaica, and a few on Cayman Brac from March 23d to the 28, 1888, but these were evidently migrating and do not remain long." Dr. Wetmore (1916) says:

In Porto Rico these birds occur at the highest altitudes (above Aibonito, at 2,000 feet), and are found in brushy growths, in pastures where there are thickets, and along the hedges of emajagua (*Paritium tiliaceum*). Dry, brushy growths back of the beaches also are favorite places, and many live in the dry forests of Vieques. In spring there was a marked diurnal movement toward the west, and on Vieques there were distinct waves of migration on March 19 and March 27. Another was noted on Culebra Island on April 9. In each case the birds were in company with many other warblers. * * * The prairie warbler is apparently much more common as a migrant than as a true winter visitant.

DISTRIBUTION

Range.—Eastern United States and the West Indies.

Breeding range.—The prairie warbler breeds **north** to northeastern Kansas (Lake Quivira); central Missouri (Columbia); southeastern Iowa (Lee County); northeastern Illinois (Peoria and Chicago); central Michigan (Berrien County and Lovells); southern Ontario (Honey Harbor, Wasaga Beach, and St. Williams); central New York (Schenectady); southern New Hampshire (Concord and Manchester); and northern Massachusetts (Haverhill). **East** to the Atlantic coast from northeastern Massachusetts (Haverhill) to southern Florida (Miami and Key West). **South** to southern and western Florida (Key West, Fort Myers, and Cedar Keys); central Georgia (Macon and Columbus); south central Alabama (Autaugaville and Greensboro; and northern Louisiana (Monroe). **West** to central northern Louisiana (Monroe); central and western Arkansas (Hot Springs, London, and Winslow); northeastern Oklahoma (Tulsa and Ponca); and northeastern Kansas (Lake Quivira). Occurrences of the prairie warbler in summer have been recorded north to central Iowa (Polk County and West Liberty); southeastern Wisconsin (Madison and Appleton); northern Michigan (Hillman); central Ontario (Frank's Bay and Lake Nipissing); north-central New York (Holland Patent); and southern Maine (Sanford and Little Green Island). The first known occurrence in Ontario was in 1900, and it now breeds to the shore of Georgian Bay.

Winter range.—The prairie warbler is found in winter **north** to southern South Carolina rarely (Beaufort and Charleston, occasionally Bulls Island); the Bahamas (Nassau, Watling, and Caicos); the Dominican Republic (Samaná); the Virgin Islands (St. Thomas); and the Lesser Antilles (Anguilla Island). **East** to the northern Lesser Antilles (**Anguilla, Barbuda, and Antigua.**) **South** to Antigua Island; Puerto Rico; Hispaniola (Gonave Island); Jamaica; the Swan Islands; Banco Chinchorro, Quintana Roo; occasionally south to Corn Island, Nicaragua. **West** to the islands off Quintana Roo (Banco Chinchorro and Cozumel); western Cuba (Isle of Pines and Habana); western Florida (Key West, Sanibel Island, Tarpon Springs, and Gainesville); and southern South Carolina (Beaufort).

The range as outlined includes two subspecies or geographic races. The northern prairie warbler (*D. d. discolor*) inhabits all the breeding range except the mangrove swamps of southern Florida from New Smyrna and Anclote Key southward where it is replaced by the Florida prairie warbler (*D. d. collinsi*).

Migration.—Last dates of spring departure from the winter home are: Virgin Islands—St. Croix, April 3. Puerto Rico—Mayagüez, April 23. Haiti—Grande Cayemite Island, April 13. Cuba—Habana, May 8. Bahamas—May 13 (struck light). Mississippi—Edwards, May 30.

Early dates of spring arrival are: Florida—De Land, March 13. Alabama—Prattville, March 30. Georgia—Savannah, March 8. North Carolina—Chapel Hill, April 1. Virginia—Lawrenceville, April 5. West Virginia—Bluefield, April 22. District of Columbia—Washington, April 12. Pennsylvania—Philadelphia, April 23. New York—New York City, April 25. Massachusetts—Danvers, May 1. Louisiana—Monroe, March 30. Mississippi—Gulfport, April 6. Arkansas—Delight, April 7. Tennessee—Chattanooga, April 5. Kentucky—Bowling Green, April 6. Missouri—St. Louis, April 11. Indiana—Wheatland, April 15. Ohio—Fremont, April 11. Michigan—Ann Arbor, May 2. Ontario—Toronto, April 17. Wisconsin—Madison, April 23. Oklahoma—Norman, April 22. Kansas—Lake Quivira, April 28.

Late dates of fall departure are: Wisconsin—Milwaukee, October 8. Missouri—St. Louis, September 23. Michigan—Detroit, September 30. Ontario—Point Pelee, September 5. Ohio—South Webster, October 8. Indiana—Waterloo, September 26. Illinois—Chicago, October 4. Kentucky—Bowling Green, October 15. Tennessee—Tate Spring, September 25. Louisiana—Monroe, September 21. Mississippi—Deer Island, October 29. New Hampshire—Jaffrey, September 1. Massachusetts—Martha's Vineyard, October 6. New York—Far Rockaway, September 28. Pennsylvania—Philadelphia, October 18 (struck city hall tower). District of Columbia—Washington, October 3. Virginia—Salem, October 9. West Virginia—Bluefield, October 13. North Carolina—Raleigh, October 10. Georgia—Fitzgerald, October 22. Alabama—Anniston, October 15. Florida—Sombrero Key, November 6 (struck light).

Early dates of fall arrival are: Mississippi—Bay St. Louis, July 22. Florida—Pensacola, July 20. Bahamas—Maraguana, August 8. Cuba—Cienfuegos, August 16. Puerto Rico—Coamo Springs, September 7. Virgin Islands—St. Croix, September 10.

Casual records.—There is a single record of the occurrence of the prairie warbler in Bermuda, a specimen collected on October 3, 1848. On October 23, 1924, a prairie warbler came aboard a ship about 300 miles north of Puerto Rico and after about five minutes aboard it flew off toward Puerto Rico.

Lighthouses.—The prairie warbler is frequently reported to strike lighthouses in Florida, usually in small numbers. At Sombrero Key they have struck during the periods from March 7 to May 12, and from August 1 to November 4, with 47 the largest number for a single night during the fall migration, but on the night of April 3, 1889, 150 struck the light of which 25 were killed. The keeper reported that the birds struck between midnight and 4 a. m. and that at the time a light rain was falling. At Alligator Reef they have been reported only in fall from August 22 to September 29. On the night of September 29, 1889, during a rainstorm, 190 struck of which 19 were killed. Many struck at Sand Key on August 13, 1902, and a few at Dry Tortugas Island on April 14, 1909.

Egg dates.—Florida: 10 records, April 23 to June 25; 5 records, May 12 to June 2.

Massachusetts: 56 records, May 29 to June 21; 36 records, June 4 to 11, indicating the height of the season.

New Jersey: 51 records, May 17 to June 13; 35 records, May 24 to June 6 (Harris).

DENDROICA DISCOLOR COLLINSI (Bailey)

FLORIDA PRAIRIE WARBLER

PLATES 55

HABITS

When Harold H. Bailey (1926) described this southern race, he called it Collins's warbler, after an old Florida collector. The A. O. U. Check-List adopted Bailey's scientific name but discarded his common name. He describes the type as having " a much lighter yellow breast, and throat almost white at base of lower mandible; with less reddish on back; which is decidedly grayish. The males lack the heavy wide black markings on sides, the heavy orange on throats; and the heavy reddish backs; all so pronounced on the northern breeding birds."

He adds: "Our Prairie Warbler of Dade and Monroe Counties, Fla., seems rather out of place as a breeding bird in our hardwood hammocks and amongst the mangrove Keys."

The 1931 A. O. U. Check-List states that it breeds "in mangrove swamps on the coast of Florida from New Smyrna and Anclote Key southward." Arthur H. Howell (1932) says of it:

The Florida Prairie Warbler lives in a habitat very different from that chosen by its northern relative (*discolor*), being almost wholly restricted to tracts of mangroves bordering the coastal sloughs or marshes. At New Smyrna, R. J. Longstreet found several nests in small mangrove bushes growing on the borders of a marsh. One observed May 3, 1925, partly finished, contained one egg on May 16, but later was deserted. The nest was composed of grayish colored plant fibers, shreds of bark, and pieces of twine, and was lined with very fine shreds of palmetto fiber of a brownish color, and a few feathers. E. J. Court collected a set of 3 eggs on Palm Key, near Cape Sable, March 29, 1925. Nevin J. Nicholson reports a nest in process of construction in the top of a 20-foot mangrove tree at Fort Lauderdale, June 6, 1925. D. J. Nicholson noted a nest at Eifers, June 16, 1929, 11 feet up in a mangrove, and a newly made nest at the same place, May 10, 1931.

On Anclote Key, May 21, 1918, we heard a dozen or more of these Warblers singing, and collected several specimens in breeding condition. The birds are rather shy during the nesting season; the males sing from near tops of small mangrove trees and manage to keep well hidden in the foliage. The song sounds to my ears essentially like that of the northern birds—a series of drawled, shrilling notes on an ascending chromatic scale, uttered rather rapidly, with the bill pointing nearly straight upward. * * *

Examination of the stomachs of 10 specimens taken in Florida showed the food of this species to consist largely of moths and their larvae, beetles, bugs, flies, and spiders. Grasshoppers, tree-hoppers, ants and other Hymenoptera, and scale insects were eaten in smaller quantities, and one bird had picked up a fragment of a small bivalve.

Charles E. Doe has sent me the data for three sets of eggs of the Florida prairie warbler, collected by him on the west coast of Florida; the nests were all in red mangroves, all over water, and from 6 to 10 feet above it.

The measurements of 16 eggs average 16.3 by 12.0 millimeters; the eggs showing the four extremes measure **16.8** by 12.1, 16.2 by **12.7, 15.9** by 11.8, and 16.0 by **11.1** millimeters (Harris).

DENDROICA PALMARUM PALMARUM (Gmelin)

WESTERN PALM WARBLER

PLATE 56

HABITS

Charles Lucien Bonaparte (1832) remarks: "This is one of those lively, transient visitants, which, coming in spring from warmer regions, pass through the middle states, on their way to still colder and more northern countries, to breed. From the scarcity of the species, its passage has hitherto been unobserved; and it is now, for the first time, introduced as a bird of the United States. Authors who have heretofore made mention of it, represent it as a permanent resident of St. Domingo, and other islands of the West Indies, and even describe its nest and habits, as observed there."

Bonaparte evidently did not notice the difference between the western and the yellow palm warblers, perhaps assuming that the latter was the spring plumage and the former the winter bird. It remained for Ridgway (1876) to point out the differences and separate the two subspecies. This is not strange, for the western bird is known to us mainly as a migrant and winter resident, its summer home being in central Canada, with a southward extension into northern Minnesota and Wisconsin. The 1931 A. O. U. Check-List does not include Wisconsin in its breeding range, but Francis Zirrer writes to me that it "is not overly rare during the summer" near Hayward, Wis. "Here the bird is a dweller in the cedar-tamarack-spruce bogs, and from its arrival in spring (early May) until its departure in fall (early October) it is rarely seen anywhere else. Probably because of this, because of the scarcity of interested observers, and because of the fact that high water in spring and early summer makes our bogs not easily accessible, the bird has more or less escaped the attention of Wisconsin ornithologists. After its arrival I see it feeding mostly in cedars and black spruces; later, when the tamaracks sprout new green, most of its searching for food is done there. Toward the end of August, when the breeding season is over and until its departure, it visits other trees, especially poplars, but even then only those close to the bog."

A. L. Rand (1944) records it as "a common summer resident, breeding, in northeastern British Columbia, 150 to 160 miles northwest of Fort Nelson along the Alaska Highway." He also mentions a specimen in the National Museum at Ottawa, "taken at Bernard Harbor, Dolphin and Union Straits, Sept. 28, 1915 by Fritz Johansen."

Spring.—The migration routes of the two races of the palm warbler are interesting. The yellow palm spends the winter in the Gulf States and crosses the more southern Alleghenies to migrate northward along the Atlantic coast to northern New England and southern Canada, while the western palm, leaving its winter home in Florida and the West Indies, crosses the Alleghenies in the opposite direction seldom as far north as the Carolinas, and migrates northward through the broad Mississippi Valley to Canada. Casual wanderers have, of course, occurred outside of these limits, but the main routes are as outlined. In Illinois, according to Ridgway (1889), "during the spring migration this is one of the most abundant of the Warblers, and for a brief season may be seen along the fences, or the borders of fields, usually near or on the ground, walking in a graceful, gliding manner, like an *Anthus* or *Seiurus*, the body tilting and the tail oscillating at each step. For this reason it is sometimes, and not inappropriately called Wag-tail Warbler."

Nesting.—The main breeding grounds of the western palm warbler are in central Canada, where only a few nests have been found. Probably the first recorded nest is the one mentioned by Ridgway (1889) in this brief statement: "Mr. Kennicott found a nest at Fort Resolution, in Arctic America. It was on the ground, on a hummock, at the foot of a small spruce tree in a swamp. When discovered (June 18), it contained five young."

In more recent years nests have been found in Alberta. A. D. Henderson writes to me: "The western palm warbler is a scarce breeder in the muskegs in the vicinity of Belvedere. Richard C. Harlow took a nest and five eggs in the moss of a muskeg on June 12, 1923. I was with Dick Harlow and Dick Rauch on June 11, 1924, in a muskeg when Rauch flushed a western palm warbler from a nest and five eggs. On June 16, 1924, Harlow took a nest and five eggs near the place he took the nest in 1923." Harlow tells me that his nest of June 11, 1924, was taken 12 miles west of Belvedere in a dry muskeg among scattered spruces and tamaracks. It was very well concealed at the base of a spruce seedling under a clump of dry grass growing near the top of a large hummock of sphagnum moss. The female flushed at about 2 feet, and the five eggs were three-quarters incubated. The nest was constructed of plant fibres, fine dry grass, and fine bark shreds, and was lined with feathers of the gray ruffed grouse.

Dr. L. H. Walkinshaw (MS.) reports a nest found at Fawcett, Alberta, "built a short distance from a bordering brushy area, in the sphagnum moss of the muskeg country, sunken into the moss at the base of a small dwarf birch." And a set of five eggs in the Doe Museum in Florida, was taken by T. E. Randall at Grassland, Alberta, on May 23, 1933, from a nest "a few inches from the ground in a tiny spruce."

Dr. T. S. Roberts (1936) mentions six cases of actual, or probable, nesting of the western palm warbler in northern Minnesota, and shows a photograph of a nest in Aitkin County. And Zirrer's notes show conclusively that the species breeds in northern Wisconsin.

Eggs.—The palm warbler lays 4 or 5 eggs; apparently 5 eggs are fully as common as 4. The eggs are ovate, sometimes tending toward short-ovate or elongate-ovate. They are only slightly glossy. The ground color is white or creamy white, and they are spotted, speckled or blotched with "chestnut," "bay," "auburn," or "Brussels brown," with undertones of "brownish drab" or "light Quaker drab." They vary from eggs delicately sprinkled to those marked with large blotches and/or a few scrawls of black. Generally the spots are concentrated and form a wreath around the large end. The eggs of one set in the Museum of Comparative Zoology are creamy white, very delicately speckled with "wood brown," and one egg is almost immaculate. The measurements of 15 eggs average 16.7 by 13.1 millimeters; the eggs showing the four extremes measure 17.5 by 13.2, 16.5 by 13.7, and 16.0 by 12.7 millimeters (Harris).

Young.—Nothing seems to have been reported on incubation, brooding or care of the young nestlings of the western palm warbler, but Zirrer writes to me: "Once out of the nest, the young birds sit scattered on convenient branches, practically always a tamarack, and as a rule not more than 4 to 8 feet above the ground, waiting for the old birds to bring food. Before long, however, they begin to move with a creeping or sliding motion along the branches, usually from near the end of the branch toward the trunk; they fly, at first clumsily, from there to the nearest convenient branch or twig and creep or slide again, all the while picking at something. Ours here must have been infested with vermin, probably Mallophaga, as they would stop every once in a while and pick vigorously at the feathers and especially under the wings. Although they are soon able to find their own food, the old birds still feed them occasionally until the end of August.

Plumages.—The plumages and molts of the western palm warbler are apparently the same as those of the yellow palm warbler, to which the reader is referred. The western bird always has less yellow than the eastern.

Food.—Zirrer (MS.) writes: "Although I have watched these birds every summer since the spring of 1940, I am still unable to tell much about their food. I see them occasionally find and eat small green caterpillars, but most of the time I see them picking something from the twigs of the tamaracks without being able to tell what it is, although I have examined a number of twigs. I see them also hang on and examine cones on tamaracks two and more years old, even those on dead, dry trees, but what they find there I am unable to say. They like various berries, especially raspberries, however."

A. H. Howell (1932), referring to Florida, says: "R. W. Williams at Tallahassee, in October, 1904, observed large numbers of Palm Warblers feeding on cotton worms. F. M. Uhler, in studying the bird's food habits in the celery fields around Sanford, found the destructive celery leaf-tyer in nearly all the 23 stomachs examined, amounting to 73 percent of the total contents. Other items found in the stomachs were flies, 12.7 per cent; Lepidoptera (mainly cutworms), 6 per cent; and Hymenoptera, 7 per cent."

Robert H. Coleman (Judd, 1902) wrote to the Biological Survey that he counted the number of insects that one of these birds caught and found that it varied from 46 to 60 per minute. He writes: "He spent at least four hours on our piazza, and in that time must have gathered in about 9,500 insects." This warbler spends much time feeding on the ground, where it probably picks up some spiders and seeds.

Behavior.—The most characteristic trait of the palm warbler is its habit of almost constantly wagging its tail up and down, like a pipit, even while flitting about in the low trees. Strangely enough, Kirtland's warbler, the only other species of the genus *Dendroica* that habitually nests on ground, has the same habit. The palm warbler spends much of its time on the ground, where it has been said to walk with a gliding motion, but to me it seems to hop or run, though its little feet move so rapidly that it is not easy to see just which it does. W. B. Barrows (1912) writes of its behavior in Michigan:

Although entirely unlike the Yellow-rumped Warbler in appearance, the two species have many points in common, and the present bird is equally fond of the ground, where it alights constantly for food, hopping about in search of seeds and insects, very much like a sparrow. It is usually found in flocks sometimes as many as fifty together, though more often in small squads of six to ten. It frequents the edges of fields, the borders of woods and the sides of hedges and roads, but is often seen frequently in open fields, particularly in the wetter parts of cattle pastures, where it perches on weed-stalks or on the ground, and when alarmed flies to the nearest fence, where it sits, wagging its tail up and down in a manner entirely unlike that of any other warbler.

Zirrer says in his notes: "For weeks after the young are able to fly, the family still roosts every night in the evergreens near where the nest was situated. They quit feeding and retire comparatively early, nearly an hour or so before dark. Any attempt to follow them there causes them to become highly nervous, to fly around and above a person's head and to chirp excitedly and loudly, until one leaves them alone and moves away."

Voice.—Several writers have likened the song of the palm warbler to that of the chipping sparrow or junco. Prof. Lynds Jones (1900) recognizes the resemblance, but remarks: "The trill remains as a prominent feature, but the note is no longer a true chip. Better *tsee tsee tsee tsee*, with a distinct swell. Each syllable should be given a half double utterance except at the middle of the swell, where the greater effort seems to completely coalesce the half double quality into one distinct syllable. There is a little similarity to the song of Myrtle Warbler, but lacking the liquid quality of that species." Dr. Leonard W. Wing (1933) gives a good description of the songs of this warbler:

On its breeding grounds, the palm warbler was heard to have two distinct songs and an ordinary warbler *chip*. The first song, which appears to be song of the mated or nesting bird, is delivered from a favorite perch, generally the tallest pine in the bird's territory. It is given with the body erect, the head thrown back and the tail pointing straight down. I have written the song as *hee''-u hee''-u hee'-u hee'-u.* The first notes are delivered slowly; the last two a little more rapidly; they are higher pitched and accented as indicated. The whole song, however, is delivered in a slow, unhurried manner. The tone is rich, soft, and liquid. It has a cool, distant quality.

The second song, which may be the courting song, is almost indistinguishable from the songs of the Pine Warbler or the Eastern Chipping Sparrow. Indeed, it bears a striking resemblance to the song of the Slate-colored Junco and Myrtle Warbler. However, the Pine Warbler sings only from the taller, older trees; the Western Palm Warbler prefers the fresh growth. The song is a trill, sweeter and more musical than the song of the Eastern Chipping Sparrow and stronger than the song of the Pine Warbler. It is generally given while the bird is moving (sometimes very rapidly) through the jack pine. The singing bird stays in the same territory, though he circles a great deal. Occasionally a feeding bird bursts out with this song. It is heard oftener than the song first described. I have written it *weet weet weet weet*, with no inflection.

Field marks.—The western palm warbler looks like a washed-out yellow palm warbler. The reddish-brown crown is duller, and there is little yellow anywhere except the paler yellow on throat and under tail coverts and the greenish-yellow rump; the brownish-gray wing bars are not conspicuous. In fall and winter birds the colors are still duller, but the rump and under tail coverts are still yellowish, and there is a whitish line over the eye. The bobbing tail is always diagnostic.

Enemies.—This northern breeding race is apparently rarely imposed upon by the cowbird. Dr. Friedmann (1934) says that "Mr. T. E. Randall found two parasitized sets in Alberta."

Fall.—Zirrer (MS.) writes of the association of these warblers with chickadees in late summer and fall: "Soon after their own breeding season is over, toward the beginning or middle of July, the chickadees make steady companions of various species of warblers with similar feeding habits, here the myrtle and, especially, the palm warbler. I do not remember a day, from the time the young palm warblers are out of the nest until their departure in fall, without seeing the chickadees as their steady companions.

"Later, when the palm and myrtle begin to stray with other warblers (and also other birds) of similar feeding habits throughout the neighborhood, the call of a chickadee means that a flock of warblers is close at hand. All one has to do is to wait a few moments, watch and listen; and there they come, palms, myrtles, magnolias, several vireos, a tree creeper, an occasional nuthatch, and, of course, a flock of chickadees. This goes on until the middle of October, when the last of the warblers, the myrtle, has gone south. This may be observed not only in our bogs and their immediate neighborhood, but throughout all of our woodlands."

N. A. Wood (1911) tells of a heavy migration of western palm warblers across Saginaw Bay, Mich. The first one was seen on August 24, and the numbers increased in successive migration waves of small birds, until the third wave "occurred on the night of September 18, and on the morning of the 19th the species was very abundant. There must have been thousands of individuals about the light-house, where they fed partly on flies that collected on the window screens and sides of the house, and apparently also on ground insects and possibly seeds of the beach grasses." These birds all passed on, and another big wave came on October 5. "Among the birds in this movement there were thousands of this species and of the myrtle, and large numbers of black-throated blue, and black-throated green warblers, American redstarts, juncos, vesper sparrows and a few horned larks."

The western palm warbler is an abundant fall migrant through the broad Mississippi Valley to the Gulf States where it turns abruptly eastward into Florida, crossing the fall route of the yellow palm warbler. Although the main route is southward, chiefly west of the Alleghenies, its trend is more eastward than the spring route. In Massachusetts it occurs fairly regularly, though rarely, in fall; and it is commoner in western Pennsylvania and in South Carolina in fall than it is in spring, though it spends some winters in small numbers in the latter State. During the fall migration it frequents old brush-grown fences, hedge rows, brushy fields, and open pastures, spending most of its time in low trees or bushes or on the ground, often in company with the flocks of migrating sparrows, juncos, and other ground feeders.

Winter.—Although the western palm warbler's winter home is mainly in Florida, Cuba, and the West Indies, it is a hardy bird and has been found in winter far north of its main winter range. Forbush (1929) gives a number of December and January records for Massachusetts, and a January record for Grand Manan, New Brunswick. As a winter visitant in South Carolina, it seems to be irregular; Wayne (1910), strangely enough, says that "it appears more frequently during severe winters than in milder ones." Dr Eugene E. Murphey (1937) calls it abundant in the middle Savannah Valley, in southern Georgia, arriving in October and departing early in April, "and is to be found in low grassy damp meadows and particularly in the cotton fields after the cotton has been picked and the leaves have fallen."

The western palm warbler is one of the characteristic small birds in all parts of Florida in winter. In the regions where I have spent the winter it is a common dooryard bird, hopping or running about on the lawns or flitting through the shrubbery and low trees, even in the city yards and gardens. It is about the only small bird to be seen so close to houses. It seems to obtain most of its food on the ground, but it also inspects the tiny yellow blossoms in the center of the circle of bright red leaves of the poinsettias, where it may find some food. It is an inconspicuous little bird while foraging among the dry, brown leaves, but the frequent wagging of its tail betrays it.

Mr. Howell (1932) writes: "The Palm Warbler is a prominent feature of winter bird life in Florida, and in many places it is the most abundant species, often occurring in loose flocks numbering 50 or more. The birds are found in a variety of situations—hammocks, prairies, marshes, pine flats, old fields, cultivated lands, town yards, and even the Gulf beaches."

Dr. Barbour (1923) calls this warbler the commonest bird in Cuba during the winter months. "Its bobbing tail may be seen by every dusty roadside, along fences, in pastures, gardens and in the very cities themselves—if there be a park with any cover. They come in September and retire late in April, the males having begun to assume the nuptial dress just as they leave. The birds seem to be such an essential part of the Cuban winter landscape that it is hard to believe that they are not natives."

The palm warbler is equally common, really abundant, in nearly all the Bahama Islands in winter, according to several observers. It frequents the vicinity of the seashore, the scrub fields and pastures, the neighborhood of houses and gardens, and even the streets of the cities and towns.

DISTRIBUTION

Range.—Canada to the West Indies.

Breeding range.—The palm warbler is known to breed at least **north** to southern Mackenzie (Simpson, Providence, and Resolution); northern Saskatchewan (north shore of Athabaska Lake near McFarlane River); northern Manitoba (Churchill); central Quebec (Fort George, Mistassine Post, and Piashti); and central Newfoundland (Grand Lake, Bever Lake, and Gander). **East** to Newfoundland (Gander) and Nova Scotia (Baddeck, Halifax, and Barrington). **South** to southern Nova Scotia (Barrington); southern Maine (Mount Desert Island and Auburn); southern Quebec (Montreal); southern Ontario (Ottawa, rarely, and Sault Ste. Marie); northern Michigan (Lovells); possibly northern Wisconsin (Ladysmith); northern Minnesota (Aitkin, Cass Lake, Itaska Park and Thief Lake); southern Manitoba (Indian Bay and Lake St. Martin); central Saskatchewan (Cumberland House, probably, Emma Lake, and Flotten Lake); central Alberta (Flat Lake, Boyle, and Glenevis); and northeastern

British Columbia (Trutch and Miniker River). **West** to northeastern British Columbia (Miniker River and Fort Nelson) and southwestern Mackenzie (Simpson). Judging from the data on migration of the palm warbler the northern limit of the breeding range is in the unexplored regions to the north, possibly the limit of trees.

The palm warblers which occupy the range as outlined are divided into two geographic races: the western palm warbler (*D. p. palmarum*) breeds **east** to central Ontario, while the eastern part of the range is occupied by the yellow palm warbler *D. p. hypochrysea*).

Winter range.—The palm warbler winters regularly **north** to central Louisiana (Alexandria); central Alabama (Prattville); northern Georgia (Atlanta and Athens); and northern South Carolina (Chester). It is casual in winter north to Bicknell, Ind.; Columbus, Ohio; Toronto, Ontario; Doylestown, Pa.; Garden City and Shelter Island, N. Y.; and Martha's Vineyard, Mass. **East** to South Carolina (Chester and Charleston); eastern Georgia (Savannah and Brunswick); eastern Florida (Fernandina, St. Augustine, New Smyrna, and Miami); the Bahama Islands (Nassau, Watling, and Caicos); Hispaniola (Sánchez); Puerto Rico (San Juan); and the Virgin Islands (St. Croix). **South** to the Virgin Islands (St. Croix); Jamaica; and Providence Island. **West** to Providence Island; northern Honduras (Roatán Island); Quintana Roo (Bauco Chinchorro); Yucatán (La Vega and Progresso); and Louisiana (Chenier au Tigre and Alexandria).

The two races of the palm warbler tend to cross each other's routes in migration. The eastern form is more abundant in the western part of the winter home, while the western form is commoner in southern Florida and the West Indies.

Late dates of departure from the winter home are: Puerto Rico—San Juan, April 8. Dominican Republic—Samaná San Thomé, May 12. Cuba—Cienfuegos, May 6. Bahamas—Andros, May 2. Florida—Daytona Beach, May 10. Alabama—Birmingham, May 8. Georgia—Darien, May 18. Louisiana—Ruston, April 22. Mississippi—Rosedale, April 30.

Early dates of spring arrival are: Virginia—Charlottesville, March 27. West Virginia—Bluefield, April 3. District of Columbia—Washington, March 26. Pennsylvania—Harrisburg, March 16. New York—New York, April 2. Massachusetts—Harvard, March 30. Vermont—Rutland, April 6. Maine—Dover-Foxcroft, April 2. Quebec—Kamouraska, April 25. Nova Scotia—Bridgeton, April 14. New Brunswick—Saint John, April 13. Prince Edward Island—Tignish, May 2. Newfoundland—Tompkins, May 11. Tennessee—Nashville, March 20. Illinois—Chicago, April 8. Indiana—Goshen, April 17. Ohio—Toledo, April 13. Michigan—Lansing, April 18.

Ontario—Toronto, April 23. Missouri—St. Louis, April 5. Iowa—Sigourney, April 17. Wisconsin—Madison, April 14. Minnesota—St. Paul, April 17. Kansas—Lawrence, April 27. Nebraska—Lincoln, April 16. South Dakota—Huron, April 16. North Dakota—Fargo, April 25. Manitoba—Aweme, April 30. Wyoming—Torrington, May 10. Montana—Great Falls, May 14. Alberta—Glenevis, May 5.

Late dates of the departure of spring transients are: North Carolina—Weaverville, May 12. Virginia—Charlottesville, May 31. District of Columbia—Washington, May 13. Pennsylvania—McKeesport, May 20. New York—Rochester, May 26. Massachusetts—Boston, May 21. Vermont—St. Johnsbury, May 28. Tennessee—Knoxville, May 31. Kentucky, Bowling Green, May 20. Illinois—Yorkville, June 1. Ohio—Austinburg, May 31. Missouri—Montgomery City, May 21. Iowa—Independence, May 26. Wisconsin—Madison, June 1. Nebraska—Stapleton, May 12. South Dakota—Sioux Falls, May 25. North Dakota—Fargo, May 24.

Early dates of fall arrival are: North Dakota—Fargo, September 7. Wisconsin—Ladysmith, August 24. Iowa—National, August 31. Michigan—Sault Ste. Marie, August 9 (bird branded). Illinois—Chicago, August 30. Indiana—Waterloo, August 31. Ohio—Leetonia, August 28. Kentucky—Bowling Green, September 4. Mississippi—Bay St. Louis, September 25. Louisiana—New Orleans, October 24. New Hampshire—Hanover, September 8. Massachusetts—Monterey, September 1. New York—Rochester, September 4. Pennsylvania—Doylestown, September 6. District of Columbia—Washington, September 4. West Virginia—Bluefield, August 28. North Carolina—Chapel Hill, September 11. South Carolina—Marion, September 2. Georgia—Atlanta, September 12. Alabama—Anniston, October 8. Florida—Fort Myers, September 4. Bahamas—Nassau, October 1. Cuba—Habana, September 20. Dominican Republic—Ciudad Trujillo, October 5. Puerto Rico—Guanica Lagoon, October 24.

Late dates of fall departure are: British Columbia—Buskwa River, near Fort Nelson, September 16. Alberta—Glenevis, October 10. Montana—Great Falls, September 18. Wyoming—Laramie, November 14. Manitoba—Aweme, October 13. North Dakota—Argusville, October 16. South Dakota—Lake Poinsett, September 27. Minnesota—Minneapolis, October 11. Wisconsin—Elkhorn, November 3. Iowa—National, October 22. Missouri—Montier, October 17. Ontario—Moosonee, September 24; Port Dover, October 25. Michigan—Calumet, September 29. Illinois—Urbana, October 31. Indiana—Indianapolis, November 16. Ohio—Toledo, November 11. Kentucky—Versailles, October 27. Newfoundland—Tompkins, October 4. Prince Edward Island—North River, September 15. Quebec—Hatley, October 16. New Brunswick—Scotch Lake, October 29. Nova Scotia—Yarmouth, October 15. Maine—Portland, October 27₄ Vermont—Wells River, October 27. Massachusetts—Martha's Vineyard, November 21. New York—Orient, November 18. Pennsylvania—Jeffersonville, November 13. District of Columbia—Washington, November 20. West Virginia—Bluefield, November 15.

Banding.—While not many palm warblers have been banded, a few interesting records have been obtained. A western palm warbler was banded on October 9, 1932, at North Eastham, Cape Cod, Mass.; and seven weeks later, November 28, 1932, it was caught in a house at Point Verde, Placentia, Newfoundland, almost 900 miles northeast of the place of banding.

A yellow palm warbler banded at Elmhurst, Long Island, N. Y., on October 13, 1932, was found on January 15, 1933, at Dunn, N. C.

A palm warbler banded at Homosassa Springs, Fla., on March 29, 1936, was recaptured at the same station on April 6, 1941. Another banded at Coral Gables, Fla., on January 17, 1943, returned to the station the following fall on October 26.

Casual records.—A palm warbler was collected at the west base of the Steens Mountains in Oregon on September 26, 1913. Two specimens have been taken in California: at Pacific Grove on October 9, 1896, and on the shore of Ferguson Lake, Imperial County, on September 22, 1942. One was collected in Baja California, at Chapala, on October 16, 1930. A specimen collected September 18, 1915, at Bernard Harbor, on the shore of Dolphin and Union Straits, Mackenzie, is the northernmost record to date.

The palm warbler has twice been recorded in Colorado: one was observed in Denver on June 20, 1891, and a specimen was collected at Limon, Lincoln County, on May 13, 1947. In Otero County, N. Mex., near the White Sands National Monument, a lone palm warbler was collected on December 6, 1935. Several specimens have been collected in Bermuda: December 17, 1847; December 3, 1848; September 4, 1899; October 3, 1902; November 14, 1903; and March 15, 1937.

Egg dates.—Alberta: 6 records, May 30 to June 16.

New Brunswick: 16 records, May 28 to June 21; 10 records, June 3 to 9.

Nova Scotia: 20 records, May 18 to June 8; 15 records, May 20 to 31.

Quebec: 17 records, June 5 to July 1; 13 records, June 7 to 15 (Harris).

DENDROICA PALMARUM HYPOCHRYSEA Ridgway

YELLOW PALM WARBLER

Contributed by WINSOR MARRETT TYLER

PLATE 56

HABITS

We may suppose that the yellow palm warbler has been moving up and down the Atlantic coast on its migrations to and from Canada for many years, perhaps since the glacier retreated and opened the road to its breeding-ground some 15,000 or 20,000 years ago, but it is only recently, a little more than two generations ago, that ornithologists have recognized that the bird was distinct from the palm warbler which breeds and migrates farther toward the west.   Robert Ridgway (1876) called attention to a marked difference in the plumage of the migrant palm warblers taken in the Mississippi Valley and those from New England and southward.   He pointed out that the latter birds were uniformly bright yellow below, streaked, especially on the sides, with chestnut, and that the back was "greenish-olive," whereas the western birds were yellowish-white beneath, only tinged with yellow, except on the throat and crissum where they were clear yellow, while the entire breast was streaked with brown, and the back was "dull olive-brown."   The eastern birds were also slightly larger in all dimensions.

The eastern form was accepted as a subspecies of the palm warbler and appears in the first edition of the A. O. U. Check-List (1886) as *hypochrysea*, golden beneath.   Subsequently it was found that the breeding ranges of the two races lie chiefly in Canada, roughly to the east and west respectively of the longitude of the southern tip of Hudson Bay.

Of the older writers, Wilson and Nuttall, who studied chiefly the birds of the northeastern United States, apparently met only the yellow palm warbler, and Audubon definitely describes it, but his remarks on the birds he saw commonly in Florida throughout the winter without much doubt apply to the western race.

Spring.—The yellow palm warbler, in spite of its small size and fragile appearance, is evidently a hardy bird.   It pushes northward into New England early in April when winter is not far behind us, at a season of uncertain weather, with perhaps even snow, and before many of the leaves have expanded fully.   The bird passes through the Transition Zone a full month before the horde of north-bound migrant warblers which brighten the treetops in mid-May; it comes even earlier than the robust myrtle warbler which has wintered not far away; and before the black and white creeper which feeds from the bark of tree trunks and branches. Only the pine warbler, returning to its home in the evergreen pitch pines, precedes it by a few days.

Those who watch the arrival of the migrant birds carefully often note that the migration of the yellow palm warbler coincides almost exactly with that of the hermit thrush and the ruby-crowned kinglet. Year after year these three birds appear on the same day, or thereabouts. The birds are not closely related to one another but they possess a trait in common: they do not depend for food on the insects found solely in widely opened flowers and leaves. Both the thrush and the kinglet are accustomed to the wintry conditions of the southern States. In April the hermit feeds on the ground among the fallen leaves; the kinglet must find most of its food in conifers or on the bare branches of trees and shrubs and in their swelling buds; and the yellow palm warbler feeds to a large extent on the ground, often in the recently burned-over patches of grassland common at this season. Here it hops about in the black, parched grass, searching for insects or seeds in the company of the robins, cowbirds, grackles, chipping sparrows, savannah sparrows, and other birds which are attracted to these areas. William Brewster (1906) says of the bird:

Yellow Palm Warblers visit the Cambridge Region [Mass.] with unfailing regularity in spring and autumn, although their numbers vary greatly from year to year. Sometimes only a very few are reported, but in spring they are usually common and occasionally really abundant. On April 25, 1868, during a brief but heavy snowstorm, I found them by hundreds at Fresh Pond where, in company with an even greater number of Yellowrumps, they had congregated on a narrow strip of bare, pebbly beach at the water's edge. It is of course exceptional to see anything like so many together, but one may often meet with fifteen or twenty in a single flock or forty or fifty in the course of a morning walk.

Nesting.—The yellow palm warbler breeds in portions of Ontario, Quebec, southern Nova Scotia, southern New Brunswick, and in northern Maine. It frequents the sphagnum bogs and open barrens of these regions, building its nest on the ground or, more rarely, on low branches of small spruce trees. Robie W. Tufts (MS.), in his notes on 61 nests found in Nova Scotia, says: "The usual number of eggs to a nest is 5. I have never found a full set with fewer than 4, nor more than 5. May 20 would appear to be the average date for a complete set of the first laying, but I have reason to believe that the birds frequently, if not regularly, raise two broods. The nests are usually built on the ground on open barrens, well concealed under the dried brakes of the previous year's growth, although frequently they are hidden away among the roots of spruce seedlings. About 1 nest in 20 is likely to be found from 1 to 4 feet above the ground close to the trunk in a small spruce seedling."

W. J. Brown has sent to A. C. Bent descriptions and photographs of nests found in the southern part of the Province of Quebec. Here the birds breed in "large tracts of open sphagnum bogs," often among the lichens which cover the ground, in situations such as the following: "at the base of a seedling spruce; sunk under a clump of cotton grass; embedded in a mass of bleached grass at the side of a mound, concealed in lichens and low plants; 6 inches from the ground in crotch of seedling spruce in center of large sphagnum bog among a thin growth of spruce; 2 feet above the ground against the trunk of a small spruce tree, at the edge of an open sphagnum bog." The nests were made of dry grass and lined with feathers.

P. B. Philipp and B. S. Bowdish (1917) found the bird breeding commonly in New Brunswick in situations similar to those mentioned but "one small breeding colony were nesting on high, dry ground, in a grove of small pines." They describe a nest as "composed of fine dead weed-stalks, strippings of dead weed bark and dead grasses, lined with the finest of same material, and with a few feathers worked into lining. The feathers in nest lining seem to be characteristic of this bird." They give the dimensions of a nest as "diameter outside 3½ inches and inside 2 inches with a depth of 2½ inches outside and 2 inches inside." They remark: "The sitting Yellow Palm Warbler usually runs, mouse fashion, from the nest, while the intruder is still some feet distant, and it is with greatest difficulty and the most acute watching that this movement is detected soon enough to serve as a clue to the immediate whereabouts of the nest. The bird remains silent until well away from the nest, usually until the intruder has been in the vicinity for a few minutes, when it commonly begins a vigorous chipping, the sharp, strong note characteristic of the species."

Ora Willis Knight (1904) discovered the yellow palm warbler breeding near Bangor, Maine, in a bog similar to the bogs in the localities mentioned. He says it "consists of large open expanses thickly carpeted with sphagnum mosses, and dotted with numerous small trees and shrubs." Among the characteristic plants, he mentions hackmatack, swamp spruce, Labrador tea, rhododendron, swamp laurel, wild rosemary, birch, orchids, and many sedges. Knight (1908) says, speaking of the same region:

Nest building must begin early in May, as well grown young have been found the first of June. I am satisfied that both parents share in the duties of incubation and both take part in caring for the young. The nests can be easily located by watching the parents carrying food to the young, but before the eggs have hatched the birds are very shy of approaching the nest when observers are about. The incubating bird will remain on its nest until almost stepped upon before flying, and practically the only way of discovering nests is by flushing birds therefrom, unless some reckless person is willing to visit the bog and spend day after day during the nest building season, fighting the voracious mosquitoes and meanwhile watching to catch the birds in the act of carrying material to the nest. * * * While Maine is the only State where this species has been found nesting, I would be inclined to predict that careful search of suitable localities in northern New Hampshire and Vermont will show that they nest there also.

Eggs.—The eggs are practically indistinguishable from those of the western palm warbler, as described under that subspecies. The measurements of 40 eggs average 17.4 by 12.9 millimeters; the eggs showing the four extremes measure **19.0** by 13.1, 18.0 **by 13.8, 16.0** by 13.0, and 16.7 by **12.5** millimeters (Harris).

Young.—O. W. Knight (1904) says that the young yellow palm warblers "leave the nest within twelve days after hatching," and after hiding a day or so in the undergrowth are able to essay short flights. Frank L. Burns (1915b) gives the incubation period as 12 days.

Plumages.—[Author's Note: Dr. Dwight (1900) describes the juvenal plumage, in which the sexes are alike, as follows: "Above, dull sepia-brown, streaked with clove-brown. Wings and tail clove-brown, edged chiefly with dull olive-green, the coverts and tertiaries with drab cinnamon-tinged; the outer two rectrices with terminal white blotches on the inner webs; no definite wing bands. Below, including sides of head, dull white with dusky spots and streaks; chin and crissum faintly tinged with yellow. Orbital ring dull white; transocular streak dusky."

A partial postjuvenal molt occurs in August, involving the contour plumage and the wing coverts, but not the rest of the wings or the tail. In his first winter plumage, the young male is "above, yellowish sepia-brown, yellowish olive-green on the rump and upper tail coverts, obscurely streaked with dull clove-brown, the crown merely tinged with concealed chestnut. Wing coverts clove-brown edged with olive-green and tipped with cinnamon *not* forming wing bands. Below, canary-yellow brightest on the crissum, obscurely streaked on throat and sides with dusky chestnut everywhere veiled by overlapping whitish edgings. Superciliary line canary-yellow, orbital ring buffy white; transocular streak dusky."

The first nuptial plumage is acquired by a partial prenuptial molt, "which involves chiefly the crown, sides of head, chin and throat and not the rest of the plumage. * * * A rich chestnut cap is assumed, contrasting sharply with the worn feathers of the occiput, the lores become dull black, the auriculars chestnut and the yellow of the chin and breast becomes brighter with rich chestnut streaks on the sides of the throat and breast. The streaking of the sides of the chin and across the jugulum are darker. Elsewhere a few stray feathers are acquired." Dr. Dwight saw this molt in progress in December and January in birds from Jamaica, in March and April in birds in Florida and Georgia, and late in April in birds near New York City.

A complete postnuptial molt in August produces the adult winter plumage, which "differs little from the first winter dress, but of richer brown above with darker wing edgings, the chestnut more abundant on the crown and the streakings below more conspicuous." Adults have a partial prenuptial molt in the spring, as in the young birds.

Of the females he says: "The sexes are very similar in all plumages, females usually a little browner and with less yellow. In first winter plumage with very little or no chestnut on the crown and later practically indistinguishable, but undergoing the same moults as the male, the prenuptial more limited."]

Food.—Ora W. Knight (1904), who studied the bird on its breeding grounds, says: "The food of this species consists largely of insects and among the contents of stomachs of birds taken in spring and summer have been found small beetles, gnats, mosquitoes, flies and the general run of small insects found on the trunks of trees or flying in the air in localities which the Warblers frequent. In late summer and fall some small amount of vegetable matter is also eaten, chiefly unidentifiable plant seeds." To this list Forbush (1929) adds mayflies, leaf beetles, ants, plant lice, and grasshoppers, and remarks: "On Cape Cod it apparently eats bayberries in winter, like the Myrtle Warbler."

Francis H. Allen (MS.) speaks of "two birds on the upper beach at Ipswich, Mass., among the beach grass, feeding on flies, which they often caught on the wing. They would squat against the bank with tail resting on the ground and look about for insects and then make a sudden run or leap into the air after one."

I have seen the birds hover beside a branch and pick off insects from it.

Behavior.—The yellow palm warbler is an inconspicuous little bird, almost insignificant; it flashes no bright color, like the redstart; it has no loud, striking song, like the yellow warbler. Indeed, few people ever see the yellow palm except those who are familiar with this tiny, pale yellow, chestnut-capped, tail-wagging, quiet bird—those who are on the watch for it as it passes unobtrusively up and down the Atlantic seaboard.

Nevertheless, it is a common bird early in spring in New England and the southern States, one of the first warblers to arrive from the south. We may see it, often in groups of half a dozen together, flitting among the shrubbery bordering the country roadsides, along stone walls, or feeding on the ground out in open fields, singing its faint song, and wagging its tail up and down wherever it goes. Delicate and fragile as the bird seems, it is journeying to a wild country to spend the summer in the cold, dank, mossy swamps far away in the north. During its migration, too, it seems attracted to moisture, to wet hollows in the woods and to the edges of streams and ponds. I have seen it feeding on the surface of a brook, held up by heavy grass lying along the water.

The bird is even commoner in the autumn migration but is no more conspicuous, for at this season, September and early October, it is moving southward in company with many other species of migrant warblers.

Francis H. Allen (MS.) reports an interesting habit of the yellow palm which he noted as he watched two birds catching flies on Ipswich beach, as previously described: "They were very active, running and hopping along over the sand. They progressed both by hopping and by running, as I saw both by watching them and by observing their tracks, but they hopped more than they ran, and they always hopped when they had longish distances to go. I watched them for a long time and was often very near them, even within 8 feet. They did not seem at all afraid of me."

Voice.—The song of the yellow palm warbler is one of the so-called trills, so common in bird music, a series of short notes rapidly repeated. Sometimes the notes are inflected slightly, giving them a doubled effect. It is an inconspicuous little song, no loud or accented notes, the tone rather flat, with no ringing quality—a feeble jingle made up of listless notes, usually all on the same pitch and with little musical charm. Walter Faxon used to say that it suggested to him the song of a debilitated chipping sparrow.

As I have listened to the bird's singing over a series of years I have sometimes noted a variation both in the delivery and quality of the song. There may be a slight swell in the middle, and on one occasion I heard it divided into short sections like the early morning singing of the chipping sparrow. Rarely, the notes are uttered slowly, no faster than a flicker's *shouting*, and while they are usually uttered with no suggestion of vigor, occasionally they are given with such a sharp, staccato delivery that they suggest (in the delivery only) the bright song of Wilson's warbler. When the pitch alternates up and down with a hint of *rotary* effect, as it does in some instances, the song might be confused for a moment with that of a myrtle warbler, singing very listlessly. The palm warbler's call note is feeble, but sharply-cut at the end, suggested by the syllable, *ship*.

Aretas A. Saunders (MS.) sends to A. C. Bent this analysis: "The song of the yellow palm warbler is a simple one, consisting of 10 to 30 notes in regular, even time, and with only slight changes in pitch.

The quality is only slightly musical and is distinctly sibilant or fricative, with sounds like the consonants *s* or *f* running all through it. It is not loud, and none of the notes is strongly accented. The average number of notes per song is 16. Of 15 records of this song, 5 are made up of single notes, 3 of 2-note phrases, while 7 begin with 2-note phrases and end in single notes. Changes in pitch average about a tone, a few songs being all on one pitch, and only 2 changing more than one and a half tones. The pitch, I believe, ranges from A flat ′ ′ ′ ′ to D ′ ′ ′ ′, a range of only 3 tones. Songs range from 1⅕ to 2⅗ seconds in length. The number of notes per second varies from 8 to 12."

The bird sings freely in New England during its northward migration, but I do not recall ever hearing the song in Florida in early spring.

Field marks.—The distinctive mark of the two races of the palm warblers is their chestnut crown. The wagging tail of the palm warblers, an almost constant movement, is a pronounced up and down sweep, through a much longer arc than the twitching tail of the blackpoll and the prairie warblers. The two subspecies of the palm warbler are very similar in plumage. The most reliable point of difference is the contrast in color between the yellowish-white breast and, by comparison, the intense yellow of the under tail coverts in the western race, a contrast the yellow palm lacks, its under parts being uniformly yellow. In the autumn, when the colors are fainter, it may sometimes be impossible to identify the races surely in the field.

Enemies.—Aside from the hazards to which its ground nests are exposed and the dangers of its fairly long migration at the seasons, both spring and fall, when the Accipiter hawks are moving, the yellow palm warbler has no especial enemies as far as we know.

Herbert Friedmann (1929 and 1934) says it is "a rare victim" of the cowbird, and cites only four nests in which cowbirds' eggs have been found.

Fall.—The yellow palm warbler is often an abundant bird during its fall migration along the Atlantic coast, generally frequenting the birch thickets where plant lice abound, a favorite food of the autumn warblers. Dr. Charles W. Townsend (1905) says: "On October 14th, 1900, in a violent northeast storm with rain, I found the Ipswich dunes swarming with these birds."

Winter.—Few yellow palm warblers leave the United States during the winter. They are rare in Cuba (Barbour, 1943). Their chief range in winter is in the Gulf States from Louisiana to Florida, but in the latter State it is almost exclusively restricted to the west coast. Hence its winter range is decidedly more to the westward and much farther north than the range of the western race.

SEIURUS AUROCAPILLUS AUROCAPILLUS (Linnaeus)

EASTERN OVENBIRD

CONTRIBUTED BY ALFRED OTTO GROSS

PLATES 57, 58

HABITS

The eastern ovenbird is an inhabitant of the woodlands and, during the breeding season, is one of our commonest and one of the most interesting warblers of our hardwood and coniferous forests. Because of its loud *staccato*, with its *crescendo* ending, its somewhat mysterious and secretive habits in the underbrush and on the leaf-covered floor, and because its well-concealed nest is so different from that of the other warblers, it is often one of the chief objectives of those in quest of unusual bird lore on strolls through the woods in May and June.

The names that have been applied to this bird emphasize some of the traits and markings of this most individualistic of all our warblers. The generally accepted common name, ovenbird, was adopted because of its peculiar nest that resembles a miniature Dutch oven. The song has given origin to the names teacher-bird and accentor; the peculiar vibratory motion of its tail and body when walking has suggested the names wood-wagtail, wagtail warbler, as well as the generic name *Seiurus*. In Jamaica it is commonly known as the land-kickup; in Florida the natives call it the night-walker, thus calling attention to its method of locomotion by walking rather than by hopping. Its golden-brown crown mark is revealed not only in the species name *aurocapillus* but also in the common name golden-crowned warbler and this marking is also coupled with other characteristics in such names as golden-crowned wagtail, golden-crowned accentor, and golden-crowned thrush.

Spring.—In the spring migration the first arrivals appear on the mainland of Florida in March, single individuals have been noted during the first week, but the migration in that State extends through April to May. The average date of arrival in North Carolina, Virginia, and Washington, D. C., is April 24–26. They reach Pennsylvania, New York, and southern New England during the first week of May, by the second week of that month they can be expected in Maine, and by the third week they reach New Brunswick and Nova Scotia, arriving in Quebec during the first week of June.

The dates of arrival in the Mississippi flyway are earlier than for the same latitudes in the east. The first individuals reach Kentucky on April 10, with extremes as early as April 3. They reach Michigan by April 27, Iowa by April 29, Minnesota by May 7, by mid-May they are in Manitoba and Alberta, and by the end of May they are at their outposts of range in Alaska.

The ovenbird arrives on its breeding grounds in the spring with great regularity, and there is much less variation in the date of arrival from year to year than is exhibited by many other birds. It appears at a certain point regardless of the weather, be it warm and summer-like, freezing, or snowing. The coming of the ovenbird is so definitely announced by its loud and easily recognized song that a factor in its apparent punctuality may be its being promptly recorded. In my own experience I more frequently hear than see the first arrivals in spring.

Harry W. Hann (1937) has clearly established by banding and careful detailed observation—

that both male and female adult birds return to their old breeding grounds, if possible. Old males have a good chance of obtaining their former territory either by arriving early or by driving out the other males. Returning females have more difficulty, however, since females probably return at more nearly the same time, and there is the additional factor in their adjustment, with the male. It seems obvious, though it was not actually observed, that the female goes first to the old territory, and if the male there already has a mate, she goes to an adjoining territory. The particular male in the territory seems to be of no consequence.

With both males and females attempting to return to the same place, there would seem to be a strong tendency for the pairs to remate in subsequent years, and this happened twice with banded birds.

Courtship.—The courtship of the ovenbird, a most interesting and remarkable affair, is intimately associated with the male's extraordinary musical performance. One may see the birds walking casually over the leaves of the forest floor, making scarcely a sound, then through some sudden impulse the male starts after the female in a frantic pursuit often terminated by a wild flight, during which he pours forth a loud and eloquent love song. After this flight he returns to the forest floor to sing his ringing "teacher" notes. Morris Gibbs (1885) gives us an excellent account of this unusual courtship of a pair of birds he observed near Grand Rapids, Mich.:

Carefully crawling through the almost impenetrable growth of small saplings and brush, I came at last to a partial clearing over which a bird, apparently in the highest transports of joy, was fluttering in irregular flight. * * * I observed another bird undoubtedly its mate, perched on the ground near, and which appeared to be a Golden-crowned Thrush and the centre of attraction to the delightful warbler overhead. Never had I heard the song before, and never have I witnessed such a scene. This was indeed making love with a spirit which I have never witnessed among our birds before. The song was almost continuous, and with an occasional interruption to the new song by the common chattering notes so well known and described by Coues as a "harsh crescendo," the notes were all of the most melodious description. The energetic unconscious fellow was meanwhile constantly flying about his inamorata, describing every form of flight except that of regular sailing; first dashing through space to the edge of the glade, which was probably twenty feet across; then rising to the tops of the bushes, he would half flutter, half fall towards his prospective mate. On a sudden he would flutter directly upward as we often see the English Sparrow or House Wren do, and on reaching a height of twenty feet or more, dash about the clearing in varying circles, ever tending in his flight toward the object of his extravagant attention. She in the meanwhile sat silent and evidently interested in the performance. Suddenly the male dropped beside her, and alternately dashing and wheeling about, but continually on the move and always revolving about her, gave evidence of his adoration by a series of hops, dignified struts, droppings of the head and tail, elevation of the wings and crest, which would have done credit to both the Turkey and the Ruffed Grouse. While on the ground the song was kept up with the usual vigor, but the interruption by the coarser, common notes was more frequent and the bird stopped in its struts in order to utter the notes which apparently caused him more effort than did the more beautiful song. The appearance of a third party on the scene, probably also a lover, caused the first performer to dash into the brush much to my disappointment.

Nesting.—The ovenbird nests in woodlands, usually where the underbrush and growth of shrubs and small trees is scanty, and the forest floor is open below and carpeted with old leaves. Here it lives in company with such birds as the true thrushes and the whippoorwill. The nest is generally located in open situations on the forest floor, allowing an approach to it from any direction, though at times a tree or shrub may be standing behind or at one side of it. In one case the nest was found built in the end of a large pine log and partially concealed by a growth of ferns. The majority of the nests are located alongside trails or woodland roads, or in partially cleared places where at certain times of the day the light can filter through. These open areas are probably an advantage to the birds in approaching their nests, certainly they are a convenience to the naturalist who wishes to observe or photograph them. I know of no case where the ovenbird has departed from its habit of nesting on the ground.

The typical nest is constructed of dry grasses, vegetable fibers, leaves, leaf and weed stems, rootlets and bits of bark, and moss. It is lined with finer materials, tiny rootlets and fibers, and varying amounts of hair. Sometimes the nest may be made almost exclusively of one material. T. S. Roberts (1936) describes and figures a nest made up entirely of fine bleached grasses very different from the usual leaf-studded structure. In nests that I have found in the pine woods of Maine pine needles made up the bulk of the structure.

The nest is generally built in a slight depression of the ground and is invariably covered over; often the leaves of the leaf-bed and the branches of small, fallen, dead trees extend over the nest at the sides and back, making a roof that sheds rain as well as conceals the nest from view. Indeed the nests are so well hidden that they are difficult to find except by flushing the bird; this often occurs by accident.

Miss Cordelia Stanwood, in an unpublished account, describes a nest and a nesting site of an ovenbird near Ellsworth, Maine, as follows: "The cavity in the ground in which the nest was located was about 1 inch deep in the center. Around the edge of the excavation were maple leaves, and pine needles. The ground was swampy, covered with sphagnum moss, white birch and maple leaves, sensitive and New York ferns. The nest was located among maples and white birches adjoining some evergreens. The growth was thick overhead but open underfoot. The saucer part of the nest, level with the ground, was made of pine needles and dead leaves. It was roofed over with pine needles, dead leaves, fern, moss, stipes of ferns and bracken, and the fruit stems of maples; it was nicely lined with horsehair. Two sensitive fern fronds had grown through the nest, and the little mound of dry leaves and moss was in no wise distinguishable from its surroundings."

The width of the nest averages about 6½ inches but the leaves and nesting materials may extend for about 9 inches. The height of the nest ranges from 4½ to 5 inches. The cavity is small as compared to the exterior, usually measuring less than 3 inches in diameter. The opening is about 1½ inches high and 2¼ inches wide.

The female is responsible for selecting the nesting site and for building the nest. While the female is busily engaged in building, the male lends moral encouragement by singing; he guards the territory and gives the alarm whenever an intruder appears. He seldom visits the nest during the course of construction but is a constant attendant and assists in feeding the young after they appear. According to H. W. Hann (1937):   .

The female clears the leaves from a circular spot, by pushing them back, raising up the edges, and perhaps removing some. She then, in some cases, digs up the ground, leaving fresh soil on the surface, and may remove some soil or push it aside. * * * Nesting material is then carried and placed around the edge of the hole, chiefly on the back side, and the covering is extended over the top. The work is done almost entirely from the inside, but evidently a few leaves are placed on top and arranged from the outside. * * * The last material to be added to the nest is the hair, and the presence of this indicates a finished nest. The hair is often added a day or more after the remainder is finished, and doubtless causes the female considerable searching.

Ovenbirds will sometimes desert their nest when disturbed, especially at the time when the nest is under construction or the eggs in the early stages of incubation. However, in correspondence received from Dr. Paul Harrington, he reports flushing a bird from a nest at Birch Point, Toronto, in which the whole dome or top had been torn off (probably by cattle) and carried about 10 feet away. The bird continued incubation apparently unconcerned by its exposed condition.

Eggs.—The eggs are laid during the morning, often before sunrise, 1 to 3 days after the nest is completed. Under normal conditions an egg is laid each day until the set is completed. The number in complete sets varies from 3 to 6 eggs. In 36 nests not disturbed by cowbirds, J. P. Norris (1892) reported 6 with 3 eggs, 13 with 4, 16 with 5, and 1 with 6, an average of slightly more than 4 eggs per set. Hann (1937) in a series of 27 nests in which the eggs were checked as laid there were 2 nests with 3 eggs, 6 with 4, 18 with 5, and 1 with 6, an average of about 5 eggs per nest. If the first attempt at nesting is a failure the second set of eggs is generally smaller in number than the first. Normally the ovenbird does not rear two broods during any one season.

The eggs have a white, slightly glossed ground color speckled and spotted with hazel, lilac-gray, and reddish-brown. In the majority of the eggs the markings form a wreath about the larger end. A series of 50 eggs had an average length of 20.2 millimeters, the extremes being 18.6 and 23.2 millimeters, and an average short diameter of 15.5 millimeters, the extremes being 14.3 and 16.7 millimeters.

Incubation.—Incubation is done entirely by the female and begins the day after the last egg is laid, regardless of the size of the clutch. When incubating, the bird sits with her side parallel to the opening of the nest, her tail bent over her back and usually toward the front of the nest. She changes her position many times during the course of the day, placing her head in the opposite direction, but the axis of her body is always in the same relative position. She exhibits considerable nervousness when about to leave the nest and on leaving does not fly but walks a considerable distance over the forest floor before taking flight.

The ovenbird does not flush from her nest readily, and when walking through the woods I have unwittingly trampled on the edge of the nest before she fluttered out. At this time the bird gave a splendid exhibition of feigned injury; she struggled seemingly helpless along the ground with her wings and tail lowered and the feathers of her crown and back uplifted in an attitude of dire distress. After leading me away for a distance of about 50 feet she arose and flew away triumphantly.

The female during the period of incubation leaves the nest voluntarily for feeding from five to a dozen times during the course of the day; spending from 8 to 17 percent of the total time away from the nest. The first trip occurs soon after daylight, and the lightest incubation is from that time until noon. Late in the evening there is a tendency for her to leave again before settling down for the night. It was found that the time off during the day was roughly proportional to daily temperature changes. In a nest which I had under daily observation at Yorktown Heights, N. Y. I saw the male bird deliver several green larvae to the female while she was on the nest incubating the eggs, but this is not of common occurrence as far as I have been able to determine.

The incubation period of two nests studied in Maine was 12 days. The exact incubation period of 76 eggs in 21 Michigan nests was determined by Hann (1937). He found the time ranged from 11 days and 12 hours to 14 days, with an average of 12 days and 5.6 hours. He states that all the eggs of a clutch including the last had about the same incubation period, and any variation of more than a few hours usually concerned all. He found no difference in incubation time with respect to warm or cool weather.

The eggs may hatch at any time during the day but rarely at night. They are pipped on the day before hatching. The shell cracks at right angles to the long axis of the egg before the shell opens to allow the young to emerge.

Young.—The young at the time of hatching have their eyes sealed shut but they readily respond to sounds as soon as they emerge from the egg. When extending their heads and opening their large mouths they seem to balance themselves by their wing tips and sprawled-out legs. Between feeding the young are brooded by the female, and at this time she is very reluctant to leave the nest, even allowing a person to stroke her feathers.

The male assists in the feeding of the young at the very start, in fact he may be seen at the nest even before the young have emerged, in apparent anticipation of his domestic role soon to follow. The adults walk to the nest in bringing food, usually along well-established routes and runways which in part are concealed from view. They often stop with food in their beaks, when near the nest, and carefully scrutinize the surroundings as if to make sure they are not being spied upon by some intruder. The male, at least at first, seems to be more wary and cautious in this respect than the female when approaching the nest.

By the second day the young reach toward the opening of the nest in soliciting food. At 4 days the eyes of the young are slightly open and the edges of the gapes have assumed a more pronounced yellow. The feather papillae in the various feather tracts show prominently. The young are much more active and move themselves about the nest more readily with the aid of their rapidly growing legs. They are also quicker in responding to the parents arriving with food. Excrement is voided by turning the rear of the body toward the opening of the nest. During the first day or two the excrement is eaten by the adult birds but as the young become older more and more of it is carried away to be dropped at a considerable distance from the nest.

By the fourth day the number of feedings required of the adults has greatly increased over those of the first day. As the young grow older it is not unusual for the adults to exceed a hundred visits to the nest with food in a single day.

The eyes are completely opened by the fifth day, and from then on the young are not easily deceived by false noises or those not concerned with the arrival of food.

After 6 days of nest life the young may be seen going through exercises, stretching their wings to gain strength and, perhaps, partly to relieve an uncomfortable feeling produced by the rapidly growing parts and feathers. They preen themselves a great deal and peck at the bases of the feathers to assist in the unsheathing process. By this time their temperature control has developed sufficiently so that there is less need of brooding by the parents.

By the eighth day the primaries are unsheathed for about three-fourths of their length and the feathers of the other tracts have proceeded to such an extent that the juvenal plumage is well established, giving a more pleasing contour to the young. There is now great competition among members of the brood when the parents arrive with food, and they utter a kind of buzzing call in concert as they stretch their necks and extend their gaping mouths out of the opening of the nest. Sometimes the young may leave the nest at this age, but in some nests I have had under observation they remained a day or two longer.

In leaving the nest the young hop out one at a time, and considerable time generally elapses before all have departed. When a nestling leaves it follows one of the adult birds, and those left behind are cared for by the mate. The parent bird leads the youngster, coaxing it along now and then with food and offering encouragement by responding to its peeps and chirps. Finally each parent goes its own way with its part of the brood, and thus nest life comes to a successful ending. Under favorable conditions young birds, especially those attended by the males, may remain in practically the same territory for several days after leaving the nest.

As soon as the feathers of the wings have completed their growth the young are able to fly when flushed. They usually alight on the ground but sometimes they are able to negotiate a landing and maintain a hold on a shrub or lower limb of a tree. After the young are 3 weeks old they are able to secure their own food although it is still supplemented by the parent birds. When the young are about 5 weeks old they are abandoned by the adults and from then on are on their own. By the time they have undergone the partial postnuptial molt and have acquired their so-called first winter plumage they are physi-

cally fit to migrate.   The adults generally disappear from the woods
as soon as the young can care for themselves.

Polyandry.—Ordinarily the male and female ovenbirds have single
mates but H. W. Hann (1937) cites a case where one male had two
mates at the same time, and another in which a female copulated with
two neighboring males in her own territory, then later visited a neighboring male in his territory during her incubation period.   In a later
paper Hann (1940) records an observation in which two males as well
as the female were carrying food to the young in the nest.   After these
complicated relations were noted a third male, not banded, appeared
on the scene.   He repeatedly came near the nest, although chased by
the other males.   His intent seemed centered chiefly in the female, as
he was not seen to feed the young, and apparently, according to Mr.
Hann, he was successful in some of his attempts at copulation.   Hence
this female had three mates, although the third might well be considered an interloper.   When the young left the nest the two banded
males took charge of one young each and the female cared for the
other three.

No one else has made such an intensive study of the family interre-
lationships of the ovenbird as has Mr. Hann, with the aid of marking
and banding the individuals.   Polyandrous matings may be more
common than has been supposed among species, such as the ovenbird,
that we have always thought to be monogamous.

Plumages.—[AUTHOR'S NOTE: According to Dr. Dwight (1900), the
natal down is "pale sepia brown."

He describes the juvenal plumage, which is partially acquired in
the nest, as follows: "Above, including sides of head, cinnamon-brown,
sparingly spotted with olive-brown, the dusky lateral stripes faintly
indicated on the crown.   Wings and tail olive-brown with olive-green
edgings, the coverts slightly tipped with pale cinnamon.   Below, pale
cinnamon, yellowish white on abdomen and crissum, faintly spotted
or streaked on the sides of the chin, on the breast and on the sides
with olive-brown."

The first winter plumage is "acquired by a partial postjuvenal
moult, beginning by the end of June, which involves the body plumage,
the wing coverts, and rarely the tertiaries, but not the rest of the wings
nor the tail.   Young and old become practically indistinguishable."
This plumage is similar to the well-known adult spring plumage, except for brownish edgings on the crown, and faint buffy or yellowish
tinges on the under parts, the dark stripes being partially veiled with
white edgings.

The first and subsequent nuptial plumages are acquired by wear,
which removes the light edgings and brightens the plumage.

A complete postnuptial molt for both young and old birds occurs
in July.]

Food.—No comprehensive study has thus far been made of the food of the ovenbird. Unlike most of the warblers, this bird is terrestrial in its habits; instead of gleaning its food from the trunks, limbs, and leaves of trees, it rustles about on the ground turning over leaves to scan the leaf mold of the forest floor, where it finds snails, slugs, myriapods, and earthworms as well as the weevils, beetles, aphids, crickets, ants, and spiders which comprise a large proportion of its food. It is also known to feed on moths and caterpillars and more rarely it may catch flying insects on the wing. It takes a few seeds and small wild fruits but these represent only a little more than one-fiftieth of its entire food. In Florida, ovenbirds have been reported as feeding on the red mulberry. In certain sections of its range it feeds freely on grasshoppers and locusts. Junius Henderson (1934) quotes Aughey as finding an average of 18 locusts in each of 6 stomachs of the ovenbird collected in Nebraska. He adds there was an average of 15 kinds of other insects present in each of the stomachs.

Sylvester D. Judd (1900) examined the stomachs of 3 half-grown ovenbird nestlings which contained "beetles of the family Lampyridae and click beetles, caterpillars, moths, spiders and snails."

In watching birds at the nest from a blind, practically all of the food I saw fed to the young during the first 3 days consisted of various small green and brown larvae. After that time I saw the adults bring spiders, snails, earthworms, centipedes, and a number of winged insects such as flies, moths, beetles, and ants to feed to their young.

Miss Cordelia Stanwood saw young ovenbirds feeding on mosquitoes at Ellsworth, Maine. In her notes she writes: "As I started for home, the female crossed my path, and a young bird followed. As I neared the youngster, he stopped to snap up a mosquito. I knelt slowly and held a mosquito, on the tip of my finger to the little fellow. After hesitating once or twice, he snapped it up. Then I put my hand flat on the ground and let the mosquitoes bite. He walked over to my hand, snapping up mosquitoes for a long time. At last he followed a mosquito across the path, and in answer to the chirps of the parent birds wandered in their direction." Miss Stanwood has also observed the young catching black flies.

Dr. Alexander Wetmore (1916) reports on the examinations of the contents of 13 stomachs of ovenbirds collected in Puerto Rico during the months from December to April, inclusive. The animal food of these birds amounted to 62.43 percent and the vegetable material 37.57 percent. He presents further details as follows:

In all of these stomachs were considerable quantities of gravel, and all animal matter was ground very fine. Weevil remains (4.8 percent) were present in four stomachs taken in April. Other beetle remains (9.63 percent) in eight stomachs were so finely ground that they could not be determined. Ants were eaten by eight birds and form the large amount of 8.5 percent. Other Hymenoptera made up only 0.4 percent. Orthopterous remains (2.17 percent) include a walking stick, a grasshopper, and others. A caterpillar (0.5 percent) was found in one stomach and spiders (2.33 percent) in three. Snails, in most instances broken up in very small pieces, were eaten by eight birds and amount to 30.17 percent. A single tree toad comprises 0.93 percent and miscellaneous animal matter 3 percent.

The oven-bird is wholly beneficial in its food habits and is remarkable for the large number of ants eaten, as well as many weevils and other beetles. Snails are much relished, and form nearly half the animal food.

Of the vegetable matter contained in these stomachs 36.9 percent was composed of seeds and 0.67 percent may be classed as rubbish. The oven-bird has a strong, muscular gizzard and takes large quantities of sand, so that the seeds are broken and ground until they are fit for digestion. None are of economic value.

Voice.—The ovenbird has the reputation of being the noisiest and least musical member of the warbler group. Its arrival in the spring is made known to us by its loud, clear, sharply accented calls. It generally keeps well concealed in the dense cover of the woodlands and its voice is frequently heard when we may not discover the singer. The song is a ringing crescendo chant which Burroughs has aptly described as "TEACHER, TEACHER, TEACHER, TEACHER", an interpretation that will definitely distinguish it from that of any other bird. It has been a question whether the first or the second syllable is accented, but now this accent is known to vary.

The call song commonly heard during the nesting season may be termed the territory song, for it is an announcement of the singer's presence to all other birds and a warning to all trespassers. During mating it is often a challenge and may sometimes serve as a battle cry when a rival appears. The birds sing regularly in definite localities and seldom wander, evidently having definite singing trees and territory. The song can be heard throughout the period of incubation, but in my experience it practically ceases after the feeding of the young demands the full attention of both parents. In Maine it is seldom heard after the middle of July. A second period of singing occurs in August or early September but the song at that time is transient and most irregular. In this supplementary period the song is to be heard for only a few days, in the early morning hours, and never reaches the precision and vigor of the true spring song.

In correspondence from Aretas A. Saunders, he states: "The territory song consists of 2-note phrases, 6 to 12, and averaging 8. In each 2-note phrase one is longer than the other, and both are commonly a tone apart in pitch. Each succeeding phrase is slightly louder than the preceding one so that the song is a crescendo throughout. In my 24 records there are various variations from the normal. A few songs vary only a half-tone in pitch, and a few more a tone and a half. Two songs change in pitch in the middle of the song, finishing with phrases a tone higher than those at the beginning. Two songs begin with single notes and end with 2-note phrases, while one begins with 2-note phrases and ends with single notes.

"The pitch ranges one octave, from C sharp ''' to C sharp ''''. One bird whose song I recorded sang two different songs, the lower one reaching C sharp ''' and the higher C sharp ''''. The song lasted from 1⅘ to 3⅕ seconds. There is some variation between individuals in the rapidity of singing, some singing about three 2-note phrases per second and others about four. The accented note in the phrases may be either higher or lower in pitch than the unaccented, and my records are about equally divided in this matter."

Albert R. Brand (1936) has analyzed the songs of birds, including the ovenbird, through a detailed study of film recordings. He writes:

The speed of bird song was found to be extremely rapid. Many songs that seemed to consist of only a few notes actually contain four or five times as many as the ear can detect, and, in several cases, songs that are assumed to be divided—that is they seem to be made up of several notes—under the microscope were found to be continuous—only one note.

Such was the case of the oven-bird film studied. This song certainly sounds to me, and I imagine to others, as if it consists of a number of separate notes, if not phrases. It is often written, TEACHER. TEACHER, TEACHER, TEACHER, each "teacher" representing one phase or group of notes. But on the film the story is different. The film tells us that this song, which to our ear seems to be made up of a number of phrases, each of which in turn consists of one note that is changing constantly in pitch, is really a continuous note. However, the pitch *is* constantly changing; on that point the ear is correct. * * * The change after the downward movement of the note (flatting) into the higher portion of the song probably causes one to assume that the song is a series of notes, which it certainly is not. Many notes in bird-song were found to be of incredibly short duration, sometimes as short as a hundredth of a second, and the pauses between the notes are even shorter, occasionally only a fraction of that time. It is physically impossible for the ear to distinguish such short notes and intervals; it is no wonder that until the microscopic film studies were made these very short notes had not even been suspected.

In his study of vibration frequencies of passerine bird songs Brand (1938) found that the vibrations per second of the highest note of the ovenbird was 5,850, the lowest 3,300, and the approximate mean about 4,000.

Apparently this song is not peculiar to the male, for Robert W. Hiatt (1943) states that he collected an ovenbird, that was singing as it walked among fallen leaves and branches, which proved to be a female. Whether it is of common occurrence for the female ovenbird to sing is not known, since the sex is difficult to determine without dissection. Better to leave such an academic question unsolved than to collect singing ovenbirds solely for such a purpose!

In addition to the ordinary song, the ovenbird has another song, much more musical and beautiful, generally sung during flight and frequently referred to as the flight song. It is not heard until about

10 days or 2 weeks after the bird's arrival in the spring, it continues through the nesting season, and it normally ceases by the time the ordinary or territory song is no longer heard, although occasionally it has been heard long after the nesting season.

Aretas A. Saunders states: "The flight song is much more variable than the territory song. It is longer, has a greater range in pitch, is sweeter and more musical in quality, and is heard more commonly later in the season. It is often heard in the dusk of evening and I have heard it on a dark night at about 2 a. m.

"I have 15 records of this song. In pitch they range from F sharp ‴ to E″″. Individual songs have a range from two and one-half to five tones, averaging about three. They occupy from 2⅖ to 4⅗ seconds.

"One can say very little about the form of this song, it varies so greatly. Warbles, 2- and 3-note phrases, slurs, single notes, and twitters are mixed together in various ways. The pitch rises or falls with no regularity. All but 3 of my records have a pause in the middle of the song, 1 record has two such pauses; and 11 contain a few repeated 2-note phrases, like a portion of the territory song, but 4 have no such phrases.

"The bird sings this song in horizontal flight, often above the tops of the forest trees, but sometimes flying through the trees, only 15 or 20 feet above the ground. When a song over the treetop is finished the bird turns about, drops lower and flies back to the starting point through the trees."

The flight song is so truly remarkable that it seems well worth while to present the interpretations of other observers: E. P. Bicknell (1884) writes: "On occasions, as if sudden emotion carried it beyond the restrictions that ordinarily beset its expression, it bursts forth with a wild outpouring of intricate and melodious song, proving itself the superior vocalist of the trio of pseudo-Thrushes of which it is so unassuming a member. This song is produced on the wing, oftenest when the spell of evening is coming over the woods. Sometimes it may be heard as an outburst of vesper melody carried above the foliage of the shadowy forest and descending and dying away with the waning twilight."

Lynds Jones (1900) has called this song of the ovenbird the passion song, which he defines: "It is an outburst of melody of such richness and fullness, such thrilling ecstasy, that the signer is lifted into the air on quivering wings to pour out his melody without a pause until the inspiration has passed. * * * I have seen the ovenbird suddenly vault into the air, mounting to the tree tops on quivering wings, then dart back and forth in a zigzag course swift as an arrow, and finally burst into song as he floated gently down. * * * Sometimes the ovenbird closes his passion song with a burst of the perfect call (territory) song."

H. E. Tuttle (1919) in writing of the night performance of the flight song of the ovenbird states:

His songs of the noon hour are but jingling alliterations besides the flood of ecstasy that he pours forth above the tree tops in the dark of night. * * * When the starlit nights are warm with the promise of June, then may you hear the first glad upward rush of that far-flung torrent of poetry. Mounting with hurried gladness, as if he feared some surcease of delight, he gains the open sky, spilling the gay notes earthward in his wake, like the tumbling drops of a mountain waterfall. While the last burst of warbled rapture haunts the still air of night, he has sheered into a swift descent, with perhaps a murmured snatch of the refrain, uttered regretfully, as if Lethe had overtaken the singer and hushed the gay chords whilst they trembled from his heart. * * * Sometimes, even when the sun is high, he falls into a reverie, perched on a horizontal bough above the glade, then, rarely, and but for a moment, as if in a day-dream, the lyric gift is restored. He darts from his perch like a mad thing, and whips through the woods with incredible speed, singing wildly his flight song with all the abandon of a Bacchante, till, as suddenly, he comes to rest upon the branch from which he started, dozes a space, and wakes to walk quietly the length of his perch, returning to the earth as if quite unconscious of what has occurred.

In addition to these songs the ovenbird has an alarm note which is a loud "*tzick*" and on certain occasions utters a softer higher pitched "*tseet*." Miss Cordelia J. Stanwood describes the calls uttered by the ovenbird when disturbed at the nest as "*cheh! chip! sptz! sptz! sptz! sptz!*" and that of a bird suddenly surprised as "*chip-ip-ip-ip*."

Enemies.—The ovenbird, as in the case of other ground nesting birds of the forest, suffers from the depredations of snakes, squirrels, skunks, weasels, and other prowlers. William Brewster (1936) gives us a very graphic account of ovenbirds and a black snake which he observed on June 21, 1886, as follows:

A low but unusual chirping attracted my attention. The sound steadily became more distinct and its authors—for there were evidently several—were plainly advancing toward me. I soon made out they were Oven Birds and that they were on or near the ground, which although free from underbrush was nevertheless well shaded by an abundant growth of sarsaparilla.

Finally the dry leaves began to rustle and the sarsaparilla stems to wave directly in front of my position and the next moment a black snake about three feet long emerged into an opening, gliding swiftly and in a perfectly direct course. On each side of the slightly raised head and within less than two feet of it, walked a pair of Oven Birds, their bills open and panting, their wings slightly raised and quivering so rapidly as to produce a hazy appearance above their bodies. They kept their distance exactly and, when the snake stopped they stopped also, apparently not looking at him but facing directly ahead. They were also seemingly ignored by the snake, although he doubtless kept a not less keen side watch on them than they did on him. The entire group, which finally halted within less than ten yards of me, presented a remarkable, not to say ludicrous spectacle and at once suggested the idea that birds were in trained attendance on the snake—a well-drilled escort, as it were, to guide or guard him during his morning crawl. I ended what was likely enough to prove a tragedy to the birds by shooting the snake.

H. W. Hann (1937) reports that a pair of adult ovenbirds exhibited great concern and were annoyed by two barred owls which were in the vicinity of a nest. An owl feather found near a freshly destroyed nest was evidence of this predator. Mr. Hann also gives an account of the red squirrel in relation to nesting ovenbirds as follows:

The loss of many eggs and young was attributed to the red squirrel. In a number of cases a part of the contents of a nest disappeared, and later the remainder was taken at one or more visits. At one nest, three out of four eggs disappeared just before noon, and I decided to watch for the robber to return. I remained until dark, and returned early the next morning. About 6:00 a. m. a red squirrel came to the nest, got the remaining egg and started off with it. When I approached, it ran up a tree and ate the egg, holding it in its paws as it ate. At another nest which contained a Cowbird nearly ready to leave, a red squirrel suddenly appeared on a tree, head downward, just above the nest. It hesitated a moment until the cowbird gave the food call, then seized it by the head and ran away with it. Red squirrels evidently discover nests by accident, as they run about looking for food. The Oven-birds often chase them away from the vicinity of nests, or the loss would be greater.

Mr. Hann also found evidence that gray squirrels and possibly that skunks and raccoons had destroyed nests he had under observation.

Miss Cordelia Stanwood found a nest of the ovenbird in which one egg had been sucked, and the other was so smeared with the albumen of the first as to be very sticky. Several hairs of a weasel glued to the egg gave evidence of the predator.

There are numerous reports that many ovenbirds are killed by striking lighthouses and towers during their migration. The light keeper at Fowey Rocks, Fla., reported to W. W. Cooke (1904) that he could have filled a mail bag with ovenbirds that struck the lighthouse on October 10 and 11, 1891.

Harold S. Peters (1936) has found five species of external parasites infesting the bodies and plumage of ovenbirds as follows: two lice, *Menacanthus chrysophaeum* (Kellogg) and *Myrsidea incerta* (Kellogg); two ticks, *Haemaphysalis leporispalustris* Packard and *Ixodes brunneus* Koch; and the mite *Liponyssus sylviarum* (Canestrini and Fauzago).

Since the ovenbird is a bird of the forests and builds a nest covered over and well concealed, it would not be expected to be greatly molested by the cowbird, yet it is quite commonly parasitized in certain sections of its range. In Iowa, Lynds Jones (1888) states that every nest of the ovenbird he found at Grinnell contained two or more cowbird's eggs. Isaac E. Hess (1910) found an ovenbird's nest in central Illinois with seven eggs of the cowbird and none of the rightful owner. J. P. Norris (1892) in a series of 40 nests taken in the east chiefly from Maine to North Carolina reported 4 nests, 3 from Pennsylvania and 1 from Connecticut, which contained cowbird's eggs.

In Ohio, Lawrence E. Hicks (1934) found 41 nests out of 112, or 36 percent, parasitized by the cowbird. According to Sage, Bishop, and Bliss (1913) 11 outof 30, or nearly 37 percent, of the nests found in Connecticut contained eggs of the cowbird. H. W. Hann (1937) reports that 52 percent of those he found in southern Michigan were parasitized. Herbert Friedmann (1929) had over 150 records of parasitized ovenbirds' nests ranging from southern New England, New York, Pennsylvania and west to Illinois, Minnesota, and Iowa. In contrast it is interesting to note that of 15 ovenbirds' nests I have seen, and of many others reported in Maine, not one contained cowbird's eggs. Although the cowbird is an abundant bird in that State the ovenbird seems to be comparatively free from molestation in this part of New England.

According to Hann (1937) the cowbird lays early in the morning before the ovenbirds lay and requires only 40 to 60 seconds to deposit the egg. In 13 cases an egg of the ovenbird was removed by the cowbird before the latter deposited an egg, and the number of eggs thus removed was 75 percent of the number of cowbirds' eggs laid. The ovenbird seems to make no attempt to remove the cowbird eggs. The incubation of the cowbird's eggs averaged 11.6 days which is 0.6 of a day less than the average period of the ovenbird. Young ovenbirds in parasitized nests grew approximately as well as those in non-parasitized nests, so that the chief loss to the ovenbird was in the removal by the cowbird of an estimated 18 percent of the total number of eggs laid by the parasitized ovenbirds. However, the survival rate of the cowbirds was low, since out of 40 cowbird's eggs laid, only 22 hatched, 10 birds left the nest, and probably not more than 5 left the woods.

Fall.—Early in August ovenbirds are to be seen just south of their breeding range, indicating that the autumn migration has started. The earliest recorded dates for the Carolinas are in the first week of August. They reach southern Florida by August 20 and by the end of August the first fall migrants arrive in Cuba and Puerto Rico. The bulk of the individuals do not pass over this route until a month later. From mid-September to mid-October waves of these warblers are to be seen passing through and leaving the Florida Peninsula.

The last individuals leave Manitoba, Ontario, New Brunswick, and other sections of these parts of the northern nesting range by the last week of September. In the northern States of the Middle West and in New England they leave by the first week of October, but some linger as late as November. The last ones are generally seen in Kentucky, Virginia, and the Carolinas during the last week of October, a few are known to winter in South Carolina. From this latitude south to Florida and the Gulf States it is difficult to determine the date when the last birds leave this region for the islands of the West

Indies or via Mexico and points south.   Likewise the arrival dates in the spring are confused because of the presence of wintering individuals.

Winter.—The normal winter range of the ovenbird extends from Louisiana eastward through the Gulf States to South Carolina and southward to the West Indies, where it is widely distributed throughout the larger islands, and to the Lesser Antilles, where it has been recorded in many of the islands.   It is found throughout the Bahamas. In Mexico its winter range extends from Mazatlán on the Pacific coast, south through Central America to Colombia, South America.   It is remarkable that the ovenbird is found as far west in Mexico as Mazatlán as it is a bird of the eastern United States and it is unusual for such birds to move westward, for generally the migration routes extend south or southeastward.   Birds wintering in that section of Mexico are those which usually come by the Pacific flyway.

There are records of the ovenbird wintering or attempting to winter as far north as New England.   For example J. L. Bagg (1941) found an ovenbird at Montague, Mass., where it regularly visited a feeding shelf, from December 17, 1940, to January 30, 1941, but adds that it may have perished in the subzero night of January 30.

In correspondence received from Alexander Skutch it is stated that the ovenbird is widely distributed on both the Caribbean and Pacific sides of Guatemala and Costa Rica, in midwinter from sea level up to an altitude of 3,000 feet or more.   "At this season," Dr. Skutch writes, "it is always alone, and is most often seen walking in its usual deliberate manner over fairly open ground beneath a second-growth thicket, or in a shady plantation.   I have not encountered it in the forest.   It is typically silent, and I have not heard its song in Central America.   It has not been recorded before the first week of October; but it lingers through most of April, and at times well into May."

In Puerto Rico Alexander Wetmore (1916) states: "The oven birds frequent thickets and second-growth forests many times in dry locations.   Here they feed on the ground, flying up to low perches when alarmed.   They were entirely silent.   In coastal regions they are frequently seen in cane fields."   In Haiti and the Dominican Republic Wetmore and Swales (1931) state: "The oven-bird is found in thickets and scrubs in both humid and arid sections, where it walks about on the ground in search for food, and though not conspicuous it is not so shy as it is in its northern breeding ground."

In Florida, A. H. Howell (1932) writes: "Never particularly shy, during their winter sojourn the birds often become so tame as to come to a doorstep to pick up crumbs, * * * and once almost walked over my shoes as I sat quietly."

Range.—Canada to northern South America.

Breeding range.—The ovenbird breeds **north** to northeastern British Columbia (Fort Nelson and Fort St. John); central southern Mackenzie (probably Fort Resolution); central Saskatchewan (Pelican Narrows and Cumberland House); southern Manitoba (Aweme, Fairfield, and Family Lake); central Ontario (Lac Seul, Port Arthur, Amyot, Kapuskasing, and probably Moose Factory); southern Quebec (Mistassini Post, Lake St. John, Godbout, and Anticosti Island); and southern Newfoundland (Tompkins and probably the Avalon Peninsula). **East** to southern Newfoundland (probably the Avalon Peninsula); Prince Edward Island; Nova Scotia (Cape Breton and Baddeck); and the Atlantic Coast States south to northern Georgia (Rising Fawn, Atlanta, and Kirkwood). **South** to northern Georgia (Atlanta); northern Alabama (Florence, Monte Sano, and Anniston); southwestern Tennessee (Fayette County); northwestern Arkansas (Winslow, Magazine Mountain, London, and Clinton); eastern Oklahoma (McCurtain County); and probably eastern Colorado (Holly and Colorado Springs). **West** to Colorado (Colorado Springs, Denver); western South Dakota (Short Pine Hills and Black Hills); southeastern Montana (Miles City, Ekalaka, Long Pine Hills); southern Saskatchewan (Muscow and probably Davidson); and central Alberta (Grand Prairie, Glenevis, and Athabaska); and northeastern British Columbia (Fort Nelson).

Winter range.—The ovenbird winters **north** to northeastern Mexico (Monterrey and Matamoros); southern Louisiana (Avery Island); southern Georgia (Fitzgerald); and southern South Carolina (Mount Pleasant). **East** to South Carolina (Mount Pleasant); north-central Florida (Gainesville and Magnolia); throughout the Greater Antilles (Cuba, Jamaica, Hispaniola, and Puerto Rico); to the Bahamas and Lesser Antilles (Virgin Islands, Anguilla, Antigua, Guadeloupe, Dominica, and Martinique). **South** to the Lesser Antilles (Martinique) and northern Venezuela (Paraguana Peninsula). **West** to northern Venezuela (Paraguana Peninsula); northern Colombia (La Bonda); Panamá (Divala, Gatún, and Darién); Cost Rica; El Salvador; Guatemala (Mazatenango); Quintana Roo (Mujeres and Cozumel Islands); Yucatán (Mérida, Silan, and Chichén-Itzá); central Veracruz (El Conejo and Tres Zapotes); and northeastern Mexico (Matamoros).

Casual records include specimens taken or observed in southwestern Wyoming, southwestern Colorado (Durango), California (Farallon Islands, Glendale, and Lavic), Greenland (Narssag and Nanortalik), and **Bermuda.**

The species as outlined is divided into three subspecies, or geographic races. The eastern ovenbird (*S. a. aurocapillus*) breeds from
northeastern British Columbia to Prince Edward Island and Nova
Scotia, south to northern Georgia, and west to Colorado; the Newfoundland ovenbird (*S. a. furvior*), as far as is known, breeds only
in the southern two-thirds of Newfoundland; while the gray ovenbird
(*S. a. cinereus*) breeds in southern Alberta, southeastern Montana,
western South Dakota, and south to central and southeastern Colorado.

Migration.—Late dates of spring departure from the winter home
are: Venezuela—Rancho Grande near Maracay, Aragua, April 22.
Panamá—Chiriquí, April 15. Costa Rica—Basin of El General,
May 14. Nicaragua—Escondido River, May 6. Guatemala—Nebaj,
May 3. Nayarit—Madre Island, May 16. Virgin Islands—Kings-
hill, St. Croix, April 18. Puerto Rico—Mayagüez, April 25. Haiti—
Île á Vache, April 30; Île de la Gonâve, May 18. Cuba—Santiago
de las Vegas, April 26; average of five years at Habana, April 19.
Bahamas—Cay Lobos Light, May 13. Florida—Dry Tortugas
Island, May 22; Fort Myers, May 29. Alabama—Decatur, May 15.
Georgia—Darien, May 20. Louisiana—University, May 16. Missis-
sippi—Gulfport, May 17.

Early dates of spring arrival are: Florida—Pensacola, April 5.
Alabama—Long Island, April 8. Georgia—Athens, April 3. South
Carolina—Clemson College, April 13. North Carolina—Raleigh,
March 29 (average of 19 years, April 13). Virginia—Lawrenceville,
April 6; Rockbridge County, April 20. West Virginia—Bluefield
and French Creek, April 22 (average of 16 years at French Creek,
April 26). District of Columbia—Washington, April 10 (average of
44 years, April 23). Maryland—Baltimore County, April 9. Dela-
ware—Kent and Sussex Counties, March 27 (average of 18 years,
April 9). Pennsylvania—Harrisburg, April 12 (average of 12 years
at Philadelphia, April 25). New Jersey—Milltown, April 22. New
York—Oneida County, April 13; Bronx, April 15. Connecticut—
New Britain, April 24. Rhode Island—Kingston, April 30. Massa-
chusetts—Springfield, April 20. Vermont—St. Johnsbury, April 24.
New Hampshire—East Westmoreland, May 2. Maine—Lewiston,
April 23; Westbrook, May 1. Quebec—Montreal, April 26. New
Brunswick—Bathhurst, May 12. Nova Scotia—Halifax and Wolf-
ville, May 17. Prince Edward Island—North River, May 19. New-
foundland—Tompkins, May 19. Louisiana—Grand Isle, April 4.
Mississippi—Gulf coast, March 31. Arkansas—Winslow, April 7.
Tennessee—Memphis, March 31; Nashville—April 1 (average of 13
years, April 15). Kentucky—Bowling Green, April 8. Missouri—

St. Louis, April 11. Illinois—Chicago region, April 6 (average May 4). Indiana—Indianapolis, March 31; West Lafayette, April 1. Ohio—Wooster, April 4; average of 19 years at Oberlin, April 27. Michigan—Grand Rapids, April 13; Sault Ste. Marie, April 28. Ontario—London, April 27; Ottawa, May 10 (average of 13 years, May 16). Iowa—Ogden, April 24. Wisconsin—Madison, April 1 (average of 15 years in Dane County, May 1); Superior, April 25. Minnesota—Lanesboro, April 27 (average of 34 years for southern Minnesota, May 7; Duluth, May 4. Texas—Cove, April 1. Oklahoma—Tulsa County, April 6. Kansas—Ottawa, April 21. Nebraska—Peru, April 17. South Dakota—Vermilion, May 5. North Dakota—Wahpeton, May 7. Manitoba—Margaret, April 25. Saskatchewan—Skull Creek, May 15; Fort McMurray, May 28. Colorado—Durango, May 12; Fort Morgan, May 12. Wyoming—Camp Sheridan, May 17. Montana—Miles City, May 18. Alberta—Glenevis, May 11. California—Amboy and Los Olivos, May 13. Alaska—Kenai Peninsula and Nulato, May 30.

Late dates of fall departure are: Alaska—Kenai Peninsula, July 15. Yukon—Lebarge, July 14. British Columbia—Muskwa, July 18. California—Glendale, October 25. Montana—Hell Gate, August 26. Colorado—Mount Morrison, August 28. New Mexico—Dona Ana County, October 13. Alberta—Glenevis, September 14. Saskatchewan—Regina, September 14. Manitoba—Aweme, September 28 (average September 15); Winnipeg, October 2. North Dakota—Cass County, September 26 (average September 20); Fargo, October 4. South Dakota—Faulkton, October 5. Texas—Cove, November 19. Minnesota—Lanesboro and Minneapolis, October 16 (average of 9 years in southern Minnesota, September 23). Wisconsin—Superior, October 23. Iowa—Wall Lake, October 26. Ontario—Ottawa, October 15. Michigan—Grand Rapids, October 18. Ohio—Jerusalem Township, November 9; central Ohio, October 16 (average October 2). Indiana—Richmond, October 20. Illinois—Chicago region, October 19 (average October 2); Urbana, October 24. Missouri—Noel, November 1. Kentucky—Danville, October 14. Tennessee—Memphis and Nashville, October 15. Arkansas—Amity, October 10. Mississippi—Gulf coast, November 1. Louisiana—St. Francisville, October 17. Greenland—Narssaq (near Godthaab), October 15. Newfoundland—Cape Anguille, October 3. New Brunswick—Grand Manan, September 16. Quebec—Montreal, September 25. Maine—South Portland, October 22. New Hampshire—Water Village, October 28. Vermont—Rutland, October 11. Massachusetts—Boston, November 14; Lincoln, December 12. Connecticut—

West Hartford, November 1. New York—New York City, November
23. New Jersey—South Mountain Reservation, November 24; Sum-
mit, December 18. Pennsylvania—Berwyn, October 30. Maryland—
Patuxent Wildlife Research Refuge, October 19. District of
Columbia—Washington, November 13 (average of 23 years, October
3). West Virginia—Bluefield, October 15. Virginia—Lexington,
October 15. North Carolina—Raleigh, October 23. South Caro-
lina—Chester, October 29. Georgia—Lybee Light, Savannah,
November 11. Alabama—Greensboro, October 19. Florida—
Clewiston, November 8. Bahamas—Cay Lobos Light, November 22.

Early dates of fall arrival are: Texas—Rockport, August 13.
Ohio—Buckeye Lake, July 30 (average, August 15). Louisiana—
Rigolets, August 9. Mississippi—Gulf coast, August 25. Massachu-
setts—Marblehead, August 14. North Carolina—Raleigh, August 5.
South Carolina—Summerton, July 7; Chester, August 7. Georgia—
Athens, August 2. Alabama—Leighton, August 10. Florida—Pensa-
cola, August 10; Dry Tortugas Island, August 16. Cuba—Santiago
de las Vegas, August 26. Puerto Rico, October 3. Antigua, October 9.
Honduras—Tela, October 9. Costa Rica—San Miguel de Desam-
parados, November 1. Colombia—Bond, October 4. Venezuela—
Paraguana Peninsula, October 22.

Egg dates.—Massachusetts: 66 records, May 17 to July 1; 37 records,
May 30 to June 6, indicating the height of the season.

Michigan: 12 records, May 16 to July 26; 6 records, May 27 to
June 14.

Quebec: 17 records, May 27 to June 21; 10 records, June 3 to 10.

Pennsylvania: 14 records, May 15 to June 3; 10 records, May 25 to
31 (Harris).

SEIURUS AUROCAPILLUS FURVIOR Batchelder

NEWFOUNDLAND OVENBIRD

HABITS

Based on a series of 19 specimens collected in Newfoundland,
Charles F. Batchelder (1918) gave the above name to the ovenbirds
of that region. He describes the subspecies as follows: "Similar to
Seiurus aurocapillus, but plumage in general deeper-colored or darker.
Tawny of crown browner, less yellowish—'amber brown', instead of
the 'ochraceous orange' of *aurocapillus;* black of sides of crown more
extensive and slightly more intense; back, from nape to upper tail
coverts, and including scapulars, duskier green; dark markings of
breast and sides heavier and blacker; brown of flanks deeper."

SEIURUS AUROCAPILLUS CINEREUS A. H. Miller

GRAY OVENBIRD

HABITS

Dr. Alden H. Miller (1942) has given the above name to the oven-birds of the eastern slope of the Rocky Mountains. He describes the race as follows: "Compared with *Seiurus aurocapillus aurocapillus* of the eastern United States and Mississippi Valley, back, rump and lateral webs of rectrices grayer and paler, less intense olive-green, the feather tips at least approaching grayish olive; green almost lacking in the tails of some individuals; auriculars and side of neck less tawny."

Of its geographical distribution, he says that it breeds "along the lower eastern slopes of the Rocky Mountains and adajacent plains from the Yellowstone River in Montana south to the Arkansas River in Colorado. Suitable habitats include streamside woodlands and yellow pine forests." It "is known as a migrant from Sinaloa and the Tres Marías Islands, Mexico, where it possibly winters."

SEIURUS NOVEBORACENSIS NOVEBORACENSIS (Gmelin)

NORTHERN SMALL-BILLED WATERTHRUSH

PLATE 59

HABITS

This brilliant songster, the northern waterthrush, is known to most of us in the United States as a spring and fall migrant. It often ap-pears in our yards or gardens walking gracefully about on the lawn or under the shrubbery, but we are much more likely to find it in the thickets along the edges of the swamps or ponds, on the banks of streams, or walking daintily over the muddy shores of some shaded woodland pool. At such times it seems rather familiar and is easily approached, but on its more northern breeding grounds it is more secretive and must be looked for in the more secluded nooks in cool bogs, along the mountain streams, or about the shores of northern lakes in the Canadian Zone. There its loud and charming song will reveal its presence and tempt the listener to invade its hidden haunts.

The breeding range of the northern waterthrush includes northern New England and much of eastern Canada, but extends southward in the mountains to Pennsylvania and Virginia. It breeds locally and rarely in southern New England and New York. I once found it breeding in Rhode Island in an extensive maple swamp where cool, clear water was flowing slowly among the stumps and upturned roots of fallen trees; there, within a radius of 100 yards, we found nests of this and the Louisiana waterthrush and the winter wren, a curious mingling of northern and southern species; the musical voices of these three famous singers produced a concert that can better be imagined than described.

Todd (1940) says that at higher altitudes in western Pennsylvania, it "is sometimes found along swift mountain streams, but as a general rule it favors isolated pools of standing water in the woods— the kind of habitat that does not attract the other species at all. Rhododendron swamps are favorite haunts." Prof. Maurice Brooks (1940) says that, in the central Allegheny Mountain region, "this species, found along some of the mountain streams and in swamps at high altitudes, reaches its known southern breeding limits at Cranberry Glades. * * * It is confined to the Canadian and upper Alleghenian zones, nesting as low as 2,500 feet at Cranesville swamp in West Virginia and Maryland. * * * These warblers show a preference for streams that are lined with spruce, hemlock, or rhododendron, or a combination of these, but they may occassionally be found in northern hardwood forest."

Spring.—From its wide winter range in the West Indies and in northern South America this species apparently migrates northward over two widely separated routes, both east and west of the Gulf of Mexico, but as most of the migration records do not distinguish between the two races and are seldom based on collected specimens, it is impossible to define the routes followed by the two subspecies. It is reasonably certain, however, that the birds that winter in the West Indies and migrate northward along the Atlantic Coast States are the eastern form, although it is possible that the birds of this race that winter in British Guiana may migrate through the Antilles to Florida and northward. We would naturally expect to find that most of the birds that take the western route through Central America, Mexico, and Texas, are of the western race, *notabilis;* but typical *noveboracensis* has been taken on migration along the coast of Mexico. I have seen waterthrushes migrating along the coast of Texas, but I have taken no specimens. Birds that take the western route apparently migrate northward through the Mississippi Valley.

Nesting.—My friend Harry S. Hathaway, who had reported (1906) the nesting of the northern waterthrush in Rhode Island, showed me in 1908 what is probably the most southeastern locality in New England where this species breeds, a corner of Kingston swamp, the main portion of which was originally a cedar swamp. Most of the cedar had been cut off and was then replaced by a heavy forest of maples, large swamp white oaks, red oaks, beeches, gray and yellow birches, a few lone pines, fine holly trees, and dense patches of rhododendron. It was a cool and shady retreat, the dense foliage of the large trees shut out the sunlight, and the atmosphere was cooled by a steady flow of clear, cold spring water, in some places nearly knee deep. It was a locality well suited for such northern birds as the winter wren and this waterthrush. The nest of the latter was neatly hidden in a little cavity in a moss-covered stump prettily overgrown with ferns, the hanging dead fronds of which partially concealed the nest; it was placed only 14 inches above the water of a small pool at the base of the stump. The nest, an attractive structure, was made mainly of sphagnum moss and skeletonized leaves and was lined with green sphagnum and the red fruiting stalks of mosses. It held four fresh eggs on May 24.

I found two nests of the northern waterthrush on the heavily wooded shores of Asquam Lake, N. H., in 1926. The first nest was under an overhanging bank at the very edge of the rocky shore of the lake; it was sunken into the soil of the bank in a sheltered hollow, and contained four fresh eggs on June 16. The nest was largely made of green mosses, mixed with a few twigs, many pine needles, a few fine strips of inner bark, and some fine, black rootlets; it was lined with very fine grasses and a little cow hair. The other nest was in a similar location, but was far in under the roots of a large dead stub overhanging in the bank on the shore of the lake; it was not quite finished on June 18.

F. H. Kennard mentions in his notes a nest found near Lancaster, N. H., on June 14, 1910, that was placed in the moss on the side of a moss-covered stump in a dark, swampy place. The nest was in plain sight beneath the arch formed by two roots of the stump. T. E. McMullen has sent me the data for eight nests found in the Pocono Mountains of Pennsylvania, all found in the upturned roots of fallen trees in swamps or along streams.

Eggs.—The northern waterthrush lays either 4 or 5 eggs to a set, apparently about evenly divided, occasionally only 3 and rarely 6. These are ovate to short ovate and have little or no gloss. The ground color is creamy white or buffy white, or rarely "pale, ochraceous-buff." The eggs are speckled, spotted, and blotched with "auburn," "argus brown," "Brussels brown," or "cinnamon-brown," with underlying spots of "light purplish gray" or "fuscous." They may be finely and sparsely speckled, or boldly blotched, but in general are more heavily marked than those of the ovenbird. They may also be decorated with small scrawls or cloudings of "wood brown." Occasionally this clouding almost entirely obscures the ground color. All types of markings are concentrated at the large end. In looking over a large series of these eggs, the gray spots seem rather less pronounced than on the eggs of the Lousiana waterthrush. The measurements of 50 eggs average 19.1 by 14.6 millimeters; the eggs showing the four extremes measures 20.8 by 15.0, 19.3 by 16.0, and 17.8 by 13.7 millimeters (Harris).

Young.—Nothing seems to be known about the incubation, or about the care and development of the young.

Plumages.—Dr. Dwight (1900) calls the natal down deep olive-brown, and describes the juvenal plumage of the northern waterthrush as "above, deep olive-brown with cinnamon edgings. Wings and tail darker, the coverts tipped with pale cinnamon. Below, primrose-yellow heavily streaked on the chin and less heavily on the throat, breast and sides with deep olive or clove-brown. Indistinct superciliary line and orbital ring buff; transocular stripe dusky."

The first winter plumage is acquired by a partial postjuvenal molt in July, which involves the contour plumage and the wing coverts, but not the rest of the wings or the tail. Young and old are now practically indistinguishable. The sexes are alike in all plumages. Dr. Dwight describes this plumage as "above, yellowish olive-brown including wing coverts, without edgings. Below, straw-yellow, palest on the crissum, the flanks washed with olive-brown, spotted on the chin and streaked, except on the mid-abdomen and crissum, with black veiled by overlapping whitish edgings. Superciliary stripe and orbital ring pale ochraceous-buff; transocular streak deep olive-brown; auriculars dusky.

"First nuptial plumage acquired by marked wear, birds becoming browner above and paler below, the veiling lost. It is possible there is a very limited growth of new feathers about the head." Year-old birds can usually be recognized by the paler and somewhat worn wings and tails.

Adults have a complete postnuptial molt in July. The adult winter plumage is like that of the first winter, but the streakings below are rather broader and the wings and tail are darker. Subsequent spring plumages are produced by wear, as in the young bird.

Food.—Forbush (1929) writes: "The food of the Water-Thrush consists more or less of aquatic insects, beetles and their larvae, and moths. It picks up dead and soggy leaves from crevices in the rocks and throws them aside, thus uncovering lurking creatures on which it feeds. According to Dr. Elliott Coues tiny molluscs and crustaceans are eaten, and Arthur T. Wayne took one that had eaten a few small minnows. Dr. B. H. Warren names small worms as one consituent of its food, and it also eats quantities of mosquitoes."

Dr. Wetmore (1916) reports on the contents of four stomachs of this species, including both races, collected in Puerto Rico, as follows:

"Fly pupae and a few adults were present in three stomachs and amount to 43 per cent of the total. Ants (24 per cent), of which one bird had eaten 40, were found in three stomachs. Water scavenger beetles were found in two instances and a hister beetle (*Hister* sp.) once. In one stomach were five water boatmen (*Plea* sp.) and another aquatic bug, and two contained the remains of small crabs (in one case of *Uca*). In single stomachs were found the jaw of an orthopteran, a lantern fly, and a bone from the head of a tiny fish."

Stuart T. Danforth (1925) reports on the 95 percent of animal food in four stomachs, also from Puerto Rico, "3 damselflies, 10 per cent; 20 large fleabeetles (*Haltica jamaicensis*), 19 percent; 2 fleabeetles (*Systena basalis*), 1.3 per cent; Carabid beetles (*Stenous* sp.), 26.2 per cent; pupa of a Sesban weevil (*Tyloderma* sp.), 1.2 per cent; other Colepterous fragments, 5 per cent; 2 Noctuid caterpillars, 5 per cent; 1 Syrphid fly (*Volucella obesa*), 2 per cent; 3 caseworms (*Tincola uterella*), 6.1 per cent; 1 slug, 2.5 per cent." He also reported a few seeds.

Behavior.—Forbush (1929) describes the behavior of the waterthrush, much better than I can, in the following words: "Though not really a thrush, the Water-Thrush is well named. It is a large wood warbler disguised as a thrush and exhibiting an extreme fondness for water.

"Like the Oven-bird it walks, and seems fond of walking on a log, but prefers to pass down a slanting log, the lower end of which enters the water. It is unlike the Oven-bird, however, in its almost continuous teetering of the body and wagging of the tail, which it seems to move up and down almost as unconsciously and regularly as it draws the breath of life; this action is accompanied by a springy motion of the legs."

Dr. Coues (1878) aptly refers to the timidity and retiring habits of the waterthrush during the nesting season and adds:

But this is only when he feels the cares and full responsibilities of home and family. Later in the season, when these things are off his mind, he is quite another fellow, who will meet you more than half-way should you chance to find him then, with a wondering, perhaps, yet with a confident and quite familiar, air of easy unconcern. Anywhere by the water's edge—in the *débris* of the wide-stretched river-bottom, in the flowery tangle of the brook, around the margins of the little pools that dot the surface where tall oaks and hickories make pleasant shade—there rambles the Water-Thrush. Watch him now, and see how prettily he walks, rustling among the fallen leaves where he threads his way like a mouse, or wading even up to his knees in the shallow miniature lakes, like a Sandpiper by the sea-shore, all intent in quest of the aquatic insects, worms, and tiny molluscs and crustaceans that form his varied food. But as he rambles on in this gliding course, the mincing steps are constantly arrested, and the dainty stroller poises in a curious way to see-saw on his legs, quite like a Titlark or a Spotted Sandpiper.

We always think of the waterthrush as living on or near the ground and in the immediate vicinity of water, in such places as those mentioned, but there are exceptions to the rule, especially during migra-

tions. Wendell Taber tells me that he heard two of them singing, and
saw one of them "sitting near the top of a birch tree which rose out of
the swamp and which towered above all other trees about except bal-
sams." He estimated that the bird was about 35 feet above the ground.
On another occasion, he saw one in a hemlock grove, a long distance
from any water. The bird was very tame, and was "walking around,
bobbing, on hemlock limbs."

Mr. Brewster (1938) gives the following account of the behavior of
a bird about a nest he was photographing:

The female was very nervous and fussy, chirping and calling up her mate the
first thing. She would not go on the nest when the camera was near it but kept
running rapidly about around the bank and the camera, examining the latter as
well as the bulb of my rubber tube which lay several yards off with evident distrust. When started from the nest she would regularly run six or eight yards,
crouching close to the ground and moving with a slow gliding motion, spreading
her tail and half spreading and quivering her wings, sometimes turning back
and gliding past me or just under the nest, making no sound nor tilting while
behaving thus, but presently flying up to some branch or root to tilt and chirp
with her mate.

Again, he writes: "As I was sitting in my canoe this afternoon in a
sheltered cove one appeared on the shore within three yards of me.
By degrees it approached even nearer running about over some driftwood, now and then pausing to look at me intently with its large dark
eyes. Even when I moved abruptly it showed no fear of me."

Voice.—Aretas A. Saunders (MS.) describes the song as follows:
"The song of the northern waterthrush is a series of rather short,
staccato notes, either all equal in time or accelerating toward the end.
The number of notes in my 30 records varies from 6 to 15 and averages about 10. The song is loud, and the notes are of sweet, musical
quality. They contain marked consonant sounds, with explosive, and
liquid, single notes sounding like *tleep*, *tlip*, or *tlap*.

"The pitch of the song varies from C''' to D'''', one tone more than
an octave. Single songs have a range of from one to three and a half
tones, the majority, 16 records, ranging two and a half tones. The
general trend of change in pitch, in all songs, is downward. In all
but 4 of my records the last note is the lowest in pitch. In all but 6
the first note is on the highest pitch of the song. In 10 of the records,
however, the downward trend of the pitch is broken by a single high
note, sometimes as high as the first note, near the end of the song, and
most frequently the next to the last note.

"Songs vary from 1⅘ to 2⅗ seconds. In a majority of the songs
the first notes are slow, and the remaining notes become gradually
more rapid, but 13 of my records show no change in time, the notes
all being of equal length.

"This song may be heard commonly from migrating birds, and, on
the breeding grounds, continues until about the middle of July. I

have little data on the summer song, however, and cannot give average dates for the time of cessation."

Francis H. Allen tells me that he has recorded the song as *"wheet wheet chip chip chip wheedleyou*, and as *wheet wheet chip chip chip chip chip'-ū*, the final *ū* rather faint. A call or alarm note is a sharp, metallic or perhaps 'stony' *chip*, thinner than that of the ovenbird, but carrying well." In 1912, in Newfoundland, I recorded the song as *chip chip chip chip chitter chitterew*.

Gerald Thayer wrote to Dr. Chapman (1907) :

At its best the song of this species is not quite so fine, perhaps, as that of *Seiurus motacilla*—it is very different, and has a rare grace and vigor of its own. Like the Oven-bird the Northern Water-Thrush makes up for a great general regularity of singing by an occasional wide lapse into variation. Its flight-song, a performance relatively far less common than the Oven-bird's (?), seems to be nearly changeless. It is like the common perch song, but quicker and longer, and "framed" in a hurried jumble of half-call-half-song notes;—the whole delivered as the bird dashes horizontally through or barely above the woods. Most notable among the few important variations of its perch-song I have heard was a long, liquid strain seemingly made up of at least three united repetitions of the regular utterances, going unusually fast, in a thinner tone, and intersprinkled with sharp notes of "chippering," unlike the common call-notes. The typical perch-song itself is hard to describe in words. A ringing, bubbling warble, swift and emphatic, made up of two parts, barely divided, the second lower-toned and diminuendo.

Dr. Sutton (1928) recognizes the song as expressed by the human words, *"Hurry, hurry, hurry, pretty, pretty, pretty."*

Albert R. Brand (1938) gives for the song of this species a range of from 2,000 to 3,850 vibrations per second, with an approximate mean of 2,925, the lowest frequency, or the lowest pitch, that he recorded in any of the other wood warblers, except the yellow-breasted chat.

Field marks.—The bird with which the northern waterthrush is most likely to be confused is its congener, the Louisiana waterthrush; the former has a buffy line over the eye and sulphur-yellow under parts, streaked with black almost up to the chin; the latter has a more conspicuous pure white stripe over the eye, a much whiter throat, and white underparts, streaked less conspicuously with olive-brown; the latter also has a larger bill. The ovenbird has no stripe over the eye.

Enemies.—Dr. Friedmann (1929) says that the waterthrush is "rarely victimized" by the cowbird; probably the latter has difficulty in finding its nest, as only four observers have reported cases of victimization.

Harold S. Peters (1936) reports one louse, *Menacanthus* sp., and two bird-flies, *Ornithoica confluenta* Say and *Ornithomyia anchineuria* Speiser, as external parasites on the northern waterthrush.

Fall.—The northern waterthrush starts on its fall migration before the end of July and passes through the Atlantic Coast States mainly in August; it has been recorded in Costa Rica as early as August 12, and generally reaches its winter home in September. P. H. Gosse (1847) records its arrival in Jamaica as early as August 5.

Waterthrushes are sometimes very abundant on the fall migrations and may be found almost anywhere, even about buildings. Taverner and Swales (1908) write of the migration at Point Pelee, Ontario: "During the height of their abundance they were the most conspicuous bird on the Point, and were seen in all kinds of places, and at all times. They were in the low, damp spots in the woods, in the high walnut timber, and in the red cedar thickets. They were common everywhere. We found them in the last outlying brush pile near the end of the final sand spit, and in patches of weeds and cotton woods along the eastern sand dune. * * * It was no uncommon sight to have four or five in the same line of vision, besides others that could be heard and not seen."

Winter.—A few waterthrushes may spend the winter in Florida, but most of them pass on to the Bahamas and the West Indies, or to Central America and northern South America. Savile G. Reid (1884) lists this species as "one of the commonest but most interesting of autumnal visitors" in Bermuda. "It appears regularly early in October and a few remain all winter." It appears to be a regular winter resident in the Bahamas. Dr. Wetmore (1916) records it as "a fairly common winter visitant in the coastal region of Puerto Rico. * * * These water-thrushes occur only in the mangroves of the coastal region, where they are found about bays and lagoons feeding on the ground, and though their sharp call notes are heard repeatedly, the birds themselves are usually hidden. * * * In April they were singing as clearly as in the North." Dr. Barbour (1923) says that, in Cuba, it is "a not uncommon winter visitor. Found about lakes, ditches and river banks, and in the mangroves along the seashore."

In El Salvador, Dickey and van Rossem (1938) record it as "fairly common in fall, winter, and spring throughout the lowlands and foothills. Dates of arrival and departure are August 31 and April 29. * * * While in winter quarters water-thrushes seem always to be solitary. They were usually to be observed walking daintily about in wet or boggy places, such as swamp holes in the forest or at the water's edge along streams and ponds."

Dr. Skutch contributes the following notes: "All three races of waterthrush occur as migrants in Central America. Griscom regards the western race as the more abundant; while Carriker considered typical *noveboracensis* as the prevalent race in Costa Rica.

"Throughout Central America, the northern waterthrush (including its western representatives, Grinnell's and McCabe's waterthrushes), is seen far more often than the Louisiana waterthrush. It occurs as an abundant spring and fall transient, and as a not very abundant winter resident. As a bird of passage, it is found in both spring and fall on both sides of the Cordillera, while in the highlands I have met it as high as 10,600 feet. As a winter resident, it is most abundant in the Caribbean lowlands, but has been recorded in mid-winter in the Pacific lowlands. It arrives in Central America in August or September, and remains until April or May, late stragglers sometimes delaying until May 30.

"Like its relatives, the Louisiana waterthrush and the ovenbird, the northern waterthrush leads a solitary existence in its winter home. Most often seen foraging along the shores of streams and lagoons, but it is by no means confined to the immediate vicinity of water, for in the Central American lowlands it will occasionally be found walking sedately through a banana plantation or an orchard where the ground is moist and not too encumbered with weeds, or on the bare ground about houses where all is quiet, or even over shady lawns, flicking fallen leaves aside with its bill. But although it will at times venture so close to the habitations of man, it is not for that reason at ease in his presence, and is always ready to fly when the inmates of the dwelling show themselves. On the Island of Jamaica, in December, 1930, I found northern waterthrushes abundant in the swamps of black mangrove (*Avicennia nitida*) along the south coast, where the naked muddy ground was covered with shallow water. Doubtless they haunt similar situations in Central America.

"Early dates of fall arrival in Central America are: Guatemala—Sierra Cuchumatanes, 10,600 feet, September 15, 1934. Honduras—Tela, October 5, 1930. Costa Rica—San José (Cherrie), September 14; Escazú (Carriker), August 13, 1902; Basin of El General, October 18, 1936.

"Late dates of spring departure from Central America are: Panamá—Barro Colorado Island, Canal Zone, April 12, 1935. Costa Rica—El Pozo de Térraba (Underwood), April 8, 1906; Basin of El General, April 23, 1936, April 27, 1939, April 17, 1940, and April 11, 1942; San José (Cherrie), May 21 and May 30. Honduras—Tela, May 9, 1930. Guatemala—Sierra de Tecpán, 8,500 feet, April 27, 1933; Motagua Valley, near Los Amates, May 18, 1932; Finca Sepacuité (Griscom), May 22."

DISTRIBUTION

Range.—North America, the West Indies, and northern South America.

Breeding range.—The waterthrush breeds **north** to north-central Alaska (valleys of the Kobuk and Yukon Rivers); northern Yukon

(La Pierre House); northwestern and central southern Mackenzie (Aklavik, Fort McPherson, Fort Good Hope, Fort Norman, Fort Simpson, Fort Rae, Fort Resolution, and Hill Island Lake); northeastern Saskatchewan (Cochrane River); northern Manitoba (north end of Lake DuBrochet, Churchill, and York Factory); northern Ontario (Seven House, mouth of the Attawapiskat River, and Moose Factory); north-central Quebec (Fort George, inland from Richmond Gulf, Lake Albanel, and probably Fort Chimo); Labrador (Davis Inlet, Cartwright, St. Peter's Bay and probably Grand Falls); and Newfoundland (Hare Bay, Canada Bay, Fogo Island, Gander, and St. John's). **East** to Newfoundland (St. John's); Nova Scotia (Bridgetown, Halifax, and probably Sable Island); central Massachusetts (Lenox, Huntington, Amherst, Ware, Boston, rarely Springfield, and Taunton); rarely in Rhode Island (Washington County and Kingston); New York (Lime Lake, Naples, Potter, Canandaigua, and Oswego); northwestern New Jersey (High Point, Newfoundland Lake, and Sparta); Pennsylvania (Eagle Rock, Warren, Hollidaysburg, Williamsport, and the Pocono Mountains); West Virginia (Bluefields, Pendleton County, and Shepherd Grade); western Virginia (Salem); and western North Carolina (Buncombe County). **South** to North Carolina (Buncombe County); Ohio (Cleveland, Austinburg, Trumbull County, and Pymatuning Swamp); northern Michigan (Brown Lake, Huron Mountains, Blaney Park, and Less Chenneaux Island); rarely Wisconsin (Dunn County, Unity, and Shiocton); northeastern Minnesota (Gull Lake, Otter Lake, and Duluth); central North Dakota (Turtle Mountains); western Montana (Fortine, Bitterroot Valley, Florence, Gallatin County, and Great Falls); northern Idaho (Coeur d'Alene and St. Maries); central Saskatchewan (Buffalo River, Carlton House, and Cumberland House); southern Alberta (Grand Prairie, Jasper Park, and Vermillion Lakes); and British Columbia (Okanagan Landing). **West** to British Columbia (Okanagan Landing, Lac la Hache, Frazer Lake, Glenora, Doch-da-on Creek, and Fort Nelson); and Alaska (Goodnews Bay, Seldovia, Tustamena Lake, Tanana Crossing, and Kobuk River Valley).

Winter range.—The waterthrush winters **north** to southern Baja California (Magdalena Bay, La Paz, San Pedro, and San José del Cabo); southern Mexico (Acapulco, Tlalpan, Guerrero, Jalapa, San Andres, Tuxtla, and Chinchorro Bank); Yucatán Peninsula (Mujeres Island); Cuba (Habana and Cienfuegos); the Bahamas (New Providence, San Salvador, and Great Inagua); Bermuda; Haiti (Tortue Island, Caracol, and Etang de Miragoâne); Dominican Republic (Monte Cristi and San Juan); and Puerto Rico (Mona Island, Mameyes, and Culebra Island). **East** to Puerto Rico (Culebra Island); throughout the Lesser Antilles (Virgin Islands, Antuilla, Barbuda, Antigua, Guadeloupe, San Lucia, the Grenadines, Tobago, and Trinidad); and French Guiana (Cayenne). **South** to French Guiana (Cayenne); British Guiana; and Ecuador (Esmeraldas). **West** to Ecuador (Esmeraldas); through Central America; Mexico (Tulancingo and Metlaltoyuca); to southern Baja California (Magdalena Bay).

Casual records include specimens taken or observed in Greenland, Texas, Michigan, Louisiana, and Mississippi.

The species as outlined is divided into three subspecies or geographic races. The northern waterthrush (*S. n. noveboracensis*) breeds in the eastern part of the range from Newfoundland to North Carolina; Grinnell's waterthrush (*S. n. notabilis*) takes up the greater part of the range from Alaska to southwestern Labrador and south through north-central Quebec, northern Michigan, northeastern Ohio, and west; while McCabe's waterthrush (*S. n. limnaeus*) breeds in central British Columbia.

Migration.—Late dates of spring departure are: Venezuela—Rancho Grande near Maracay, Aragua, April 22. Colombia—Santa Marta region, April 30. Panamá—San Miguel Island, April 29. Costa Rica—San José, May 21. Nicaragua—southeastern, May 5. Honduras—near Tela, May 9. Guatemala—Uaxactún, May 7. Vera Cruz—Presidio, May 21. Baja California—Puerto Balandra, May 18. Virgin Islands—St. Croix, May 5. Puerto Rico—Fortuna, May 10. Haiti—Île à Vache, May 6. Cuba—Habana, May 20.. The Bahamas—Cay Lobos Light, May 17.

Early dates of spring arrival are: The Bahamas—Cay Lobos Light, April 11. Florida—Miami, March 15; Pensacola, March 16. Alabama—Sylacauga, April 16. Georgia—Macon, March 15. South Carolina—Mount Pleasant, March 24. North Carolina—Raleigh, April 4 (average of 15 years, April 27). Virginia—Rockbridge County, April 16. West Virginia—Bluefield, April 22. District of Columbia—Washington, April 16 (average of 36 years, April 27). Maryland—Plummers Island, April 18. Pennsylvania—Sandy Lake, Mercer County, April 22; State College, April 24 (average, April 26). New Jersey—Fort Lee, April 21. New York—Cold Spring Harbor, Long Island, April 14; Ithaca, April 23. Connecticut—Portland, April 27. Rhode Island—Kingston, April 21. Massachusetts—Nahant, April 22. Vermont—Rutland, April 26. New Hampshire—Hancock, April 29. Maine—Phillips, April 28. Quebec—Montreal, April 30. New Brunswick—Scotch Lake, May 4. Nova Scotia—Wolfville, May 3. Prince Edward Island—Mount Herbert, May 13. Newfoundland—Stephenville Crossing, May 22. Louisiana—New Orleans, April 7. Mississippi—Deer Island, April 19. Tennessee—

Memphis, April 19. Kentucky—Bowling Green, April 27. Missouri—St. Charles, April 21. Illinois—Chicago region, April 7 (average, April 20). Indiana—Richmond, April 25. Ohio—Oberlin, April 16; central Ohio, April 15 (average, April 28). Michigan—Ann Arbor and Detroit, April 27. Ontario—London, April 23; Ottawa, May 8. Iowa—Ames and Hudson, April 30. Wisconsin—Sheboygan, April 25; Madison, April 26. Minnesota—Minneapolis, April 22 (average of 32 years for southern Minnesota, May 3). Texas—Atascosa County, March 28. Kansas—Lake Quivira, April 25. Nebraska—Omaha, April 24. South Dakota—Sioux Falls, April 30. North Dakota—Argusville, April 30 (average, May 16). Manitoba—Aweme, May 4 (average, May 14). Saskatchewan—Indian Head and Lake Johnston, May 11. Mackenzie—Fort Simpson, May 14; Mackenzie Delta, May 31. New Mexico—Silver City, May 6. Arizona—Tucson, April 26. Colorado—Denver, May 12. Utah—Uinta Basin, May 8. Wyoming—Lake Como and Torrington, May 10. Idaho—Pocatello, May 13. Montana—Fortine, May 12. Alberta—Glenevis, May 12. California—Altadena, May 15 (only spring record). British Columbia—Okanagan Landing, May 2; Nulki Lake, May 26. Yukon—Forty Mile, May 20. Alaska—head of North Fork of Kuskokwim River, May 16; Bethel, May 27.

Late dates of fall departure are: Alaska—Nunivak Island, August 22; St. Michael, August 25. Yukon—Dawson, August 29; Macmillan Pass, September 4. British Columbia—Mushwa, September 8; Arrow Lakes, September 24. Washington—Prescott, September 11. California—Rodeo Lagoon, Marin County, October 18. Alberta—Glenevis, September 1. Montana—Fort Keogh, September 12. Wyoming—Laramie, September 13. Utah—Zion National Park, September 22. Colorado—Clear Creek, September 3. Arizona—Phoenix, September 16. New Mexico—Glenrio, October 21. Mackenzie—Mackenzie Delta August 15; MacTavish Bay, August 22. Saskatchewan—Redberry, September 1. Manitoba—Treesbank, October 13. North Dakota—Lower Souris Refuge, Upham, October 4; Cass County, September 23 (average, September 18). South Dakota—Faulkton, September 30. Nebraska—Minden, October 19. Texas—Anahuac, October 18; Glenrio, Deaf Smith County, October 21. Minnesota—Minneapolis, October 15 (average of 17 years for southern Minnesota, September 24). Wisconsin—Madison, October 19. Iowa—National, October 15. Ontario—Ottawa, September 17; Sundridge, October 18. Michigan—Sault Ste. Marie, October 13. Ohio—Ashtabula County, October 18; Buckeye Lake, October 13 (average, October 1). Indiana—Lake and Porter Counties, October 12. Illinois—Chicago region, October 21. Missouri—St. Louis, October 17. Kentucky—Bowling Green, October 8. Tennessee—Memphis, October 6. Louisiana—Baton Rouge region, October 24. Mississippi—Gulf coast, October 24. Newfoundland—Tompkins, September 18. Nova Scotia—Bridgetown, September 30. New Brunswick—Grand Manan, September 16. Quebec—Quebec, September 23. Maine—Winthrop, October 22. New Hampshire—Monroe, September 20. Vermont—Woodstock, September 20. Massachusetts—Worcester, October 16; Swampscott, November 17. Rhode Island—Providence, October 8. Connecticut—West Hartford, October 24. New York—Schenectady, October 25; Rhinebeck, November 16; Brooklyn, November 30. New Jersey—Union County, October 23 (average of 12 years, October 8). Pennsylvania—Renovo, October 15. Maryland—Cambridge, October 22; Solomons, December 12. District of Columbia—Washington, October 16 (average of 15 years, September 25). West Virginia—Bluefield, October 11. Virginia—Rockbridge County, October 27. North Carolina—Louisburg, October 13; Raleigh, October 12 (average of 9 years, September 29). South Carolina—Mount Pleasant, October 22. Georgia—Augusta, October 22. Alabama—Brewton, October 8. Florida—Pensacola, October 22; Fort Myers, October 24. Bahamas—Cay Lobos Light, October 30.

Early dates of fall arrival are: Yukon—Sheldon Lake, Canol Road, August 7. California—Marin County, August 13; Cactus Flat, San Bernardino County, August 16. Montana—Chief Mountain Lake, and west of Sweet Grass Hills, and Billings, August 12. Wyoming—Fort Steele, Carbon County, August 9. Utah—Uinta Basin, August 11. Colorado—Estes Park, July 16. Arizona—Mormon Lake, August 17; Camp Verde, August 27. New Mexico—Glenrio, August 25. Manitoba—Treesbank, August 21. North Dakota—Cass County, August 13 (average August 16). South Dakota—Faulkton, August 10. Kansas—Doniphan County, August 23. Oklahoma—Fort Sill, August 29. Texas—Mission, August 5. Minnesota—Minneapolis, August 14 (average of 11 years for southern Minnesota, August 27). Wisconsin—Beloit, August 14. Iowa—National, August 14. Ontario—Sundridge, July 13. Michigan—McMillan, August 6. Ohio—Lucas County, July 23 (1932); Buckeye Lake, August 14 (average August 24). Indiana—Whiting, August 10. Illinois—Chicago region, August 1 (average August 20). Missouri—La Grange, August 14. Tennessee—Quebec and Nashville, August 21. Louisiana—Baton Rouge region, August 15. Mississippi—Biloxi, August 11. New Brunswick—Kent Island, July 31. Maine—Seguin Island Light, August 5. Massachusetts—Belmont, August 1. Rhode Island—Block Island, July 29. Connecticut—Hartford, July 17. New York—Elmhurst, Long Island, July 20. New Jersey—Cape May, July 23. Pennsylvania—Berks County, August 7. Maryland—Kensington, July 21. District of Columbia, Washington, July 28

(average of 13 years, August 12).   Virginia—Fort Belvoir (10 miles
south of Alexandria), August 16.   North Carolina—Raleigh, July 21
(average of 7 years, August 3).   South Carolina—Clarendon County,
July   7.   Georgia—Athens,   August   18.   Alabama—Greensboro,
August 25.   Florida—Pensacola, August 19, Boca Chica Key, August
26.   Cuba—Cienfuegos, July 8 and August 20; Batabano, Habana,
August   20.   Jamaica—August   5.   Puerto   Rico—Mona   Island,
August 18.   Barbuda—August 25.   Senora—Bernardina River, Sep-
tember 4.   Guatemala—Sierra Cuchumatanes, September 15.   Nica-
ragua—near Bluefields, September 19.   Costa Rica—base of Volcán
Turialba, August 12.   El Salvador—Lake Olomega, August 31.
Panamá—east coast of Panamá, September 18.   Colombia—Santa
Marta region, September 8.   Venezuela—Tucacas, Estado Falcón,
October 19.   French Guiana—Cayenne, October 14.

Egg dates.—Alaska: 5 records, May 29 to June 20.

British Columbia: 5 records, June 5 to 27.

Maine: 30 records, May 28 to June 13; 23 records, May 30 to June 6,
indicating the height of the season.

Pennsylvania: 16 records, May 25 to June 22; 11 records, May 31
to June 7.

Quebec: 8 records, May 22 to June 27; 5 records, May 26 to June
1 (Harris).

SEIURUS NOVEBORACENSIS NOTABILIS Ridgway

GRINNELL'S SMALL-BILLED WATERTHRUSH

HABITS

This northwestern race is described by Ridgway (1902) as similar
to the eastern race, but "larger, especially the bill; coloration of upper
parts less olive (more grayish sooty), that of under parts less yellowish usually white, with little if any yellow tinge.   Young much darker
above than that of *S. n. noveboracensis*, the feathers entirely dusky
(except the buffy tip), instead of olive with a subterminal bar of
dusky."   He gives as its range—

western North America; breeding from Minnesota (north of Red Wing), western
Nebraska (Sioux County), and probably the more northern Rocky Mountain
districts of the United States to Alaska (whole of wooded districts), and East
Cape, Siberia; southward during migration throughout western United States
(including Mississippi Valley), more rarely through Atlantic coast States (New
Jersey, District of Columbia, Virginia, South Carolina, Florida, etc.), to the
Bahamas (New Providence Island, February), Cuba (Santiago, November 18),
island of Old Providence, Caribbean Sea, Cozumel Island, Yucatan, through
Mexico and Central America to Colombia (Chirua, province of Santa Marta,
February), and to Cape St. Lucas.

Dr. Nelson (1887) says of its range in northern Alaska: "In the
wooded interior, as at the Yukon mouth, it is abundant, and, in fact,

is one of the most common bush-frequenting birds throughout the entire fur countries, extending north even beyond the tree limit."

Its migration route seems to be mainly east of the Rocky Mountains, as it is apparently only accidental in California and farther south along the Pacific coast of Central America.

Nesting.—Baird, Brewer, and Ridgway (1874) give us the following short account of what were probably the first reported nests of Grinnell's waterthrush: "Among other memoranda given me by the late Mr. Kennicott was one furnished him by Mr. Lockhart, to the effect that, at Yukon River, June 21, 1859, he had shot a female Water Thrush as she flew from her nest. This contained five eggs, and was concealed under a small pile of drift, close to the river, but under large willow-trees. This was not lined with down. At the same locality another nest with six eggs was also obtained. This also was on the ground at the foot of some willows near the water. It was made of moss, and lined with very fine grass."

Henry C. Killingstad writes to me from Mountain Village, Alaska: "These birds nest wherever there is brush or tree growth. The presence of water is a foregone conclusion here where everything is wet. I found one nest on June 13, 1943, under the upthrust end of a piece of driftwood 20 feet from the Yukon. Earlier in the same month I saw several birds carrying nesting material along a spring-fed trickle through the alders north of the village. This little stream is not more than 2 feet across, but where it cuts into the tangled alders it makes many tunnels and labyrinths through which the birds can be found feeding day and night."

Richard C. Harlow has sent me the data for a nest that he found north of Belvedere, Alberta, on June 17, 1926; it was well-hidden in the overhanging upturned roots of a spruce tree, a foot above stagnant water, on the edge of a wet, swampy portion of the woods; it was made of leaves, weed stalks, mosses, and fern stalks.

Eggs.—Grinnell's waterthrush lays from 4 to 6 eggs to a set. These are apparently indistinguishable from those of the northern waterthrush. The measurements of 21 eggs average 19.1 by 14.4 millimeters; the eggs showing the four extremes measure 20.7 by 15.3, 19.8 by 15.4, and 16.0 by 12.7 millimeters (Harris).

Voice.—Although he never made a record of it, Aretas A. Saunders tells me that, from his limited experience with it, he believes that the song of Grinnell's waterthrush is "distinctly different from that of the northern waterthrush." But published accounts indicate that there is a decided similarity in the songs of the two subspecies, which one would naturally expect to find. And H. C. Killingstad adds: "At Mountain Village, this bird does not act as it does in the States. Its loud, clear, and pleasing song is heard from bush and tree tops, one of the most characteristic voices in the bird chorus. This song is a pleasant surprise to one accustomed only to its metallic alarm note. For the past two summers, 1942 and 1943, a favorite singing perch of one of these birds has been the top of a 30-foot radio antenna pole in the middle of the village and only a few feet from an Eskimo cabin door. From this perch the song rings to both ends of the village, a half mile distant each way."

Fall.—William T. Shaw (MS.) thus pleasantly portrays an early stage in the fall migration of Grinnell's waterthrush: "When mid-August nights are cool in Saskatchewan and one awakens to morning sunrays slanting over low, wild meadows that glisten lightly with the white of frost, presently there comes from the margin of the sedge-grown, spring-fed lakelet nearby the sharp, evenly spaced call note of the waterthrush, early reminder of the southern drift of migration. Here, on August 20, 1943, this bird first came down out of the northern territory on its way out. It is water-loving and inhabits moist rims of streams and lakelets, comfortably shaded by trembling aspen, black poplar, and willow. It is noticeably solitary, more rarely coming in pairs during migration. Through the past few years, it has arrived with dependable regularity beside my camp at Livelong, in northwestern Saskatchewan, remaining a week or ten days through storm or shine as the weather happens to come, before it passes on. To find it, look low by the water's edge, among the outer radiating willow stems, now lightly touched with yellow tints of Autumn, where shade has all but banished grass growth, and dark, damp prairie soil soon emerges into the waters of the pool; there is found this oddly marked, graceful bird of trim sparrow size, but in mannerism and habit one uniquely set aside unto itself."

Arthur T. Wayne (1920) evidently considered Grinnell's waterthrush to be the prevailing form in South Carolina on migrations. He writes: "On one occasion during a heavy rain storm one night in September—I think on September 12, 1912—I saw vast hosts of Water-Thrushes in a swamp near my house on the morning of that day, there being in sight hundreds in the area of a hundred square feet, and I estimated that there must have been certainly twenty-five thousand or even more birds in the portion of the swamp I explored that day."

SEIURUS NOVEBORACENSIS LIMNAEUS McCabe and Miller

BRITISH COLUMBIA SMALL-BILLED WATERTHRUSH

HABITS

Thomas T. McCabe and Alden H. Miller (1933) have published a study of the geographic variation in the northern waterthrushes, to which the reader is referred, as it is too long to include here. From their study of the characters involved in these variations they conclude that a new name is desirable for the waterthrushes that breed in British Columbia. They summarize the subspecific characters of the new race as follows: "Dorsum between olivaceous black and dark grayish olive; underparts with yellowish averaging less than in *S. n. noveboracensis* but more than in *S. n. notabilis;* wing and tail averaging small; tarsus as in *notabilis.*"

They give the breeding range as "central interior British Columbia, extending with some diminution of characters through northern British Columbia."

Its migration extends as far south as Panamá.

SEIURUS MOTACILLA (Vieillot)

LOUISIANA WATERTHRUSH

PLATES 60, 61

HABITS

The earlier ornithologists confused the two waterthrushes. Neither Wilson nor Nuttall recognized two species, and their accounts evidently referred partly to one and partly to the other. For example, Wilson (1832) speaks of one as passing through Pennsylvania to the north, and mentions the other as living in the cane brakes and swamps of Louisiana; both of these he called "Water Thrush—*Turdus aquaticus*"; but his description fits the Louisiana waterthrush, as we now know it. Nuttall's (1832) account is similar, though he uses the name *noveboracensis*, and his description follows Wilson. Audubon (1841) evidently recognized and figured both species, though his figure of the northern bird is apparently *notabilis*, and most of his remarks seem to refer to *motacilla*. Both species, however, had been recognized and named previously by European ornithologists, as shown in their present names.

The haunts of the Louisiana waterthrush have been variously described. Dr. Edgar A. Mearns (1879) writes: "Its notes cannot be dissociated from the sound of gurgling, rushing waters. * * * Even a casual allusion to this little bird recalls, to the mind of the collector, a bright picture of clear mountain streams, with their falls and eddies, their dams of rocks and fallen tree-trunks, their level stretches flowing over bright, pebbly bottoms, with mossy banks and rocky ferneries, and their darting minnows and dace; for only in such wild localities is the Water Wagtail at home."

Baird, Brewer, and Ridgway (1874) state that in the Wabash Valley, where it is an abundant summer resident, "it inhabits the dampest situations in the bottom-lands, the borders of creeks, lagoons,

and swamps, living there in company with the Prothonotary Warbler."
And in Knox County, Ind., William Brewster (1878) found it breeding on "the edge of a lonely forest pool in the depth of a cypress
swamp." Although this species apparently shows a preference for the
vicinity of running water, it seems content to live in surroundings
where such streams are not to be found; however, the presence of
water seems to be a decided necessity, hence it deserves its name.

Richard C. Harlow tells me that, "in the Pocono Mountains of Pennsylvania, where the northern waterthrush is very common and the
Louisiana a common breeder, the normal nesting habitat of the
northern species is in rhododendron bogs amid damp surroundings,
but where water is slow-moving or stagnant, and where upturned roots
of fallen, moss-covered trees abound. The Louisiana is here normally
a bird of the fast-flowing trout streams, nesting in the banks or gullies
near by. Both species may nest in overlapping zones, but they are
much more frequent in the respective habitats indicated above."

Nesting.—One of the earliest, and one of the best, accounts of the
nesting of the Louisiana waterthrush is by Mr. Brewster (1878) ; in
Knox County, Ind.—

a large tree had fallen into the shallow water, and the earth adhering to the
roots formed a nearly vertical but somewhat irregular wall about six feet in
height and ten or twelve in breadth. Near the upper edge of this, in a cavity
among the finer roots, was placed the nest, which, but for the situation and the
peculiar character of its composition, would have been exceedingly conspicuous. * * * The nest, which is before me, is exceedingly large and bulky,
measuring externally 3.50 inches in diameter, by 8 inches in length, and 3.50
inches in depth. Its outer wall, a solid mass of soggy dead leaves plastered
tightly together by the mud adhering to their surfaces, rises in the form of a
rounded parapet, the outer edge of which was nicely graduated to conform to the
edge of the earthy bank in which it was placed. In one corner of this mass, and
well back, is the nest proper, a neatly rounded, cup-shaped hollow, measuring
2.50 inches in diameter by 2.50 inches in depth. This inner nest is composed of
small twigs and green mosses, with a lining of dry grasses and a few hairs of
squirrels or other mammals arranged circularly.

A second nest was found 2 days later on the opposite side of the same
pond; it was similarly located and constructed, but square in shape to
fit the hollow. Another was found "on the shore of an isolated little
woodland pond. The site, in this instance, was at the foot of a huge
stump, the nest being placed in a cavity in the rotten wood."

A very different nesting site, in a gorge near Ithaca, N. Y., is thus
described in some notes sent to me by Dr. Alexander F. Skutch: "At
length, I entered a very narrow and deep portion of the gorge, into
which the stream poured by way of a murmuring fall, and then proceeded along the bottom through a trough in the rock. The walls of
the chasm rose steeply up to a height of 40 or 50 feet, either in precipi-
tous slopes overgrown with hemlock, spiked maple and Canadian yew,

or else in quite vertical cliffs of bare rock, their faces broken into a myriad fragments by the shattered edges of the strata. Here and there, rooted in a deeper niche in the cliff, a belated columbine held its nodding scarlet blossoms.

"As I passed downward through the narrow defile, an inconspicuous brown bird darted out from a niche almost at the foot of the wall to my left, and flew quietly downstream ahead of me. The brown feathers which concealed them gone, the whitish eggs caught my eye in a twinkling; and there, in plain view, was my first Louisiana waterthrush's nest, scarcely concealed in its little niche in the moss-covered cliff. It was a firm, well-made but shallow cup constructed, on a foundation of dead leaves, of fine herbaceous stems, more half-decayed leaves interspersed with a little moss, and lined up fine rootlets and fibers, I believe, from decayed fern stipes."

Of 14 Pennsylvania nests, for which T. E. McMullen has sent me the data, all but one were over or close to water along the banks of streams, either in the banks or under the roots of trees; the other was in the upturned roots of a tree in a swamp.

I have seen but two nests of the Louisiana waterthrush in southern New England. The first was near the eastern limit of the breeding range of the species, in Kingston swamp, R. I., a locality described under the northern waterthrush, and was within 100 yards of occupied nests of the northern species and of the winter wren. Located in the upturned roots of a fallen tree, 12 inches above the pool of water that filled the cavity left by the uprooted tree, it was made of dead leaves, moss, and rootlets, and was lined with finer pieces of the same materials and with some white deer hair.

At Hadlyme, Conn., on May 19, 1934, while following two companions along the banks of a small, quiet brook that wound its way through some low, swampy woods of maples, black and yellow birches, oaks, beeches, dogwoods, ironwoods, laurels, and azaleas, with plenty of skunkcabbages, I saw a bird flush out behind them and fly across the brook. Its nest was soon found deeply hidden between the roots of and directly under the trunk of a large yellow birch within a yard of the brook. The nest, on a foundation of dead leaves, was made of fine grasses and rootlets, and was lined with the reddish, fruiting stems of mosses.

A nest found by Clarence F. Stone near Branchport, N. Y., was beautifully concealed under a mass of ferns that overhung a bank.

Eggs.—From 4 to 6 eggs constitute the usual set for the Louisiana waterthrush, 5 being the commonest number. The nest described above by Dr. Skutch held the remarkable number of 10 eggs, but these were probably the product of two females, for, otherwise, we have no

record of more than 6 eggs in a nest, except where cowbirds' eggs
had been added.

The eggs are ovate to short ovate and more or less glossy, usually
only slightly lustrous. The ground color is white or creamy white,
and the egg is speckled, spotted or blotched with "bay," "auburn,"
"chestnut," or "hazel," with under spottings of "light vinaceous-drab,"
"pale purplish drab," or "purplish gray." The eggs vary considerably,
and may be almost immaculate, very finely speckled, or boldly
blotched. In some cases the speckles are confluent over the entire
egg and practically obscure the ground color, giving it a buffy white
appearance. In general the markings are heavier at the large end.
The gray spottings seem to be somewhat more prominent than on the
eggs of the northern waterthrush. The measurements of 50 eggs
average 19.9 by 15.5 millimeters; the eggs showing the four extremes
measure 22.1 by 15.6, 21.0 by 16.3, 17.8 by 14.8, and 18.3 by 14.7 millimeters (Harris).

Young.—The period of incubation is said to be about 14 days.
The female probably does all of the incubating and brooding, but
both parents assist in feeding and caring for the young, which are said
to remain in the nest about 10 days. When partially fledged the colors
of the young match their surroundings so well and they keep so still,
with eyes closed, that they are easily overlooked, even in an open nest.
The young are cared for by their parents for some time after they leave
the nest and while they remain hidden in the surrounding underbrush.

Plumages.—Dr. Dwight (1900) records the natal down of the
young Louisiana waterthrush as deep olive-brown, and describes the
juvenal plumage as "above, deep olive-brown, without cinnamon
edgings [thus differing from the young of *noveboracensis*]. Wings
and tail darker, the coverts faintly tipped with cinnamon. Conspicuous line above and behind the eye dull white. Below, yellowish
white, washed on the sides and crissum with cinnamon and narrowly
streaked on the chin, throat, breast and sides with dull olive-brown."

The postjuvenal molt, involving the contour plumage and the wing
coverts but not the rest of the wings or the tail, begins early in July.
This produces the first winter plumage, which is similar to that of the
juvenal. Dr. Dwight describes the first winter plumage as "above,
deep olive-brown, much darker on the crown, which is bordered by
conspicuous white superciliary stripes. The wing coverts are dark
and without edgings. Below, white, buffy tinged and strongly
washed on sides of the throat, flanks and on crissum with ochraceous
buff. The chin is faintly flecked, the breast and sides streaked with
olive-brown. Lower eyelid white; anteorbital spot and postocular
streak dusky."

The first nuptial plumage is "acquired by marked wear through
which the buff tints are largely lost, the flecks of the chin and the

breast streaks diminished." Subsequently plumages are acquired by a complete postnuptial molt in July and by wear during the winter, the winter plumages of old and young birds being practically indistinguishable.

The sexes are alike in all plumages, and the molts are the same.

Food.—"Examination of the stomachs of 4 birds of this species from Florida showed their food to consist chiefly of insects and spiders. The insects included dragon flies, crane-fly larvae, grouse locusts, beetles, bugs, ants, caterpillars, and scale insects. Two of the birds had eaten small mollusks, and one had taken a killifish" (Howell, 1932).

Five stomachs, collected in Puerto Rico by Dr. Wetmore (1916), contained 98 percent animal matter and 2 percent vegetable food. "Remains of flies (33 percent) were present in three stomachs. Water beetles (Parnidae and others) were found in three stomachs and leaf beetles in two. In one bird was a tree hopper and in two others were indeterminate bug remains. A dragon fly was found once and spider remains and bits of a scorpion twice. Three-fourths of the contents of one stomach was composed of fragments of a snail, and in another was found a tree toad (*Eleutherodactylus* sp.). Two birds had eaten seeds, in one case those of the aji (*Capsicum* sp.)."

Behavior.—The two species of waterthrushes are much alike in their habits and movements; both of them are walkers and both have the peculiar habit of tilting the tail upward as if a spring holding it down had been suddenly released; both spend most of their time on or near the ground walking gracefully along the margins of streams or pools, or even in the shallow water, seemingly as devoted to the vicinity of water as is the water ouzel to the western mountain streams. Dr. Mearns (1879) describes the behavior of the Louisiana waterthrush very aptly as follows:

It *runs* about (never hopping) over the stones and moss, gleaning along the sandy margin of the stream. Occasionally you may see it alight upon the witch-hazel, or alder bushes, that border the water, running dexterously along their branches. It always accompanies every employment with a Sandpiper-like, tilting motion of its body. Now it starts off in pursuit of one of its fellows. They fly through the forest with astonishing velocity, uttering a sharp twittering note, that sounds like the noise produced by striking two pebbles together. As they emerge higher up the stream, the chase is relinquished for the time, and you are surprised as they fly past to hear the clear notes of its song uttered as distinctly in mid-air as when perched; then the chase is renewed, but as they fly back again, one of the birds rises high up in the air above its pursuer, and then flutters slowly downward, pouring out its sweet song as it descends, mingling its cadence with the sound of the brook—the whole effect in perfect harmony with the spirit of the place. These performances take place oftenest early in the morning, about sunrise.

Voice.—Aretas A. Saunders sends me the following study of the song:

"The song of the Louisiana waterthrush is a loud, high-pitched one, exceedingly pleasing in its wild, sweet quality. Songs in my records vary from 6 to 19 notes, averaging about 11. The song is distinctly divisible into two parts. The first part consists of 2 to 4 rather slow notes or slurs, usually on or near the highest pitch, the notes most frequently being slurred upward. The second part consists of a series of 3 to 17 very rapid, twittering notes quite variable in form but usually descending in pitch. The average number of these notes is 8, and they are delivered two to three times as fast as those of the first part. The first part is distinctly sibilant and the second rather chattery, with rarely any of the liquid consonants that characterize the northern waterthrush.

"The pitch of the songs varies from C sharp ′′′ to E ′′′′. Single songs vary from two tones to an octave in range, averaging about three tones. The song begins high and usually becomes lower at or near the end. In all but 6 of my 49 records the first notes are on the highest pitch. In 30 of the records the last note is the lowest. The pitch of the rapid notes in the second part of the song is exceedingly variable, rarely with two notes in succession on the same pitch. The pitch varies up and down between single notes, though the general trend is usually downward.

"The song, in my timed records, varies from 2 to 3⅕ seconds, but several records that were not timed may have been somewhat longer. The notes of the first part are delivered at a rate of only two or three to the second, but those of the second part may be at a rate of six to ten; however, individual notes in the second part vary in length, so that the time is very irregular.

"Louisiana waterthrushes sing abundantly when they first arrive. As nesting starts the song is less frequent. I believe that individual birds cease singing for a time, perhaps for the period of incubation. In June the song seems to be longer and more elaborate. Most of my June records have more notes than those of April and May. The song ceases in late June, but I have too few records to give average dates. It is sometimes revived in July, evidently after the molt."

Albert R. Brand's (1938) records of frequencies in bird songs show the song of this species to be somewhat higher in pitch than that of the northern waterthrush, the vibrations per second varying from 6,600 to 2,475, with an approximate mean of 4,000, about the average of passerine song.

Two impressions of the song are worth noting. Dr. Skutch says of hearing it in a gorge near Ithaca, N. Y.: "A Louisiana waterthrush, perching upon a twig of a hemlock tree far above the stream, was singing in a ringing voice that rose above the murmur of the falling waters. *Chirp, chirp, chirp, chirp*, his song began boldly; then, as though he were suddenly confused in his recitation, broke into a lisping and incoherent garble impossible to paraphrase in human sounds. Such is always the character of their song; they have never learned the end of it." And Dr. George M. Sutton (Todd, 1940) describes the startling song as follows:

> Three distinctly repeated notes introduce this striking volley, which is entirely unlike the song of other warblers and much stronger and more prolonged than that of the species' near relative, the Northern Waterthrush. It is delivered either from the ground or from a tree, and sometimes even during flight. The head of the singer is thrown well back, his whole body is shaken with energy, and his usually restless tail is for the moment allowed to hang at an easy, downward angle. * * * The evening flight song, as I have heard it in Greene County, is a memorable performance. In the gathering dusk the singer himself is not seen. The song seems to be dashing here and there. It sweeps downward in jerking stages as the final measures decrease in volume. It is prolonged, and the latter half is a repetition of tinkling notes that fade away to nothingness as the bird plunges back into the darkness whence he came.

Field marks.—The Louisiana waterthrush most closely resembles the northern waterthrush, from which it can be distinguished by its broad, white superciliary stripe and its whiter under parts with less and duller streaking, its chin and throat being nearly immaculate. It looks a little like its relative, the ovenbird, but the latter has an eye ring and no stripe over the eye.

Enemies.—This waterthrush is a frequent victim of the cowbird, except in heavily wooded regions, where the cowbird is less likely to penetrate. Dr. Friedmann (1929) lists 3 nests that contained 4 eggs of the cowbird, 7 containing 3, and 45 other nests that held 1 or 2 eggs of this parasite. Three or four eggs of the cowbird are likely to cause the waterthrush to desert the nest.

Harold S. Peters (1936) lists only one tick, *Haemaphysalis leporis-palustris* Packard, as an external parasite.

Winter.—Dr. Skutch contributes the following account: "In Central America, the Louisiana waterthrush is a moderately abundant fall and spring transient, but in most parts at best a rare winter resident. During the southward migration, at least, it passes along both sides of the Cordillera, but in greater numbers on the Caribbean side, from late August well into October. As a winter resident, it appears to be confined to the Caribbean lowlands in both Guatemala and Costa Rica. For the spring months, there are records for the Caribbean lowlands and the central highlands, but apparently none for lower elevations on the Pacific side—a gap which may some day be filled. This, at least, is the story told by the few records before me as I write; but it is likely that some modifications of statement would be made necessary by a greater number of observations. Both the Louisiana and the northern waterthrushes are shy and difficult to approach while in Central America. It is not easy to see them sufficiently well to distinguish them in the field, especially where the presence of *Seiurus noveboracensis notabilis*, with its white superciliary lines, adds to the possibility of confusion with the Louisiana waterthrush. As a result, I have seen far more waterthrushes than I have distinguished as to species and set down in my records.

"While in Central America, the Louisiana waterthrush is usually seen foraging along the shores of streams or other bodies of water, whether rocky, sandy, or muddy. It is always alone and usually silent.

"Central American occurrences are: Guatemala—Motagua Valley near Los Amates, not uncommon spring transient, April 20 to May 2, 1932; Sierra de Tecpán, 8,500 feet, rare transient, February 12 and 28, 1933 (probably same individual on both dates). Honduras—Tela, abundant fall transient, arriving August 25, rare winter visitant, January and February. Costa Rica—Caribbean lowlands to 2,000 feet: fairly abundant fall transient, Río Sicsola, September 3, 1904, and El Hogar, August 28, 1906 (Carriker); rare winter resident, Pejivalle, January 23, 1934. Central highlands: Volcán Irazú, October 13 (Underwood) and San José, March 9, 1889 (Cherrie). Basin of El General, 2,000–3,000 feet, uncommon fall transient, September 30, 1936 and October 14, 1942."

From Central America, the three waterthrushes extend their winter ranges southward into northern South America and eastward to the Bahamas and the West Indies. In Florida, they seem to be rare or casual in winter.

Dr. Wetmore (1916) says: "The Louisiana water-thrush is a fairly common winter visitant to Porto Rico. The birds may arrive in September, though there are no positive records, and the first that I saw were at Cayey January 17. They were common in the mangrove swamps along the coast and inland followed the rapid streams, frequenting the parts bordered by brushy growth or running through coffee and banana plantations. The call note is noticeably higher than that of the other waterthrush, from which it can readily be distinguished."

DISTRIBUTION

Range.—Eastern Canada and the United States, the West Indies, Central America, and northwestern South America.

Breeding range.—The Louisiana waterthrush breeds **north** to southeastern Minnesota (Hutchinson, Minneapolis, and southern Pine County); central Wisconsin (probably Durand, Reedsburg, and **New**

London); southern Michigan (Grand Rapids, Lansing, Flint, South Lyon, and probably Port Huron); southern Ontario (Komoka, London, and Webster's Falls); central and eastern New York (Medina, Rochester, Canandaigua, Utica, Point Comfort, Warren, and Port Henry); southern Vermont (rarely Brattleboro); and central-southern New Hampshire (Harrisville and Dublin). East to New Hampshire (Dublin); more regularly to central-southern Massachusetts (Sheffield, Springfield, and Ware); Rhode Island; central New Jersey (Crosswick, Princeton, and Elizabeth); central Maryland (Patuxent Wildlife Research Refuge and Wildacres); eastern central Virginia (Lawrenceville and Ashland); central and northeastern North Carolina (Clinton, Garner, Greenville, and Walke); central South Carolina (Aiken and Columbia); and southwestern and central Georgia (Blakely and Macon). South to Georgia (Blakely); southern Alabama (Abbeville); southern Mississippi (Brooklyn); northern and southeastern Louisiana (Mansfield, Bienville, Como, Bains, and Baton Rouge); and northeastern Texas (Corsicana). West to northeastern Texas (Corsicana); eastern Oklahoma (Tulsa County, Washita River, and Kiowa Agency); eastern Kansas (Manhattan, Topeka, and Neosha River); eastern Nebraska (London and Fontanelle Forest); central western and central northern Iowa (Pottawattamie County and Emmetsburg); and southeastern Minnesota (Hutchinson).

Winter range.—The Louisiana waterthrush winters **north** to southern Mexico; Jalisco (Mazatlán); Morelos (Cuernavaca); Puebla (Metlatoyuca); Veracruz (Jalapa, Motzorongo); Tabasco (Frontera); and Yucatán (Mérida); Cuba (Bahia Honda, Isle of Pines, Trinidad, and Guamo); the eastern Bahamas (Bimini and Berry); and Puerto Rico. East to Puerto Rico; the Virgin Islands; and the northern Lesser Antilles (Barbuda, Antigua, Montserrat, Guadeloupe, and Dominica). South to the Lesser Antilles (Dominica); central and northeastern Colombia (Santa Marta, Villavincencia, La Bonda); and western Panamá (Permé). West to western Panamá (Permé); and southern Mexico (Jalisco). Also winters in Bermuda, and there is one sight record from Trinidad. Accidental in California (Mecca).

Migration.—Late dates of spring departure are: Colombia—Fusugasugá, March 24. Costa Rica—El General, March 23. Guatemala—near Quiriguá, May 2. Yucatán—Mérida, March 29. Veracruz—Arroyo del Sitio, March 25. San Luis Potosí—Valles, March 25; Tamaulipas—Gómez Farías region, April 4; Chihuahua—Alamos, March 28. Trinidad—April 23. Puerto Rico—Cartagena Lagoon, April 22. Haiti—Rivière Seche near Fonds des Nègres, April 2. Cuba—Villalba, April 18.

Early dates of spring arrival are: Florida—Lower Suwannee River, March 10; Pensacola, March 16. Alabama—Woodbine, March 9. Georgia—Atlanta and Fitzgerald, March 9. South Carolina—Spartanburg, March 20. North Carolina—Raleigh, March 14 (average of 23 years, March 29). Virginia—Naruna, March 8; Rockbridge County, April 2. West Virginia—French Creek, March 19 (average of 17 years, March 31). District of Columbia—Washington, March 25 (average of 31 years, April 9). Maryland—Forest Glen, March 26. Delaware—Kent and Sussex Counties, April 1 (average of 16 years, April 10). Pennsylvania—Sewickley, March 30. New Jersey—Newark, March 28. New York—New York City, April 2; Ithaca, April 4. Connecticut—Kensington, March 30. Rhode Island—Hopkinton, April 10. Massachusetts—Easthampton, April 5. Vermont—West Dummerston, April 24. New Hampshire—New Hampton, May 5. Louisiana—Baton Rouge region, March 14. Mississippi—Saucier, March 8. Arkansas—Rogers, March 10. Tennessee—Nashville, March 16 (average of 12 years, March 22). Kentucky—Barbourville and Bardstown, March 20. Missouri—southeastern, March 12; St. Louis, March 29. Illinois—Forest Park, March 28; Murphysboro and Springfield, March 31. Indiana—Monroe County, March 20; Helmsburg, March 30. Ohio—central Ohio, March 7 (average April 7). Michigan—Battle Creek, April 6. Ontario—Toronto, April 1 (1950); London, April 22. Iowa—Iowa City, April 2. Wisconsin—Milwaukee, April 4 (1948), April 7 (1947); St. Croix Falls, April 15. Minnesota—Lanesboro and Minneapolis, April 17 (average of 21 years for southern Minnesota, April 25). Texas—Refugio County, March 17; Gainesville, March 21. Oklahoma—Tulsa County, April 8. Kansas—Independence, April 1. Nebraska—Peru, April 20. South Dakota—Sioux Falls, April 28.

Late dates of fall departure are: South Dakota—Sioux Falls, September 8. Nebraska—Lincoln, September 30. Minnesota—Minneapolis, September 20 (average of 8 years for southern Minnesota, August 27). Wisconsin—Reedsburg, September 27. Iowa—Wall Lake, September 29. Ontario—Credit Run, Peel County, August 23; Point Pelee, August 28. Michigan—Kalamazoo, October 18. Ohio—Hillsboro, October 10; central Ohio, October 11 (average, September 18). Indiana—Indianapolis, October 23. Illinois—Evanston, September 28. Missouri—Columbia, October 24. Kentucky—Bowling Green, October 18. Tennessee—Elizabethton, October 30. Arkansas—northwestern, October 4. Mississippi—Gulfport, October 29. Louisiana—Baton Rouge region, October 25. Massachusetts—Lenox, August 23. Connecticut—Groton, August 15. New York—New York City, October 3 and November 24. New Jersey—Morristown, October 20. Pennsylvania—Renovo, October 10. Delaware—Kent and

Sussex Counties, September 28 (average, September 15). Maryland—Baltimore County, September 24. District of Columbia—Washington, October 4 (average of 8 years, September 19). West Virginia—French Creek, October 7. Virginia—Lawrenceville, October 19. North Carolina—Waynesville, September 29. Georgia—Macon, October 12. Alabama—Leighton, October 12. Florida—Alachua County, October 27; Fowey Rocks, November 2.

Early dates of fall arrival are: California—Mecca, August 17 (only record for State. Oklahoma—Tulsa County, August 9. Texas—Cove, August 29. Wisconsin—Racine, August 9. Ohio—Buckeye Lake, August 27 (average, September 1). Illinois—La Grange, August 18; average for Chicago region, September 3. Tennessee—Elizabethton, August 23. Mississippi—Bay St. Louis, July 4. Louisiana—Mandeville, August 18. New York—New York City, August 4. South Carolina—Mount Pleasant, July 13. Florida—Pensacola, July 13; Old Town, July 23; Fort Myers, August 4. Bermuda—September 4. Cuba—Habana, August 10. Jamaica—Trelawney, September 5. Dominican Republic—Puerto Plata, August 12. Puerto Rico—Mona Island, August 18. Antigua—September 19. Dominica—September 25. Tamaulipas—Río Sabinas, August 5. Guatemala—Peten, August 11. Honduras—Lancetilla, August 24. Nicaragua—Escondido River, October 23. Costa Rica—El Hogar, August 28. Panamá—Cricamola, August 24.

Egg dates.—Connecticut: 43 records, May 7 to June 6; 25 records, May 12 to 25, indicating the height of the season.

New Jersey: 26 records, May 11 to June 24; 21 records, May 17 to 22.

North Carolina: 10 records, April 2 to May 14.

Pennsylvania: 26 records, May 6 to June 6; 13 records, May 11 to 17 (Harris).

OPORORNIS FORMOSUS (Wilson)

KENTUCKY WARBLER

PLATE 62

HABITS

Wilson (1832) discovered this handsome warbler and named it for the State in which he found it most abundant. The name is not inappropriate, for Kentucky is not far from the center of its abundance in the breeding season. Its summer range covers most of the eastern half of the United States, chiefly in the Mississippi Valley, but it extends northward to southern Minnesota, southern Ontario, Ohio, and Pennsylvania, and southward to the Gulf States. Eastward, it breeds locally from the lower Hudson Valley, New York, to North

Carolina, but it is rare east of the Alleghenies in the southeastern States.

The Kentucky warbler is a woodland bird, a lover of deep shade and dense, damp thickets. Ridgway (1889) says that it "is one of the most abundant of birds in the rich woods of southern Illinois. As far north as Wabash, Lawrence, and Richland counties, it is even more abundant than the Golden-crowned Thrush, though the two usually inhabit different locations, the latter preferring, as a rule, the dryer upland woods, while the present species is most abundant in the rich woods of the bottom-lands."

Franklin L. Burns wrote to Dr. Chapman (1907) from Berwyn, Pennsylvania: "It is here an inhabitant of the overgrown clearings, swampy thickets, and the borders of woodland; a bird of the south, loving the luxuriant undergrowths of spicewood, ferns, mandrake, skunk cabbage, and other shade-loving plants of rank growth."

Andrew Allison wrote to Dr. Chapman (1907) that, in Mississippi, this warbler inhabits "undergrowth in damp, or, at least, heavily shaded, woods. It may frequent the thickets of rose-bay (*Illicium*) and the tangle of bamboo briers on the Gulf coast, the varied tangled growth along the creeks and rivers of the higher regions, or the brakes of switch-cane; but it always selects a low, thick growth, where it feeds almost entirely on the ground."

In the central Allegheny Mountain region, according to Prof. Maurice Brooks (1940), "the birds seem at home in a number of forest types, southern mixed hardwoods, scrub and pitch pine mixtures, oak-hickory, and northern hardwoods. * * * As with many other sylvan birds, ravines seem especially to attract them."

Spring.—From its winter home, from southern Mexico to Colombia, the Kentucky warbler moves northward mainly in April. While a few individuals may cross from Yucatán and Cuba to Florida, it is evidently rather rare on that side of the Gulf of Mexico. The main migration route of the great bulk of these birds is northward and northeastward through Texas to the Mississippi Valley, where its center of abundance in summer is in the bottom-land forests of the great rivers, mainly west of the Alleghenies and east of the great plains. M. A. Frazar (1881) saw "large numbers" of Kentucky warblers migrating across the Gulf of Mexico, when his ship was about 30 miles south of the mouth of the Mississippi River; they had apparently come from Yucatán and were flying due north.

Nesting.—Dr. Alexander F. Skutch writes to me: "A nest found near Baltimore, Md., on May 31, 1934, was concealed among a vigorous stand of *Sanicula marilandica* in low and moist but not swampy ground in light woods. The bottom of the nest was about 2 inches above the ground. In form, the structure was a bulky, open cup. The very thick outer layer contained about 200 dead leaves which were whole or nearly whole, chiefly medium-sized leaves of oak, beech, and red maple. The inner lining, very thin in comparison with the bulky outer wall, consisted of fine rootlets and other fibrous material. The nest contained two proper eggs and one of the cowbird.

"The female, if she happened to be incubating or, later, brooding the nestlings at the time of my visits, would sit bravely facing me while I looked down at her with my head scarcely more than a foot distant from her. When I tried to touch her, she jumped abruptly from the nest and walked slowly over the ground with the tips of her wings dragging, chirping excitedly.

"I have another record of a nest found near Baltimore on June 22, 1934. It was in weedy open woods, on the ground at the foot of a bush. It contained four newly laid eggs."

F. L. Burns (Chapman, 1907) says:

The nest is often placed in the most unexpected places: It may be on top of the ground at the foot of a beech, spice-bush, dog-wood, sweet birch, or black haw sprout; under a fallen bough, or perhaps just off the wet earth between the ground forks of a bunch of spice-wood, winter fern, Spanish needles or other weeds; or less frequently, in the midst of a patch of wild sarsaparilla, mandrake or other annuals, with nothing to turn aside the crushing foot of man or beast. It is usually well concealed by the surrounding vegetation while in a comparatively open spot, and if not directly in an abandoned cartroad, not far from some woodland footpath, public road, or the edge of the woods.

A rather bulky and loosely constructed nest, outwardly of somewhat ragged dead leaves of the chestnut, beech, cherry, maple, white, black and chestnut oak, a few weed or grass stems, an occasional strip of wild grapevine bark, and, once, many green leaves of the dogwood, and, in another example, several oak blossoms; usually followed by an inner layer of bright, clean dead leaves of the beech, lined with black rootlets and in fully half of the nests examined, a few long black horse-hairs. In one instance the lining was of light-colored rootlets. Another nest, so well hidden in a patch of woodplants that I accidentally trod upon it while actually searching for it, was a most frail affair built exclusively of grasses, lined with black rootlets, however.

During the nest building period the birds are so extremely jealous and watchful, deserting the site rather than be spied upon, that I have been unable so far to follow this interesting period to a finish. The male unquestionably aids his mate.

Charles F. De Garis (1936) has published an interesting paper describing six nests of the Kentucky warbler, among which was one peculiar nest in an unusual situation. It was placed in a fence corner of a garden in an open situation.

There was no trace of logs or lichens, ferns or vines, no shelter of any kind, in fact nothing but a heap of clods and leaves raked from the garden. * * *

With the purpose of offering her a choice of artificial materials, I worked till dark assembling bits of plain and colored string, thread, cotton and wool, and such fragments of ribbon and rayon as I could find. When the female came, the next morning, she "made several trips for grass before taking any notice of my bargain counter display. Finally she became interested in a bit of brown sweater wool, which she promptly conveyed to the nest. Then followed white string, green string, yellow ribbon and the like, taken with little or no deliberation. A piece of pale blue rayon gave her pause, but after shredding it a while she took it on to the nest. However, she eschewed all materials of carmine, scarlet and purple.

The only nest of the Kentucky warbler that I have ever found was in a typical situation in a large tract of heavy, deciduous, upland woods in Delaware County, Pa., on June 8, 1896. I had been hunting carefully and thoroughly over a limited area in which the male had been singing and flitting about in an apparently unconcerned manner, when I flushed the female from her nest almost at my feet; she fluttered along the ground as if with a broken wing. The nest was only partially concealed beneath the leaves of two very small spice-wood saplings. It was built up some 4 or 5 inches above the ground between the two saplings with a great mass of beech and other hardwood leaves; the inner nest was made of weed stems and rootlets and was lined with finer rootlets and a little cowhair. It held five half-incubated eggs.

Eggs.—The Kentucky warbler lays from 3 to 6 eggs to a set; sets of 3 are perhaps incomplete and sets of 6 are rare. In a typical series of 30 sets there are 13 sets of four, 10 sets of 5, and only 2 sets of 6. The shape varies from short ovate to elongated ovate, and they are only slightly lustrous. The white or creamy white ground color is speckled, spotted, and sometimes blotched with shades of "bay," "auburn," or "chestnut," with undertones of "Quaker drab" or "light mouse gray." Although some eggs are rather boldly marked with blotches, the majority seem to be speckled or finely spotted. On some the speckles are very dense, on others they may be sparsely scattered over the entire surface or concentrated at the large end. The measurements of 50 eggs average 18.6 by 14.3 millimeters; the eggs showing the four extremes measure **20.4** by **15.7**, **16.8** by 13.7, and 17.8 by **12.7** millimeters (Harris).

Young.—At a nestful of eggs, marked and carefully watched, Mr. De Garis (1936) found that "after twelve days' incubation all four eggs hatched, and after ten days of nest-feeding the vigorous brood of four was brought off. * * * I found that each egg was turned on its long axis once, sometimes twice, every twenty-four hours, and that the relative position of the eggs to each other was variously altered from time to time."

Evidently, all the incubating and brooding was performed by the female, and "the burden of feeding the young was assumed very unequally by male and female. The male continued to devote most of his waking hours to musical exercise, and only rarely passed on a small moth or fly to his mate." When the time came for the young to leave the nest, the female came near the nest with tempting food, but would not feed the crying young until she had persuaded them to leave. After that they were fed by both parents for as much as 17 days. At other nests, he found incubation to last 13 days, and the young were nest-fed 8½ days.

Mr. Burns (Chapman, 1907) says that "the eyes of the young are opened on the fifth day and in two instances birds left the nest on the eighth day. If the too inquisitive observer is noticed lurking around, the female will frequently drive the young from the nest prematurely. The male, while protesting vigorously, seldom approaches as closely as the female."

Dr. Skutch (MS.) relates the following interesting experience: "At about noon on June 16, 1934, while following up a small rivulet flowing through an extensive woodland in Baltimore County, Md., I entered a low, swampy area surrounding the channel, almost devoid of trees, but overgrown with spice-bush and skunk cabbage. As I came into this natural clearing, a pair of Kentucky warblers flitted nervously about, uttering loud, full chirps. I suspected they had a nest in the low ground, and stood quietly at one side, hoping that they would eventually reveal its location to me. After a period of excited chirping, one of them found a larva and flew with it to the far side of the opening. After hesitating a minute or so, it flew down and disappeared among the herbage with its burden. I crossed the swamp and began to search among the skunk cabbages and sedges in the spot where the parent had disappeared. When I had gone beyond the area where I expected to find the nest—the parents meanwhile flitting excitedly around me—I was brought suddenly to a halt by a loud explosion of small bird voices that seemed to arise from my very feet. Looking downward, I beheld three or four little olive birds hopping rapidly away in as many directions, while the parents were driven to renewed chirping and excitement. Not two inches from my right foot was the nest, now entirely deserted, a bulky open cup of dead leaves lined with fibrous material. It rested upon the ground at the base of a skunk cabbage plant at the edge of the swamp.

"I pursued one of the little birds, who tried to escape by hopping, and finally capturing it, found that it bore little resemblance to its parents. * * * Meanwhile one of the parents, probably the mother, crept slowly and painfully over the ground at a safe distance from me, dragging her relaxed wings and her tail; while the other flitted about holding in his bill a larva which he was too excited to deliver to a youngster."

Plumages.—Dr. Dwight (1900) describes the juvenal plumage of the Kentucky warbler, in which the sexes are alike, as "above, including sides of head rich olive-brown. Wings and tail rather darker, edged with deep olive-green, the wing coverts with wood-brown. Below, pale raw umber-brown, Naples-yellow on the abdomen and crissum."

A partial postjuvenal molt in July, involving the contour plumage and the wing coverts but not the rest of the wings or the tail, produces the first winter plumages, in which the sexes are recognizable. In this plumage, the young male is "above, olive-green including the wing coverts. Below, including superciliary stripe, bright canary-yellow. The forehead, crown, lores and auriculars are partly black much veiled by smoke-gray edgings." The first nuptial plumage is acquired by a partial prenuptial molt "which involves a part of the head, chin and throat, but no other areas. The black crown with plumbeous edgings, the black lores, auriculars and a short extension on the sides of the neck are assumed, together with the yellow feathers of the chin and superciliary stripe. Young and old become indistinguishable."

A complete molt in July produces the adult winter plumage, which "differs from first winter in the crown being grayer, the black areas more defined and the edgings clear plumbeous gray, veiling the black much less." He says that the adult nuptial plumage is "acquired apparently by a partial prenuptial moult, as in the young bird, although wear alone may modify the winter plumage after the first year." Females differ from males in all the later plumages, the black markings being duller and more restricted.

Food.—No extensive study of the food of the Kentucky warbler is available. Forbush (1929) says: "The food of this bird consists in part of grasshoppers and locusts, caterpillars and the larvae of other insects, moths, plant-lice, grubs, spiders and other animal food that it finds chiefly on or near the ground, or in bushes, vines or the lower parts of trees. In summer it takes some berries." A. H. Howell (1924) reports that the stomachs of two birds, taken in Alabama, contained remains of bugs, beetles, ants, and other Hymenoptera.

Behavior.—The Kentucky warbler is essentially a ground warbler, and, like others of similar habits, it walks gracefully along rather than hopping; it shares to some extent with the waterthrushes the habit of bobbing its tail, though this habit is no more pronounced than it is with the ovenbird. John Burroughs (1871) classes him with the ground warblers and says that "his range is very low, indeed lower than that of any other species with which I am acquainted. He is on the ground nearly all the time, moving rapidly along, taking spiders and bugs, overturning leaves, peeping under sticks and into crevices and every now and then leaping up eight or ten inches, to take his game from beneath some overhanging leaf or branch. Thus each species has its range more or less marked. Draw a line three feet from the ground, and you mark the usual limit of the Kentucky warbler's quest for food." Ridgway (1889) writes:

In its manners it is almost a counterpart of the Golden-crowned Thrush, but is altogether a more conspicuous bird, both on account of its brilliant plumage and the fact that it is more active, the males being, during the breeding season, very pugnacious, and continually chasing one another about the woods. * * * Considering its great abundance, the nest of this species is extraordinarily difficult to find; at least this has been the writer's experience, and he has come to the conclusion that the female must slyly leave the nest at the approach of the intruder and run beneath the herbage until a considerable distance from the nest, when joined by her mate, the pair by their evident anxiety mislead the collector as to its location. However this may be, the writer has never found a nest of this species except by accident, although he has repeatedly searched every square foot of ground within a radius of many yards of the spot where a pair showed most uneasiness at his presence.

Other observers have commented on this same trait. And Amos W. Butler (1898) refers to its resemblance to the ovenbird in its actions, saying: "It carries its body evenly balanced, apparently, and the equilibrium is only maintained with much difficulty by using its tail as a balance, causing that appendage to bob up and down. Hopping about a steep, springy bank, it reminds one of the Worm-eating Warbler, as it climbs over roots, sticks and logs, now disappearing from view in a hole beneath the roots, then behind a log, here stopping to peck at an insect, and there turning over the leaves."

Voice.—Dr. Chapman (1912) writes:

His song is entirely unlike that of any other Warbler. It is a loud, clearly whistled performance of five, six, or seven notes—*tur-dle, tur-dle, tur-dle*—resembling in tone some of the calls of the Carolina Wren. Even in the woods it may be heard at a distance of about one hundred and fifty yards. In the height of the breeding season this Warbler is a most persistent singer. On one occasion, at Englewood, N. J., I watched a male for three hours. During this period, with the exception of five interruptions of less than forty-five seconds each, he sang with the greatest regularity once every twelve seconds. Thus, allowing for the brief intervals of silence, he sang about 875 times, or some 5,250 notes. I found him singing, and when I departed he showed no signs of ceasing.

F. L. Burns wrote to Dr. Chapman (1907):

The song is a loud, clear and sweetly whistled peer-ry, repeated rapidly four or five times. Often, though less frequently, a *che che che peer-ry peer-ry peer-ry*. When first heard it is suggestive of the song of the Cardinal or Carolina Wren. During the nesting season it is an incessant singer from the lower branches of the sapling in which it is constantly moving or as often from the ground where it is at its best, walking about with an air and dignity not often attained by small birds. The song continues from arrival until June 27–June 23, and one was heard August 7, (1902). * * * A flight song is sometimes delivered about dusk during the height of the breeding period. It is indescribable. The alarm note is a metallic *chip, check,* or *chuck*, more or less rapidly repeated, and to a critical ear easily recognizable."

A. D. Du Bois tells me that the song reminds him of the *pe-to* note of the tufted titmouse; Francis H. Allen gives me his impression of it as sounding like *wittly wittly wittly wittly wittly wittly;* other recorded renderings are similar, but those I have cited are sufficient to give a good idea of the striking and characteristic song of the Kentucky warbler.

Field marks.—The olive-green upper parts, with no white in wings or tail, the under parts wholly bright yellow, and the black markings on the crown and sides of the head and neck are all distinctive field marks. In females and fall birds the colors are duller, and the black markings are more restricted and veiled but they show similar patterns.

Enemies.—This warbler is a common victim of the cowbird. Dr. Friedmann (1929) had 65 records, and says: "In Greene County, Pennsylvania, the Kentucky Warbler seems to be the commonest victim of the Cowbird. Jacobs found eggs of the parasite in 47 nests of this warbler, as follows: 39 nests with 1 Cowbird egg each; 7 nests with 2 Cowbird eggs each; 1 nest with 3 Cowbird eggs."

Snakes and prowling predators have been known to rob the nests of this and other ground-nesting species. Harold S. Peters (1936) recorded only one external parasite as found on this warbler, a tick (*Haemaphysalis leporis-palustris*).

Winter.—Dr. Skutch contributes the following: "Of all the wood warblers, resident or migratory, the Kentucky warbler is the species most often seen in the undergrowth of the heavy lowland forests of Central America. The one member of the family that breeds among the loftier forests of the lowlands, the buff-rumped warbler, haunts the rocky streambeds, and is rarely found among the undergrowth at a distance from water. The migrant warblers that winter in some abundance in these forests, as the chestnut-sided warbler and the American redstart, are birds of the tree-tops. This leaves the Kentucky warbler, with occasionally a worm-eating warbler, to represent its family in the company of antbirds, manakins, wood-wrens, and wintering russet-backed thrushes in the underwood.

"Not that the Kentucky warbler is abundant in these forests, even at the height of the northern winter. I have rarely seen as many as two, and still more rarely three, in a day's wandering through the forest. Nor is it restricted to the forest; for it haunts also the heavier, more humid second-growth. But in either habitat, it is always seen moving restlessly through the vegetation near the ground, often clinging to slender upright stems, ant-bird-fashion. It is always alone, unless in chance company with small birds of other kinds; it shows no true sociability at this season. It is silent, save for its reiterated, sharp call note.

"Arriving in September, the Kentucky warbler spreads over the length of Central America, including the lowlands of both coasts, wherever suitably humid conditions prevail, and winters at altitudes up to 3,500 or perhaps 4,000 feet above sea-level. It appears to depart early; until the present year I had only two records as late as April, one for the third and the other for the twelfth of the month. But this year, 1943, it was for a brief period in late March and early April rather abundant in the forests of this region of southern Costa Rica; and I saw it repeatedly until April 9.

"Early dates of fall arrival in Central America are: Guatemala—Chimoxan (Griscom), September 13. Honduras—Tela, September 11, 1930. Costa Rica—San José (Cherrie), October 7; Río Sicsola (Carriker), September 21; Basin of El General, October 8, 1936, and October 12, 1942.

"Late dates of spring departure are: Panamá—Barro Colorado Island, Canal Zone, March 28, 1935. Costa Rica—Basin of El General, April 3, 1936, February 26, 1937, March 11, 1939, April 12, 1940, February 23, 1942, April 9, 1943."

DISTRIBUTION

Range.—Central and eastern United States, Mexico, Central America, and northern South America.

Breeding range.—The Kentucky warbler breeds **north** to southeastern Nebraska (Lincoln and Omaha); eastern Iowa (Grinnell and Waukon Junction); southwestern and central southern Wisconsin (Wyalusing, Mazomaine, and Janesville); northeastern Illinois (rarely Chicago area); central Indiana (Rockville, Crawfordsville, and Indianapolis); southern and eastern Ohio (Oxford, Wilmington, Columbus, Corning, Wooster, Hartville, and Youngstown); and southeastern New York (rarely Ossining and Bronx). **East** to New York (Bronx); north-central New Jersey (probably Princeton and Elizabeth); southeastern Pennsylvania (Philadelphia); Delaware (Wilmington); southeastern Maryland (Plummers Island and Easton); eastern Virginia (Lawrenceville, Petersburg, and Ashland); central North Carolina (Charlotte and Raleigh); central South Carolina (Aiken and Summertown); central Georgia (Macon, Round Oak, and Carmichaels Pond); and northwestern Florida (Chipley). **South** to northwestern Florida (Chipley and Pensacola); southern Alabama (Mobile, Castleberry, and Dothan); southern Mississippi (Saucier, Gulfport, and Woolmarket); southern Louisiana (Sulphur, Iowa, Lottie, and Thibodaux); and southeastern Texas (Orange, Houston, Matagorda County). **West** to central Texas (Matagorda County, San Antonio, Kerrville, Waco, and Rhome); eastern Oklahoma (Copan, Stillwater, Fort Reno, Moore, and Kiowa Agency);

eastern Kansas (Blue Rapids, Fort Riley, Emporia, and Burlington) ; and southeastern Nebraska (Lincoln)·

Winter range.—The Kentucky warbler winters in southern Mexico; (Isthmus of Tehuantepec, probably) ; Campeche (Apazote and Pacaytún) ; south through Central America to Panamá (Santa Fe, Paracote, Gatún, and Chepo) ; and northern Colombia (Río Frío, Bonda, and Don Diego).

Migration.—Late dates of spring departure are: Panamá—Loma del León, March 29. Costa Rica—San Isidro del General, April 19. British Honduras—Mountain Cow, April 13. Guatemala—Peten, April 15. Veracruz—Tres Zaptoes, April 8. Sonora—Rancho Santa Barbara, June 12.

Early dates of spring arrival are: Florida—Dry Tortugas Island and Pensacola, March 29. Alabama—Birmingham, April 5 (average for 10 years, April 7). Georgia—Macon, March 27; Atlanta and Kirkwood, April 1. South Carolina—Columbia, April 10. North Carolina—Old Fort, April 14; Raleigh, April 15 (average of 17 years, April 30). Virginia—Cape Henry, April 3. West Virginia—Kayford, April 21; French Creek, April 25 (average of 16 years, May 1). District of Columbia—Washington, April 25 (average of 30 years, May 2). Maryland—St. Marys City, April 19. Delaware—Kent and Sussex Counties, March 30 (average of 19 years, April 8)· Pennsylvania—Swarthmore, April 28. New Jersey—New Brunswick, May 3. New York—Ossining, May 2; Orient, May 4. Connecticut—Kent, May 5. Massachusetts—Cambridge, April 28. Louisiana—Baton Rogue region, March 19. Mississippi—Bay St. Louis, April 1. Arkansas—Saline County, March 24. Tennessee—Nashville, April 15 (average of 12 years, April 17). Kentucky—Eubank, April 15. Missouri—southeastern, April 9. Illinois—Anna, April 12; Beecher, April 24. Indiana—Bloomington, April 17. Ohio—Columbus, April 17 (average, May 4). Michigan—Petersburg, May 4. Ontario—Hamilton, May 3. Iowa—Keokuk, April 26. Wisconsin—Winneconne, Madison, and Milwaukee, May 7. Texas—Corpus Christi, April 7; Houston, April 11. Oklahoma—Copan, April 19. Kansas—Manhattan, April 25. Nebraska—Omaha, May 7.

Late dates of fall departure are: Kansas—Lawrence, September 14. Oklahoma—Tulsa, September 19. Texas—Rockport, October 28. Wisconsin—Eau Claire, September 17. Iowa—Polk County, September 13. Ontario—Lynn Valley, September 9. Ohio—Buckeye Lake, September 29 (average, September 20). Indiana—Richmond, September 9. Illinois—Mount Carmel, October 15. Missouri—Columbia, September 18. Kentucky—Bardstown, September 28. Tennessee—Elizabethton, October 2. Arkansas—Saline County, October 5. Mississippi—Gulf coast, October 6. Louisiana—New Orleans, October 19. Nova Scotia—Sable Island, September 1 (only record). Massachusetts—Northampton, September 21. Connecticut—Hartford, September 26. New York—Belmont Lake, Long Island, October 2; Buffalo, October 1. New Jersey—Elizabeth, September 21. Pennsylvania—Jeffersonville, September 18. Delaware—Kent and Sussex Counties, September 18 (average of 19 years, September 5). Maryland—Baltimore County, October 11. Cumberland, September 28. District of Columbia—Washington, September 5. West Virginia—Bluefield, August 26. Virginia—Cape Henry, August 31. North Carolina—Raleigh, October 13 (average of 9 years, August 29). South Carolina—October 24. Georgia—Fitzgerald, September 28. Alabama—Birmingham, September 29. Florida—Pensacola, September 29; Chokoloskee, October 25.

Early dates of fall arrival are: Texas—Cove, July 17. Mississippi—Deer Island, July 31. South Carolina—Mount Pleasant, July 31. Georgia—Savannah, August 6. Florida—Jefferson County, August 6; Key West, August 24. Tamaulipas—Matamoros, August 26. Guatemala—Chimoxan, September 13. Honduras—Lancetilla, September 1. Salvador—Lake Olomega, September 1. Costa Rica—Río Sicsola, September 21. Panamá—Changuinola, Almirante Bay Region, October 4. Colombia—Bonda, Santa Marta region, October 7.

Egg dates.—Missouri: 6 records, May 10 to June 6.

Pennsylvania: 32 records, May 15 to June 28; 20 records, May 24 to June 2, indicating the height of the season.

OPORORNIS AGILIS (Wilson)

CONNECTICUT WARBLER

PLATE 63

HABITS

Wilson (1822) discovered this interesting warbler in Connecticut, described it, and named it for the State in which he first found it. He gave it the specific name *agilis*, because it "seemed more than commonly active, not remaining for a moment in the same position." Both names now seem inappropriate, for Connecticut is far from either its breeding range or its winter home; furthermore, recent studies of its habits show that it is not necessarily "more than commonly active", as it often remains perched for considerable periods.

Not much was known about it by either Wilson or Audubon, who regarded it as a very rare bird. For some 70 years after its discovery, nothing was known about its breeding range and nesting habits, until Ernest T. Seton (1884) found the first nest in 1883 in Manitoba. And for some years thereafter its home life and migrations remained clouded in mystery, but its life history and its ranges are now fairly well known. It is now known to breed in the Canadian Zone from central Alberta and southern Manitoba to central Minnesota, southern Wisconsin, perhaps northern Michigan, and southern Ontario; it spends the winter in South America, from Venezuela to southeastern Brazil, and perhaps in Colombia.

The locality in which Seton (1884) found it breeding is thus described by him: "A few miles south of Carberry, Manitoba, is a large spruce bush, and in the middle of it is a wide tamarack swamp. This latter is a gray mossy bog, luxuriant only with pitcher plants and Droseræ. At regular distances, as though planted by the hand of man, grow the slim straight tamaracks, grizzled with moss, but not dense, nor at all crowded; their light leafage casts no shade."

In Alberta the Connecticut warbler seems to prefer the small, dry, well-drained ridges, or the vicinity of poplar woods, at least such were haunts in which Richard C. Harlow and A. D. Henderson found their nests. The latter tells me that this was formerly a quite common breeding bird around Belvedere, but that now it is extremely rare. The general locality where they found it breeding "was one of small prairies, a few acres in extent, scattered through groves of poplars. I have also heard the call of the Connecticut warbler many times in poplar woods, in the Fort Assiniboine District, but never in the muskegs either there or at Belvedere. The Connecticut warbler in this locality is a bird of the poplar woods."

According to Dr. Roberts (1936), in Minnesota the Connecticut warbler "so far as discovered, makes its summer home in cold tamarack and spruce swamps of typical *Canadian Zone* character. Such places are numerous and wide-spread in northern Minnesota." But it has evidently not been found there in anything like the numbers found in Alberta under the conditions described. On the other hand, Ian McT. Cowan (1939) found it, in the Peace River District of British Columbia, established in its "territory in a grove of young aspens below an open stand of large poplars, aspens and white spruce."

Spring.—The Connecticut warbler is one of the few small birds that follow different migration routes in spring and fall. The spring route is through the West Indies and Florida, northwesterly across the southern Alleghenies, and then northward through the broad Mississippi Valley. It is rarely seen in spring east of these mountains and north of South Carolina and western North Carolina (Asheville). There are, however, scattering spring records, mostly sight records, as far north as Pennsylvania, New Jersey, New York, and Massachusetts. Todd (1940) lists only three spring specimens for western Pennsylvania, and says: "During its spring sojourn the Connecticut Warbler keeps in the shelter of low brush and thick undergrowth, especially in swampy places. Rarely does it venture more than a few feet above the ground, and it pays little or no attention to 'squeaking.' " Forbush (1929) mentions only one spring specimen for Massachusetts, but adds several sight records that he considers reliable.

Brewster (1906) says, however: "They never appeared in spring, nor is there a single record in which I have full confidence of their occurrence at that season in any part of Massachusetts."

In the Mississippi Valley, it is a common spring migrant, occurring rarely as far east as extreme western Pennsylvania, and more commonly from Ohio westward. At Buckeye Lake, Ohio, Milton B. Trautman (1940) calls it "among the last of the warbler transients to appear," and says: "In spring this warbler was found almost entirely in brush tangles of the remnant swamp forests, and on only 2 occasions was an individual seen in the upland type of woodlands."

George H. Lowery, Jr. (1945), advances some grounds for assuming that this and the mourning warbler "are at least in part" migrants across the Gulf of Mexico to the Mississippi Valley.

Nesting.—Seton (1884) tells of finding the first nest of the Connecticut warbler: "As I went on, a small bird suddenly sprang from one of the gravelike moss-mounds. It seemed distressed, and ran along with its wings held up, like a Plover just alighting. On seeing that I would not be decoyed away, it ran around me in the same attitude. Recognizing that it was the Connecticut Warbler, I took it, and then sought out the nest in the moss. It was entirely composed of dry grass, and sunken level with the surface."

Forty years elapsed before any more nests were reported. These were found by Richard C. Harlow, with the help of A. D. Henderson, near Belvedere, Alberta. The latter writes to me: "In 1923, Mr. Richard C. Harlow took at least two and, if I remember rightly, three nests with eggs near Belvedere. I helped him hunt the last of these nests on June 19, 1923, and secured a picture of the nest and eggs. The nest, which contained four eggs, was well concealed at the side of a bunch of dry grass, which overhung the nest, and it was a slight hollow in the ground lined with dry grass, with an inner lining of finer grass. The nest was in the open in rather short grass and weeds, near the edge of poplar woods. The females are very secretive and keep mostly to the ground or near it, and are difficult to observe. Previous to finding this nest, I had started the female from the nest, or close to it, and she crept away along the ground much after the manner of a mouse."

Another nest, found June 25, after Mr. Harlow had left, was on a ridge covered with an open growth of fire-killed poplars, small bushes, and weeds. "It was made of a few leaves on the outside, a few bark strips and vine stems, and was lined with fine fibres and horsehair. It was completely hidden and was attached to rose bush canes 6 inches from the ground."

Mr. Harlow now tells that, up to 1926, he has found 8 nests of the Connecticut warbler, 2 sets of 3 eggs, 5 sets of 4, and 1 set of 5 eggs, all in the vicinity of Belvedere. What he describes in his notes as a typical nest was found in open poplar woods on a ridge above a small slough, surrounded by a growth of willows, into which the female always went when flushed. The nest was at the base of a small, spreading wild rose bush, well under the spreading lower branches, entirely concealed, well sunken in a scratch in the ground, and draped about by fine, dead grass. He describes the nest as much more frail than that of the mourning warbler and made of fine grasses and plant fibres.

According to Dr. Roberts (1936) and several other observers, for which he gives the references, the Connecticut warbler, in Minnesota, always nests in spruce or tamarack bogs, in sphagnum moss or among other northern bog vegetation. One of the best accounts for this region is given by N. L. Huff (1929). He describes a swamp in Aitkin County, northern Minnesota, in which he found this warbler breeding, as follows:

This swamp is perhaps half or three-quarters of a mile wide and two miles or more in length. Much of its area is covered with a pure stand of a small black spruce, some parts with an equally pure stand of tamarack, but in places these two species are more or less mixed together. The pitcher plant and the sundew thrive here, as do the buckbean and the wild calla, the coral root, the moccasin flower, and that rare and gorgeous orchid, the dragon's mouth (*Arethusa bulbosa*). * * *

The spot chosen for the nesting site was a little opening among the black spruce trees, not more than 30 yards from the margin of the swamp. A luxuriant growth of sphagnum covered the ground everywhere to a depth of several inches. The nest was a rather deep, rounded cup, compact and well made. Inside it measured an inch and a half in depth, and two inches in width. The wall of the nest was approximately half an inch in thickness, and was composed entirely of fine dry grasses, except for a few black plant fibers resembling horse hairs, woven into the lining of the bottom. It was sunken in a mossy mound, the top of the nest being level with the top of the moss. Labrador tea and swamp laurel, low bog shrubs that formed a dense tangle throughout the little opening, over-topped the moss by a foot or more and offered ample protection for the otherwise open nest.

Eggs.—Four or five eggs make up the usual set for the Connecticut warbler. The eight eggs in the Thayer collection in Cambridge are ovate and have a slight gloss. The creamy white ground color is speckled, spotted and blotched with "auburn," "bay," and "chestnut," with underlying spots of "brownish drab," "light vinaceous drab," and "light Quaker drab." They seem, generally, to be more boldly marked than those of the Kentucy warbler. Some eggs are heavily blotched or clouded with "wood brown."

The eggs of one such set are all clouded with large patches of brown, which merge with the undertones of drab, and one egg has the large end entirely covered. The markings tend to be concentrated, but do not form a wreath as often as with the eggs of many other warblers. The measurements of 39 eggs average 19.5 by 14.3 millimeters; the eggs showing the four extremes measure **21.3** by 14.3, 19.9 by **15.6, 17.3** by 14.0, and 18.8 by **13.2** millimeters (Harris).

Young.—We have no information on the incubation of the Connecticut warbler nor on the development and care of the young while in the nest. But Francis Zirrer (MS.) has sent me the following account of the behavior of the young after leaving the nest, as observed near his woodland dwelling near Hayward, Wis.: "A pair breeding nearby in 1942 was hardly ever seen until July 20, when the whole family appeared among the tamaracks in the rear of the dwelling and remained there for nearly 2 weeks, part of the time within sight of our windows. At first the young kept close to the ground, in small tamaracks, other evergreens and bog shrubbery, but most of the time, and apparently preferably, in the piles of treetops and other coniferous slashings of which there are several nearby. There the birds moved in and out, after the manner of wrens. Time and again I saw the old birds feeding young on the top of these slashings and saw the young disappear out of sight again after being fed. A few days later, however, the young birds were moving about freely, coming at times quite close to the dwelling. Although most of the searching for food and feeding the young was done in the tamaracks when they were near the dwelling, the old birds every once in a while would disappear among the dense brambles on the edge of the bog and feed the young, mostly with raspberries, with an occasional green caterpillar.

"On August 2, for the first time, they disappeared entirely out of sight of the windows, but after a short search I found them about 80 yards away. From then on every day I found them farther away, but until August 20 the birds remained within a narrow belt of evergreens. * * * After August 20 the birds had apparently begun to band with others of their kind into larger flocks, for a flock of about 20 to 25 was seen several times."

Plumages.—Kilgore and Breckenridge (1929) give us the only account we have of the juvenal plumage of the Connecticut warbler: "The nestling, which was just passing from the downy to the juvenile plumage and was probably far enough advanced to leave the nest within 2 or 3 days, shows the following characters. Upper parts dark olive-brown, breast and sides snuff-brown merging into buffy-yellow on the belly, legs and feet very light flesh color."

Dr. Dwight (1900) describes the first winter plumage of the male as "above, including wings and tail, brownish olive-green almost exactly like *G. trichas*, but usually greener and grayer. Below, unlike *G. trichas*, being canary-yellow, washed on the sides with pale olive-brown, and with broccoli-brown on the throat often concealing cinereous gray, the chin wood-brown. The orbital ring conspicuously pale buff."

He says that the first nuptial plumage is acquired by a partial prenuptial molt, "involving much of the head and throat, which become clear plumbeous or ashy gray instead of brown, slightly veiled with olive-brown on the pileum and with drab-gray on the throat, the orbital ring white."

A complete postnuptial molt in summer produces the adult winter plumage, which "differs from the first winter dress in being cinereous gray instead of brown on the head and throat, palest on the chin, and slightly veiled with drab-gray on the throat, and olive-green on the crown. The back is greener and the yellow below rather brighter. The orbital ring is white. The birds with deeper plumbeous throats are probably still older. This dress differs but little from the nuptial, a fact not generally known."

The adult nuptial plumage is "acquired perhaps by a partial prenuptial moult as in the young bird or possibly by wear alone."

The female, in first winter plumage, is "browner above and on the throat than the male, but often indistinguishable. The first nuptial is acquired chiefly by wear. The adult winter is similar to the first winter but rather grayer on the throat resembling the male in first winter dress. The adult nuptial and later plumages are never as gray as those of the male."

Food.—Very little seems to be known about the food of the Connecticut warbler. Audubon (1841) observed two "chasing a species of spider which runs nimbly over the water, and which they caught by gliding over it, as a Swallow does when drinking. * * * On opening them I counted upwards of fifty of the spiders mentioned above, but found no appearance of any other food."

Dr. B. H. Warren (1890) says that it "feeds on beetles, larvae, spiders, snails and sometimes on small seeds and berries."

Behavior.—While with us on the fall migration, the Connecticut warbler is not particularly shy, though rather retiring. As we find it in the swampy thickets or in damp meadows among scattered bushes, we may see it walking quietly on the ground, or starting up when disturbed, it stops to perch on some low branch, watching us intently for several seconds before seeking the seclusion of the denser shrubbery. These birds are excessively fat in the fall, so fat in fact that it is difficult to make a good specimen of one. Huff (1929), however, writes:

In his summer home the Connecticut Warbler is a shy and elusive bird, so secretive in his manner that he would rarely be seen here, even by those looking for him, were it not for his betraying song. * * *

When driven from his song perch by too close approach of his observer he escapes, often unseen, from the opposite side of the tree, and the first indication of his departure may be his jubilant, triumphant song gushing from a tree several yards away. If one is fortunate enough to see him enter another tree nearby, one is impressed with the remarkable facility with which he creeps, half hidden, through the tree until he reaches a secure position, separated from his observer by a limb or a small mass of foliage. More than once as he scampered along a branch, his body low, his head extended, seeking a suitable hiding place, I have seen him pause an inch beyond the coveted spot. With head and shoulders visible he takes a hasty peep at his observer, then suddenly retreats a step or two and adjusts his position until he is wholly obscured. * * *

If one remain perfectly still or in hiding for a while, the singer forgets one's presence and sooner or later will move out of his hiding place, walking along on a limb or occasionally hopping to a nearby branch, taking some tiny insect or other tidbit that meets his fancy, all the while repeating his song several times a minute. His relative inactivity, his rather deliberate movements, now afford an excellent opportunity for observation. * * *

Whether he had forgotten my presence or merely regarded me now as a part of the landscape, I do not know, but he no longer sought to conceal himself. He often sat motionless for several minutes, except for the shaking and quivering of his body which always accompanied his singing.

Mr. Harlow tells me that a female that he watched returned to her nest three times within an hour; she always walked back to the nest.

Voice.—In his first account of the nesting of the Connecticut warbler, Seton (1884) says of its song: "It may be suggested by the syllables, *beecher-beecher-beecher-beecher-beecher-beecher*. It is like the song of the Golden-crowned Thrush, but differs in being in the same pitch throughout, instead of beginning in a whisper and increasing the emphasis and strength with each pair of notes to the last." Later (1891), he recorded another type of song which "nearly resembled the syllables '*Fru-chapple fru-chapple fru-chapple whoit*,' and is uttered in a loud, ringing voice, quite unlike the weak, hurried lisping of the Wood Warblers, which are nesting abundantly in the adjoining dry spruce woods." Mr. Harlow (MS.) refers to its song as heard on the breeding grounds as "very distinctive, *whíp-pity, whíp-pity, whíp*, clear, ringing, deliberate and resonant, with a definite accent on the first syllable." Various other renderings of the song have been given in syllables, all of which give similar impressions of it, and some of which suggest the song of the Maryland yellowthroat as well as that of the ovenbird. The carrying power of the song is shown by the fact that Mr. Trautman (1940) "heard a male singing more than 300 yards away.   Even at that distance the song was readily heard above a brilliant morning bird chorus"

Huff (1929) writes: "The song of the Connecticut Warbler varies with different individuals, and at times with the same individual.   The volume may be changed, and certain syllables may be changed or omitted, but the quality of his tone is unique and practically invariable, especially as regards two syllables, '*freecher*,' always included in his song.   So characteristic is his voice that one having heard him may identify him more quickly by his song than by sight.   His voice is sharp, piercing, penetrating, rather shrill yet pleasing, and is one that I always associate with the wild swampy wilderness where he sings."

This warbler sings nearly as freely on the spring migration as on its breeding grounds.   Trautman (1940) says: "More than 80 per cent of all identified birds were singing, and had it not been for the singers the species would have been considered very rare rather than uncommon."

In the fall it is usually silent except for its distinctive call notes. Dr. Chapman (1907) calls this "a sharp, characteristic *peek*."   Francis H. Allen writes to me: "I have recorded an autumn note as a sharp chip like the syllable *witch;* that is, it seems to have both a *w* and a *ch* in it.   It struck me as a distinctive note."   Gerald Thayer wrote to Dr. Chapman (1907): "The only note I have ever heard from it is a very quick, sharp call, with a clipped-short metallic ring, *plink*, easily remembered and differentiated among warbler chips."

Dr. Tyler and Walter Faxon, two expert and careful observers, were confident that they heard several Connecticut warblers singing on September 25, 1910, in the swamp referred to below.   Dr. Tyler has sent me the following account of it: "When we entered the swamp our attention was at once attracted by a bird song which was new to us; it came from the high trees deep in the swamp.   My notes, speaking out of this dim past, record that the song suggested to both of us, but rather faintly, that of a parula warbler, but neither of us was satisfied with our provisional diagnosis.

"Later we heard the song repated many times from birds near at hand, and we were impressed again by its novelty, but now by its distinct dissimilarity from the parula's buzzing voice.   The notes were far too loud for a parula, too clear and full-voiced, but they had suggested *Compsothlypis* to us because they were given with a sort of rotary effect as opposed to a to-and-fro rhythm.

"The song—clear, ringing, and very loud—was made up of four notes, all strongly emphasized, sounding like *three, three, three, three*, pronounced in two or three syllables each.   The pitch ran up the scale slightly, and the quality suggested to both of us the mourning warbler's voice.   On this notable morning Connecticut warblers were scattered throughout the swamp, an area of twenty acres or so. We must have seen a dozen, perhaps twice that number, during the two hours we spent there. On one occasion three jumped up from the ground into the same shrub, and time after time from one end of the swamp to the other we started single birds. A few days later we heard the song here again. The Connecticut warblers were still present, but we never actually saw a bird in the act of singing, although once we heard the song from a shrub from which, a moment later, jumped one of the birds. Nevertheless, because of the large number of Connecticut warblers gathered here on these two days, because we could ascribe this song to no other species of bird, and because it fitted well the published descriptions of the bird's song, we had little doubt in our minds that we had heard Connecticut warblers singing during their autumn migration. This was the only time in his life that Mr. Faxon ever heard the song, although we often saw the birds afterwards, and in all the years since I have never heard it again."

Field marks.—The Connecticut is a rather large warbler and rather plainly colored, with no white in the wings and tail, but with a pronounced eye ring, white in the adult and buffy or yellowish in the young. The adult male is olive-green above and yellow below, with a broad, light-gray throat. The female and young are browner. The adult male might be confused with the mourning warbler, but it is larger, has no black on the breast and has a complete and conspicuous eye ring; the latter is the best field mark in any plumage, regardless of age or season.

Fall.—On its return to its winter quarters the Connecticut warbler follows a partially different route from that taken in the spring. From its breeding range in central Canada it migrates almost due east to New England, largely avoiding the Mississippi Valley south of northern Illinois and Ohio, and thence southward along the Atlantic coast through Florida and the West Indies to its winter home in South America.

Mr. Trautman (1940) says of the fall migration in Ohio: "In this migration the species was not recorded as frequently nor in as large numbers as in spring, and seldom more than 3 birds were seen in a day. It is probable that the species was as numerous as it was in spring, since the nonsinging birds appeared in equal numbers in both seasons. In fall this warbler was not confined to dense tangles of remnant swamp forests, but also inhabited brushy, weedy, and fallow fields."

The following note from Dr. Winsor M. Tyler is typical of our experience with this warbler in Massachusetts in the fall: "There used to be a wooded swamp in Lexington, Mass., not unlike the region near Fresh Pond where, in the 1870's, the Cambridge ornithologists often observed the Connecticut warblers. In the Lexington swamp, years later, Walter Faxon and I used to find the birds in the fall, starting them from among the beds of jewel weed which grew profusely there. I spoke of this locality when writing of the veery and of the golden-winged warbler, for both of these birds bred in it commonly every year.

"The Connecticut warbler, as we see it in the fall migration, is a very distinctive bird. It starts up from nearly underfoot and, alighting for a moment at short range, often in full view, jerks about in the shrubbery, peering inquisitively at us, its eye ring giving the odd effect of a man looking over his spectacles with eyebrows raised. If really startled, the bird retires to the high trees where it walks sedately over the branches. Its throat at this season varies from brownish yellow to smoky gray, and a striking character, as we look up at the bird, is the long under tail coverts which come nearly to the tip of the tail."

William Brewster (1906) used to find these warblers very abundant in certain swamps near Cambridge during September, and writes:

We used to find Connecticut Warblers oftenest among the thickets of clethra, *Andromeda ligustrina*, shad-bush, and black alder, which formed a dense undergrowth beneath the large maples that shaded the wooded islands of this swamp, and in the beds of touch-me-not (*Impatiens*) that covered some of its wetter portions. They were also given to frequenting the banks of the numerous intersecting ditches, especially where the deadly nightshade, clinging to the stems of the bushes, trailed its gray-green foliage and coral-red berries over the black mud or coffee-colored water. In such places they often literally swarmed, but so retiring and elusive were they that by any one unacquainted with their habits they might easily be overlooked. They spent most of their time on the ground under or among the rank vegetation, where they would often remain securely hidden until nearly trodden on.

DISTRIBUTION

Range.—Southern Canada and north-central United States south to central South America.

Breeding range.—The Connecticut warbler breeds **north** to central eastern British Columbia (probably Tupper Creek) ; central Alberta (Manly, Athabaska, Lac la Nonne, Battle River, probably Grand Prairie, Peace River, and Lac la Biche) ; and probably central and northeastern Ontario (Moose Factory, Lowbush, Gargantua, Sundridge, and Algonquin Park). **East** to northeastern Ontario (Moose Factory) and northern Michigan (Porcupine Mountains, Huron Mountains, Munising, McMillan, and Bois Blanc Island). **South** to northern Michigan (Bois Blanc Island) ; northern Wisconsin (Orienta and Wascott) ; northern Minnesota (Itasca Park, Gull Lake, Aitkin County, Cambridge, and Tower) ; southern Manitoba (Duck

Mountain, Lake Saint Martin, Carberry, Aweme, Shoal Lake, and Sandilands); and southern Alberta (Glenevis). West to southern Alberta (Glenevis) and central eastern British Columbia (probably Tupper Creek).

Winter range.—The winter range of the Connecticut warbler is known only through specimens from central western Brazil (Alliança and Rio San Lourenço); and probably north to central Venezuela (Cumbre de Valencia and Carabobo).

Migration.—Late dates of spring departure are: Brazil—Tonantins, April 9 and Venezuela—Rancho Grande, near Maracay, Aragua, April 29.

Early dates of spring arrival are: Bahamas (casual)—Cay Lobos Light, May 9. Florida—Stock Island in lower Florida Keys, and Mosquito Inlet, May 9. Georgia—Atlanta, May 5. South Carolina—Chester, May 10. North Carolina—Asheville, May 12. West Virginia—Ritchie County, April 25. District of Columbia—Washington, April 30. Maryland—Baltimore County, May 5. Pennsylvania—Crystal Lake in Crawford County, May 18. New Jersey—Makania Swamp, May 6. New York—Keene, May 15. Massachusetts—Wachusett Mountain, May 10. Louisiana—Monroe, April 27. Arkansas—Monticello and Hot Springs National Park, April 28. Tennessee—Memphis, April 23. Kentucky—Bowling Green, April 21. Missouri—Columbia, May 4. Illinois—Chicago region, May 3 (average May 15). Indiana—Bloomington, April 27. Ohio—Oberlin, May 3; Columbus, May 3 (average for central Ohio, May 12). Michigan—Muskegon County, May 4. Ontario—Guelph, May 9. Iowa—Polk County, Hillsboro, and Wall Lake, May 5. Wisconsin—Ripon, May 10. Minnesota—Minneapolis, May 11 (average of 16 years for southern Minnesota, May 25). Texas—Houston, April 20. North Dakota—Fargo, May 23. Manitoba—Aweme, May 18 (average, May 27). Alberta—Edmonton, May 20.

Late dates of fall departure are: Alberta—Glenevis, September 5. Manitoba—Shoal Lake, September 6; Aweme, September 3 (average, August 30). North Dakota—Fargo, October 1. Texas—Cove, November 5. Minnesota—Minneapolis, September 19. Wisconsin—Madison, October 4. Iowa—Polk County, October 1. Ontario—Point Pelee, October 2. Michigan—Detroit and vicinity, October 8. Ohio—Youngstown, October 16; Columbus area, October 12 (average, October 2). Indiana—Richmond, October 9. Illinois—Chicago region, October 13. Kentucky—Bardstown, October 11. Arkansas—Washington County, October 14. Louisiana—Monroe, October 9 (only fall record). Quebec—Hudson, October 4. Nova Scotia—Sable Island, October 6. Maine—Westbrook, September 20. New Hampshire—Jefferson region, October 6. Vermont—Woodstock, October 2. Massachusetts—Boston, October 29. Rhode Island—Green Hill, October 5. Connecticut—New Haven, October 13. New York—Idlewild, Long Island, November 6; East Hampton, Long Island, November 26. New Jersey—Union County, October 18 (average of 9 years, October 1). Pennsylvania—Jeffersonville, October 16. Maryland—Patuxent Wildlife Research Refuge, October 29; College Park, November 7. District of Columbia—Washington, October 22 (average of 13 years, October 12). West Virginia—Bluefield, October 1. Virginia—Rosslyn, October 24. North Carolina—Raleigh, October 24. Florida—Sombrero Key, October 9.

Early dates of fall arrival are: North Dakota—Cass County, August 16. Texas—Commerce, August 28. Minnesota—Hutchinson and Frontenac, August 29. Wisconsin—New London, August 24. Iowa—Marshalltown, August 22. Ontario—King, August 21. Michigan—Sault Ste. Marie, August 19. Ohio—Waverly, August 10; central Ohio, August 27 (average, September 8). Indiana—Lake County, August 31. Illinois—Glen Ellyn, August 14. Quebec—Hudson, August 18. Maine—Cape Elizabeth, August 30. New Hampshire—Randolph, August 18. Vermont—St. Johnsbury and Wells River, August 21. Massachusetts—Belmont and Martha's Vineyard, August 19. Connecticut—East Hartford and Litchfield, September 1. New York—Frost Valley in southern Catskills, August 16; Alley Pond, Long Island, August 17. New Jersey—Passaic, August 24. Delaware—Delaware City, September 3. Maryland—Patuxent Wildlife Research Refuge, September 9. District of Columbia—Washington, August 28 (average of 21 years, September 21). West Virginia—Bluefield, September 10. Virginia—Rockbridge County, August 31. North Carolina—Raleigh, September 28. Florida—St. Marks, September 21. Bahamas—Nassau, October 12. Costa Rica—San José, October 6. Colombia—Bonda, Santa Marta region, October 22. Venezuela—La Trilla, October 23. Brazil—Alliança, Rio Madeira, November 16.

Egg dates.—Alberta: 8 records, June 15 to 25.

Manitoba: 2 records, June 12 to 21.

Minnesota: 2 records, June 12 and 13 (Harris).

OPORORNIS PHILADELPHIA (Wilson)

MOURNING WARBLER

PLATE 64

HABITS

Alexander Wilson (1832) discovered this warbler "on the border of a marsh, within a few miles of Philadelphia," hence the scientific name *philadelphia*; he called it the mourning warbler on account of the black markings on its breast, which suggested a symbol of mourning. The name is not happily chosen, however, for as Forbush (1929) says, "this crêpe-like marking about the breast is the only thing about the bird that would suggest mourning, for it seems as happy and active as most birds, and its song is a paean of joy." Wilson never saw another specimen, and Audubon handled very few; Nuttall was apparently not sure that he even saw a single one. This is not strange, for it is not common in the Eastern States, where it occurs as a late migrant and is not easily detected in the dense shrubbery that it frequents at a time when vegetation is in full leaf.

Spring.—From its winter home in Central and South America, the mourning warbler enters the United States on a front extending from Florida to Texas; it is apparently very rare in Florida, where Howell (1932) gives only two spring records. There is probably a heavy migration directly across the Gulf of Mexico, from Yucatán to the Gulf States, for M. A. Frazar (1881) saw "large numbers" flying northward on a line from Yucatán to the mouth of the Mississippi, when his ship was about 30 miles south of the Louisiana coast. It has been reported by various observers as migrating regularly through eastern Texas, where I have observed it in the passing waves of migrants. Thence it spreads out northeastward along the Alleghenies, as well as migrating northward through the Mississippi Valley. It is comparatively rare east of the Alleghenies, but decidedly commoner to the west of that range. Milton B. Trautman (1940) says of the spring migration in Ohio:

In spring the Mourning Warbler inhabited chiefly the dense shrub layer of the remnant swamp forests, and, occasionally, the dense tangles of hilly woodlands. The birds in the upland woods were almost invariably in the wetter sections, such as in the lower third of a ravine. The females and some males were very secretive, remaining in dense shrubbery, except when flying in a skulking manner from one tangle to another, or when scolding for an instant upon some terminal branch in response to much "Screech Owl" whistling. The high-plumaged males, however, seemingly sang each morning, and while singing were most conspicuous. The males usually remained quiet during the early morning warbler chorus. About 7 a. m. their sharp, "chip" note could be heard in tangles, and shortly thereafter they appeared singly and in small groups. They perched on small twigs, peered about for a moment, flew upward a few feet, and alighted upon the twigs of small, rather isolated bushes or saplings. There they perched quietly for a few moments before beginning to sing. After singing in loud clear voices several times they hopped upward to the next branches and repeated the song, and then continued alternately to perch higher and sing until the tops of the shrubs or saplings were reached.

From the fan-shaped migration route the breeding range spreads out from Newfoundland on the east to Alberta on the west, including southern Canada and some of the Northern States, and extends southward in the mountains to New York, Pennsylvania, and West Virginia. On its breeding grounds, the mourning warbler shows a preference for old clearings and cut-over lands or slashings, often on the uplands, where dense thickets of raspberries or tangles of blackberry vines have covered the open ground; it is also partial to patches of nettles and is especially fond of extensive growths of jewelweed and other rank herbage. It seldom ventures far into the shady woods but may be found around the edges, along old brush fences and in lowland thickets, such as are frequented by northern yellowthroats, even where the ground is damp.

Nesting.—The rather bulky nest of the mourning warbler is placed on or near the ground, usually not over 6 inches above it, though sometimes as much as 30. It is generally built in tangles of raspberry, blackberry, or other briery shrubs, sometimes in a bunch of ferns, in a clump of goldenrod or other rank herbage, or even in a tussock of grass. Ora W. Knight (1908) describes a nest found in Maine:

The nest was quite a bulky affair and placed at the base of a clump of coarse weed stocks about six inches from the ground. The outer nest was of dry leaves and vine stalks. The nest proper was made up with a thick outer wall of dead, coarse, flat-bladed grass, with finer grasses and a few weed stalks, and all through this outer wall was interwoven a few small, dead, white maple leaves. The inner wall was composed of fine grasses, and the inner lining contained a few horsehairs. It was a very neat, compact nest, well built to protect the eggs from dampness from the moist ground where it was placed. It measured, outside diameter, five inches; inside diameter, two inches; outside depth, three and one-half inches; inside depth, two inches.

E. H. Eaton (1914) quotes Verdi Burtch, of Branchport, N. Y., as follows:

In Potter swamp, where the timber has been well thinned out, where the ground is wet and springy, where the ferns, skunk cabbage, tall rue, spice bush, bishop's cap, false Solomon's seal, white baneberry and marsh marigold mingle, and poison ivy and woody nightshade cover the stumps and dead tops, and here and there a tall dead stub towers above the bushes, here the Mourning warbler makes its summer home, nesting along the abandoned wood roads and more open places that are now grown up with grass, ferns, skunk cabbage, rue and marsh marigolds. * * * These swamp nests are usually situated in a grassy place among the brush and tops that were left by the lumbermen, in a bunch of weeds, or in the middle of a bunch of skunk cabbage or ferns. One nest was placed on top of a thick vine that ran over the ground and there was scarcely any attempt at concealment. Another was in a very wet place in the heart of a marsh marigold. Another was in a bunch of weeds on a rotted moss and dirt-covered log. The nests are usually very well concealed and very near the ground. * * *

The Mourning warbler also nests in an entirely different situation near Branchport. June 4, 1903, a nest was found in a dry bush lot clearing along a large gully at an elevation of 250 feet above the valley. It was placed in a small beech bush 18 inches from the ground among wild blackberry bushes, beech stumps and sprouts. * * * A nest found June 13, 1909, was a little farther up this same hill and was placed on the ground in a clump of oxeye daisies close by the highway through some woods and it was less than 2 feet from the beaten track.

Eggs.—The mourning warbler lays from 3 to 5 eggs to a set, more often 4. They are ovate with a tendency toward short ovate and have a slight gloss. The ground color is white, or creamy white, and is speckled, spotted, or blotched with "bay," "chestnut," and "auburn," with underlying spots of "light vinaceous drab," "brownish drab," or "drab-gray." In addition to these markings, many eggs have a few scattered spots, or very small scrawls of black. Although there is a tendency toward concentration of markings at the large end, many eggs are finely and delicately speckled over the entire surface. The measurements of 50 eggs average 18.2 by 13.8 millimeters; the eggs showing the four extremes measure **20.0** by 14.2, 19.9 by **14.7, 16.5** by 13.7, and 17.7 by **13.2** millimeters (Harris).

Plumages.—Dr. Dwight (1900) says that the juvenal plumage of the mourning warbler is "very similar to *G. trichas* but darker. Above deep olive-brown. Wings darker, edged with olive-green, the coverts faintly edged with pale cinnamon. Tail deep olive-green. Below, very deep grayish tawny-olive, abdomen and crissum pale brownish Naples-yellow. Inconspicuous orbital ring pale buff."

The postjuvenal molt, which involves the contour plumage and the wing coverts, but not the rest of the wings or the tail, occurs in August and is completed before the birds reach their winter home. Dr. Dwight describes the male as "above similar to *G. trichas* and to *G. agilis* but greener than either, with a plumbeous tinge about the head, and the yellow below brighter. There is usually a little concealed black on the throat; the chin is yellowish white. The conspicuous orbital ring and a supraloral line are pale canary-yellow, the lores dusky."

The first nuptial plumage is "acquired by a partial prenuptial moult which involves chiefly the head and throat. The plumbeous cap, the black throat veiled with cinereous, the dusky lores and the white orbital rings are assumed, the rest of the plumage showing a good deal of wear." This and subsequent prenuptial molts occur in late February and March, before the birds come north.

Adults have a complete postnuptial molt in August and a partial prenuptial molt as in the young birds. Of the female, he says: "The plumages and moults correspond to those of the male. In first winter plumage the throat is browner and in but slight contrast to the breast, scarcely distinguishable from the male first winter dress of *G. agilis*. The first nuptial plumage is acquired chiefly by wear. The adult winter plumage resembles the somewhat grayer first winter male." No black is assumed on the throat.

Food.—No one seems to have made a study of the food of this warbler. Dr. B. H. Warren (1890) mentions beetles and spiders in the food of two that he examined. The bird is doubtless mainly insectivorous and probably obtains most of its food on or near the ground. An interesting item of food is mentioned in Dr. Skutch's account of winter habits.

Behavior.—In a general way the behavior of the mourning warbler is much like that of the northern yellowthroat, though it is rather more timid and retiring, plunging into the densest thickets on the slightest alarm. It is especially secretive on the fall migration, skulking through the thickest underbrush on the edges of the woods or along old brush fences. But, in the spring, the males are often quite conspicuous, mounting to the tops of bushes or small trees to sing. William Brewster (1938) writes: "A male among fallen tree-tops behind the house eluded me in the most provoking manner, creeping about like a Wren among the debris. Sometimes he would appear within a few yards of me, disappearing almost instantly, and when next seen would be perhaps forty or fifty yards away. His gait was distinctly a 'hop' but in other respects he resembled the Connecticut Warbler, especially in flight and in attitude when perched."

Voice.—Aretas A. Saunders contributes the following study of the song:

"The song of the mourning warbler is quite short, and averages a little lower in pitch than most warbler songs. It is loud, musical in quality and contains marked explosive and liquid consonant sounds. It is usually in two distinct parts.

"The first part consists of 2 to 5 notes, slurs, or 2-note phrases, sounding, when a single note, like *tleet or tseet*, and when of 2-notes like *tolee* or *choree*, varying in individual birds. The majority of songs have 3 such notes or slurs. Of my 30 records 20 slur upward, 6 slur downward, and 4 are single notes. When they slur downward the sound is like *teelo*. The second part is short, and the notes faster, especially when there are many. The number of notes varies from 1 to 9, averaging 3. In 5 records there is no second part. The notes of the second part vary considerably. In some songs they are all equal and on one pitch, sounding like *to to to* or *tsit tsit*. When there are more notes they vary in pitch and are often connected giving an effect like *totletoleeto*. The second part is two to three tones lower in pitch than the first.

"The pitch varies from C''' to B''', a half tone less than an octave. Individual songs range from one to three and a half tones, averaging two tones. Songs are from 1 to 2 seconds in length. The notes of the first part occur about three a second; those of the second part about five a second.

"The mourning warbler also sings a flight song which is somewhat longer, contains several *choree* notes, usually at the beginning, and several groups of rapid twitters. The bird rises from the ground or a low perch, singing as it rises, terminates the song at a height of about 20 feet, and drops silently back to the ground.

"My records of 14 years in Allegany State Park, N. Y., show that the song ceases in July, averaging July 14, the earliest date being July 7, 1932 and the latest date July 22, 1935. The song is sometimes revived in August, especially the flight song."

Francis H. Allen (MS.) sets the song down as "*wee surree surree surree surree*, with a falling inflection. Three or four *thur-rees* are often followed by a pretty warble, which I once recorded as *thur-réedloo*. Sometimes there are two or three introductory notes, and a bird at Underhill, Vt., used to address my companion with a greeting that sounded much like *kiss me Charrlie, Charrlie, Charlie*. Birds on the spring migration sang very distinctly *wee-three wee-three we-three*. The song, in my experience, is always distinctive and easily identified. A call or alarm note is a sharp, rough *chip* that seems to be diagnostic."

A. D. Du Bois (MS.) writes the song as "*chooy, chooy, chooy, choo-choo-choo*. The first three notes are alike, beginning at the same pitch, and each slurred upward to the same extent." In some notes sent to me a long time ago, Dr. Harrison F. Lewis records nine different renderings of the song in syllables; six of these are different combinations of *yeee, yeee, yeee, churr, churr, churr*, varying from two to four of each of the two syllables in the different songs; others are *yeee, yeee, churry-urry-urry*, and three or four repetitions of the *churry* note. The song reminded him of the songs of the house wren and Lincoln's sparrow. I recorded it in Newfoundland in 1912 as *we zrrée, we zrrée, we zrrée-u*. Many other similar renderings have been published. Wendell Taber refers in his notes to the persistent singing of a male mourning warbler on its breeding grounds; he counted 49 songs in 12 minutes between 7:30 and 7:42 p. m., the songs being regularly spaced.

Field marks.—The mourning and MacGillivray's warblers are very much alike, but the adult male of the latter has a white spot above and another below the eye, which are lacking in the former. The young male and the female of these two species are almost impossible to distinguish, as the young mourning warbler has an indication of an eye ring, but it has a shorter tail than the MacGillivray's. Fortunately, the ranges of the two do not overlap to any great extent. In some plumages, the mourning warbler resembles the Connecticut warbler, though it is decidedly smaller, and the under tail coverts of the latter are decidedly longer. The adult male mourning is distinguished by its black throat and by the absence of the white eye ring, but females and young males have an incomplete eye ring in the fall, making their recognition difficult.

Enemies.—This warbler is evidently a rare victim of the cowbird; I can find only four records of such parasitism.

Fall.—The autumnal migration route of the mourning warbler is apparently a reversal of the spring route. The bird is an early migrant, leaving its breeding range in July and August, and appearing in Central America early in September. It seems rarer in the fall than it probably is, for it is very secretive, skulking through dense thickets and rank herbage; it is mainly silent, also, which helps to make it seldom observed.

Winter.—Dr. Alexander F. Skutch contributes the following account: "The mourning warbler is an abundant winter resident in the lowlands of Costa Rica, up to an altitude of about 4,000 feet. It is numerous on the lower Caribbean slope, and equally so in the basin of El General on the Pacific slope, where at an elevation of 3,000 feet it is still one of the most abundant of wintering warblers. But in the drier northwestern province of Guanacaste, it is rare or absent. Avoiding the woodlands, it frequents low, dense thickets and fields overgrown with tall weeds and rank grass, where it reveals its presence by its constantly repeated sharp call-note, yet is difficult to glimpse. It is solitary during the winter months.

"During the exceptionally wet year of 1937, a mourning warbler, who lived in a weedy field close by my cabin, sang repeatedly, especially on rainy or darkly overcast and threatening afternoons. I first heard him on February 15, and then at intervals until late in March. As he flitted about through the wet vegetation in search of insects, he would sing a low but full, smoothly flowing, long-continued warble—an exceptionally beautiful song, much like that of the Central American ground-chat. On April 24 of the same year, I heard another mourning warbler sing, but this time only a few detached syllables. This bird then proceeded to eat the protein bodies from the leaf-bases of a young Cecropia tree. These tiny, white, beadlike corpuscles, produced in numbers on the brown, velvety bases of the long petioles of the broad Cecropia leaves, are the special food of the Azteca ants that dwell in the hollow stems of this fast-growing tree. When the tree is occupied by its usual colony of ants, the corpuscles are removed as fast as they ripen; but if the tree chance to remain untenanted, they accumulate and become a dainty food for a variety of small birds.

"Although it passes on migration through northern Central America, the mourning warbler has been rarely recorded there. It arrives in Costa Rica in September, usually late in the month, and remains until the end of April or May, sometimes delaying its departure until the middle of May.

"Early dates of fall arrival in Central America are: Guatemala—Panajachel (Griscom), September 20. Costa Rica—San José (Cherrie), September 1, 1890; Río Sicsola (Carriker), September 24; Basin of El General, September 23, 1936 and October 4, 1942.

"Late dates of spring departure from Central America are: Costa Rica—Boruca (Underwood), April 27; Basin of El General, April 27, 1936, May 1, 1937, May 14, 1939, May 5, 1940, April 24, 1942 and April 29, 1943; San José (Cherrie), April 27, 1890; Jejivalle, April 16, 1941. Honduras—Tela, May 10, 1930. Guatemala—La Carolina (Griscom), May 15."

DISTRIBUTION

Range.—Southern Canada and eastern United States south to northwestern South America.

Breeding range.—The mourning warbler breeds **north** to probably northeastern British Columbia (Fort Nelson and Dawson Creek); central Alberta (Athabaska, Camrose, Nevis; probably: Grand Prairie, Peace River, Egg Lake, and Fort MacMurray); probably central Saskatchewan (Big River, Emma Lake, and Hudson Bay Junction); Manitoba (Duck Mountain, Fairford, and Hillside Beach); central Ontario (Kenora, Lac Seul, Missinaibi, Kapuskasing, and Lake Abitibi); southern Quebec (Mistassini Post, Notre Dame de la Doree, Val Jalbert, Cross Point, and Magdalen Island); and Newfoundland (Nicholsville and probably Lewisporte). **East** to Newfoundland (probably Lewisporte); central Nova Scotia (Wolfville and Halifax); central western and southeastern Maine (Andover, Waterville, and Machias); central New Hampshire (Mount Moosilauke); northwestern and central Massachusetts (Mount Graylock and Princeton); southeastern New York (Kortright and Roxbury); northeastern Pennsylvania (Harvey Lake and Laanna); western Maryland (Backbone Mountain); and eastern West Virginia (Cheat Bridge, Cherry River Glades, Top of Allegheny, and Spruce Knob). **South** to West Virginia (Spruce Knob); northwestern Ohio (Spencer and Toledo); Michigan (Montcalm County and Lansing); northeastern Illinois (La Grange Park); central and eastern Wisconsin (Unity, New London, and Germantown); northwestern and central eastern Minnesota (eastern Polk County, Leech Lake, Gull Lake, and Isanti County); and central northern and northeastern North Dakota (Turtle Mountains, Pembina, and Grand Forks). **West** to central northern North Dakota (Turtle Mountains); southern Alberta (Glenevis); and northeastern British Columbia (Fort Nelson).

The mourning warbler winters **north** to southern Nicaragua (Greytown) and western Venezuela (Encontrados). **East** to western Venezuela (Encontrados); Colombia (Ocana and Bogotá); and Ecuador (Mapoto, Papallacta, and Oyacachi). **South** to Ecuador (Oyacachi). **West** to Ecuador (Oyacachi); Costa Rica (Beruca, Juan Viñas, and Cerro de Santa María); and Nicaragua (Greytown).

Migration.—Late dates of spring departure are: Venezuela—Rancho Grande near Maracay, Aragua, April 9. Colombia—Santa Marta region, April 11. Panamá—Gatún, April 28. Costa Rica—San Isidro del General, May 8. Salvador—Lake Chanmica, May 14. Honduras—near Tela, May 10. Guatemala—La Carolina, May 15. Tabasco—Reforma, May 22; Veracruz—Buena Vista, May 13.

Early dates of spring arrival are: Puerto Rico—Santa Isabel, March 21. Florida—St. Augustine, March 13. Virginia—Lexington, April 27. West Virginia—Cabell County, May 7. District of Columbia—Washington, May 4 (average of 16 years, May 15). Maryland—Elk River, May 7. Pennsylvania—Carlisle, May 3; Berwyn, May 5. New Jersey—Bernardsville, May 5. New York—Buffalo and Syracuse, May 2; Hempstead, Long Island, May 8. Connecticut—Glastonbury, May 6. Rhode Island—Cranston, May 21. Massachusetts—Manchester, May 11. Vermont—Wells River, May 10. New Hampshire—East Westmoreland, May 8. Maine—Winthrop and Big Lyford, May 10. Quebec—Montreal, May 20. Nova Scotia—Antigonish, May 30. Newfoundland—Gander, June 7. Gulf of Mexico—30 miles south of mouth of Mississippi River, April 2. Louisiana—Oak Grove, April 18. Mississippi—Edwards, April 28. Arkansas—Helena, May 2. Tennessee—Memphis, May 5. Missouri—Columbia, April 30. Kentucky—Bowling Green, April 20. Ohio—Columbus area, May 1 (average, May 12). Indiana—Terre Haute, May 2. Michigan—Ann Arbor, May 5. Ontario—Ottawa, May 10 (average of 8 years, May 24). Illinois—Chicago region, May 8 (average, May 16). Wisconsin—Dane County, May 3. Iowa—Sac County, May 4. Minnesota—Minneapolis, May 8 (average of 24 years for southern Minnesota, May 18). Texas—Rockport, April 31; San Antonio and Kemah, April 24. Oklahoma—Copan, May 16. Kansas—Lawrence, May 12. Nebraska—Plattsmouth, May 6. South Dakota—Mellette, May 14. North Dakota—Lower Souris Refuge, Upham, May 13; Cass County, May 22 (average May 25). Manitoba—Margaret, May 13; Aweme, May 20 (average June 3). Saskatchewan—Lake Johnston, May 25. Alberta—Glenevis, May 24.

Late dates of fall departure are: Alberta—Glenevis, September 2. Manitoba—Treesbank, September 25; Aweme, September 5 (average, August 29). North Dakota—Fargo, September 21; Cass County, September 18 (average, September 13). Nebraska—Hastings, October 8. Kansas—Washington Creek and Lawrence, September 14. Oklahoma—Norman and Oklahoma City, October 6. Texas—Harlingen, October 27. Minnesota—Minneapolis, October 5 (average of 5 years, September 20). Iowa—Osage, September 12. Wisconsin— Madison area, October 5. Illinois—Chicago region, September 29. Ontario—Ottawa, August 28; Port Dover, September 2. Michigan— Ottawa County, September 27. Indiana—Whiting and Richmond, September 19. Ohio—central Ohio, November 1 (average, September 30). Kentucky—Bowling Green, October 2. Louisiana—Baton Rouge region, October 18. Newfoundland—Cape Anguille, September 24. Quebec—Bird Rock, Magdalen Islands, September 7. Maine—Monhegan Island, October 21. New Hampshire—Monroe, September 21. Vermont—Wells River, September 21. Massachusetts—Nauset, October 1. Connecticut—West Hartford, October 7. New York—Rye, October 12. New Jersey—Union County, October 7. Pennsylvania—Jeffersonville, October 7. Maryland—Patuxent Wildlife Research Refuge, October 13. District of Columbia—Washington, October 1. Virginia—Charlottesville, October 4. North Carolina—Asheville, October 4. Florida—Chokoloskee, September 30. Mexico—Tamaulipas—Guiaves, September 22.

Early dates of fall arrival are: North Dakota—Fargo, August 17; Cass County, August 22 (average, August 30). Nebraska—Red Cloud, August 23. Kansas—Lake Quivira, Johnson County, August 31. Oklahoma—Pittsburg County, August 23. Texas—Austin region, August 17; Brownsville, August 28. Minnesota—Minneapolis, July 31 (average of 11 years, August 22). Iowa—Osage, August 24. Wisconsin—near Neillsville, August 7. Illinois—Glen Ellyn, August 17. Michigan—Sand Point, Huron County, August 17. Indiana— Lake County, September 3. Ohio—South Webster, August 7; central Ohio, August 23 (average, September 5). Kentucky—Bowling Green, September 19. Tennessee—Quebec, August 18. Mississippi— Edwards and Bolivar Counties, September 1. Maine—Muscongus Bay, July 20. New Hampshire—Monroe, August 29. Vermont— Northfield, July 22. Massachusetts—Swampscott, July 20; Northampton, August 9. Connecticut—Hartford and East Windsor Hill, September 7. New York—Bronx, August 5. New Jersey—Englewood region, August 21. Pennsylvania—Pittsburgh, August 14. Maryland—Laurel, August 17. District of Columbia—Washington, August 21. Virginia—Rosslyn, August 19. North Carolina— Montreat, July 31; Asheville, August 23. Tamaulipas—Matamoros, August 16. Guatemala—Panajachel, September 20. Salvador— Divisadero, September 29. Nicaragua—near Bluefields, October 8. Costa Rica—San José, September 1. Panamá—Almirante, October 12. Colombia—Cauca Valley, October 11.

Egg dates.—New York: 44 records, May 24 to July 3; 24 records, June 3 to 20, indicating the height of the season (Harris).

Quebec: 10 records, June 9 to 20.

OPORORNIS TOLMIEI TOLMIEI (Townsend)

NORTHERN MacGILLIVRAY'S WARBLER

PLATE 65

HABITS

Westerners seem to prefer to call this bird the Tolmie warbler, a most appropriate name, on which W. L. Dawson (1923) makes the following pertinent comment:

J. K. Townsend discovered the bird and really published it first, saying, "I dedicate the species to my friend, W. T. Tolmie, Esq., of Fort Vancouver." Audubon, being entrusted with Townsend's specimens, but disregarding the owner's prior rights, published the bird independently, and tardily, as it happened, as *Sylvia macgillivrayi*, by which specific name it was long known to ornithologists. Macgillivray was a Scotch naturalist who never saw America, but Tolmie was at that time a surgeon and later a factor of "the Honorable the Hudson Bay Company," and he clearly deserves remembrance at our hands for friendly hospitality and cooperation which he invariably extended to men of science."

This pretty warbler closely resembles the eastern mourning warbler in general appearance; it frequents similar haunts and is much like it in all its habits. Its breeding range covers a large part of western North America from southeastern Alaska to central California and New Mexico, including the Rocky Mountains and their foothills. Over most of this region it seems to be more abundant than is the mourning warbler in the East.

Samuel F. Rathbun, of Seattle, Wash., says in his notes that MacGillivray's is "a rather common warbler throughout the region, but of unusual distribution. It is partial to localities more or less covered with new growth, particularly if this happens to be scattered among a confusion of dead and fallen trees, through which a fire has swept at some little time previously, and over which nature is beginning to throw a covering of young growth, this having a somewhat open exposure. If such spots are contiguous to low ground, they seem more apt to be frequented by this warbler; but at times it will be found in dry sections of this same rough nature."

In Montana, according to Aretas A. Saunders (1921), it is "a common summer resident of the western half of the state, ranging east to the easternmost mountains, and occurring occasionally in migrations to the more eastern parts of the state. Breeds in the Transition zone in clumps of willow and alder, wild rose or other shrubs, mainly in moist situations along the foothills or lower mountain canyons."

Gabrielson and Jewett (1940) say: "In western Oregon, it frequents the blackberry patches and dense thickets of *Spiraea* or *Salal*, and in the eastern part of the State, it is equally at home in the dense growth of willow about the springs and along the stream bottoms."

Dawson (1923) says of its California haunts: "Brushy hillsides not too remote from water, or dense shrubbery partially shaded by trees, afford ideal cover for this handsome warbler and his all but invisible spouse. Mere chaparral will not do either, for the bird loves mois-ture, and a certain tang in the atmosphere, found in California in the humid coastal counties and on the middle levels of the northern Sier-ras. Variety, also, is his delight; and after temperature, variety in cover seems to be the bird's requirement; and a great confusion of shrubs, willow, alder, ceanothus, chokecherry, serviceberry, chinqua-pin, or mountain mahogany suits him best."

Mrs. Amelia S. Allen writes to me: "About 500 feet beyond our house in Strawberry Canyon in Berkeley, Calif., there is a little draw, running down an oak-covered north slope, in which are many thimble-berries, trilliums, ferns, and brakes. It is occupied each summer by a pair of Tolmie warblers, and I hear their notes from my bedroom window. I always expect to hear it on the seventh of April. In 1940, it was singing on April 2, and I have a few firsts on the fourth, sixth, and eighth. A walk up the canyon the second week of April usually shows four or five singing males, each one in its regular location year after year."

Nesting.—Rathbun has sent me his notes on several nests of Mac-Gillivray's warbler found near Seattle, Wash., all of which were built in salal bushes at heights varying from 2 to 3 feet above the ground. One was "on a somewhat open side-hill not far from an old path. It was very much concealed, and found only by carefully examining each bit of growth thoroughly." Another was "near an old path running through a somewhat open spot in a forest, overgrown with salal shrubs, the ground being littered with old logs above which many of these shrubs thrust their tops"; it was quite plainly seen as he stood on one of the logs. He describes a third as follows: "The loca-tion of this nest was in a small clearing on a rather open hillside with scattered second growth, mostly of small firs, with stunted salal shrubs growing about. In one of these latter the nest was built about a foot above the ground and quite plainly to be seen, having the ap-pearance of an old nest, apparently because it was so carelessly con-structed. It was outwardly composed of dry weed-stalks, next to which were finer weed-stalks and straws; the lining was of soft dry grasses, fine rootlets, and a few horsehairs. On the top of the nest, effectually concealing the eggs from view, was placed a dead salal leaf, its point and the end of its stem being lightly caught just under the inside edge of the nest, this being, in our opinion, done by the bird with the intent of concealing the eggs on account of the exposure of the nest; it could not have fallen and assumed any such position."

He refers to another nest in which some fine twigs were used. He gives the measurements of two nests in inches; the outside diameters, respectively, were 5½ and 4½, outside height 2¼ and 3, inside diameter 2½ and 2, and inside depth 1⅛ and 1½. Three other nests were in *Spiraea* bushes, and one was in a little fir.

A. D. Du Bois has sent me the data for three nests found in Flathead County, Mont.; one of these was 2 feet from the ground in a yew bush at the side of a tie-hauling road, in the edge of some woods at the base of a foothill; another was 4½ feet from the ground in a balsam fir sapling at the side of a trail.

J. Stuart Rowley writes to me: "On June 16, 1938, while trout fishing along Mammoth Creek, Mono County, Calif., I found two nests of this warbler located in the same general situation and each contained four fresh eggs. The nests were well concealed in thick shrubs along the wet creek bottom and were placed about a foot from the ground. Both females scolded when flushed from the eggs, whereupon the respective males immediately joined in the chirping. It is my firm belief that one will find more warbler eggs while trout fishing than while actually looking for nests."

In the Yosemite region, Miss Margaret W. Wythe (1916) found a nest of the Tolmie warbler, nine inches above the ground in a clump of blossoming chokecherry.

The structure was placed between four stalks of the chokecherry, and was supported below by several short twigs growing from the root stock. The materials were not woven around the four upright stalks, although several grass blades passed behind one of them. Materials of which the nest was composed were fine dry grass blades and stems, and several shreds of bark about three-eighths of an inch wide. These latter were woven into the outer part of the structure, where a single oak leaf also lay embedded, whether purposely or by accident, I cannot say. The lining was of fine grasses and a few black horsehairs. Some loose grass arched over the top, attached to the nest a little on one side. Later on the two openings thus made by these arching grasses made a sort of entrance and exit, the bird invariably entering on one side and leaving on the other.

Although, most of the nests of MacGillivray's warbler are placed near the ground, some of them practically on the ground, a few have been found from 3 to 5 feet up in bushes, scrub oaks and alders.

Eggs.—MacGillivray's warbler lays from 3 to 5 eggs in a set, most often 4 and very rarely 6. The eggs are ovate and slightly glossy. The white, or creamy white, ground color is speckled, spotted or blotched with "auburn," "chestnut," "bay," or "cinnamon," with spots or undertones of "light brownish drab," "pale vinaceous-drab," or "Quaker drab." Some eggs are delicately marked, while others may be clouded. On many, even the delicately marked types, are often scattered a few spots, or small scrawls, of very dark brown or even black. Occasionally, these scattered dark spots or scrawls are the only apparent markings, the lighter browns lacking and the undertones almost imperceptible. While the markings are generally concentrated at the large end, there is not as great a tendency to form a wreath as in many of the warblers' eggs. The measurements of 50 eggs average 17.8 by 13.6 millimeters; the eggs showing the four extremes measure **19.4** by **15.1,** and **16.4** by **12.7** millimeters (Harris).

Young.—The nest watched by Miss Wythe (1916) held four eggs on June 13, on which the female had been incubating for an unknown period; on the twenty-third two of the eggs had hatched, and the third egg hatched the following day; the incubation period was, therefore, at least ten days. When first hatched, the nestlings had "scarcely a trace of down on them." One the following day, they "were now scantily covered with down, a patch showing on top of the head, a line down the middle of the back, and a tuft on the wings. * * * On June 27 I spent an hour during the morning timing the feeding of the three young birds, from a point about twelve feet distant. I found that the female warbler came with food at intervals of from three to five minutes throughout the hour. On the fourth day after hatching, "juvenal feathers had appeared over most of the head, down the center of the back, and on the wings. The eyes of one bird were open. On the following day the eyes of the second bird were open. * * * The sixth day showed juvenal feathers appearing on the lateral tracts, and tail feathers just beginning to grow out. On the seventh day, June 30, the wing feathers had broken through the sheaths for about one-half an inch. The birds' heads were well covered with feathers, but the sheaths still adhered to the bases. The contour feathers were in a similar condition. The tail feathers did not show any further development. On July 2, the ninth day after hatching, the two older birds left the nest, followed later the same day by the third bird, the latter having been in the nest only eight days.

Based on the findings at four nests, Grinnell and Storer (1924) state that "eggs are laid on successive days, incubation begins immediately upon the laying of the last egg or possibly before, and is completed in 13 days, the young hatch on the same day, or on two successive days, and leave the nest 8 or 9 days after hatching. The male seems to participate but little in caring for the brood."

Plumages.—The molts and plumages of MacGillivray's warbler parallel those of the mourning warbler and need not be repeated here. In the juvenal plumages the two species are practically indistinguishable, except that the former has a longer tail. The differences in later plumages are referred to under field marks. Dickey and van Rossem

(1938) have this to say about the prenuptial molt: "In February and March there is a body molt, apparently much more extensive in the young than in adults. The former at this time take on the bluish head and chest of maturity. There is some individual variation, but in general it may be said that the extreme richness of coloration is not attained until the second year. The spring plumage of older birds is the result of a limited renewal plus the wearing away of the paler colored tips of the fall plumage. It takes place in February and March at the same time as that of the younger birds."

Food.—Mrs. Bailey (1928) lists in the food of this warbler "insects, including the click beetle, dung beetle, flea beetle, caterpillars, and the alfalfa weevil." No comprehensive study of its food seems to have been made.

Behavior.—MacGillivray's is the same timid, shy, and elusive little bird as its eastern counterpart, the mourning warbler. Gabrielson and Jewett (1940) write: "The birds are much in evidence in their chosen haunts in late April and early May while the courtship is in progress, but when household cares occupy the daylight hours they become as elusive as field mice, slipping about through the thickets like shadows, only the sharp alarm note betraying their presence to an intruder."

Voice.—Rathbun says in his notes: "Its song begins with three or four quickly given notes on nearly the same key, followed by several on a lower key, but this may be varied at times. It is a quite distinctive song and when once learned is not easily forgotten. Throughout there seems to be a minor key; the song lacks smoothness and when heard at a distance has somewhat of a roughness; but, like so many of the songs of birds, it is heard at its best when one is close to the singer. Should its chosen territory be infringed upon, the intruder becomes aware of its presence by hearing a rapid, harsh alarm note, which may be repeated many times." Du Bois tells me that the song of MacGillivray's warbler "resembles the syllables *te-te-te-te-cheweet-cheweet-cheweet*, the first part being about a note higher than the latter part. It is uttered rapidly, the whole song requiring about a second and a half. Sometimes there are only three *te's*, followed by four *cheweet's*."

Mrs. Amelia S. Allen writes to me: "The song of the Tolmie warbler is more musical than most warbler songs. The first half of the song is composed of double notes with a rising inflection; the second half with a falling inflection: *Swee-eét, swee-eét, swee-eét, peáchy, peáchy, peáchy*. But I hear also: *Peáchy, peáchy, peáchy, twit twit twit*, the first half with a falling inflection." Grinnell and Storer (1924) write:

At Hazel Green, on May 14, 1919, a bird was observed fully 50 feet above the ground on one of the lower branches of a large incense cedar. * * * This bird sang ten times in two minutes, changing position usually after singing twice on one perch. The song was rendered by the observer *sizik, sizik, sizik, lipik, lipik,* little change being detected in successive songs. In the first three "words" the "z" sounds were strong, whereas the last two were more liquid. In singing, the bird would throw its head back, and put much bodily effort into the process of utterance. Soon the bird dropped close to the ground and sang from within the shrubbery, changing his position frequently. The sharp *tsip* of the female was heard at this time. After a few songs the male flew up to a perch 30 feet above the ground, sang twice, and then went below again. * * * Other individuals studied and timed while they sang gave their songs at intervals of 10 to 14 seconds. Song production is not continuous, however. * * *

The "z" sounds heard from the bird at Hazel Green are entirely lacking in other songs studied. Two of these clearer utterances we wrote as follows: *syr-pit, syr-pit, syr-pit, syr-sip-sip-sip-sip* (J.G.), and another *cheek-a, cheek-a, cheek-a, cheek-a, chee-e-e-e* (T.I.S.). The first syllables are loud, clear, and set off from one another, while the shorter ones (*sip*) are given rapidly, faster than a person can pronounce them, and sometimes are run almost into a trill.

Field marks.—MacGillivray's warbler is quite unlike any other western warbler. Its dark gray head, neck, and upper breast, the latter almost black, its olive-green back and its bright yellow under parts are distinctive in the adult male. The female and young are similarly marked, but the gray is much paler, sometimes grayish white. Where its range approaches that of the mourning warbler, the two white spots above and below the eye of the adult male will distinguish it. The young bird is less easily recognized, but in all plumages the tail of the western species is the longer.

Enemies.—This warbler is seldom bothered by the cowbird; I can find only four published records of such parasitism.

Winter.—Dr. Alexander F. Skutch contributes the following: "MacGillivray's warbler is an abundant winter resident over the whole highland area of Guatemala, from 10,000 feet down to at least 2,000 feet on the Pacific slope. Avoiding the forest, it lurks near or on the ground on bushy mountainsides and in low, dense thickets— just such habitats as, at lower altitudes in Costa Rica, are chosen by the closely similar mourning warbler. So well do these birds remain concealed, as they forage screened by the foliage, that the bird-watcher must learn to recognize their distinctive, sharp *tuc, tuc* in order to gain a just motion of their abundance; were he to rely upon sight alone, he would call them everywhere rare. Like nearly all birds of similar habits, they live in solitude rather than in flocks.

"MacGillivray's warbler arrives in Guatemala during the second half of September, and departs early in May. On the Sierra de Tecpán, they were much more in evidence at the end of April than they had been earlier in the year, suggesting that the population of wintering birds had been augmented by transients from farther south, for the species winters southward to Colombia. In Costa Rica they appear to be very rare, in sharp contrast to their abundance farther northward.

"Early dates of fall arrival in Central America are: Guatemala—
passim (Griscom), September 23; Sierra de Tecpán, September 26,
1933; Huehuetenango, September 19, 1934; Colomba, September 24,
1934. Costa Rica—San José (Underwood), September 25, 1898.

"Late dates of spring departure from Central America are: Guatemala—passim (Griscom), April 26; Sierra de Tecpán, May 10, 1933."

In El Salvador, Dickey and van Rossem (1938) record MacGillivray's warbler as a—

common midwinter visitant and spring migrant to the upper foothills and mountains, from 2,300 feet on the Arid Lower Tropical Zone to 8,000 feet in the
Humid Upper Tropical. * * * MacGillivray's warblers did not arrive until
much later than *O. philadelphia*, but after the first week of December they
were to be found everywhere in underbrush in the higher foothills and mountains. On Mt. Cacaguatique they were noted in ravine growth along watercourses; on Volcán de Conchagua among the pines in company with black-
throated green warblers; on Volcán de San Miguel in the head-high grass of
the lava gullies; and on Los Esesmiles in clearings and in natural open spaces
in the cloud forest. A fairly cool temperature rather than any particular plant
association seems to be the primary factor governing their choice of winter
quarters.

DISTRIBUTION

Range.—Southern Alaska, western Canada, and the United States
south to northwestern South America.

Breeding range.—MacGillivray's warbler breeds **north** to southern
Alaska (Port Snettisham); central Alberta (probably Peace River
Landing, Lesser Slave Lake, and Edmonton); and southwestern Saskatchewan (Cypress Hills). **East** to southwestern Saskatchewan
(Cypress Hills); southwestern South Dakota (Black Hills); and
through the mountains of central Colorado to New Mexico (Alto and
Arroyo Hondo Canyon). **South** to southeastern New Mexico (Alto);
central Arizona (San Francisco Mountains and White Mountains);
northern and central Nevada (Galena Creek, Toyabe Mountains, and
Baker Creek); and central California (Paicines, Placerville, Yosem-
ite, Sequoia National Park, Kern River, White Mountains, and
Berkeley). **West** to central California (Berkeley); northeastern Ore-
gon (Powder River Mountains); northwestern and central British
Columbia (Telegraph Creek, Doch-da-on Creek, Hazelton, Summit
Lake, and Yellowstone Lake); and southern Alaska (Boca de Quadra,
Bradfield Canal, and Port Snettisham).

Winter range.—The species winters **north** to southern Baja California (La Paz, El Triunfo, and Cabo San Lucas); southern Sonora
(rarely Alamos); and Nuevo León (rarely Monterrey). **East** to
Nuevo León (Monterrey); Guatemala (Lake Atitlán, Cobán, Patulul,
and Dueñas); Costa Rica (San José, Barranca, Buenos Aires); Panamá (Volcán de Chiriquí and Colón); and northern Colombia (Antio_
quia, Santa Elena, and Bogotá). **South** to Colombia (Bogotá); El

Salvador (Volcán de San Miguel, Volcán de Conchagua, and Volcán de Santa Ana); and Oaxaca (Tehuantepec). **West** to Oaxaca (Tehuantepec); Michoacán (Patambán and Zamora); Colima; Sinaloa (Mazatlán and Escuinapa); and southern Baja California (La Paz).

Casual in northeastern British Columbia (Lower Liard Crossing); southwestern Manitoba (Aweme); southwestern North Dakota (Buffalo Springs Lake); eastern South Dakota (Aberdeen); Nebraska (Stapleton, North Platte, and Hastings); Kansas (Blue Rapids); and northwestern Texas (Gainesville).

The range as outlined is for the entire species, of which two subspecies are recognized. The northern MacGillivray's warbler (*Oporornis tolmiei tolmiei*) is found from southern Alaska, British Columbia, north-central Alberta, southwestern Saskatchewan, and southwestern South Dakota south to southern Baja California, throughout Mexico (except the Yucatán Peninsula), Guatemala, El Salvador, Costa Rica, Panamá, and northern Colombia; the southern MacGillivray's warbler (*Oporornis tolmiei monticola*) is found from northeastern California, southern Oregon, southern Idaho, southern Wyoming, northern and central Nevada, central Arizona, and through central Colorado to south-central New Mexico south to Colima, Michoacán, Morelos and Guatemala.

Migration.—Late dates of spring departure are: El Salvador—Volcán de Santa Ana, May 15. Guatemala—above Tecpán, May 10. Tamaulipas—Gómez Farías region, May 3. Sonora—Rancho la Arizona, May 22.

Early dates of spring arrival are: Sonora—Chinobampo, March 7. Texas—El Paso, April 21; Los Fresnos, Cameron County, May 4. Oklahoma—Cheyenne, May 13. Nebraska—North Platte and Hastings, May 7. North Dakota—Wilton, May 22. Saskatchewan—Wiseton and Conquest, May 25. New Mexico—Fort Bayard, April 1. Arizona—Tucson, March 23. Colorado—Denver, May 1. Utah—Pine Valley, Washington County, May 11. Wyoming—Torrington, May 7. Idaho—Meridian, May 5. Montana—Fortine, May 11. Alberta—Onoway and Waterton Lakes Park, May 25. California—Berkeley, April 2 (average for 18 years in San Francisco Bay region, April 13). Nevada—Pioche, May 12. Oregon—Salem, April 17. Washington—Shelton, April 15; Walla Walla, April 28. British Columbia—Courtenay, Vancouver Island, April 14. Alaska—Wrangell, June 9.

Late dates of fall departure are: Alaska—Point Barrow, September 12. British Columbia—Okanagan Landing, October 2. Washington—Kamiak Butte, Whitman County, September 27. Oregon—Eugene area, November 2; Multnomah County, October 12. Nevada—south end of Belted Range, Nye County, September 28. California—San Francisco Bay region, November 27; Los Angeles, October 24. Montana—Fortine, September 11. Idaho—Moscow area, September

30. Wyoming—Laramie, October 15 (average of 7 years, September 17). Utah—Boxelder County, September 19. Colorado—Weldon, October 20. Arizona—Keams Canyon, October 12. New Mexico—Apache, October 12. Saskatchewan—Last Mountain Lake, August 25. Manitoba—Aweme, September 9. Oklahoma—Cimarron County, September 24. Texas—El Paso, October 8. Mexico—Sonora, Cajon Bonito Creek, September 28.

Early dates of fall arrival are: Utah—Salt Lake City, August 10. Arizona—Tucson, August 6. New Mexico—Apache, August 3. Oklahoma—Cimarron County, August 16. Texas—El Paso County, August 21. Mexico—Sonora, Cerro Gallardo, August 14. Guatemala—Dueñas, September 17. Costa Rica—San José, September 25.

Egg dates.—California: 39 records, May 2 to July 7; 21 records, June 2 to 20, indicating the height of the season.

Washington: 42 records, May 29 to June 22; 23 records, June 1 to 10 (Harris).

OPORORNIS TOLMIEI MONTICOLA Phillips

SOUTHERN MacGILLIVRAY'S WARBLER

This race was named by Dr. Allan R. Phillips (1947) and described as having the tail the "relatively longest" of the species; the "color dull, differing from *O. t. tolmiei* in darker and grayer (less yellowish) green upper parts and paler and greener (less orange) yellow under parts. The difference in color of the under parts is less constant in fall females of unknown age, perhaps due to variation with age and to erroneous sexing of some young birds."

He says that it breeds "in dense deciduous brush of the Canadian Zone from southeastern Oregon (Steens and Mahogany Mts.) and southwestern Wyoming (Ft. Bridger and Steamboat Mt.) south to central Arizona (White and San Francisco Mts.) and central New Mexico (Alto)."

It evidently winters in Mexico and Guatemala.

GEOTHLYPSIS TRICHAS BRACHIDACTYLA (Swainson)

GEOTHLYPIS TRICHAS TRICHAS (Linnaeus)

NORTHERN AND MARYLAND YELLOWTHROATS

CONTRIBUTED BY ALFRED OTTO GROSS

PLATES 66–68

HABITS

While the following account applies primarily to the northern yellowthroat *Geothlypsis trichas brachidactyla*, for practical reasons it also includes the Maryland yellowthroat *Geothlypsis trichas trichas*, as the breeding and winter ranges overlap and the literature pertaining to these two forms is so intermixed that they are not easily separated.

The species of *Geothlypis* respond more readily to the influences of the environment than do other American warblers. As a result 12 subspecies of *trichas* have been recognized by the 1931 A. O. U. Check-List and subsequent supplements. Of these, 4, *trichas*, *brachidactyla*, *ignota*, and *typhicola* are in eastern United States and the other 8, *occidentalis*, *campicola*, *sinuosa*, *chryseola*, *scirpicola*, *arizela*, *insperata*, and *modesta* are represented in the western part of the country.

The color pattern of the 12 subspecies is similar; and they vary chiefly in minor differences of size and intensity of color. In a number of instances, the great individual variation which characterizes these birds so obscures their subspecific differences that determination of skins is often difficult and positive identification in the field, especially where the ranges overlap, is impossible.

Of the two forms included in this life history, the northern yellow-throat differs from the Maryland yellowthroat, in the male, in its larger size, and by reason of its more greenish upper surface, more whitish frontal band of grays, more extensively yellow posterior parts, and its usually brownish flanks. The female of the northern is similar to the Maryland but is larger, more greenish above, and slightly paler.

The breeding range of the northern yellowthroat extends from Newfoundland, Labrador and Quebec south to New Jersey, northern Pennsylvania and West Virginia, while that of the Maryland extends from southern Pennsylvania south to eastern Texas and northern parts of Georgia and Alabama.

Throughout most of its breeding range the yellowthroat ranks as one of the abundant warblers. Because of the striking and easily recognized plumage of the male, especially the bright yellow throat and contrasting black mask, and its characteristic syllabic and easily memorized song it is one of our best-known birds. The modestly colored female is more difficult to identify, as it may be confused, by the beginner, with other similarly colored warblers. The yellowthroat seldom visits the habitation of man; it prefers wild lands, especially those grown up with briers and low brush. Its favorite nesting haunts are in the tangled vegetation of brook-sides or margins of swamp woodlands or among the grass and sedges of the marshes, where it frequently shares the company of such birds as the swamp sparrow and the marsh wrens.

When invading its haunts one is impressed with the vigorous personality of the male. He nervously raises his alarm with a variety of scolding, interrogative chirps and chattering notes and his dark inquisitive eyes sparkle with excitement through the black masks.

He darts with nervous animation from place to place, then disappears in the dense cover only to appear again to denounce the intrusion. He displays many wrenlike characteristics, suggesting to Bartram the name olive-colored wren.

Although seemingly secretive and shy, they are unsuspecting and will often allow an approach to within a few feet of them. When finally convinced that no harm is meant, the male may even pour out his song from an elevated perch above his retreat, well-exposed to view. At times he will sing as he proceeds with his serious search for insects among the grass and shrubs.

Spring.—It is impossible to separate the records on the migration of the subspecies of the yellowthroat occurring on the Atlantic coast. The earliest spring migrants appearing in Florida are said to be the Florida yellowthroat (*ignota*) whereas the northern (*brachidactyla*) follows at later dates. The earliest records for North Carolina have been reported as the Maryland yellowthroat (*trichas*). The matter is further complicated by the fact that southern representatives of the yellowthroat are almost non-migratory, being more or less permanent residents in Florida, whereas the northern yellowthroats which breed as far north as Newfoundland and Labrador pass over southern United States, going directly over the home of their southern relatives to spend the winter in the West Indies.

The earliest dates of its appearance at the Florida lighthouses occur during the first week in March, the numbers increase during April, and it is one of the few warblers that are common migrants in southern Florida during the month of May. The migration of the yellowthroat is thus one of the most extended.

The first yellowthroats arrive in North Carolina during the last week of March, by the middle of April they arrive in New Jersey and Maryland, and late in April they are in New York state. The first arrivals appear in southern New England during the first week of May, and the vanguard of northern yellowthroats can be expected in Maine before the middle of the month, although the bulk of the birds do not appear until a week or so later. They reach the northern limits of their nesting range in Newfoundland by the last week of May.

The subspecies *brachidactyla*, according to H. C. Oberholser (1938), is a winter resident in Louisiana from October 8 to April 1. Records, presumably of the northern yellowthroat, reach Arkansas and Kentucky about the middle of April, and St. Louis, Mo., a few days later. They arrive in Ohio during the last week of April, Minnesota the first week of May, and by the middle of the month they are on their breeding grounds in North Dakota and Ontario. The progress of the birds on the Atlantic and Mississippi flyways during the spring migration is at approximately the same rate.

Nesting.—Unlike many of our warblers, the yellowthroat does not nest in the interior of our dense forests and is seldom seen in the upper branches of tall trees, being more or less restricted to low growths of vegetation. However, it is not strictly terrestrial in its habits, as in the ovenbird. It is partial to wet situations but these need not be great in extent. While it may be found on the borders of large marshes and especially on little islands in marshes and swamps it is also met with near springs and small brooks. An extreme wet situation for a nesting site of the Maryland yellowthroat is described by W. I. Whitehill (1897) as follows: "While collecting in a large slough in Jackson County, Minnesota, on June 9, 1897, amid the green rushes where Long- and Short-billed Marsh Wrens were breeding, I ran across a pair of Yellow-throats * * * in some high rushes in about four feet of water, and upon investigating I found the nest placed almost level with the water in a thick clump of cat-tails, over fifty feet from shore, and right in the midst of a colony of Marsh Wrens."

Often individuals take up their residence in dry upland situations remote from water. They may be found along old fence rows grown up with weeds and tangles of briers and shrubbery, in huckleberry or raspberry or blackberry patches, and along the margins of woodlands and neglected country roadsides. Maurice Brooks (1940) reports that in the central Allegheny Mountain region where the spruces have been cut, the northern yellowthroats have invaded the highest mountains and are now abundant at all altitudes.

I have found it a very common nesting bird on many of the small outer islands off the coast of Maine. Some of these islands are without any source of fresh water and the only apparent attraction is a growth of rank grass and weeds and briers, and the extreme isolation from enemies, that such sites provide. For example, on Outer Green, a tiny islet of a few acres, there is a bit of tall grass and weeds only a few square yards in area, but it is sufficient to serve each year as the home of a pair of northern yellowthroats. On some of the larger islands where there is no fresh water other than rain I have seen as many as four pairs, all of which apparently were nesting.

The nest of the yellowthroat is frequently placed on or a few inches above the ground and is securely lodged in tussocks of grass, reeds, cattails, briers, and sometimes in herbaceous plants such as skunk-cabbage and similar vegetation. Quite often the grass in which the nest is built is backed by a shrub or small tree. The nest is always well concealed from view until the grass or shrubs are parted. This in addition to the secretive habits of the birds makes the task of locating the nest most difficult. All I have seen were accidently found by flushing the bird from the nest when scouting through masses of vegetation in search of other birds.

Although the yellowthroat's nest is commonly located on or within a few inches of the ground there are numerous instances in which the nest is secured to tall weed stalks or shrubs well above the ground. I. D. Campbell (1917) describes a nest of the Maryland yellowthroat that he found at Bernardsville, N. J., which was located in an alder, 3 feet above the ground. R. B. Simpson (1920) found a nest in the top of a cluster of laurels that was growing among a growth of hemlock trees. Mr. Simpson states that this nest was more like that of a mourning warbler than of a Maryland yellowthroat. William Brewster (1906) writes: "I have twice found it nesting in ground junipers in perfectly dry upland pastures near Arlington Heights" [Massachusetts]. Others have found nests in a diversity of situations indicating a great deal of individual variation as far as the selection of the nesting site is concerned.

One most unusual situation for a nest is described by A. W. Brockway (1899) of Old Lyme, Conn., as follows:

The locality chosen was near a back entrance to a house situated on the main street of town. A pair of shoes, which were the property of my friend, were placed outside of the door on the under pinning which projected out from the side of the house about two feet. One day he had occasion to wear them and went out and brought them into the house; * * * he discovered something in one of them, and upon examination found it to be a nest. The other shoe contained a few dry grasses and other fine material but for some reason the bird gave up the idea of building in that, and took up housekeeping in shoe No. 2. My friend immediately put the shoes back, thinking that she would return, and upon glancing into the shoe the next day was surprised to see that it contained an egg.

The yellowthroat continued laying until she had deposited five eggs.

P. G. Howes (1919) found a nest of the Maryland yellowthroat near his house in Stamford, Conn., which was effectively guarded by a nest of large hornets. According to Mr. Howes, the birds did not bother the wasps and the wasps respected the birds; a case of symbiosis.

The nests of the yellowthroat are not always isolated from others of their kind. For example Isaac E. Hess (1910) found 17 nests in a half-acre swamp in central Illinois. This small swamp was in an extensively cultivated agricultural area, a region where suitable nesting sites are few in number. This unusual concentration of nesting birds was probably due to necessity rather than to choice.

The nest is a rather large, bulky structure composed of dead grass, weed stems, dead leaves, grape vine bark, dead ferns, etc. all loosely put together. The lining consists of fine grasses, tendrils, delicate fibers of bark, and often a quantity of hair.

The external parts of a nest, located in a meadow, was made up of wide blades of fresh grass lined with moss. Nests in cattail marshes had a foundation of cattail shreds, dried leaves, and grass stems and were lined with fine grasses only.

The nest is cup-shaped but in some instances loosely attached material extends above the main rim and may partially roof over the top of the structure. The average measurements of several typical nests, not including protruding materials, are outside diameter $3\frac{1}{4}$ inches, outside depth $3\frac{1}{2}$ inches, inside diameter of the cup $1\frac{3}{4}$ inches, and its depth $1\frac{1}{2}$ inches.

All nests that I have seen were completed when found, and I have no information as to the time required or the manner in which the nest is built. The female apparently builds the nest, but on one occasion I saw a male bird carrying nesting material and it is probable that he sometimes assists his mate in its construction.

Eggs.—The usual set of the northern yellowthroat is four eggs but complete sets vary from three to five, and as many as six eggs have been reported. The eggs have a ground color of white or creamy white specked chiefly at the larger end with reddish brown, umber and black and with shell markings of stone gray. As in any large series of eggs of a species there is more or less variation from the typical. In some eggs the markings are in a distinct wreath near the larger end, in a few, some of the marks are in the form of small streaks and in still others the marks are faint and much reduced. The average size of two sets of four eggs each is .69 by .52 inch.

[AUTHOR'S NOTE: The measurements of 50 eggs of the northern yellowthroat average 17.5 by 13.3 millimeters; the eggs showing the four extremes measure **19.4** by **14.5**, and **14.2** by **11.7** millimeters. The measurements of 26 eggs of the Maryland yellowthroat average 16.7 by 13.2 millimeters; the eggs showing the four extremes measure **18.3** by 13.8, 17.5 by **14.0,** and **15.4** by **12.1** millimeters.]

Incubation.—The incubation of the eggs requires 12 days and is performed entirely by the female. The male sings throughout the incubation period and is ever alert in defending his territory. He sometimes delivers foods to the female while she is incubating the eggs.

H. Mousley (1917) has found that although the eggs of different individual northern yellowthroats are subject to great variation, the successive sets of any one bird are strikingly alike in shape, size, and markings. Mr. Mousley did not succeed in getting the yellowthroat to lay a third set of eggs after the first two sets had been taken. It is doubtful if the yellowthroat rears more than two broods a year, although Aretas A. Saunders (1938) believes that some of them do, since he has found the last birds leaving the nest in August. Usually an egg is laid each day until the set is completed but L. H. Porter (1908) reports finding a nest on June 4 in which the set of four eggs was not completed until June 12, a case, according to Porter, in which the deposit of the eggs was greatly prolonged by cold weather.

Unlike many birds, the northern yellowthroat usually leaves the nest unobtrusively when a human intruder comes near and does not betray its location by scolding. In the case of one nest the female sat very closely, and by exercising care I was able to almost touch her before she slipped off, mouse-fashion. She crept silently through the grass to the shelter of the neighboring vegetation and from there watched me intently. On another occasion the reaction of a yellow-throat was very different in respect to a small dog. Both birds made a wild demonstration, calling and scolding loudly and even making passes at the intruder in their efforts to drive him away from the vicinity of the nest.

The birds readily adapt themselves to a blind placed close to the nest, although their suspicions may be aroused at first. A day after the blind is in place they pay little attention to it, and I have had the bird return within 20 minutes after I had entered the structure.

Young.—The young at the time of hatching are nearly naked, having only scant tufts of grayish or mouse-colored down on the crown and dorsal tracts of the body and wings. The eyes are sealed shut. Soon after emerging from the eggs the young are active and open wide their mouths in anticipation of food, which arrives before many minutes have elapsed. In one nest under observation the male delivered the first food in the form of a small, green insect larva. During the first day the male did the major part of the feeding, since the female remained at the nest much of the time to brood the delicate young. She was seen to leave the nest but twice during the first day, probably in search of food. During the first few days the male frequently delivered food to the female at the nest, and she in turn fed it to the young.

By the third day the papillae of the developing feathers of the primaries, secondaries, and tertials, and to a minor degree those of the dorsal tract, have pierced the integument. The remainder of the body remains naked except for the persisting tufts of down.

On the fourth day the eyes are open for the first time. The response of the young to the presence of the adults is much more marked than during the first days. Both male and female now share about equally in the arduous task of feeding the young, the food still consisting chiefly of insect larvae or soft-bodied adult insects. In feeding, at one nest I had under observation, the adult birds approached the nest silently, except for low twitters. They sneaked through the grass, selecting definite pathways more or less hidden by the vegetation, thus giving an observer little warning of their approach. The female did all of the brooding, but by the fourth day she spent less time at the nest and took more excursions in search of food.

The young usually emit a fecal sac after they are fed, and this is immediately seized by the parent that chances to be present. During the first few days the fecal sacs are usually eaten, but in later nest life they are more often carried away some distance from the nest and dropped. I have seen the female eagerly keep watch for fully 5 minutes in anticipation of the fecal sac, even stimulating the youngsters with the tip of her bill to make them respond. The birds also removed all other foreign material such as a pellet of gum, small wads of paper, or rolled-up leaves purposely dropped into the nest as an experiment. The eggshells were removed at the time of hatching by the female. Nelle E. Shaver (1918) gives an interesting account of the removal of an addled egg as follows:

The nestlings had crept to one side of the nest to escape the rays of the sun, so that the addled egg remained alone and in plain view. The male Yellow-throat came first to the nest with food. Seeing the addled egg he picked it up between the mandibles and carried it away, without breaking it and with no slips or unsuccessful trials. The bird, carrying the egg, disappeared in the foliage of the trees at a distance of about twenty-five feet from the nest. It is possible that the ridge formed by the shell fragment may have furnished a "grip" by which the egg was firmly held in the mandibles. On the other hand, the mandibles are capable of opening to a surprising degree, and the whole behavior of the bird in this act seemed to proceed without uncertainty or experimentation.

This behavior is probably unusual, as in nests that I have had under observation the infertile egg remained until after the young normally left the nest.

By the fifth day the papillae of the larger feathers are bursting from their tips and this process is considerably advanced by the following day. At times the adult birds peck at the feathers apparently to facilitate the process of unsheathing. On the sixth day the young exhibit evidence of fear when a human observer examines the nest. The food delivered at this time consists of many adult insects such as small moths, spiders, beetles, and grasshoppers. A. C. Redfield (1911) made a unique observation concerning the order in which the young are fed, as follows: "On one occasion the male fed two of the young. Before he had left, the female arrived with an insect. He held his bill toward her as though wishing to take the food from her. Not heeding him she proceeded to feed the young one last favored by the male. Quickly her mate removed the food from the young one's mouth and thrust it into the bill of the third young one, which had received nothing. This would make it appear that the parent birds do actually keep account of which young they have last fed." Mr. Redfield's interpretation may be correct, but it is rare for birds to exhibit such intelligence or to detect the sequence in which the young are fed.

By the eighth day the feathers have proceeded in the unsheathing process to such an extent that the young present a smooth and pleasing contour. A few tufts of down, however, still cling to the ends of some of the contour feathers. Now that the young have a substantial protective covering and have acquired a temperature control, continuous brooding is not essential, but during extreme weather conditions, such as a cold rain or when the nest is exposed to the direct rays of the sun, the female protects the young by shielding them with her half-spread wings.

On the ninth day the young are ready to leave the nest and the least disturbance at the nest is a signal for them to leave. Under normal conditions they remain at the nest until the tenth day.

On June 10, 1945, I flushed a juvenal northern yellowthroat from the tall grass on Cone Island, off the coast of Maine. It flew but a few yards and alighted on a limb of a small dead shrub. The bird then allowed me to approach very near and exhibited not the least fear of my presence or that of the three other observers who stood nearby staring at the little creature. When we continued on our way the bird persisted in following us alighting again and again within a few feet of us. The youngster followed us in this manner for nearly a mile, until finally it joined company with an adult male, possibly its parent, and together they disappeared in the dense vegetation.

A. D. DuBois sends notes of his observations of a northern yellowthroat caring for a young cowbird and of its own young at Lincoln, Illinois, on June 21, 1913: "Found a female yellowthroat caring for a young cowbird which could fly very well and was about twice her own size. The cowbird flew to a bush near me. Its foster mother was nearby with food in her bill but she became agitated at my presence and flitted about, chirping. I suddenly clapped my hand over the young cowbird and thus caught it. The cowbird cried out with its squeaky voice and both male and female yellowthroats were immediately on the scene of the disturbance, fully as much concerned as though this young rascal were their own flesh and blood. The male, particularly, spread and fluttered his wings in a little bush 10 or 15 feet away, exhibiting great excitement, while the female chirped nervously from beneath a bush on the other side. They did not flutter along the ground as many birds do but remained in the weeds and bushes while doing all in their power to attract my attention. Sometimes the male held up his wings in a very pretty fashion. When I released the young cowbird it flew probably 100 feet, the foster mother following after it.

"Later, in the same bushy, weedy pasture, I caught a young yellow-throat, with much difficulty—a pretty little fellow much like the adult female, but with its tail just sprouting. I think this belonged to other parents. They made much less fuss about their own offspring than did the other pair about the young cowbird."

The young are cared for by the adults for an unusually long period after they leave the nest, this being especially true of the second brood of the season, when parent birds may be seen feeding young that are able to fly as well as the adults, and apparently long after the young are capable of caring for themselves; in fact, they have been seen feeding their young up to the time of the fall migration. It is possible that the fall migration starts as a family group.

Plumages.—The juvenal plumage which is acquired by a complete molt of the natal down is described by Dr. Dwight (1900) as follows: "Above, pale olive-brown of variable depth, greenish on the upper tail coverts. Wings olive-brown edged with olive-green, the median and greater coverts faintly tipped with cinnamon. Tail bright olive-green. Below, tawny wood-brown, Naples-yellow on the abdomen and olive-yellow on the crissum. Inconspicuous orbital ring pale buff. Bill and feet pinkish buff becoming deep sepia with age."

The following plumages of the Maryland yellowthroat are also described by Dr. Dwight: The first winter plumage is acquired "by a partial postjuvenal molt, beginning about the middle of July, which involves the body plumage and the wing coverts, but not the rest of the wings nor the tail." It is unlike the previous plumage in being "above, deep olive-brown, greener on the upper tail coverts, the crown and forehead tinged with Mars-brown, the forehead frequently with a very few feathers black basally. The wing coverts chiefly olive-green. Below, bright lemon on the chin, throat and crissum, pale straw-yellow on the abdomen, the flanks washed with olive-brown, and a very faint buffy pectoral band." Dr. Dwight notes that "the malar and auricular regions show traces of the black mask varying from a few black feathers to a considerable area always veiled by ashy edgings. The black seldom invades the lores and forehead and never the orbital ring as in the adult. The orbital ring is buffy white."

The first nuptial plumage, he says, is acquired "by a partial prenuptial moult which involves chiefly the forehead, crown, sides of head and chin and not the rest of the plumage. These areas are somewhat worn, as a rule, when the birds reach New York in May, but specimens from Jamaica, West Indies, taken December 2nd, January 9th, 22d and 24th and February 4th show actual moult in progress. It is not surprising that the feathers assumed should show considerable wear before May. The black feathers of the 'mask' are acquired."

He says that those of the upper margin of this area are broadly
tipped with pearl-gray, which becomes ashy with wear. "This gray
band, posteriorly on the crown, has its feathers tipped with Mars-
brown and the basal black gradually diminishes more posteriorly as
the extent of brown on each feather increases. There is a yellow tinge
in some of the feathers. The width of the band varies greatly. The
bright yellow chin is also acquired and young birds and old become
indistinguishable."

The adult winter plumage is acquired "by a complete post-nuptial
moult in July and August. It differs from the first winter dress in
possessing a complete black 'mask', which includes the forehead, lores,
orbital ring and auriculars, only the forehead and the auriculars being
slightly veiled. The 'mask' has a distinct cinereous posterior border
veiled on the crown with Vandyke-brown. The yellow below is deeper
and the brown wash on the flanks darker in most cases." He reports
that 6 specimens out of 22 in this plumage show a few white feathers
in the orbital ring, usually confined to the lower eyelid, and 3 out of 23
spring males show the same peculiarity, which seems to be purely
individual and possibly peculiar to the younger birds.

The adult nuptial plumage is "acquired by wear," although he thinks
there must be only a limited prenuptial molt, for he examined specimens of this species taken every month in the year, but found "only a
few young birds showing actual moult in February, March and April."
He adds that "the adult nuptial and winter plumages are so extremely
similar that wear alone might convert the latter into the former,"
although even with the large series he examined positive conclusions
were not possible.

In the female "the plumages and moults correspond to those of the
male. In juvenal plumage the sexes are alike. In first winter plumage the female is much browner, the yellow of the lower surface is
wholly replaced by buff, and there is no black about the head. The
first nuptial dress is assumed by a limited prenuptial moult (sometimes suppressed) illustrated by a specimen of February 4th. Later
plumages differ little, except in yellowness, from the first winter dress
and no black is ever assumed about the head."

Albinistic plumages of the yellowthroat have been reported.

Food.—In the case of the yellowthroat, as of other birds which
usually inhabit places remote from agricultural areas, no studies
based on the stomach contents of a large and representative number
of individuals has been made. However, from various field observations and the few stomachs that have been examined we know the
yellowthroat is insectivorous in its food-eating habits. In its nesting
haunts it has been observed feeding on beetles, grubs, larvae and
adults of moths and butterflies, flies, ants, spiders, plant lice, and such

insects as leafhoppers and leaf rollers which are abundant among the grass and low-growing herbage that it frequents.

E. H. Forbush (1907) writes: "I watched a Maryland yellowthroat on the low willow sprouts, and saw him pick off fifty-two gipsy moth larvae before flying away." Mr. Forbush concluded in his study of the gipsy moth infestation in Massachusetts that the yellowthroat ranked among the efficient enemies of this pest. At another time Mr. Forbush saw one eat 89 aphids during the course of one minute.

S. A. Forbes (1883), in the examination of three stomachs of the yellowthroat, found four-fifths of the food consisted of canker worms and other undetermined caterpillars, 8 percent consisted of Coleoptera (beetles), gnats amounted to 4 percent, and a small hemipteran (*Piesma cinerea*) was found. Others have reported yellowthroats in orchards where their chief food seemed to be cankerworms. A. W. Butler (1898) gives the summary of food eaten by 11 specimens of the yellowthroat examined by Prof. F. H. King as follows: 22 case-bearing caterpillars, 5 other larvae, 6 small dragonflies, 3 moths, 3 dipterous insects, 3 small hymenopterous insects, 3 beetles, 3 spiders, 2 small grasshoppers, 1 leafhopper, 2 hemipterous insects, and 2 insect eggs. J. Henderson (1934) quotes Aughey as having reported 8 locusts in the stomach of a single Maryland yellowthroat. C. W. Townsend (1905) found beetles, flies, and small seeds in the stomach of a Maryland yellowthroat he collected at Ipswich, Mass., on December 6, 1903.

Under ordinary conditions the yellowthroat secures its food in an environment remote from agricultural areas, orchards, and gardens; thus it may be thought to be of little economic importance. However, since many destructive insects breed in areas inhabited by these birds, and from there spread to cultivated areas, the yellowthroat can be considered a useful insectivorous bird in its food-eating habits.

Nelle E. Shaver (1918) who made a nest study of the Maryland yellowthroat at the Iowa Lakeside Laboratory on Lake Okoboji has presented detailed and painstaking observations on the food delivered to the young by the adult birds. Miss Shaver summarized the results of 1,694 observations made over the entire nesting period from the time the young hatched until they left the nest. The food delivered was as follows: Unidentified insects 376, moths 347, various larvae 290, spiders 280, mayflies 116, flies 61, unrecognized material 92, caterpillars 20, damselflies 54, beetles 13, chrysalids 13, butterflies 11, seeds 10, caddisflies 3, grasshoppers 6. Miss Shaver states further:

The birds gleaned their food from the ground and the shrubbery close to the ground. The greater amount of the food for the young was such as must have been picked from low bushes around the nest. The small moths which were so numerous in the grass, seemed to afford an unfailing source of supply. * * *

The "worms" were the usual miscellaneous assortment, mostly with a greenish color. These were, of course, gleaned from the foliage. The number of spiders taken by these birds was an interesting fact. * * * Sometimes the food morsel was large, and the time required by the young in swallowing made identification possible. At other times the food was small and the feeding process was so rapid that identification was impossible. Much of the small stuff may have consisted of plant lice, etc.

Voice.—The northern yellowthroat may be heard in full song soon after the arrival of the males in spring. Although the song is subject to great individualistic and local variations its characteristic rhythm and the loud, clear, and strongly accented syllables make it distinctive and easily identifiable. But while the song of the yellowthroat lends itself readily to syllabification, few interpreters agree as to what the bird seems to say. It utterances have been rendered as: *I beseech you, I beseech you, I beseech you; witchity, wichity, wichity; witch-a-wee-o, witch-a-wee-o, witch-a-wee-o; peachity, peachity, peachity,* etc. Witmer Stone (1937) in his study of the Maryland yellowthroat at Cape May, N. J., emphasizes the idividual variation of the song. He states that no two appeared alike, although each carries a similar phrase that is characteristic and gives to all songs an impression of identity. He offers 13 interpretations of songs he recorded and claims that it was very easy to identify individual birds after their songs were memorized.

Aretas A. Saunders has given us his interpretation of the song as follows: "The song of the yellowthroat consists of 3 or 4 repetitions of a phrase of 2 to 6 notes, with 1 note of the phrase strongly accented. The phrases vary greatly in different songs and individual birds. Some phrases are very common, while others are comparatively rare. 3- or 4-note phrases are much commoner than others. In 106 records of the song of this species, only 1 is of 2-note phrases; 7 are of 5 notes and 3 of 6. The remainder are almost equally divided between 3 and 4. In 5 of these records the phrase is sung only twice; in 67 records three times, in 32 four times, and in 2 five times.

"Probably the commonest phrase is one of three notes, the first highest in pitch, and the last lowest; the first note the one usually accented. This is commonly sung with three full phrases and the first note of a fourth, *wit'ato-wit'ato-wit'ato-wit.* This is sometimes varied by making it a phrase of four notes, each lower in pitch than the preceding one, making the phrase *wee'titato.* In the Allegany State Park this is the commonest yellowthroat song. Another common song has the second note highest, and accented, *witee'to,* and this is varied by two notes on the same pitch before the accented note *titiway'to.* There are many other variations, but they seem to be less common than these. In all these, however, the song is readily recognized, for it is much more definite and distinctive than most warbler songs.

"The pitch of songs varies from D′′′ to D′′′′, or one octave. Single songs commonly have a range of one and one half to two and one half tones, a very few only one tone, and a few others up to three and one half tones. Songs vary in the rapidity of the phrases and range from 1⅖ to 2⅖ seconds in length. Usually about two phrases occuy 1 second of time."

The song of the northern yellowthroat may be heard throughout the nesting season but in the last weeks of July and the first week of August singing is less general and less spirited. I have never heard the song in Maine after the last week of July, but observers in other sections of its range have heard it throughout the month of August and as late as the second week of September, although this late singing is unusual. M. B. Trautman (1940) in his intensive study of the birds of Buckeye Lake, Ohio, writes: "The song period began with the first male arrivals in the spring, reached its height in mid-May, and continued undiminished until late June. There was less singing in early July, and by August it had ceased almost entirely. A few birds continued to sing throughout summer and fall, especially in the early morning. An individual on Lieb's Island sang during late October and until November 2, 1929, the last day on which it was observed." Others have reported individual birds remaining throughout the winter, as far north as Toronto, Canada, that were heard singing their characteristic song in spite of snow and severe weather conditions.

Aretas A. Saunders writes that the northern yellowthroat sings until August 1, an average based on 14 seasons in Allegany State Park. The latest date on which the song was heard was August 8, 1929. Frank L. Burns (1937) states that the approximate duration of the yellowthroat's song is 87 days, extending from May 5 to July 31. Of this time the two nesting cycles were in progress for a period of 77 days. In Arkansas W. J. Baerg (1930) writes that in a 5-year period of study the average singing period extended from April 15 to August 10, or 117 days, about a month longer than the determinations made by Burns in Pennsylvania.

The northern yellowthroat seems to exhibit some ability in imitating the song of other birds. E. M. S. Dale, of London, Ontario, writes to us: "For several days in early May 1933, we heard a chipping-sparrow-like song coming from the edge of Spettique's Pond (a mile or two south of London). We were unable to catch a glimpse of the singer until the fifteenth, when we got a good look at it in the very act, and were much surprised to find that it was a northern yellow-

throat. We were wondering if it had been listening to swamp sparrows and had copied them. In 1936 a similar case occurred, when
we heard what we took to be a short-billed marsh wren singing, only
to find that it was the yellowthroat again. I guess we would have all
put it down for a wren without thinking a second time, but one of the
party took the trouble to look it up. On May 14, 1937 we heard what
was without doubt the same bird singing the same wren song from
the same location. Here are two instances of a marsh bird whose
song imitated very closely the songs of two other marsh birds, the
normal songs of the three species being about as unlike as it is possible
to get them."

H. Mousley (1919) has determined that the "singing tree," or the
place selected by the male for singing, was near the nest; in five nests
the distance varied from only 7 to 11 yards. He found this information useful in locating the nests.

H. W. Wright (1912) found that the awakening song of the Maryland yellowthroat at Jefferson Highland, in the White Mountains of
New Hampshire, begins on an average at 3:51 a.m. but varied from
3:41 to 3:55 a.m.

The yellowthroat in its haunts is generally well concealed from
view, and since it is readily excited and disturbed by our approach,
the first indication to us of his presence is a sharp *tchch*, *schick*, or
chit note which is excitedly uttered as he hops nervously about in the
thicket closely scrutinizing our movements to determine whether we
are friend or foe. At other times he may be heard to utter a slight
chip or *tip* note.

In addition to the ordinary, or territory, song the yellowthroat has
a so-called flight song which is more generally heard late in the season
after the birds have begun nesting. The flight song is not so highly
developed in the yellowthroat as it is in the true flight singers of the
open grass areas, nor is it as spectacular as the performance of two
other warblers, the ovenbird and the yellow-breasted chat. The flight
song of the yellowthroat is merely an outburst of ecstasy consisting
of short, confused, and sputtering notes, but generally including
phrases of the common song. It is uttered as it gracefully flies up
from the ground to a height of 15 to 20 feet. The song ends while
the bird is at its highest point of the flight. He then silently drops to
the place from which it started. The flight song is more often heard
in the late afternoon or toward evening than it is during the early
part of the day.

E. H. Forbush (1929) presents an account of a flight song of the
yellowthroat, which was most unusual for the height at which the
bird flew during the performance, as follows:

There is an occasional song-flight that goes far beyond the ordinary. I recall
but one high-flyer, and probably a high flight is very unusual. One such is de-

scribed by Miss Florence M. Pease as follows: "On May 14, 1914, I saw a
Maryland yellow-throat fly very high, then spiral down and then fly off toward
the church, where it was still a good distance from the ground. I was not able to
estimate accurately how many feet the bird flew up, but I noted that when it
began to spiral down it was far, far above the church steeple. I had always
supposed that the flight-song of the Maryland yellow-throat was given from a
height of a few feet."

Enemies.—The yellowthroat is subject to the usual enemies of birds
that nest near or on the ground. I remember finding a nest of the
yellowthroat in a grassy area near a meandering meadow brook in
central Illinois where snakes were common. During a second visit
to the nest, when the young were 3 days old, I saw a large water moccasin disappearing into the vegetation as I approached. Two of
the young were missing and I presume, judging from the behavior of
the adults, they were victims of the unwelcome visitor.

A. L. Rand (1943) cites a report from Lake Okeechobee, Fla., in
October 1942, where a 3-pound large-mouthed bass was found to
have a yellowthroat in its stomach. These fish often feed in shallow
water among the water-hyacinth where they could easily capture a
bird as they do various insects on or near the surface. Mr. Rand
mentions reports of other birds captured by black bass and since
yellowthroats are frequent visitors to such situations in quest of insects, it may not be a rare incident. Turtles have been known to
capture small birds and may also prove to be an enemy of the yellowthroat.

However, the number of yellowthroats that fall victims to natural
enemies are insignificant when compared with the appalling losses
suffered by this species during the migration, especially when the
great migration waves meet with severe storms and foggy weather.
D. E. Culver (1916) gives an account of a large number of birds that
were killed on May 21 and 22, 1915, by flying into public buildings and
the City Hall in Philadelphia. On May 21 there was a heavy mist or
fog prior to the storm, but this was later cleared away by falling
rain. Many of the birds became exhausted from continuous fluttering about the lights and later succumbed to exposure, but the death
of the majority was caused by dashing into the structures. The
Maryland yellowthroat suffered the greatest mortality, Mr. Culver
recovering 130 of this species of which three-fourths were females.
This sex ratio was due to the lateness of the season, as the males are
the first to migrate. Culver also reports that during a migratory
wave, October 17 and 18, 1915, the yellowthroat was again killed in
large numbers, the total being exceeded only by that of the myrtle
warbler.

Robert Overing (1938) on September 12, 1937, between 10:30 p. m.
and midnight identified 576 individuals of 24 species which struck

the Washington Monument.   There was a slight mist enveloping the top of the shaft and the wind velocity was 8 to 10 miles an hour. Mr. Overing identified 189 Maryland yellowthroats and other subspecies of *Geothlypis trichas.*

W. E. Saunders (1930) writes of the great loss of bird life at Long Point lighthouse, Ontario, during certain nights of September 1929. Out of 2,060 birds killed on September 7, 9, and 24–29, 254 of them were Maryland yellowthroats, this being the most frequent victim of the 55 species reported.

A. M. Frazar (1881) reports a great destruction of birds on April 2, 1881, during a sea trip from Texas to Mobile, Ala.   Land birds including a great number of Maryland yellowthroats were seen to perish.   Even those that came aboard the boat were washed into the sea again.

The yellowthroat is a frequent victim of parasitism by the cowbird. L. E. Hicks (1934) reports that out of 41 nests of the northern yellowthroat he has found 19, or 41 percent, that were parasitized by the cowbird.   Dr. Friedmann (1929) states that at Ithaca, N. Y., the yellowthroat stands seventh in order of the birds most frequently imposed upon by the cowbird.   There are many instances on record where the cowbird has been successful in having the yellowthroat accept its eggs and of rearing the young to maturity.   However, some circumvent the intrusion by building a second nest over the first containing the egg of the cowbird, a method frequently employed by the yellow warbler.   A. W. Butler (1898) writes of a 3-story nest of the yellowthroat as follows: "Mr. E. R. Quick has in his collection a three-story nest of this bird, taken near Brookville, Ind.   Two additional nests were built upon the original structure, burying beneath each the egg of the cowbird (*Molothrus ater*).   Thus it outwitted the detestable parasite, and in the third nest deposited her complement of eggs.   Similar nests have been found elsewhere, showing that this is not an individual peculiarity, but others of its kind had experimented along the same line."

The northern yellowthroat is host to a number of external parasites of which Harold S. Peters (1936) has identified the louse *Ricinus vallens* (Kellogg) and the two flies *Ornynoica confluenta* Say and *Ornithomyia anchineuria* Speiser.

Fall.—There are so many breeding birds on the migration range of the yellowthroat that it is not easy to mark the beginning of the southward migration in the autumn.   The bulk of the birds leave their northern breeding grounds in September, but even in these northern sections many birds linger well into October, a few as late as November.   Indeed there are a number of records of birds seen throughout the winter months.

M. B. Trautman (1940) writes of the fall migration at Buckeye Lake, Ohio, as follows: "Upon a few occasions the *chip* note of night migrating birds was recognized as early as late July, and a few apparent transients were seen dropping earthward in the early mornings. Evidence of migration was always apparent by August 10. The peak of migration took place between late August and late September, and then the species was as abundant as in spring. It disappeared between October 5 and November 2." At Oneida Lake, N. Y., according to D. Stoner (1932) fall migration begins in September and by mid-October practically all of the birds have left the territory.

At the Florida lighthouses, where specimens have been recovered, thus making it certain that individuals of the northern yellowthroat are migrating, the first birds appear about the middle of September. They are reported to reach Cuba during the last two weeks of the month. The earliest arrivals reach Jamaica the first week of October and have been reported in Nicaragua during the last week of October.

Winter.—The winter ranges of the northern and Maryland yellowthroats overlap to a great extent. The records are confusing in certain cases, and we cannot be sure that the races are properly designated. The northern yellowthroat winters from southern United States to the Bahamas and the West Indies and through eastern Mexico to Costa Rica. The Maryland winters from North Carolina and Louisiana to Florida, the Bahamas and Haiti. An adult male was taken by Todd (1922) as far south as the Santa Marta region, Colombia.

Dickey and Van Rossem (1938) have found the northern yellowthroat a common midwinter visitant in El Salvador. They write as follows:

The northern yellowthroat was not detected in the fall, even in localities where later in the year it was present in numbers. It is safe to say that few, if any, reach El Salvador before about January 1, after which date the species is common and generally distributed in marshland, shrubbery along streams, and even in fern bracken up to 8,000 feet in the Arid Upper Tropical Zone.

The northward migration is chiefly during early April. At Lake Olomega from April 1 to 8, 1926, and at San Salvador until April 17, 1912, yellowthroats were very common, much more so than during the winter. However, some individuals remain very late in spring; indeed, locally, they are sometimes actually common in the middle of May. An instance of this is the fact that at Lake Chanmico from May 13 to 17, 1912, *brachidactyla* was frequently noted in the grass and mimosa scrub about the edge of the lake. A peculiarity of this occurrence was that the birds were usually in pairs. The two males taken were in breeding condition, and the single female had rapidly developing ova.

Dr. Alexander F. Skutch has sent us the following notes concerning the yellowthroat (races not designated) in Central America: "Like so many of the warblers that winter in Central America, the yellowthroats are abundant in the north but rare in the south. In Panamá and Costa Rica it has been very rarely recorded; I have seen it only once during eight years in these countries. In Guatemala, it winters in fair numbers at lower elevations, on both sides of the Republic, upward to at least 3,000 feet above sea level. I saw two at Panajachel, 5,000 feet above sea level, in late October; but it is possible that at this date they had not yet settled down for the winter. This single bird I met on the Sierra de Tecpán, at 8,500 feet, on March 7, 1933, was obviously only a transient—I saw no other of the kind during the course of the year. In the lower Motagua Valley, I found the yellowthroat an abundant winter resident; and it was not rare on the great coffee plantations of the Pacific slope. It frequents low-lying pastures where the grass is tall, moist thickets, and the brakes of giant cane along the rivers. Always solitary, it shows no tendency to flock.

"The yellowthroat arrives late and apparently has not been recorded before October. In April, when the migratory movements begin, these birds become exceedingly abundant in the Motagua Valley of Guatemala. They linger into May, rarely past the middle of the month; and I have recorded males as late as females. On May 7, 1932, I heard a male, the last of his kind I saw that year, sing repeatedly but rather weakly, among tall, lush grass in the Motagua Valley."

Dr. Barbour (1923) states the northern yellowthroat is a common winter visitant in Cuba, where it is found about marshes, in cane brakes and reed beds, and in lowland thickets of vines and lianas.

In the Isle of Pines, W. E. C. Todd (1916) states that the Maryland yellowthroat is a common winter resident throughout the northern part of the island where it inhabits the low, wet thickets.

In Haiti and the Dominican Republic Wetmore and Swales (1931) state: "The yellow-throat is found in numbers at the proper season in weed-grown fields, and the borders of marshes in the lowlands, and also ranges widely into the higher altitudes where there is suitable cover for it. It lives near the ground concealed in the dense growths that it affects, coming out on open perches for a few seconds and then dodging quickly out of sight, or flushing with tilting flight to fly for a few yards before disappearing again into its coverts. Attention often is directed to it by its harsh call note, a low *chimp*, as it scolds whenever disturbed."

So many individuals of yellowthroats have been found wintering well north of the usual winter range of these birds that it has become something more than an accidental occurrence. A few representative records in this connection are of interest. Baillie and Thompson (1928) report that a Maryland yellowthroat was seen December 25, 1927, in a sheltered ravine of Hyde Park, Toronto, Canada. It was a male in good plumage; it was active and uttered its characteristic

song. M. B. Trautman (1933) saw a male northern yellowthroat
during a severe cold snap during mid-March at Buckeye Lake, Ohio.
It was wintering in the cattails which stood beside a 2-foot snow drift
at the time it was seen   The bird was collected and upon examination
was found to be fat and in apparently good condition.

C. W. Townsend (1905) writes: "I found a Maryland yellow-throat
on December 6th, 1903, in the sand dunes just back of Ipswich Beach,
among some bayberry bushes and goldenrod stalks.   There was about
an inch of snow on the ground and the thermometer early in the
morning was only 15° F.   The bird proved to be a young male, quite
fat, with its stomach filled with insects, mostly beetles and flies, and
a few small seeds.   Its plumage was interesting, as it had partially
assumed the first nuptial plumage." Since Dr. Townsend's winter
record there have been numerous winter records of the northern yellowthroat in Massachusetts as well as in other sections of New England.   The yellowthroat is a regular winter resident from North
Carolina southward.

DISTRIBUTION

Range.—North America, Central America, and the West Indies.

Breeding range.—The yellowthroat breeds **north** to southeastern
Alaska (Chickamin River) ; southern Yukon (Jarvis River at Alaska
Highway, Champagne, and Pelly River) ; northern Alberta (Peace
River area, and the Athabaska Delta) ; south-central Saskatchewan
(Manito Lake, Emma Lake, and Yorkton) ; southern Manitoba
(Brandon, Aweme, Pembina, Lake St. Martin, Shoal Lake, and Car-
man) ; central and northern Ontario (Kenora, Lac Seul, Roseport,
Amyot, and Moose Factory) ; central and southeastern Quebec (Mis-
tassini Post, Lake Albanel, Godbout, Mingan, Natashquan, and
Anticosti Island) ; and southern Newfoundland (Lewis Hills, Grand
Lake, Pushthrough, possibly Gooseberry Island, and Exploits River).
East to Newfoundland (Exploits River) ; Connecticut; New York;
eastern Pennsylvania; western Maryland (Cranesville) ; Virginia
(Emporia, Pungo, and Dismal Swamp) ; North Carolina (Wadesboro
and Raleigh) ; South Carolina (Greenwood, Lancaster) ; Georgia (At-
lanta, Athens, Newton, and Saint Marys) ; and eastern Florida
(Gainesville, Micanopy, Deep Lake, Royal Palm Hammock, and
Miami).   **South** to Florida (Miami, Tallahassee, and Pensacola) ;
southeastern Alabama (Abbeville and Dothan) ; southern Mississippi
(Gulfport and Biloxi) ; southern Louisiana (Pilot Town, Houma.
Vermillion Bay, and Sunset) ; southern Texas (Brownsville) ; north-
western Chihuahua (probably San Diego) ; and Colima (Colima and
Manzanillo).   **West** to Colima (Manzanillo) ; Nayarit; Sinaloa;
Sonora (Tepopa Bay and Kino Bay) ; Baja California (San Ramón,

Rosario, San Felipe) ; coastal California (Santa Barbara, San Rafael, San Francisco Bay) ; western Oregon (Portland, Salem, and Corvallis) ; western Washington (Sumas, Seattle, Grays Harbor, Tacoma) ; western British Columbia (Kispiox Valley, Hazelton, Comax, and Chilliwack) ; to southeastern Alaska (Chickamin River).

Winter range.—The yellowthroat winters **north** to northern California (Eureka) ; southern Arizona (Yuma and Tucson) ; southern Texas (Brownsville and Beaumont) ; southern Louisiana (Chenier au Tigre, Grand Isle, and New Orleans) ; southern Mississippi (Biloxi) ; and North Carolina (Raleigh and Lake Mattamuskeet). **East** to North Carolina (Lake Mattamuskeet) ; Georgia (Atlanta and Savannah) ; throughout Florida; Cuba (Isle of Pines) ; Jamaica; the Bahamas (Bimini, Andros, Nassau, and Hog Island) ; Haiti (Gonâve) ; Dominican Republic (Fort Liberté) ; and Puerto Rico (Guajatico Reservoir). **South** to Puerto Rico (Guajatico Reservoir) ; and Panamá (Volcán de Chiriquí). **West** to Panamá (Volcán de Chiriquí) ; Costa Rica (San José) ; Nicaragua; Honduras; El Salvador; Guatemala; Quintana Roo; Oaxaca (Huajuapan) ; Guerrero (Coyuca) ; Baja California (Cabo San Lucas, Miraflores) ; and along the California coast to Eureka.

The range as outlined is for the entire species of which 12 subspecies are recognized. The northern yellowthroat (*G. t. brachidactyla*) breeds from southeastern Manitoba, central and northeastern Ontario, central and southeastern Quebec, and the southwestern half of Newfoundland south to western North Carolina and west to central and northeastern Oklahoma, Kansas, and central Nebraska; the Maryland yellowthroat (*G. t. trichas*) breeds from southern Pennsylvania south to northern parts of Georgia and Alabama, and to eastern Texas; the Florida yellowthroat (*G. t. ignota*) is a permanent resident in southeastern Louisiana, southern Mississippi, and Florida; the Athens yellowthroat (*G. t. typhicola*) breeds from southeastern Virginia to central Alabama; the western yellowthroat (*G. t. occidentalis*) breeds from central northern and southeastern Oregon, southern Idaho, southwestern Wyoming, central northern Colorado, southwestern Nebraska, and southwestern and central southern Kansas, south to central eastern California, south-central Nevada, central southern Utah, northern and central eastern Arizona, northern and central eastern New Mexico, and northern Texas; the Pacific yellowthroat (*G. t. arizela*) breeds along the Pacific coast in southeastern Alaska, to northwestern, central northern, and central California; the salt marsh yellowthroat (*G. t. sinuosa*) breeds in the salt-water marshes of the San Francisco Bay area of central western California; the Sonora yellowthroat (*G. t. chryseola*) breeds and is probably resident in southeastern Arizona, southern central and southeastern New Mexico, and western Texas, south to northeastern Sonora and northwestern Chihuahua; the tule yellowthroat (*G. t. scirpicola*) is a resident race in southern California, southeastern Nevada, southwestern Utah, and westernmost Arizona, south to northern Baja California; the Brownsville yellowthroat (*G. t. insperata*) is a resident race of the Rio Grande delta region below Brownsville, Texas; the San Blas yellowthroat (*G. t. modesta*) is a resident race along the western coast of Mexico from central western Sonora through Sinaloa and Nayarit to Colima; and the northern plains yellowthroat (*G. t. campicola*) breeds in southern Yukon, northeastern British Columbia, northern Alberta, south-central Saskatchewan, and southwestern Manitoba; south to southeastern Alaska, central Oregon, central Idaho, northeastern Colorado, and North Dakota.

Migration.—Late dates of spring departure are: Colombia—Lake Macotama, Santa Marta region, April 21; Baudó Mountains, near Nuqui, June 16. El Salvador—Lake Chanmico, May 17. Costa Rica—Basin of El General, May 2. Honduras—near Tela, April 28. Guatemala—near Quiriguá, May 7. Tabasco—Balancán, May 9. Puerto Rico—Desengano, April 18. Dominican Republic—May 8. Jamaica—Spanishtown, May 10. Cuba—Cienfuegos, May 12. Bahamas—May 10. Florida—Lower Florida Keys, May 21. Arizona—Tucson, June 7. California—Pasadena, May 20.

Early dates of spring arrival are: Bahamas—Cay Sal, March 13. Florida—Sombrero Key Light, March 3. Alabama—Greensboro and Shelby, March 11; Birmingham, March 14 (average of 10 years, March 17). Georgia—Savannah, March 12. South Carolina—Columbia, March 11. North Carolina—Raleigh, High Rock, and Washington, March 20 (average of 30 years at Raleigh, March 28). Virginia—Cape Henry, March 7 (average, April 7); Rockbridge County, April 18. West Virginia—Bluefield, April 14; French Creek, April 27 (average of 17 years, May 1). District of Columbia—Washington, April 11 (average of 57 years, April 22). Maryland—Baltimore and Patuxent Wildlife Research Refuge, April 12. Delaware—Kent and Sussex Counties, March 4 (average of 21 years, March 20). Pennsylvania—Carlisle, April 3; Kennett Square, April 15. New Jersey—Camden, April 3; Trenton, April 20. New York—Staten Island, April 10; Poughkeepsie, April 14; Watertown, April 22. Connecticut—Carrollton, April 25. Massachusetts—Woods Hole, April 17. Vermont—St. Johnsbury, May 1. New Hampshire—East Westmoreland, May 3. Maine—Waterville, April 18; South Harpswell, May 4. Quebec—Montreal, May 4. New Brunswick—Fredericton, April 30. Nova Scotia—Yarmouth, May 9. Newfoundland—St. Andrews, May 27. Louisiana—Bains, March 30. Mississippi—Edwards,

March 10. Arkansas—Monticello, March 26. Tennessee—Nashville,
April 6 (average of 12 years, April 8); Elizabethton, April 1.
Kentucky—Bowling Green, April 8. Missouri—Pemiscot County,
April 8. Illinois—Murphysboro, April 15; Chicago region, April 20
(average May 4). Indiana—Carlisle, April 17. Ohio—Oberlin, April
13; Columbus, April 17 (average for central Ohio, April 25). Michi-
gan—Ann Arbor (University), April 17. Ontario—London, April
25; Ottawa, May 4 (average of 9 years, May 16). Iowa—Elkader,
April 19. Wisconsin—Prairie du Sac, April 10; Madison, April 24.
Minnesota—Lanesboro, April 30 (average of 40 years for southern
Minnesota, May 9). Texas—White Rock, March 9. Oklahoma—
Adair County, April 7. Kansas—Wichita, April 12. Nebraska—
North Platte, April 18. South Dakota—Yankton, April 30. North
Dakota—Devil's Lake region, May 3. Manitoba—Treesbank, May 13.
Saskatchewan—Regina, May 7. New Mexico—San Antonio, March
28. Utah—Wendover, March 15. Arizona—Tucson Valley, Febru-
ary 29. Colorado—Colorado Springs, April 2. Wyoming—Douglas,
April 16; Laramie, May 2 (average of 10 years, May 10). Idaho—
Moscow, May 1. Montana—Fortine, May 9. Alberta—Banff Na-
tional Park, May 5. California—San Clemente Island and Colorado
River Valley, March 23. Nevada—Millett, April 26. Oregon—Jack-
son County, March 22. Washington—Yakima County, March 29.
British Columbia—Courtenay, Vancouver Island, April 15.

Late fall departure dates are: Alaska—Taku River, September 9.
British Columbia—Okanagan Landing, October 10; Comox, Vancouver Island, October 12. Washington—Bellingham, October 1. Oregon—Eugene area, October 18. Nevada—Indian Springs, Charleston
Mountains, October 11. California—Coalinga, October 22. Alberta—
Glenevis, October 8. Montana—Bozeman, October 8. Idaho—Mos-
cow, October 4. Wyoming—Douglas, October 16; Laramie, October
12 (average of 7 years, September 18). Colorado—Boulder, Septem-
ber 30. Arizona—Tucson, November 11. Utah—Deep Creek, October
5. Saskatchewan—Eastend, September 28. Manitoba—Brandon,
October 5; Aweme, September 26 (average, September 17). North
Dakota—Fargo, October 18. South Dakota—Yankton, October 15.
Nebraska—Hastings, October 8. Kansas—Lake Quivira, Johnson
County, September 27. Oklahoma—Oklahoma City, October 16;
Copan, November 29. Texas—El Paso, October 26. Minnesota—
Hutchinson, October 26 (average of 14 years for southern Minnesota,
September 27). Wisconsin—Mazomanie, October 18; Madison, De-
cember 21. Iowa—Osage, October 26. Ontario—Fort Albany, James
Bay region, September 22; Ottawa, September 27; Hamilton, Decem-
ber 19; Toronto, December 25 and 26. Michigan—Erie, November

29; Sault Ste. Marie, December 1. Ohio—Toledo, November 23; Buckeye Lake, November 2 (average, October 14). Indiana—Bloomington, November 4. Illinois—Chicago, October 28 (average of 15 years, October 9). Missouri—St. Louis, October 19. Kentucky—Bowling Green, October 29. Tennessee—Elizabethton, October 27. Mississippi—Oxford, October 10. Newfoundland—Cape Anguille, October 3. Nova Scotia—Wolfville, October 4. New Brunswick—Saint John, October 15. Quebec—Montreal, October 14; November 29. Maine—Bath, October 21, November 10; Portland, December 8. New Hampshire—Hanover and Sandwich, October 22. Vermont—Rutland, October 23. Massachusetts—Cambridge, November 26; East Orleans, December 10. Rhode Island—Little Compton, November 5. Connecticut—Portland, November 7; West Hartford, November 12. New York—Rochester, October 28; numerous November and December records near the coast. New Jersey—Union County, November 24 (average, October 21). Pennsylvania—Renovo, October 24; Jeffersonville, November 1. Maryland—Baltimore County, October 27. District of Columbia—Washington, November 2 (average of 20 years, October 6). West Virginia—Bluefield, October 21. Virginia—Rockbridge County, October 21. North Carolina—Raleigh, October 24 (average of 8 years, October 13). South Carolina—Spartanburg, October 16. Georgia—Tybee Light, October 21; Demarest, November 30. Alabama—Birmingham, October 22 (average of 10 years, October 19).

Early dates of fall arrival are: California—Cactus Flat, San Bernardino Mountains, August 16. Arizona—Huachuca Mountains, August 25. Illinois—Chicago, August 21 (average, August 29). New York—New York City, August 13. Maryland—Patuxent Wildlife Research Refuge, August 12. Georgia—Tybee Light, September 23. Florida—Sombrero Key, September 12. Cuba—Cienfuegos, September 5. Dominican Republic—Ciudad Trujillo, September 30. Puerto Rico—Monte Grande, October 31. Yucatán—Chichén-Itzá, October 8. Honduras—near Tela, October 3. Nicaragua—Escondido River, October 28.

Egg dates.—Arizona: 11 records, May 30 to July 22; 7 records, June 1 to 9.

California: 66 records, April 4 to July 10; 33 records, May 1 to 20, indicating the height of the season.

Florida: 11 records, April 22 to July 20; 6 records, April 26 to May 7.

Massachusetts: 97 records, May 23 to June 27; 55 records, May 30 to June 8.

Nova Scotia: 9 records, June 4 to 26 (Harris).

GEOTHLYPIS TRICHAS IGNOTA Chapman

FLORIDA YELLOWTHROAT

CONTRIBUTED BY ALFRED OTTO GROSS

PLATE 69

HABITS

The Florida yellowthroat was first described by Frank Chapman (1890) based on an adult male in breeding plumage taken at Tarpon Springs, Fla., May 19, 1887. His description is as follows:

Above olive green with a slight rusty tinge, somewhat lighter on the rump and tail; wings brownish, the feathers edged with the color of the back, the outer web of the first primary whitish, the carpal bend yellow. A broad black facial mask includes laterally the eyes, auriculars, and sides of the throat, reaching on the forehead to near the posterior margin of the eyes, and is bordered by a band of hoary ash, which has no abrupt posterior termination but, suffusing the crown, changes gradually into the color of the back. Under parts rich yellow, whitish on the centre of the abdomen; flanks rich ochraceous brown, the sides of the breast slightly washed with the same color. *Measurements:* Wing 2.26; tail, 2.32; tarsus, .84; exposed culmen, .50 inch. * * *

Adult female in breeding plumage. * * * Similar in color to the male, but without the black mask and ashy border, the crown being rusty brownish, paler on the forehead. * * *

Adult male in winter. Similar to adult male in the spring but darker above, the ashy band bordering the black mask restricted to a narrow line; crown rich rusty brown, brighter anteriorly, where also the feathers have more or less ashy and yellowish bases, and fading gradually into the color of the back; abdomen somewhat paler. * * *

Adult female in winter. Similar to adult fall specimens of *trichas*, but darker above, with the yellow of the breast and underparts washed with brownish.

Immature birds. Immature birds of both sexes are not readily distinguishable from wintering northern specimens, and from the nature of the case there are at this season specimens showing every degree of intergradation, both as regards size and coloration. Generally speaking the resident birds are slightly darker above, with the marking of the under-surface deeper in color and of greater extent.

The Florida yellow-throat is similar to the Maryland yellow-throat, but with a longer tarsus, tail, and bill; yellow of underparts of a deeper shade and greater extent; flanks of a much darker color; the upper parts browner; the facial mask wider, with its ashy border (in summer specimens) slightly paler and of greater extent. First primary shorter, equalling the eighth instead of the sixth, as in the Maryland yellow-throat.

The breeding range of the Florida yellowthroat as formerly defined included the region from the Dismal Swamp region of Virginia, the coast of South Carolina, central Alabama, and central Georgia to Florida and along the Gulf coast to Louisiana. Since the Athens yellowthroat (*typhicola*) has been recognized, the breeding range does not extend farther north on the Atlantic coast than northern

Florida (Burleigh, 1937). In a later paper Burleigh (1944b) states the Florida yellowthroat has an extremely limited range on the coast of Mississippi. Specimens were taken every month of the year except July along a narrow southeastern coastal area but it was noted only once, during the summer, on any of the islands off the coast. Breeding birds taken only 22 miles inland north of Gulfport were found to be intermediate in their characters between the Florida and the Athens yellowthroat. The Florida yellowthroat breeds throughout Florida and is practically resident except in the more northern parts of its breeding range. Possibly a few migrate south of Florida to Cuba, since *ignota* as well as the two northern forms have been found dead at stations in southern Florida during the migration season.

According to Holt and Sutton (1926) it is abundant in all suitable places throughout southern Florida, but particularly numerous at " 'Gator Lake, in the salt-marsh inhabited by the Cape Sable Seaside Sparrows at East Cape, and along New River near Miami. Common also on the keys off East Cape." Frank M. Chapman (1907) writes: "In Florida this resident form of the Yellow-throat is so commonly found only in scrub palmettos that it is known as the 'Palmetto Bird.' I have also found it about the bushy borders of 'bay-galls' surrounded by scrub palmetto, while in the Kissimee region it lives in the lower growth (largely young palms) of cabbage palms." According to A. H. Howell (1932) :

The Florida yellow-throat inhabits thickets and brier patches, being especially partial to wet situations, such as the borders of streams, lakes, and sloughs. The birds are common along the canals in the Everglades, and in the floating vege-tation on the upper St. Johns River near Lake Washington, and are found in smaller numbers in dry palmetto thickets on the prairies or in the forests. They are rather shy, and on being disturbed take refuge in the depths of the thickets in which they live, and voice their alarm with a characteristic burring *chink*. In singing they usually come out to the edge of the thicket or fly to a low perch on a bush or tree.

In winter the Florida yellowthroat is common about cultivated lands, in thick scrub and tall switch grass on the prairies and in grassy, marshy situations. Since there is no marked increase in spring, it is another indication that this form is not strongly migratory.

Nesting.—The nesting habits of the Florida yellowthroat are similar to those of the northern subspecies. It is interesting that it breeds as late in the season (April 10 to June 9) as do the birds in the middle Atlantic states. The nests are placed in clumps of grass in marshy situations and sometimes in weeds, bushes, and thickets on dry ground. They are loosely woven of dry grasses, stems, and bits of wide blades of swamp grass, and lined with fine grasses; they are seldom placed more than a few inches above the ground.

Eggs.—Most of the sets of eggs are four in number but a few with five eggs have been reported. The color and markings of the eggs are similar to those of the Maryland yellowthroat. The measurements of 29 eggs average 17.7 by 13.4 millimeters; the eggs showing the four extremes measure **19.2** by 13.5, 18.6 by **14.0,** and **16.1** by **12.4** millimeters.

Food.—The yellowthroat is said to be a very beneficial insect-eating bird in Florida, in regions where tomatoes and other vegetable produce is reared. But like the other subspecies of yellowthroats the majority of the birds occupy habitats where the destruction of insects is of less importance to agriculture.

The contents of the stomachs of seven yellowthroats collected in Florida were found by the United States Biological Survey to consist mainly of insects, with a few spiders and small mollusks and a small number of seeds of the sweetgale. Of the insects eaten, Orthoptera (chiefly grasshoppers) and crickets comprise the largest amount, with Hymenoptera (ants, wasps, bees) next in importance. Other forms well represented were beetles, bugs, flies, and caterpillars.

Voice.—The song of the yellowthroat as it is heard in Florida is full and strong, and while having the same characteristics, is nevertheless recognizably different from that of the northern yellowthroat we hear in New England. The song has been interpreted as *witcher-cheree, witcher-cheree, witcher-cheree,* but there is considerable individual variation in the renditions. The song may be heard throughout the spring and summer but in spring it seems to be more spirited and perhaps more elaborate.

The flight song begins as the singer launches forth from his thicket, reaches a climax at a height of 15 or 20 feet, when the head is thrown b..ck as when singing at rest, and gradually dies away as the bird sinks down with rapidly vibrating wings. The flight song resembles the following: *Chee, chee, chee, chee, che-witchery, witchery, witchery, witchery.*

Enemies.—The Florida yellowthroat like that of its near relatives is subject to parasitism by the cowbird. It is seldom that the young of the yellowthroat survive more than a few days before they are starved or suffocated to death by the much larger and more aggressive cowbird.

Various observers have reported that it frequently falls prey to snakes, turtles, and even fish. This might reasonably be expected of individuals that frequent the swamps and marshlands of semitropical Florida where such enemies are abundant.

Harold S. Peters (1936) has found the tick, *Haemaphysalis leporispalustrus* Packard a parasite of the Florida yellowthroat. It is of interest that he found no ticks infesting either the Maryland or the northern yellowthroats.

Since the Florida yellowthroat does not migrate to the extent of the northern yellowthroat it does not meet with the extraordinary hazards of a long migration which has been the cause of the death of so many of the northern species.

GEOTHLYPIS TRICHAS TYPHICOLA Burleigh

ATHENS YELLOWTHROAT

CONTRIBUTED BY ALFRED OTTO GROSS

HABITS

The Athens yellowthroat bears a superficial resemblance to the Florida race but can be readily separated from it by its distinctly smaller bill, and less brownish under parts and flanks. The northern yellowthroat can be differentiated from the Athen's yellowthroat by its larger bill and olive green rather than brownish upper parts.

The Athens yellowthroat is distributed from southeastern Virginia to Georgia and Alabama and in migration to eastern Mexico. Burleigh (1937), in an account of the yellowthroats of Georgia, writes:

> The Athens yellow-throat is the most abundant of the yellow-throats occurring in the state, and in fact it is one of the most characteristic birds of Georgia. Except for the limited area occupied by the Maryland yellow-throat it can be found throughout the state, and, while less numerous during the winter months is to a large extent resident as far north as Athens. In severe winters it is perceptibly scarcer in the northern half of the state, but even with snow on the ground and the temperature well below freezing an occasional bird can be seen in the thickets and stretches of underbrush. All winter records based on actual specimens taken have without exception been found to refer to this race alone.

Specimens of the Athens yellow throat were previously referred to the Florida yellowthroat, a race, as now restricted, that is confined largely to the peninsula of Florida and the coastal regions of southeastern Georgia.

The nesting habits and behavior of the Athens and Florida yellowthroats are similar.

GEOTHLYPIS TRICHAS OCCIDENTALIS Brewster

WESTERN YELLOWTHROAT

CONTRIBUTED BY ALFRED OTTO GROSS

HABITS

The western yellowthroat is a large form of *Geothlypis trichas* first described by William Brewster in 1883 (Allen and Brewster, 1883). An adult male collected at Truckee River, Nev., May 4, 1881, was described as follows: "Upper parts nearly uniform pale yellowish-olive, with a tinge of brown on the occiput; throat, jugulum, breast, anterior portion of abdomen, and under tail-coverts rich, pure yellow; sides of body warm ochraceous brown strongly tinged with yellow; middle of abdomen anteriorly creamy white; a black mask on the front and sides of the head bordered behind by a broad band of creamy white, slightly tinged with bluish; much concealed yellow on the feathers of the crown." In comparing *G. trichas occidentalis* with *G. t. trichas* he states it "is somewhat larger * * * and its tail is disproportionately longer. Its upper parts always paler and usually yellower; the yellow of the under parts is decidedly richer and purer, and extends much farther down on the abdomen, frequently tinging nearly all of the body beneath; the flanks are paler and more ochraceous; the white of the head purer and generally broader."

W. Palmer (1900) in comparing the western with the northern yellowthroat states:

> The western bird, *occidentalis*, is a little larger than *brachidactyla*, but grayer in dorsal coloration with a broad white posterior edging of the facial black. The yellow of the throat is more intense and the black of the forehead is relatively narrower. Freshly molted adult birds are but slightly paler dorsally than eastern birds, but immature birds are fully as dark and as brown above as in similar aged eastern birds. The females in summer are as a rule less yellowish and paler than eastern birds. A few have decidedly yellow throats but it is far from the rule. The immature females are browner and duller above and beneath with a much browner tinge across the breast than in either *trichas* or *Brachidactyla*.

The wing formula and the relative length of the primaries exhibit distinct differences from those of the eastern forms.

The western yellowthroat breeds from Oregon, southern Idaho, and the western portion of the Great Plains (North and South Dakota and Texas) south to northern New Mexico. The distribution of the western yellow-throat in California where there are also the two forms *G. t. sinuosa* and *G. t. scirpicola* represented, is complicated. According to Grinnell and Miller (1944) : "In breeding season, valleys of northern California from the coast east to the Nevada line; in central California south to northern Sonoma County, thence east of San Francisco Bay through Solano and eastern Contra Costa counties to the Monterey Bay area and the Salinas Valley; extends south into central San Joaquin Valley where intergradation with *scirpicola* takes place; similarly east of the Sierra Nevada intergradation becomes apparent in Owens Valley, Inyo County."

In winter the western yellowthroat is found in the Sacramento and San Joaquin Valleys, Calif., from Tehama County southward to southern California, and through Baja California and western Mexico as far south as Cape San Lucas and Tepic, Nayarit. In California migrants appear in all sections of the State, even up the middle elevations in the mountains.

Specimens of the western yellowthroat have been taken as far east as Erie, Mich. (Van Tyne, 1944), and Gulfport, Miss. (Burleigh, 1944).

In Washington, according to correspondence from Samuel F. Rathbun, the western yellowthroat is decidedly localized in its distribution, being restricted to brushy borders of swamps, marshes, lakes, and streams, but very often it is absent from these localities. When seen among the rushes along the edge of some rush-bordered piece of water, climbing actively among the stalks, its actions are reminiscent of those of the tule wrens.

At Fort Klamath, Oreg., J. C. Merrill (1888) writes: "The habits of the Western Yellow-throat in this vicinity, as regards its favorite resorts, are quite unlike what I have elsewhere observed. Though the numerous streams offer it the same rank undergrowth along their swampy edges that it in other places prefers, yet it is rarely seen in such situations. A few are found among the low willows growing in the marsh, but its favorite haunt, and one in which it is very common, is among the tules in company with Marsh Wrens and Yellow-headed Blackbirds."

In California, Grinnell and Miller (1944) state that its habitat is in the "low thick tangles of plant growth in or about fresh- or brackish-water marshes and sloughs; extremely small areas of flooded ground in river bottoms * * * may suffice. Important is continuous cover for concealment in foraging down to the mud or water surfaces. The sphere of activity is within six feet of the water and principally within three feet."

In Montana, according to A. A. Saunders (1921) the western yellow-throat is—

a very common summer resident in the western half of the state, east to the western part of the prairie region. Apparently rare in the more eastern part of the prairie region, and occuring there only in migration. Breeds throughout the Transition zone, on the prairies, and in the mountain valleys and foothills. Nests in thickets of willow, wild-rose and similar shrubs, in moist places along the streams. The breeding range of the Western Yellowthroat in Montana is almost exactly coincident with that of the MacGillivray Warbler, both being found east of Fergus County and the Musselshell River, but the Yellowthroat is much commoner at low elevations in valleys, and much less common in the mountain foothills. In many localities, however, the two species are found together.

In Utah where the western yellowthroat is a common resident, except in the southwestern part of the state, W. H. Behle (1944) writes:

"[it] occurs in cattail and tule marshes and in willow-cottonwood association bordering valley streams."

Nesting.—In his Birds of California, William Leon Dawson (1923) writes:

Nests of the yellow-throats are the commonplace of all swampy localities— commonplace, yet never without interest, because of their varied architecture and their diverse setting. A nest may be sunk firmly into a tussock of grass barely clear of the ground or water, or it may be lashed firmly to stalks of an investing clump of cattails, or it may be deftly hidden under a canopy of weed-tops a hundred feet from water. The nest may be composed chiefly of brittle weathered leaves or grass or sedge, so coherent as to be scarcely removeable, or else it may be settled into a veritable fortress of coiled cattail leaves sturdy and dependable. The lining too, may be of coiled grasses almost as light in color as the speckled white eggs which they support, or it may be of black horsehair, throwing the jewels into prized relief.

Grinnell and Miller (1944) write: "nests are placed low down, often over the water. Plant associations most likely to meet these requirements: growths of cattails, tules and other sedges, especially where tangled and matted; thickets of young willows; blackberry vines, accompanied by nettles and dock."

A nest collected at Fairbank, Ariz., is described by A. C. Bent (MS.) as follows: "Bulky, loosely built nest made up entirely of coarse strips of sacaton grass and other grasses; no plant down or other soft material. The dimensions were, outer height 3 inches, diameter 4½ inches, inner depth 2 inches and inner diameter 2¼ inches."

W. L. Dawson (1923) states the nest is "of course coiled grasses, or, more rarely, leaves of *Typha angustifolia;* lined with fine grasses or horse hair." Others have mentioned that a lining of horsehair is sometimes used, as is also the case of many nests built by the eastern forms of the yellowthroat.

Eggs.—The eggs vary from three to five in number but the majority of the nests contain four eggs. They are similar in their markings to those of other forms of yellowthroat, having a ground color of white or creamy white, dotted and spotted or rarely streaked with black, shades of brown, and lavender or vinaceous gray. The markings are usually concentrated about the larger end of the egg.

Food.—F. E. L. Beal (1907) in an investigation of the food of the western yellowthroat examined the contents of 114 stomachs of birds taken in California during every month but January. He found the yellowthroat to be practically wholly insectivorous and the insects it eats to be either harmful or of little economic value. It eats no fruit or grain, or, as far as known, any other useful product. Beal states further:

The animal matter amounted to 99.8 percent of the total food. The largest item is Hymenoptera, amounting to 35 percent, of which about half is ants and the remainder wild bees, wasps, etc. Hemiptera amount to 28 percent, and are made up of leaf-bugs, leaf-hoppers, tree-hoppers, plant lice, scales, and probably some others not identifiable. The black olive scale was found in a few stomachs and plant-lice in one, but the other families were a pretty constant component of the food in every month. Beetles were eaten to the extent of nearly 15 percent, and are mostly harmful species.—The three orders of insects [Hymenoptera, Hemiptera, and Coleoptera] mentioned above form the greatest bulk of the food of the yellowthroat, and are regularly eaten throughout the year.

Caterpillars and moths comprise 5 percent, Diptera 12 percent, spiders 4 percent. Grasshoppers were found in four stomachs.

The vegetable food was incidental and was probably taken accidentally when other food was being secured. It consisted of only a few seeds and vegetable rubbish.

Voice.—The song of the western yellowthroat is similar to that of the eastern forms but William Leon Dawson (1923) has presented some interesting and unusual interpretations as follows:

Mounting a weed-stalk, he rubs out, *Rees'iwitte, rees'iwitte, rit,* or *I beseech you, I beseech you, I beseech.* Rhythm is the chief characteristic of this song, and although a given bird appears to be confined to a single type, the variety of feet offered by a swamp is most entertaining. *Chit'ooreet, chit'ooreet chu';* heard on the edge of a northern pond, reminded me of the Kentucky warbler (*Oporornis formosus*); while another, less ambitious, lisped, *O-tis twiss'-pe, o-tis twiss' pe.* Returning to the typical rhythm, one indignant swain near Los Angeles, shouted, *Greas'y wittles, greas'y wittles, grit!* * * *

But by far the most remarkable song in my experience came from a locality in eastern Washington. We had just been listening to the unwonted notes of a Desert Sparrow * * * some hundreds of miles out of its usual range, and we were not unprepared for shocks, when *Hoo hee, chink i woo chu tip* fell upon our ear. Again and again came the measured accents, clear, strong and sweet. Not till I had seen the mandibles of a Western Yellow-throat, and that repeatedly, moving in perfect rhythm to music, could I believe so small a bird the author of this song. For fifteen minutes the Warbler brought forth this alien strain, *Hee-o chiti wo, chu tip,* or *Hee oo chitiwew chu tipew,* without once lapsing into ordinary dialect.

Mr. Dawson also describes a harsh accusing note uttered by the western yellowthroat which he describes as "a sort of Polish consonantal explosion, *wzschthub,*—a sound not unlike that made by a guitar string when struck above the stop."

Richard Hunt (1919) describes and presents an excellent analysis of the song of the western yellowthroat he heard on the campus at Berkeley, Calif., as follows:

As I listened from an office window, a single clear and near example of the song reached my ears. It was an utterance in four sections, the first three being four syllabled and exactly alike: *pritisitta, pritisitta, pritisitta, prit,* with accent on the *prit.* I had never heard a Yellowthroat song of this exact syllabification, but the chief and important distinguishing character of the song of the species is, after all, its exact repetition of some sort of two- or three or four-syllabled word. Every individual Yellowthroat has quite a stock of different words, and some are likely to be different from any words one would hear another individual sing. Timbre, to be sure, is also a character of the Yellowthroat song—

though it varies among and in individuals as widely as does the word-form. The timbre of this song was hardly typical: it was unusually loose and liquid. The utterance was comparatively slow.

Samuel F. Rathbun writes that in Washington the western yellow-throat sings from the time of its arrival, during the last week of April, until nearly the end of July.

Like its eastern relatives, the western yellowthroat has a characteristic flight song which has been noted by various observers but I have seen no published accounts of the details of the performance.

Enemies.—The western yellowthroat is frequently parasitized by the cowbird, and several writers claim that it is one of the most frequent victims in their respective localities. The records range from Colorado to Utah, the latter probably referring to the sagebrush cowbird. In California this yellowthroat has been reported as being parasitized by the dwarf cowbird.

While the yellowthroat resides in a habitat where it would not be expected to be molested, nevertheless, according to various reports, it is often a victim of predatory birds. W. L. Finley (1907) relates an experience in which a Cooper's hawk attempted to strike the birds he was observing.

Migration.—The dates of migration of the western yellowthroat seems to vary greatly in different parts of the west, depending on the altitude, climate, and temperature of the regions traversed. W. W. Cooke (1904) states: "The birds arrive at just about the same time— second week in May—on the plains of north-central Colorado and at Great Falls and Columbia Falls, Mont., the latter place almost 600 miles farther north, but enjoying at this period of the year an equal degree of warmth with the Colorado plains. But almost a month earlier than this, southern British Columbia is reached by the yellow-throats that wintered in the warm valleys of California lying as far north as the plains of north-central Colorado which during the winter season can support no warbler life."

It is difficult to follow the migration of the western yellowthroat, as it passes through regions where it is resident and where other sub-species are also resident. In Arizona it is a common migrant in April and May (throughout May at Shiprock, N. Mex.) and has been reported at Rinconada May 5, 1904. It has been recorded as late as May 10 at Ortez, Sonora, Mexico. Spring dates in California are: Colorado River Valley and San Clemente Island, March 23; Pasadena, March 25; Berkeley, May 21; and Yosemite Valley, May 25. The western yellowthroat arrives in Oregon during April, the earliest date for Jackson County is March 22 and the earliest date for Lake County is April 9. In Washington it reaches Seattle April 17–21; Hoquiam, April 27; Ocosta, April 30; Tacoma, April 6–12; and Yakima County, March 29.

Migration in the autumn begins in August and continues through October. There are numerous winter records of the western yellowthroat in California, so that fall as well as spring records mean little in following migration. It has been recorded at San Bernardino Ranch, Sonora, Mexico, August 26 to September 8, 1892; and at San Pedro River, October 7 to 15, 1892.

GEOTHLYPIS TRICHAS CAMPICOLA Behle and Aldrich

NORTHERN PLAINS YELLOWTHROAT

CONTRIBUTED BY JAMES LEE PETERS

HABITS

The breeding yellowthroat of the northern Rocky Mountains and northern Great Plains region was named by Behle and Aldrich (1947) who characterized the race as follows:

Similar to *Geothlypis trichas occidentalis* of the Great Basin, but upper parts grayer, less yellowish olive green; yellow of underparts less extensive posteriorly; belly and flanks grayer, averaging more whitish, less buffy. Similar to *G. t. arizela* of the humid coast belt west of the Cascade Range, but also grayer on upper parts; white frontal stripe broader; yellow of under parts slightly paler and less extensive; posterior underparts whiter, less buffy. The range assigned to this race by its describers is as follows: "Breeds east of the Cascade Mountains in northern Oregon, Washington, and British Colombia, thence east through northern Idaho, Alberta, Saskatchewan, Montana, northern Wyoming to northern North Dakota. In migration occurs southward in Utah, Colorado, and Arizona. Winter range undetermined.

GEOTHLYPIS TRICHAS SINUOSA Grinnell

SALT-MARSH YELLOWTHROAT

CONTRIBUTED BY ALFRED OTTO GROSS

HABITS

The salt-marsh yellowthroat is known also as the San Francisco yellowthroat because of its restricted distribution chiefly in the region about that city. This form was described by Joseph Grinnell (1901) as follows: "Similar to *Geothlypis trichas occidentalis*, but dorsally and laterally darker in color, and size much less. Thirteen specimens (males) from the marshes of San Francisco Bay measure: Wing 51 mm. to 54.6 mm. averaging 53 mm.; tail 52.6 to 56.6 mm. averaging 55 mm."

Grinnell and Miller (1944) give an account of its status, range, and habitat as follows:

Status—Resident; but to some degree scatters or migrates from breeding range in San Francisco Bay region to appear, fairly commonly, as a winter visitant in southern California from late September to mid-March. Common through-out year on breeding grounds.

Geographic range—In breeding season vicinity of San Francisco Bay, Marin County, and Napa sloughs, southern Sonoma County, on the north, east to Carquinez Strait, and south to vicinity of San Jose, Santa Clara County. In winter, coastal marshes from San Francisco Bay region south to San Diego; also, twice recorded north to Humbolt Bay. Life-zones, Upper Sonoran and Transition; localities of nesting all below 1,000 feet elevation. * * *

Habitat—In summer, fresh and salt water marshes, but chiefly the former. More commonly found near salt and brackish water in fall and winter. Requires plant cover similar to that frequented by the race *Geothlypis trichas occidentalis* [the western yellow-throat]. * * * Tall grasses, tule patches and willow thickets provide normal plant environment for nesting activity.

Milton S. Ray (1916) found three nests of the salt-marsh yellow-throat in the Lake Merced region of San Francisco County on April 22, 1911. Two of the nests had four eggs each in advanced stages of incu-bation and one contained three fresh eggs. All three nests were about two feet up in wiregrass and were made of coarse flat weed stems lined with fine light-colored grasses, loosely put together. Mr. Ray states this yellowthroat does not inhabit the salt marshes exclusively but is much more abundant along fresh-water lakes and streams and in wet meadow land. However, one nest with 4 eggs was found in a salt marsh north of San Rafael on April 12, 1914. This nest was on high ground not subject to overflow. An excellent account of the nest-ing habits of the salt-marsh yellowthroat in the Lake Merced region has been written by G. W. Schussler (1918), as follows:

The nesting period ranges from middle April until June, fresh eggs having been taken on April 2 and June 18. The yellowthroats, habitually suspicious, become doubly vigilant during the breeding season and I think only twice in all the years I have studied them have I surprised the female in the act of carrying nesting material. It has been my experience that if any unfinished structure not containing eggs is located, the birds promptly abandon it. The nest, a cup-shaped, fairly compact receptacle is usually composed of lengths of dried grass well interwoven with the supporting stems. It is commonly hidden in bunches of wire grass or weeds among willows and placed from six to twenty-four inches above the ground. The bowl-like interior is often lined in rather a loose manner with dried grass or thin fiber. The usual complement is four though a set of three, particularly when laid late in the season, is not rare. The eggs are taperingly oval in shape, white, with a decided pink tinge when fresh, and circularly splotched about the larger end with dots and dashes of black, brown, and deep lavender, varying in size from minute markings on some specimens to a pronounced ring of color on others. Incubation, which is performed by the female, usually occupies about fourteen days.

While incubating, the females show remarkable shyness in slipping off the nest and keeping well ahead of the observer, with short undulating flight. Oc-casionally as evening approaches they are apt to flush from directly beneath one's feet, particularly should he beat quietly up toward them against the wind. When startled from her nest the female disappears and maintains silence for some moments but if the intruder remains in the vicinity, or removes the nest or eggs, her sharp *chack* of alarm will rapidly summon the male and the pair will flit nervously about in the underbrush, often fearlessly approaching within a few yards of the observer.

The young when hatched are naked, but gradually become sparsely covered with light down. Feeding, which is participated in by both parents, takes place at short intervals during the greater part of the day, until the young are ready to leave the nest. So far as I have been able to observe, the parent birds appear to entice the ambitious nestlings into the tule and willow thickets away from the open flats where they may have been hatched. This is probably in order to afford them the shelter of the branches and, by removing them some little distance from the ground, to protect them against small predatory mammals.

[AUTHOR'S NOTE: The measurements of 28 eggs average 17.1 by 13.2 millimeters; the eggs showing the four extremes measure **18.5** by 13.5, 18.2 by **13.8, 15.9** by 12.9, and 16.3 by 12.4 millimeters.]

Voice.—G. W. Schussler (1918) states that in the winter the salt-marsh yellowthroats are in the seclusion of the high tules standing in deep water. At this season the birds flit out of sight in advance of one's approach, uttering their solitary *chack* of protest and suspicion. With the approach of spring they leave the tules to make incursions into the shorter grasses and among the willows. At this period Mr. Schussler has heard them utter a short grating call resembling *k-r-r-r-r* in addition to their familiar *chack*. He writes of the song as follows:

It is usually not until some warm, sunny morning in late February that the clear ringing *wreech-ity wreech-ity, wreech-ity, wreech-ity* of the male is heard. The song varies considerably with the season and individual, those in early spring often sounding sadly out of tune, and some are even rendered in a condensed form of two syllables; but the power of it rises rapidly as the year advances until by the end of March its nuptial gladness pours forth in full-throated volume. Sometimes as evening approaches, one of the little black-faced birds will leap into the air with fluttering wings and expanded tail and as it slowly tumbles down into the grass again, will execute an exquisite series of melodious runs and trills not unlike the vocal accomplishments of the chat.

In September the summer songs of the males have ceased and a great diminution in their numbers is noticeable. By November, *sinuosa* has again largely retired to the tule jungle and with his added winter air of distrust is once more the shy flitting figure of the December marshlands.

GEOTHLYPIS TRICHAS CHRYSEOLA Van Rossem

GOLDEN YELLOWTHROAT

CONTRIBUTED BY ALFRED OTTO GROSS

HABITS

The golden yellowthroat was described from a breeding adult male, taken June 12, 1929 at Saric, north-central Sonora, Mexico, by A. J. Van Rossem (1930), who says of its subspecific characters: "Compared with *Geothlypis trichas scirpicola*, both sexes are brighter and more yellowish above, the yellow of the underparts is brighter and more extensive (the flanks of the males are only slightly, or not at all, tinged with grayish), and the post-frontal white band in the males is even wider and is noticeably suffused with yellow." Its range, he says, is "north-central Sonora, northeast to the San Pedro River in Cochise County, Arizona; east to northwestern Chihuahua and south, in spring at least, to Tecoripa, east-central Sonora."

Three of the four localities from which the Sonora yellowthroat is known indicate an upland habitat, and its range, when finally worked out, will probably be found to center in the northern part of the Mexican plateau.

Van Rossem (1945), speaking of Mexico, writes: "Evidently a fairly common resident in suitable localities along fresh water streams from the vicinity of Rancho La Arizona (and very probably from the Altar River valley) eastward across the northern part of the State nearly or quite to the Chihuahua boundary. The southernmost breeding station known at the present time is Pilares in the Bavispe River valley. * * * One specimen taken at Tecoripa, March 3, 1929, indicates a seasonal movement by part, at least, of the population."

Monson and Phillips (1941) state that *chryseola* is common at Feldon, Ariz., and that birds taken at Tucson and Bisbee are of this race. Burleigh and Lowery (1940) collected a male 10 miles east of Guadalupe Peak, Tex., at an elevation of 4,500 feet in an arroyo in the open desert on April 29, 1939. Sutton and Burleigh (1939) collected a male several miles north of Victoria, northeastern Mexico on February 25, 1938.

GEOTHLYPIS TRICHAS SCIRPICOLA Grinnell

TULE YELLOWTHROAT

Contributed by Alfred Otto Gross

HABITS

The tule yellowthroat was described by Grinnell (1901) as "similar to *Geothlypis trichas occidentalis*, but brighter colored and larger throughout with especially longer tail. Twenty-five males from the Pacific slope of Los Angeles County measure: Wing, 55 mm. to 60.3 mm. averaging 57 mm.; tail, 56 mm. to 64 mm. averaging 60 mm. *Scirpicola* is the brightest and deepest colored of all [the western yellowthroats], the yellow of the under parts being more extended posteriorly and having a hint of an orange tint, while the upper parts are brighter brown or green according to age and wear." A. J. Van Rossem (1930), in comparing the tule with the western yellowthroat, states that it has a brighter coloration and a slightly larger bill. "In *scirpicola* the dorsal plumage is greener (less grayish) ; the yellow of the underparts extends farther over the abdomen and is, in a series definitely brighter; the flanks are more brownish (less grayish) and the post-frontal band of white in the males is wider."

The range of the tule yellowthroat "extends along the Pacific slope from about 30° in Lower California north to Santa Barbara, California, the southern San Joaquin Valley and Walker Basin on the south fork of the Kern River. The Colorado River drainage colony which is (apparently) isolated from that on the Pacific extends from the mouth of the Colorado River north along that stream, and its tributary the Virgin River, to Washington, Washington County, Utah, west through the Imperial Valley to Mecca, Riverside County, and east up the Gila and Santa Cruz rivers at least to Tucson, Arizona." In California, according to Grinnell and Miller (1944), the altitudes of occurrence are chiefly below 1,500 feet, but birds may range up to 4,200 feet, as at Julian, San Diego County.

The measurements of 40 eggs average 17.3 by 13.3 millimeters; the eggs showing the four extremes measure 18.9 by 12.5, 18.0 by 14.0, and 16.0 by 12.5 millimeters.

The ecology and nesting habits of the tule and western yellowthroats are similar.

GEOTHLYPIS TRICHAS ARIZELA Oberholser

PACIFIC YELLOWTHROAT

HABITS

Some fifty years after it was originally described, the Pacific race was officially admitted to the A. O. U. Check-List as a recognizable form.

The original describer, Dr. Harry C. Oberholser (1899) gives a detailed description of the type, an adult spring male from Fort Steilacoom, Wash., and writes: "From *occidentalis* the present race may be readily distinguished by its much narrower white frontal band, and also by its appreciably smaller size; though the former character is of course not available for determination of females and young. It differs from *trichas* as does *occidentalis*, but in dimensions not to so marked a degree. Intermediates between *trichas* and *occidentalis* such as occur on the Great Plains, come sometimes rather close to *arizela*."

He gives for this form the following distribution: "Pacific coast region from southern British Columbia to northern Lower California; east to the Cascade Mountains and the west slope of the Sierra Nevada; south in winter to Cape St. Lucas and Tepic."

GEOTHLYPIS TRICHAS INSPERATA Van Tyne

BROWNSVILLE YELLOWTHROAT

CONTRIBUTED BY ALFRED OTTO GROSS

HABITS

The Brownsville yellowthroat was described by Josselyn Van Tyne (1933) from an adult male secured in the Rio Grande Delta below Brownsville, Tex., on June 11, 1930:

Subspecific characters.—Similar to *Geothlypis trichas trichas* (Linnaeus) but bill larger, forehead more whitish, and general coloration paler. Compared with *Geothlypis trichas occidentalis* Brewster it is smaller (wing of male 55–56 mm. instead of 55–60 mm.) but has a larger bill. The belly and flanks are more whitish, but the forehead is less extensively white. Compared with *Geothlypis trichas brachidactyla* (Swainson) it is paler and has a shorter wing but an even larger bill. The ninth primary of *insperata* is shorter than the fourth, instead of longer as in *brachidactyla*. Two juveniles of the new form, taken June 2 and 4, are much paler and have larger bills than any of a series of *brachidactyla* with which I have compared them.

Geothlypis trichas insperata has the ninth primary shorter than the fourth, as in *Geothlypic trichas ignota* Chapman, but is much paler and has a very much larger bill. The larger bill alone is sufficient to separate *insperata* from the Pacific coast forms.

The Brownsville yellowthroat is known only from the type locality. It leaves the region during the winter but its winter home is not at present known, nor is anything known of its nesting habits.

GEOTHLYPIS TRICHAS MODESTA Nelson

SAN BLAS YELLOWTHROAT

CONTRIBUTED BY ALFRED OTTO GROSS

HABITS

The San Blas yellowthroat was described by E. W. Nelson in 1900. The description of a male taken at San Blas, Tepic, Mexico, June 12, 1897, is as follows: "Smaller than typical *G*[*eothlypis*] *trichas* from the eastern United States, with the green of back darker, more brownish olive and brownish flanks; black frontlet and white border to same nearly as in *Geothlypis trichas occidentalis*. * * * The young as well as the adults are distinguishable by their dark color."

A. J. Van Rossem (1930) states: "In typical form *modesta* is a dark colored race. It is much like *Geothlypis trichas sinuosa* of the San Francisco Bay region, but is slightly grayer (less olive) and has a longer tail and decidedly larger bill." Were it not for the larger bill it would be difficult to distinguish these two races, although their ranges are separated by a gap of over a thousand miles.

The San Blas yellowthroat is resident in a narrow strip of Tropical Zone salt-water associations of western Mexico, from southern Sinaloa northward to Tepopa Bay, and is accidental in Baja California (Magdalena Bay and San José Island). Its typical habitat is the mangrove–salicornia association. Nothing is known concerning its habits and nesting.

GEOTHLYPIS BELDINGI BELDINGI Ridgway

BELDING'S PENINSULAR YELLOWTHROAT

HABITS

This large handsome yellowthroat was discovered in southern Baja California in 1882 by that famous naturalist Lyman Belding, and was named for him by Ridgway (1882). It is considerably larger and much more richly colored than the yellowthroats of the *G. trichas* group. Belding (1883) found it "common in the few suitable localities around San José, Miraflores, and cañons of the Miraflores and Santiago Peaks."

Walter E. Bryant (1890b) found it on the west coast "at lower Purisima cañon, and as far north as San Ignacio." He says that "the birds kept mainly within the bullrushes and bushes of the creek," at Comondú on the east coast.

William Brewster (1902) writes: "Mr. Frazar saw his first Belding's Yellowthroat on April 21 at Triunfo, in a small, deep arroyo where the stream had been dammed for irrigating purposes, making a little pool of water around which grew a quantity of canes and rank grasses, the whole covering an area of about forty yards square. Here were found three pairs, the females of which were apparently incubating, although no nests were discovered. The species was next met with at San José del Cabo, where it proved to be one of the most abundant birds. It was also very common about the lagoon at Santiago, frequenting rushes, often where the water was three or four feet deep."

Nesting.—Bryant (1890a) was the first to find and positively identify the nest of Belding's yellowthroat. He found, or had shown to him, five nests near Comondú in 1889. A nest found on March 25 is thus described:

"The nest was loosely woven in a clump of 'cat-tails' (*Typha*) one metre above running water. It is composed outwardly entirely of dry leaves of the 'cat-tail,' and thinly lined with fine fiber and a few horsehairs. It measures externally (as nearly as can be determined from its rough shape) not less than 150 mm. in height by about 115 mm. in diameter. The receptacle is about 55 mm. in depth, with a diameter at the top of 50 mm. The general appearance is almost

identical with some song sparrows' nests." Another nest, found on
March 27, was in a similar situation but was only half as high. And
a third was found on March 28, "in a heavy growth of 'cat-tails' near
the outer edge of the clump, and placed one and one-half metres high.
This nest, like the others, is composed of 'cat-tail' leaves, but is
lined almost exclusively with black horsehairs, so few being used that
they do not even hide the structural material." It should be noted
that the birds breeding near Comondú are somewhat intermediate
between the two races, but, as we have no nesting information from the
Cape region, it seems best to include these quotations here.

Eggs.—Two or three eggs seem to make up the set for Belding's
yellowthroat; 3 seems to be the commonest number. The 12 eggs in
the Thayer collection are ovate and slightly glossy. The ground color
is white or creamy white, which is rather sparingly speckled, spotted
or blotched with "light vinaceous-drab," "light mouse gray," "pale
brownish drab," or "Quaker drab," with fewer spots of "Hay's brown,"
"Dresden brown," or black. The markings are generally concentrated
at the large end, often leaving the small end immaculate. The wreath,
which may be made up of fine, dense specklings or spots, often has
over-writings of black which circle the egg. The measurements of
32 eggs of the species, some of which may be intermediate between the
two races, average 19.5 by 15.0 millimeters; the eggs showing the
four extremes measure **21.0** by **16.0, 18.0** by 14.5, and 20.1 by **14.0** millimeters (Harris).

Plumages.—Brewster's fine series probably illustrates all the regular plumages of this yellowthroat. He (1902) describes the juvenal
plumage from a specimen taken on September 5, just before the postjuvenal molt, as follows: "Above dull brownish drab, the wings
faintly, the tail distinctly, tinged with olive; greater and middle wing
coverts edged and tipped with rusty, forming obscure wing bands;
below pale brownish buff, deepest on the sides, abdomen, and upper
portion of the breast, unmixed with yellow save on the chin, where
there are a few bright yellow feathers, evidently those of the first
winter plumage; bend of wing slightly yellowish; under surface of
wing ashy white; lores with a faint yellowish tinge."

This and other specimens indicate that the postjuvenal molt of the
body plumage and the wing coverts occurs in late August and September. The male in first winter plumage differs from the adult "only
in having the feathers of the black mask slightly tipped with grayish
or yellowish, especially on the forehead; the yellow border of the
mask more restricted and mixed with brownish; the breast and under
tail coverts tinged with brownish saffron; the flanks and sides rich
purplish cinnamon." The female in first winter plumage differs from
the adult female in autumn "only in having the upper parts tinged

with reddish brown, the throat and breast with brownish saffron, the flanks and sides, as well as the anal region, with cinnamon."

The series indicates that the spring plumage is acquired mainly, if not wholly, by wear in both young and old birds; and there is probably a complete postnuptial molt in late summer. He describes the adult male in fall as "differing from the spring male in having the yellow of the crown paler and tinged with grayish white; the upper parts of a deeper, browner olive, tinged slightly on the occiput and nape with purplish brown; the yellow of the under parts richer with more decided brownish on the sides and flanks; the base of the lower mandible flesh colored; the remainder of the bill dark horn colored instead of black. The black mask is wholly unmixed with any lighter color." The adult female in autumn differs "from the spring female only in being slightly grayer above."

Voice.—Bryant (1890) writes: "I frequently heard them singing, sometimes in the top of a low tree. Their notes are rather loud and quite clear, an interval of a few seconds occurring between each song. The three songs which I heard sung by the same individual March 31, were noted on the spot. In different places of the song occurred a low, short buzz, represented by stars in the following. The first song occupied about five seconds.

1. *Sweet, sweet * * * ear * * * sweet, sweet ear * * * sweet, sweet ear.*
2. *Sweet, sweet ear * * * sweet, sweet ear.*
3. *Sweet, sweet ear * * * sweet, sweet ear * * *.*"

According to Brewster (1902), Frazar told him that "the song resembles that of the Maryland Yellow-throat, but is so much heavier and fuller that it can be easily recognized." Brewster says further that the bird occasionally mounts into the air and sings on the wing.

DISTRIBUTION

Range.—Resident in the southern half of Baja California.

Breeding range.—The peninsular yellowthroat is resident in Baja California from San Ignacio south to San José del Cabo. Two subspecies are recognized; Belding's peninsular yellowthroat (*G. b. beldingi*) is found only in the extreme southern part of the peninsula (Todos Santos, Triunfo, Santiago, Miraflores, and San José del Cabo); Goldman's peninsular yellowthroat (*G. b. goldmani*) occupies a range in central Baja California (San Ignacio, Santa Igueda, San Joaquin, Purissima, and Comondú).

Egg dates.—Baja California: 9 records, March 25 to May 17; 4 records, May 2 to 9.

Mexico: 6 records, April 9 to June 1; 3 records, May 4 to 18, indicating the height of the season (Harris).

GOLDMAN'S PENINSULAR YELLOWTHROAT

PLATE 70

HABITS

Dr. Harry C. Oberholser (1917) described the more northern race of *beldingi*, Goldman's peninsular yellowthroat, from the central portion of Baja California, as—

similar to *Geothlypis beldingi beldingi*, but male with the upper surface much duller, more brownish or grayish (less yellowish) throughout; crown behind the black mask largely or wholly grayish or whitish instead of yellow; yellow of under parts somewhat lighter and confined to throat and breast; lower abdomen white or whitish, instead of usually deep yellow, as in *Geothlypis beldingi*; sides and flanks paler and more grayish. Female similar to the female of *Geothlypis beldingi*, but upper parts and sides of head paler, more grayish (less yellowish); yellow of lower parts paler and less extensive, confined to throat and upper breast, the abdomen being dull whitish, slightly or not at all washed with yellow; sides and flanks paler, more grayish.

He gives its distribution as "central Lower California, from San Ignacio to Comondú." But he remarks: "Birds from San Ignacio, which represents the northern limit of its range, are, as would be expected, most extreme in their characters. Two males and two females from Comondú, some distance south of San Ignacio, are intermediate between *Geothlypis beldingi goldmani* and *Geothlypis beldingi beldingi*, the females being more like the latter than are the males, which are but slightly different from *Geothlypis beldingi goldmani*. As a whole the Comondú birds are certainly referable to the northern race."

From the more northern portion of its breeding range, Griffing Bancroft (1930) reports that Goldmans yellowthroat is—

resident in Santa Agueda, San Ignacio, and San Joaquim, the only localities where there is tule. These birds do not appear to care for willow associations. They are fairly common, especially in San Ignacio, where they nest in the heart of the heaviest tule patches. Their nests are strips of dead tule leaves, well woven and tied around several living stalks. The linings show individual variations but are usually of palm fibre. The nests are decidedly larger than those of more northerly birds. * * *

The eggs of *goldmani* are a dull white, heavily spotted about the larger end, but otherwise almost immaculate. The decorative scheme is complicated. There are blotches, up to a millimeter in diameter, and a few hair lines which are jet black. A majority of the spots, many three millimeters long, are so weakly pigmented that they are gray and even have a suggestion of a lavender cast. Mixed throughout are specks of either color.

He gives the measurements of 13 eggs as averaging 18.7 by 14.5 millimeters. The measurements of 8 other eggs, apparently of this race, average 19.0 by 14.5 millimeters; the eggs showing the four extremes measure **19.7** by 14.5, 19.3 by **14.8,** and **17.8** by **14.0** millimeters (Harris).

CHAMAETHLYPIS POLIOCEPHALA POLIOCEPHALA (Baird)

RIO GRANDE GROUND-CHAT

HABITS

When Baird (1865) described and named the Rio Grande ground-chat he placed it in the genus *Geothlypis* and gave it full specific rank. Since then allied races have been named in Mexico and Central America. The subject of this sketch belongs to the northern race, found in northern and central Mexico, and is known to extend its range across our border only in the valley of the lower Rio Grande and the vicinity of Brownsville, Tex., where it seems to be rare.

This genus seems to be intermediate between *Geothlypis* and *Icteria*. Ridgway (1902) calls it "Ralph's ground-chat," and characterizes it as "similar in general appearance to *Geothlypis*, but tail longer than wing, graduated; bill very stout, with culmen strongly curved (much as in *Icteria*) ; tarsus nearly half as long as wing, or at least much nearer one-half than one-third as long; no black on forehead nor auriculars in adult males; sexes alike, or at least not very different in color." From *Icteria* it "differs in its shorter and more rounded wing, more graduated tail with pointed rectrices, longer tarsi, and stouter feet."

Nesting.—Very little seems to be known about the nesting habits of the Rio Grande ground-chat. A nest and four eggs are in the Thayer collection in Cambridge, collected by Gerald Thomas at Paisano, Tex., on May 1, 1902. The nest was in a clump of coarse grass near a road. The exterior was formed of dry grass and the interior with finer grass, with an inner lining of horsehair. Externally it measures 3¼ inches high by 3¾ in diameter; the inner cup is 2¼ inches deep and 1⅞ wide.

Eggs.—The four eggs are ovate and slightly glossy. They are creamy white, rather sparingly speckled, spotted and blotched with "auburn," "bay," "chestnut," and "raw umber," and with undermarkings of "pale brownish drab" and "light brownish drab." Some of them have small scrawls of very dark brown, almost black. The markings are somewhat concentrated at the large end, but none of the eggs could be termed heavily marked. The measurements of 16 eggs average 17.5 by 13.8 millimeters; the eggs showing the four extremes measure **18.5** by 13.7, 18.0 by **14.5, 16.9** by 13.2, and 17.8 by **12.7** millimeters (Harris).

Plumages.—The sexes are nearly alike in all plumages. The nestling plumage has apparently never been described. Ridgway (1902) describes the immature plumage as "similar in general to the adult plumage, but duller, the pileum concolor with back, or nearly so, and lores dull brownish gray or dusky, not distinctly different from color of pileum." The adults in fall and winter are "similar to the spring and summer plumage, but plumage softer, more blended; back, etc., more buffy olive or light olive-brown; feathers of pileum (at least the occiput) tipped with brown, and flanks more decidedly buffy."

Chapman (1907) says of the adult spring plumage: "Crown slaty with a slight olive wash, lores black, this color extending below the eye; a white mark on eye-ring above and below the eye; back, wings and tail olive-green without white markings, bend of wing yellow; throat and breast bright yellow becoming paler on the belly and brownish on the flanks."

In the adult female the black on the lores, so prominent in the male, is much restricted or nearly or quite lacking.

Dr. Wetmore (1943) writes of this species in southern Veracruz:

This is a resident species, common in the Tres Zapotes region wherever bushes are scattered through the grasslands. They kept under cover ordinarily, flying out occasionally as I passed, or were seen as they sang from the tops of bushes or tall grass stems. The song is a low, rather inconsequential warble of several notes. I had a better view of them at times in crossing these savannas on mule back, as then from the elevation of the saddle I could see about more, and the birds were less wary. They tend always to be inconspicuous and to slip aside. They suggested the yellowthroats of the north in most of their habits. * * *

On comparison of material in the U. S. National Museum it is evident that specimens from near Brownsville, Tex., in the lower Rio Grande Valley, differ from typical *poliocephala* in significantly paler color, with less yellow on the lower surface. They are to be separated therefore as *Chamaethlypis poliocephala ralphi* (Ridgway) in spite of the fact that Ridgway in his last account of the species placed the Texas birds under typical *poliocephala*. With a good series of skins the differences are clearly evident.

In his earlier description of *ralphi*, Ridgway (1894) calls it similar to "*G. poliocephala* Baird, but larger (the bill especially), upper parts grayer (the tail particularly), and the edge of the wing and under tail coverts much paler yellow."

DISTRIBUTION

Range.—Resident from southern Texas south through Mexico and central Mexico to Panamá. One race, the Rio Grande ground-chat (*C. p. poliocephala*), is found from southernmost Texas (Harlingen, Lomita, and Brownsville) south to Michoacán (Querendero) Morelos (Cuernavaca) and southern Tamaulipas (Aldama).

Egg dates.—Texas: 2 records, April 3 and May 1.

ICTERIA VIRENS VIRENS (Linnaeus)

EASTERN YELLOW-BREASTED CHAT

PLATES 71, 72

HABITS

This curious bird seems somewhat out of place among the wood warblers, on account of its large size, different proportions, and strikingly different behavior. There were confused ideas among the earlier writers as to where it belongs. Audubon classed it with the manakins, and others have placed it with the vireos or with the honeycreepers, but structurally it seems to be most closely related to the wood warblers, with its nine primaries, partly booted tarsus, and deeply cleft inner toe. It differs from the vireos, which also have nine primaries, in having no notch in the bill. But it also differs from the wood warblers in having a larger, heavier and more curved bill, shorter and more rounded wings, and relatively longer and more graduated tail.

During the breeding season the species *Icteria virens* occupies practically all the United States, except Florida, the Gulf coast, and northern New England. Its range extends into southern New England, where it is rare and irregular north and east of Connecticut, and into some southern portions of central Canada, where it is also irregular in its occurrence. Throughout all this range it is perhaps commoner than we suppose, on account of its secretive habits. Its favorite resorts are the very dense thickets and briery tangles that grow in profusion on low, damp ground, along small streams, or about the borders of ponds or swamps. But it also finds a congenial home in isolated patches of thick, tangled shrubbery on high, dry ground, in old, neglected pastures and along the edges of woodlands. Especially attractive are such upland thickets where small trees and bushes are entwined with an almost impenetrable tangle of catbrier, Virginia creeper, poison ivy, and wild grape vines. In such unattractive places for exploration, the bird is often overlooked by the casual observer, for it is a past master in the art of keeping out of sight. But a medley of strange sounds, musical and otherwise, catcalls, whistles, and various bird notes coming from points now here, now there in the bushes will betray the presence of this furtive and elusive clown among birds. Then, if we sit down quietly and squeak in imitation of a wounded bird, curiosity will prompt this versatile performer to show himself for a moment, after which he will disappear, to scold us from some remote corner of his retreat.

Courtship.—Chats are not much in evidence on their spring migration; they apparently do not often make long sustained flights in the open, but move along by short stages, keeping concealed for the most part in the dense thickets of shrubbery and vines, and are largely silent. But when they reach their chosen breeding grounds, the males proclaim their presence and advertise their home territory by the medley of whistling, chuckling, barking, and mewing sounds, coupled with the curious eccentricities that have made them famous.

When the females arrive, about a week later, the males greet them with a richer, more musical, and more pleasing performance, which P. A. Taverner (1906) describes very well, as follows:

His love-song is a woodland idyl and makes up for much of his shortcomings. From some elevated perch from which he can survey the surrounding waste for a considerable distance, he flings himself into the air—straight up he goes on fluttering wings—legs dangling, head raised, his whole being tense and spasmodic with ecstasy. As he rises he pours fourth a flood of musical gurgles, and whistles that drop from him in silvery cascades to the ground, like sounds of fairy chimes. As he reaches the apex of his flight his wings redouble their beatings, working straight up and down, while the legs hanging limply down remind the observer of those drawings we sometimes see from the brushes of Japanese artists. He holds his hovering position for an instant, then the music gradually dies away; and, as he sinks toward the ground, he regains his natural poise, and seeks another perch like that from which he started. What mistress could turn a deaf ear to such love-making as that? And we can rest assured that his does not.

Nesting.—Although the eastern yellow-breasted chat has nested a number of times, rather irregularly, in Massachusetts, I have never found it farther north and east than Connecticut, where it is a regular and common breeder.

I find three typical nests recorded in my notes, found near New Haven, Conn., on June 3 and 4, 1910. The first was 3 feet from the ground in a clump of dogwood and hawthorn bushes; and the second was in a thicket of small black birches overgrown with catbriers, 30 inches above ground; both of these nests were rather insecurely attached to their supports; the locality was a large neglected tract of cut-over land, grown up to scattered clumps of bushes and sprouting stumps. The third nest was only 2 feet up in a small huckleberry bush in a scrubby field, full of underbrush and scattered red cedars. The three nests were all much alike, consisting of a foundation of dead leaves, coarse straws, and weed stems, on which was built a firmly woven inner nest of grapevine bark, thinly lined with fine weed stems and grasses.

A. Dawes Du Bois has sent me his notes on two nests found in Sangamon County, Ill., on May 30, 1908. The first of these was "two feet from the ground in a clump of blackberry briers, in a pasture thicket. It was constructed outwardly of small vine and weed stems, then a thick layer of dried oak leaves which formed the body of the nest. There was a slight lining of grasses and fine plant stems, inside the layer of leaves. A few shreds of coarse grass were added just before the layer of leaves was put in. There were 32 oak leaves and one elm leaf in the body of the nest, all smoothly laid in place. The dimensions were: Internal diameter 3 inches, depth 2; external diameter 5 inches, depth 3." The second nest was "3 feet from the ground in a wild gooseberry bush intergrown with blackberry briers, amid dense foilage, in a thicket-grown pasture." He mentions seven other nests, seen in Tompkins County, N. Y.; most were from 2½ to 5 feet up in various bushes, but one was "about 8 feet from the ground, loosely supported on a drooping young elm tree in a dense thicket."

T. E. McMullen's notes record data on 34 New Jersey and Pennsylvania nests found at heights from 18 inches to 5 feet; 21 of these were in blackberries, the others being in various bushes and vines; 3 were in hollies.

Nests of the yellow-breasted chat have doubtless been found in many other small trees and bushes, but the notes I have cited give a good idea of its usual nesting habits. Dr. Chapman (1907) says that he has known chats to nest in a village when favorable cover was available. A most unusual nesting site is recorded by Charles F. Batchelder (1881); a pair of chats began building a nest in a wren box on a piazza; a violent windstorm blew down the box, which was replaced, but the chats did not return.

Eggs.—The number of eggs laid by the yellow-breasted chat varies from 3 to 5 to a set, commonly 5, but as many as 6 have been recorded. The eggs are ovate and rather glossy. The white, or creamy white, ground color is speckled and spotted with "bay," "chestnut," "auburn," "argus brown," or "chestnut-brown," with underspottings of "brownish drab," "light vinaceous-drab," or "pale brownish drab." The markings, usually sharply defined, are generally scattered over the entire egg with some concentration at the large end. Often the brown and the drab markings are equally intermingled, and then again the drab spots may be entirely lacking. Some of the more attractive eggs are marked with blotches, often of two or three shades of brown mixed with the drabs. The measurements of 50 eggs average 21.9 by 16.9 millimeters; the eggs showing the four extremes measure 25.4 by 17.3, 22.1 by 18.3, 18.3 by 17.3, and 22.1 by 15.8 millimeters (Harris).

Young.—F. L. Burns (1915b and 1921) recorded the incubation period as 15 days, which is probably unusual, for George A. Petrides (1938) determined it to be 11 days "from the appearance of the full clutch." Burns gives 11 days for the young to remain in the nest, but Petrides says that they spent 8 days in the nest before leaving. The latter continues:

The young were born naked. Brooding of both eggs and young was accomplished by the female alone during the period of observation, although both sexes evidently feed the young. * * *

The food of the young consisted almost entirely of soft-bodied orthoptera and larval lepidoptera. The only insect definitely identified was the large green mantis (*Paratenodera sinensis*), two half-grown specimens of which were fed the four-day old young. An unknown species of brown, almost hairless caterpillar was the greatest capture in numbers. A small green long-horned locust and a small brownish grasshopper also were fed the youngsters.

Four-day old young were fed only six times in five hours by the female, although the male attempted unsuccessfully to feed them several times. Copeland (1909), however, records a feeding time average of once every thirty-four minutes for the four-day old young over a thirteen-hour period.

The nest was kept very clean and the female, after feeding the young, would look carefully about the nest and if any excretory capsules were present she would pick them up in her bill and eat them. On one occasion, after swallowing the excretory sacs of two of the young she pulled a third capsule from the anus of the third and flew off with it.

Plumages.—The yellow-breasted chat seems to be the only wood warbler that develops no natal down, and the only one that has a complete postjuvenal molt, characteristics that suggest a wrong classification!

Dr. Dwight (1900) describes the juvenal plumage as "above, grayish olive-brown. Wings and tail olive-brown, edged with dull brownish olive-green. Below, ashy gray washed with olive-gray across the jugulum and on the sides. Auriculars grayish and lores dusky with a trace of white above the eye. * * * This plumage has been figured in colors (*Auk*, XVI, 1899, pp. 217–220, pl. III)."

The first winter plumage is "acquired by a complete postjuvenal moult after the middle of July. Two specimens examined show a complete moult in progress and the color and shape of rectrices in the limited material at my disposal points to this unusual moult, for this is the only Warbler known to me that renews wings and tail at this time."

He describes the first winter plumage of the male as "above, brownish olive-green, the wings and tail darker than in juvenal plumage and with greener edgings. Below, bright lemon-yellow, somewhat veiled with olive-gray, the abdomen and crissum dull white, the sides washed with olive-brown. Lores, suborbital region and postocular stripe dull black, veiled with ashy feather tips. Superciliary, suborbital and malar stripes white. Young and old become practically indistinguishable although young birds are rather duller."

The first and subsequent nuptial plumages are assumed by wear and slight fading of the browns and greens. Adults have a complete postnuptial molt in July, producing the adult winter plumage, which differs but little from that of the first winter, the black areas about the head averaging blacker.

Females have the same molts and similar plumages, the colors being only lighter or duller.

Food.—Probably all of the items mentioned above in the food of the young are also eaten by adult chats. A. H. Howell (1932) writes: "The Chat feeds largely on insects, including beetles, bugs, ants, weevils, bees, wasps, May flies, and various caterpillars, such as tent caterpillars and currant worms. It is said to be fond of wild strawberries and takes considerable other wild fruit, such as blackberries, raspberries, whortleberries, elderberries, and wild grapes. The stomachs of 7 specimens taken on Amelia Island in May and June contained insects and fruit pulp in about equal proportions, with a few spiders and small crustaceans. The insects included moths and their larvae, beetles, bugs, ants, wasps, and grasshoppers. The fruit consisted of blueberries and blackberries." Elsewhere (1907) he lists the chat among the birds that eat the cotton-boll weevil.

Behavior.—Next to its astonishing vocal performances, the eccentric, ludicrous, almost clownish, behavior is one of the chat's most outstanding characteristics. Although a bit fanciful and imaginary, Dr. J. M. Wheaton's (1882) account is a good character study of this buffoon of the brier patch.

If he discovers the approach of a human being, even at a considerable distance, he prepares to resent the intrusion; and giving three short, loud whistles, very low in tone, as a warning, he advances toward him, all the while careful that he should be heard and not seen. Then follows a medley of sputtering, cackling, whispering and scolding notes, frequently interspersed with loud whistles, and continued as the bird runs, hops, or flies in the densest thicket, with a pertinacity that knows no fatigue. He tells you that your gun won't shoot, that it is a flint-lock, that your ramrod is broken, that you shot it at a buzzard, that you haven't got a gun; that you are a bald-headed cripple; that there is a horrid suicide in the bushes, and a big snake and a nasty skunk; that your baby is crying, your house is afire and the bridge broken down; that you have missed the road to the reform farm, and that the poor house is over the creek, and he calls the dogs; says that you have gone to seed; go west and grow up with the country; that you are taking up too much of his valuable time, and that you must excuse him for a moment.

During all this time he remains invisible, or at most, his black eye and mask, or golden breast, appear for a moment as he peers at you from the tangled branches of the brambles, or flashes from branch to branch, dancing an accompaniment to his fantastic notes. And at last, he suddenly appears on the top of a bush not ten feet from you, makes a profound bow, and with a derisive whisk of his long tail, exposes his immaculate white crissum and dives again into the deepest thicket. You take a long breath and wipe your face, and he returns to the assault from the rear. Should you move on, he follows, and if you approach, he retires, and, keeping at a respectful distance, he laughs defiance, shouts mockery and tantalizing sarcasm. He is a fearful scold, and it is no wonder the inside of his mouth is black.

And Taverner (1906) gives the following character sketch:

With his stealthy elusiveness, wild outpourings of song and fund of vituperation, the Chat is a droll imp. * * * He is full of life and boiling over with animation. It bubbles out of his throat in all manner of indescribable sounds.

He laughs dryly, gurgles derisively, whistles triumphantly, chatters provokingly, and chuckles complacently, all in one breath. He throws himself about through the bush regardless of consequences, never still, scrutinizing the intruder in all attitudes. Viewing him now from under a branch, and then from over it, talking always exictedly, rather incoherently and usually indelicately. In fact, one throat is not sufficient to relieve the pressure of his feelings, and he presses into service his long tail, and with it wig-wags things such as even he, irresponsible little sprite that he is, dare not say out loud.

The chat has a well-deserved reputation for shyness and elusiveness. When the nest is approached, the incubating female will usually slip off it and away without being observed; and she has been said to desert her eggs, or even her young, on slight provocation. But this is not always the case, as is shown by the many excellent photographs that have been taken of the bird at its nest. A. D. Du Bois tells me that on three out of nine of the nests examined by him, the sitting bird was quite tame, allowing him to approach quite closely and, in one case, almost to touch her. Gradual and careful approach to the nest gave Petrides (1938) an opportunity to take some fine pictures and to study the home life of the chat. "The blind, a green umbrella tent six and one-half feet high, was first erected some eighteen feet from the nest and moved forward about four feet every other day until, when the eggs were hatched, the tent was only two and one-half feet from the nest. On each visit several leaves were plucked from before the nest until it was well exposed."

His second nest "was approached noisily through the underbrush on six different occasions and the contents lifted out and handled," but the birds did not desert it.

Voice.—To the comments already made on the chat's vocal performances must be added the more serious contribution of Aretas A. Saunders, who says: "The song of the yellow-breasted chat is not only entirely unlike that of any other warbler, but unlike that of any other bird with which I am acquainted. It is long-continued, and consists of a variety of notes and phrases delivered in an irregular, mixed order, with pauses between them. The phrases vary greatly in quality, consisting of whistles, harsh cackles, squawks, squeals, and various explosive noises, not always easy to describe. Some of these are single short notes, short series of notes, or long series, often retarded in time.

"The pitches of these various sounds range from B′ to A‴, almost two octaves. Songs of individual birds range from three and a half tones to seven and a half, averaging about an octave. The songs are sometimes fairly rapid, and at other times slow. I have one song recorded as 7 phrases in 9 seconds, and another where the average pause between phrases was 6 seconds.

"I have records from 20 different birds, but only those of 11 are believed to be complete, that is, all the phrases commonly used are recorded. These 11 birds each had from 6 to 10 phrases in their song, averaging about 7. Only one bird had 10 phrases; of these 5 were single notes, 3 being whistles, 1 harsh, and 1 like a note on an organ; 2 other phrases were of several notes repeated in even time, one whistled, the other very harsh; the other 3 were long series of notes, retarded at the end, two of them whistled but on different pitches, the other like a long rattle. I recorded the singing of this bird, and the order of phrases, as it sang 48 phrases. There was great variety in the arrangement. One phrase was used 11 times, another 10, while 2 other phrases were sung only once, and the others from 2 to 8 times each.

"Not only is the song unusual, but also the manner of singing, for the bird frequently flies from one bush to another while singing, flapping its wings up and down and pumping its tail, with its legs dangling, the line of flight being exceedingly jerky.

"This bird is reported to imitate other birds. I have never heard any thing I believed was an actual imitation, but there are often sounds that suggest the sounds of other birds. I recorded one such as 'like the *chuck* of a robin,' and another as 'like a note of the yellow-throated vireo,' but I did not consider them to be imitations.

"The chat sings from the time of its arrival in spring until about the third week in July, but I have too few observations to give average dates of cessation."

The yellow-breasted chat, according to Albert R. Brand (1938), has the lowest-pitched voice of any of the warbler family, its highest note being but little above the average frequency of all passerine song; he recorded the highest note as having a frequency of 4,400 vibrations per second, the lowest 1,275 (the lowest of all but the starling and the catbird), and the approximate mean 2,600 vibrations per second (lower than all but three or four others).

Several observers have classed the chat as a mimic, and it certainly gives that impression, but its own vocabulary is so extensive and varied that perhaps it is only an impression; it does not need to learn much from others.

It is a most versatile vocalist and a most persistent singer at times; its voice may be heard at any hour of the day or night, especially on moonlit nights. To try to express its varied notes in syllables is almost hopeless. Mr. Forbush (1929) suggests the following: "*C-r-r-r-r-r, whrr, that's it, chee, quack, cluck, yit-yit-yit, now hit it, tr-r-r-r, when, caw,caw, cut,cut, tea-boy, who, who, mew, mew,* and so on till you are tired of listening." Dr. Witmer Stone (1937) heard one give a rapid call like that of a kingfisher. "One singing from inside a wild cherry bush had a trill like that of a tree toad, a *pheu, pheu,* call like a Greater Yellow-legs, and a strange note resembling a dis tant automobile horn. One of the other birds sat on the top of a dead bush in full view, all hunched up as if its back were broken and with tail hanging straight down. Every now and then it would stretch up its neck, which appeared very thick and out of proportion, with feathers all ruffled up on end, and utter a triple note *hoo-hoo-hoo*."

The chat usually sings within the dense thickets in which it hides, or perhaps from the top of some small tree or bush only a few feet above the thicket, but Clarence F. Stone mentions in his notes, sent to me by Verdi Burtch, one that he heard and saw singing in the top of a large tree, 45 feet above the ground.

Dr. Daniel S. Gage tells me that he heard a chat give a number of times "a note which we could liken only to the sweet tone of a silver bell."

Field marks.—Its large size, heavy bill, and long tail will distinguish the eastern yellow-breasted chat from any of the other wood warblers, also from the yellow-throated vireo, which it suggests in color pattern, though the chat has no white wing bars. The olive-green upper parts, with no white in wings or tail, the white stripe over the eye, the bright yellow throat and breast, and the pure white abdomen are all diagnostic. Its behavior and, above all, its vocal performances are unlike those of any other bird; as it is more often heard than seen, it is most easily recognized by its noisy voice.

Enemies.—The yellow-breasted chat is a common victim of the cowbird, but it will often desert its nest after the alien egg is deposited. Dr. Friedmann (1929) gives about one hundred records of such parasitism, and mentions only three cases of tolerance, though doubtless there have been many other cases where chats have accepted the eggs, which are about the same size as its own, and have raised the young. He says: "Apparently there is considerable variation in the sensitiveness of Chats around their nests, but the bulk of the evidence goes to show that normally a Cowbird's egg has little chance of ever being hatched by a Yellow-breasted Chat."

Winter.—Dr. Skutch contributes the following account: "During the winter, the yellow-breasted chat spreads over Central America, including both coasts and the lower parts of the highlands, as far as southern Costa Rica. In this country it is rare and I have never seen it; but I knew it as a rather abundant winter resident in the Caribbean lowlands of Honduras, and on both sides of Guatemala. Here I found it on the coffee plantations of the Pacific slope, up to about 3,500 feet above sea-level, in January; and while I have no midwinter record for higher altitudes, on the shore of Lake Atitlán, at 4,900 feet, during the last week of October, I saw two—a number which, considering the retiring habits of the bird, indicates fair abundance.

"The chats arrive in northern Central America toward the end of September. On October 1, 1930, they suddenly became exceedingly numerous in the narrow valley of the Tela River in northern Honduras. As I passed from a dense second-growth thicket to the comparatively open vegetation of the flood-plain of the river, I was greeted by a chorus of chucks and cackles, which reminded me strongly of the sound of a distant flock of purple grackles or red-winged blackbirds; the voices were by no means so loud as those of the blackbirds when chattering close at hand, yet in aggregate they created much the same impression. A numerous party of garrulous yellow-breasted chats had spread out among the trees and vine-tangles of the stony plain. Although they so loquaciously proclaimed their presence, the birds were yet so wary, lurking among the densest tangles, that they were by no means easy to glimpse; but during the course of an hour I saw a number, and watched them forage among the Cecropia and other trees. Among their varied utterances were harsh *clucks*, as a man makes by clacking his tongue far back in his mouth, to urge a laggard horse, and nasal notes like those of the catbird. How unexpected to come upon a warbler with a voice like a grackle! Soon the chats were well distributed over the valley; and their calls sounded from every side all through the day.

"While migrating, yellow-breasted chats may at times appear in the most surprising situations. On October 5, 1934, I found one among the open shrubbery of the central plaza of the town of Retalhuleu, on the Pacific coast of Guatemala. Without much doubt, this bird used the little park only as a temporary place of rest, and soon moved on to a more sequestered spot.

"When well settled in their winter home, the chats gradually grow less loquacious. The flocks in which they apparently arrive soon disperse; and they live in solitude through the winter months. Avoiding the forest, they hunt through the most tangled thickets, where their presence would scarcely be suspected but for their harsh notes occasionally voiced. They are at all times so secretive that to glimpse one is a feat—or an accident. They linger deep in their vine-smothered thickets until about the middle of April, then return northward.

"Early dates of fall arrival in Central America are: Guatemala—passim (Griscom), September 24; Colomba, September 29, 1934. Honduras—Tela, October 1, 1930.

"Late dates of spring departure from Central America are: Costa Rica—El Pozo de Térraba (Underwood), April 9, 1906. Guatemala—passim (Griscom), April 7; Motagua Valley, near Los Amates, April 17, 1932."

DISTRIBUTION

Range.—Southern Canada, the United States, Mexico, and Central America.

Breeding range.—The yellow-breasted chat breeds **north** to southern British Columbia (Sumas, probably Penticton, Vancouver, and Kamloops); central southern Alberta (Milk River Valley); southern Saskatchewan (Cypress Lake and East End, probably Tregarva); northwest and central northern North Dakota (Minot, Charlson, and Rice Lake); southern Minnesota (Hendricks and Wilder); southern Ontario (Harrow, Port Burwell, probably Coldstream, Hamilton, and Oshawa); central New York (Rochester, Geneva, Holland Patent, and Schenectady; probably Granville); southern Vermont (Bennington); and southern New Hampshire (South Hooksett). **East** to southern New Hampshire (South Hooksett) and south along the Atlantic coast to northern Florida (Tallahassee); rare breeder on Coastal Plains. **South** to northern Florida (Tallahassee, Amelia Island, and Pensacola); Texas (Fort Worth, Houston, Kerrville, Hidalgo, and Brazos County); southern Tamaulipas (probably Tampico); Mexico (Mexico City); Jalisco (Ocotlán and Lagos); southern Sonora (Lower Río Yaqui and Quiriego); and south-central Baja California (Comondú). **West** to Baja California (Comondú) and the Pacific coast (except Oregon and Washington west of the coastal ranges) to southern British Columbia (Vancouver).

Winter range.—The yellow-breasted chat winters **north** to southern Baja California (Cabo San Lucas); southern Sinaloa (Esquinapa); and southern Texas (Laredo). **East** to southern Texas (Laredo); central Tamaulipas (Arroyo de la Presa); Veracruz (Motzorongo and Tres Zapotes); Tabasco (Frontera); Yucatán (Mérida, and Chichén-Itzá); Quintana Roo (Xcopén, Chunyaxché, and Cozumel Island); Honduras (Ceiba and Yaruca); Nicaragua (Greytown); Costa Rica (San José); and western Panamá (Almirante). **South** to western Panamá (Almirante); El Salvador (Puerto el Triunfo and Lake Olomega); Guatemala (Volcán de Fuego, Cobán, and Choctum); Oaxaca (Llano Grande and Tehuantepec City); and Colima (Colima and Manzanillo). **West** to Colima (Manzanillo); southern Sinaloa (Esquinapa); and southern Baja California (Cabo San Lucas).

Chats have been recorded casually north to southern Manitoba (Brandon); northeastern North Dakota (Fort Union); central Minnesota (Brainerd and Saint Cloud); southwestern Maine (North Bridgton, Eliot, and Portland); and south on peninsular Florida (Dunedin, Fort Myers, and Key Largo). They are accidental in New Brunswick (Saint Andrews and Grand Manan); rare in southwestern British Columbia (Comox and Courtenay); and north to southwestern California (San Diego).

The range as above outlined is for the entire species, which has been separated into two geographic races. The eastern yellow-breasted chat (*Icteria virens virens*) breeds west to South Dakota, Nebraska, Kansas, and eastern Texas, wintering from eastern Mexico south through Central America to western Panamá; the western yellow-breasted chat (*Icteria virens auricollis*) occupies the western part of the range to the Pacific coast, wintering in western Mexico and Central Guatemela.

Migration.—Late dates of spring departure are: Costa Rica—Pozo del Rio Grande, April 9. El Salvador—Lake Olomega, April 12. British Honduras—Mountain Cow, April 7. Guatemala—near Quirigua, April 17. Texas—Cove, May 12; Dallas, May 13.

Early dates of spring arrival are: Florida—Titusville, April 19; Pensacola, April 17. Alabama—Greensboro, April 8; Birmingham, April 14 (average of 10 years, April 19). Georgia—Round Oak, April 9. South Carolina—Summerville, April 9. North Carolina—Charlotte, April 14; Raleigh, April 17 (average of 29 years, April 25). Virginia—Cape Henry, April 16; Rockbridge County, April 22. West Virginia—Wheeling area, April 23; French Creek, April 26 (average of 17 years, April 30). District of Columbia—Washington, April 16 (average of 52 years, April 30). Maryland—Chevy Chase, April 14. Delaware—Kent and Sussex Counties, March 29 (average of 18 years, April 10). Pennsylvania—Mercer County, April 21; Renovo, April 24 (average of 25 years, May 7). New Jersey—Montclair and Livingston, April 30. New York—Bronx, April 28; Ithaca, May 4 (average, May 12). Connecticut—New Haven, May 1. Rhode Island—Providence, May 2. Massachusetts—Amherst, April 22 (1929); East Longmeadow, May 7. Vermont—Bennington, May 11. New Hampshire—East Westmoreland, May 8. Maine—Kittery and Falmouth, May 16. Louisiana—Bains, April 4. Mississippi—Bay St. Louis and Oxford, April 11. Arkansas—Helena, April 7 (average, April 20). Tennessee—Nashville, April 16 (average of 12 years, April 21). Kentucky—Eubank, April 19. Missouri—Kansas City, April 14. Illinois—Murphysboro, April 19; Chicago region, May 6 (average, May 16). Indiana—Wheatland and Columbus, April 22. Ohio—Hamilton County, April 18; Barnesville, April 24 (1929) (average for central Ohio, May 2). Michigan—Kalamazoo, May 2. Ontario—Oshawa, May 5. Iowa—Fairfield and Waubonsie State Park, May 9. Wisconsin—Mazomanie, May 4. Minnesota—Red Wing, May 14. Texas—Victoria, March 15. Oklahoma—Oklahoma City, April 5; Tulsa, April 12. Kansas—Manhattan, April 22. Nebraska—Nebraska City, and Dunbar, April 29. South Dakota—Yankton, May 5. North Dakota—Wilton, May 15. Manitoba—Brandon, May 25. Saskatchewan—Skull Creek, May 11. New Mexico—Socorro, May 1. Arizona—Topock, April 11. Colorado—Lytle, May 6. Utah—Washington County, April 27; Salt

Lake, May 8. Wyoming—Guernsey and Torrington, May 10. Idaho—Meridian, May 13. Montana—Kirby, May 16. California—Los Angeles County, April 1; San Francisco Bay region, April 14. Nevada—Vegas Wash, May 3. Oregon—Oswego, Portland, and Eugene area, April 28. Washington—Yakima and Walla Walla, May 4. British Columbia—South Vancouver, May 9.

Late dates of fall departure are: Washington—Touchet, September 12. Oregon—Weston, October 2. Nevada—Indian Springs, Charleston Mountains, September 15. California—Azusa, October 9. Idaho—Moscow, September 10. Wyoming—Careyhurst, September 11. Utah—Uinta Basin, September 25. Colorado—Yuma, September 24. Arizona—Keams Canyon, October 12; San Pedro River, October 15. New Mexico—Apache, September 15. Saskatchewan—East End, August 14. North Dakota—Stutsman County (September 22; Fargo, October 11. South Dakota—Faulkton, October 20. Nebraska—Lincoln, September 26. Kansas—Lawrence, October 23. Oklahoma—Oklahoma City, September 17. Texas—Cove, November 10. Wisconsin—Mazomanie, September 3. Iowa—Sioux City, October 2. Michigan—Locke, October 2. Ohio—Hillsboro, October 16; central Ohio, September 22, (average, August 27). Indiana—Bloomington, September 28. Illinois—Murphysboro, September 12. Missouri—Creve Coeur Lake, September 25. Kentucky—Fulton County and Bowling Green, September 23. Tennessee—Elibabethton, October 8. Arkansas—Saline County, September 19. Mississippi—Deer Island, October 19 and 29. Louisiana—Baton Rouge region, October 22, December 28. New Brunswick—Grand Manan, December 1; St. Andrews, December 11. Maine—Seguin Light, October 5; Kittery, December 10. New Hampshire—Boar's Head, September 19. Massachusetts—Essex County, October 27 (more than 20 November and December records in the past 5 years). Rhode Island—Little Compton, November 12. Connecticut—New Haven County, October 3, November 23; South Norwalk, January 1. New York—Mastic, Long Island, October 31; Jones Beach, Long Island, November 13. New Jersey—Cape May Light, September 29; Long Branch, December 15. Pennsylvania—Renovo, October 2; Norristown, November 28. Delaware—Kent and Sussex Counties, September 30 (average of 18 years, August 30). Maryland—Ocean City, October 5; Patuxent Wildlife Research Refuge, November 1. District of Columbia—Washington, October 4 (average of 8 years, September 19). West Virginia—Bluefield, October 6. Virginia—Rockbridge County, October 2; Cape Henry, October 22. North Carolina—Weaverville, October 1; Raleigh, September 19 (average of 8 years, August 8). Georgia—Athens, October 18. Alabama—Birmingham, October 30 (average of 10 years, September 24). Florida—Pensacola, October 12.

Early dates of fall arrival are: California—Azusa, August 31. Mississippi—near Biloxi, August 27. Rhode Island—Block Island, August22. Guatemala—Colomba, Quezaltenango, September 29. Honduras—near Tela, October 7. Nicaragua—Escondido River, October 14. El Salvador—Divisadero, October 10. Costa Rica—San José, October 26.

Egg dates.—Arizona: 29 records, April 26 to Aug. 1; 16 records, May 21 to June 9; 7 records, July 15 to 25.

California: 62 records, May 4 to July 13; 32 records, May 13 to June 4, indicating the height of the season.

Georgia: 18 records, May 9 to June 2; 10 records, May 13 to 20.

Pennsylvania: 31 records, May 19 to June 25; 18 records, May 30 to June 12.

Texas: 39 records, April 10 to June 25; 20 records, May 6 to 26 (Harris).

ICTERIA VIRENS AURICOLLIS Lichtenstein

WESTERN YELLOW-BREASTED CHAT

HABITS

The western race of the yellow-breasted chat is only slightly differentiated from its well-known eastern relative. Ridgway (1902) describes it as "similar to *I. v. virens*, but wing, tail, and bill longer, the tail always, or nearly always, longer than wing, instead of the reverse; upper parts more grayish olive-green, usually more nearly gray than olive-green; white of malar region much more extended, frequently occupying entire malar area; yellow of under parts averaging deeper."

It is well distributed, generally common, and locally abundant over much of North America during the breeding season from the Pacific coast to the Plains, and from British Columbia and extreme southern Saskatchewan to the Mexican plateau. Only within comparatively recent years has the chat been known to breed across the southern boundary in Saskatchewan, south of the Cypress Hills. Although Dr. Bishop, Dr. Dwight, and I did considerable field work in this region and in southern Alberta in 1906, we failed to find it. Some years later, Laurence B. Potter wrote to me: "Since the first discovery of the yellow-breasted chat by Taverner, in 1921, in southwestern Saskatchewan, the species has established itself as a regular, and not uncommon, summer visitant. For twenty years previous to Taverner's taking the first specimen, I had lived in the same district, watching and hearing birds; but it was not until 1922, a year later, that I first heard a chat, the male bird of a pair that certainly were nesting. And I feel quite sure the species was, at that time, a newcomer." Some thirteen years later, Mr. Potter (1935) established the chat as a breeding bird in that vicinity by finding a nest with eggs.

The western yellow-breasted chat, as it is now called, has evidently permanently extended its breeding range slightly north of the international boundary in southwestern Saskatchewan. J. Dewey Soper (1942) writes:

From June 15 to 18, 1941, I camped at the Frenchman River about 200 yards from the International Boundary. The valley here is several miles wide and between 300 and 400 feet deep, the bottom of which is approximately 2,500 feet a. s. l. It exhibits pronounced arid characteristics such as sparse, short-grass cover, an abundance of cacti, broad sagebrush and greasewood flats, rattlesnakes, horned lizards, etc. A few miles up the valley are several towns of the Black-tailed Prairie Dog. The river is bordered by rather extensive and very dense thickets of willows, buckthorn, green ash, wild rose, snowberry, gooseberry and sagebrush. Zonal conditions lean conspicuously to the Upper Sonoran.

No sooner was the locality entered than Long-tailed Chats were heard on every hand. This was at once recognized as an unusual experience. As the bottomland thickets were carefully explored in the days that followed, it was increasingly realized that *longicauda* was not only common, but actually abundant. * * * I hesitate to express an opinion as to the number of chats in the neighborhood, but they may have totaled between fifty and one hundred. If the former figure should approximately apply (which strikes me as very conservative), then the average would have been about one pair to every 140 yards.

In the Great Basin region, in Nevada, according to Dr. Jean M. Linsdale (1938), "The large, dense thickets of buffalo berry, intertwined with willow and rose provided satisfactory home sites for this bird; in Smoky Valley in favorable stretches of a mile 3 or 4 pairs could be detected. Year after year noises made by this bird came from exactly the same spots. Either these were more suitable than other spots which appeared to be similar, or the birds exhibited an especially strong tendency to return to the same bushes."

In the Lassen Peak region of California, Grinnell, Dixon, and Linsdale (1930) say that "chats were limited closely to the tangles of tall weeds, brush (willow, rose, blackberry, elder) and grapevines that bordered the lower stream-courses."

Nesting.—The western chat does not seem to differ materially from its eastern relative in its nesting habits, or in any of its other habits.

The nests are usually not over 2 or 3 feet from the ground in thickets of willows, wild rose bushes, or other shrubs, often overgrown with grapevines or other tangles. Grinnell, Dixon, and Linsdale (1930) record one that "was slightly over two meters above the ground in a vine that covered a dead tree. A large cottonwood close by furnished shade. The site was about on a level with the top of the undergrowth of willows, weeds, and elders."

Eggs.—The eggs are indistinguishable from those of the eastern chat. The measurements of 50 eggs average 21.8 by 16.6 millimeters;

the eggs showing the four extremes measure 25.4 by 17.8, 20.3 by **19.1,** **18.3** by 15.2, and 19.3 by **14.7** millimeters (Harris).

Young.—Mrs. Wheelock's observations (1904) indicate rather rapid feeding by both parents at a nest that she watched:

On one day, which seemed to be a fair average, when the young were eight days old, they were fed twenty times between five and six a.m., eight times between nine and ten a.m., eleven times between three and four p.m., and seventeen times between five and six p.m. For the first four days there was no visible food in the bill of the adult, and the feeding seemed to be by regurgitation. After that, parts of insects could be seen protruding from his bill, and were given to the young in a fresh state. Beetles, grasshoppers, and butterflies were all in the dietary, and were brought indiscriminately; but hairless caterpillars seemed to be the favorite food. The adults are said to eat berries, but I saw none brought to the nest for the young.

Behavior.—Chat behavior is much the same in the west as in the east, but the following observations on the territorial behavior and daily routine of the long-tailed western chat, by Eric Campbell Kinsey (1934), are of interest:

The usual territorial rights, enforced by breeding birds generally, so far as their own species is concerned, obtained markedly with the chats. Each breeding pair appeared to stay strictly within its own territory except when there was a general alarm emanating from a particular territory (such as that occasioned by pilfering jays or hawks), when a number of chats would congregate at that spot to aid in driving away the would-be despoilers.

Each chat followed a very definite schedule each day. For example, a certain male would appear at dawn on a particular dead branch some fifty feet up in a cottonwood tree and, after a short song, would then fly down to a definite spot in an adjacent flooded meadow, whereupon satisfying his appetite he would return to the original perch. After remaining there for several minutes, singing, he would repair to a particular branch in the middle of a nearby elderberry bush, drop from there to a certain nettle stalk, cross to the nest where his mate was brooding eggs, and after (presumably) feeding her would again return to the dead branch in the cottonwood. Then he would fly to the irrigation ditch for his early morning plunge, return again to the cottonwood branch, preen and complete his toilet; then down into the meadow for more insects, back to the original cottonwood, again to the elderberry patch, down to the nest, etc. This routine was followed out with little variation throughout the morning. Immediately after mid-day he would descend from the cottonwood to another patch of elderberries on the opposite side and to an adjacent dry meadow where grasshoppers were quite plentiful; then would again return to the cottonwood, from there drop down to the nest, and, after being satisfied that all was as it should be, would once again return to the cottonwood. The same procedure would be followed all during the afternoon, broken only by a bath in the irrigation ditch just before dusk. The nest was situated due east of the cottonwood and it was the eastern part of the territory, upon which the sun shone, that he foraged in the morning. In the afternoon the sun was on the west of the cottonwood and it was the western section of the territory that then received his attention.

This species is apparently as casual as are hummingbirds, so far as their mates are concerned. Again, to illustrate, a certain female was trapped late one afternoon whereupon her mate appeared next forenoon with a new female and, on the succeeding day, this pair started constructing a new nest near the site of the old one. On the following day the male was trapped and on the next day what we assumed was the remaining female appeared with a new male and afforded every evidence of mating. This particular pair was located at one of the extreme ends of the territory covered. Another pair was under observation at the other end of the territory, where the male was first trapped; two days later the female appeared with a new mate whereupon she was trapped and, on the following day, the same male appeared with a new female.

Voice.—Many writers have referred to chats as mimics; whether the various notes heard from chats are really imitations or are parts of the birds' own elaborate vocabularies is open to question. However that may be, we have the following list of possible imitations heard by Grinnell, Dixon, and Linsdale (1930):

Facsimiles that were heard and checked within a few days in late May and early June were as follows: gray squirrel (the "coughing" note); young turkey (of which many were herded around the ranch at Dale's to feed on grasshoppers); willow woodpecker (the high-pitched "whinnying"); Bullock oriole (the harsh call-note only); crow (the caw, repeated four to six times, or, sometimes, just once, accurately given); ash-throated flycatcher (call-note); wren-tit (without the terminal trill, but accurate in pitch and timbre—no wren-tits were seen within six miles of this place [Dale's]); Pacific nighthawk (*pe-ärk,* perfectly rendered); California jay (one of the staccato calls); Steller jay (a staccato note); flicker (the *kuk-kuk-kuk* note); yellow-billed magpie (perfect, though magpies were not found by us in the near neighborhood); meadow-lark (a call-note); slender-billed nuthatch (*yank,* loud nasal note); robin (*cluck-cluck,* note of mild alarm).

EUTHLYPIS LACRIMOSA TEPHRA (Bonaparte)

WESTERN FAN-TAILED WARBLER

HABITS

The casual occurrence of this species at Santo Domingo, northern Baja California, where, according to Grinnell and Lamb (1927) a single specimen was taken by Lamb on December 31, 1925, entitles this primarily Mexican species to a place on our list. The bird "was on the ground in a damp spot beneath a pepper tree on the Hamilton ranch. Had been seen several times previously the same day, flying nervously from object to object on the ground, at times flirting its tail sidewise and uttering a single lisping whistle."

The following description of the juvenal plumage, which Ridgway (1902) did not describe, is given by Dickey and van Rossem (1938):

"Upperparts, including sides of head and wing coverts, uniform 'dark neutral gray'; chin, throat, and chest, 'hair brown' or 'fuscous'; flanks similar but more sooty; median underparts, including under tail coverts, pale 'primrose yellow,' mingling with the color of the chest in the form of broad streaking or mottling; wings and tail essentially as in adult, but rectrices more pointed.

"The postjuvenal body plumage is apparently identical with that of the adult. The juvenal remiges and rectrices are retained through the following breeding season. There is no evidence of more than one molt a year."

In El Salvador, they found the fan-tailed warbler a—

fairly common resident of the foothills and mountains in the Arid Lower Tropical Zone. Although found from elevations varying from 200 to 3,500 feet, the species is relatively rare below 500 feet.

"Rock warbler" would be a name fully as appropriate as fan-tailed warbler, for throughout its El Salvador range this species is an inhabitant of rocky ravines and jungle-covered lava flows. In addition there appear to be other requirements such as thin undergrowth beneath tall forest so that, although the species has a wide range, the distribution is necessarily spotty in character.

The general appearance of this warbler is very similar to that of a redstart—a resemblance due in no small measure to the continual nervous fanning of the tail. Living as these birds do in heavily shaded situations among dark rocks, they would be nearly invisible were it not for this curious habit. In life the brightly colored underparts are not often noticeable, and the tail movement, in which the white terminal spots are alternately flashed out and concealed, is the most betraying character. When this bird works over rocks and through leaf litter, it has, except for the tail movements, no jerky motions. The birds steal about quickly, taking full advantage of all cover. They do not hop like thrushes and most sparrows, but walk after the manner of larks and the North American oven-birds.

Rocks being their preference these warblers are never found on the flat portions of the coastal plain, although they descend to very low levels where there are old lava flows. The deep, gloomy ravines so numerous on the Colinas de Jucuarán and Volcán de Conchagua, provide an ideal environment, and fan-tailed warblers are perhaps more common in these two localities than in any others.

Ten stomachs examined contained insects exclusively.

DISTRIBUTION

The fan-tailed warbler is a resident species ranging south from southern Sonora (Guirocoba); southern Chihuahua (Hacienda de San Rafael); and southern Tamaulipas; south through the Isthmus of Tehuantepec to southwestern Guatemala and Nicaragua. It is accidental in northern Baja California (Santo Domingo).

CARDELLINA RUBRIFRONS (Giraud)

RED-FACED WARBLER

PLATE 72

HABITS

This well-marked and striking species is a Mexican bird that has extended its range into southern Arizona and southwestern New Mexico. Since the bird is common in the mountains of Mexico, it is not surprising that it should follow the trends of these ranges into the United States, as some other species have done. Early reports of the occurrence of the red-faced warbler in Texas having been discredited as probably erroneous, it was definitely added to our fauna by Henry W. Henshaw (1875), who "met with the species at two points, near Camp Apache, and again on Mount Graham, a point some two hundred miles to the south. At the former place, several specimens were captured, including the young in nesting plumage, thus indicating that they breed in the vicinity."

The northern red-faced warbler is essentially a bird of the mountain canyons, breeding quite commonly from 7,000 feet upward in probably all of the mountain ranges of southeastern Arizona and southwestern New Mexico. Dr. Edgar A. Mearns (1890) found it to be "a summer resident from near the lower border of the pine belt to the summit of the Mogollon Mountains. It was not seen in the San Francisco Mountains, but was found breeding about thirty miles south of them," in Arizona. We found it common in Ramsay Canyon in the Huachuca Mountains, mainly between 6,000 and 8,000 feet, where the sloping sides of the canyon were clothed with spruces, firs, and, higher up, with pines. Here the bright red faces of the otherwise sombre-colored males flashed like glowing embers in the dark shadows of the conifers and quickly caught the eye.

Dr. George M. Sutton (1943) found it common in the Santa Rita Mountains, south of Tucson, where "every open aspen copse visited by the writer sheltered a pair of these handsome birds." Mrs. Bailey (1928) mentions a number of localities in New Mexico where it has been observed or found breeding.

Spring.—The red-faced warbler may eventually be found breeding farther north than is now known, as it seems to be more abundant in southern Arizona on the spring migration than during the breeding season, suggesting that some may be passing through that region. O. W. Howard (1899) says: "These birds are quite common in the mountains of Southern Arizona, especially during the spring migration. I have seen as many as four or five feeding in one tree. They become scarcer as the season advances and at the time of breeding comparatively few of them remain." And Harry S. Swarth (1904) says that, in the Huachucas, it is "found during the breeding season from 7000 feet upwards, and in the migrations as abundant in the higher pine regions as anywhere. The first arrival was noted April 20th, and up to the middle of May they were seen in considerable numbers along the canyons, often in company with other migrating warblers. During the breeding season their numbers seem to be greatly decreased, but this is probably more apparent than real, as at this time they are very quiet and inconspicuous; and as soon as the young begin to appear, about the middle of August, they are as numerous as ever."

Nesting.—Although not the first to report it, Dr. Mearns (1890) was the first naturalist to find the nest of the red-faced warbler. He describes the event as follows:

On the 19th of June, 1886, I was encamped on a southern slope of the Mogollon Mountains, about five miles within the pine belt, in what has been designated the Great San Francisco Forest. Following a small stream into a little cañon between whose rocky walls stood groups of towering spruces and of aspens, the ground beneath thickly sprinkled with violets, strawberries, honeysuckles, and columbines, I entered a side ravine and had stooped to gather some flowering honeysuckles when a little bird was flushed from its nest upon the side of the bank, close to the trunk of a large spruce. Alighting in a young spruce tree, it uttered a sharp, hard *chip*. It was the first Red-faced Warbler I had ever seen; and its red face, black cap, gray back, and white rump suggested to my mind a miniature of the European Bulfinch. The bird was so fearless, and the place so confined, that I had some difficulty in securing the specimen in good condition. The male was not seen. After a close search an old nest was discovered on the ground; and I was about to conclude that it belonged to my bird and was as yet unfinished, when I descried a small opening close beside it among the stones and pine needles; on parting some blooming honeysuckles (*Lonicera ciliosa*) and moss, I discovered the nest,—most artfully concealed. In it were four eggs, containing small embryos which were easily extracted, the shells being thick and hard. The nest rested on a mass of dry leaves and spruce needles, and was entirely covered up and concealed by the honeysuckles. It is well built, being composed of a neatly felted mass of plant-stems and strips of fine bark, lined with soft vegetable fibres and cow-hairs.

W. W. Price (1888) was the first to report and describe a nest of the red-faced warbler, which he found in Ramsey Canyon in the Huachucas on May 31, 1888; his nest "was placed on sloping ground in a slight hollow and contained four fresh eggs." He had seen the bird fly to a clump of columbine which grew on the bank of a creek.

A few sprays of the columbine hid the nest so completely that had not the bird been frightened and directly off from it, I should not have found it. * * * The structure was a very poor attempt at nest-building, and made of such loose material that it crumbled to fragments on being removed. The chief substance was fine fibrous weed stalks, while the lining consisted of fine grass, rootlets, plant fibres, and a few hairs. Skeleton leaves and bits of fine bark were scattered sparingly throughout the nest. Leaves and other rubbish had drifted with the wind or had been scratched up all around, to a level with the rim, so that one could hardly see where the nest proper left off. Inside the nest was about two and one half inches wide by one and one half inches in depth; outside it was about five inches wide by three inches in depth. The ground on which the nest was placed was so damp that the bottom part of it was badly decayed.

In the same region, Swarth (1904) found a nest that "was well concealed under an old rotten log, on a steep bank by the side of a trail, and could never have been seen had not the bird darted from the nest when it was approached." Howard's (1899) first nest was "on a side hill under a tuft of grass." The only nest that I have ever seen was also in a branch of Ramsey Canyon; we had previously seen the bird go to the nest while building it, and on May 26, 1922, we photographed (pl. 72, lower) and collected the nest with a set of four fresh eggs. The nest was located on a wooded open slope, close to a trail, and was in a depression in the ground at the foot of a tiny oak sprout, among a litter of fallen leaves and partially under some grass and other herbage, but it was not any too well hidden. It was made of dead leaves, dry grasses and fine strips of inner bark of cedar, and was lined with fine grass and horsehair. All of these Huachuca Mountains nests were at elevations ranging from 7,000 to 8,500 feet.

In the Santa Rita Mountains, Dr. Sutton (1943) found the red-faced warbler nesting in the aspen copses at an elevation of about 8,000 feet; a nest containing small young was found on May 29 "on the ground in a low bank under aspens."

One of the five nests of this warbler in the Thayer collection in Cambridge, was taken by Virgil W. Owen in the Chiricahua Mountains, Ariz., from the side of a bank in a narrow canyon, "in a depression under a projecting rock, which was overhung by a bunch of grass which entirely concealed both rock and nest." The main body of the nest is made externally of a large number of coarse pine needles and internally of grasses; it is lined with the finest of plant fibers and a quantity of reddish brown and white cow hair. Another is made externally of many coarse strips from heavy weed stalks, and still another was made mainly of strips of cedar bark, the latter composing most of each nest. I suspect that the lining in some of these nests may be deer hair, as these animals are fairly common there.

Eggs.—The red-faced warbler seems to lay three or four eggs to a set. The eggs are ovate, some tending to short ovate or elongate ovate, and have only a slight gloss. They are white, finely and delicately speckled with "auburn," "Mars brown," or "snuff brown," with undermarkings of "dusky drab." In general the markings are very fine and few seem to be large enough to be called spots or blotches; sometimes they are so light as to be almost imperceptible. The speckles are frequently scattered over the entire egg, although there is usually a concentration at the large end. The measurements of 44 eggs averaged 16.5 by 12.7 millimeters; the eggs showing the four extremes measure 17.9 by 13.0, 16.6 by 13.5, 14.3 by 12.2, and 15.3 by 12.0 millimeters (Harris).

Young.—We have no information on the incubation of the eggs or on the care and development of the young.

Plumages.—I have seen no small nestlings, but the fully grown young bird in the juvenal plumage is very dull-looking, with no trace of the red face. The upper parts, including the top and sides of the head and the back are uniform sooty brown, sometimes browner on the crown or more buffy on the nape; the rump is white; the wings and tail are as in the adult, except that the middle and greater wing coverts are tipped with buff, forming two narrow wing-bars; the throat and breast are brownish gray, becoming whitish on the abdomen.

The postjuvenal molt begins in June; a specimen taken June 13 shows a few black feathers coming in the crown and a few red feathers on the forehead, chin and sides of the neck. I have seen this molt in progress on birds taken June 21 and July 6 and 9; and I have a bird in my collection, taken July 13, that has completed the molt into the first winter plumage. This molt apparently involves all the contour plumage and the wing coverts, but not the rest of the wings or the tail. The sexes are alike in the juvenal plumage.

The first winter plumage is much like the winter plumage of the adult of the same sex, but the plumages of the young birds are always duller than those of the corresponding adults, the red being much paler or inclining to flesh color, the nuchal patch tinged with buff and the gray of the upper parts browner. We have no specimens showing a prenuptial molt; what specimens we have indicate that the dull, first winter plumage is worn until the following July; at least, I have seen what were apparently one-year-old birds molting out of a first winter plumage on June 27 and on July 9. If there is a partial prenuptial molt, it must occur while the birds are in winter quarters, and specimens from there are scarce.

Adults have a complete postnuptial molt in June, July, and August; I have seen the beginning of it as early as June 10; Swarth (1904) says it takes place in August. The June birds I have seen are all in worn plumage, and the August birds I have examined are in fresh plumage. In the fresh fall plumage the white of the nape, rump, and under parts are often tinged with pink, which gradually fades or wears away during the spring.

Food.—Nothing seems to have been published on the food of the red-faced warbler, which is probably largely, if not wholly, insectivorous. Its method of feeding, as described under "Behavior," indicates a diet similar to that of other wood warblers.

Behavior.—H. W. Henshaw (1875) wrote in his notebook:

While collecting in the early evening in the pine woods, a few angry chirps coming from the thick foliage of a spruce attracted my attention, and in a moment a robin flew out in hot haste closely followed by a small bird, which after a short chase returned, and with a few satisfied chirps called together several young, whose presence I for the first time was thus made aware of. The old bird immediately began to search for food, moving like a Chickadee over the limbs, and flying out now and then for a short distance to snap up an insect, which was instantly given to one or the other of the several young that, with beseeching notes and cries, followed the old one about as it moved from one part of the tree to another. * * *

Just a month later [in August], on visiting Mount Graham, I not only saw the species again, but it proved to be a common bird of this locality, flocks of ten or fifteen not being unusual among the pines and spruces; it frequented these trees almost exclusively, only rarely being seen on the bushes that fringed the streams. Its habits are a rather strange compound, now resembling those of Warblers, again recalling the Redstarts, but more often perhaps bringing to mind the less graceful motions of the familiar Titmice. Their favorite hunting places appeared to be the extremities of the limbs of the spruces, over the branches of which they passed with quick motion, and a peculiar and constant sidewise jerk of the tail.

When thus engaged, especially when high overhead, they might easily be passed by, as a busy group of Titmice intent only on satisfying their hunger. They appear to obtain most of their food from the branches, seizing the insects when at rest; but they are abundantly able to take their prey on the wing, and accomplish this much after the style of the Redstarts. Their disposition seems to prompt them to sociability with other species, and occasionally I found them accompanying the Audubon's Warblers, and imitating them in their short flights from tree to tree, occasionally paying flying visits to the fallen logs and even to the ground.

Dr. Walter P. Taylor tells me that the red-faced warbler is not shy, and "is characterized by a curiosity that usually discloses it to view and enables one to really see it much more easily than is the case with many or most other warblers." He saw one hawking for insects, making two sorties in the air while he watched it; it has a peculiar "flitty" flight. The birds that he saw in the Catalina Mountains stayed more in the aspens than in the pines. But he noted one in the Chiricahua Mountains in the oak brush just below the pines.

Voice.—Dr. Taylor refers to the song in his notes as quite close to that of the yellow warbler; he calls it a whistled song with variations, "*a link a tink a tink tsee tsee tswee tsweep*," and says that it is "more ringing and bell-like than that of Grace's warbler, which is often associated with it in the yellow pines." He says that the *chip* call-note is conspicuous, and he mentions another note as *psst.* Henshaw (1875) says: "Save in being rather louder and harsher, their chirps resemble the notes of the Yellow-rump Warblers."

Field marks.—A gray bird with a black cap, a red face and throat, a white rump, and white wing bars, could not be mistaken for anything but a red-faced warbler. No other North American bird looks at all like it.

Winter.—Dr. Alexander F. Skutch contributes the following notes: "On the Sierra de Tecpán, in west-central Guatemala, the red-faced warbler wintered in small numbers from September 13 to March, chiefly in the mixed forests of pine, oak, alder, arbutus and other broad-leafed trees, between 7,000 and 9,000 feet above sea level. These pretty warblers were usually found in the mixed flocks of Townsend's warblers and other small birds, only one or more rarely two in a flock. When there was a single red-faced member of the company, it was nearly always silent; but when two chanced to be together, they would usually be singing. On September 29, 1933, soon after the return of the red-faced warblers to the Sierra, I came upon two of them foraging in the same alder tree. They sang over and over a clear, mellow warble, as fine a song as I have heard of any member of the family, and twice welcome in those dreary, misty, rain-drenched days at the height of the wet season, when scarcely any bird sang. They continued to repeat their songs as they foraged, sometimes simultaneously, sometimes answering each other, and kept this up for perhaps half an hour. Just as I started to walk away from them, I noticed that they had flown together and were fighting. After a few moments, they separated and each went his own way, repeating his song.

"On a number of other occasions I found two individuals together; one or both—doubtless depending on their sexes—would be singing; and usually, if I waited long enough, one would drive the other away. The victorious bird might sing a little hymn of triumph upon the retreat of his rival, but soon would fall silent, and forage in peace among his companions of other species. These singing bouts were all staged during the fall months; from December onward, when the birds were well settled in their winter home, I found them alone and silent; until in March they resumed their beautiful song in anticipation of their departure for their northern nesting grounds.

"Such singing in rivalry has been paralleled in my experience by other migratory birds which are solitary during the winter months, including the yellow warbler, the black and white warbler, the blue-headed vireo and the blue-gray gnatcatcher, and by the males of non-migratory warblers which are solitary at this season, as Kaup's redstart (*Myioborus miniatus*), or of those which remain paired and continue to defend their territory, as Delattre's warbler (*Basileuterus delattrii*).

"In March, long before the majority of the migratory warblers, the red-faced warbler vanished from the Sierra de Tecpán. Except on the plains of Chimaltenango at the foot of the Sierra, I have not met this bird in other parts of Guatemala."

DISTRIBUTION

Breeding range.—The red-faced warbler breeds **north** to central and central eastern Arizona (30 miles south of San Francisco Mountains, Mogollon Plateau, and Camp Apache) and southwestern New Mexico (Mogollon Mountains, Powderhorn Canyon, and probably Fort Bayard). **East** to southwestern New Mexico (Fort Bayard) and northwestern Chihuahua (probably Barranca). **South** probably through the highlands of Mexico to southern Guatemala.

Winter range.—It winters in southern Mexico from Morelos (Cuernavaca) and Veracruz (Jalapa) to northern Oaxaca (La Parada and Cinco Senores).

Migration.—A late date of spring departure is: Guatemala—above Tecpán, March 5.

Early dates of spring arrival are: Texas—Water Canyon of the Magdalena Mountains, April 19. New Mexico—35 miles northeast of Silver City, April 19. Arizona—Tucson area, April 9; Willow Creek, May 3.

An early date of fall arrival is: Guatemala—above Tecpán, September 13.

Late dates of fall departure are: Arizona—San Francisco Mountains, September 4; Chiricahua Mountains, September 21. New Mexico—Little Rocky Creek, August 21.

Egg dates.—Arizona: 12 records, May 6 to June 19; 12 records, May 29 to June 7, indicating the height of the season (Harris).

WILSONIA CITRINA (Boddaert)

HOODED WARBLER

PLATES 73–75

HABITS

Dr. Chapman (1907) introduces this pretty warbler with the following words of well-deserved praise: "Its beauty of plumage, charm of voice, and gentleness of demeanor, make it indeed not only a lovely, but a truly lovable bird. Doubtless, also, the nature of the Hooded Warbler's haunts increase its attractiveness, not merely because these well-watered woodlands are in themselves inviting, but because they bring the bird down to our level. This creates a sense of companionship which we do not feel with the birds ranging high above us, and at the same time it permits us to see this exquisitely clad creature under most favorable conditions."

The hooded warbler makes its summer home almost entirely within the eastern half of the United States, extending its range only slightly into Canada, in southern Ontario. Being a forest-loving bird, it is much less common between the Mississippi River and the Plains than it is in the more heavily forested regions east of that river. It reaches its eastern limit in extreme southern New England, beyond which it occurs only casually. I have found it breeding commonly in southern Connecticut, where the forested slopes and the valleys of small streams support a luxuriant growth of mountain laurel and other undergrowth.

I know of another place in Rhode Island where a few pairs breed in a fine old, mature mixed forest, watered by tiny streams, that protects in its shady ravines and hollows a similar undergrowth; in this same cool forest retreat, we find the Canada warbler breeding near the southern limit of its summer range, save at the higher elevations of the Alleghenies.

Samuel F. Rathbun writes to me: "When my home was in west-central New York, about thirty miles from Lake Ontario, a friend and I made a camping stay of ten weeks in July and August, on the end of a projection of the mainland which was bounded on two sides by enclosed bays. This extension of land, about three-quarters of a mile long and in places a quarter of a mile wide, was heavily clothed with a forest of hardwood trees of the highest type, beech, hard maple, basswood, hickory, and here and there a little hemlock. Inside the forest were many open spaces, large and small, thickets of all sizes, some dense and some sparse, and many vistas where the wind and sunshine had free play. We soon found that the hooded warbler showed a predilection for this type of forest, for about fifteen pairs of birds used it as a summer home. During our stay we were never out of hearing or sight of a hooded warbler."

In the central Allegheny Mountain region, according to Maurice Brooks (1940), "these birds show a preference for areas of deciduous timber, light or heavy. They occur in southern mixed hardwoods, oak-hickory, northern hardwoods, and in 'chestnut sprout' areas. On Cheat Mountain they nest at 3,500 feet, and in Giles Co., Va., they breed at 4,000 feet."

Dr. Arthur B. Williams, of Cleveland, Ohio, has very kindly sent me some extensive notes on the habits of the hooded warbler, based on 15 years of observation in the Cleveland region, where the species is evidently abundant and is increasing in numbers and expanding its range. "In the Cleveland region the hooded warbler may be found during the breeding season in most mature beech-maple woodlands, seeming to prefer those which border on the river valleys where there is an abundance of moisture. It nests not only in the ravines and gulches in such woodlands, but also throughout the more level and open stretches of woodland where there is an understory of small beech and maple seedling trees. Characteristics of this forest are reduction of light, reduction of wind movement to a minimum, reduction of evaporation rate by 55 percent as compared with adjoining open field, and a high relative humidity of from 80 to 90 percent during the breeding season.

"In the forest community I studied most thoroughly, an average of 14 pairs of hooded warblers nest in an area of approximately 65 acres. In this community the warbler takes its place in a group of

18 species of nesting birds, the most common of which are the red-eyed vireo, wood thrush, redstart, ovenbird and scarlet tanager. In this group the hooded warbler usually ranks third or fourth in abundance."

The above accounts are fairly typical of the more northern habitats, but near the southern limits of its breeding range the hooded warbler seems to favor more swampy environment. Andrew Allison wrote to Dr. Chapman (1907) that, in Mississippi, it inhabits "low, heavily shaded woods, with thick undergrowth. Where convenient cover, such as a brake of switch-cane, extends to the border of the woods, the bird has no objection to an open, light, situation; and along the Gulf coast, where the only swampy situations are the narrow 'baygalls,' the thickets of rose-bay (*Illicium*) and azalea afford sufficient seclusion for a few. Damp woods such as are afforded by river and creek bottoms, however, are more favored."

S. A. Grimes (1935) says of its haunts in northern Florida: "A good-sized, poorly drained swamp, heavily forested with ash and maple, with a dense undergrowth mainly of fetterbush, red titi, and the seedlings and sprouts of several species of lowland trees, and such vines as Virginia creeper, smilax, and ivy, is evidently best suited to the hooded warbler's requirements. In such places it is usually the most abundant bird throughout the spring and summer, and it is not exceptional to hear, from one point, as many as five or six males singing at one time. In the swamps most favored there is commonly a breeding pair every fifty to one hundred yards in any direction. I have found occupied nests only fifty yards apart."

Spring.—Dr. Chapman (1907) says that the hooded warbler "reaches the United States by a flight across the Gulf of Mexico, avoiding the West Indies and (for the most part) southern Florida." This statement is doubtless correct, for there seems to be only scattering records for Key West, the Tortugas and points on the west coast of Florida. Howell (1932) calls it an "abundant migrant and a common summer resident in northwestern Florida south to the lower Suwannee River." Furthermore, M. A. Frazar (1881) reported "large numbers" seen 30 miles south of the mouth of the Mississippi, flying north toward the river, suggesting that they may have come straight across the Gulf from Yucatán. There seems to be a heavy migration, also, along the coast of Texas.

In northern Ohio, according to Dr. Williams (MS.), "the first week in May usually sees the arrival of the first hooded warblers from the south and within a few days thereafter the entire nesting population is present. The males appear first, but the females are close upon their heels. The males are in song from the moment of their arrival, though their first songs are not so complete or well-developed as they shortly become. Nesting territories are immediately occupied, and the limits of these correspond closely from year to year. The male patrols the territory regularly. His presence and movements are advertised by his song, which in May and June is almost continuous. He has no regular singing post, but sings as he moves back and forth within the limits of his chosen territory. This is a regular part of his behavior and is thoroughly done. If you approach, he will attempt to lead you away by singing ahead of you. If you sit down and remain motionless, he will quietly approach to look you over. Nesting territories which I have measured vary from 300 by 400 feet to 300 by 700 feet.

"While the male is easily seen and his progress followed by ear, the behavior of the female is quite the opposite. She drops out of sight immediately, and unless she is especially sought for and routed out, the record of observed birds is likely to include only males. She does not sing, but if alarmed or anxious will betray her presence by the characteristic *chip* note, often repeated at regular intervals. Since the male uses the same note however, one must actually see the female to be sure of her presence.

"Both birds will defend the nesting territory. I have seen them unite to drive out such an innocent intruder as a migrating black-throated blue warbler. The hooded warbler holds very closely to its chosen territory, and second or third nests are located not far from the first. The last birds to be found in the area without young in late September are still resident in the territories occupied by them in May."

Nesting.—Rathbun (MS.) says of its nesting habits in western New York: "All the nests of the hooded warbler found by me were placed at an average height of from 2 to 3 feet above the ground, with the exception of two which were about twice that height. In every case the nests were placed in the lowest fork of a beech sapling well within a small thicket. Invariably, at first sight, it resembled a small cluster of dead leaves caught up by the wind and lodged in the fork. On this platform of dead leaves the nest was securely placed. In each case the nest could not be detected by looking directly at the thicket. I found the easiest way to locate a nest was to place my head close to the ground, scan the low open spaces and look for a clump of leaves, which sooner or later proved to be a nest.

"The hooded warbler builds a neat, compact, and nicely woven nest, outwardly constructed of dry plant fibers, some quite long and some shorter, from the outside of dead plants. The substantial lining is composed of fine, dry, soft grasses, bits of plant fibers and other soft material, with occasionally a few horsehairs, to aid in holding the lining in place."

In southern Connecticut, the nests of the hooded warbler are usually built in the low, dense thickets of mountain laurel (*Kalmia latifolia*), which is locally abundant there, often in extensive patches, in well-shaded spots. Judge J. N. Clark (1882) gives the following good description of such a nest:

Pieces of yellow birch bark, beech and chestnut leaves carefully matted and bound together and to the triangular crotch, formed the base of the structure, rounded and neatly finished at the top with the inner bark of chestnut and cedar, with fine grass and scales from beech buds and a little fern down mixed in, and all secured compactly together with spider webs. I speak advisedly having seen the bird diligently gather the webs. Inside the nest was neatly and smoothly lined with mixed horsehair and very fine grass. Largest outer diameter three inches and a half, inner diameter two inches, and depth two inches, and built in a little kalmia bush about fifteen inches from the ground. This description will answer for most of the many nests I have found of the species, with varying quantities of birch bark and fern down, invariably in a kalmia bush.

T. E. McMullen has sent me the data on 20 New Jersey nests; 14 were in small hollies in thick, dry or swampy woods; others were in pepper or huckleberry bushes, or in laurels; the heights above ground varied from 10 inches to 3½ feet. Dr. George M. Sutton (1928) mentions a very unusual nest in Pymatuning Swamp, Pa., "at the surprising height of eighteen feet from the ground in a slender upright shoot growing out from the trunk of a large beech tree."

In my collection are 22 sets of eggs from North Carolina; 5 of these were in oak saplings, 3 in myrtles, and 2 each in alders and hollies; the others were in various saplings, bushes, and brier patches; they were found at heights varying from 10 inches to 4 feet. In Georgia and South Carolina, the nests are often built in canes, as well as in low bushes, seldom as much as 5 feet up. In northern Florida, according to Grimes (1935)—

the site of the nest may vary considerably, but one feature of the nest itself is quite consistent—its inconspicuousness. I have seen many nests of this species in northeastern Florida and believe I am safe in saying that nine out of ten are built in the fetterbush (*Pieris nitida*) in this region. I cannot name a second choice, but have found nests in such other shrubs as the button-bush, swamp blackberry, wax myrtle, and red titi, and in seedlings of the laurel oak, water oak, swamp ash, and red bay. * * * I have seen one nest in a low fetterbush directly beneath the center of a large horizontal palmetto frond that shielded it from rain as well as from view.

There is a good deal of variation in the size, shape, and even the general tone of the exterior of the nest. The type most often met with is small, compact, rather dark in appearance, and an inconspicuous object in its natural surroundings. Such a nest is made outwardly of dead leaves of swamp ash, red maple, smilax, and water elm held together with strips of bark, spider web, and the black, hairlike heart of dried Spanish moss, these materials forming the foundations and shell of the structure. The shell or framework is reinforced with a strong lining of bark of the wild grape vine and cypress tree tightly bound together with spider web and threads of moss, like the outer wall. The inner-most lining, on which the eggs rest, ordinarily consists entirely of the black, skeletonized Spanish moss, somewhat more generously supplied at the bottom of the nest than up the sides.

Dr. Williams (MS.) gives me the following account of nesting hooded warblers in Ohio: "The first nest of the season is carefully made and is a real work of art. It is made without hurry and may take as long as a week for completion. Preferred nesting sites may be grouped under four heads:

"1. Rather isolated sites in more open woods where suckers from the roots of beech or sour gum trees, young sugar maple saplings, plants of red-berried elder or maple-leaved viburnum, or even blackberry canes, which may occasionally be found growing in open places in the woods, furnish the actual support for the nest, while the birds seem to rely on the natural camouflage of construction to make the nest inconspicuous. These nests resemble so closely a wad of woods rubbish caught by accident in the low growth near the ground that they escape the attention of most woods prowlers.

"2. Already existing camouflage in the shape of dead leaves hanging near the ground seems to exert a real fascination for the nest-builder, and frequently determines the exact location of the nest. The nest itself simulates such litter so closely that it easily escapes attention if built in such a situation. It is interesting to note that a nest which I discovered in a dead beach top lying on the ground had its exact counterpart over 40 years previously in New York State, as described by J. H. Langille.

"3. Small ravines seem to offer attractive nesting sites, a favorite location being just over the edge so that the nest is just below the level of the surrounding ground. Thus it is well out of the way of the beaten paths which woodland animals often make along the ravine edges and it is well-screened by vegetation above it.

"4. Thickets of spicebush, choke-cherry, grape tangles, or luxuriant vegetation of herbaceous plants are sometimes chosen, and in such a situation the nest is screened from view on all sides. One such nest was discovered in the forked stem of a plant of blue cohosh, 16 inches from the ground.

"In the case of 99 nests which I have studied, the average distance from the ground to the rim of the nest was 25 inches. The highest was 63 inches, but this nest was in a small sugar maple growing in a ravine in such a way that the nest was practically at ground level at the ravine edge. The lowest nest was 7 inches from ground to rim. This was in a small Y-shaped sugar maple seedling in which the dead cane of a blackberry had become lodged.

"Nest construction conforms to a very definite pattern. First there is a wad of loose dead leaves or long plant fibers like the strips of inner bark of dead chestnut or the inner bark of small sugar maples stripped off by squirrels, though beech leaves and the skeletonized leaves of sugar maples most frequently enter into this foundation. This wad of loose material may be long if there is a long narrow crotch to be filled up, or relatively flat if the location includes some sort of platform or cradle as a nest support. Usually the location is in a fork, and often includes a dead branch which has fallen across the fork, thus providing additional support. In a depression in the center of this loose collection of leaves a thin but strong basket is woven, the materials most frequently used being the strong, flat strips of bark of the wild grape. Other materials may sometimes be used, but they all have the common characteristics of flatness and strength. There is always a well-formed rim, carefully worked, of long plant fibers bound about the upper part of the structure, and well fastened in most cases with insect or spider silk, to which, sometimes, masses of the scales of beech buds or dried catkins of oak or hickory, or the dried staminate blossoms of the beech, adhere. The lining is always of springy, rather hard, finely shredded plant material, quite often hair-like in character. Probably much of this is finely shredded inner bark of grape vine. Many of the attachments of the nest to its supports will be of spider webbing or at least be reinforced by spider silk. Often long streamers will be left hanging from the bottom of the nest or from the rim. Second or third nests are apt to be much more hurriedly constructed than the first ones of the season, and lack the care and attention to details bestowed upon the earlier ones. Of 84 nests studied, measurements averaged as follows: height (from bottom to rim) 75 mm.; outside width, 79 mm.; inside width, 36.5 mm.; depth (inside), 52.5 mm."

Eggs.—Three or four eggs, often only three, make up the set for the hooded warbler, very rarely as many as five. These are usually ovate, sometimes tending toward short ovate or elongate ovate, and they are only slightly glossy. The creamy white ground is blotched, spotted or speckled with "bay," "chestnut," "auburn," "carob brown," or "russet," with undermarks of "vinaceous-brown," or "brownish drab." The markings on some eggs are scattered over the entire surface, but generally they are more or less confined to the large end, where they tend to form a wreath. Some have such pale spots that they appear as freckles, or, again, they may be so dark as to appear almost black. The measurements of 50 eggs average 17.6 by 13.6 millimeters; the eggs showing the four extremes measure 19.1 by 13.8, 18.5 by 14.5, and 15.2 by 12.7 millimeters (Harris).

Young.—Grimes (1935) says:

> The hooded warbler ordinarily rears only one brood each season in this area, but I have known some to build again a week or ten days after the young left the first nest and successfully bring off a second brood. * * * While the female hooded seems to assume the whole task of building the nest, the male has a part in incubating the eggs and brooding the nestlings. [See remarks under plumages.] They share equally the work of supplying food for the young, and when a second nest is started, the male takes over the care of the fledglings of the first brood until they are able to shift for themselves. It is a rather common occurrence to find a male being trailed all over the swamp by a clamorous brood of young as large as the parent himself. But I have noticed that they do not receive as much attention as they demand.

Eugene P. Odum (1931) made some observations on a nest near Chapel Hill, N. C., of which he writes:

> During the first three days after the young had hatched, the male fed on the average of six times per hour, and the female fed three times and brooded three times per hour, during the five hours of observation. The average length of brooding periods was about ten minutes. During the remaining days that the young were in the nest brooding was discontinued, and the male fed on the average of every ten and one-half minutes, and the female every fourteen minutes, in eight hours of observation. The nest was somewhat infested with lice, and the female often spent several minutes eating. The excretus was usually carried away.
>
> The young were hatched almost naked, but soon were clothed in a coat of gray down. By the eighth day, when their eyes opened, they were partly feathered, and were beginning to utter audible food cries, resembling those of other young warblers. Their food seemed to be entirely insects, many of which were caught on the wing. Large brown crane-flies formed an important item in the fare.

Dr. Williams (MS.) contributes the following information: "The incubation period is 12 days, and it is quite usual to find one infertile egg. The life of the young in the nest is 8 days or a little over. The young come off the nest before they are able to fly at all well, but they have remarkably well-developed legs and feet, are very active as climbers and scramblers, and seem to be quite self-reliant. At first they seek places where fallen tree tops or a tangle of decaying logs on the forest floor offer them a refuge. Here both parents continue to feed them, but they are soon on the wing and may be seen following the parent birds about begging for food.

"By no means are all pairs successful in rearing a brood at the first attempt. In a four-year study of the birds of a 65-acre tract it appeared that only one seventh of the pairs were successful in the first attempt. Nests are frequently disturbed or destroyed, apparently by predators. But the hooded warbler is a persistent nester. Second and third attempts are made if necessary, and I am of the opinion that only the advance of the season finally puts an end to the bird's efforts to get a family of young on the wing if previous efforts are not successful. One young hooded warbler in juvenal plumage and in a dying condition was found at a considerable distance from any known occupied nesting territory on August 22, apparently abandoned by the parent birds at this late date.

"During the nesting period the interest of both parent birds in the welfare of the nest and its contents is intense. Frequent visits are made to it, apparently with no other purpose than to assure themselves that everything is all right. Cooperation between the two parents in the care of the nest and young is developed to a high degree. In the case of one pair held under close observation during the entire nesting period, it seemed to be the job of the male to clean the nest. Sometimes the female, brooding the young, would signal for the male by giving a call, and on his arrival would stand on the rim of the nest watching him while he performed this duty. During incubation the male frequently brought food to the female, and she in turn would pass them on to the young beneath her. As to whether the male ever assists the female in incubating the eggs I am unable to say. Early in my acquaintance with the hooded warbler I thought I saw a male in the act of incubating the eggs in the nest, and I so recorded it. As I gained in experience and in familiarity with the species, I noted that some females had much more black on the head than others, and I am not sure that the incubating bird may not have been one of these well-marked females."

Plumages.—The downy young are described as gray, but Dr. Dwight (1900) calls the natal down pale sepia-brown. He describes the juvenal plumage, in which the sexes are alike, as "above, pale yellowish wood-brown, edged with Mars-brown, drab when older. Wings and tail deep olive-brown, edged with olive-green, brightest on the secondaries and tertiaries, the wing coverts edged with pale wood-brown, often darker. Below, primrose-yellow, washed with wood-brown on the throat, breast and sides. The three outer rectrices largely white on their inner webs."

He says that the first winter plumage is "acquired by a partial postjuvenal moult beginning the end of June which involves the body plumage and the wing coverts but not the rest of the wings nor the tail. Young and old become practically indistinguishable."

In the young male in first winter plumage, "the crown occiput, sides of neck, whole throat and part of the chin are jet-black veiled with narrow edgings of lemon-yellow most marked on the throat. The rest of the upper surface and the sides are bright olive-green; the forehead, sides of head, anterior part of chin, breast, abdomen and crissum are rich lemon-yellow; the forehead partly veiled with olive-green or dusky tips, the lores with black ones."

The first nuptial plumage is "acquired by wear which is not very obvious, the black areas losing the veiling yellow tips. The olive-green above becomes grayer and wear brings into prominence a slight grayish collar bordering the black 'hood.' " The adult winter plumage is "acquired by a complete post-nuptial moult the last of June and in July. In some cases scarcely distinguishable from the first winter but usually the yellow edgings are absent or very obscure. The black occupies the whole chin up to its apex and the yellow below is richer." The adult nuptial plumage is acquired by wear as in the young bird.

Of the female Dwight says:

The plumages and moults correspond to those of the male, from which indistinguishable until the first winter plumage is assumed. This lacks the black of the male and is uniform olive-green above and lemon-yellow below, occasionally one or two black feathers being assumed on the crown. The first nuptial plumage acquired by wear is, of course, plain olive-green and yellow. The adult winter plumage assumed by a complete moult shows a variable amount of black about the head and throat. How much of the black is due to individual vigor and how much to successive postnuptial moults is a question not easily answerable. We know that some females in the breeding season are almost indistinguishable from males, and there are all sorts of intermediates from these mature birds down to those of the worn first winter dress, which are guiltless of black.

The fact that very old, or very vigorous, females sometimes assume a plumage that is scarcely distinguishable from that of the male casts some doubt on the statements made by some observers that both sexes incubate the eggs. Apparently, most, if not all, fully adult females have more or less black in the crown and throat. In this connection the reader is referred to remarks by Ridgway (1889) and to descriptions of the adult female by Ridgway (1902) and by Chapman (1907), all of which refer to this subject. For a detailed description of the immature plumages and molts, the reader is referred to an interesting paper by William Palmer (1894).

Food.—Forbush (1929) says: "Little is known of the food of this bird. Grasshoppers, locusts, caterpillars and plant-lice are taken by it, and it takes many small insects upon the wing, but what they are we know not." A. H. Howell (1932) states that "examination of the stomachs of 6 specimens from Florida showed the food to consist of flies, ants, wasps, beetles, bugs, moths and their larvae, caddis flies, round-worms, and spiders."

Most of the food of the hooded warbler is obtained on or near the ground in the forest undergrowth where it lives, but it subsists largely on insects caught in the air. It is an expert fly-catcher, an activity for which its bill and bristles are well developed, and it may often be seen darting up into the air for a passing insect, or, if not successful on the first dash, following the insect in its erratic flight until it is captured, much after the manner of the true flycatchers.

Behavior.—Mr. Rathbun writes to me: "The hooded warbler does not spend its life far above the ground. Rarely have I found it over

15 feet above ground, and then only when startled. Neither is it often seen on the ground. It prefers small semi-open thickets of beech and maple, where it nests. It is a lively bird, and is constantly moving from one thicket to another, at times following the edges and again in the densest part. It seems to have much curiosity, for if a person sits quietly in the woods, he will hear the constantly nearing sound of its sharp alarm note until finally the bird will peer from the foliage, from which it quickly flies if disturbed. It is an exceedingly active bird in every way and one may be sure that, if there is a hooded warbler in any wood, sooner or later its alarm note will be heard and the bird glimpsed."

Although this warbler spends most of its life in the lower story of the forest, it often rises to the treetops to sing, as William Brewster (1875) observes: "As the day advanced the males would frequently ascend to the tops of the forest trees, and sing many times in succession sitting perfectly motionless in one place, then with expanded wings and tail would sail to the next tree and sing again. * * * When among the low thickets they are restless and shy, keeping a considerable distance ahead however fast you may walk, and were it not for the loud song they would be most difficult to procure. At such times they have a habit, observable in others of the genus, of flirting up six or eight feet after an insect and dropping almost perpendicularly again with closed wings."

I should call the hooded warbler more retiring than shy. If actively pursued, it retires to the seclusion of its leafy retreats, but it can be approached quietly, and has been photographed successfully at its nest, where the male seems to be less timid than the female. Forbush (1929) tells of one that even followed a man about for a while; and he quotes Aretas A. Saunders as saying that "he saw a pair of these birds acting as if their nest was near-by, but he could not find it. He stayed to eat his lunch, and as he finished and was about to rise, the male bird suddenly dropped to a low bush and then flew directly at his head; as Mr. Saunders dodged, the bird's wing brushed his face. This seems remarkable, as this bird usually seems to be of a gentle disposition, though some rival males fight fiercely in the mating season."

Mr. Allison told Dr. Chapman (1907) of "a very interesting fight between two male Hooded Warblers, for the possession of a female; the two began the contest in a tree, fluttering down into the mud and water, and the upper one, who had the other by the head, was in a fair way to drown or disable his opponent, when we frightened them off."

A conspicuous habit of the hooded warbler, so common with the redstarts and some other fly-catching warblers, is the frequent fanning in and out of its showy tail feathers, making a striking display of the white areas, a directive rather than a concealing action. Referring to this, Francis H. Allen writes to me: "The constant opening and shutting of the hooded warbler's tail, showing the areas of white, is extraordinary. Sometimes the bird switches its whole body to right or left, and sometimes the tail is jetted up and down slightly, but the opening and shutting is constant and very rapid. It is a graceful bird, and the tail action is as easy as the flickering of a flame."

Voice.—Aretas A. Saunders contributes the following study of the song of this warbler: "The song of the hooded warbler is one of the loudest of the warbler songs, and clearest in musical quality. It is short, consisting of 5 to 11 rather rapid notes, averaging 7. A typical song begins with two or three 2-note phrases or single notes, and ends with two longer, strongly accented notes, the first high in pitch and the second low; *tawit tawit tawit tée tóo.*

"In 25 of my 38 records the last two notes are the highest and lowest pitches of the song. In 26 records these two notes are simple and distinct; in 7 records they are connected by a slur, *teeyoo.* In 3 records the last note is a downward slur, so that the ending is *tee toyo;* while in 2 records the last note is highest of the song, the ending being *tay tee.* The first notes are regular 2-note phrases in 21 records and single notes in 9, while the remaining 8 records are quite irregular.

"Pitch of the song varies from D''' to E flat''''. Individual songs have a range of pitch from one and a half to four tones, the average being about two and a half tones. Songs vary from 1 to 2⅗ seconds, mainly according to the number of notes they contain.

"The birds sing on spring migration and from arrival on the breeding grounds till July. The average date of the last song heard in 12 seasons in Allegany State Park, N. Y., is July 16; the earliest July 8, 1930, and the latest July 24, 1938. But the bird is rather uncommon and local there, and could not be heard daily, so that the average may be somewhat later than this. The song is occasionally resumed in late August and September."

Albert R. Brand (1938) found that the number of vibrations per second in the song of the hooded warbler varied from 5,850 on the highest notes to 2,925 on the lowest notes, with an approximate mean of 4,000.

Wayne (1910) says that, in South Carolina, the song period is portracted for more than 5 months; and Grimes (1935) hears the males singing "throughout the sultry days of July and August and until late September."

Dr. Chapman (1907) writes: "The song of the Hooded Warbler is distinguished by an easy, *sliding* gracefulness. To my ear the words *you must come to the woods or you won't see me,* uttered quickly,

and made to run one into the other exactly fit the bird's more prolonged vocal efforts, though they are far from agreeing with the
attempts at syllabification of others.   The call is a high, sharp *cheep*,
easily recognized after it has been learned."   He quotes from Allison's notes: "There are two common songs, both uttered on every
possible occasion in spring, when the woods are ringing with them.
The most frequent is a short one of four syllables, *Se-whit, se-wheer;*
the longer song may be rendered, *Whee-whee-whée-a-whée*, accented
as marked.   A sharper, very clear-cut *chirp* is sometimes to be heard
late in the evening, about dusk."

To John N. Clark's (1882) ear the bird seems to say *Pe-ter Pe-ter
Re-gis-ter*, sometimes repeating the *Pe-ter* three times, or only once,
again saying just *Re-gis-ter*, with the accent on the *Re*.

Rathbun (MS.) writes: "The song of this warbler signals its arrival, and on any soft June morning which has a rising temperature
and rather high humidity, this warbler's song will be given more or
less incessantly and at its very best, the forest fairly ringing with
its lovely song.   As nesting time draws near, the song improves
in quality and frequency; this will continue until shortly after the
eggs are hatched, when a decline begins, ceasing altogether by August
1.   The bird has two songs, each consisting of clear, lively and
sprightly notes.   One song is decidedly longer than the other and,
in my opinion, is much the better of the two.   It is composed of seven
notes, quite rapidly given, the last note having a strong rising inflection and often ending abruptly.   It is essentially a carefree song,
musical, and often spiced with a little jauntiness, which in many
ways perfectly reflects the actions of the bird.   It also has a quality
which enables it to be heard for a long distance.   This warbler has
an abrupt alarm note which is much used by both sexes not only as
a warning note, but also to hold the members of the family group
together."

Dr. Williams says in his notes: "In addition to the full song, and
its variations and modifications, the hooded warbler on occasion uses
a song of a *chip-chip-chippity* nature, somewhat comparable to the
redstart's well-known vocal effort, and quite unlike the more usual
song.   When first heard, it seems as if it must come from the throat
of quite another bird.

"The quite characteristic *chip* note, used by both male and female,
has been described by most authors who have written about the hooded
warbler.   Some say that it has a metallic ring at the end, while others
quite definitely say that it has not.   The fact is that both are correct.
The *chip* note may be delivered either with or without the ringing
ending, and it more often lacks the ring late in the season than earlier.
It may be distinguished from the cardinal's well known *chip* because

it is louder and less sparrowlike, and has a ring at the end which the cardinal's note lacks. From the note of the Louisiana waterthrush it may be separated by the fact that it is not so loud. And it may be told from the chipmunk's *chip* because of its more even spacing, and its more usual ring, which the chipmunk's note lacks.

"During May and June the hooded warbler is one of the most consistent singers of the woods which he frequents. He is one of the last to stop at night as darkness comes on, sometimes continuing longer than the wood thrush, the scarlet tanager or the wood pewee."

Field marks.—The adult male hooded warbler is unmistakable, with its black hood and throat surrounding its bright yellow cheeks in marked contrast with its olive-green black and yellow under parts. There are no white wing-bars, but the outer tail feathers are largely white and are almost constantly displayed. The fully adult female is often much like the male in general appearance, as noted under Plumages, but young birds are mainly plain olive above and yellow below. The seasonal plumages are not strikingly different. The song is quite distinctive.

Enemies.—Dr. Friedmann (1929) says that this warbler is a rather uncommon victim of the cowbird; he had only ten records.

Harold S. Peters (1936) lists one louse, two bird-flies, and one tick as external parasites on the hooded warbler. Dr. Williams (MS.) says: "The raccoon, skunk, opossum, red squirrel, and pilot black-snake are all regular prowlers throughout the areas where the hooded warbler nests. The barred owl and the blue jay have young to feed while the warblers are incubating their eggs and feeding their own young in the nest. The cowbird is a frequent visitor to hooded warblers' nests, slightly over 50 percent of nests found with eggs or young containing from one to three cowbird's eggs or young."

Winter.—Dr. Skutch contributes the following: "Very rarely recorded in southern Central America, the hooded warbler is one of the less abundant winter residents in the lowlands of Honduras and Guatemala. In northern Central America it is found on both the Caribbean and Pacific sides of the mountains, and in midwinter ranges upward to at least 3,000 feet above sea level. On September 28, 1933, I met a male on the Sierra de Tecpán at an altitude of 8,500 feet; but he was obviously a transient and did not linger; nor have I any other record of the species at so high an altitude. The hooded warbler frequents low, moist thickets and second-growth woodland, and like practically all birds of similar habitat, is found singly rather than in flocks. Wearing his bright nuptial attire through the year, the male hooded warbler is always a delightful bird to meet amid the low second-growth, and is sufficiently rare to make the encounter a memorable event. The birds arrive in Guatemala in September and remain until early April.

"Early dates of fall arrival in Central America are: Guatemala—
Hacienda California (Griscom), September 22; Sierra de Tecpán,
8,500 feet, September 28, 1933; Colomba, September 29, 1934. Hon-
duras—Tela, September 3, 1930. Late dates of spring departure from
Central America are: Guatemala—Motagua Valley, near Los Amates,
April 6, 1932."

DISTRIBUTION

Range.—Eastern United States, eastern Mexico, and Central
America.

Breeding range.—The hooded warbler breeds **north** to extreme
southeastern Nebraska (rarely); central Iowa (mouth of the Des
Moines River; probably Grinnell, Mahoska County, and Burlington);
central and northeastern Illinois (Havana, Glen Elyn, and probably
Waukegan); southwestern Michigan (Kalamazoo County; probably
Macataw, and Grand Rapids); northern Ohio (rarely Toledo, Oberlin,
Cleveland, and Painesville); northwestern Pennsylvania (Erie);
western and central New York (Gaines, Rochester, Oswego, Baldwins-
ville, Stockbridge, and Cincinnatus); rarely to southern Massachu-
setts (Springfield and Dighton); and southern Connecticut (Newton,
New Haven, and Preston). **East** to southern Connecticut (Preston);
southeastern New York (Greenwood Lakes, Highland Falls, and
Palenville); and south along the Atlantic coast to northern peninsular
Florida (Old Town, Palatka, and Hastings). **South** to northern
Florida (Hastings); the shores of the Gulf of Mexico, and southeastern
Texas (Brazoria County, Kountz, and probably Matagorda). **West**
to southeastern Texas (probably Matagorda); eastern Oklahoma
(Cherokee Nation, Le Flore County, and McCurtain County); eastern
Kansas (probably Fort Leavenworth and Burlington); and south-
eastern Nebraska.

Winter range.—It winters in southern Tamaulipas (Altimira);
Veracruz and the Yucatán Peninsula south to southern Guatemala
(Quetzaltenango, Patlul, and Ocós) and Costa Rica (Mount Cacagu-
atique, Volcán de Conchagua, and Guácimo; rarely central Panamá
(Canal Zone).

The species is rare in southern Wisconsin (North Freedom, Apple-
ton, Green Bay, and Two Rivers); and in southern Ontario (Ron-
dreau, Woodstock, Toronto, and Cataraqui), and is only casual in
South Dakota (Faulkton); North Dakota (Kenmare); Minnesota
(Heron Lake and Minneapolis); Vermont (Rutland and St. Johns-
bury); Maine (Fryeburg and Falmouth); and New Brunswick
(Saint John). It is accidental in Jamaica; the Bahamas (Cay
Lobos); Bermuda; Puerto Rico (Barrio Miradero); and the Virgin
Islands (Saint Croix).

Migration.—Late dates of spring departure are: Volcán de Conchagua, March 3. Guatemala—Uaxactún, Petén, April 11. British Honduras—Mountain Cow, April 13. Mexico—Veracruz, Los Tuxtlas, March 30. Bahamas—Cay Lobos Light, April 15.

Early dates of spring arrival are: Virgin Islands, St. Croix, March 16, Cuba—El Guama, near Pinar del Río, March 25. Florida—Pensacola, March 16 (1947). Alabama—Mobile, March 24; Birmingham, March 28 (average of 10 years, March 30). Georgia—Atlanta, March 17. South Carolina—Yemassee, March 24. North Carolina—Windsor, March 31; Raleigh, April 5 (average of 26 years, April 17). Virginia—Cape Henry, April 9 (average, April 17); Rockbridge County, April 22. West Virginia—Bluefield, April 20; French Creek, April 24 (average of 17 years, May 1). District of Columbia—Washington, April 13 (average of 35 years, April 29). Maryland—Whaleysville, April 16; Patuxent Wildlife Research Refuge, Laurel, April 17. Delaware—Kent and Sussex Counties, April 3 (average of 14 years, April 15). Pennsylvania—Chambersburg, April 23. New Jersey—Cape May, April 25. New York—Niagara Falls, April 6 (1947); Westchester County, April 28 (1929). Connecticut—Fairfield and Hartford, May 1. Massachusetts—Martha's Vineyard, April 22 (1929); Northampton, May 2, (1929). Vermont—Rutland, May 4. Maine—Gorham, May 18. Louisiana—New Orleans, March 8. Mississippi—Deer Island, March 14. Arkansas—Huttig, March 19; Helena, March 31. Tennessee—Elizabethton, March 29 (1950); Nashville, March 31 (average of 13 dates, April 12). Kentucky—Bowling Green, April 13. Missouri—Dunklin County, April 2; St. Louis, April 17. Illinois—Chicago, March 27 (1950); Crab Orchard Lake, March 30 (1950); Blue Island, April 6 (1947); Rockford, April 6 (1950). Indiana—Lake County, April 14. Ohio—Put-in-Bay, March 28 (1950); Columbus, March 30, (1950); Toledo, April 9 (1947); average for central Ohio, May 2. Michigan—Detroit, April 6 (1947); Ann Arbor, April 7. Ontario—Toronto, March 28 (1950); Hamilton, March 30 (1950); Point Pelee, April 23. Iowa—Keokuk, May 7. Wisconsin—Milwaukee and Madison, March 27 (1950). Minnesota—Minneapolis, May 17. Texas—Cove, February 29; Houston, March 2. Oklahoma—Adair County, April 9. Nebraska—Omaha, May 7.

Late dates of fall departure are: Texas—Harlingen, November 7. Wisconsin—Dane County, September 12. Ohio—Columbus, October 10 (average for central Ohio, September 20). Indiana—Brookville and Lebanon, October 20. Illinois—Rockford, September 19. Missouri—St. Charles County, September 20; Dunklin County, September 28. Kentucky—Bowling Green, October 15. Tennessee—Athens, October 18. Arkansas—Arkansas County, October 7. Louisiana—

Baton Rouge region, October 26. Maine—Fryeburg, September 18. Massachusetts—Framingham, October 15; Marblehead, November 7. Rhode Island—Green Hill, September 17. Connecticut—Fairfield, September 22. New York—Orient, Long Island, September 28. New Jersey—Grantwood, Bergen County, November 8. Pennsylvania—Renovo, October 4. Maryland—Patuxent Wildlife Research Refuge, October 3. District of Columbia—Washington, October 1 (average of 10 years, September 14). West Virginia—Bluefield, October 8; Mount Lookout, Nicholas County, November 9. Virginia—Lynchburg, October 10; Cape Henry, October 16 (average, September 20). North Carolina—Raleigh, October 1 (average of 8 years, September 13). South Carolina—Charleston, November 11. Georgia—Savannah and Atlanta, October 28. Alabama—Birmingham, October 22 (average of 10 years, October 8). Florida—Pensacola, November 8. Cuba—Habana, September 24.

Early dates of fall arrival are: Texas—Galveston, August 27. Kentucky—Bowling Green, August 20. Mississippi—Deer Island, July 30. New York—New York City, July 19. Florida—Alligator Point, July 19; Key West, September 19. Cuba—Habana, August 27. Guatemala—Hacienda California, September 22. Honduras—near Tela, September 3. Nicaragua—Escondido River, September 24. Costa Rica—Guácimo, October 26.

Egg dates.—Connecticut: 42 records, May 22 to June 15; 23 records, May 27 to June 2, indicating the height of the season.

Georgia: 10 records, April 30 to June 13; 5 records, May 6 to 31.

New Jersey: 35 records, May 23 to June 14; 22 records, May 27 to 31.

South Carolina: 10 records, April 25 to June 26; 6 records, May 7 to 18 (Harris).

WILSONIA PUSILLA PUSILLA (Wilson)

WILSON'S PILEOLATED WARBLER

CONTRIBUTED BY WINSOR MARRETT TYLER

PLATE 76

HABITS

Wilson (1832) and Audubon (1941) knew little about Wilson's pileolated warbler. Wilson apparently saw only a few migrating birds in New Jersey and Delaware, and Audubon, although he "found the birds abundant in Newfoundland," evidently did not discover its nest, as he describes it "amongst the thick foliage of dwarf firs, not more than from three to five feet from the ground."

Spring.—Wilson's warbler is one of the less common transients which pass through southern New England on the way to their more northern breeding grounds. We find the birds most commonly, perhaps, in swampy thickets or roadside shrubbery, although often they frequent well-grown woodlands. They are also at times fairly common visitors to our city parks—the Public Garden in Boston, for example—during the height of the spring migration, at which time they seem to be in full song.

In the open country the birds as a rule appear singly, but in the parks they may collect in considerable numbers; Horace W. Wright (1909) reports 10 birds in the Public Garden on a single day.

Whenever we meet the little bird our attention is sure to be drawn to it by its bright song, and then the eye is caught by the quick sprightliness of its demeanor, and a flash of sunny gold.

Nesting.—When we meet Wilson's warblers during the spring migration they may be on their way to the far north, for they breed to the limit of trees in northwestern and central Mackenzie as well as in the more southern Provinces of Canada and in northern Maine and New Hampshire.

In the southern part of its breeding range, where it has been studied carefully, it chooses for nesting the moist sphagnum bogs which are characteristic of this region—lonely, mosquito-infested wastes where, often associated with yellow palm and Tennessee warblers, it builds its nest on the ground.

Philipp and Bowdish (1917) thus describe a typical nest found in New Brunswick. "On June 16, a nest with five eggs, in which incubation was well commenced, was found in a boggy and quite wet clearing, surrounded by woods, with a considerable growth of small cedar, tamarack, spruce, and balsam saplings. This nest was built in the side of a moss tussock, resting in the angle formed by the abrupt side of the tussock and a little cedar, at the base of which the nest was placed. It was composed of moss, dead leaves, fine weed stalks and grasses, a little hair being mingled with the lining of fine, dead grass. It measured 3.50 x 1.50 inches in depth and 3.50 x 1.75 inches in diameter." Of the several nests found they say: "The nests are typical and readily distinguishable from other ground nesting warblers of the region, being very bulky for such a small bird."

W. J. Brown (MS.) sends this interesting account of the habitat of Wilson's warbler and the behavior of the birds at the nest, drawn from his long "friendship" with the bird, and his intimate knowledge of some 75 of their nests. "In the County of Matane, Gulf of St. Lawrence there is a sphagnum bog three miles in circumference and over a mile across. It is hidden on the west, east, and south by heavy evergreen woods, while the north end extends to the seacoast. Throughout this bog the ground is covered with deep moss, while black spruce, tamarack, and pine saplings are scattered over the whole region. The undergrowth is mostly Laborador tea and blueberry plants. Along the sides of this delightful barren are extensive open runs of alder, birch, and other mixed small timber, with many beautiful mounds interspersed. This region is the home of Wilson's warbler, and the bird is not only abundant in this bog, but throughout the entire County of Matane. I use the word 'friendship' advisedly in the case of the Wilson's because it is a confiding little bird, entirely lacking in fear during the nesting season. Should a warbler be flushed from a nest and you are in doubt as to its identity, wait a few seconds, and if it be a Wilson's, the bird will immediately return and exhibit a mild curiosity and a look of inquiry, flitting about noiselessly, and probably will enter the nest while the intruder is standing near by. I have never seen this warbler fail to return at once to its nest after being flushed. This action is characteristic and quite contrary to that of Nashville and Tennessee warblers.

"At the end of June, 1930, I flushed a Wilson's warbler from a nest in a hummock well-sheltered by a thick bunch of Labrador tea, and near a fringe of alders. The nest contained five young a few days old. I sat down 3 feet from the nest for 2 hours, with an old hat on my head. The bird, returning with insects, perched on my hat, then on my shoulder, and into the nest. This happened 20 times while I was anchored at the nest. The bird was fearless and tame and no doubt took it for granted that I was going to be a part of the landscape. Each time, on leaving the nest, she flew directly away. I did not see the male bird, but I heard him singing as he patrolled along the fringe of alders. I have found a nest of Wilson's warblers in this same mound every season for the past 10 years and I believe they become attached to old haunts. While I have been shuffling about with my camera and tripod, the birds are either perched on the camera and its base or are in the nest, sitting. This applies to most of the nests which I have observed.

"The majority of nests are sunk in moss at the base of alders or tamarack saplings at the edge of second growth. They are well hidden, and the bird sits close until almost trodden upon. They are sociable little birds with their own kind; three or four pairs may nest near together in a line of alders not over 75 yards long. The nests are simple affairs composed inside and out of a compact mass of fine, bleached grasses. After the young are hatched the male is often seen at the nest; before this time he patrols the alders, feeding and singing in a lazy way, with an occasional long flight to feed the sitting bird."

Of the occurrence of Wilson's warbler as a breeding bird in Maine, Knight (1908) says:

That the species breeds frequently in the Canadian life areas of northern and central Maine seems well established, and that it has not been more often discovered during the nesting season is on account of the favorite habitats being rarely visited by ornithologists. Full sets of eggs may be sought between June first and June nineteenth. There seems to be no doubt at all that a person acquainted with the habits of the present species and the Yellow Palm Warbler as well, can go into territory in northern and central Maine and find both species in many localities where other observers have failed to see them, provided that suitable tracts of spruce and hackmatack bog exist in the region.

Horace W. Wright (1911) speaks of the bird as "a rare summer resident, but becoming less rare" in Jefferson, N. H. He found the birds settled in Jefferson in the summer of 1905, and during the following 5 years, a little colony of six males was established. He reports also a nest and eggs found in 1909 by F. B. Spaulding in the neighboring town of Lancaster.

Eggs.—Wilson's warbler lays from 4 to 6 eggs to a set, most commonly five. These are ovate, with some tending toward short ovate, and they have only a slight lustre. They are white, or creamy white, finely speckled or spotted with "chestnut," "auburn," or "russet," with underlying markings of "light brownish drab" or "pale brownish drab." Sometimes the markings are scattered well over the egg, but there is a tendency to concentrate at the large end, often forming a distinct wreath of fine specklings. On the more boldly marked eggs the drab tones are quite prominent, whereas on the finely marked eggs they are often absent. The measurements of 44 eggs average 15.9 by 12.4 millimeters; the eggs showing the four extremes measure 17.3 by 12.7, 16.8 by 13.2, and 14.0 by 11.4 millimeters (Harris).

Young.—Two nests under the observation of W. J. Brown (MS.) at Matane County, Quebec, contained five fresh eggs on June 18, 1939. "The young appeared in both nests in the early morning of June 29. On July 10 both nests were empty. On the basis of these records, the incubation period lasts 10 to 11 days, and the young remain in the nest for the same length of time."

Plumages.—Dr. Dwight (1900) describes the juvenal plumage, in which the sexes are alike, as follows: "Above, sepia or hair brown, mottled with sepia. Wings and tail dull olive-brown, edged with olive-green; wing coverts paler and indistinctly edged with buff. Below, primrose-yellow washed with pale wood-brown on the throat and sides."

The first winter plumage is acquired in July and involves a molt of all the body plumage and the wing coverts, but not the rest of the wings or the tail. The black cap is acquired, veiled with brownish feather tips; the upper parts become bright olive-green; the forehead, sides of the head, and the under parts become lemon-yellow.

The first nuptial plumage is acquired by a partial prenuptial molt, chiefly about the head and throat, young and old birds becoming indistinguishable.

A complete postnuptial molt occurs in July, at which an adult winter plumage is assumed that differs only slightly from the first winter plumage.

These remarks refer to the male. The plumages and molts of the female are similar, but the black cap is wholly lacking in the first winter plumage and more restricted afterward.

Food.—No comprehensive study of the food of Wilson's warbler has appeared in the literature, and practically nothing has been published in detail on the food of our eastern bird. Prof. Beal (1907) examined the contents of 53 stomachs of one of the western races of the species and found that 93 percent of the food was animal matter and only 7 percent of it vegetable. There is no reason to suppose that the eastern race has not a somewhat similar diet. Moreover, since our Wilson's warbler has been seen repeatedly foraging among the twigs and foliage of trees and shrubs, presumably in search of insects and their eggs and larvae, or darting out into the air to capture flying insects, it may be safely regarded as primarily insectivorous and hence mainly a beneficent species.

Dr. Alexander F. Skutch (MS.), speaking of the bird in Central America, says: "Among the peculiar foods of the Wilson's warblers in their winter home are the little, white, beadlike protein corpuscles which they daintly pluck from the furry cushions at the bases of the long petioles of the Cecropia tree. These minute grains, the chief nourishment of the Azteca ants that dwell in myriads in the hollow stems of the tree, are also sought by a number of other small birds, both resident and migratory."

Mrs. Edith K. Frey tells me that she has seen Wilson's warblers and several other species of wood warblers feeding on aphids in her shrubbery day after day until the pests were gone.

Behavior.—Wilson's warbler is a bright spot to bird watchers at the full tide of migration in May, and again in late summer, although we meet the bird less frequently during its southerly retreat from its breeding ground. It is a bright spot not solely because of brilliancy of plumage, but rather because it appears as a lively personality, standing out sharply as an individual among the quieter warblers. It gives us the impression of extreme alertness as it flits about in the trees and shrubbery, fluttering among the foliage, dashing into the air to capture flying insects, restless, full of energy, symbolizing, in spring, its characteristics by its brisk, vivid song. William Brewster (1936) thus pictures the bird:

Wilson's Blackcap is a most interesting little bird, very like the Canadian Warbler in general behavior, but fussier and more animated. It feeds chiefly among low bushes (especially willows) near water and is incessantly in motion. It is much given to making short, abrupt upward flights to seize insects from the under sides of the leaves. It jerks its tail upward every few seconds and also

waves it from side to side much after the manner of a Gnatcatcher. It frequently darts out after flying insects and not infrequently descends to the ground
to search for food among the fallen leaves. When on the ground it hops about
briskly and often flutters its wings.

J. Merton Swain (1904) says of the bird on its breeding ground:
"They feed in briery thickets, picking up insects very nimbly. They
have the talents of a Flycatcher, and capture much of their food on
the wing, but do not, like the Flycatcher, return to the same perch."

Voice.—Like most wood warbler's songs, which in the main are
little more than a series of squeaky notes, or at most shrill whistles,
the song of Wilson's warbler is neither beautiful nor artistic. Yet
it stands out by reason of its brightness; the notes are delivered so
emphatically, are so sharply cut and staccato, and follow each other
in chattering haste so rapidly that the song has a distinctive quality
and is easily distinguished from those of those other warblers which
sing on about the same pitch. At times the song may suggest that of
the yellow warbler, but the latter, in comparison, has almost a drawl-
ing delivery; at other times it may suggest that of the Nashville, but
here again the staccato quality marks it; it sometimes recalls for a
moment the song of the northern waterthrush, but as all the notes are
very short and never isolated, the resemblance at once vanishes;
occasionally there is a hint of the goldfinch's voice (I find this point
mentioned more than once in my notes of the last quarter of a century), but the tone is too flat for a goldfinch—it lacks the sweet,
musical ring.

The song is more or less varied, but there are not two distinct songs
as in the case of some warblers. In a common form the pitch drops
in the second half when, the notes becoming faster and more emphatic,
the song changes into a sort of chatter. I have heard this form given
over and over for half an hour or more with little or no change. More
rarely the pitch at the end may return to the original pitch, thus
dividing the song into three parts. Occasionally the song ends with
a single, emphasized note, and frequently neither pitch nor tempo
varies—a perplexing song at first, but the extreme liveliness of the
notes soon identifies the author.

Gerald Thayer (Eaton, 1914) gives this accurate description: "Its
song suggests somewhat in miniature that of the Northern water
thrush although it is itself quite loud and rich, a bright, hurried,
rolling twitter, suddenly changed into more of a trill, richer and
somewhat lower in tone. The first portion of the song varies in
length and richness, sometimes longer and fuller in tone, more often
shorter and weaker than the second, while some individuals omit it
altogether, uttering only the trill when the song is rather difficult
to recognize. * * * The call note is a weak but ringing *tschip*."

Aretas A. Saunders (MS.) sends the following: "The song of Wilson's warbler is mainly a series of rapid chatterlike notes, dropping downward in pitch toward the end. It is not especially musical in quality. The notes are short, staccato, and with marked explosive consonant sounds. I have had opportunity to record only songs heard on migration, and since the song is not often heard then, I have only 12 records. These have from 8 to 15 notes, averaging about 10. They vary from F''' to C'''' in pitch, and from 1⅖ to 1⅘ seconds in length. Individual songs have a pitch range from one to two and a half tones, averaging about one and a half. In most of the records the notes are all on the same pitch and of equal length at the beginning, only the last 3 or 4 notes dropping in pitch, and sometimes becoming faster in time. In all but 2 records the last note is lowest in pitch, and in these exceptions it is the next to the last note that is lowest. A typical song would sound like *wititititititititatoo*."

Ralph Hoffmann (1899) reports: "On the 2d of November I found a female Wilson's Blackcap in Belmont [Mass.]; the bird stayed in the same locality till Nov. 20, and uttered when startled a curious wren-like *kek,kek*, which I have never before heard."

Field marks.—Although the identification points in the plumage of Wilson's warbler are mostly negative—absence of wing bars and tail spots, and no streaks or lines in the plumage—the tiny bird is distinctive in the field. The black skull cap is often difficult to see, but the contrast between the plain darkish back and the brilliant, plain under parts is an aid in identification, and even more helpful is the unmarked, bright yellow side of the head with the black eye, a dot in the center.

Enemies.—Wilson's warbler presumably has few enemies aside from danger during its long migration and the hazards of a ground nest. Wilson's warbler, like the Tennessee and yellow palm, is apparently rarely molested by the cowbird. The three species breed in the same environment, often in the same swamps, where, it may be supposed, cowbirds seldom go. Friedmann (1929) does not list the bird, but records the race *chryseola* as "a not uncommon victim of the Dwarf Cowbird in southern California."

Fall.—Of the bird in Cambridge, Mass., in the fall, William Brewster (1906) says: "During their return migrations, which begin late in August, Wilson's Blackcaps are decidedly less numerous—or at least conspicuous—than in spring, and also more given to haunting dry places. Indeed I have seen them oftenest at this season among oaks or pines growing on high ground. Most of them pass southward before the middle of September, but Mr. Ralph Hoffmann has reported finding a young bird in Belmont as late as November 20 (1898)."

Winter.—Dr. Alexander F. Skutch (MS.) sends to A. C. Bent the following comprehensive account of the bird as he has seen it during the winter in Central America: "All three forms of Wilson's warbler pass the winter months in Central America. Of these, the race that breeds in the Rocky Mountains, the pileolated warbler, appears from the determination of specimens to be far the most numerous. Yet since all three may occur in the same locality and it is difficult or impossible to distinguish them in the field, it seems best to treat them all under the name of the typical form.

"Arriving early in September in Guatemala, and about the middle of the month in Costa Rica, Wilson's warblers rapidly increase in numbers until they are among the most abundant of wintering warblers. They settle down for their long sojourn in a great variety of situations, from the warm lowlands up to the bushy summits of the higher mountains that are so cold and frosty during the nights of the northern winter. I have found them abundant even at 11,000 feet above sea level. They are far less common in the Caribbean lowlands than they become above 1,500 feet, and are distinctly uncommon on the Pacific side of Central America below 2,000 feet. But from these levels up to the tree line, there seems to be slight variation in their midwinter abundance, which is associated with the type of vegetation rather than with altitude. Everywhere the blackcaps haunt the bushy abandoned fields, neglected pastures, openings in the forest, hedgerows, and at times even the dooryard shrubbery. They avoid the sunless undergrowth of heavy forests, yet frequent the lighter woods of oak and pine in the highlands, and the thinner of the woodlands at lower elevations. Restless and sprightly, they flit tirelessly among the bushes in pursuit of tiny insects, constantly advertising their presence with their emphatic nasal *chip.*

"The period of absence of Wilson's warbler from Central America is brief. On the Sierra de Tecpán in the Guatemalan highlands, I saw the last one of the season on May 22, 1933. The first fall arrival was encountered on September 3 of the same year; four were seen on the following day, and by the fifth of the month, they were so numerous that it was hopeless to try to keep count of them. They had been absent only 3 months and 12 days. At Vara Blanca on the Cordillera Central of Costa Rica, the first appeared on September 18, 1937, and the last was seen on May 5 of the following year. They were present through the year, save for a period of 4 months and 13 days.

"Although at times Wilson's warblers are present on the bushy mountain slopes in such great numbers that they give the impression of being gregarious, they are in fact evenly distributed through the bushes. Where less abundant, they are seen singly rather than in flocks, for they are intolerant of the company of their own kind during

the winter months. At times, in the highlands, a single individual
of the species will attach itself to a mixed flock of warblers and other
small birds. On the central plateau of Costa Rica, I would sometimes
find a single Wilson's warbler keeping company among the coffee
bushes with a pair of the pretty, chestnut-headed Delattre's warblers
(*Basileuterus delattrii*), a resident species which remains paired and
maintains a territory throughout the year. But perhaps more often
the blackcaps pass the winter quite alone. On October 12, 1933, I came
upon two male Wilson's warblers fighting earnestly on the ground in
the garden of the house in which I dwelt on the Sierra de Tecpán.
While I did not witness the beginning of the conflict and can only
surmise its cause, it seems probable that this was a struggle for the
possession of the garden in which it was staged. They separated a
few moments after I came upon them; and I did not hear them sing,
as migratory warblers will sometimes do under similar circumstances.
As the date for their departure approaches, these long-solitary
warblers tend to draw together in flocks for their northward flight.

"On April 27, 1933, I heard a Wilson's warbler singing in the
Guatemalan highlands. Five days later, I found another caroling far
more whole-heartedly, repeating several times over his simple but
happy little lay, a rapid chipping gradually ascending in pitch. These
songs hearalded their northward departure. By the latter part of
April, few Wilson's warblers remain in Costa Rica, although they have
been recorded as late as May 5. In Guatemala they linger somewhat
later, a few individuals tarrying until past the middle of May. Long
before they depart from Central America as a whole, these warblers
appear to withdraw from the lower altitudes at which they are not
uncommon earlier in the year, probably merely ascending the mountains to higher levels. Thus, in the lower Motagua Valley in Guatemala, at about 500 feet above sea level, I found them fairly abundant
in January and February, but did not record them later. In the
Pejivalle Valley of Costa Rica at 2,000 feet, I found a number in
February, 1934, but failed to see a single one when I revisited the
locality in April, 1941. In the Basin of El General, on the Pacific
side of the same country, they may be exceedingly numerous at an
altitude of 3,000 feet from their fall arrival until the following March,
when they rapidly grow more silent and become fewer. In dry years
they are seen in April only as rare transients, while in abnormally
wet years they may remain somewhat more numerous. This local
movement, well in advance of the main northward migration, is
paralleled by that of the Tennessee warbler; it appears to be caused
by increasing dryness or higher temperatures, or by the two in combination.

"Early dates of fall arrival in Central America are: Guatemala—
passim (Griscom), September 11; Sierra de Tecpán, 8,500 feet, Sep-

tember 3, 1933; San Juan Atitán, September 8, 1934; Huehuetenango, September 11, 1934. Costa Rica—La Hondura (Carriker), September 22; Vara Blanca, September 18, 1937; San Miguel de Desamparados, September 20, 1935; El General, September 18, 1936.

"Late dates of spring departure from Central America are: Costa Rica—El General, April 22, 1936 and April 24, 1937; Vara Blanca, May 5, 1938; Juan Viñas (Carriker), April 19. Guatemala—passim (Griscom), April 26; Sierra de Tecpán, May 22, 1933."

DISTRIBUTION

Range.—North America and Central America.

Breeding range.—The pileolated warbler breeds **north** to northern Alaska (Kotzebue Sound, probably Barrow, and Fort Yukon); northern Yukon (La Pierre House); northwestern and central eastern Mackenzie (Fort MacPherson, Mackenzie Delta, and Fort Anderson); northeastern Manitoba (probably York Factory); northern Ontario (probably Moose Factory); central Quebec (Mistassini Post, Mingan Islands, and Mutton Bay); southern Labrador (probably Hamilton River, Cartwright, and Squasho Run); and Newfoundland (Saint Anthony, Lewisport, and Trinity). **East** to Newfoundland (Trinity); central Nova Scotia (Kings County and Halifax); and Maine (Machias). **South** to Maine (Machias, Augusta, and Fryeburg); northern New Hampshire (Lancaster and Jefferson); northeastern Vermont (Saint Johnsbury); southern Quebec (Sherbrooke); southern Ontario (Sudbury, Madoc, and Ottawa); northern Michigan (Baraga and Blaney Park); northern Minnesota (Mud Lake and Duluth); western Texas (probably Guadalupe, Davis, and Chisos Mountains); north-central New Mexico (Santa Fe Canyon); and southern California (Julian and Escondido). **West** to California (Escondido, Riverside, Mount Whitney, Eagle Lake, and Edgewood); western Oregon (Mount Hood and Fort Klamath); western Washington (Bellingham, Seattle, and Mount Rainier); British Columbia (Victoria); and Alaska (King Cove, Kodiak Island, Cordova Bay, Chitina Moraine, Sitka, Gravina Island, Norton Sound, and Kotzebue Sound).

Winter range.—This species winters **north** to southern Baja California (La Paz); southern Sonora (Tesia, and Alamos); Nuevo León (Monterrey, and Linares) and southernmost Texas (Santa Maria). **East** to southernmost Texas (Santa Maria); Tamaulipas (Victoria); Costa Rica (Guayabo, San José, and Cerro de Santa María); and Panamá (Veraguas). **South** to Panamá (Veraguas, Chiriquí, and Boquete); and Guerrero (Chilpancingo). **West** to Guerrero (Chilpancingo) and southern Baja California (San José del Cabo and La Paz).

The range as outlined is for the entire species of which three sub-species are recognized. The Wilson's pileolated warbler (*Wilsonia pusilla pusilla*) breeds from northwestern and central Mackenzie to Nova Scotia and New England, northern Michigan, northern Minnesota, southern Manitoba, central Saskatchewan and central eastern Alberta; the northern pileolated warbler (*W. p. pileolata*) breeds in northern Alaska, northern Yukon and northwestern Mackenzie, Montana, eastern Wyoming, southwestern Colorado, north-central New Mexico, and western Texas, and south from Alaska through the Rockies and mountains of the Great Basin to northeastern and central eastern California; and the golden pileolated warbler (*W. p. chryseola*) breeds along the coasts and coastal ranges from southwestern British Columbia, south through western Washington, western Oregon, to eastern and southern California.

Casual in Florida (Tallahassee, Sharpes, and Fort Myers); Missouri (Independence); and Mississippi (Gulfport).

Migration.—Late dates of spring departure are: Costa Rica—Basin of El General, April 24. Guatemala—above Tecpán, May 22. Baja California—Sierra San Pedro Mártir, May 21; Sonora—Rancho La Arizona, western foothills of Pajaritos Mountains, May 25.

Early dates of spring arrival are: Alabama—Florence, May 1. Georgia—Milledgeville region, April 13. South Carolina—Chester, May 10. North Carolina—Salisbury, May 8. Virginia—Charlottesville, May 4. West Virginia—Bee, April 24; French Creek, May 7 (average of 10 years, May 12). District of Columbia—Washington, May 1 (average of 38 years, May 8). Maryland—Baltimore County, May 4. Pennsylvania—Renovo, May 1. New Jersey—Long Valley, May 5; Union County, May 12 (average, May 15). New York—New York City, April 30. Connecticut—Hartford, May 3. Rhode Island—Kingston, May 8. Massachusetts—Huntington, May 1. Vermont—Wells River, May 6. New Hampshire—Monroe, May 5. Maine—Lewiston and Winthrop, May 7. Quebec—Montreal, May 13. New Brunswick—Saint John, May 15. Nova Scotia—Halifax, May 18. Newfoundland—St. Andrews, May 27. Labrador—Grand Falls, Hamilton River, May 31. Louisiana—Monroe, April 16. Arkansas—Rogers, April 27. Tennessee—Elizabethton, May 4. Kentucky—Bowling Green, April 18. Missouri—St. Louis, and St. Charles, April 29. Illinois—LeRoy, April 27; Chicago, May 6 (average, May 11). Indiana—Marion County, April 28. Ohio—South Webster, April 25; central Ohio, May 2 (average, May 11). Michigan—Ann Arbor, May 11. Ontario—Toronto, May 10; Ottawa, May 14 (average of 17 years, May 20). Iowa—Buchanan County, May 7. Wisconsin—Madison, May 4. Minnesota—Lanesboro and Minneapolis, May 2 (average of 39 years for southern Minnesota, May 10).

Texas—Brewster County and Victoria, April 1; El Paso, April 6. Oklahoma—Gate, April 22. Kansas—Douglas County and Lake Quivira, Johnson County, May 2. Nebraska—Hastings, April 26. South Dakota—Sioux Falls, May 3. North Dakota—Fargo, May 8; Cass County, May 11 (average May 17). Manitoba—Aweme, May 3 (average, May 18). Saskatchewan—Indian Head, May 14. Mackenzie—Mackenzie Delta, May 28. New Mexico—Glenrio, April 15. Arizona—Tucson, March 7; Holbrook, May 4. Colorado— Monon, Baca County, May 3. Utah—Uinta Basin, May 12. Wyoming—Laramie, May 2. Idaho—Moscow, May 11. Montana—Anaconda and Fortine, May 14. Alberta—Medicine Hat, May 17. California—El Cajon, March 8; San Francisco Bay area, March 12 (average of 22 years, March 24). Nevada—Charleston Mountains, April 30. Oregon—Newport, April 13. Washington—Lapush, April 10. British Columbia—Comox, Vancouver Island, April 14. Yukon— Carcross and Ross Post, May 22. Alaska—Kake, May 5; Nushagak, May 10; Kotzebue Sound region, June 3.

Late dates of fall departure are: Alaska—Nome, August 27; Nunivak Island, September 7. Yukon—Macmillan River region, September 16. British Columbia—Okanagan Landing, September 22. Washington—Seattle, September 25; Pullman, September 18. Oregon—Eugene area, September 24; Government Island, December 11. Nevada—Montello, and West Humboldt Mountains, Pershing County, September 20. California—Hastings Reservation, Monterey County, November 1; Eureka, November 20. Alberta—Warner, September 30. Montana—Sun River, October 7. Idaho—Moscow area, October 21. Wyoming—Parco, October 18; Laramie, October 16, November 10 and 11. Utah—North Creek, Beaver, September 26. Colorado—Pueblo, October 20. Arizona—Tucson, October 28; average of 5 years for Parker, Topock area, September 30. New Mexico—Apache, October 15. Mackenzie—Artillery Lake, September 5. Saskatchewan—East End, September 29. Manitoba—Aweme, September 21. North Dakota—Fargo, October 20; Cass County, September 19 (average, September 15). South Dakota—Faulkton, October 10 and 30. Nebraska—Red Cloud, September 28. Kansas—Gore County, October 9. Oklahoma—Cimarron County, September 23. Texas—Victoria, November 14; Cove, November 16, January 1. Minnesota—Montevideo, October 5; Minneapolis, October 20 (average of 10 years for southern Minnesota, September 21). Wisconsin—Racine, October 8. Iowa—Tabor, October 3. Ontario—Ottawa, September 25 (average, September 19). Michigan—Grand Beach, October 18; Hillsdale, December 8. Ohio—central Ohio, September 30 (average, September 24). Indiana—Monroe County, October 3. Illinois—Chicago, October 5 (average, September 19); Port Byron, October 11. Missouri—

Columbia, September 30. Kentucky—Bowling Green, October 1. Tennessee—Nashville, October 10. Arkansas—Rogers, October 7. Mississippi—Saucier, October 12. Louisiana—Cameron, November 21; Baton Rouge, October 24, December 20. Newfoundland—Tompkins, September 30. Quebec—Quebec, September 15. Maine—Jefferson, October 11. New Hampshire—Warren, October 3. Vermont—Clarendon, September 29. Massachusetts—Belmont, November 20; Groton, November 27; West Gloucester, November 29; Boston, December 3. Connecticut—Hartford, October 1; Windsor Hill, November 3. New York—New York City, October 31, November 22 and 25; Orient Point, Long Island, November 24. New Jersey—Sandy Hook, October 7; Union County, September 29 (average, September 25); Princeton, December 23. Pennsylvania—Laceyville, October 15; Radnor, December 7. Maryland—Baltimore County, and Patuxent Wildlife Research Refuge, Laurel, September 23; Snow Hill, December 22. District of Columbia—Washington, October 13 (average of 8 years, September 19). West Virginia—French Creek, September 30. Virginia—Charlottesville, October 6. North Carolina—Piney Creek, October 11. South Carolina—Mount Pleasant, November 9. Georgia—Fitzgerald, October 31. Alabama—Birmingham, October 6. Florida—Pensacola, November 11; Lake Jackson, December 19; Tallahassee, January 1. Sonora—San José Mountains, October 25.

Early dates of fall arrival are: Washington—Seattle area, August 14. Nevada—Charleston Mountains, August 13. California—Santa Cruz Island, August 29. Montana—Great Falls, August 17. Idaho—Moscow area, August 10. Arizona—Tucson, July 31. New Mexico—Willis, August 8; Cooney, August 20. North Dakota—Wilton, August 15; Cass County, August 16 (average, August 21). Nebraska—Gresham, August 20. Kansas—Douglas County, and Geary, Doniphan County, August 23. Oklahoma—Cimarron County, August 25. Texas—Austin region, August 6; El Paso region, August 27. Minnesota—Hibbing, August 13; Minneapolis, August 15 (average of 9 years for southern Minnesota, August 24). Wisconsin—Mazomanie, August 26. Iowa—Winnebago, August 17. Michigan—Sault Ste. Marie, August 24. Ohio—central Ohio, August 20 (average, August 27). Indiana—Lake County, August 28. Illinois—Chicago, August 17 (average, August 24). Missouri—La Grange, August 16. Kentucky—Versaille and Bowling Green, September 6. Tennessee—Knoxville area, August 12. Arkansas—Winslow, September 7. Mississippi—Bolivar County, September 10. Louisiana—Baton Rouge, September 11. Maine—Hog Island, August 6. New Hampshire—Hancock and Monroe, August 16. Vermont—Wells River, August 20. Massachusetts—Lynnfield, August 19. Connecticut—New Haven and West Hartford, August 27. New York—New

York City, July 26; Bayside, Long Island, July 31. New Jersey—Englewood region, August 15; Union County, August 20 (average, September 1). Pennsylvania—Crawford County and Pittsburgh, August 28. Maryland—Patuxent Wildlife Research Refugee, Laurel, August 17. District of Columbia—Washington, August 22. Virginia—Shenandoah National Park, August 19. North Carolina—Piney Creek, September 4. Georgia—Athens, September 2. Alabama—Birmingham, August 23. Florida—Pensacola, September 23. Cuba—western Cuba, September 24. Mexico—Sonora, Rancho La Arizona, western foothills of Pajaritos Mountains, August 16; Baja California—San José del Cabo, August 25. Guatemala—above Tecpán, September 3. Salvador—Monte Mayor, Volcán de Sociedad, October 6. Costa Rica—Basin of El General, September 18.

Egg Dates.—Alaska: 10 records, May 20 to July 3; 5 records, June 15 to 18.

California: 82 records, April 27 to July 4; 41 records, May 10 to June 10, indicating the height of the season.

Colorado: 17 records, June 2 to July 1; 9 records, June 12 to 20.

Maine: 2 records, June 4 and 22.

New Brunswick: 7 records, June 6 to 21 (Harris).

WILSONIA PUSILLA PILEOLATA (Pallas)

NORTHERN PILEOLATED WARBLER

PLATE 77

HABITS

The western representatives of *Wilsonia pusilla* are divided into two subspecies, the northern pileolated warbler (*W. p. pileolata*) and the golden pileolated warbler (*W. p. chryseola*). The former breeds from the northern tree limit in Alaska, southward along the coast to the Queen Charlotte Islands, and farther southward, mainly in mountain regions, as least as far as New Mexico and perhaps central-western Texas. Dr. E. W. Nelson (1887) calls it "one of the commonest of the brush-frequenting species in the north and extends its breeding range to the shores of the Arctic Ocean, where it is found breeding about Kotzebue Sound as well as along the eastern coast of Norton Sound wherever shelter is afforded." Dr. Herbert Brandt (1943) says: "In the Hooper Bay area the Pileolated Warbler confines itself to the brushy flanks of the Askinuk Mountains where it is a rather common breeder. Along the lower Yukon River, however, during early July I recorded it at every landing that we made as far up as Mountain Village."

Referring to its status in Montana, Aretas A. Saunders (1921) writes: "A common summer resident of the mountains in the western

half of the state, and a common migrant in the mountain valleys and
at the edge of the prairie region near the mountains. A rare migrant
in the eastern part of the state. Breeds in the Canadian zone, in
willow thickets along the mountain streams or bordering mountain
lakes. West of the divide the Pileolated Warbler breeds in arbor-
vitae forests."

It probably breeds in eastern Oregon, but Gabrielson and Jewett
(1940) say that "the first actual Oregon nest remains to be discovered."
According to Prof. Cooke (1904), "in Colorado it breeds commonly
at timber line, ranging from 12,000 down to 6,000 feet."

The northern pileolated warbler is much like the eastern Wilson's
warbler, but it is somewhat larger on the average and its coloration
is brighter, the upper parts being more yellowish olive-green and the
yellow of the under parts brighter. It is, however, not so brightly
colored as the golden pileolated warbler that breeds in California.

Spring.—From its winter home in Mexico and Central America
this subspecies makes a long flight to northern Alaska, and over a
wide range, from the Pacific coast to the eastern foothills of the
Rocky Mountains. It is a later migrant in California than the local
breeding form. Mrs. Amelia S. Allen tells me that the golden pileolated warblers generally arrive on their breeding grounds in March
or very early in April, sometimes as early as March 11. She says in
her notes: "About the middle of May, after the breeding birds are
busy nesting, migrating birds pass through on the way north."

Harold S. Gilbert writes to me: "On June 11, 1933, Mr. Everett
Darr, of the Mazamas, found 200 frozen pileolated warblers scattered
over the snow and ice at about 10,000 feet elevation, in the crater
of Mt. St. Helens, Wash. He brought some of these birds to my office
for identification. Apparently, during migration they had been
swept up in a storm and frozen."

Nesting.—Herbert Brandt (1943) found five nests of this warbler in
Alaska, of which he says:

The nest of the Pileolated Warbler in the Hooper Bay area is found only in
the vicinity of the willow and alder thickets that decorate the lower mountain
slopes. Out in the cleared defiles and under the matted dead grass that never
again rises from its supine position after being beaten down by winter's pressure, this little bird builds its home. The nest may be sunken flush with the
mossy sod, or it may be built in the center of a large grass tuft, in which case
it may be elevated a few inches above the surrounding floor. However, so
closely hidden is it that considerable search is required to discover the dainty
abode.

The nest is made entirely of short grass straws that are not interwoven, and
the structure is therefore so fragile that it will scarcely retain its form when
removed. The lining may be entirely of fine, thread-like grass shreds, or there
may be admixed therewith considerable coarse dog hair. If the latter is used,
each hair is laid in separately, and none of the wool-like tufts of the dog's under

coat is employed. The measurements of five nests are: height, 2.00 to 3.50; outside diameter, 3.00 to 4.00; inside diameter, 1.75 to 2.00; and inside depth, 1.50 to 1.75 inches.

H. D. Minot (1880) thus describes a Colorado nest: "The nest was sunken in the ground, on the eastern slope or border of the swamp, at the end of a partly natural archway of long dry grass, opening to the southward, beneath the low, spreading branch of a willow. It is composed of loose shreds, with a neat lining of fine stalks and a few hairs, and with a hollow two inches wide and scarcely half as deep."

Dr. Joseph Grinnell (1909) writes: "A nest of the Alaska pileolated warbler was found by Stephens on the 7th of June near Hasselborg Lake, Admiralty Island. It was in the thick moss growing among the roots of an uprooted tree in a creek bottom. The nest was about five feet from the ground and occupied a niche in the mass of moss which overhung and hid it. The nest consists externally of moss, weathered leaves, and bark strips; internally of deer hair."

Eggs.—All of the 5 nests found by Brandt in Alaska contained 6 eggs each, but farther south the numbers run from 3 to 5, four being the commonest number. The eggs are apparently indistinguishable from those of Wilson's warbler. Dr. Brandt (1943) describes his eggs as follows: "The spots are irregular in shape, angular, and range in size from the finest pepperings to small dots. These are often confluent at the larger end, forming a broad zone or wreath. A few weak markings are scattered towards the small end which is almost unmarked. The markings are of two types: the richer one which is more frequent is of red colors, ranging from brick red to Indian red, with the weaker underlying markings vinaceous lavender. The latter are inconspicuous and often just peer out from beneath the bolder overlying spots." The measurements of 40 eggs average 15.8 by 12.2 millimeters; the eggs showing the extremes measure 17.2 by 12.6, 16.0 by 13.1, 14.7 by 12.2, and 15.2 by 10.7 millimeters.

Plumages.—The molts and plumages of the two western races correspond to those of the eastern race and their food is probably similar; in fact, the three do not differ materially in any of their habits, except as these are affected by their environment.

Behavior.—Mrs. Bailey (1902) writes attractively:

Seen in migration when the dainty pileolated warbler has plenty of leisure, his airy ways are peculiarly charming. He usually hunts in low bushes, and as he suddenly appears through a chink in the dull chaparral wall the intense brilliant yellow of the little beauty set off by his shining jet black crown gives you a thrill of surprise and delight.

He is winningly trustful and will come close to you and with wings hanging turn his head and look up to you from under his jaunty cap, then whip along with a jerk of his tail. As he goes he stops to run up a twig, leans down to peck under a leaf, flutters under a spray like a hummingbird, and then flies off singing his happy song.

Fall.—This warbler seems to be more abundant, or more conspicuous, on the fall migration east of the Rocky Mountains, where it is often the commonest of all the wood warblers, even as far east as western Nebraska.

Winter.—Of its winter haunts in Mexico, Dr. Beebe (1905) writes:

> The Pileolated Warbler and the Western Gnatcatcher were two small friends which we first met at the edge of the *barranca*. They were cheerful little bodies, forever busy searching leaves and twigs and flowers for tiny insects. Perhaps to this unflagging activity was due the fact that they seemed able to find a substantial living in all sorts and conditions of places. The Pileolated Warbler— so like our Wilson Black-cap, but of brighter yellow—never became common, and yet in every list of birds we made, whether of upland, marsh, cactus desert, *barranca*, or tropical jungle, he was sure to have a place. He was not particular as to his winter home, but found everywhere enough to keep his black-crowned little head busy picking and picking, interpolating a sharp *chip!* now and then, between mouthfuls.

In El Salvador, according to Dickey and van Rossem (1938), "the northern pileolated warbler was found to be a rather common winter visitor between the elevations of 3,500 and 8,500 feet. * * * In its winter home this warbler is chiefly an inhabitant of low growth beneath the forest. Coffee groves are particularly favored in the lower elevations. On Los Esesmiles many were noted in the cloud forest, but there were even more in the arid associations such as oak scrub, bracken beneath the pines, and blackberry tangles along small watercourses."

WILSONIA PUSILLA CHRYSEOLA Ridgway

GOLDEN PILEOLATED WARBLER

PLATES 77, 78

HABITS

This brilliantly golden race of the pileolated warbler is confined in the breeding season to the Pacific coast district, from southern British Columbia to southern California, mainly west of the mountain ranges. Ridgway (1902) describes it as similar to Wilson's warbler, "but slightly smaller and much more brightly colored; olive-green of upper parts much more yellowish, almost olive-yellow in extreme examples; yellow of forehead and superciliary region (especially the former) inclining more or less to orange; yellow of under parts purer, more intense."

Samuel F. Rathbun tells me that in western Washington this is "probably the most common of all the warblers and occurs all through the region, from the foothills of the Cascades to the Pacific Ocean."

In the Lassen Peak region of California, according to Grinnell, Dixon, and Linsdale (1930), "this race of pileolated warbler in summer was limited closely to alder and willow thickets bordering ponds, along streams and in and around the edges of moist meadows. These two plants, alder and willow, appeared to furnish the chief factors favoring the initial choice of this habitat, rather than any of the plants associated with them." Such haunts seem to be favored by the species in other parts of its western range.

Spring.—Rathbun tells me that it arrives in western Washington about the first of May. "It differs in some ways from the rest of the warblers: there is no straggling in their arrival; a goodly number come all at once, followed by the regular run of the birds until all have settled down. In the Olympic region, at least, they stick quite close to the tidewater. Sometimes one can stand on the beach facing the ocean and hear the warbler's song directly behind in the woods; this is one of the very few birds of which this can be said."

Nesting.—Rathbun describes in his notes two nests found near Seattle. One was located about a foot above the ground "in a salal shrub that grew by the side of an old path through the rather dense forest, with a quite heavy undergrowth. The nest consisted, outwardly, entirely of dry, dead leaves, next to which were finer and softer ones of the same character and a little shredded inner bark of a cedar, the lining being fine rootlets and a few horsehairs." The other was "built quite close to the ground on a slight elevation in a mass of dead bracken, being so well concealed that it was found only by flushing the female. It was composed outwardly of dead leaves and decayed weed stalks with a little green moss interwoven, this forming a base on which rested the main part of the nest, consisting of fine, dry weed stalks and shredded strips of the soft inner bark of a cedar, next being very soft, dry leaves, with a lining of fine, dry grasses. The whole structure was beautiful, the material being well interwoven and the construction neat. The outside height was 4 inches, outside diameter 6, inside diameter 2, and inside depth 1¾ inches. The location was well within a growth of young firs, widely scattered so that rather open spaces existed, overgrown with bracken."

James B. Dixon tells me that he found the golden pileolated warbler nesting in Mono County, Calif., at elevations betwen 7,000 and 9,200 feet. And in the Yosemite region, Grinnell and Storer (1924) found a nest that "was in a depression in an earth bank at the base of two azalea stems. It was overhung by these stems and also by a mat of dead brakes, which concealed the eggs from view above. The foundation of the nest was of loosely laid dead leaves, and this graded into the rest of the structure, which was composed of leaves and grass blades. The fine lining was chiefly of deer hair. The structure measured about 3½ inches in diameter outside, and the cavity was 2 inches across and 1¼ inches deep."

J. Stuart Rowley writes to me: "The nests which I have found were all well-made, deep-cupped affairs and were all placed on the ground, either at the base of a clump of skunk cabbage or of a small sapling or shrub."

Eggs.—From 3 to 5 eggs, most often 4, make up the set for the golden pileolated warbler. These are, apparently, indistinguishable from those of other races of the species. The measurements of 40 eggs average 16.2 by 12.4 millimeters; the eggs showing the four extremes measure **17.0** by **13.0**, and **15.0** by **11.9** millimeters.

Young.—Mrs. Amelia S. Allen says in her notes: "I flushed a female from her nest about a foot from the ground in dense bracken. I sat down 6 feet from the nest and she returned almost immediately and regurgitated food, then brooded the three young that had been hatched recently. Then she spent 4 minutes hunting for food, returned, fed the young, and brooded 8 minutes." A few days later torrential rains fell for 4 days, after which she found "a water-soaked nest containing five naked young that had been drowned."

Mrs. Wheelock (1904) says:

The first brood is usually hatched early in May, and is fed by regurgitation by both parents until four or five days old, when the usual food of small insects and little green worms is given to them in the fresh state. As soon as their nursery days are over, the male takes entire charge of the nestlings, feeding them for ten days or two weeks longer.

For the second brood a locality slightly higher up the mountain may be chosen, but oftener the little mother builds her second nest within a hundred yards of the first, commencing it alone, while the male is still occupied with the first series. Incubation lasts twelve days, and is, I think, attended to solely by the female, although the male is frequently at the nest both to feed her and to watch over—but not brood—the eggs.

Food.—Prof. Beal (1907) examined 52 stomachs of the golden pileolated warbler, and says:

Animal matter amounts to over 93 percent, vegetable to less than 7 percent. Of the former, the larger item is Hemiptera, which aggregates over 35 percent. The black olive scale was found in four stomachs, but leaf-hoppers make up the bulk of this portion of the food. Hymenoptera stand next in importance, with 31 percent, made up of both wasps and ants. Flies are eaten to the extent of 11 percent, and in connection with the Hymenoptera proves what observations of its habits indicate, that this bird gets much of its food when on the wing. A good many of the insects were the tipulids, or crane-flies. Beetles of half a dozen different families were eaten to the extent of about 9 percent. They were mostly leaf-beetles (Chrysomelidae), with a few weevils and one or two others. No coccinellids were found. Somewhat less than 5 percent of the food consists of caterpillars. They do not appear to be favorite food, for they are eaten very irregularly. Spiders also are taken only sparingly, and form but little more than 1 percent of the total food.

The vegetable food, less than 7 percent of the total, is made up almost entirely of fruit pulp, and was eaten in the months of September and October.

Behavior.—Grinnell and Storer (1924) write:

Pileolated Warblers do most of their foraging within 6 feet of the ground and practically never ascend far into trees even to sing. They keep within the cover of the lower stratum of foliage and are therefore only to be caught sight of momentarily. The birds are noted for their habit of darting out after flying insects; indeed one book name of the eastern relative of the pileolated is "black-capped fly-catching warbler." Of all our other warblers only the Tolmie is likely to be found in the same cover inhabited by the Pileolated Warbler. The Tolmie often forages out into the drier chaparral, whereas the present species adheres closely to damp situations, either over boggy ground or else within a few yards of a stream. In favorable country, pairs of Pileolated Warblers may occur as frequently as eight or even more to a linear mile.

Voice.—On this subject Grinnell and Storer (1924) say:

The song of the Pileolated Warbler is far less shrill than that of the Yellow Warbler and is less clear and more mechanical than that of several other warblers. The syllables are given all on about the same pitch and about as rapidly as a person can pronounce them, but with the intervals shortening and the emphasis decreasing toward the end of the series; *tshup, tshup, tshup-tshup-tshup-tshup.* The call note is not nearly so sharp as that of other warblers, but, on occasion, appeals to one as surprisingly loud for the size of the bird. It has an unmistakable quality of its own. Singing is done largely within the cover of the shrubbery; in other words this species does not, as do so many brush dwellers, seek out prominent song perches.

Mrs. Allen writes to me: "The song of this warbler is a series of rather sharp staccato notes without much change of pitch. It is not a trill, but rather a rapid series of *chips.* The call note is easily recognized because it is not a *chip,* but a thin wiry *chee-ee,* with some of the quality of the call note of the western winter wren."

Ralph Hoffmann (1927) says: "Beginners find it difficult to distinguish the song of the Pileolated from that of the Lutescent, with which it is often associated. The distinction lies in the sharpness and staccato quality of the Pileolated's notes, and the final crescendo. There is of course much individual variation, but the typical song may be written: *chit-chi, chit-chi, chit-chi, chit-chi, chit-chi CHIT CHIT CHIT;* the song of the Lutescent is softer, more trilled and generally trails off at the close into weaker notes in a lower pitch. The call note of the Pileolated is diagnositic, a husky *tsik* or *tschek,* suggesting a Yellow-throat's but not so heavy."

Field marks.—This species can be recognized by its black cap, very prominent in the male and usually more or less in evidence in the female; young females, in which the black cap is missing, and juvenals resemble female or young yellowthroats, but the latter are more suffused with brownish, the olive and yellow colors in the former being clearer. It is the only western warbler that is wholly olive above and wholly yellow below, with a black cap and with no white in wings or tail. The golden pileolated warbler can be easily distinguished from the northern by its much brighter colors. The song and the call notes are quite distinctive.

Enemies.—According to Friedmann (1929) this warbler is "a not uncommon victim of the Dwarf Cowbird in southern California."

Fall.—Rathbun (MS.) writes from Seattle: "About the middle of August, the golden warbler will often be seen about the city, this being an indication of the fall migration; individuals continue to be noted until about the middle of September. At this time the only note given is a harsh squeak, and the males are very beautiful in their bright, fresh plumage. They will generally be found in the company of the California yellow warbler, one or two of the golden with a number of the yellow warbler."

The fall migration through California, in company with other warblers and vireos, occurs mainly in September. Ralph Hoffmann (1927) says: "the Pileolated Warbler is one of the commonest birds in migration; at times every oak tree or tangle of low bushes seems alive with their bright and active forms."

WILSONIA CANADENSIS (Linnaeus)

CANADA WARBLER

PLATES 78–80

HABITS

In spite of its name, this pretty, necklaced warbler is not confined to Canada, but finds congenial haunts in many of the cooler spots in the Northern States and at the higher altitudes in the Alleghenies as far south as northern Georgia. Gerald Thayer wrote to Dr. Chapman (1907) : "It is a bird of rich deciduous undergrowth in the deep, damp forest,—a ranger between the bush-tops and low tree-branches and the ground. It avoids purely coniferous woods, and so is almost wholly wanting from the closely-spruce-clad northern slopes of Mt. Monadnock [New Hampshire], though abundant in the deep mixed timber all about its northern base. On the *eastern* slopes of the mountain, where the forest is more largely deciduous, the Canada is fairly common almost up to the rocky backbone ridge, at heights of from 2,300 to 2,700 or so feet."

In southeastern Massachusetts, where I live, the Canada warbler breeds regularly, but not abundantly, in the cool, damp, heavy woods of mixed growth, mainly around the borders of the extensive cedar swamps, but also in mature forests where large trees furnish cool shade and where rocky ravines are watered with spring-fed streams.

Rev. J. J. Murray tells me that this is the most common warbler on the higher mountains of West Virginia, abundant above 3,000 feet. Prof. Maurice Brooks (1936) says that it "has found an apparently satisfactory home in the deciduous second growth. This species shares with the Magnolia the claim to being the most abundant northern warbler in West Virginia. There is not a mountain area where it may not be found." Elsewhere, he says (1940) : "A favorite haunt is a ravine with dense hemlock overstory and an understory of tangled rhododendron."

In northwestern North Carolina, Thomas D. Burleigh (1941) found it on Mount Mitchell, "a plentiful breeding bird in the cut-over area to an altitude of approximately 6,300 feet, appearing early in May and lingering until the first of September. Not known to nest in the fir and spruce woods at the top of the mountain until the year 1934 when two pairs were found there May 23." He had previously (1925) found it breeding in northeastern Georgia on the north slope of Brasstown Bald above an elevation of 4,000 feet. He felt sure "that at least ten pair must have nested there among the moss-covered boulders and tangled rhododendron thickets."

Spring.—From its winter haunts in South America the Canada warbler migrates through the eastern United States in May, covering a period of 3 or 4 weeks in passage. Prof. Cooke (1904) writes: "The great bulk of the species passes along the Atlantic coast and westward to and including the valley of the Ohio. In the interior the bird is a rare migrant from eastern Texas, eastern Kansas, eastern Nebraska, through the valley of the Red River of the North to Manitoba. Accidental occurrences are reported from central Texas, southern New Mexico, and eastern Colorado."

On the spring migration, we generally see the Canada warbler in the lower stories of the swampy woods, or in the denser underbrush, much such places as are frequented by Wilson's warblers. Referring to Ohio, Milton B. Trautman (1940) says: "In spring the species was found in the greatest numbers in the profuse shrub layer of the larger upland and lowland remnant forests. This lovely warbler had a decided preference for the spicebushes (*Benzoin aestivale*) of the swamp forest, and it fed and sang its pleasing song among these newly leaved flowering shrubs."

Nesting.—The Canada warbler builds its nest on or near the ground, often in a mossy hummock, on a moss-covered log or stump, or in a cavity in a bank or the upturned roots of a fallen tree. Robie W. Tufts' notes mention a Nova Scotia nest that was "built among the roots of an upturned tree over a pool of water, in thick, swampy land in coniferous woods." F. H. Kennard records in his notes two nests, found near Lancaster, N. H., that were placed on the sides of moss-covered stumps. In Owen Durfee's journal I find the descriptions of five nests of this warbler, found in the same locality; these were all well hidden in sphagnum moss, or green tree moss, on hummocks, old stumps or fallen logs; two were in a wet swamp and less than a foot above water. The nests were well inside the concealing moss with an entrance about 2 inches wide; one nest measured 4½ inches in outside diameter, 2½ in inside diameter, and 1½ inches in inside depth.

Miss Cordelia J. Stanwood (MS.) describes a nest she found near Ellsworth, Maine, placed in a rather open situation on the ground between a moss-covered stump and the roots of a gray birch. "The outside was composed of leaves—poplar, dwarf cornel and gray birch—with the addition of the inner bark fibre of such young dead trees as poplar, soft maple, and willow, and also a few white pine needles, several decayed fern stipes, and a number of skeletonized leaves. The lining consisted of minute threads of inner bark fibre and a few black horsehairs. Aside from the large, dry leaves on the outside, the stuff of which the structure was composed was fine, even minute, in texture."

Of the nesting of the Canada warbler in western Pennsylvania, W. E. Clyde Todd (1940) mentions situations such as those described above and adds: "R. B. Simpson, who has found many nests in Warren, reports that they are also placed under the projecting banks of streams and among the ferns and moss on the sides of large rocks and ledges. One nest referred to by Burleigh was built in a mass of dry leaves at the base of a huckleberry bush; the brim was flush with the ground. Wherever located, the nest is a more or less bulky, formless structure; it is composed of dry (often skeletonized) leaves, shreds of bark, dry grass, and weed stalks, with a lining of finer vegetable fibers, among which the black rootlets of the maidenhair fern (*Adiantum*) are a conspicuous element."

T. E. McMullen has sent me the data for eight sets of eggs, found in the Pocono Mountains, Pa.; two of these were in upturned roots, two in rotten stumps, one 3 feet up on the side of a 10-foot creek bank, and the others were on the ground, one of which was among rhododendrons.

I found my first and only nest of the Canada warbler in Bridgewater, Mass., on June 9, 1924. While walking through some mixed moist woods, mostly white pines with a few oaks and other deciduous trees, near a swampy place, I flushed the warbler from its nest almost under foot; it was in plain sight at the foot of a clump of brakes (*Pteridium aquilinum*); the nest contained three fresh eggs; two days later, I photographed the bird on its nest. The nest, now before me, is rather bulky and loosely made externally of dry and skeletonized leaves, coarse strips of weeds and inner bark, stems and fronds of ferns and weed tops; it is lined with very fine plant fibers, fine rootlets, and hair. The outside diameter is about 4 by 5 inches, the height about 2½, the inside diameter 2¼ by 2½, and the inside depth 1¾ inches.

Eggs.—From 3 to 5 eggs, usually 4, constitute the set for the Canada warbler. They are ovate, some tending toward short ovate, and are slightly glossy. The white, or creamy white, ground color is speckled, spotted and sometimes blotched with "chestnut," "bay," or "chestnut-brown," with undertones of "light Quaker drab," or "light purplish gray." On many, the markings are confined to speckles which may be scattered all over the eggs, although they are generally concentrated at the large end, where frequently they form a distinct wreath. Occasionally eggs may have spots of "Hay's brown" and black, instead of the usual red-browns. One set of eggs which I collected is boldly marked with blotches of rich red-browns instead of the usual smaller spots. The measurements of 50 eggs average 17.2 by 13.1 millimeters; the eggs showing the four extremes measure 18.4 by 12.6, 18.0 by 14.0, 16.1 by 12.9, and 17.1 by 12.2 millimeters (Harris).

Young.—The period of incubation for the Canada warbler does not seem to have been determined, nor do we know just how long the young remain in the nest. Data on the development and growth of the young seem to be lacking. The female probably does all, or most, of the incubating and the brooding. Both parents feed the young and remove the excretal sacs.

Miss Stanwood placed a blind within a few feet of a nest and watched the birds feed the young. Her notes indicate that they are fed at frequent intervals, sometimes as often as once a minute, but more often at intervals of from 3 to 6 minutes; occasionally an interval of 15 or 20 minutes may elapse between feedings. She saw the male feed several nestlings with a large beakful of yellow grubs that had probably been found in rotten wood. He was seen to catch mosquitoes on the wing and feed them to small young by regurgitation. Green and gray caterpillars and brown measuring worms were fed to the young, and once a large gray moth. If the nest was left long unguarded, it was overrun with insects, but the female usually cleared the nest of such vermin by burrowing under the young and removing them.

Plumages.—Dr. Dwight (1900) calls the natal down of the Canada warbler sepia-brown, and describes the juvenal plumage, in which the sexes are alike, as "above sepia and, when older and faded, hair-brown. Wings and tail dull olive-brown, faintly edged with dull olive-green; wing coverts paler and indistinctly edged with buff. Below, primose-yellow washed with pale wood-brown on the throat and sides. * * * Practically indistinguishable from *S. pusilla* except by duller wing edgings."

The first winter plumage is acquired by a partial postjuvenal molt, beginning early in July, which involves the contour plumage and the wing coverts, but not the rest of the wings or the tail. The sexes are recognizable in this plumage. Dr. Dwight describes the young male as "above, cinereous gray, browner on the back, the crown yellow-tinged and sometimes flecked with black; wing coverts uniform with the back. Below, including supraloral line lemon-yellow, the orbital ring paler, a narrow 'necklace' of small black spots on the jugulum the black extending to the auriculars and lores, slightly veiled by overlapping yellow edges; the crissum dull white." The first winter female plumage "is a little paler than that of the male without black on the crown which is brownish in contrast to the back and the 'neck-lace' consists of obscure grayish lines."

The first nuptial plumage is acquired mainly by wear, but there is a limited prenuptial molt about the head, chin, and throat. Young birds are now like the adults, except for the worn wings and tail, which have been carried over from the juvenal plumage. Adults have a complete postnuptial molt in July. The adult winter plumage of the male is "quite different from first winter dress, the black 'necklace' being of heavy streaks and the black area on the lores and crown larger; black feathers with broad grayish edgings are assumed on the crown, and the wing edgings are apt to be grayer and bluish instead of greenish." In the female, "the adult winter plumage differs slightly it any from the first winter; it has a bluer gray tint on the back and the crown is yellow-tinged rather than brown."

The adult nuptial plumage in both sexes is acquired mainly by wear, with possibly some new growth. The female is always duller in coloration than the male, but she usually shows some traces of the "necklace."

Food.—Ora W. Knight (1908) says of the food of the Canada war-bler: "They eat moths, flies, beetles, grubs, caterpillars of the smooth, hairless type such as canker worms, the eggs of insects, spiders, mos-quitoes and similar insects." Prof. Aughey (1878) found five locusts and 29 other insects in a stomach examined in Nebraska. The items mentioned above as the food of the young are doubtless also included in the food of the adults. Of three specimens examined by F. H. King (1883) in Wisconsin, "two had eaten flies; one, a hymenopterous insect; one, beetles; and one larvae." Although the Canada warbler obtains most of its food on the branches and foliage of trees, as well as on the ground, it feeds largely on the wing, catching its insect prey in the air. It is one of the most expert of the warblers in this pursuit, hence it was formerly called the Canada flycatching warbler, or Can-ada flycatcher.

Behavior.—Gerald Thayer wrote to Dr. Chapman (1907): "The Canadian is a sprightly, wide-awake, fly-snapping Warbler, vivid in movement and in song; clearly marked and brightly colored. In actions it is like the Wilson's, a sort of mongrel between a *Dendroica*, an American Redstart, and a true Flycatcher. It darts after flying insects like one of the Tyrannidae, and its bill may sometimes be heard to 'click' when it seizes something; it has much of the Redstart's insistent nervousness of motion, but it is a less airy 'flitter'; and, finally, it glides and gleans among leaves and twigs like a true gleaning Warbler."

But, with all its nervous activity, it is not particularly shy nor timid; I had no difficulty in photographing it on its nest, and Miss Stanwood observed at short range a pair feeding their young.

Voice.—Aretas A. Saunders has contributed the following account: "The song of the Canada warbler is a series of rather rapid notes and 2-note phrases, varying greatly and most irregularly in pitch and time. There seems to be no general rule about the form of the song, except that two notes in succession are rarely on the same pitch. The quality of the notes is fairly musical and rather similar to that of the yellowthroat. Not only is the song variable in different individuals, but the same bird often varies it greatly. I have records of 7 songs by one individual, and 11 by another, all more or less distinct.

"The number of notes in the song varies from 5 to 15, averaging about 10. The length of song varies from 1 to 2⅗ seconds. The pitch ranges from E''' to F'''', and single songs have ranges from one and one half to three and one half tones, averaging two and one half. These are results from 47 records of the song.

"The length of individual notes varies, as well as the pitch, short and long notes being mixed irregularly. Occasional notes are accented. Explosive consonant sounds are fairly clear. No one rendition will fit more than one song, but one may give a general idea of the songs. *Tsip chitawee tita wee'ti tipa tupa tee* is an example of one written in the field as I listened to the bird. I have heard a flight song from this bird; it is like the regular song but more prolonged.

"The Canada warbler sings on the breeding grounds till the middle of July. Records of 14 summers in Allegany State Park give an average date of July 16; the earliest are July 11 (1929 and 1939) and the latest is July 31 (1937). The song is resumed after a rather short interval, in late July or August. This bird sings more frequently after the molt than any other warbler I know of. The song is about as common in the first half of August as in early July."

The animated song of the Canada warbler is regularly heard on migration. Many years ago, I recorded it in Taunton in May as a striking, variegated warble, rapidly uttered and fairly well indicated by such syllables as *ker, chicharew, chichew, chicherew, chew,* or *chick-*

arew, chicarie, cherwee. Again, on its breeding grounds in Maine, I wrote it as *cher, whit, whit, whe'o,* or *cher, whit, whit, whe'o, whe'o,* with many variations, sometimes a continuous warble, but always rich in tone, strongly accented, loud and striking.

A. D. Du Bois writes it in his notes as *te wichi tichy—te wich chu,* or *te wichi tichi—te wichi wee,* or *te wich e wee.* Francis H. Allen (MS.) writes: "The characteristic song of this warbler is of a warbling character but ends with an emphatic *wip.* I have been in the habit of writing it (unrealistically) as *te-widdle-te-widdle, te-widdle-te-wip'.* I once heard one reverse the order of the two parts, singing repeatedly *te-widdle-te-wip', te-widdle-te-widdle.* On June 2, 1929, in Newton, Mass., I heard one give a continuous performance of singing, one song following another immediately, the whole interspersed with *chips* and short trills. It was restless and flew ahead of me as I walked, finally perching on a small dead limb near the top of a small tree, where it constantly shifted its position as it sang, turning its head this way and that, and frequently facing about. It seemed to be in a frenzy of excitement."

Field marks.—The adult Canada warbler can always be recognized by the plain gray of the upper parts, without any white markings in wings or tail, by its yellow eye ring, and especially, by the pretty necklace of black spots on the yellow breast. The female is marked like the male, but her colors are somewhat duller. The young bird, in juvenal plumage, is much like the young Wilson's warbler.

Fall.—The general trend of the fall migration from eastern Canada and New England, is southwestward, and more directly southward from central Canada. Professor Cooke (1904) says:

The birds from the northeastern section of the United States appear to follow the general trend of the mountains to the Gulf Coast, being found in the fall apparently not east of Mississippi. Thence they cross the Gulf of Mexico to southern Mexico and Guatemala, reaching the Pacific coast at Tehuantepec. They probably then turn southeast and follow the mountains through Costa Rica and Panama to their principal winter home in Ecuador and Peru."

It is doubtful if all regularly migrate across the Gulf; probably some of them migrate through Texas, for Dr. W. P. Taylor tells me that two were collected in Polk County, on September 7, 1937; they were in cut-over longleaf pine timber; one was in an association of blue-gray gnatcatchers, chickadees, titmice and one Carolina wren; the other was alone in a sweet gum tree near a cornfield. Again, two days later, "this warbler was found to be quite numerous here in the river bottom. Seemed to show little preference for the tall trees over the shrubs, being seen equally often in both. I flushed several off the ground."

Dr. Alexander F. Skutch writes to me: "The Canada warbler is known in Central America only as a rather rare transient, journeying between its breeding ground in the north and its winter home in South America. It has been seen far more often in the fall than in the spring; and in Costa Rica, although there are a number of fall records, it has apparently never been noted in the spring. On its southward migration through Central America it spreads over both coasts as well as the central highlands up to 6,500 feet or more. The extreme dates of its fall passage are September 8 to October 7 in Guatemala, and to October 20 in Costa Rica. It appears to travel singly rather than in flocks—at least, while resting and feeding it is almost always found alone; and I have only rarely seen two together. At this time it is found either in the woodland or among scattered trees."

Dickey and van Rossem (1938) write: "The Canada warbler is by no means a common species in El Salvador, even during the height of the migration. All those that were noted were either in forest undergrowth or in the lower levels of foliage. Not one individual was detected during the spring mingrations—a circumstance which indicates that El Salvador is somewhat off the main migration route of this species."

Winter.—Professor Cooke (1904) gives the following account of this warbler's winter haunts:

The winter home of the Canadian warbler lies a long distance from Canada. The species is found in greatest abundance in Peru, especially in the northern portion, and in the neighboring regions of southern Ecuador. In these sections it is found through the winter in flocks, which wander over the country on both the eastern and western slopes of the Andes. The extremes of the normal altitudes attained by the bird are 3,700 and 7,000 feet. Most of the records of its occurrence were made at an elevation of 4,000 to 5,000 feet. One specimen was secured at Quito, Ecuador, at 9,500 feet altitude. The extreme southeastern point at which it has been recorded is in the mountains east of Lima, where Jelski took a male and two females on the eastern slope of the Andes at over 10,000 feet elevation. These individuals were 5,700 miles distant from Labrador by the principal route of migration followed by the species.

DISTRIBUTION

Range.—South central and southeastern Canada, eastern United States south to northwestern South America.

Breeding range.—The Canada warbler breeds **north** to central eastern Saskatchewan (Hudson Bay Junction and probably Cumberland House); central Manitoba (probably the head of Lake Winnipegosis); central western and northwestern Ontario (Kenora and Moose Factory); central Quebec (Mistassini Post, Inlet, Matamek, and Anticosti Island); and Newfoundland. **East** to Newfoundland; Massachusetts (Bristol County); Rhode Island (Noyes Beach); rarely

Connecticut (North Cornwall, Hartford, and Hadlyme); southeastern New York (Putnam County); northern New Jersey; central Pennsylvania (State College, Pottsville, and Mauch Chunk); western Maryland (Dans Mountain); western Virginia (Roanoke and Blue Ridge Mountains); western North Carolina (Highlands, Black Mountain, and Boone); and northeastern Georgia (Brasstown Bald). **South** to northeastern Georgia (Brasstown Bald) and eastern Tennessee (Cosby Knob). **West** to eastern Tennessee (Cosby Knob); eastern Kentucky (Black Mountain); eastern West Virginia (Terra Alta, Watoga, and White Sulphur Springs); northeastern Ohio (Pymatuning Swamp); southern Ontario (Listowel, Elora, and Hallowell); northern Michigan (Blaney Park, Weketonsing, and Bois Blanc Island); northern Wisconsin (Ladysmith, Unity, and Kelley Brook); central Minnesota (Cass Lake, and Mille Lacs); southern Manitoba (Aweme and Portage la Prairie); and central eastern Saskatchewan (Cumberland House).

Winter range.—The Canada warbler winters in western Colombia (Alto Bonito, Río Frío, and San Antonio) south through Ecuador to central Perú (Lima region and La Merced).

The species is casual in Colorado (Clear Creek and Parker Lake); and is accidental in Alaska (Forrester Island); California (Santa Barbara); and Greenland.

Migration.—Late dates of spring departure from the winter home are: Peru—Tambillo, March 28. Ecuador—San José, April 2. Colombia—San Agustín, April 10. Panamá—Gatún, April 28. Guatemala—above Tecpán, April 29. Florida—Wakulla County, May 5.

Early dates of spring arrival are: Florida—Princeton, March 17. Alabama—Birmingham, April 24. Georgia—Milledgeville region, April 7; Atlanta, April 23. South Carolina—Spartanburg, April 30. North Carolina—Highlands, April 29. Virginia—Charlottesville, April 30 (average, May 3); Rockbridge County, May 6. West Virginia—French Creek, April 27 (average of 16 years, May 1). District of Columbia—Washington, May 2 (average of 38 years, May 8). Maryland—Baltimore, April 26. Pennsylvania—Brookville, May 2; Beaver, May 3 (average, May 7). New Jersey—Morristown, May 2; Union County, May 7 (average, May 11). New York—Rochester, May 1; Ballston Spa and Westchester County, May 2. Connecticut—Portland, May 1. Rhode Island—Cranston, May 3. Massachusetts—Nahant, May 1. Vermont—Woodstock, May 10. New Hampshire—Charlestown, May 6. Maine—Brunswick, April 24; Bangor, April 25. Quebec—Montreal, May 4. New Brunswick—Bathurst, May 12. Louisiana—Monroe, April 27. Mississippi—Tishomingo County, May 3. Arkansas—Delight, April 25. Tennessee—Memphis, April 24; Athens, April 27 (average of 7 years, April 30). Kentucky—Bowling Green, April 28. Missouri—New Madrid County, April 10; St. Louis, April 28. Illinois—Chicago region, April 30 (average, May 9). Indiana—Wheatland, April 18; Holland, April 22. Ohio—Oberlin, April 28; central Ohio, May 2 (average, May 7). Michigan—Petersburg and Ann Arbor, May 1. Ontario—Walton and Hamilton, May 3; Ottawa, May 15 (average of 14 years, May 21). Iowa—La Porte City, May 6. Wisconson—Milwaukee and Madison, May 6. Minnesota—Fairmont, May 4 (average of 25 years for southern Minnesota, May 13). Texas—Victoria, April 1. Kansas— Harper, April 24. Nebraska—Greeley, May 3. South Dakota— Sioux Falls, May 18. North Dakota—Wilton, May 11. Manitoba, Aweme, May 18 (average, May 28). Saskatchewan—McLean, May 14. Alberta—Edmonton, May 29.

Late dates of fall departure are: Alberta—Glenevis, August 29. Saskatchewan—Last Mountain Lake, September 3. Manitoba— Winnipeg, September 11; Aweme, September 4 (average, August 28). North Dakota—Jamestown, September 14; Cass County, September 6 (average, September 1). Kansas—Lake Quivira, Johnson County, September 7. Texas—Dallas region, October 17. Minnesota—Hutchinson, September 30. Wisconsin—Milwaukee, October 10. Iowa—Davenport, October 4. Ontario—Ottawa, September 5; Welland County, October 10. Michigan—Detroit, September 30. Ohio—central Ohio, October 2 (average, September 21). Indiana— Richmond, October 9. Illinois—Chicago region, September 22; (average, September 11); Rockford, October 17. Missouri—St. Louis, October 5. Kentucky—Bowling Green and Letcher County, September 25. Tennessee—Elizabethton, October 22. Mississippi— Ariel, October 14. Louisiana—Baton Rouge, October 17. Quebec— Gaspé County, September 25. Maine—Pittsfield and Winthrop, September 12; Cutler, October 31. New Hampshire—Monroe, September 18. Vermont—Wells River, September 21. Massachusetts—Hamilton, October 16. Rhode Island—Watchaug Pond, October 8. New York—New York City, October 29, November 13. New Jersey— Union County, October 2 (average, September 21). Pennsylvania— Pittsburgh, October 3; York, October 7. Maryland—Plummers Island, October 23. District of Columbia—Washington, October 11 (average of 16 years, September 18). West Virginia—Bluefield, September 31. Virginia—Charlottesville, September 28 (average, September 25). South Carolina—Clemson, October 28. Georgia— Atlanta, September 24. Alabama—Birmingham, October 1. Florida—Dade County, October 14. Guatemala—Colomba, Quezaltenango, October 7.

Early dates of fall arrival are: North Dakota—Fargo and Cass County, August 16 (average for Cass County, August 24). Texas— Cove, August 18. Minnesota—Minneapolis, August 13 (average of 9 years for southern Minnesota, August 22). Wisconsin—Racine, August 16. Iowa—Emmetsburg, August 13. Ontario—Toronto, August 5. Michigan—Sault Ste. Marie, July 29. Ohio—Dayton region, August 12 (average for central Ohio, August 27). Indiana—Richmond, August 15. Illinois—Chicago region, August 3 (average, August 19). Missouri—St. Louis, August 15. Tennessee—Lebanon, August 21. Arkansas—Winslow, August 26. Mississippi—Gulfport, August 30. Louisiana—Saint Francisville, August 13. Massachusetts—Northampton and Belmont, August 2. Connecticut—Fairfield, August 11. New York—New York City, August 6. New Jersey—Essex County, August 2; Union County, August 10 (average, August 16). Pennsylvania—Pittsburgh, July 25 and 27. Maryland—Middle River, August 7. District of Columbia—Washington, July 31 (average of 15 years, August 19). West Virginia—Bluefield, August 13. Virginia—Charlottesville, July 24 (average, August 14). North Carolina—Chapel Hill, August 29. Georgia—Atlanta, August 6. Alabama—Leighton, August 18. Mexico—Tamaulipas, Matamoros, August 19. Guatemala—Colomba, Quezaltenango, September 23. El Salvador—Lake Olomega, September 1. Costa Rica—San Miguel de Desamparados, September 14. Panamá—Almirante, September 22. Colombia—Chicoral, October 12. Ecuador—below Oyacachi, August 9. Perú—Huachipa, October 1.

Egg dates.—Maine: 10 records, May 30 to June 21.

New York: 25 records, May 25 to June 26; 15 records, June 1 to 8.

Pennsylvania: 19 records, May 27 to June 25; 12 records, May 30 to June 8 (Harris).

SETOPHAGA RUTICILLA RUTICILLA (Linnaeus)

SOUTHERN AMERICAN REDSTART

PLATES 81–83

HABITS

CONTRIBUTED BY ALFRED OTTO GROSS

The southern redstart is one of the commonest warblers in New England, perhaps second in abundance only to the yellow warbler. It is a resident of our forests, but unlike the ground-inhabiting oven-bird it is strictly an arboreal species and is much more frequently seen. Because of the brilliant, contrasting colors of the male and its extreme vivaciousness it is better known, and to many it has proven to be a favorite warbler. The bright flashes of orange-red which it proudly displays in its frequently spread tail and fluttering wings has suggested to the imaginative Cubans the beautiful name Candelita, the "little torch," which in such unusual numbers brightens the dark shadows of their tropical forests.   In the Province of Quebec, the Canadian French know it as "La Fauvette à Queue Rousse," another allusion to the bright red patches in the male's tail.   Like many other American birds the name redstart was given it by the earlier settlers who bestowed upon it the name of a familiar Old World form which also has an orange-red tail but is otherwise very different in coloration and belongs to another family.

One of the most pleasant experiences I have had with warblers in the Maine woods, occurred on a bright morning in May when I suddenly came upon three male redstarts.   One of them was working along a horizontal birch limb with its wings lowered in characteristic fashion and eagerly scanning every twig in its quest of insects.   The other two were whirling about, darting upward, floating downward displaying their gorgeous colors, then snapping up their victims as they dashed again and again through a haze of midges hovering in the sunshine of the clearing.   This scene, as it was enacted against a contrasting background of rich green hemlocks and firs, always comes to my mind when I think of redstarts.

The redstart's manner of catching insects, as well as the shape of its bill and the well-formed rictal bristles, suggests the flycatchers; but instead of perching and patiently waiting for his prey to come near, as does a true flycatcher, the redstart is continually in action, dashing here and there after flying insects or perhaps snapping up larva dangling in midair at the end of its long silken fiber.

Spring.—The redstart, which spends the winter in the West Indies and Central and South America, makes its first appearance in spring on the Florida Peninsula and coasts of the other Gulf States during the first week of April.   By the middle of the month the vanguard reaches North Carolina, Kentucky, and Missouri.   During the last week of April they progress as far as Maryland, Pennsylvania, and Indiana.   We may expect the first arrivals in New England, New York, Ohio, Michigan, and Iowa during the first week of May.   By the middle of the month they reach Quebec, Ontario, and Manitoba; and before the end of May they arrive at the outposts of their summer range in northern British Columbia.

After the redstarts leave their winter quarters early in April, they cross the Gulf of Mexico, following no particular route, or proceed from the West Indies via Florida.   They thus enter the United States on a wide front extending westward a distance of some 2,000 miles to Texas.   From this wide area of entry they spread out fanlike, as do members of many other species, until they reach across the widest part of the North American Continent from Newfoundland on the east to British Columbia on the Pacific.   The migration from the winter quarters to the extreme northwestern section of its nesting range requires somewhat less than two months.

Milton B. Trautman (1940) from many years of observations at Buckeye Lake, Ohio, finds that the first redstarts arrive there in April. A marked increase in numbers occurs during the first week of May, the period of maximum abundance extending from May 10 to May 20. A marked decrease occurs after May 22, and a few days later virtually all that remain are summer residents. This condition seems to be typical throughout this belt of the redstart's range. At points farther south or north the dates would be correspondingly earlier and later.

Courtship.—The males are the first to appear and can be heard singing at the time of their arrival. The females come a few days or a week later. Although the first redstart arrivals in Maine may be expected early in May, it is several weeks before the bulk of the resident birds are to be found on their breeding grounds. The males exhibit unusual aggressiveness and indulge in a good deal of fighting in defending their chosen territories. Sometimes two males may be seen hovering in flight as they peck viciously at each other and then perhaps dart into cover with their tails spread and their whole being in a quivering belligerent state. Again, the strutting antics of the amorous males may be seen as they display before the females.

Joseph J. Hickey (1940) as a result of a very intensive and thorough study of the redstarts on a 40-acre area in Westchester County, N. Y., gives us an excellent account of their courtship and territorial aspects. The redstart, he says—

is a highly territorial species. Males advertised their presence by their typical well-known song and by formalized territorial displays that apparently served to define boundaries and reduce fighting. These displays consisted of short, horizontal, semicircular flights made with stiffened wings and out-spread tails. These performances were frequently observed between males, less commonly between females and never between a male and a female where a question solely of territory was involved. Hingston's interpretation of the function of warning coloration in plumages seemed to be particularly applicable in these cases. Low, repeated *quit, quit* notes could be heard when the displays were concluded and the birds returned to their perches. As far as could be observed, the same performances seemed to serve as some part of the male's courtship of the females. On all exciting occasions, of course, both sexes spread their tails like many other wood warblers. Flight songs appeared to be absent. Singing perches, if present, were largely undetected by the observer. One male which took up territory in a blackberry-locust association sang frequently on April 30 and May 8 only one to two feet from the ground. Three males were once watched for an entire morning before females had arrived in the area: one was quite obviously patrolling the boundaries of his territory, the two others seemed to be moving back and forth on an indefinite and irregular axis, which approximated the length of their territories.

A special effort was made in 1937 to learn the number of unmated males. Twenty-four occupied rigidly fixed territories on the study area. Twenty of these birds were definitely mated. Of the remaining four, one held a territory until at least June 13, another until at least June 19, a third until June 20, and a fourth until June 26. If all four, or even half of these were unmated, the percentage of paired birds would be between 83 and 91. * * * An indeterminate number of unmated wandering males also exist. * * *

A male in the immature plumage spent the entire morning softly singing and gradually working its way along 800 yards at the top of the ridge. This bird was furiously driven off by males and females whenever it passed through their territories. Plumage notes on 48 males on territory showed that only four (8.3 per cent) were in immature plumage. All four were paired and possessed territories of the same size as those of the adult males.

The size of territories was about one acre or less, but in one instance was compressed to about half an acre. Approximately twenty-two pairs (or males) each year occupied the 39.93 acres under investigation. Their boundaries were observed in two cases to break down on June 17, when young were being fed in the nest. Interspecies competition or jealousy were seldom in evidence. Redstarts and Ovenbirds were the two most dominant species of the slope and both would sing in the same tree without the slightest evidence of hostility. The former was once seen briefly fighting with a Black and White Warbler.

Nesting.—In Maine the redstart is an inhabitant of the hardwood or mixed deciduous and coniferous woodlands. These may be in low, damp situations but many of them are found in the second growth of trees and brush of our dry sandy plains. Often the nests are found in the thick growth of small trees which border the forest of larger trees, as well as in places where trees have sprung up along the roadsides. Others may be found in alder and willow thickets bordering our streams and ponds. In New York, it nests in low, damp woods; it has been found in mixed woodland with a considerable growth of pine and hemlock; and in the Adirondacks its nesting site is often in places where spruces predominate. In Ohio, Michigan, and other sections of the Middle West it frequents the maple, elm, ash, and pin-oak association of the larger, more mature swamp forests, although sometimes found among similar trees and brush in the larger upland woods. In the far Northwest it shows a decided preference for willow trees and alder thickets.

There is a tendency for the redstart to forsake the seclusion of the woodlands and, like the yellow warbler, to build its nest in trees and shrubbery adjacent to human habitations. It may even use the exterior of a human dwelling for a nesting site. Annie Lyman Sears of Waltham, Mass., reports that a nest was built on a bracket above a Venetian ironwork lantern hanging before the front door of her home The redstart has also taken up its residence in the parks located in the midst of some of our densely populated cities.

The most usual site of the nest of the redstart is an upright, 3- or 4-pronged crotch of a dead or live hardwood sapling, such as a maple, elm, ash, or birch. The majority of the nests range from 4 to 20 feet above the ground with an average height of about 7 feet. However, in many instances the redstart has selected other than typical nesting sites.

J. Claire Wood (1904) reports finding a nest in Wayne County, Mich., that was partly sunken into the ground at the base of a gooseberry bush between two logs, a very unusual situation. Verdi Burtch has sent us a photograph of a redstart's nest, found near Branchport, N. Y., May 31, 1929, that was built in the forks of a bush only a few inches above the ground. Richard C. Harlow reported that he found a nest at Tabusintac, New Brunswick, June 26, 1919, that was 20 inches above the ground; it straddled and was near the tip of the horizontal limb of a spruce standing on the edge of a bog in rather open woods. On June 25, 1927, at Squam Lake, N. H., Arthur C. Bent found a nest 5 feet up in the fork of a dead branch that had fallen and was leaning upright against a striped maple sapling. At Brunswick, Maine, I discovered a nest held by a thick cluster of branches growing upward from the side of the main trunk of a large elm tree more than 2 feet in diameter at the base. This nest was not less than 30 feet from the ground. Nests placed in crotches formed by limbs branching from the main trunk of large trees are not rare. J. Claire Wood (1904) also reports an extreme case of a redstart's nest built 70 feet above the ground in a large oak tree.

The redstart may also choose a small shrub or bush for its nesting place. A. C. Bent found a nest with three eggs, at Squam Lake, N. H., built in a small mountain laurel among a large clump growing in deep woods. The nest was not over 2 feet above the ground, a situation often selected by the black-throated blue warbler.

In June 1942 a pair of redstarts built their nest in a lilac shrub next to a house on Boody Street, Brunswick, Maine. It was saddled in a cluster of branches about 5 feet above the ground and was only a foot from a front window. Pedestrians frequently passing by on a walk only a few feet distant did not seem to disturb the birds in the least, and the birds even allowed me to take motion pictures of them as I stood only 4 feet away, completely exposed to view. During the same month another pair occupied a mockorange bush growing in the yard of a home only a short distance from this nest. Their nest rested on a horizontal branch about an inch in diameter and was securely anchored by three small upright branches. M. B. Trautman (1940) found six nests of the redstart in the Buckeye Lake region, Ohio, all in grapevine tangles 10 to 20 feet above the ground. J. Claire Wood (1904) describes an interesting nest in a grapevine in Wayne County, Mich., as follows: "This vine reached downward about ten feet from the first limb of a large oak tree and thence upward to within a foot of the starting point, forming a swing, and at the bottom of the loop the nest was placed. It was a windy day and the nest swung over a space of five feet, but madam clung to her treasures perfectly unconcerned."

Another curious departure from the usual nesting habits of the redstart is its use of old or deserted new nests of other species such as the vireos. On June 5, 1898, in Yates County, N. Y., Verdi Burtch (1898) found a red-eyed vireo's nest which had been newly lined with red bark fibers that the redstart usually uses to line its nests in that locality. The nest contained three fresh eggs of the redstart. Others have come to my attention: Three in which red-eyed vireo's nests were used, one in which a yellow-throated vireo's nest was used, and another in which a nest started by a yellow warbler was used. Since these instances were in widely separated places, it indicates the practice is not isolated or merely local. The nest is built entirely by the female, which exhibits more than ordinary architectural ability. It is a firm, compact structure composed of various plant and bark fibers, small rootlets, and flexible grass stems. The outside walls are covered with plant fibers, ornamented with small lichens, bits of birch bark, bud scales, seed pods, and vegetable down firmly bound in with a liberal use of spider web. The interior is lined with fine grasses, weed and bark fibers, and often with the hair of horse or deer.

Feathers of various kinds are frequently used, apparently as an added decoration. These may be ordinary small chicken feathers, but sometimes those of highly colored birds such as the tanager or indigo bunting are chosen. Ernest H. Short (1893) gives an account of a redstart's nest made up almost entirely of the feathers of a wood thrush that had been killed by an owl near the nesting site.

Each nesting season I put out masses of cotton and tow for various birds to use as nesting material. A redstart which built its nest in a tall, slender maple nearby not only used some of the long delicate fibers of tow but studded the whole structure of the nest with small tufts of cotton, giving it a most unusual appearance, not unlike many similarly decorated yellow warbler's nests I have seen. The nest of the redstart somewhat resembles that of the yellow warbler but it is a neater structure with thinner walls, especially at the rim. It is higher than wide and in this respect differs from the goldfinch's nest, which is wider than high.

The average dimensions of a series of nests are as follows: outside diameter $2\frac{7}{8}$ inches, inside diameter $1\frac{1}{2}$ inches; outside depth 3 inches, and inside depth of the cup $1\frac{1}{2}$ inches. The chief departure from these dimensions are of nests that are built in very narrow crotches where the upright supporting branches are close together at their point of origin. In such cases the birds continue to build until a sufficient height is reached to give a satisfactory width. The height of such nests may exceed 5 inches and are acutely V-shaped in section. High nests also occur when the redstart builds over cowbird's eggs deposited before its own eggs have been laid.

It requires a week or ten days for the industrious female to build the nest. The task is performed in a most expert manner. The outside framework is first constructed, and then she enters the nest to adjust the lining, turning around and around and pressing her breast against the sides until the desired symmetry is attained. The final bits are dextrously manipulated by the bird's bill and seem to be pasted on, according to various observers, with the aid of her own saliva.

Louis Sturm (1945) observed the building of one nest, which he states was completed in the course of 2½ to 3 days. He estimated that the bird made 650 to 700 trips in building the nest. The first egg in this case was laid 2 days after the completion of the nest.

William Brewster (1936) presents a detailed account of the building of a redstart nest that is interesting and informative:

At about 6 A. M. on May 17th a female redstart brought a long, transparent, silky-looking fiber—apparently that of a milkweed stalk—to a gray birch in front of the cabin and, placing it at the intersection of a rather stout branch with the main stem, began moving it about until its position suited her, when she pressed it down firmly by rubbing it with the side of her head which she turned slowly from side to side. This was literally the first bit of nest material that was put into the crotch. Many others of an apparently similar kind were brought during the forenoon and treated in the same way, although the bird had to use her bill rather vigorously in tamping some of the more refractory ones into place. She worked busily and steadily until noon when the foundation of the nest was finished.

At about 2:30 P. M. she began the frame by attaching one end of a strand of fibrous material to the right hand side of the trunk a little above the branch on which the foundation was laid and fastening the other end to the foundation on the same side, the strand inclining downward at an angle of about 30° or 40°. Next, another strand was placed on the left side in the same position as the first, the ends of the two overlapping on the trunk. Then a third piece was brought and one end rubbed lightly against the center of the strand on the right, the opposite end being carried a little beyond that of the left hand strand. Next a fourth strand was rubbed on the trunk a little above the upper end of the left hand guy, to the middle of which the opposite was fastened by rubbing the two together. Each piece of fiber was fashioned into the general shape of the nest as soon as it was attached to both ends and more were brought and carried from point to point until a complete framework of about the size and shape of the half of a hen's egg was erected around and resting on the foundations. This framework was so delicate that it looked as if the merest breath of wind would blow it away. During its construction, the bird worked entirely from the outside, standing on the branch and shaping each piece of fiber with her head.

The next day (May 18th) she began using cocoon fibers as well as milkweed bark. The former she obtained from a groove near the top of the cabin door in front of which she would hover on rapidly vibrating wings until the exertion compelled her to alight for a moment to rest and regain breath, either on top of the door or its hand knob. As soon as she had filled her bill, she would fly to the birch, alight on the branch and distribute her load around the inside of the nest; then, hopping into it and squatting down with her head and tail raised and back deeply hollowed, she would move slowly around to the right and then to the left, making usually a half but sometimes a whole turn and, with her head and breast, pressing the materials which she had brought into the meshes of the framework until they were completely filled. Working thus, always from the inside, she modeled and remodeled until by the constant application of fresh material she had transformed the original skeleton framework into a compact, firmly-woven nest. Occasionally she would drop directly into the nest without first alighting outside but she did not attempt to perch on its rim until it was nearly completed.

After putting in the lining, which consisted of horse hair, dry grass, and shreds of birch, grapevine and mullein bark, she drew the loose ends which had been left projecting or hanging down around the outside of the nest. These ends were drawn and tucked in to bind the lining and were held down by the bird's breast until all within her reach were secured. She then managed to rub them still more firmly into place by craning her head over the rim of the nest and bringing her bill, throat and neck to bear on its top and inner and outer surfaces at one and the same time.

After this nest was finished, it was frequently visited by Black and White Creepers, Yellow Warblers and Red-eyed Vireos, all of whom attempted to appropriate some of its component materials for their own domiciles. They sometimes succeeded in getting away with a few strands despite the vigilance of the Redstart, who defended her castle with the greatest spirit.

Eggs.—The usual number of eggs in a complete set of the redstart is 4 but the total ranges from 2 to 5 (I have never found a set containing more than 4 eggs); this number seems to vary in different sections of its range. J. Claire Wood (1904) reported that out of 143 nests with eggs 9 of them had 5 eggs; other observers have reported finding 5 eggs, but sets of more than 4 eggs are not common. Although the first set generally consists of 4 eggs, if these are destroyed the second set seldom exceeds 3 eggs and very often there may be but 2.

The eggs are subject to considerable variation in their size and markings; the average short diameter of a series of 50 eggs is 12.3 millimeters and the average long diameter 16.2 millimeters. They are ovate but some tend toward short ovate. They have a slightly glossy texture with a ground color that varies from white to creamy-white, greenish white, or grayish white. The eggs are speckled, spotted, and frequently blotched with various shades of brown with undertones of gray and drab. There is generally a concentration of markings at the larger end, forming a distinct wreath. The amount and intensity of the markings vary; some eggs may be almost free of markings, on others the markings are so dense as to nearly conceal the ground color.

Incubation.—The period of incubation is 12 days, and is performed entirely by the female. Normally only one brood is reared during any one season.

B. W. Baker (1944) in 3 hours of observation at a nest during the morning noted that the female left the nest seven times, the length of her absence varying from 2 to 10 minutes, while the time spent on the nest was 144 minutes or 80 percent of the observation time. In nests that I have had under observation in Maine, the male was seen to deliver food to the female at frequent intervals and perhaps for this reason these females left the nest less often.

A. D. DuBois writes to me of an interesting reaction of a nesting female to a mirror: "The spunky little female flew at a small mirror which I held over the nest on the end of a stick; she snapped her bill and even grew bold enough to peck at it. On June 3 she again fought the small mirror as I held it up to look into the nest, but she returned to her eggs immediately when I withdrew the obnoxious looking-glass."

Young.—In one nest under observation at Brunswick, Maine, the first egg hatched while the adults were away from the nest. The male was the first to return to greet the youngster and his first act after an inspection of the nest was to remove the eggshells. The male also delivered the first food, a small minced larva, when the young was about 2 hours old. When the female returned, which was shortly after the male's first visit, she carefully inspected the nest, then immediately settled down to brood the young and the three eggs. The male never brooded but he was very attentive in feeding the young. If the female was at the nest when he arrived, the food was presented to her and she in turn fed it to the young, but if she was away the male fed the young directly. On the first day the youngster was brooded 75 percent of the time. There were three young on the following day, and the fourth egg proved to be sterile. The amount of time required for brooding was more or less dependent on weather conditions. On a cool, rainy day more time was spent on the nest than when a moderate temperature prevailed. When it rained the female extended her wings over the edge of the nest and her head was directed upward toward the oncoming rain drops. She thus provided an effective roof to shield the helpless young from a disastrous soaking. The brooding instinct is very strong and if the young were removed from the nest for purposes of study and photography, the female mechanically brooded the empty nest the entire time the young were out, seemingly unaware of their absence. In the afternoon the nest was exposed to the direct rays of the sun and on hot days the female perched on the edge of the nest with her wings half spread and her back toward the sun. At such times she panted incessantly in order to control her temperature through her intricate air-sac system. It is just as necessary for the adult to protect the young from heat as it is to keep them warm on cool days. The amount of time spent in brooding becomes much reduced as the young grow older, and by the time they have attained their covering of feathers and acquire a temperature control there is little need for brooding.

The male, if it is an old bird, usually exhibits greater wariness in approaching the nest than does the female. Miss Cordelia Stanwood has found the reverse to be true of one first-year male, which seemed to show no fear at all of her presence at the nest, whereas the female hesitated to feed the young at such times. Perhaps the older bird's wariness is due to more experience in life.

The part played by the two sexes in feeding the young varies with different individuals; usually both take an equal part, but at times either the male or the female may take the major responsibility. Miss Stanwood studied a nest of the redstart in which the female had disappeared, apparently killed. In this case the male took over all of the arduous duties of feeding the family and of caring for them after they left the nest. Since the young are fed 8 to 10 times every hour it takes the resourcefulness of both parents, let alone one, when a mate is lost.

At the time of hatching, the young have their eyes closed and are naked except for limited tufts of down found on the dorsal tracts including the crown. By the third day the eyes show slightly through very narrow slits and the papillae of the wing feathers make their appearance. By the sixth day the tips of the feathers are unsheathed; from this time on the young preen their feathers a great deal and they may be seen picking at the growing feathers, an action that apparently accelerates the unsheathing process. By the eighth day the juvenal plumage is well established, and the young may leave the nest but if not disturbed or excited usually remain a day longer.

Bernard W. Baker (1944) found the weight of a young on the day of hatching was 1.1 gm. and at 7 days the same young had increased its weight to 7.5 gm. The tarsus of the same bird was 6 mm. in length on the first day and 17 mm. on the seventh day.

As with other warblers, the nest is kept scrupulously clean not only of vermin but of the feces, which are anticipated and disposed of as soon as they appear. During the first two days the fecal sacs are swallowed by the adults, but as the young grow older, more and more of them are carried away and dropped at some distance from the nest. This task, like that of feeding the young, is performed by both parents.

J. Claire Wood (1904) presents an interesting account of a nest of seven eggs which was shared by two pairs of birds, as follows: "When found one female was upon the nest and the other perched close beside it. They were equally demonstrative of anxiety as I ascended the tree. The eggs were in two layers and slightly incubated. Being of two distinct types there was no difficulty in separating them into sets of three and four. This was not a case of polygamy, as both males were present. All four were living in perfect harmony and understanding, which is remarkable from the fact that the males are inclined to pugnacity and firmly attack all intruders of their kind that invade their chosen territory." Whether or not polygamy ever exists among redstarts, as with the ovenbird, to my knowledge has never been determined.

Dr. A. F. Skutch describes an injury feigning performance of a pair of adult redstarts which he observed at Ithaca, N. Y., on June 13, 1931. These birds apparently had young in the vicinity. He writes: "While passing through a tract of low, swampy woods, I was led by the excited chirping of a pair of American redstarts to the discovery of their nest in the crotch of an elderberry bush about 9 feet above the ground. When I attempted to learn by feeling with my finger-tips what it contained, the birds gave such a demonstration as I have seldom witnessed. The female approached the closer to me, advancing within easy reach as she chirped her distressed reproaches; but the male, although he remained at a somewhat greater distance, was more active in his efforts to lead me away. Although I felt that to them it was a most anxious occasion, I confess that I deliberately prolonged their agony that I might delight my eyes with the gorgeous display of the male redstart as he perched on a long twig with tail spread and wings fully extended, vibrating—it seemed to me—as rapidly as a humming-bird's. What a splendid color-contrast in the full black and the orange-salmon of the wings flashing into a blur, while the rich colors of the relatively motionless tail showed so clearly! Descending to the broad surface of a skunk-cabbage leaf, he continued his manifestations of distress—but how can so airy and refulgent a creature convincingly express despair? Next, falling to the ground, he danced over it with spread tail and fluttering wings; but it impressed me rather as some fairy dance than a wounded bird attempting to avert grave danger from his nest. The female redstart's display was similar but less intense, while her paler colors made it less spectacular. When next I returned my attention to the nest, I found it empty. Since it is inconceivable that the birds should have become so excited over an empty nest, I had no doubt that fledglings were hiding close by, possibly having scrambled to safety while my delighted eyes were fastened upon the parents. The attendants of tender nestlings in a nearby nest made no such demonstration upon my approach."

Adults feeding young out of the nest are commonly seen throughout the month of July. There is a tendency for them to remain in the vicinity of the nesting site, but they are less noisy than the young of other species and hence are much less in evidence.

Plumages.—The plumage of the redstart is distinctive and can be easily distinguished from those of other warblers. The young males, even those in the first nuptial plumage, are similar to the females;

and, hence, the identification of the sexes of the younger individuals is more difficult.

The natal plumage is hair-brown and is present as small tufts located on the crown and various tracts of the dorsal part of the body.

The juvenal plumage is well established at the time the young leave the nest and in the course of a few weeks is completed with all of the feathers unsheathed. Jonathan Dwight, Jr. (1900), has described the juvenal plumage as follows: "Above, including the sides of the head, deep sepia-brown. Wings and tail deep olive-brown, the basal portion of the primaries, secondaries and outer rectrices pale lemon-yellow, the secondaries and tertiaries edged with dull olive-green, the coverts with wood-brown paler at the tips. Below, pale primrose-yellow, hair brown on the chin, throat and breast. Bill and feet dusky pinkish buff darkening to brownish black when older."

George A. Petrides (1943b) studied the plumage of a young redstart which he kept in captivity after it had left the nest. He found that at 10 days of age the tail feathers began breaking out of their sheaths; at 13 days the yellow areas on the wings first appeared and by 20 days the yellow patches of the tail became completely exposed. It was not until the young were 26 days old that the yellow patches of the wings were fully visible.

When the bird was 22 days old the slate-gray juvenal plumage of the occipital and dorsal tracts was being replaced in quantity by the olive-green first winter plumage. The yellow underwing coverts also began to appear at this time; previously the underwing areas had been naked. The postjuvenal molt was thus begun before the juvenal plumage was fully acquired.

The first winter plumage involves changes in the body feathers and wing coverts but not the rest of the wings or the tail. Dwight (1900) describes this plumage as follows:

Unlike the previous plumage. Above, the pileum, nape and sides of neck mouse-gray, the back olive-green, often tinged with brownish orange, the upper tail coverts clove-brown. The wing coverts become dull olive-green. Below, dull white, ashy and pinkish buff suffusing the chin and throat, and orange-ochraceous or deep chrome-yellow area on either side of the breast, the color tinging the breast and sides. Orbital ring, white.

First nuptial plumage acquired by a partial prenuptial moult, which involves chiefly the head and throat, where a few black feathers in patches are acquired. A few may be found scattered sparingly elsewhere and new white feathers on the chin are the rule. Abrasion and fading make birds paler above and whiter below. In this species, which is unique among our warblers during the first breeding season in wearing an immature dress strikingly different from the adult, the renewal is reduced to a minimum.

Adult winter plumage acquired by a complete postnuptial moult in July. The black and orange-red dress is assumed, the black feathers often having a faint buffy edging. Sometimes the orange basal part of the primaries or of the rectrices fails to develop and yellow, as in the first winter, takes its place.

Adult nuptial plumage acquird by wear. The abrasion of the black plumage is in places so slight that there might be some replacement by new feathers, but it is not apparent. Fading is not obvious, except of the flight feathers.

The plumages and moults [of the female] correspond to those of the male. First differs in first winter plumage which is browner, the breast patches merely yellow tinged and the basal part of the rectrices much paler yellow, this color usually absent from the base of the primaries and reduced in extent on the secondaries. Some specimens are much like males. The first nuptial plumage is acquired by a very limited, sometimes suppressed prenuptial moult. The adult winter plumage is scarcely different from the first winter, a little grayer on the back and the yellow area on the wings greater. The adult nuptial plumage is apparently the previous plumage plus wear.

Pure and partial albinistic and melanistic forms of the redstart have been reported.

Thos. D. Burleigh (1944a) describes a hybrid between the redstart (*Setophaga ruticilla*) and the parula warbler (*Composothlypis americana*) which he secured on Cat Island, Miss., 9 miles offshore from Gulfport:

This specimen bears a superficial resemblance to the female Redstart but close scrutiny reveals marked differences. The bill is not broadly wedge-shaped as in the Redstart, and the rictal bristles are developed only to the same degree as in the Parula Warbler, in this respect differing markedly from the genus *Setophaga*. The wings have the middle and greater wing-coverts broadly tipped with dull white, forming two distinct bands, and there is a complete absence of the speculum on the inner remiges. The tail, although noticeably longer than in the genus *Compsothlypis*, lacks the yellow characteristic of *Setophaga;* this basal portion of the outer rectices is dull white instead. The color pattern of the upper parts is distinctly that of the Parula Warbler, and while duller in hue, the olive green of the mantle is in contrast to the color of the lower back. On the other hand, the under parts suggest the Redstart, the throat being dull white rather than yellow, with the median portion of the breast tinged with light salmon.

Food.—There has been no comprehensive study made of the food of the redstart based on an examination of the contents of a representative number of stomachs, but many field observations clearly indicate that it is strictly insectivorous in its food-eating habits. The insects it eats are extremely varied; it gleans them in the form of eggs, larvae, pupae, and adults from the trunks, limbs, twigs, and leaves of trees; and it is most adept in capturing insects in the air. There are few small forest insects, whatever their stage of development, that escape this active and resourceful warbler, so busy is it in pursuit of its prey. Even the caterpillars that escape from other slower warblers by hanging by their silken fibers are readily snatched up by this aerial acrobat. It feeds on insects injurious to deciduous trees and in Maine it frequents the coniferous forests to supplement its food supply. I have frequently seen it snap up flies and tiny midges, mosquitoes, and black flies, all of which, though not injurious to vegetation, are most annoying to human beings. It feeds upon a great variety of caterpillars including the smaller hairy types. It may be seen in orchards, where various observers have noted its fondness for cankerworms, and it has also been seen to feed on brown-tail and gipsy moths. Forbush (1907) saw one redstart eat 31 gipsy moth larvae before it left the clump of willows in which he was able to watch it at close range. At another time he saw a redstart take 11 brown-tail larvae from an apple tree in the course of 5 minutes.

W. L. McAtee (1926) in his study of the relation of birds to wood-lots in New York State writes: "Rations for the Redstart consist entirely of insects, spiders, and daddy-long-legs. Beetles, including flea beetles, leaf beetles, and round-headed wood borers; caterpillars and moths; and such true bugs as spittle insects, tree hoppers, and leaf hoppers are commonly taken. The Redstart devours also some hymenoptera, mayflies, and diptera including craneflies. Busy at all times in the pursuit of insect prey, the Redstart in the long run must account for vast numbers of the forms injurious to trees."

While the vast majority of the insects eaten by the redstart are harmful to man's interest it must be admitted that it does feed on a few beneficial insects such as the parasitic Hymenoptera and Diptera as well as an occasional ladybird beetle which are classed as useful.

Although the redstart is preeminently an insect destroyer it has been known to eat berries and seeds on rare occasions. Aretas A. Saunders (1938) reports that in Allegany State Park, N. Y., they feed on shadbush berries; George A. Petrides (1943) reported them feeding on the berries of *Berberis bealei;* and A. H. Howell (1932) states that in addition to its usual food, while the birds are migrating through Florida, it feeds on magnolia seeds as well as on spiders, plant lice, and scale insects.

Alexander Wetmore (1916) reported on his examination of the food found in 13 stomachs of redstarts, which he collected in Puerto Rico during the months of December, January, February, and April, as follows:

In these animal food amounts to 100 per cent. Small lantern flies (*Fulgoridae*) occur nine times and form 37.23 per cent of the total. Longicorn beetles make up 0.57 per cent, snout beetles 1.5 per cent and miscellaneous species 2.54 per cent. All are classed as injurious species save a single ladybird beetle, so small that it is lost in the bulk of the others. Moth remains amount to 11.75 per cent, while no caterpillars were eaten. Hymenoptera remains (6.67 percent) were found in five stomachs. Approximately two-thirds of these small species, probably of parasitic habit. One that parasitizes ants was definitely identified as a species of *Kapala*. Diptera (39.24 per cent) were present in eight of the stomachs examined. One bird had eaten a spider, and another insect eggs, both amounting to only 5 per cent.

Though present only in winter, this small warbler is a bird of economic importance. It destroys thousands of lantern flies, abundant in the trees and shrubbery, as well as many beetles, moths, and flies. A very small percentage of its food is taken from beneficial species of insects, the remainder being entirely injurious. This bird is entirely insectivorous and does not feed upon any of the abundant wild berries, a fact which increases its importance, as it destroys proportionately more insects than do the more or less vegetarian resident species of similar habit.

Small larvae and tiny insects are fed to the young by the adults during the first days of nest life but as the young become older and their demands for food correspondingly greater they are fed larger insects such as adult moths, beetles, locusts, and craneflies. Bernard W. Baker (1944) in observations made of nesting redstarts in northern Michigan writes: "Various kinds of insects and larvae were fed to the young—Mayfly (*Ephemera*), Rosy Maple Moth larvae (*Dryocampa rubicnda*), House Fly (*Musca domestica*), and many others I could not identify. During a Mayfly hatch 90 per cent of the insects brought to the nests were Mayflies. It was not unusual for the male to bring in two or three Mayflies and feed two young on one trip. On one occasion a male brought four Mayflies at once and fed three young."

The young are usually fed from 4 to 15 times during the course of an hour. At one nest under observation the young were fed by the female 28 times and by the male 22 times during the course of 9 hours. The feeding intervals varied from 1 to 25 minutes, with an average of about 10 to 11 minutes between feedings. Ira N. Gabrielson (1922) who observed a nest of young at Marshalltown, Iowa, states that during the course of 5½ hours the nestlings had 30 feedings, 10 of which were by the female and 20 by the male. During these feedings he recognized 22 winged insects, 16 larvae, 1 fly, and 1 spider, but in some cases he was unable to determine the character of the food.

It is obvious that the redstart can be classed as a bird very useful to man's interests because of its destruction of many harmful insects.

Voice.—The song of the redstart is not especially pleasing nor is there any outstanding feature of the song except its extreme variation and the different versions in which it occurs. It is a short monotonous *weechy* type and of a high-pitched sibilant quality. I have often been mystified by the vagaries of this versatile singer. The beginner may at first confuse the song with that of the yellow warbler, which it resembles, but the latter is longer and has a different ending. The fundamental difference between the two is a tendency of the song of the yellow warbler to accelerate while that of the redstart retards. Sometimes the redstart will emit a series of notes that are weak and *buzzy* and suggest the parula's song, and again they will be like the shrill notes of the blackpoll or the loud *wheeze* of the black-throated blue warbler.

Aretas A. Saunders has sent us his interpretation and analysis of the redstart's songs, as follows: "The song of the redstart is not loud, but certain notes are sometimes strongly accented. In 59 records, the songs contain from 4 to 11 notes, averaging about 7. They occupy from 3/5 to 1 2/5 seconds.

"The song varies in pitch from G ′ ′ ′ to E ′ ′ ′ ′. Individual songs vary from no change in pitch to a change of three tones. Three of my records are all on the same pitch. Four change pitch only a half tone. Only one has a range of three tones. The average range is just about one and a half tones.

"Songs begin with a series of simple notes or of 2-note phrases. The former sounding like *tseet, tseet, tseet* and the latter *tseeta, tseeta, tseeta*. Songs may end in three different ways; the first just as it began, without change to the end; the second with a single, strongly accented, higher-pitched note; and the third by a downward slur, strongly accented at the beginning. These two latter forms may be represented as *tsita, tsita, tsita, tseet* and *tsit, tsit, tsit, tsit, tseeo*. Of my records, 15 are of the first form, 18 of the second, and 26 of the third.

"These three different songs may all be sung by one individual and there is nothing seasonal about their use. The bird frequently alternates two or more songs, sometimes regularly, sometimes one is sung three or four times as often as the other. One bird sang four different songs one after another, but the order varied with each repetition. So far as I know, this is the only warbler that sings different songs in alternation.

"The redstart sings from the time of its arrival until the middle of July. The average date of the last song, based on 14 years of observation in Allegany State Park, is July 14. The earliest is July 2 (1927) and the latest July 25 (1937)."

In northern New York, A. Sidney Hyde (1939) states that no songs of the redstart are heard in late July but that songs were regularly heard from August 1 until September 2. Several birds were singing with almost full springtime vigor at Irondequoit Bay on August 20.

Eugene P. Bicknell (1884), in writing of the late singing of the redstart, says:

In some years I have found this species songless soon after the beginning of July. In seasons when it thus early becomes silent singing is resumed in the first part of August, and continues for two or three weeks. But the period of July silence is inconstant, and sometimes singing is little interrupted through the month. When this is the case singing seems to cease finally at the end of the month or early in August, and is followed by no supplementary song period. * * * My dates of last songs are limited by the third week of August, except in one exceptional instance when one of the birds was heard to sing on September 5.

A number of observers have reported seeing the female sing, the song being about the same in quality and length as that of the male.

It has been suggested by critics that these reports were based on
seeing the first-year male, which has a plumage similar to that of
the female and could be easily mistaken for a female.   The male
breeds the first year in this plumage and this adds to the confusion.
However, it has been definitely proved that the females do sing at
times.   J. L. Baillie, Jr. (1926) collected a female at Lowbush, Lake
Abitibi, Ontario, on June 3, 1925, which was singing one of the usual
songs of the male, including the usual *swee-a, swee-a* notes.   The
specimen was carefully sexed and was found to have enlarged ovaries;
hence, no mistake was possible.   On June 22, F. W. Braund (Braund
and McCullah, 1940) heard what appeared to be a singing male on Anticosti island.   When seen it was thought to be a young male in immature plumage in full song, but after it was collected and sexed it
proved to be an adult female.   These and other similar cases indicate
that some females sing the full song of the males, although it is
unusual for them to do so.

Albert R. Brand (1938) has determined the vibration frequencies
of the songs of many passerine birds from motion-picture film recordings.   The highest note in the song of the redstart had a frequency of 7,300 vibrations per second, the lowest 4,400, and the
approximate mean of 6,200 vibrations per second.   It is of interest
to compare the mean of the redstart with that of the blackpoll warbler,
which has a mean of 8,900, whereas the mean of the yellow-breasted
chat is only 2,600 vibrations per second.

Horace W. Wright (1912) has observed the early morning awakening of birds at Jefferson Highlands in the White Mountains of New
Hampshire.   Of the redstart he writes: "If the Ovenbird is excepted,
the Redstart introduces the warbler singing.   All warbler song is
delayed on the average until 3.29, when the Ovenbird begins to
sing.   The Redstart based on ten records, averages to sing seventeen minutes later, or at 3.46 o'clock.   It has been heard once as
early as 3.26, but on three other occasions was first heard at 3.55,
3.56, and 3.58 respectively.   Two and sometimes three birds sing
within hearing.   On June 28, 1911, the first bird began to sing at 3.41,
the second was heard at 3.49, the third at 3.52, and the three continued singing much of the time up to 5.15 o'clock."   He states further
that the Redstart was one of only three warblers which were heard to
sing after sunset, which at the time the records were taken was at 7.30
p. m.

Enemies.—The redstart's habit of nesting in rather tall slender
trees, usually at a considerable distance from the ground, frees it from
most of the enemies to which ground-nesting birds are subject.
However, I know of one nest of the redstart, built in a shrub about
4 feet above the ground, that was destroyed by a cat, and of another,

also located in a shrub near a house, that was quite probably destroyed by one. However, since the vast majority of redstarts build in locations remote from human habitations, cats are not an important factor in affecting the redstart population as a whole.

John and James M. Macoun (1909) cite a case of a redstart's nest, built in an exposed position, that was presumably destroyed by an olive-sided flycatcher that had a nest on an overhanging branch a few rods away.

C. H. Morrell (1899) states that two redstart nests which he observed were deserted after the eggs had been laid because caterpillars had taken possession of the nesting tree and had completely overrun the nests. E. H. Forbush (1907) in connection with a gipsy moth infestation at Medford, Mass., writes: "There was a nest of the American redstart and the tree had been stripped of leaves by the caterpillars. There were four young in the nest. I saw the old birds take but one very small gipsy moth caterpillar to the young, but they would pick the large ones off the nest and drop them to the ground very often. There were no pupae near the nest that I could see." Mr. Forbush does not state whether the redstarts succeeded in winning their fight against this caterpillar infestation.

Louis Sturm (1945) says that one nest that he observed "was robbed by a small fox snake (*Elaphe vulpina gloydi*) which had swallowed all three eggs when discovered coiled in the nest."

The redstart, like most birds, is host to a number of external parasites, of which Harold S. Peters (1936) has identified the three species of lice *Menacanthus* sp., *Myrsidea incerta* (Kellogg), and *Philopterus subflavescens* (Geoffroy) and the tick *Haemaphysalis leporis-palustris* Packard.

Perhaps the greatest menace to the redstart is the parasitic cowbird, of which this warbler is one of the commonest victims. According to Herbert Friedmann (1929) at Ithaca, N. Y., the redstart was the most imposed upon species. Out of 34 nests he found 23 of them contained one or more of the parasitic eggs and it was not uncommon to find sets composed of but one or two of the rightful eggs, the rest being the cowbird's.

Occasionally the redstart builds a new floor over the cowbird's eggs, as is often done by the yellow warbler. This procedure is especially likely to take place if the cowbird succeeds in laying its eggs before the redstart's eggs are present. More often the redstart does not seem to be annoyed by the strange eggs but goes on laying its own. It is unusual for the redstart to desert its nest because of the presence of cowbird's eggs.

A nest was found on June 9, 1922, with two young cowbirds 5 days old, completely filling and covering the nest. In the bottom beneath the young parasites were four addled eggs of the warbler. If some of the rightful eggs hatch, the young are usually starved or suffocated by the young cowbirds, although nests are occasionally found in which one or more of the young survive along with the interloper.

In discussing the effect of this parasitism on the redstart Friedmann adds: "When a cowbird is raised by a one-brooded species such as the redstart it represents the total product of its pair of foster-parents for the year. The loss here is a very decided one if we consider the food consumed by one cowbird and that which would have been eaten by four Redstarts. However, judging from the constancy of the numerical status of the Redstart from year to year it seems as though three of the four young would succumb anyway to various dangers before the next year. Also we must remember that the Redstart is in many places more abundant than the cowbird."

Joseph J. Hickey (1940) writes: "Males were silent in the presence of female Cowbirds, but females reacted with sharp hisses, a rapid snapping of the bill and much spreading of the tail." Friedmann (1929) writes: "On July 2, 1921, a young Cowbird, full grown in size and fully fledged was seen following a Redstart and begging for food from it. The Redstart paid absolutely no attention to it although several times the two were very close together. All this time the Redstart was busy gathering food and when it had as much as it could carry it flew off and the young Cowbird did not follow."

Dayton Stoner (1932) gives an account of an interesting experience of the behavior of redstarts as follows: "I saw one female carrying food for young. Another female was seen feeding a young cowbird that was out of the nest and able to fly, while an adult female cowbird sat on a limb nearby and apparently watched the proceedings. The female cowbird did not offer the young one any food, but after the latter's wants had been satisfied in some measure by the diminutive redstart, she moved close to the young one and at least *appeared* to be solicitous of its welfare. But any maternal solicitude involving real care of the young was utterly foreign to this parasitic bird."

Fall.—The redstarts start migrating from the most northern sections of their nesting range in August but it is well into September before the last individuals leave these outposts. The individuals breeding in British Columbia near the Pacific Ocean do not follow the Pacific flyway but retrace their path across the mountains to the interior and leave the United States between Texas and Florida, their point of entry. In recent years an increasing number of redstarts have nested in Washington and Oregon, and there are many records of occurrence, especially during the time of migration, throughout California and southward. This may mean a building up of a tendency of the individuals nesting in the northwest to use the Pacific flyway, which in the course of a few hundred years may become a regular migration route for these Redstarts.

At Point Pelee, Ontario, according to Taverner and Swales (1908) the bulk of the redstarts pass through during the first week of September but are fairly common during the latter part of the month. In Maine the bulk of the redstarts leave by the middle of September but in southern New England and New York there are many records of redstarts throughout the month of October.

In Ohio and the Middle West there is a distinct movement of redstarts early in August and the peak of the migration takes place from August 20 until September 25. A sharp decrease takes place during the last few days of September, and by October 5 the species disappears except for an occasional straggler.

Thomas D. Burleigh (1944b) in discussing the fall migration on the Mississippi Gulf coast writes: "The first birds to appear are always young of the year, and although a few females are seen early in August, it is not until after the middle of the month that the males are observed. During September the Redstart occurs in its greatest numbers, and there is usually an occasional day after the middle of the month * * * when these warblers are found literally everywhere." Mr. Burleigh's latest fall record is November 10, 1937. In Florida the largest flights also occur about the middle of September, and at this time many are reported killed at the lighthouses. Many are seen throughout October and some late fall records are: Pensacola November 19, 1929; Fort Pierce November 2, 1918; Fort Drum November 3, 1888; and Sombrero Key November 4, 1888.

According to F. C. Lincoln (1935), redstarts, evidently the more southern breeders, are seen returning southward on the northern coast of South America just about the time that the earliest of those breeding in the North reach Florida on their way to winter quarters.

Winter.—The redstart may be found in the West Indies from August until the following April. In Cuba, according to Thomas Barbour (1923), "the Redstarts are the first sign to the Cubans that the migration is on, and they probably are the very last northern visitor to leave in the spring. They are excessively abundant in thickets and woods everywhere, even in the cities. Except for the Palm Warbler, no bird is more in evidence during the winter than the Candelita— the little flame. The North American observer never would dream that there could be enough redstarts gathered together from all the bird's range to make up the hordes which come to Cuba."

Alexander Wetmore (1916), in his account of the birds of Puerto Rico, writes of the redstart: "These birds frequent the mangroves, forest growths, and coffee plantations, and sometimes shade trees about houses. The greater portion seen were immature birds and females, though occasionally males in full plumage were observed. As always, these birds were very active, searching through the limbs for insects, and expertly catching insects on the wing. On El Yunque, in the dense forests, they were seen up to 1,500 feet altitude, and elsewhere in more open locations were found in the highest elevations. Next to the parula warbler this is the most common of the wintering warblers." In Haiti and the Dominican Republic, Wetmore and Swales (1931) found that "the redstart frequents shrubbery, groves and forests, where it is a most active flycatcher, pursuing its living prey with dash and vigor among the branches with much display of its brilliantly marked, fan-shaped tail. It ranges from coastal thickets to the summits of the mountains."

Todd and Carriker (1922), in their account of the birds of the Santa Marta region of Colombia, state that the redstart is "an abundant bird during the winter months in the mountains, but much rarer in the lowlands. Its habits are practically the same as in the north, except that it does not sing. Simon speaks of finding it in the densest forest in the tops of the highest trees, where it is hard to see." The earliest fall arrival date reported by the authors was August 24, 1898, and the latest spring date May 1, 1913.

Dr. A. F. Skutch has written us an account of the redstart as he found it wintering in Central America as follows: "First appearing in Central America in mid-August, the redstart spreads rapidly over the lower portions of the whole great isthmus. Although during its periods of migratory flight it is at times met in the highlands, even up to an altitude of 8,000 feet, like the majority of the warblers that breed in the Austral region of North America it prefers the warmth of the lowlands. Once it has settled down in its winter home, it is only rarely found as high as 5,000 feet. At lower altitudes, it is a fairly common winter resident throughout the length and breadth of Central America. Although not rare on the Pacific side, it is more numerous in the Caribbean lowlands. In the northern lowlands of Honduras and Guatemala, it is very much in evidence during the winter months, and may be expected wherever it can find trees in which to forage. Incessantly active, it retains in the Tropics the same sprightly ways that make it a favorite of northern bird-lovers, and as it weaves skillfully through the boughs of the trees in pursuit of insects on the wing, conspicuously displays the bright orange or yellow areas on its sides, wings and tail. Like nearly all of the warblers that winter in the lowlands, it is quite solitary during its sojourn in Central America, never associating with others of its own kind. I have not heard it sing while in the Tropics.

"Like the black-and-white warbler, the redstart begins to withdraw from Central America considerably earlier than many other of the wintering warblers. As a rule, it disappears from Costa Rica before the end of March. I have April records for only two individuals, one of which, a female, lingered as late as the sixth. In Guatemala, however, it has been reported as late as May 6."

DISTRIBUTION

Range.—North America, south to the West Indies and northern South America.

Breeding range.—The redstart breeds **north** to northern British Columbia (Atlin, Telegraph Creek, and Liard Crossing); Yukon; central western and central southern Mackenzie (Fort Norman, Fort Wrigley, Fort Simpson, and Fort Resolution); central Saskatchewan (Emma Lake and Cumberland House); southern Manitoba (Duck Mountain and Berens Island); central and northeastern Ontario (Kenora, Lac Seul, Rossport, and Moose Factory); central western and southeastern Quebec (probably Rupert House, Mistassini Post, Godbout, Matamek, Mingan, and Anticosti Island); and Newfoundland (Bay of Islands, Twillingate, and Fogo Island). **East** to Newfoundland (Fogo Island); Nova Scotia; New Brunswick; Maine (Andover and Auburn); New Hampshire (Hollis); Vermont (Newfane); Massachusetts; New York; southeastern Virginia (Dismal Swamp); central North Carolina (Charlotte and Raleigh); and central Georgia (Atlanta, Macon, rarely Americus, and once in Savannah. **South** to central Georgia (Savannah); central Alabama (Greensboro, Booth, and Seale); central Mississippi (Edwards); northwestern, central and southeastern Louisiana (Mansfield, Natchitoches, Lottie, and Diamond); central and southeastern Oklahoma; central northern Colorado (Central City, Longmont, and Boulder); and central Utah (Provo). **West** to central Utah (Provo and Parleys Park); northeastern Oregon (probably Minan); central northern Washington (Winthrop and Chelan); and western British Columbia (Hagensborg, Pemberton, and Atlin).

Winter range.—The redstart winters **north** to southern Baja California (Miraflores); Veracruz (Presido and Tres Zapotes); Yucatán (Chichén-Itzá); Quintana Roo (Holbox Island and Cozumel Island); Cuba (Mariel, Guamo, and Gibara); rarely the Bahamas (Green Cay, Andros, New Providence, and Great Inagua); Hispaniola (Fort Liberté, Sousa, and Sánchez); and Puerto Rico (Mona Island, Mayagüez, and Culebra Island). **East** to Puerto Rico (Culebra Island); the Lesser Antilles (Virgin Islands, Barbuda, Antigua, Dominica, Santa Lucia, Grenada, Tobago, and Trinidad); and British Guiana (Mount Roraima and Bartica). **South** to British Guiana (Bartica); northwestern Brazil (Sierra Imeri); and Ecuador (Zamora). **West** to Ecuador (Zamora, Quito, and Esmeraldas) ; Puebla (Metlatoyuca) and southern Baja California (San José del Cabo and Miraflores).

The range as outlined is for the two recognized races. The Southern redstart (*Setophaga ruticilla ruticilla*) breeds from North Dakota to Maine, south to Georgia, Louisiana, and central and southeastern Oklahoma; while the northern redstart (*S. r. tricolora*) breeds from northern British Columbia to Nova Scotia, south to central northern Colorado, and west to central northern Washington and northeastern Oregon.

Migration.—Late dates of spring departure are: Ecuador—below San José, March 15. Venezuela—Rancho Grande near Maracay, Aragua, May 5. Colombia—La Tigrera, Santa Marta region, May 1. Panamá—Gatún, April 28. Costa Rica—El General, April 6. British Honduras—Mountain Cow, April 14. Swan Island—April 19. Guatemala—Chuntugui, May 3. Tabasco—Balancan, May 16. Virgin Islands—Kingshill, St. Croix, April 30. Puerto Rico—Cabo Rojo Light, April 26. Haiti—Île de la Gonâve, May 20. Cuba—Cienfuegos, May 13; Habana, May 11 (average of 8 years, May 4). Bahamas—Nassau and Cay Lobos Light, May 13.

Early dates of spring arrival are: Venezuela—Rancho Grande near Maracay, Aragua, February 27. Florida—Key West, March 6; Fort Myers, March 12; Pensacola, April 4. Alabama—Birmingham, April 1. Georgia—Milledgeville region, March 16; Athens, April 7. South Carolina—Clarendon County, March 24; Marion, April 2. North Carolina—Raleigh, April 2 (average of 27 years, April 12). Virginia—Charlottesville, April 13 (average, April 22). West Virginia—Kayford, April 10; French Creek, April 22 (average of 17 years, April 29). District of Columbia—Washington, April 16 (average of 53 years, April 22). Maryland—Largo, Prince Georges County, April 15. Delaware—Kent and Sussex Counties, February 28 (average of 22 years, March 20). Pennsylvania—Berwyn, April 3; Pittsburgh, April 21; Renovo, April 29 (average of 25 years, May 4). New Jersey—Bridgeton, April 23. New York—Bronx County, April 24; Ithaca, April 29. Connecticut—Hartford, April 22. Rhode Island—Providence, April 29. Massachusetts—Springfield, April 28. Vermont—Bennington, Wells River, and Bakersfield, May 4. New Hampshire—South Hooksett, May 2. Maine—Bowdoinham, May 3. Quebec—Montreal, May 4. New Brunswick—St. Stephen and Bathurst, May 12. Nova Scotia—Wolfville, May 3. Prince Edward Island—North Bedeque, May 24. Newfoundland—Tompkins, May 29. Louisiana—New Orleans and Grand Isle, April 7. Mississippi—Edwards, March 23. Arkansas—Helena, March 31. Tennessee—Nashville and Chattanooga, April 12 (average of 10 years at Nashville, April 20). Kentucky—Bowling Green, April 4. Missouri—southeastern Missouri, April 11. Illinois—Addison, April 9 (average for Chicago region, May 7). Indiana—Bloomington, April 12. Ohio—Oberlin, April 7; Buckeye Lake, April 25 (average May 2). Michigan—Ann Arbor, April 25. Ontario—London, April 30; Ottawa, May 3 (average of 17 years, May 16). Iowa—Wall Lake, April 21. Wisconsin—Milwaukee, March 20; Berlin, April 28. Minnesota—Lanesboro and Red Wing, May 2 (average of 45 years for southern Minnesota, May 10). Texas—Port Arthur, March 23. Oklahoma—Tulsa, April 16. Kansas—Manhattan, April 22. Nebraska—Red Cloud, April 5, April 17 (average of 20 years, May 12). South Dakota—Yankton, May 3. North Dakota—Cass County, May 7 (average, May 14). Manitoba—Brandon, May 8; Aweme, May 11 (average, May 15). Saskatchewan—Indian Head, May 12. Mackenzie—Fort Simpson, May 20. Arizona—Yuma, April 30. Colorado—Fort Morgan, May 5. Utah—Ogden, May 22. Wyoming—Careyhurst, April 30; average of 8 years for southern Wyoming, May 17. Idaho—Rathdrum, May 11. Montana—Billings, May 12. Alberta—Camrose, May 9. Nevada—Las Vegas, May 21. Washington—Cheney, May 19. British Columbia—Okanagan Landing, May 20. Alaska—Wrangell, June 9.

Late dates of fall departure are: British Columbia—Shuswap Falls, September 22. California—Verdugo, Los Angeles County, November 23; Pasadena, December 27. Alberta—Glenevis, September 22. Montana—Great Falls, October 3. Idaho—Moscow, September 4. Wyoming—Laramie, September 12 (average of 5 years, September 4). Utah—Uinta Basin, September 20. Colorado—Yuma, October 22. Arizona—Imperial National Wildlife Refuge, September 22. Saskatchewan—Wiseton, October 2. Manitoba—Aweme, September 28 (average, September 18); Winnipeg, October 26. North Dakota—Cass County, September 23 (average, September 17); Rice Lake, September 25; Fargo, November 1. South Dakota—Faulkton, October 15. Nebraska—Omaha, September 16. Kansas—Harper, September 21. Oklahoma—Tulsa, September 25. Texas—Cove, November 6, December 26. Minnesota—Virginia and Faribault, October 12 (average of 14 years for southern Minnesota, September 23). Wisconsin—La Crosse, October 11. Iowa—Sigourney, October 12. Ontario—Ottawa, October 3; Point Pelee, October 15; Toronto, November 28. Michigan—Detroit, October 11. Ohio—central Ohio, October 27 (average, October 6); Hillsboro, November 1. Indiana—Lake or Porter County, October 11; Carlisle, October 29. Illinois—Chicago, October 31 (average, October 8). Missouri—Keokuk, October 20. Kentucky—Danville, October 23. Tennessee—Elizabethton, October 19. Mississippi—Gulf coast, November 10. Louisiana—Baton Rouge region, November 7. Newfoundland—Stephenville,

September 21. Prince Edward Island—North River, September 7.
Nova Scotia—Yarmouth, August 31. New Brunswick—Saint John,
September 25. Quebec—Montreal, October 6. Maine—Jefferson,
October 11. New Hampshire—New Hampton, October 9. Ver-
mont—Wells River, October 17; Bennington, November 11. Massa-
chusetts—Cambridge, November 7; Belmont, November 16. Rhode
Island—Little Compton, October 22. Connecticut—West Hartford,
October 24; Windsor, November 25. New York—Ithaca, October
18; New York City, November 22 and 23, December 27. New Jersey—
Englewood region, October 19. Pennsylvania—Sewickley, November
28; Lakemont, Blair County, December 25. Delaware—Kent and
Sussex Counties, October 16 (average, September 10). Maryland—
Patuxent Wildlife Research Refuge, October 16; White Marsh,
December 6. District of Columbia—Washington, November 16
(average of 33 dates, September 20). West Virginia—Bluefield,
October 12. Virginia—Cape Henry, November 28 (average, Septem-
ber 28). North Carolina—Raleigh, October 13 (average of 12 years,
October 3) ; Statesville, October 16. South Carolina—Clarendon
County, October 21. Georgia—Athens, October 27. Alabama—
Birmingham, October 22, December 17. Florida—Pensacola, Novem-
ber 19. Bahamas—Cay Lobos Light, October 20.

Early dates of fall arrival are: British Columbia—Francois Lake,
August 5. California—Monterey Park, August 30. Idaho—Jerome,
July 7; Jensen, August 20. Colorado—Yuma, August 26. Arizona—
Oracle, August 12. New Mexico—Kingston, August 24. North Da-
kota—Cass County, August 20 (average, August 27). South Da-
kota—Faulkton, August 15. Nebraska—Red Cloud, August 21.
Oklahoma—Norman, August 30. Texas—Austin region, August 17;
Brownsville, August 31. Iowa—Osage, August 11. Ohio—Buckeye
Lake, July 23 (average, August 4). Illinois—La Grange, August 2;
Chicago, August 9 (average, August 14). Mississippi—Gulfport,
July 16. Maine—Bailey Island, July 30. Massachusetts—Chatham,
August 27. New York—New York City, August 2. New Jersey—
Milltown, August 6. Maryland—Patuxent Wildlife Research Refuge,
August 12. Virginia—Cape Henry, September 3 (average, September
10). North Carolina—Washington, August 10. South Carolina—
Clarendon County, July 18. Georgia—Athens, July 22. Alabama—
Leighton and Birmingham, August 23. Florida—Alligator Point,
Franklin County, July 19; Fort Myers, July 28. Cuba—Cienfuegos,
August 6. Jamaica—St. Elizabeth, August 10. Dominican Repub-
lic—Constanza, September 22. Puerto Rico—Cabo Rojo, September
17. Barbuda, August 10. Guatemala—Puerto Barrios, August 21.
Salvador—Lake Olomega, August 27. Honduras—near Tela, August
19. Costa Rica—El Hogar, August 16. Panamá—Almirante Bay
region, August 27. Colombia—Santa Marta region, August 24.

Venezuela—Rancho Grande, near Maracay, Aragua, August 31.
Ecuador—Esmeraldas, October 18.

Egg dates.—Illinois: 32 records, May 25 to July 21; 16 records,
May 29 to June 6, indicating the height of the season.

Michigan: 14 records, May 25 to July 12; 7 records, May 30 to
June 8.

Maine: 20 records, June 5 to 24; 11 records, June 10 to 17.

Massachusetts: 64 records, May 22 to June 30; 40 records, May
30 to June 6.

Nova Scotia: 13 records, June 3 to 25; 7 records, June 15 to 18.

Pennsylvania: 7 records, June 2 to 16 (Harris).

SETOPHAGA RUTICILLA TRICOLORA (Müller)

NORTHERN AMERICAN REDSTART

CONTRIBUTED BY JAMES LEE PETERS

HABITS

The name *Motacilla tricolora* was applied by Müller (1776) to a
colored figure of a redstart in Daubenton's Planches Enluminées (1765,
pl. 391, fig. 2), Müller apparently not recognizing that this figure
actually represented the bird named *Motacilla ruticilla* by Linnaeus
in 1758. Müller's name remained in the synonymy of *ruticilla* until
resurrected by Oberholser (1938) who applied it to a western race of
redstart which he characterized as differing "from the eastern form in
smaller size, smaller orange or yellow wing spot; in the female also
paler, more grayish, less conspicuously olivaceous, upper surface."

As breeding range he assigned northern British Columbia, Mackenzie, and central Manitoba, south to Oregon, northern Utah, and
Wisconsin; he believed that it migrated through the greater part of
the United States and wintered in South America to Ecuador and
French Guiana. Wetmore (1949) found that the characters given
by Oberholser for distinguishing *S. r. tricolora* from *S. r. ruticilla*
did not hold, and the range of the former was more extensive than
supposed. As a result of his investigations Wetmore found that the
size of the wing patch was variable and hence not a subspecific character; in fact he could find no constant differences between the adult
males of the two races, but found that females and immature males of
tricolora differ from *ruticilla* in being "somewhat darker above, washed
with duller green in immature dress."

The breeding range for *tricolora* given by Wetmore extends from
Yukon, Mackenzie, Saskatchewan, central Ontario, and Quebec to
Newfoundland, south to west-central Washington, northern Utah,
Montana, northern Maine, New Brunswick, and Nova Scotia.

Both forms appear to migrate and winter together.

NORTHERN PAINTED REDSTART

HABITS

One of the most attractive birds to be found in the mountain canyons of southern Arizona is this pretty little redstart, painted in striking contrasts of shining black, pure white, and brilliant red. It seems well aware of its beauty, as it flits about the rocky slopes and in the low undergrowth, constantly fanning its pretty tail, spreading its wings, and fluffing out its plumage to show off its colors in a charming display. We found it very common in the canyons of the Huachuca Mountains, from 5,000 up to 7,000 feet, but most abundant in the narrow, damp, shady parts near the mountain streams. H. W. Henshaw (1875) says: "It appears not to inhabit the high mountains nor the extreme lowlands, but to occupy an intermediate position, and to find the rocky hills covered with a sparse growth of oak most congenial to its habits." William Brewster (1882) reports that Frank Stephens found this redstart in the Chiricahua and the Santa Rita Mountains at an elevation of fully 7,000 feet; they occurred most frequently among pines in a canyon, where they had been seen in April.

Mrs. Bailey (1928) says: "Those seen by Major Goldman in the Burro Mountains [in New Mexico] in the fall were found 'among the oaks and pines on the northeast slope from 7,000 feet to the summit. One was working over the face of a cliff, its location and motions suggesting those of a Canyon Wren.'"

Josselyn Van Tyne (1929) added the painted redstart to the avifauna of Texas by finding it breeding in the Chisos Mountains, where a young bird was seen that was barely able to fly. "The species was seen only in the heavy pine and cedar forest at 7,000 [feet]. As they hunted insects in the pine trees their actions were often very Creeperlike, but with the additional spreading of the tail so characteristic of *S. ruticilla.*" Later (1937), he writes:

Great fluctuations in the numbers of a species of bird in an apparently unchanged habitat are difficult to explain. The case of this species in the Chisos Mountains is especially interesting. In 1901 Bailey, Fuertes, and Oberholser saw no Painted Redstarts during their three weeks' exploration of these mountains. In 1928 Van Tyne and Gaige found the species fairly numerous at Boot Spring, and yet Van Tyne, Peet, and Jacot spent the whole of May at the same locality four years later without getting more than an unsatisfactory glimpse of one; and the Carnegie Museum party, in 1933 and 1935, did not record the species at all. On June 24, 1936, however, Tarleton Smith saw an adult male at the head of Blue Creek Canyon.

Spring.—The painted redstart belongs to a Mexican and Central American species. The northernmost of the two subspecies extends its breeding range across our border into southern New Mexico and Arizona. They arrive early in spring. H. S. Swarth (1904) noted the first arrivals in the Huachuca Mountains on March 15, "and a week or so later they were quite abundant. At all times rather a solitary bird, they are never to be seen in the mixed flocks of migrating warblers, but prefer rather to forage for themselves." During migration they are quite widely distributed over the mountains and down to the foothills. Those that Major Bendire saw near Tucson, and those that others have seen in April among the pines and oaks were probably migrating. Mrs. Bailey (1928) says that they arrive in New Mexico before the end of March. As the breeding season arrives, they settle down in their favorite canyons for the summer.

Nesting.—Eight years after the painted redstart was added to our avifauna the first nest was discovered by Herbert Brown, on June 6, 1880. A second nest was found by Frank Stephens in May of the next year, in a canyon between the two peaks of the Santa Rita Mountains. "It was under a small boulder in the side of a nearly perpendicular bank, which was but two or three feet high. The vicinity was heavily timbered with oak and sycamore."

This nest, with its three eggs was sent to Brewster (1882) who describes it as follows: "The nest, which is now before me, is large, flat and shallow. It is composed of bark, coarse fibres from weed-stalks, and fine, bleached grasses, the latter, with a few hairs, forming a simple lining. The cup measures 2.10 inches in width by 1 inch in depth; while the external diameter of the whole structure is rather more than 5 inches, and its depth about 1.50."

Since then quite a number of nests have been found in the Chiricahua and Huachuca Mountains, all somewhat similar to the above in location and in construction, differing widely in both respects from the nesting sites and the nests of the well-known eastern species, the American redstart. With one exception, all the nests of which we have any record have been placed on the ground, under a projecting rock, beneath the roots of a tree or shrub, or under a tuft of grass, and on the side of some steeply sloping bank or the rocky side of a mountain canyon, usually where grasses and ferns grow luxuriantly not far from a small stream or spring.

We found three painted redstart nests with eggs in the Huachucas on May 11, 16, and 28, 1922. Two of these were quite typical of the species, built on the ground on the sloping, rocky sides of canyons and well hidden under tufts of long grass; they were made of grasses and leaves and lined with finer grasses and hair. Both were found by watching the birds while they were building them; and neither was far from the little mountain stream that drained the canyon.

The third nest was most exceptional, I believe, in its location. We made our headquarters for the month of May in a little 2-room cabin that stood over the stream that flowed down through Ramsey Canyon. When we arrived on May 1, we were delighted to see that a pair of painted redstarts had begun building their nest in an ivy vine growing thickly over one side of our cabin. They were very tame and confiding and did not seem to be disturbed in the least by our frequent coming an going, but continued to build their nest and to lay and incubate the eggs. The nest was 10 feet above the ground in the thickest part of the vine, under the eaves; it was a bulky affair, made of the usual materials, as named. It held three eggs on May 16.

Eggs.—From 3 to 4 eggs, usually 4, make up the full set for the painted redstart. The eggs are ovate and slightly glossy. Those in the three sets in the Museum of Comparative Zoology are creamy white, very finely and delicately speckled with "chestnut," "auburn," or "russet," with almost imperceptible under markings of "deep brownish drab" or "light brownish drab." On some, the specklings are sharply defined and on others so faint as to hardly show. While the markings are concentrated at the large end, they do not seem to form a distinct wreath, as in so many warblers' eggs, but instead gradually dissipate toward the small end. The measurements of 50 eggs average 16.5 by 12.8 millimeters; the eggs showing the four extremes measure 17.6 by 13.2, 16.0 by 13.5, 14.5 by 12.7, and 16.8 by 11.7 millimeters (**Harris**).

Plumages.—The painted redstart is one of the few wood warblers in which the young bird assumes a practically adult plumage at the postjuvenal molt and in which the sexes are hardly distinguishable in any plumage.

In the juvenal plumage, the upper parts are sooty black and the lower parts are largely sooty grayish, passing into dull whitish on the center of the abdomen; the breast is spotted or streaked with sooty black; the wings and tail are black, as in the adult; the white patch on the wing and the white of the abdomen are usually tinged with yellowish or brownish buff.

The postjuvenal molt involves all the contour plumage and the wing coverts, but not the rest of the wings or the tail, and occurs mainly in July and August; I have seen the beginning of the molt as early as June 27, being well along on the head and back and only just beginning on the breast; on the other hand, I have seen a bird in full juvenal plumage as late as August 7, and another that had not quite completed the molt on October 31.

The complete postnuptial molt of adults occurs in July and August, but most birds that I have seen are in full, fresh plumage in August. There is little or no sexual difference in adults, though some females are slightly duller (less glossy) than males.

Food.—Nothing of consequence seems to have been published on the food of the painted redstart, but, as it is known to be an expert flycatcher, and as it has been seen frequently gleaning food from the trunks of trees and from the surfaces of rocks, it is evidently largely, if not wholly, insectivorous.

Behavior.—The actions of the painted redstart are strikingly reminiscent of the movements of the American redstart, to which of course it is closely related. It is one of our most active birds, almost constantly in motion, seldom remaining in one spot for more than a few seconds, and hardly to be exceeded in its nervous activity by the most restless of our little wrens. In spite of the striking colors that make it so conspicuous, it is not at all shy and seems to show no fear of humans; in fact it seems to court attention as it displays before us the beauties of its plumage, spreading its wings and tail to show the white areas and fluffing out its feathers to expose the brilliant carmine of its lower breast.

Swarth (1904) says that—

he can be seen clambering over tree trunks or mossy rocks, turning now this way and now that, as if conscious and proud of his beautiful appearance even when engaged in the commonest duties of life, gathering insects for the young or material for the nest. Females, as well as males, strut about in the same ostentatious manner, for in color and appearance the sexes are absolutely indistinguishable; and even the dull colored juveniles adopt the same style as soon as they are able to fly. * * * Though feeding to some extent in the underbrush, and even on the ground and over the rocks, they do not stick closely to such places as do the Tolmie Warblers and Yellow-throats; nor on the other hand do they frequent the extreme tree tops and tips of the limbs as the Townsend, Hermit and other Warblers do, but preferring rather the medium between the two extremes, they can be seen clambering about the sides of the tree trunks and over the larger limbs, examining the crevices and interstices in the bark in search of food, and occasionally flying out a short distance after some passing insect.

Mrs. Bailey (1928) writes:

In catching insects they often dropped through the air or made downward swoops in conventional Redstart and Flycatcher-manner, and once one dropped about twenty feet to catch on a hanging rope and then on a vine that swung with it prettily; but in the main they hunted in the sycamore and live oak tops and markedly and perhaps preferably on the great slanting trunks of the live oaks where the crevices of the bark seemed to supply a ready feast. Even in the mesquites, a Painted Redstart was seen flying from one trunk to another. On the oaks, when the long black and white fan tail was outspread against the bark the suggestion was of a museum specimen, a pinned-out gorgeous butterfly. Another interesting pose of the Redstart's suggesting a close scrutiny for insects was a forward tilt of the body with the black crest raised enquiringly.

Voice.—Swarth (1904) says: "A call note is uttered at frequent intervals, not unlike the peep of a young chicken, and occasionally the short, low song of the male can be heard. Though this is usually given utterance to between intervals of feeding, I have once or twice, usually in the early morning, seen the male ascend to the top of a tall tree, and from the tip of some dead limb repeat his song, sometimes for half an hour before descending."

According to Mrs. Bailey (1923), "their song begins with an ordinary warbler *whee-tee, whee-tee,* but ends unusually, both call and song having individual rich contralto quality."

Dr. Alexander F. Skutch contributes the following note on the habits of the Guatemalan subspecies:

"I first made the acquaintance of the painted redstart on the Sierra de Tecpán in west-central Guatemala, where I studied the bird life during the year 1933. I had been on the Sierra many months before I saw a painted redstart. It was keeping company with a Kaup's redstart (*Myioborus miniatus*) in the lighter oak woods on the lower part of the mountain, at an altitude of about 7,500 feet. These two warblers are rather similar in color pattern; but the hues of the painted redstart were even more brilliant than those of its companion. The methods of foraging of the two birds formed an interesting contrast. The painted redstart sought its food chiefly on the bark of the trunks, branches, and coarser twigs; the other caught its insects on the finer twigs, the foliage, and in the air. The painted redstart worked along the larger branches of the oak trees, often hung head downward from their sides while it peered beneath them, and not infrequently clung in an inverted position while it plucked some insect from the underside of a horizontal limb. It also ascended erect trunks, to which it clung with perfect ease, and moved upward by a series of quick, irregular, jumping flights. An allied woodhewer accompanied the two redstarts, and at one time it hunted on the same trunk with the painted redstart. It was instructive to compare their modes of procedure. The woodhewer worked up the tree in its slow, methodical fashion, and probably found every insect and spider that lurked in the crevices of the bark over which it passed. The redstart ascended in a rapid, impulsive manner, touching the bark only here and there, taking only a fraction of the time consumed by the woodhewer in covering the same distance, but without much doubt missing a number of morsels which the patient brown bird would have discovered. Sometimes, too, the painted redstart hunted among the foliage, but not nearly so much as on the bark.

"I must have watched the redstarts for more than an hour, rarely having seen two more attractive birds in the same tree; and they kept together the whole time. The painted redstart had been molting; its two outermost tail feathers were considerably shorter than the others and served as a mark of recognition. Two hours after I had left these birds, I returned to the part of the woods where I had first encountered them, and found the two still together. Since a Kaup's redstart was almost never to be found in company with another of its own kind at this season—it was then the first of August—I thought it strange that it should associate so intimately with a member of another species of rather similar habits. After this date, the painted redstarts became more numerous on the Sierra de Tecpán; and not infrequently I saw one of each of these two species in a mixed flock of small birds. The painted redstart appeared to be just as intolerant of its own kind at that season as the Kaup's redstart; but the two species got along very well together.

"On the same morning when I met my first painted redstart, I found a second bird in perfect plumage who was singing. His loud, ringing *weecher weecher weecher* was wonderfully rich and mellow, surpassing in fullness of tone even the *ch'ree ch'ree ch'ree* of Kaup's redstart.

"These two lovely redstarts are found separately more often than together. The painted redstart, which ranges much farther to the north, prefers dry, open woodlands of pine and oak, and is very much at home in some of the dry interior valleys in the highlands of Guatemala, where one will look in vain for Kaup's redstart. The latter lives in heavier and more humid forests where the other rarely ventures; but in intermediate types of woodland the two species may meet. In the latter part of the rainy season, the painted redstarts seemed to wander about a good deal; and I frequently saw them on parts of the Sierra de Tecpán where I am sure they had not been during the breeding season. All did not forage so exclusively upon the bark as the first which I met; but usually they devoted considerable attention to this source of food. At times they wove among the branches and darted out into the air with a sprightliness almost equal to that of Kaup's redstart, or the American redstart. Like their relatives, they often kept their tail spread as they hunted, revealing its contrasting areas of black and white, and adding greatly to their appearance.

"Later in the year, after the American redstarts came down from the north, I once encountered a single member of each of the three species foraging together in a little grove on the plateau near Tecpán. The American redstart was a male in perfect plumage. Since the sexes of the other two species are alike, it was impossible to decide whether they were male or female; but each was an excellent representative of its own kind. It was indeed difficult to judge which of the three was the most beautiful; but the painted redstart, with its deep, contrasting colors, most took my eye."

C. Russell Mason contributes the following remarkable record of the winter wandering of the far-western species:

"On October 18, 1947, while casually birding at Marblehead Neck, Mass., Mrs. Heyliger deWindt, of Boston, and Mrs. David H. Searle, of Marblehead, were attracted to a small bird, strikingly marked in black, white, and bright red, that was actively feeding in a tree above

them. It was a species entirely new to them, and examination of their
eastern bird books on returning home failed to place it. The bird
was watched intermittently in the same neighborhood over a 5-hour
period, and every detail of color and marking was noted. A call
to the executive director of the Massachusetts Audubon Society and
a further check on the bird by the discoverers and by Herbert Caswell,
of the Essex County Ornithological Club, Salem, identified the visitor
as a painted redstart. The bird was still present in the same area
the following day, when it was observed by Ludlow Griscom, of the
Museum of Comparative Zoology at Harvard University, and many
parties of bird enthusiasts, including fifty members of the Massachusetts Audubon Society on a regularly scheduled field trip.

"In the Audubon party, a graduate student at Harvard who was
equipped with a motion picture camera having a telephoto lens
secured color motion pictures of this western redstart as it posed
obligingly for minutes between its active feeding and preening
periods. The bird was last seen in midafternoon of that day.

"So far as can be determined by the records, this is the first occurrence of the painted redstart in the United States outside of its usual
range, which includes Arizona, New Mexico, and the Chisos Mountains of western Texas, except for somewhat recent reports of the
species from southern California. How the bird happened to reach
New England must remain a mystery, though other western and
southwestern species have been reported in increasing numbers in
recent years. The possibility of its being an escaped cage bird seems
remote, since birds with food habits of the warblers are seldom, if
ever, caged, even by cage-bird enthusiasts living in Mexico and Cuba."

DISTRIBUTION

Range.—Southeastern Arizona, southwestern New Mexico, western
Texas, central Nuevo León, and central Tamaulipas; south through the
Mexican highlands to Guatemala, El Salvador, and central Honduras.

Breeding range.—Only the northern painted redstart (*Setophaga
picta picta*) reaches our borders. It breeds **north** to southeastern
Arizona (Santa Catalina Mountains, Seven Mile Canyon, Fort
Apache, and Bear Canyon); southwestern New Mexico (Alma,
Cooney, and Monticello); and western Texas (Chisos Mountains).
East to western Texas (Chisos Mountains); through the Sierra Madre
Oriental to Hidalgo (probably La Placenta); and probably Vera-
cruz. **South** to probably Veracruz; and Oaxaca. **West** to Oaxaca;
Guerrero; and southeastern Arizona (Santa Catalina Mountains).
It has been seen or collected during the nesting season in north-central
Arizona (Wheeler Canyon, near Flagstaff, and the Mogollon Pla-

teau); southwestern Utah (Zion National Park); and northwestern New Mexico (Zuni Mountains).

Winter range.—It winters in the southern part of its breeding range north to central Sonora (Huerachi); central western Chihuahua (Guanopa); central Nuevo León (Mesa del Chipinque); and central Tamaulipas (Río Martínez and Victoria); casually north to southern Arizona (Pena Blanca Canyon).

Casual in southern California (Altadena); accidental in Massachusetts (Marblehead Neck).

Early dates of spring arrival are: New Mexico—Anthony, March 25. Arizona—Huachuca Mountains, March 14. Utah—Zion National Park, April 26 (only Utah record).

Late dates of fall departure are: New Mexico—San Luis Mountains, September 29. Arizona—Oracle, October 17.

Egg dates.—Arizona: 18 records, April 28 to July 2; 9 records, May 17 to June 7, indicating the height of the season.

New Mexico: 2 records, March 30 and May 30 (Harris).

LITERATURE CITED

ABBOTT, CLINTON GILBERT.
  1926. Peculiar nesting site of a dusky warbler. Condor, vol. 28, pp. 57–60.
AIKEN, CHARLES EDWARD HOWARD, and WARREN, EDWARD ROYAL.
  1914. Birds of El Paso County, Colorado. Colorado College Publ., gen ser. No. 74 (sci. ser., vol. 12, No. 13, pt. 2), pp. 497–603.
ALLEN, GLOVER MORRILL.
  1903. A list of the birds of New Hampshire. Proc. Manchester Inst. Arts and Sci., vol. 4, pp. 23–222.
ALLEN, JOEL ASAPH.
  1870. Notes on some of the rarer birds of Massachusetts. Amer. Nat., vol. 3, pp. 568–585.
  1880. Destruction of birds by light-houses. Bull. Nuttall Orn. Club, vol. 5, pp. 131–138.
ALLEN, JOEL ASAPH, and BREWSTER, WILLIAM.
  1883. Lists of birds observed in the vicinity of Colorado Springs, Colorado, during March, April and May, 1882. Bull. Nuttall Orn. Club, vol. 8, pp. 151–161.
ALLISON, ANDREW.
  1907. Notes on the spring birds of Tishomingo County, Mississippi. Auk, vol. 24, pp. 12–25.
AMERICAN ORNITHOLOGISTS' UNION.
  1886. The code of nomenclature and check-list of North American birds adopted by the American Ornithologists' Union.
  1931. Check-List of North American birds. Ed. 4.
ANDERSON, RUDOPH MARTIN.
  1909. Breeding of *Dendroica striata* at Great Slave Lake. Auk, vol. 26, p. 80.
ATTWATER, HENRY PHILEMON.
  1892. List of birds observed in the vicinity of San Antonio, Bexar County, Texas. Auk, vol. 9, pp. 337–345.
AUDUBON, JOHN JAMES.
  1839. Ornithological biography, vol. 2.
  1841. The birds of America, vol. 2.
AUGHEY, SAMUEL.
  1878. Notes on the nature of the food of the birds of Nebraska. First Report of the United States Entomological Committee. Hayden Survey of the Territories, Appendix 2.
AXTELL, HAROLD HAMILTON.
  1938. The song of Kirtland's warbler. Auk, vol. 55, pp. 481–491.
BAERG, WILLIAM J.
  1930. The song period of birds of northwest Arkansas. Auk, vol. 47, pp. 3240.
BAGG, AARON CLARK, and ELIOT, SAMUEL ATKINS, Jr.
  1937. Birds of the Connecticut Valley in Massachusetts.
BAGG, J. L.
  1941. [Note on ovenbird.] Bull. New England Bird Life, vol. 5, p. 6.
BAILEY, ALFRED MARSHALL, and NIEDRACH, ROBERT JAMES.
  1938. Nesting of Virginia's warbler. Auk, vol. 55, pp. 176–178.

BAILEY, FLORENCE MERRIAM.
  1902. Handbook of birds of the Western United States.
  1923. Birds recorded from the Santa Rita Mountains in southern Arizona.
          Pacific Coast Avifauna, No. 15.
  1928. Birds of New Mexico.
BAILEY, HAROLD HARRIS.
  1913. The birds of Virginia.
  1925. The birds of Florida.
  1926. The prairie warbler in south Florida. Bailey Mus. Nat. Hist., Bull. 3.
BAILLIE, JAMES LITTLE, Jr.
  1926. Female redstart singing at Hamilton. Can. Field-Nat., vol. 40, p. 184.
BAILLIE, JAMES L., Jr., and THOMPSON, STUART L.
  1928. Canadian Christmas bird census, 1927. Can. Field-Nat., vol. 42, pp.
          101–106.
BAIRD, SPENCER FULLERTON.
  1852. Description of a new species of *Sylvicola*. Ann. Lyc. Nat. Hist., New
          York, vol. 5, pp. 217–218.
  1865. Review of American birds in the museum of the Smithsonian Insti-
          tution. Part 1, North and Middle America. Smithsonian Misc.
          Coll. vol. 12, art. 1.
BAIRD, SCENCER FULLERTON; BREWER, THOMAS MAYO; and RIDGWAY, ROBERT.
  1874. A history of North American birds, vol. 1. Land birds.
BAIRD, SPENCER FULLERTON; CASSIN, JOHN; and LAWRENCE, GEORGE NEWBOLD.
  1860. Birds of North America.
BALDWIN, SAMUEL PRENTISS, and KENDEIGH, SAMUEL CHARLES.
  1938. Variations in the weight of birds. Auk, vol. 55, pp. 416–467.
BANCROFT, GRIFFING.
  1930. The breeding birds of central Lower California. Condor, vol. 32,
          pp. 20–49.
BANGS, OUTRAM.
  1918. A new race of the black-throated green wood warbler. Proc. New
          England Zool. Club, vol. 6, pp. 93–94.
  1925. The history and characters of *Vermivora crissalis* (Salvin and God-
          man). Auk, vol. 42, pp. 251–253.
BARBOUR, THOMAS.
  1923. The birds of Cuba. Mem. Nuttall Orn. Club, No. 6.
  1943. Cuban ornithology. Mem. Nuttall Orn. Club, No. 9.
BARLOW, CHESTER.
  1899. Nesting of the hermit warbler in the Sierra Nevada Mountains, Cal-
          ifornia. Auk, vol. 16, pp. 156–161.
  1901. A list of the land birds of the Placerville–Lake Tahoe stage road.
          Central Sierra Nevada Mountains, Cal. Condor, vol. 3, pp. 151–
          184.
BARNES, RICHARD MAGOON.
  1889. Nesting of the prothonotary warbler. Ornithologist and Oologist, vol.
          14, pp. 37–38.
BARROWS, WALTER BRADFORD.
  1912. Michigan bird life. Spec. Bull. Dept. Zool. and Physiol. Michigan Agr.
          College.
BATCHELDER, CHARLES FOSTER.
  1918. Two undescribed Newfoundland birds. Proc. New England Zool.
          Club, vol. 6, pp. 81–82.
BEAL, FOSTER ELLENBOROUGH LASCELLES.
  1907. Birds of California in relation to the fruit industry, Pt. I. Biol.
          Surv. Bull. 30.

BEEBE, CHARLES WILLIAM.
    1905.   Two bird-lovers in Mexico.
BEHLE, WILLIAM HARROUN.
    1944.   Check-List of the birds of Utah. Condor, vol. 46, pp. 67–87.
BEHLE, WILLIAM HARROUN, and ALDRICH, JOHN WARREN.
    1947.   Description of a new yellow-throat (*Geothlypis trichas*) from the northern Rocky Mountain–Great Plains region. Proc. Biol. Soc. Washington, vol. 60, pp. 69–72.
BERGTOLD, WILLIAM HARRY.
    1913.   A study of the house finch. Auk, vol. 30, pp. 40–73.
BICKNELL, EUGENE PINTARD.
    1884.   A study of the singing of our birds. Auk, vol. 1, pp. 209–218.
BIGGLESTONE, HARRY C.
    1913.   A study of the nesting behavior of the yellow warbler (*Dendroica aestiva aestiva*). Wilson Bull., vol. 25, pp. 49–67.
BONAPARTE, CHARLES LUCIEN.
    1832.   *In* Wilson's American ornithology, vol. 3.
BOND, JAMES.
    1937.   The Cape May warbler in Maine. Auk, vol. 54, pp. 306–308.
BONHOTE, JOHN LEWIS.
    1903.   On a collection of birds from the northern islands of the Bahama group. Ibis, pp. 273–315.
BOWDISH, BEECHER SCOVILLE.
    1906.   Some breeding warblers of Demarest, N. J. Auk, vol. 23, pp. 16–19.
BOWDISH, BEECHER SCOVILLE, and PHILIPP, PHILIP BERNARD.
    1916.   The Tennessee warbler in New Brunswick. Auk, vol. 33, pp. 1–8.
BOWLES, CHARLES WILSON.
    1902.   Notes on the black-throated gray warbler. Condor, vol. 4, pp. 82–85.
BOWLES, CHARLES WILSON, and BOWLES, JOHN HOOPER.
    1906.   The Calaveras warbler in western Washington. Condor, vol. 8, pp. 68–69.
BOWLES, JOHN HOOPER.
    1906.   The hermit warbler in Washington. Condor, vol. 8, pp. 40–42.
    1908.   A few summer birds of Lake Chelan, Washington. Condor, vol. 10, pp. 191–193.
BRAND, ALBERT RICH.
    1936.   Bird-song study problems. Bird-Lore, vol. 38, pp. 187–194.
    1938.   Vibration frequencies of passerine bird song. Auk, vol. 55, pp. 263–268.
BRANDT, HERBERT.
    1940.   Texas bird adventures.
    1943.   Alaska bird trails.
BRAUND, FRANK WILLIAM, and McCULLAGH, ERNEST PERRY.
    1940.   The birds of Anticosti Island, Quebec. Wilson Bull., vol. 52, pp. 96–123.
BREWSTER, WILLIAM.
    1875.   Some observations on the birds of Ritchie County, West Virginia. Ann. Lyc. Nat. Hist. New York, vol. 11, pp. 129–146.
    1876.   Description of a new species of *Helminthophaga*. Bull. Nuttall Orn. Club, vol. 1, pp. 1–2.
    1877.   The black-and-yellow warbler (*Dendroica maculosa*). Bull. Nuttall Orn. Club, vol. 2, pp. 1–7.
    1878a.   The prothonotary warbler (*Protonotaria citrea*). Bull. Nuttall Orn. Club, vol. 3, pp. 153–162.

BREWSTER, WILLIAM—Continued

1878b. Nesting of the large-billed water-thrush (*Siurus motacilla* (Vieill.) Bp.) Bull. Nuttall Orn. Club, vol. 3, pp. 133–135.

1879. On the habits and nesting of certain rare birds in Texas. Bull. Nuttall Orn. Club, vol. 4, pp. 79–80.

1881. On the relationship of *Helminthophaga leucobronchialis*, Brewster, and *Helminthophaga lawrencei*, Herrick; with some conjectures respecting certain other North American birds. Bull. Nuttall Orn. Club, vol. 6, pp. 218–225.

1882a. Notes on some birds and eggs from the Magdalen Islands, Gulf of St. Lawrence. Bull. Nuttall Orn. Club, vol. 7, pp. 253–256.

1882b. On a collection of birds lately made by Mr. F. Stephens in Arizona. Bull. Nuttall Orn. Club, vol. 7, pp. 135–147.

1885a. Swainson's warbler. Auk, vol. 2, pp. 65–80.

1885b. Additional notes on the nest and eggs of Swainson's warbler (*Helinaia swainsoni*). Auk, vol. 2, pp. 346–348.

1886. Bird migration. Mem. Nuttall Orn. Club, No. 1.

1887. Discovery of the nest and eggs of the western warbler (*Dendroica occidentalis*). Auk, vol. 4, pp. 166–167.

1888. Notes on the birds of Winchendon, Worcester County, Massachusetts. Auk, vol. 5, pp. 386–393.

1889. Descriptions of supposed new birds from western North America and Mexico. Auk, vol. 6, pp. 85–98.

1891. Notes on Bachman's warbler (*Helminthophila bachmani*). Auk, vol. 8, pp. 149–157.

1895. A ground nest of the black-throated green warbler. Auk, vol. 12, pp. 184–185.

1896. Descriptions of a new warbler and a new song sparrow. Auk, vol. 13, pp. 44–47.

1902. Birds of the Cape region of Lower California. Bull. Mus. Comp. Zool., vol. 41, No. 1.

1905. Notes on the breeding of Bachman's warbler, *Helminthophila bachmanii* (Aud.), near Charleston, South Carolina, with a description of the first plumage of the species. Auk, vol. 22, pp. 392–394.

1906. The birds of the Cambridge region of Massachusetts. Mem. Nuttall Ornith. Club, No. 4.

1936. October Farm.

1938. The birds of the Lake Umbagog region of Maine, part 4. Compiled by Ludlow Griscom. Bull. Mus. Comp. Zool., vol. 66, pp. 525–620.

BRIGGS, GUY H.

1900. Black and white warbler. Journ. Maine Ornith. Soc., vol. 2, pp. 40–41.

BRIMLEY, CLEMENT SAMUEL.

1943. Birds rebuild when nest is destroyed. Chat, vol. 7, pp. 41–44.

BRIMLEY, HERBERT H.

1941. Unusual North Carolina records. Auk, vol. 58, pp. 106–108.

BROCKWAY, ARTHUR WILLIAM.

1899. Odd nesting of Maryland yellow-throat. Auk, vol. 16, pp. 360–361.

BROOKS, ALLAN.

1934. The juvenal plumage of Townsend's warbler (*Dendroica townsendi*). Auk, vol. 51, pp. 243–244.

BROOKS, MAURICE.

1933. Cape May warblers destructive to grapes. Auk, vol. 50, pp. 122–223.

1936. The Canadian component of West Virginia's bird life. Cardinal, vol. 4, pp. 53–60.

BROOKS, MAURICE—Continued
1940. The breeding warblers of the central Allegheny mountain region. Wilson Bull., vol. 52, pp. 249–266.
BROOKS, MAURICE, and CHRISTY, BAYARD HENDERSON.
1942. Sutton's warbler again. Cardinal, vol. 5, pp. 187–189.
BROOKS, MAURICE, and LEGG, WILLIAM CLARENCE.
1942. Swainson's warbler in Nicholas County, West Virginia. Auk, vol. 59, pp. 76–86.
BROWN, JOHN CLIFFORD.
1889. Unusual nesting site of *Dendroica virens*. Auk, vol. 6, p. 74.
BROWN, NATHAN CLIFFORD.
1878. A list of birds observed at Coosada, central Alabama. Bull. Nuttall Orn. Club, vol. 3, pp. 168–174.
BRYANT, WALTER [PIERC]E.
1890a. Descriptions of the nests and eggs of some Lower California birds, with a description of the young plumage of *Geothlypis beldingi*. Proc. California Acad. Sci., ser. 2, vol. 2, 1889, pp. 20–24.
1890b. A catalogue of the birds of Lower California, Mexico. Proc. California Acad. Sci., ser. 2, vol. 2, 1889, pp. 237–320.
BURLEIGH, THOMAS DEARBORN.
1923. In the haunts of the Swainson's warbler. Murrelet, vol. 4, pp. 5–7.
1925. Notes on the breeding birds of northeastern Georgia. Auk, vol. 42, pp. 70–74.
1927a. Further notes on the breeding birds of northeastern Georgia. Auk, vol. 44, pp. 229–234.
1927b. Notes from La Anna, Pike County, Pennsylvania. Wilson Bull., vol. 39, pp. 159–168.
1934a. A critical study of the distribution and abundance of *Dendroica castanea* and *Dendroica striata* in the southeastern States during the spring and fall migrations. Wilson Bull., vol. 46, pp. 142–147.
1934b. Description of a new subspecies of yellow-throat, *Geothlypis trichas* from Georgia. Proc. Biol. Soc. Washington, vol. 47, pp. 21–22.
1937. The yellow-throats of Georgia. Oriole, vol. 2, pp. 32–33.
1941. Bird life on Mt. Mitchell. Auk, vol. 58, pp. 334–345.
1944a. Description of a new hybrid warbler. Auk, vol. 61, pp. 291–293.
1944b. The bird life of the Gulf coast region of Mississippi. Occas. Pap. Mus. Zool., Louisiana State Univ., No. 20, pp. 329–490.
BURLEIGH, THOMAS DEARBORN, and LOWERY, GEORGE HINES, Jr.
1940. Birds of the Guadalupe Mountain region of western Texas. Occas. Pap. Mus. Zool., Louisiana State Univ., No. 8.
1942. Notes on the birds of southeastern Coahuila. Occas. Pap. Mus. Zool., Louisiana State Univ., No. 12.
BURNS, FRANKLIN LORENZO.
1905. The worm-eating warbler. Bird-Lore, vol. 7, pp. 137–139.
1915a. The Cape May warbler (*Dendroica tigrina*) as an abundant autumnal migrant and as a destructive grape juice consumer at Berwin, Pa. Auk, vol. 32, pp. 231–233.
1915b. Comparative periods of deposition and incubation of some North American birds. Wilson Bull., vol. 27, pp. 275–286.
1921. Comparative periods of nestling life of some North American Nidicolae. Wilson Bull., vol. 33, pp. 4–15.
1937. The song periods of some common southeastern Pennsylvania birds in comparison with their seasonal reproductive cycles. Oologist, vol. 54, pp. 111–130.

BURROUGHS, JOHN.
    1871. Wake robin.
    1895. Locusts and wild honey.
BURTCH, VERDI.
    1898. Curious nesting of American redstart. Auk, vol. 15, p. 332.
BUTLER, AMOS WILLIAM.
    1898. The birds of Indiana. Indiana Dept. Geol. and Nat. Res., 22nd Ann.
        Rep.
    1928. Nesting of the sycamore warbler. Auk, vol. 45, pp. 224–225.
BYERS, GEORGE W.
    1950. Black and white warbler's nest with eight cowbird eggs. Wilson
        Bull., vol. 62, pp. 136–138.
CAIRNS, JOHN SIMPSON.
    1896. The summer home of *Dendroeca caerulescens*. Paper presented to
        the World's Congress in Ornithology, Chicago, 1896, pp. 136–138.
CAMPBELL, I. D.
    1917. A day's outing. Oologist, vol. 34, pp. 160–161.
CAMPBELL, LOUIS WALTER.
    1930. Unusual nesting sites of the prothonotary warbler. Wilson Bull.,
        vol. 42, p. 292.
CARRIGER, HENRY WARD.
    1899. Elevated nest of the lutescent warbler. Bull. Cooper Orn. Club, vol. 1,
        p. 72.
CHAMBERLAIN, MONTAGUE.
    1885. The nesting habits of the Cape May warbler (*Dendroeca tigrina*).
        Auk, vol. 2, pp. 33–36.
CHAPMAN, FRANK MICHLER.
    1890. On the eastern forms of *Geothlypis trichas*. Auk, vol. 7, pp. 9–14.
    1905. Note on the migration of warblers from the Bahamas to Florida.
        Bird-Lore, vol. 7, p. 140.
    1907. The warblers of North America.
    1912. Handbook of birds of eastern North America.
CHUBB, S. HARMSTED.
    1919. The cerulean warbler (*Dendroica cerulea*) in the Catskills. Auk,
        vol. 36, pp. 582–583.
CLARK, JOHN NATHANIEL.
    1882. Hooded warblers. Nesting in southern Conn. Ornithologist and
        Oologist, vol. 6, pp. 9–10.
COALE, HENRY KELSO.
    1887. Description of a new species and subspecies of the genus *Dendroica*.
        Bull. Ridgway Orn. Club, No. 2, pp. 82–83.
COOKE, MAY THACHER.
    1929. Birds of the Washington, D. C., region. Proc. Biol. Soc. Washington,
        vol. 42, pp. 1–79.
COOKE, WELLS WOODBRIGE.
    1904. Distribution and migration of North American warblers. Biol. Surv.
        Bull. 18.
COPELAND, W. F.
    1909. An exercise in bird study. Wilson Bull., vol. 21, pp. 40–45.
COBY, CHARLES BARNEY.
    1879. Capture of Kirtland's warbler (*Dendroeca kirtlandi*) in the Bahama
        Islands. Bull. Nuttall Orn. Club, vol. 4, p. 118.

COUES, ELLIOTT.
  1878. Birds of the Colorado Valley. U. S. Geol. Geogr. Surv. Terr. Misc.
    Publ. No. 11.
  1888. Nesting of the prairie warbler (*Dendroica discolor*) in the vicinity
    of Washington, D. C. Auk, vol. 5, pp. 405–408.
  1897. Characters of *Dendroica caerulescens cairnsi.* Auk, vol. 14, pp.
    96–97.
COWAN, IAN MCTAGGART.
  1939. The vertebrate fauna of the Peace River District of British Columbia.
    Occas. Pap. British Columbia Prov. Mus., No. 1.
CRIDDLE, NORMAN.
  1922. A calendar of bird migration. Auk, vol. 39, pp. 41–49.
CROSBY, MAUNSEL SCHLIFFELIN.
  1912. The golden-winged warbler at Rhinebeck, N. Y. Bird-Lore, vol. 14,
    pp. 145–146.
CULVER, DELOS EVERETT.
  1916. Mortality among birds at Philadelphia. Cassinia, No. 19, pp. 1–136.
DALL, WILLIAM HEALEY.
  1915. Spencer Fullerton Baird.
DANFORTH, STUART TAYLOR.
  1925. Birds of the Cartagena Lagoon, Porto Rico. Journ. Dept. Agr. Porto
    Rico, vol. 10, No. 1, pp. 1–136.
DARLINGTON, PHILIP JACKSON, Jr.
  1931. Notes on the birds of Rio Frio (near Santa Marta), Magdalena,
    Colombia. Bull. Mus. Comp. Zool., vol. 71, pp. 349–421.
DAWSON, WILLIAM LEON.
  1903. The birds of Ohio.
  1923. The birds of California, vol. 1.
DAWSON, WILLIAM LEON, and BOWLES, JOHN HOOPER.
  1909. The birds of Washington, vol. 1.
DE GARIS, CHARLES FRANCIS.
  1936. Notes on six nests of the Kentucky warbler (*Oporornis formosus*).
    Auk, vol. 53, pp. 418–428.
DICKEY, DONALD RYDER, and VAN ROSSEM, ADRIAAN JOSEPH.
  1938. The birds of El Salvador. Publ. Field Mus. Nat. Hist., zool. ser.,
    vol. 23.
DICKEY, SAMUEL S.
  1934. The worm-eating warbler. Cardinal, vol. 3, pp. 179–184.
DINGLE, EDWARD VON SIEBOLD.
  1926. Spotted eggs of Swainson's warbler. Auk, vol. 43, p. 376.
DUGMORE, A. RADCLYFFE.
  1902. The increase in the chestnut-sided warbler. Bird-Lore, vol. 4, pp.
    77–80.
DUTCHER, WILLIAM.
  1888. Bird notes from Long Island, N. Y. Auk, vol. 5, pp. 169–183.
DWIGHT, JONATHAN, JR.
  1900. The sequence of plumages and moults of the passerine birds of New
    York. Ann. New York Acad. Sci., vol. 13, pp. 73–360, pls. 1–7.
EATON, ELON HOWARD.
  1914. Birds of New York. New York State Mus. Mem. 12, pt. 2.
EMBODY, GEORGE C.
  1907. Bachman's warbler breeding in Logan County, Kentucky. Auk,
    vol. 24, pp. 41–42.

FAXON, WALTER.
  1911. Brewster's warbler. Mem. Mus. Comp. Zool., vol. 40, pp. 57–78.
  1913. Brewster's warbler (*Helminthophila leucobronchialis*) a hybrid
          between the golden-winged warbler (*Helminthophila chrysoptera*)
          and the blue-winged warbler (*Helminthophila pinus*). Mem. Mus.
          Comp. Zool., vol. 40, pp. 311–316.
FINLEY, WILLIAM LOVELL.
  1904a. Two Oregon warblers. Condor, vol. 6, pp. 31–35.
  1904b. The lutescent warbler. Condor, vol. 6, pp. 131–133.
  1907. American birds.
FORBES, STEPHEN ALFRED.
  1883. The regulative action of birds upon insect oscillations. Illinois State
          Lab. Nat. Hist. Bull. 6, pp. 1–32.
FORBUSH, EDWARD HOWE.
  1907. Useful birds and their protection.
  1929. Birds of Massachusetts and other New England states, pt. 3. Land
          birds from sparrows to thrushes.
FRAZAR, MARSTON ABBOTT.
  1881. Destruction of birds by a storm while migrating. Bull. Nuttall Orn.
          Club, vol. 6, pp. 250–252.
FRIEDMANN, HERBERT.
  1929. The cowbirds.
  1934. Further additions to the list of birds victimized by the cowbird.
          Wilson Bull., vol. 46, pp. 25–36, 104–114.
  1943. Further additions to the list of birds known to be parasitized by the
          cowbirds. Auk, vol. 60, pp. 350–356.
GABRIELSON, IRA NOEL.
  1922. Short notes on the life histories of various species of birds. Wilson
          Bull., vol. 34, pp. 193–210.
GABRIELSON, IRA NOEL, and JEWETT, STANLEY GORDON.
  1940. Birds of Oregon.
GALBRAITH, CHARLES S.
  1888. Bachman's warbler (*Helminthophila bachmani*) in Louisiana.
          Auk, vol. 5, p. 323.
GIBBS, MORRIS.
  1885. Song of the golden-crowned thrush (*Siurus auricapillus*). Orni-
          thologist and Oologist, vol. 10, pp. 191–192.
GILMAN, MARSHALL FRENCH.
  1909. Nesting notes on the Lucy warbler. Condor, vol. 11, pp. 166–168.
GOSS, NATHANIEL STICKNEY.
  1891. History of the birds of Kansas.
GOSSE, PHILIP HENRY.
  1847. The birds of Jamaica.
GREENE, EARLE ROSENBURY.
  1942. Golden warbler nesting in lower Florida Keys. Auk, vol. 59, p. 114.
  1944. Notes on certain birds of the lower Florida Keys. Auk, vol. 61,
          pp. 302–304.
GRIMES, SAMUEL ANDREW.
  1935. The hooded warbler in Florida. Florida Naturalist, vol. 8, pp. 16–22.
  1936. "Injury feigning" by birds. Auk, vol. 53, pp. 478–480.
GRINNELL, JOSEPH.
  1898. Birds of the Pacific slope of Los Angeles County. Pasadena Acad.
          Sci., Publ. 1.

GRINNELL, JOSEPH—Continued

1900. Birds of the Kotzebue Sound region. Pacific Coast Avifauna, No. 1.

1901. The Pacific coast yellowthroats. Condor, vol. 3, pp. 65–66.

1903. The California yellow warbler. Condor, vol. 5, pp. 71–73.

1908. The biota of the San Bernardino Mountains. Univ. California Publ. Zool., vol. 5, pp. 1–170.

1909. Birds and mammals of the 1907 Alexander expedition to southeastern Alaska. The birds. Univ. California Publ. Zool., vol. 5, pp. 181–244.

1914. An account of the mammals and birds of the lower Colorado Valley. Univ. California Publ. Zool., vol. 12, pp. 51–294.

GRINNELL, JOSEPH; DIXON, JOSEPH; and LINSDALE, JEAN MYRON.

1930. Vertebrate natural history of a section of northern California through the Lassen Peak region. Univ. California Publ. Zool., vol. 35, pp. 1–594.

GRINNELL, JOSEPH, and LAMB, CHESTER CONVERSE.

1927. New bird records from Lower California. Condor, vol. 29, pp. 124–126.

GRINNELL, JOSEPH, and MILLER, ALDEN HOLMES.

1944. The distribution of the birds of California. Pacific Coast Avifauna, No. 27.

GRINNELL, JOSEPH, and STORER, TRACY IRWIN.

1924. Animal life in the Yosemite. Contr. Mus. Vert. Zool., Univ. California.

HALLER, KARL WILLIAM.

1940. A new wood warbler from West Virginia. Cardinal, vol. 5, pp. 49–52.

HANN, HARRY WILBUR.

1937. Life history of the oven-bird in southern Michigan. Wilson Bull., vol. 49, pp. 145–237.

1940. Polyandry in the oven-bird. Wilson Bull., vol. 52, pp. 69–72.

HARDING, KATHARINE CLARK.

1931. Nesting habits of the black-throated blue warbler. Auk, vol. 48, pp. 512–522.

HATHAWAY, HARRY SEDWICK.

1906. The water-thrush (*Seiurus noveboracensis*) nesting in Rhode Island. Auk, vol. 23, p. 463.

HENDERSON, JUNIUS.

1927. The practical value of birds.

HENNINGER, WALTHER FRIEDRICH.

1918. Notes on Ohio birds. Wilson Bull., vol. 30, pp. 19–21.

HENSHAW, HENRY WETHERBEE.

1875. Report upon the ornithological collections made in portions of Nevada, Utah, California, Colorado, New Mexico, and Arizona during the years 1871, 1872, 1873, and 1874. Wheeler's Rep. Expl. Surv. West 100th Merid.

1881. On some of the causes affecting the decrease of birds. Bull. Nuttall Orn. Club, vol. 6, pp. 189–197.

HERRICK, HAROLD.

1874. Description of a new species of *Helminthophaga*. Proc. Philadelphia Acad. Nat. Sci., 1874, p. 220.

HESS, ISAAC ELMORE.

1910. One hundred breeding birds of an Illinois ten-mile radius.

HIATT, ROBERT WORTH.

1943. A singing female oven-bird. Condor, vol. 45, p. 158.

HICKEY, JOSEPH JAMES.

1940. Territorial aspects of the American redstart.

700   BULLETIN 203, UNITED STATES NATIONAL MUSEUM

HICKS, LAWRENCE EMERSON.
    1934. A summary of cowbird host species in Ohio. Auk, vol. 51, pp. 385–386.
    1945. Some West Virginia breeding-season records. Wilson Bull., vol. 57, pp. 129–131.
HIX, GEORGE EDWARD.
    1905. A year with the birds in New York City. Wilson Bull., vol. 17, pp. 35–43.
HOFFMANN, RALPH.
    1899. Late migrants and stragglers in eastern Massachusetts. Auk, vol. 16, p. 196.
    1904. A guide to the birds of New England and eastern New York.
    1927. Birds of the Pacific States.
HOLT, ERNEST GOLSAN.
    1920. Bachman's warbler breeding in Alabama. Auk, vol. 37, pp. 103–104.
HOLT, ERNEST GOLSAN, and SUTTON, GEORGE MIKSCH.
    1926. Notes on birds observed in southern Florida. Ann. Carnegie Mus., vol. 16, pp. 409–439, pls. 39–44.
HOWARD, OZRA WILLIAM.
    1899. Summer resident warblers of Arizona. Bull. Cooper Orn. Club, vol. 1, pp. 37–40, 63–65.
HOWARD, WILLIAM JOHNSTON.
    1937. Bird behavior as a result of emergence of seventeen year locusts. Wilson Bull., vol. 49, pp. 43–44.
HOWELL, ALFRED BRAZIER.
    1917. Birds of the islands off the coast of southern California. Pacific Coast Avifauna, No. 12.
HOWELL, ARTHUR HOLMES.
    1907. The relation of birds to the cotton boll weevil. Biol. Surv. Bull. 29.
    1924. Birds of Alabama.
    1930. Description of a new subspecies of the prairie warbler, with remarks on two other unrecognized Florida races. Auk, vol. 47, pp. 41–43.
    1932. Florida bird life.
HOWES, PAUL GRISWOLD.
    1919. Birds and wasps. Oologist, vol. 36, pp. 12–13.
HUEY, LAURENCE MARKHAM.
    1924. The natural end of a bird's life. Condor, vol. 26, pp. 194–195.
    1927. The bird life of San Ignacio and Pond Lagoons on the western coast of Lower California. Condor, vol. 29, pp. 239–243.
HUFF, NED L.
    1929. The nest and habits of the Connecticut warbler in Minnesota. Auk, vol. 46, pp. 455–465.
HUNT, RICHARD.
    1919. A western yellow-throat on the University of California campus. Condor, vol. 21, p. 236.
HYDE, ARTHUR SIDNEY.
    1939. The ecology and economics of the birds along the northern boundary of New York State. Roosevelt Wildlife Bull., vol. 12, No. 2.
INGRAHAM, SYDNEY E.
    1938. Instinctive music. Auk, vol. 55, pp. 614–628.
JACOBS, JOSEPH WARREN.
    1904. The haunts of the golden-winged warbler. Gleanings, No. 3.
JENSEN, JENS KNUDSON.
    1923. Notes on the nesting birds of northern Santa Fe County, New Mexico. Auk, vol. 40, pp. 452–469.

JEWETT, STANLEY GORDON.
    1934. Nesting of the orange-crowned warbler in Oregon Condor, vol. 36,
        p. 242.
    1944. Hybridation of hermit and Townsend warblers. Condor, vol. 46, pp.
        23–24.
JONES, LYNDS.
    1888. Nesting of the golden-crowned thrush. Ornithologist and Oologist,
        vol. 13, p. 133.
    1900. Warbler songs. Wilson Bull., vol. 12, pp. 1–57.
JUDD, SYLVESTER DWIGHT.
    1900. The food of nestling birds. Yearbook U. S. Dept. Agr., 1900, pp.
        411–436.
    1902. Birds of a Maryland farm. Biol. Surv. Bull. 17.
KALMBACH, EDWIN RICHARD.
    1914. Birds in relation to the alfalfa weevil. U. S. Dept. Agr. Bull. 107.
KENDEIGH, SAMUEL CHARLES.
    1941. Birds of a prairie community. Condor, vol. 43, pp. 165–174.
KILGORE, WILLIAM, and BRECKENRIDGE, WALTER JOHN.
    1929. Connecticut warbler nesting in Minnesota. Auk, vol. 46, pp. 551–552.
KING, FRANKLIN HIRAM.
    1883. Economic relations of Wisconsin birds. Geology of Wisconsin, vol.
        1, pp. 441–610.
KINSEY, ERIC CAMPBELL.
    1934. Notes on the sociology of the long-tailed yellow-breasted chat. Con-
        dor, vol. 36, pp. 235–237.
KIRKWOOD, FRANK COATES.
    1901. The cerulean warbler (Dendroica caerulea) as a summer resident in
        Baltimore County, Maryland. Auk, vol. 18, pp. 137–142.
KIRN, ALBERT JOSEPH BERNARD.
    1918. Observations on Swainson's warbler. Oologist, vol. 55, pp. 97–98.
KNIGHT, ORA WILLIS.
    1904. Contributions to the life history of the yellow palm wabler. Journ.
        Maine Orn. Soc., vol. 6, pp. 36–41.
    1908. The birds of Maine.
KOPMAN, HENRY HAZLITT.
    1904. Bird migration phenomena in the extreme lower Mississippi Valley.
        Auk, vol. 21, pp. 45–50.
    1905. Warbler migration to southeast Louisiana and southern Mississippi.
        Auk, vol. 22, pp. 280–296.
    1915. List of the birds of Louisiana. Part 7. Auk, vol. 32, pp. 183–194.
KUMLIEN, LUDWIG, and HOLLISTER, NED.
    1903. The birds of Wisconsin. Bull. Wisconsin Nat. Hist. Soc., new ser.,
        vol. 3, Nos. 1–3.
LADD, SAMUEL BRAGG.
    1887. Nesting of the worm-eating warbler. Ornithologist and Oologist,
        vol. 12, p. 110.
    1891. Description of nests and eggs of Dendroica graciae and Contopus
        pertinax. Auk, vol. 8, pp. 314–315.
LAMB, CHESTER CONVERSE.
    1925. The Socorro warbler added to the A. O. U. Check-list. Condor, vol.
        27, pp. 36–37.
LANGILLE, JAMES HIBBARD.
    1884. Our birds in their haunts.

LA PRADE, WILLIAM H., Jr.
　　1922. Breeding warblers around Atlanta, Georgia. Wilson Bull., vol. 34, pp. 80–83.
LAWRENCE, LOUISE DE KIRILINE.
　　1948. Comparative study of the nesting behavior of chestnut-sided and Nashville warblers. Auk, vol. 65, pp. 204–219.
LEOPOLD, NATHAN FREUDENTHAL, Jr.
　　1924. The Kirtland's warbler in its summer home. Auk, vol. 41, pp. 44–58.
LINCOLN, FREDERICK CHARLES.
　　1935. The migration of North American birds. U. S. Dept. Agr. Circ. 363.
　　1939. The migration of American birds.
LINSDALE, JEAN MYRON.
　　1938. Environmental responses of vertebrates in the Great Basin. Amer. Midl. Nat., vol. 19, pp. 1–206.
LOOMIS, LEVERETT MILLS.
　　1887. *Helinaia swainsonii* near Chester C. H., S. C. Auk, vol. 4, pp. 347–348.
　　1901. An addition to the A. O. U. Check-list. Auk, vol. 18, pp. 109–110.
LOWERY, GEORGE HINES, Jr.
　　1945. Trans-Gulf spring migration of birds and the coastal hiatus. Wilson Bull., vol. 57, pp. 92–121.
MACFARLANE, RODERICK ROSS.
　　1891. Notes on and list of birds and eggs collected in Arctic America, 1861–1866. Proc. U. S. Nat. Mus., vol. 14, pp. 413–446.
　　1908. Notes on the mammals and birds of northern Canada. *In* "Through the Mackenzie Basin," by Charles Mair.
MACOUN, JOHN, and MACOUN, JAMES MELVILLE.
　　1909. Catalogue of Canadian birds.
MAILLIARD, JOSEPH.
　　1937. Hybridism between myrtle and Audubon warblers. Condor, vol. 39, pp. 223–225.
MAYNARD, CHARLES JOHNSON.
　　1896. The birds of eastern North America, ed. 2.
　　1906. Directory to the birds of eastern North America.
MCATEE, WALDO LEE.
　　1904. Warblers and grapes. Auk, vol. 21, pp. 489–491.
　　1912. Bird enemies of the coddling moth. Yearbook U. S. Dept. Agr., 1911, pp. 237–246.
　　1926. The relation of birds to woodlots in New York State. Roosevelt Wild-life Bull., vol. 4, pp. 7–152.
MCCABE, THOMAS TONKIN, and MILLER, ALDEN HOLMES.
　　1933. Geographic variation in the northern water-thrushes. Condor, vol. 35, pp. 192–197.
MCGREGOR, RICHARD CRITTENDEN.
　　1899. The myrtle warbler in California and description of a new race. Bull. Cooper Orn. Club, vol. 1, pp. 31–32.
MEARNS, EDGAR ALEXANDER.
　　1879. A list of the birds in the Hudson Highlands, with annotations. Bull. Essex Inst., vol. 11, pp. 154–168.
　　1890. Observations on the avifauna of a portion of Arizona. Auk, vol. 7, pp. 251–264.
MENDALL, HOWARD LEWIS.
　　1937. Nesting of the bay-breasted warbler. Auk, vol. 54, pp. 429–439.

MERRIAM, CLINTON HART.
  1885. Nest and eggs of the Blackburnian warbler. Auk, vol. 2, p. 103.
MERRIAM, HENRY FRANKLIN.
  1917. Nesting of the Cape May warbler at Lake Edward, Quebec. Auk, vol.
        34, pp. 410–413.
MERRILL, JAMES CUSHING.
  1878. Notes on the ornithology of southern Texas, being a list of birds
        observed in the vicinity of Fort Brown, Texas, from February,
        1876, to June, 1878. Proc. U. S. Nat. Mus., vol. 1, pp. 118–173.
  1888. Notes on the birds of Fort Klamath, Oreg. Auk, vol. 5, pp. 357–366.
  1898. Notes on the birds of Fort Sherman, Idaho. Auk, vol. 15, pp. 14–22.
MEYER, HENRY, and NEVIUS, RUTH REED.
  1943. Some observation on the nesting and development of the prothonotary
        warbler, *Protonotaria citrea*. Migrant, vol. 14, pp. 31–36.
MILLER, ALDEN HOLMES.
  1942. Differentiation of the oven-birds of the Rocky Mountain region.
        Condor, vol. 44, pp. 185–186.
MILLER, WALDRON DeWITT, and GRISCOM, LUDLOW.
  1925. Notes on Central American birds, with descriptions of new forms.
        Amer. Mus. Nov., No. 183, pp. 1–14.
MINOT, HENRY DAVIS.
  1877. The land birds and game-birds of New England.
  1880. Notes on Colorado birds. Bull. Nuttall Orn. Club, vol. 5, pp. 223–232.
MONSON, GALE, and PHILLIPS, ALLAN ROBERT.
  1941. Bird records from southern and western Arizona. Condor, vol. 43,
        pp. 108–112.
MOORE, ROBERT THOMAS.
  1942. New records of the Colima warbler from Mexico. Auk, vol. 59, p. 315.
MOORE, WILLIAM HENRY.
  1904. Notes concerning New Brunswick warblers. Ottawa Nat., vol. 18,
        pp. 97–103.
MORRELL, CLARENCE HENRY.
  1899. Caterpillars disturbing the birds. Journ. Maine Orn. Soc., vol. 1,
        p. 28.
MOUSLEY, HENRY M.
  1916. Five years personal notes and observations on the birds of Hatley,
        Stanstead County, Quebec—1911–1915. Auk, vol. 33, pp. 168–186.
  1917. A study of subsequent nestings after the loss of the first. Auk,
        vol. 34, pp. 381–393.
  1918. Further notes and observations on the birds of Hatley, Stanstead
        County, Quebec, 1916–1917. Auk, vol. 35, pp. 289–310.
  1919. "The singing tree," or how near to the nest do the male birds sing?
        Auk, vol. 36, pp. 339–348.
  1924. A study of the home life of the northern parula and other warblers
        at Hatley, Stanstead County, Quebec. Auk, vol. 41, pp. 263–288.
  1926. A further study of the home life of the northern parula and of the
        yellow warbler and ovenbird. Auk, vol. 43, pp. 184–197.
  1928. A further study of the home life of the northern parula warbler
        (*Compsothlypis americana usneae*). Auk, vol. 45, pp. 475–479.
  1940. Food of the sharp-shinned hawk. Condor, vol. 42, pp. 168–169.
MOYER, JOHN WILLIAM.
  1933. Bird life along the Kankakee. Wilson Bull., vol. 45, pp. 135–138.
MULLER, PHILIP LUDWIG STATIUS.
  1776. Natursystem, Suppl. und Register Band, 1776, p. 175.

MURPHEY, EUGENE EDMUND.
    1937. Observations on the bird life of the middle Savannah Valley, 1890–
           1937. Contr. Charleston Mus., No. 9.
MURRAY, JAMES JOSEPH.
    1932. Wayne's warbler, an addition to the Virginia avifauna. Auk, vol. 49,
           pp. 487–488.
    1935. Breeding of Swainson's warbler in Robeson County, North Carolina.
           Auk, vol. 52, p. 459.
NELSON, ARNOLD LARS.
    1933. Golden-winged warbler feeding on larvae of *Talponia plummeriana*.
           Auk, vol. 50, pp. 440–441.
NELSON, EDWARD WILLIAM.
    1887. Report upon natural history collections made in Alaska. U. S. Signal
           Serv., Arctic ser., No. 3.
    1900. Descriptions of thirty new North American birds, in the Biological
           Survey collection. Auk, vol. 17, pp. 253–270.
NICE, MARGARET MORSE.
    1926. A study of the nesting of magnolia warblers (*Dendroica magnolia*).
           Wilson Bull., vol. 38, pp. 185–199.
    1930a. Observations at a nest of myrtle warblers. Wilson Bull., vol. 42,
           pp. 60–61.
    1930b. A study of a nesting of black-throated blue warblers. Auk, vol. 47,
           pp. 338–345.
    1931. The birds of Oklahoma. Revised edition. Publ. Univ. Oklahoma,
           vol. 3.
    1932. Habits of the Blackburnian warbler in Pelham, Massachusetts. Auk,
           vol. 49, pp. 92–93.
NICE, MARGARET MORSE, and NICE, LEONARD B.
    1932. A study of two nests of the black-throated green warbler. Bird-Band-
           ing, vol. 3, pp. 95–105, 157–172.
NICHOLS, JOHN TREADWELL.
    1908. Lawrence's and Brewster's warblers and Mendelian inheritance.
           Auk, vol. 25, p. 86.
NICHOLSON, DONALD JOHN.
    1929. Nesting of the yellow-throated warbler in Volusia County, Florida.
           Wilson Bull., vol. 41, pp. 45–46.
NIETHAMMER, GÜNTHER.
    1937. Handbuch der deutschen Vogelkunde, vol. 1.
NORRIS, JOSEPH PARKER.
    1890a. A series of eggs of the black-poll warbler. Ornithologist and Oologist,
           vol. 15, pp. 41–43.
    1890b. A series of eggs of the prothonotary warbler. Ornithologist and
           Oologist, vol. 15, pp. 177–182.
    1892. A series of eggs of the oven-bird. Ornithologist and Oologist, vol. 17,
           pp. 65–67.
NORRIS, JOSEPH PARKER, Jr.
    1902. Nesting of the Tennessee warbler in British Columbia. Auk, vol. 19,
           pp. 88–89.
NUTTALL, THOMAS.
    1832. A manual of the ornithology of the United States and of Canada.
           Land birds.
    1833. Remarks and inquiries concerning the birds of Massachusetts. Mem.
           Amer. Acad. Arts and Sci., vol. 1, pp. 91–106.

OBERHOLSER, HARRY CHURCH.

1899. Description of a new *Geothlypis*. Auk, vol. 16, pp. 256–258.

1905. The forms of *Vermivora celata* (Say). Auk, vol. 22, pp. 242–247.

1917. A new subspecies of *Geothlypis beldingi*. Condor, vol. 19, pp. 182–184.

1938. The bird life of Louisiana. Louisiana Dept. Conserv., Bull. 28.

ODUM, EUGENE PLEASANTS.

1931. Notes on the nesting habits of the hooded warbler. Wilson Bull., vol. 43, pp. 316–317.

OSGOOD, WILFRED HUDSON.

1896. Nest and eggs of the Calaveras warbler. Nidologist, vol. 3, pp. 140–141.

OVERING, ROBERT.

1938. High mortality at the Washington monument. Auk, vol. 55, p. 679.

PALMER, WILLIAM.

1894. Plumages of the young hooded warbler. Auk, vol. 11, pp. 282–291.

1900. Ecology of the Maryland yellow-throat and its relatives. Auk, vol. 17, pp. 216–242.

PARKES, KENNETH CARROLL.

1951. The genetics of the golden-winged × blue-winged warbler complex. Wilson Bull., vol. 63, pp. 5–15.

PEARSON, THOMAS GILBERT; BRIMLEY, CLEMENT SAMUEL; and BRIMLEY, HERBERT HUTCHINSON.

1919. Birds of North Carolina.

1942. Birds of North Carolina. Revised edition.

PERRY, TROUP D.

1887. Some additional notes on Swainson's warbler. Ornithologist and Oologist, vol. 12, pp. 141–142.

PETERS, HAROLD SEYMOUR.

1936. A list of external parasites from birds of the eastern part of the United States. Bird-Banding, vol. 7, pp. 9–27.

PETERSON, ROGER TORY.

1939. A field guide to the birds.

PETRIDES, GEORGE ATHAN.

1938. A life history of the yellow-breasted chat. Wilson Bull., vol. 50, pp. 184–189.

1943a. *Berberis beali* as a spring food of songbirds. Auk, vol. 60, pp. 99–100.

1943b. Notes on a captive redstart. Wilson Bull., vol. 55, pp. 193–194.

PHILIPP, PHILIP BERNARD.

1925. Notes on the summer birds of the Magdalen Islands. Can. Field-Nat., vol. 39, pp. 75–78.

PHILIPP, PHILIP BERNARD, and BOWDISH, BEECHER SCOVILLE.

1917. Some summer birds of northern New Brunswick. Auk, vol. 34, pp. 265–275.

1919. Further notes on New Brunswick birds. Auk, vol. 36, pp. 36–45.

PHILLIPS, ALLAN ROBERT.

1947. The races of Macgillivray's warbler. Auk, vol. 64, pp. 296–300.

PITELKA, FRANK ALOIS.

1939. Flight song of the blue-winged warbler. Auk, vol. 56, pp. 340–341.

1940a. Nashville warbler breeding in northeastern Illinois. Auk, vol. 57, pp. 115–116.

1940b. Breeding behavior of the black-throated green warbler. Wilson Bull., vol. 52, pp. 3–18.

PORSILD, A. E.
1943. Birds of the Mackenzie Delta. Can. Field-Nat., vol. 57, pp. 19–35.
PORTER, LOUIS HOPKINS.
1908. Nesting habits of birds at Stamford, Connecticut, as affected by the cold spring of 1907. Auk, vol. 25, pp. 16–21.
POTTER, LAURENCE BEDFORD.
1935. Nesting of the yellow-breasted chat in Saskatchewan. Condor, vol. 37, p. 287.
PREBLE, EDWARD ALEXANDER.
1908. A biological investigation of the Athabaska-Mackenzie region. North American Fauna, No. 27.
PRESTON, JUNIUS WALLACE.
1891. A glimpse of the Nashville warbler. Ornithologist and Oologist, vol. 16, pp. 89–90.
PRICE, WILLIAM WIGHTMAN.
1888. Nesting of the red-faced warbler (*Cardellina rubrifrons*) in the Huachuca Mountains, southern Arizona. Auk, vol. 5, pp. 385–386.
1895. The nest and eggs of the olive warbler (*Dendroica olivacea*). Auk, vol. 12, pp. 17–19.
RAND, AUSTIN LOOMIS.
1943. Bass eats yellowthroat, young stilts, and young ducks. Auk, vol. 60, p. 95.
1944. Notes on the palm warbler, *Dendroica palmarum* (Gmelin), in Canada. Can. Field-Nat., vol. 58, pp. 181–182.
RAWSON, CALVIN L. (J. M. W.).
1888. The parula warbler—its nest and eggs. Ornithologist and Oologist, vol. 13, pp. 1–5.
RAY, MILTON SMITH.
1916. More summer birds of San Francisco County. Condor, vol. 18, pp. 222–227.
READING, D. K., and HAYES, S. P., Jr.
1933. Notes on the nesting and feeding of a pair of black-throated green warblers. Auk, vol. 50, pp. 403–407.
REDFIELD, ALFRED C.
1911. A yellow-throat family. Bird-Lore, vol. 13, pp. 196–197.
REED, J. HARRIS.
1888. An albino blackpoll warbler. Auk, vol. 5, p. 432.
REID, [PHILIP] SAVILE GREY.
1884. Contributions to the natural history of Bermuda. Pt. 4, Birds. U. S. Nat. Mus. Bull. 25, pp. 163–279.
RICHARDSON, RUSSELL, Jr.
1926. Black-throated green warbler in the Dismal Swamp. Auk, vol. 43, pp. 552–553.
RIDGWAY, ROBERT.
1876. On geographical variation in *Dendroeca palmarum*. Bull. Nuttall Orn. Club, vol. 1, pp. 81–87.
1877. United States geological exploration of the fortieth parallel, pt. 3: Ornithology.
1882. Descriptions of some new North American birds. Proc. U. S. Nat. Mus., vol. 5, pp. 343–346.
1885. A review of the American "golden warblers." Proc. U. S. Nat. Mus., vol. 8, pp. 348–350.
1887. A manual of North American birds.
1889. The ornithology of Illinois.

RIDGWAY, ROBERT—Continued

1894. Description of a new *Geothlypis* from Brownsville, Texas. Proc. U. S. Nat. Mus., vol. 16, 1893, pp. 691–692.

1897. Description of the nest and eggs of Bachman's warbler. Auk, vol. 14, pp. 309–310.

1902. The birds of North and Middle America. U. S. Nat. Mus. Bull. 50, pt. 2.

RILEY, JOSEPH HARVEY.

1905. List of birds collected and observed during the Bahama Expedition of the Geographic Society of Baltimore. Auk, vol. 22, pp. 349–360.

RIVES, WILLIAM CABELL.

1890. A catalogue of the birds of the Virginias. Proc. Newport Nat. Hist. Soc., Document 7.

ROBERTS, THOMAS SADLER.

1936. The birds of Minnesota, ed. 2, vol. 2.

SAGE, JOHN HALL; BISHOP, LOUIS BENNETT; and BLISS, WALTER PARKS.

1913. The birds of Connecticut.

SAUNDERS, ARETAS ANDREWS.

1921. A distributional list of the birds of Montana. Pacific Coast Avifauna, No. 14.

1938. Studies of breeding birds in the Allegany State Park. New York State Mus. Bull. 318.

1941. A guide to bird songs.

SAUNDERS, WILLIAM EDWIN.

1900. Nesting habits of the cerulean warbler. Auk, vol. 17, pp. 358–362.

1930. The destruction of birds at Long Point light-house, Ontario, on four nights in 1929. Auk, vol. 47, pp. 507–511.

SAY, THOMAS.

1823. *In* Long, Account of an expedition to the Rocky Mountains, vol. 1, p. 169.

SCHRANTZ, FREDERICK GEORGE.

1943. Nest life of the eastern yellow warbler. Auk, vol. 60, pp. 367–387.

SCHUSSLER, GEORGE W.

1918. The salt marsh yellowthroats of San Francisco. Condor, vol. 20, pp. 62–64.

SCOTT, WILLIAM EARLE DODGE.

1885. Winter mountain notes from southern Arizona. Auk, vol. 2, pp. 172–174.

1890. A summary of observations on the birds of the Gulf coast of Florida. Auk, vol. 7, pp. 14–22.

1905. On the probable origin of certain birds. Science, vol. 22, pp. 271–282.

SENNETT, GEORGE BURRITT.

1878. Notes on the ornithology of the lower Rio Grande of Texas, from observations made during the season of 1877. Bull. U. S. Geol. and Geogr. Surv., vol. 4, pp. 1–66.

1879. Further notes on the ornithology of the lower Rio Grande of Texas, from observations made during the spring of 1878. Bull. U. S. Geol. and Geogr. Surv., vol. 5, pp. 371–440.

SETON, ERNEST THOMPSON (ERNEST EVAN SETON-THOMPSON).

1884. Nest and habits of the Connecticut warbler (*Oporornis agilis*). Auk, vol. 1, pp. 192–193.

1891. The birds of Manitoba. Proc. U. S. Nat. Mus., vol. 13, pp. 457–643.

1901. Lives of the hunted.

SHARP, CLARENCE SAUGER.
     1903.   *Dendroica auduboni* a raisin eater.   Condor, vol. 5, p. 79.
SHAVER, NELLE E.
     1918.   A nest study of the Maryland yellow-throat.   Univ. Iowa Studies,
              No. 23.
SHEPPARD, ROY WATSON.
     1939.   A very late Blackburnian warbler.   Auk, vol. 56, p. 341.
SHORT, ERNEST H.
     1893.   A study in orange and black.   Oologist, vol. 10, pp. 197–199.
SILLOWAY, PERLEY MILTON.
     1901.   Flathead Lake findings.   Condor, vol. 3, pp. 4–7.
SIMMONS, GEORGE FINLAY.
     1925.   Birds of the Austin region.
SIMPSON, RALPH B.
     1920.   The Maryland yellowthroat.   Oologist, vol. 37, pp. 43–45.
SKINNER, MILTON PHILO.
     1928.   A guide to the winter birds of the North Carolina sandhills.
SMITH, WENDELL PHILLIPS.
     1943.   Some yellow warbler observations.   Bird-Banding, vol. 14, pp. 57–63.
SOPER, JOSEPH DEWEY.
     1942.   The long-tailed chat in Saskatchewan.   Can. Field-Nat., vol. 56,
              pp. 83–85.
SPRUNT, ALEXANDER, Jr.
     1932.   Some emendations to the ranges of the new Check-list.   Auk, vol. 49,
              pp. 237–239.
STACKPOLE, RICHARD.
     1939.   Black-poll warbler.   New England Bird life, vol. 3, p. 8.
STANWOOD, CORDELIA JOHNSON.
     1910a. A lowly home.   Nest and young of the Nashville warbler.   Journ.
              Maine Orn. Soc., vol. 12, pp. 28–33.
     1910b. The black-throated green warbler.   Auk, vol. 27, pp. 289–294.
     1910c. The black and white warbler.   Journ. Maine Orn. Soc., vol. 12,
              pp. 61–66.
STEWART, ROBERT EARL.
     1943.   Post-breeding pugnacity of the pine warbler.   Auk, vol. 60, p. 271.
STOCKARD, CHARLES RUPERT.
     1905.   Nesting habits of birds in Mississippi.   Auk, vol. 22, pp. 273–285.
STONE, WITMER.
     1937.   Bird studies at Old Cape May, vol. 3.
STONER, DAYTON.
     1932.   Ornithology of the Oneida Lake region: With reference to the late
              spring and summer seasons.   Roosevelt Wild Life Annals, vols. 2,
              Nos. 3 and 4.
STURM, LOUIS.
     1945.   A study of the nesting activities of the American redstart.   Auk,
              vol. 62, pp. 189–206.
SUTTON, GEORGE MIKSCH.
     1928.   The birds of Pymatuning Swamp and Conneaut Lake, Crawford
              County, Pennsylvania.   Ann. Carnegie Mus., vol. 18, pp. 19–239.
     1935.   An expedition to the Big Bend country.   Cardinal, vol. 4, pp. 1–7.
     1943.   Records from the Tucson region of Arizona.   Auk, vol. 60, pp. 345–350.

SUTTON, GEORGE MIKSCH, and BURLEIGH, THOMAS DEARBORN.
 1939. A list of the birds observed on the 1938 Semple expedition to north-eastern Mexico. Occas. Pap. Mus. Zool., Louisiana State Univ. No. 3.
SUTTON, GEORGE MIKSCH, and PETTINGILL, OLIN SEWALL, Jr.
 1942. Birds of the Gomez Farias region, southwestern Tamaulipas. Auk, vol. 59, pp. 1–34.
SWAIN, JOHN MERTON.
 1904. Contributions to the life history of the Wilson's warbler. Journ. Maine Orn. Soc., vol. 6, pp. 59–62.
SWALES, BRADSHAW HALL, and TAVERNER, PERCY ALGERNON.
 1907. Recent ornithological developments in southeastern Michigan. Auk, vol. 24, pp. 135–148.
SWARTH, HARRY SCHELWALDT.
 1904. Birds of the Huachuca Mountains, Arizona. Pacific Coast Avifauna, No. 4.
 1905. Summer birds of the Papago Indian Reservation and of the Santa Rita Mountains, Arizona. Condor, vol. 7, pp. 22–28, 47–50, 77–81.
 1914. A distributional list of the birds of Arizona. Pacific Coast Avifauna, No. 10.
 1926a. Report on a collection of birds and mammals from the Atlin region, northern British Columbia. Univ. California Publ. Zool., vol. 30, pp. 51–162.
 1926b. The Audubon's warbler. Bird-Lore, vol. 28, pp. 82–85.
TAVERNER, PERCY ALGERNON.
 1906. The yellow-breasted chat. A character sketch. Bird-Lore, vol. 8, pp. 131–133.
TAVERNER, PERCY ALGERNON, and SWALES, BRADSHAW HALL.
 1908. The birds of Point Pelee. Wilson Bull., vol. 20, pp. 79–95.
TAYLOR, WALTER PENN, and SHAW, WILLIAM THOMAS.
 1927. Mammals and birds of Mount Rainier National Park.
TERRES, JOHN KENNETH.
 1940. Birds eating tent caterpillars. Auk, vol. 57, p. 422.
THAYER, JOHN ELIOT.
 1909. Some rare birds and sets of eggs from the Cape region of Lower California. Condor, vol. 11, pp. 10–11.
TODD, WALTER EDMOND CLYDE.
 1916. The birds of the Isle of Pines. Ann. Carnegie Mus., vol. 10, Nos. 1, 2, art 11, pp. 146–296, pls. 22–27.
 1940. Birds of western Pennsylvania.
TODD, WALTER EDMOND CLYDE, and CARRICKER, MELBOURNE ARMSTRONG.
 1922. The birds of the Santa Marta region of Colombia: A study in altitudinal distribution. Ann. Carnegie Mus., vol. 14, pp. 3–611.
TORREY, BRADFORD.
 1885. Birds in the bush.
TOWNSEND, CHARLES HASKINS.
 1883. Some albinos in the museum of the Philadelphia Academy. Bull. Nuttall Orn. Club, vol. 8, p. 126.
 1890. Birds from the coasts of western North America and adjacent islands, collected in 1888–'89, with descriptions of new species. Proc. U. S. Nat. Mus., vol. 13, pp. 131–142.

TOWNSEND, CHARLES WENDELL.
    1905. The birds of Essex County Massachusetts. Mem. Nuttall Orn. Club, No. 3.
    1908. On the status of Brewster's warbler (*Helminthophila leucobron-chialis*). Auk, vol. 25, pp. 65–68.
TRAUTMAN, MILTON BERNARD.
    1933. Some recent Ohio records. Auk, vol. 50, pp. 234–236.
    1940. The birds of Buckeye Lake, Ohio. Univ. Michigan Mus. Zool. Misc. Publ. 44.
TROTTER, SPENCER.
    1909. An inquiry into the history of the current English names of North American land birds. Auk, vol. 26, pp. 346–363.
TUFTS, ROBIE WILFRID.
    1927. Banding yellow warblers in Nova Scotia. Bull. Northeastern Bird-Banding Assoc., vol. 3, pp. 3–5.
TUTTLE, HENRY EMERSON.
    1919a. The night warbler. Bird-Lore, vol. 21, p. 229.
    1919b. The warbler in stripes. Bird–Lore, vol. 21, pp. 296–298.
TWOMEY, ARTHUR CORNELIUS.
    1936. Climographic studies of certain introduced and migratory birds. Ecology, vol. 17, pp. 122–132.
TYLER, JOHN GRIPPER.
    1913. Some birds of the Fresno District, California. Pacific Coast Avifauna, No. 9.
TYLER, WINSOR MARRETT.
    1937. A note used during migration by the yellow warbler. Auk, vol. 54, pp. 395–396.
VAN ROSSEM, ADRIAAN JOSEPH.
    1922. The salt marsh yellow-throat in southern California. Condor, vol. 24, p. 134.
    1930. Critical notes on some yellowthroats of the Pacific southwest. Condor, vol. 32, pp. 297–300.
    1931. Report on a collection of land birds from Sonora, Mexico. Trans. San Diego Soc. Nat. Hist., vol. 5, No. 19, pp. 287–304.
    1936. Birds of the Charleston Mountains, Nevada. Pacific Coast Avifauna, No. 24.
    1945. A distributional survey of the birds of Sonora, Mexico. Louisiana State Univ. Occas. Pap. Mus. Zool., No. 21.
VAN TYNE, JOSSELYN.
    1929. Notes on some birds of the Chisos Mountains of Texas. Auk, vol. 46, pp. 204–206.
    1933. Some birds of the Rio Grande Delta of Texas. Univ. Michigan Occas. Pap. Mus. Zool., No. 255, pp. 1–5.
    1936. The discovery of the nest of the Colima warbler (*Vermivora crissalis*). Univ. Michigan Mus. Zool. Misc. Publ. 33.
    1944. A specimen of the western yellow-throat from Michigan. Auk, vol. 61, p. 475.
VAN TYNE, JOSSELYN, and SUTTON, GEORGE MIKSCH.
    1937. The birds of Brewster County, Texas. Univ. Michigan Mus. Zool. Misc. Publ. 37.
WALKINSHAW, LAWRENCE HARVEY.
    1938. Nesting studies of the prothonotary warbler. Bird-Banding, vol. 9, pp. 32–46.

WALKINSHAW, LAWRENCE HARVEY—Continued
1941. The prothonotary warbler, a comparison of nesting conditions in Tennessee and Michigan. Wilson Bull., vol. 53, pp. 3–21.

WARREN, BENJAMIN HARRY.
1890. Report on the birds of Pennsylvania, with special reference to their food-habits.

WAYNE, ARTHUR TREZEVANT.
1886. Nesting of Swainson's warbler in South Carolina. Ornithologist and Oologist, vol. 11, pp. 187–188.
1901. Bachman's warbler (*Helminthophila bachmanii*) rediscovered near Charleston, South Carolina. Auk, vol. 18, pp. 274–275.
1904. Kirtland's warbler (*Dendroica kirtlandi*) on the coast of South Carolina. Auk, vol. 21, pp. 83–84.
1907. The nest and eggs of Bachman's warbler, *Helminthophila bachmani* (Aud.), taken near Charleston, South Carolina. Auk. vol. 24, pp. 43–48.
1910. Birds of South Carolina. Contr. Charleston Mus., No. 1.
1918. Some additions and other records new to the ornithology of South Carolina. Auk, vol. 35, pp. 437–442.
1919. Nest and eggs of Wayne's warbler (*Dendroica virens waynei*) taken near Mount Pleasant, S. C., Auk, vol. 36, pp. 489–492.
1920. Notes on seven birds taken near Charleston, South Carolina. Auk, vol. 37, pp. 92–94.
1925. A late autumnal record for Bachman's warbler (*Vermivora bachmani*). Wilson Bull., vol. 37, p. 41.

WELLMAN, GORDON BOIT.
1905. A black and white creeper family. Bird-Lore, vol. 7, pp. 170–172.

WETMORE, ALEXANDER.
1916. Birds of Porto Rico. U. S. Dept. Agr. Bull. 326.
1920. Observations on the habits of birds at Lake Burford, New Mexico. Auk, vol. 37, pp. 393–412.
1936. The number of contour feathers in passeriform and related birds. Auk, vol. 53, pp. 159–169.
1937. Observations on the birds of West Virginia. Proc. U. S. Nat Mus., vol. 84, pp. 401–441.
1939. Notes on the birds of Tennessee. Proc. U. S. Nat Mus., vol. 86, pp. 175–243.
1943. The birds of southern Veracruz, Mexico. Proc. U. S. Nat. Mus., vol. 93, pp. 215–340.
1949. Geographical variation in the American redstart (*Setophaga ruticilla*). Journ. Washington Acad. Sci., vol. 39, pp. 137–139.

WETMORE, ALEXANDER, and SWALES, BRADSHAW HALL.
1931. The birds of Haiti and the Dominican Republic. U. S. Nat. Mus. Bull. 155.

WHEATON, JOHN MAYNARD.
1882. Report on the birds of Ohio. Rep. Geol. Surv. Ohio. Part 1, Zoology, pp. 187–628.

WHEELOCK, IRENE GROSVENOR.
1904. Birds of California.

WHITE, STEWART EDWARD.
1893. Birds observed on Mackinac Island, Michigan, during the summers of 1889, 1890, and 1891. Auk, vol. 10, pp. 221–230.

WHITEHILL, WALTON I.
  1897. Peculiar nesting of the Maryland yellow-throat. Auk, vol. 14, pp. 408–409.
WHITTLE, CHARLES LIVY.
  1922. A myrtle warbler invasion. Auk, vol. 39, pp. 23–31.
WIDMANN, OTTO.
  1897. The summer home of Bachman's warbler no longer unknown. A common breeder in the St. Francis River region of southeastern Missouri and northeastern Arkansas. Auk, vol. 14, pp. 305–310.
WILLARD, FRANCIS COTTLE.
  1910. The olive warbler (*Dendroica olivacea*) in southern Arizona. Condor, vol. 12, pp. 104–107.
WILLIAMS, ELLISON ADGER.
  1935. Swainson's warbler in the North Carolina mountains. Auk, vol. 52, pp. 458–459.
WILLIAMS, GEORGE G.
  1945. Do birds cross the Gulf of Mexico in spring? Auk, vol. 62, pp. 98–110.
WILSON, ALEXANDER.
  1832. American ornithology.
WING, LEONARD WILLIAM.
  1933. Summer warblers of the Crawford County, Michigan, uplands. Wilson Bull., vol. 45, pp. 70–76.
WITHERBY, HARRY FORBES, and others.
  1920. A practical handbook of British birds, vol. 1.
WOOD, JOHN CLAIRE.
  1904. Some notes on the life history of the American redstart, Bull. Michigan Orn. Club, vol. 5, pp. 33–35.
WOOD, NORMAN ASA.
  1904. Discovery of the breeding area of Kirtland's warbler. Bull. Michigan Orn. Club, vol. 5, pp. 3–13.
  1911. The results of the Mershon expedition to the Charity Islands, Lake Huron. Wilson Bull., vol. 23, pp. 78–112.
  1926. In search of new colonies of Kirtland warblers. Wilson Bull., vol. 38, pp. 11–13.
WRIGHT, HORACE WINSLOW.
  1909a. Birds of the Boston Public Garden.
  1909b. A nesting of the blue-winged warbler in Massachusetts. Auk, vol. 26, pp. 337–345.
  1911. The birds of the Jefferson region in the White Mountains of New Hampshire. Proc. Manchester Inst. Arts and Sci., vol. 5, part 1.
  1912. Morning awakening and even-song. Auk, vol. 29, pp. 307–327.
  1917. The orange-crowned warbler as a fall and winter visitant in the region of Boston, Massachusetts. Auk, vol. 34, pp. 11–27.
WYTHE, MARGARET WILHELMINA.
  1916. Nesting of the Tolmie warbler in Yosemite Valley. Condor, vol. 18, pp. 123–127.
YARRELL, WILLIAM.
  1876–1882. A history of British birds, edition 4. Revised and enlarged by Alfred Newton.
ZOTTA, ANGEL.
  1932. Notas sobre el contenido estomacel de algunas aves. El Hornero, vol. 5, pp. 77–81.

INDEX

Abbott C. G., *on* dusky orange-crowned
  warbler, 104.
aestiva, Dendroica, 19, 80, 182, 186.
  Dendroica petechia, 160, 180, 184,
    185, 189.
agilis, Geothlypis, 527.
  Oporornis, 513.
Aiken, C. E. and Warren, E. R., *on*
  Virginia's warbler, 121, 123.
Alaska myrtle warbler, 258.
Alaska pileolated warbler, *see* **northern**
  pileolated warbler, 641.
Alaska yellow warbler, 179, 184.
albilora, Dendroica dominica, 358, 359.
Allen, Amelia S., *on* California yellow
  warbler, 186, 188.
    on golden pileolated warbler, 644,
      645.
    on hermit warbler, 322.
    on northern MacGillivray's warbler
      535, 538.
    on northern pileolated warbler, 640.
    on Pacific Audubon's warbler, 262,
      266.
    on Townsend's warbler, 283, 287,
      288.
Allen, C. A., 323, 324.
Allen, F. H., *on* black-and-white war-
  bler, 10, 11.
    on Blackburnian warbler, 344.
    on blue-winged warbler, 63.
    on Canada warbler, 652.
    on Cape May warbler, 220.
    on cerulean warbler, 333.
    on chestnut-sided warbler, 375.
    on Connecticut warbler, 520.
    on eastern myrtle warbler, 248, 249.
    on eastern Nashville warbler, 112.
    on eastern orange-crowned war-
      bler, 92.
    on eastern yellow warbler, 173.
    on golden-winged warbler, 54.
    on hooded warbler, 621.
    on Kentucky warbler, 510.
    on magnolia warbler, 206.
    on mourning warbler, 529.
    on northern black-throated blue
      warbler, 227, 232.
    on northern black-throated green
      warbler, 301.
    on northern pine warbler, 413.
    on northern prairie warbler, 433,
      434.
    on northern small-billed water-
      thrush, 483.
    on Tennessee warbler, 83.

Allen, F. H.—Continued
    on worm-eating warbler, 43.
    on yellow palm warbler, 454, 455.
Allen, G. M., *on* bay-breasted warbler,
  380.
    on black-polled warbler, 392.
Allen, J. A., *on* golden-winged warbler,
  47.
Allison, Andrew, *on* black-and-white
  warbler, 11.
    on hooded warbler, 612, 620, 622.
    on Kentucky warbler, 504.
    on northern parula warbler, 140.
    on Sycamore yellow-throated war-
      bler, 360, 362.
American Museum of Natural History,
  XI.
American Ornithologists' Union, X.
American redstart, 651, 683, 685, 687.
americana, Compsothlypis, 72, 135, 668.
  Compsothlypis americana, 135.
  Parula, 37, 150.
  Parula americana, 135, 147.
Ammann, G. A., X.
amnicola, Dendroica petechia, 179, 182,
  184.
Anderson, R. M., *on* black-polled war-
  bler, 394.
Anderson, W. W., 119.
arizela, Geothlypis trichas, 543, 562, 575,
  579.
arizonae, Peucedramus taeniatus, 153.
Athens yellowthroat, 562, 566, 569.
Atkins, J W., *on* Bachman's warbler, 72,
  73.
Attwater, H. P., 364.
    on golden-cheeked warbler, 316, 317,
      319, 320.
Audubon, J. J., 39, 47, 75, 105, 135, 195,
  212, 329, 380, 408, 429, 450, 513.
    on Bachman's warbler 67.
    on black-and-white warbler, 6.
    on blue-winged warbler, 4.
    on chestnut-sided warbler, 373.
    on Connecticut warbler, 518.
    on eastern yellow-throated warbler,
      353.
    on golden-winged warbler, 4.
    on hermit warbler, 321.
    on Louisiana waterthrush, 493.
    on prothonotary warbler, 25.
    on Swainson's warbler, 30.
    on Wilson's pileolated warbler, 626.
auduboni, Dendroica, 260, 266, 268, 273,
  274.
  Dendroica auduboni, 260, 272.

O

PLATES

PLATE 45

Dutchess County, N. Y.

CHESTNUT-SIDED WARBLER

PLATE 46

Carter County, Tenn., June 7, 1942   B. P. Tyler

NEST OF CHESTNUT-SIDED WARBLER

PLATE 47

H. L. Mendall

W. G. F. Harris

MALE BAY-BREASTED WARBLER AND NEST

PLATE 48

Torbay, Newfoundland, July 12, 1943   W. H. Carrick

Magdalen Islands, Quebec   B. S. Bowdish

BLACK-POLLED WARBLERS, ADULT MALE AND YOUNG, AND NEST

PLATE 49

S. A. Grimes

Duval County, Fla., May 11, 1930

FLORIDA PINE WARBLER'S NEST

PLATE 50

Oscoda County, Mich., June 23, 1932

Crawford County, Mich., June 24, 1938

KIRTLAND'S WARBLER. FEMALES

PLATE 51

B. W. Baker

L. H. Walkinshaw

Crawford County, Mich., June 19, 1944

Crawford County, Mich., July 21, 1944

KIRTLAND'S WARBLER, MALES

PLATE 52

Montmorency County, Mich., June 16, 1936 Josselyn Van Tyne

Michigan, July 4, 1941 E. M. Brigham, Jr.

NESTING SITE AND NEST OF KIRTLAND'S WARBLER

PLATE 53

Tennessee, June 21, 1944   H. O. Todd

NEST OF NORTHERN PRAIRIE WARBLER
(In winged elm, 42 inches from ground)

PLATE 54

Crawford County, Mich., June 18, 1944   L. H. Walkinshaw

NORTHERN PRAIRIE WARBLER

PLATE 55

St. Johns County, Fla., June 12, 1922　　　　　　　　　　　　　　S. A. Grimes

FLORIDA PRAIRIE WARBLER'S NEST IN A BLACK MANGROVE

PLATE 56

W. V. Crich   Matane County, Quebec, June 15, 1939   W. J. Brown

WESTERN PALM WARBLER (LEFT) AND NEST OF YELLOW PALM WARBLER (RIGHT)

PLATE 57

Nest as originally found

Johnson City, Tenn., May 16, 1943   B. P. Tyler

Nest opened (note cowbird egg)

NEST OF EASTERN OVENBIRD

PLATE 58

EASTERN OVENBIRD AND NEST

PLATE 59

Verdi Burtch

Potter Swamp, N. Y., May 23, 1909

W. J. Brown

Matane County, Quebec, June 1925

NORTHERN SMALL-BILLED WATERTHRUSH AND NEST

PLATE 60

Leechburg, Pa., June 19, 1943   H. H. Harrison

LOUISIANA WATERTHRUSH

PLATE 61

Armstrong County, Pa., May 20, 1943

H. H. Harrison

NEST OF LOUISIANA WATERTHRUSH

PLATE 62

R. E. Lawrence

KENTUCKY WARBLER

Patuxent Wildlife Research Refuge, Md., July 8, 1945

PLATE 63

Aitkin County, Minn., June 13, 1929   N. L. Huff

HABITAT AND NEST OF CONNECTICUT WARBLER

PLATE 64

Yates County, N. Y., June 7, 1908   Verdi Burtch

NESTING SITE AND NEST OF MOURNING WARBLER

PLATE 65

A. Walker

W. L. Finley

Mulino, Oreg., May 29, 1912

Oregon

NESTS OF NORTHERN MACGILLIVRAY'S WARBLER

PLATE 66

H. H. Harrison

NORTHERN YELLOWTHROAT, MALE

Pymatuning, Pa., June 10, 1944

PLATE 67

Eliot Porter

Maine, 1945

NORTHERN YELLOWTHROAT, FEMALE, WITH YOUNG

PLATE 68

Logan County, Ill., June 6, 1913   A. D. Du Bois

NORTHERN YELLOWTHROAT'S NEST
(One cowbird egg showing)

PLATE 69

S. A. Grimes

S. A. Grimes

Duval County, Fla., May 22, 1932

Duval County, Fla., May 4, 1932

NESTING SITE AND NEST OF FLORIDA YELLOWTHROAT

PLATE 70

San Ignacio, Baja California, May 1928   Griffing Bancroft (Courtesy of *The Condor*)

EGGS AND NEST OF GOLDMAN'S PENINSULAR YELLOWTHROAT

PLATE **71**

Eliot Porter

EASTERN YELLOW-BREASTED CHAT, FEMALE, WITH YOUNG

Illinois, June 19, 1942

PLATE 72

Tennessee, July 9, 1944   H. O. Todd, Jr.

Huachuca Mountains, Ariz., May 26, 1922   A. C. Bent

NESTS OF EASTERN YELLOW-BREASTED CHAT (UPPER) AND RED-FACED WARBLER
(LOWER)

PLATE 73

Johnson County, Tenn., June 14, 1942   B. P. Tyler

NEST OF HOODED WARBLER
(Upper picture shows side of nest)

PLATE 74

H. H. Harrison

Armstrong County, Pa., June 8, 1942

HOODED WARBLER, MALE, WITH YOUNG

PLATE 75

Morristown, N. J.   R. T. Peterson

HOODED WARBLER, FEMALE

PLATE 76

Tabusintac, New Brunswick

B. S. Bowdish

NESTS OF WILSON'S PILEOLATED WARBLER

PLATE 77

Askinuk Mountains, Alaska, June 17, 1924   Herbert Brandt   Mono County, Calif., June 1940   J. S Rowley

NESTS OF NORTHERN PILEOLATED WARBLER (LEFT) AND GOLDEN PILEOLATED WARBLER (RIGHT)

PLATE 78

A. M. Bailey and R. J. Niedrach (Courtesy Colorado Museum of Natural History)

Yates County, N. Y., June 6, 1910   Verdi Burtch

GOLDEN PILEOLATED WARBLER (UPPER) AND NEST OF CANADA WARBLER (LOWER)

PLATE 79

Sand Lake, Ontario, June 24, 1945   H. M. Halliday

CANADA WARBLER, MALE

PLATE 80

Sand Lake, Ontario, June 24, 1945   H. M. Halliday

CANADA WARBLER, FEMALE

PLATE 81

Washington County, Tenn.   B. P. Tyler

Genesee County, N. Y., June 7, 1927   S. A. Grimes

NESTS OF SOUTHERN AMERICAN REDSTART

PLATE 82

Maine, June 1945   Eliot Porter

SOUTHERN AMERICAN REDSTART, MALE

PLATE 83

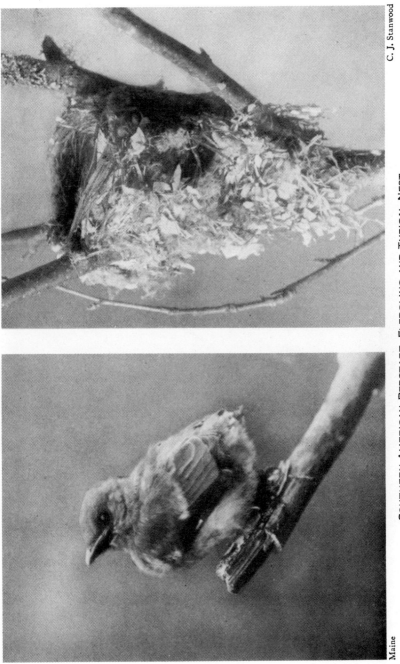

C. J. Stanwood

Maine

SOUTHERN AMERICAN REDSTART, FLEDGLING AND TYPICAL NEST

A CATALOGUE OF SELECTED DOVER BOOKS
IN ALL FIELDS OF INTEREST

A CATALOGUE OF SELECTED DOVER BOOKS
IN ALL FIELDS OF INTEREST

THE DEVIL'S DICTIONARY, Ambrose Bierce. Barbed, bitter, brilliant witticisms in the form of a dictionary. Best, most ferocious satire America has produced. 145pp. 20487-1 Pa. $1.50

ABSOLUTELY MAD INVENTIONS, A.E. Brown, H.A. Jeffcott. Hilarious, useless, or merely absurd inventions all granted patents by the U.S. Patent Office. Edible tie pin, mechanical hat tipper, etc. 57 illustrations. 125pp. 22596-8 Pa. $1.50

AMERICAN WILD FLOWERS COLORING BOOK, Paul Kennedy. Planned coverage of 48 most important wildflowers, from Rickett's collection; instructive as well as entertaining. Color versions on covers. 48pp. 8¼ x 11. 20095-7 Pa. $1.35

BIRDS OF AMERICA COLORING BOOK, John James Audubon. Rendered for coloring by Paul Kennedy. 46 of Audubon's noted illustrations: red-winged blackbird, cardinal, purple finch, towhee, etc. Original plates reproduced in full color on the covers. 48pp. 8¼ x 11. 23049-X Pa. $1.35

NORTH AMERICAN INDIAN DESIGN COLORING BOOK, Paul Kennedy. The finest examples from Indian masks, beadwork, pottery, etc. — selected and redrawn for coloring (with identifications) by well-known illustrator Paul Kennedy. 48pp. 8¼ x 11. 21125-8 Pa. $1.35

UNIFORMS OF THE AMERICAN REVOLUTION COLORING BOOK, Peter Copeland. 31 lively drawings reproduce whole panorama of military attire; each uniform has complete instructions for accurate coloring. (Not in the Pictorial Archives Series). 64pp. 8¼ x 11. 21850-3 Pa. $1.50

THE WONDERFUL WIZARD OF OZ COLORING BOOK, L. Frank Baum. Color the Yellow Brick Road and much more in 61 drawings adapted from W.W. Denslow's originals, accompanied by abridged version of text. Dorothy, Toto, Oz and the Emerald City. 61 illustrations. 64pp. 8¼ x 11. 20452-9 Pa. $1.50

CUT AND COLOR PAPER MASKS, Michael Grater. Clowns, animals, funny faces ... simply color them in, cut them out, and put them together and you have 9 paper masks to play with and enjoy. Complete instructions. Assembled masks shown in full color on the covers. 32pp. 8¼ x 11. 23171-2 Pa. $1.50

STAINED GLASS CHRISTMAS ORNAMENT COLORING BOOK, Carol Belanger Grafton. Brighten your Christmas season with over 100 Christmas ornaments done in a stained glass effect on translucent paper. Color them in and then hang at windows, from lights, anywhere. 32pp. 8¼ x 11. 20707-2 Pa. $1.75

MOTHER GOOSE'S MELODIES. Facsimile of fabulously rare Munroe and Francis "copyright 1833" Boston edition. Familiar and unusual rhymes, wonderful old woodcut illustrations. Edited by E.F. Bleiler. 128pp. 4½ x 6⅜. 22577-1 Pa. $1.00

MOTHER GOOSE IN HIEROGLYPHICS. Favorite nursery rhymes presented in rebus form for children. Fascinating 1849 edition reproduced in toto, with key. Introduction by E.F. Bleiler. About 400 woodcuts. 64pp. 6⅞ x 5¼. 20745-5 Pa. $1.00

PETER PIPER'S PRACTICAL PRINCIPLES OF PLAIN & PERFECT PRONUNCIATION. Alliterative jingles and tongue-twisters. Reproduction in full of 1830 first American edition. 25 spirited woodcuts. 32pp. 4½ x 6⅜. 22560-7 Pa. $1.00

MARMADUKE MULTIPLY'S MERRY METHOD OF MAKING MINOR MATHEMATICIANS. Fellow to Peter Piper, it teaches multiplication table by catchy rhymes and woodcuts. 1841 Munroe & Francis edition. Edited by E.F. Bleiler. 103pp. 4⅝ x 6.
22773-1 Pa. $1.25
20171-6 Clothbd. $3.00

THE NIGHT BEFORE CHRISTMAS, Clement Moore. Full text, and woodcuts from original 1848 book. Also critical, historical material. 19 illustrations. 40pp. 4⅝ x 6. 22797-9 Pa. $1.00

THE KING OF THE GOLDEN RIVER, John Ruskin. Victorian children's classic of three brothers, their attempts to reach the Golden River, what becomes of them. Facsimile of original 1889 edition. 22 illustrations. 56pp. 4⅝ x 6⅜.
20066-3 Pa. $1.25

DREAMS OF THE RAREBIT FIEND, Winsor McCay. Pioneer cartoon strip, unexcelled for beauty, imagination, in 60 full sequences. Incredible technical virtuosity, wonderful visual wit. Historical introduction. 62pp. 8⅜ x 11¼. 21347-1 Pa. $2.00

THE KATZENJAMMER KIDS, Rudolf Dirks. In full color, 14 strips from 1906-7; full of imagination, characteristic humor. Classic of great historical importance. Introduction by August Derleth. 32pp. 9¼ x 12¼. 23005-8 Pa. $2.00

LITTLE ORPHAN ANNIE AND LITTLE ORPHAN ANNIE IN COSMIC CITY, Harold Gray. Two great sequences from the early strips: our curly-haired heroine defends the Warbucks' financial empire and, then, takes on meanie Phineas P. Pinchpenny. Leapin' lizards! 178pp. 6⅛ x 8⅜. 23107-0 Pa. $2.00

WHEN A FELLER NEEDS A FRIEND, Clare Briggs. 122 cartoons by one of the greatest newspaper cartoonists of the early 20th century — about growing up, making a living, family life, daily frustrations and occasional triumphs. 121pp. 8½ x 9½.
23148-8 Pa. $2.50

THE BEST OF GLUYAS WILLIAMS. 100 drawings by one of America's finest cartoonists: The Day a Cake of Ivory Soap Sank at Proctor & Gamble's, At the Life Insurance Agents' Banquet, and many other gems from the 20's and 30's. 118pp. 8⅜ x 11¼. 22737-5 Pa. $2.50

THE ART DECO STYLE, ed. by Theodore Menten. Furniture, jewelry, metalwork, ceramics, fabrics, lighting fixtures, interior decors, exteriors, graphics from pure French sources. Best sampling around. Over 400 photographs. 183pp. 8⅜ x 11¼.
22824-X Pa. $4.00

THE GENTLEMAN AND CABINET MAKER'S DIRECTOR, Thomas Chippendale. Full reprint, 1762 style book, most influential of all time; chairs, tables, sofas, mirrors, cabinets, etc. 200 plates, plus 24 photographs of surviving pieces. 249pp. 9⅞ x 12¾.
21601-2 Pa. $5.00

PINE FURNITURE OF EARLY NEW ENGLAND, Russell H. Kettell. Basic book. Thorough historical text, plus 200 illustrations of boxes, highboys, candlesticks, desks, etc. 477pp. 7⅞ x 10¾.
20145-7 Clothbd. $12.50

ORIENTAL RUGS, ANTIQUE AND MODERN, Walter A. Hawley. Persia, Turkey, Caucasus, Central Asia, China, other traditions. Best general survey of all aspects: styles and periods, manufacture, uses, symbols and their interpretation, and identification. 96 illustrations, 11 in color. 320pp. 6⅛ x 9¼.
22366-3 Pa. $5.00

DECORATIVE ANTIQUE IRONWORK, Henry R. d'Allemagne. Photographs of 4500 iron artifacts from world's finest collection, Rouen. Hinges, locks, candelabra, weapons, lighting devices, clocks, tools, from Roman times to mid-19th century. Nothing else comparable to it. 420pp. 9 x 12.
22082-6 Pa. $8.50

THE COMPLETE BOOK OF DOLL MAKING AND COLLECTING, Catherine Christopher. Instructions, patterns for dozens of dolls, from rag doll on up to elaborate, historically accurate figures. Mould faces, sew clothing, make doll houses, etc. Also collecting information. Many illustrations. 288pp. 6 x 9. 22066-4 Pa. $3.00

ANTIQUE PAPER DOLLS: 1915-1920, edited by Arnold Arnold. 7 antique cut-out dolls and 24 costumes from 1915-1920, selected by Arnold Arnold from his collection of rare children's books and entertainments, all in full color. 32pp. 9¼ x 12¼.
23176-3 Pa. $2.00

ANTIQUE PAPER DOLLS: THE EDWARDIAN ERA, Epinal. Full-color reproductions of two historic series of paper dolls that show clothing styles in 1908 and at the beginning of the First World War. 8 two-sided, stand-up dolls and 32 complete, two-sided costumes. Full instructions for assembling included. 32pp. 9¼ x 12¼.
23175-5 Pa. $2.00

A HISTORY OF COSTUME, Carl Köhler, Emma von Sichardt. Egypt, Babylon, Greece up through 19th century Europe; based on surviving pieces, art works, etc. Full text and 595 illustrations, including many clear, measured patterns for reproducing historic costume. Practical. 464pp.
21030-8 Pa. $4.00

EARLY AMERICAN LOCOMOTIVES, John H. White, Jr. Finest locomotive engravings from late 19th century: historical (1804-1874), main-line (after 1870), special, foreign, etc. 147 plates. 200pp. 11⅜ x 8¼.
22772-3 Pa. $3.50

AUSTRIAN COOKING AND BAKING, Gretel Beer. Authentic thick soups, wiener schnitzel, veal goulash, more, plus dumplings, puff pastries, nut cakes, sacher tortes, other great Austrian desserts. 224pp. USO 23220-4 Pa. $2.50

CHEESES OF THE WORLD, U.S.D.A. Dictionary of cheeses containing descriptions of over 400 varieties of cheese from common Cheddar to exotic Surati. Up to two pages are given to important cheeses like Camembert, Cottage, Edam, etc. 151pp. 22831-2 Pa. $1.50

TRITTON'S GUIDE TO BETTER WINE AND BEER MAKING FOR BEGINNERS, S.M. Tritton. All you need to know to make family-sized quantities of over 100 types of grape, fruit, herb, vegetable wines; plus beers, mead, cider, more. 11 illustrations. 157pp. USO 22528-3 Pa. $2.00

DECORATIVE LABELS FOR HOME CANNING, PRESERVING, AND OTHER HOUSEHOLD AND GIFT USES, Theodore Menten. 128 gummed, perforated labels, beautifully printed in 2 colors. 12 versions in traditional, Art Nouveau, Art Deco styles. Adhere to metal, glass, wood, most plastics. 24pp. 8¼ x 11. 23219-0 Pa. $2.00

FIVE ACRES AND INDEPENDENCE, Maurice G. Kains. Great back-to-the-land classic explains basics of self-sufficient farming: economics, plants, crops, animals, orchards, soils, land selection, host of other necessary things. Do not confuse with skimpy faddist literature; Kains was one of America's greatest agriculturalists. 95 illustrations. 397pp. 20974-1 Pa. $2.95

GROWING VEGETABLES IN THE HOME GARDEN, U.S. Dept. of Agriculture. Basic information on site, soil conditions, selection of vegetables, planting, cultivation, gathering. Up-to-date, concise, authoritative. Covers 60 vegetables. 30 illustrations. 123pp. 23167-4 Pa. $1.35

FRUITS FOR THE HOME GARDEN, Dr. U.P. Hedrick. A chapter covering each type of garden fruit, advice on plant care, soils, grafting, pruning, sprays, transplanting, and much more! Very full. 53 illustrations. 175pp. 22944-0 Pa. $2.50

GARDENING ON SANDY SOIL IN NORTH TEMPERATE AREAS, Christine Kelway. Is your soil too light, too sandy? Improve your soil, select plants that survive under such conditions. Both vegetables and flowers. 42 photos. 148pp.
USO 23199-2 Pa. $2.50

THE FRAGRANT GARDEN: A BOOK ABOUT SWEET SCENTED FLOWERS AND LEAVES, Louise Beebe Wilder. Fullest, best book on growing plants for their fragrances. Descriptions of hundreds of plants, both well-known and overlooked. 407pp.
23071-6 Pa. $3.50

EASY GARDENING WITH DROUGHT-RESISTANT PLANTS, Arno and Irene Nehrling. Authoritative guide to gardening with plants that require a minimum of water: seashore, desert, and rock gardens; house plants; annuals and perennials; much more. 190 illustrations. 320pp. 23230-1 Pa. $3.50

How to Solve Chess Problems, Kenneth S. Howard. Practical suggestions on problem solving for very beginners. 58 two-move problems, 46 3-movers, 8 4-movers for practice, plus hints. 171pp.   20748-X Pa. $2.00

A Guide to Fairy Chess, Anthony Dickins. 3-D chess, 4-D chess, chess on a cylindrical board, reflecting pieces that bounce off edges, cooperative chess, retrograde chess, maximummers, much more. Most based on work of great Dawson. Full handbook, 100 problems. 66pp. 7⅞ x 10¾.   22687-5 Pa. $2.00

Win at Backgammon, Millard Hopper. Best opening moves, running game, blocking game, back game, tables of odds, etc. Hopper makes the game clear enough for anyone to play, and win. 43 diagrams. 111pp.   22894-0 Pa. $1.50

Bidding a Bridge Hand, Terence Reese. Master player "thinks out loud" the binding of 75 hands that defy point count systems. Organized by bidding problem—no-fit situations, overbidding, underbidding, cueing your defense, etc. 254pp.   EBE 22830-4 Pa. $2.50

The Precision Bidding System in Bridge, C.C. Wei, edited by Alan Truscott. Inventor of precision bidding presents average hands and hands from actual play, including games from 1969 Bermuda Bowl where system emerged. 114 exercises. 116pp.   21171-1 Pa. $1.75

Learn Magic, Henry Hay. 20 simple, easy-to-follow lessons on magic for the new magician: illusions, card tricks, silks, sleights of hand, coin manipulations, escapes, and more —all with a minimum amount of equipment. Final chapter explains the great stage illusions. 92 illustrations. 285pp.   21238-6 Pa. $2.95

The New Magician's Manual, Walter B. Gibson. Step-by-step instructions and clear illustrations guide the novice in mastering 36 tricks; much equipment supplied on 16 pages of cut-out materials. 36 additional tricks. 64 illustrations. 159pp. 6⅝ x 10.   23113-5 Pa. $3.00

Professional Magic for Amateurs, Walter B. Gibson. 50 easy, effective tricks used by professionals —cards, string, tumblers, handkerchiefs, mental magic, etc. 63 illustrations. 223pp.   23012-0 Pa. $2.50

Card Manipulations, Jean Hugard. Very rich collection of manipulations; has taught thousands of fine magicians tricks that are really workable, eye-catching. Easily followed, serious work. Over 200 illustrations. 163pp. 20539-8 Pa. $2.00

Abbott's Encyclopedia of Rope Tricks for Magicians, Stewart James. Complete reference book for amateur and professional magicians containing more than 150 tricks involving knots, penetrations, cut and restored rope, etc. 510 illustrations. Reprint of 3rd edition. 400pp.   23206-9 Pa. $3.50

The Secrets of Houdini, J.C. Cannell. Classic study of Houdini's incredible magic, exposing closely-kept professional secrets and revealing, in general terms, the whole art of stage magic. 67 illustrations. 279pp.   22913-0 Pa. $2.50

THE JOURNAL OF HENRY D. THOREAU, edited by Bradford Torrey, F.H. Allen. Complete reprinting of 14 volumes, 1837-1861, over two million words; the sourcebooks for Walden, etc. Definitive. All original sketches, plus 75 photographs. Introduction by Walter Harding. Total of 1804pp. 8½ x 12¼.
20312-3, 20313-1 Clothbd., Two vol. set $50.00

MASTERS OF THE DRAMA, John Gassner. Most comprehensive history of the drama, every tradition from Greeks to modern Europe and America, including Orient. Covers 800 dramatists, 2000 plays; biography, plot summaries, criticism, theatre history, etc. 77 illustrations. 890pp. 20100-7 Clothbd. $10.00

GHOST AND HORROR STORIES OF AMBROSE BIERCE, Ambrose Bierce. 23 modern horror stories: The Eyes of the Panther, The Damned Thing, etc., plus the dream-essay Visions of the Night. Edited by E.F. Bleiler. 199pp. 20767-6 Pa. $2.00

BEST GHOST STORIES, Algernon Blackwood. 13 great stories by foremost British 20th century supernaturalist. The Willows, The Wendigo, Ancient Sorceries, others. Edited by E.F. Bleiler. 366pp. USO 22977-7 Pa. $3.00

THE BEST TALES OF HOFFMANN, E.T.A. Hoffmann. 10 of Hoffmann's most important stories, in modern re-editings of standard translations: Nutcracker and the King of Mice, The Golden Flowerpot, etc. 7 illustrations by Hoffmann. Edited by E.F. Bleiler. 458pp. 21793-0 Pa. $3.95

BEST GHOST STORIES OF J.S. LEFANU, J. Sheridan LeFanu. 16 stories by greatest Victorian master: Green Tea, Carmilla, Haunted Baronet, The Familiar, etc. Mostly unavailable elsewhere. Edited by E.F. Bleiler. 8 illustrations. 467pp. 20415-4 Pa. $4.00

SUPERNATURAL HORROR IN LITERATURE, H.P. Lovecraft. Great modern American supernaturalist brilliantly surveys history of genre to 1930's, summarizing, evaluating scores of books. Necessary for every student, lover of form. Introduction by E.F. Bleiler. 111pp. 20105-8 Pa. $1.50

THREE GOTHIC NOVELS, ed. by E.F. Bleiler. Full texts Castle of Otranto, Walpole; Vathek, Beckford; The Vampyre, Polidori; Fragment of a Novel, Lord Byron. 331pp. 21232-7 Pa. $3.00

SEVEN SCIENCE FICTION NOVELS, H.G. Wells. Full novels. First Men in the Moon, Island of Dr. Moreau, War of the Worlds, Food of the Gods, Invisible Man, Time Machine, In the Days of the Comet. A basic science-fiction library. 1015pp. USO 20264-X Clothbd. $6.00

LADY AUDLEY'S SECRET, Mary E. Braddon. Great Victorian mystery classic, beautifully plotted, suspenseful; praised by Thackeray, Boucher, Starrett, others. What happened to beautiful, vicious Lady Audley's husband? Introduction by Norman Donaldson. 286pp. 23011-2 Pa. $3.00

MANUAL OF THE TREES OF NORTH AMERICA, Charles S. Sargent. The basic survey of every native tree and tree-like shrub, 717 species in all. Extremely full descriptions, information on habitat, growth, locales, economics, etc. Necessary to every serious tree lover. Over 100 finding keys. 783 illustrations. Total of 986pp.
20277-1, 20278-X Pa., Two vol. set $8.00

BIRDS OF THE NEW YORK AREA, John Bull. Indispensable guide to more than 400 species within a hundred-mile radius of Manhattan. Information on range, status, breeding, migration, distribution trends, etc. Foreword by Roger Tory Peterson. 17 drawings; maps. 540pp.
23222-0 Pa. $6.00

THE SEA-BEACH AT EBB-TIDE, Augusta Foote Arnold. Identify hundreds of marine plants and animals: algae, seaweeds, squids, crabs, corals, etc. Descriptions cover food, life cycle, size, shape, habitat. Over 600 drawings. 490pp.
21949-6 Pa. $4.00

THE MOTH BOOK, William J. Holland. Identify more than 2,000 moths of North America. General information, precise species descriptions. 623 illustrations plus 48 color plates show almost all species, full size. 1968 edition. Still the basic book. Total of 551pp. 6½ x 9¼.
21948-8 Pa. $6.00

AN INTRODUCTION TO THE REPTILES AND AMPHIBIANS OF THE UNITED STATES, Percy A. Morris. All lizards, crocodiles, turtles, snakes, toads, frogs; life history, identification, habits, suitability as pets, etc. Non-technical, but sound and broad. 130 photos. 253pp.
22982-3 Pa. $3.00

OLD NEW YORK IN EARLY PHOTOGRAPHS, edited by Mary Black. Your only chance to see New York City as it was 1853-1906, through 196 wonderful photographs from N.Y. Historical Society. Great Blizzard, Lincoln's funeral procession, great buildings. 228pp. 9 x 12.
22907-6 Pa. $6.00

THE AMERICAN REVOLUTION, A PICTURE SOURCEBOOK, John Grafton. Wonderful Bicentennial picture source, with 411 illustrations (contemporary and 19th century) showing battles, personalities, maps, events, flags, posters, soldier's life, ships, etc. all captioned and explained. A wonderful browsing book, supplement to other historical reading. 160pp. 9 x 12.
23226-3 Pa. $4.00

PERSONAL NARRATIVE OF A PILGRIMAGE TO AL-MADINAH AND MECCAH, Richard Burton. Great travel classic by remarkably colorful personality. Burton, disguised as a Moroccan, visited sacred shrines of Islam, narrowly escaping death. Wonderful observations of Islamic life, customs, personalities. 47 illustrations. Total of 959pp.
21217-3, 21218-1 Pa., Two vol. set $7.00

INCIDENTS OF TRAVEL IN CENTRAL AMERICA, CHIAPAS, AND YUCATAN, John L. Stephens. Almost single-handed discovery of Maya culture; exploration of ruined cities, monuments, temples; customs of Indians. 115 drawings. 892pp.
22404-X, 22405-8 Pa., Two vol. set $8.00

150 MASTERPIECES OF DRAWING, edited by Anthony Toney. 150 plates, early 15th century to end of 18th century; Rembrandt, Michelangelo, Dürer, Fragonard, Watteau, Wouwerman, many others. 150pp. 8⅜ x 11¼.   21032-4 Pa. $3.50

THE GOLDEN AGE OF THE POSTER, Hayward and Blanche Cirker. 70 extraordinary posters in full colors, from Maîtres de l'Affiche, Mucha, Lautrec, Bradley, Cheret, Beardsley, many others. 9⅜ x 12¼.   22753-7 Pa. $4.95
21718-3 Clothbd. $7.95

SIMPLICISSIMUS, selection, translations and text by Stanley Appelbaum. 180 satirical drawings, 16 in full color, from the famous German weekly magazine in the years 1896 to 1926. 24 artists included: Grosz, Kley, Pascin, Kubin, Kollwitz, plus Heine, Thöny, Bruno Paul, others. 172pp. 8½ x 12¼.   23098-8 Pa. $5.00
23099-6 Clothbd. $10.00

THE EARLY WORK OF AUBREY BEARDSLEY, Aubrey Beardsley. 157 plates, 2 in color: Manon Lescaut, Madame Bovary, Morte d'Arthur, Salome, other. Introduction by H. Marillier. 175pp. 8½ x 11.   21816-3 Pa. $3.50

THE LATER WORK OF AUBREY BEARDSLEY, Aubrey Beardsley. Exotic masterpieces of full maturity: Venus and Tannhäuser, Lysistrata, Rape of the Lock, Volpone, Savoy material, etc. 174 plates, 2 in color. 176pp. 8½ x 11.   21817-1 Pa. $3.75

DRAWINGS OF WILLIAM BLAKE, William Blake. 92 plates from Book of Job, Divine Comedy, Paradise Lost, visionary heads, mythological figures, Laocoön, etc. Selection, introduction, commentary by Sir Geoffrey Keynes. 178pp. 8½ x 11.
22303-5 Pa. $3.50

LONDON: A PILGRIMAGE, Gustave Doré, Blanchard Jerrold. Squalor, riches, misery, beauty of mid-Victorian metropolis; 55 wonderful plates, 125 other illustrations, full social, cultural text by Jerrold. 191pp. of text. 8⅛ x 11.
22306-X Pa. $5.00

THE COMPLETE WOODCUTS OF ALBRECHT DÜRER, edited by Dr. W. Kurth. 346 in all: Old Testament, St. Jerome, Passion, Life of Virgin, Apocalypse, many others. Introduction by Campbell Dodgson. 285pp. 8½ x 12¼.   21097-9 Pa. $6.00

THE DISASTERS OF WAR, Francisco Goya. 83 etchings record horrors of Napoleonic wars in Spain and war in general. Reprint of 1st edition, plus 3 additional plates. Introduction by Philip Hofer. 97pp. 9⅜ x 8¼.   21872-4 Pa. $2.50

ENGRAVINGS OF HOGARTH, William Hogarth. 101 of Hogarth's greatest works: Rake's Progress, Harlot's Progress, Illustrations for Hudibras, Midnight Modern Conversation, Before and After, Beer Street and Gin Lane, many more. Full commentary. 256pp. 11 x 14.   22479-1 Pa. $6.00
23023-6 Clothbd. $13.50

PRIMITIVE ART, Franz Boas. Great anthropologist on ceramics, textiles, wood, stone, metal, etc.; patterns, technology, symbols, styles. All areas, but fullest on Northwest Coast Indians. 350 illustrations. 378pp.   20025-6 Pa. $3.50

JEWISH GREETING CARDS, Ed Sibbett, Jr. 16 cards to cut and color. Three say "Happy Chanukah," one "Happy New Year," others have no message, show stars of David, Torahs, wine cups, other traditional themes. 16 envelopes. 8¼ x 11.
23225-5 Pa. $2.00

AUBREY BEARDSLEY GREETING CARD BOOK, Aubrey Beardsley. Edited by Theodore Menten. 16 elegant yet inexpensive greeting cards let you combine your own sentiments with subtle Art Nouveau lines. 16 different Aubrey Beardsley designs that you can color or not, as you wish. 16 envelopes. 64pp. 8¼ x 11.
23173-9 Pa. $2.00

RECREATIONS IN THE THEORY OF NUMBERS, Albert Beiler. Number theory, an inexhaustible source of puzzles, recreations, for beginners and advanced. Divisors, perfect numbers. scales of notation, etc. 349pp.   21096-0 Pa. $2.50

AMUSEMENTS IN MATHEMATICS, Henry E. Dudeney. One of largest puzzle collections, based on algebra, arithmetic, permutations, probability, plane figure dissection, properties of numbers, by one of world's foremost puzzlists. Solutions. 450 illustrations. 258pp.   20473-1 Pa. $2.75

MATHEMATICS, MAGIC AND MYSTERY, Martin Gardner. Puzzle editor for Scientific American explains math behind: card tricks, stage mind reading, coin and match tricks, counting out games, geometric dissections. Probability, sets, theory of numbers, clearly explained. Plus more than 400 tricks, guaranteed to work. 135 illustrations. 176pp.   20335-2 Pa. $2.00

BEST MATHEMATICAL PUZZLES OF SAM LOYD, edited by Martin Gardner. Bizarre, original, whimsical puzzles by America's greatest puzzler. From fabulously rare Cyclopedia, including famous 14-15 puzzles, the Horse of a Different Color, 115 more. Elementary math. 150 illustrations. 167pp.   20498-7 Pa. $2.00

MATHEMATICAL PUZZLES FOR BEGINNERS AND ENTHUSIASTS, Geoffrey Mott-Smith. 189 puzzles from easy to difficult involving arithmetic, logic, algebra, properties of digits, probability. Explanation of math behind puzzles. 135 illustrations. 248pp.   20198-8 Pa. $2.00

BIG BOOK OF MAZES AND LABYRINTHS, Walter Shepherd. Classical, solid, and ripple mazes; short path and avoidance labyrinths; more — 50 mazes and labyrinths in all. 12 other figures. Full solutions. 112pp. 8⅛ x 11.   22951-3 Pa. $2.00

COIN GAMES AND PUZZLES, Maxey Brooke. 60 puzzles, games and stunts — from Japan, Korea, Africa and the ancient world, by Dudeney and the other great puzzlers, as well as Maxey Brooke's own creations. Full solutions. 67 illustrations. 94pp.   22893-2 Pa. $1.25

HAND SHADOWS TO BE THROWN UPON THE WALL, Henry Bursill. Wonderful Victorian novelty tells how to make flying birds, dog, goose, deer, and 14 others. 32pp. 6½ x 9¼.   21779-5 Pa. $1.00

THE FITZWILLIAM VIRGINAL BOOK, edited by J. Fuller Maitland, W.B. Squire. Famous early 17th century collection of keyboard music, 300 works by Morley, Byrd, Bull, Gibbons, etc. Modern notation. Total of 938pp. 8⅜ x 11.
ECE 21068-5, 21069-3 Pa., Two vol. set $12.00

COMPLETE STRING QUARTETS, Wolfgang A. Mozart. Breitkopf and Härtel edition. All 23 string quartets plus alternate slow movement to K156. Study score. 277pp. 9⅜ x 12¼.   22372-8 Pa. $6.00

COMPLETE SONG CYCLES, Franz Schubert. Complete piano, vocal music of Die Schöne Müllerin, Die Winterreise, Schwanengesang. Also Drinker English singing translations. Breitkopf and Härtel edition. 217pp. 9⅜ x 12¼.
22649-2 Pa. $4.00

THE COMPLETE PRELUDES AND ETUDES FOR PIANOFORTE SOLO, Alexander Scriabin. All the preludes and etudes including many perfectly spun miniatures. Edited by K.N. Igumnov and Y.I. Mil'shteyn. 250pp. 9 x 12.   22919-X Pa. $5.00

TRISTAN UND ISOLDE, Richard Wagner. Full orchestral score with complete instrumentation. Do not confuse with piano reduction. Commentary by Felix Mottl, great Wagnerian conductor and scholar. Study score. 655pp. 8⅛ x 11.
22915-7 Pa. $10.00

FAVORITE SONGS OF THE NINETIES, ed. Robert Fremont. Full reproduction, including covers, of 88 favorites: Ta-Ra-Ra-Boom-De-Aye, The Band Played On, Bird in a Gilded Cage, Under the Bamboo Tree, After the Ball, etc. 401pp. 9 x 12.
EBE 21536-9 Pa. $6.95

SOUSA'S GREAT MARCHES IN PIANO TRANSCRIPTION: ORIGINAL SHEET MUSIC OF 23 WORKS, John Philip Sousa. Selected by Lester S. Levy. Playing edition includes: The Stars and Stripes Forever, The Thunderer, The Gladiator, King Cotton, Washington Post, much more. 24 illustrations. 111pp. 9 x 12.
USO 23132-1 Pa. $3.50

CLASSIC PIANO RAGS, selected with an introduction by Rudi Blesh. Best ragtime music (1897-1922) by Scott Joplin, James Scott, Joseph F. Lamb, Tom Turpin, 9 others. Printed from best original sheet music, plus covers. 364pp. 9 x 12.
EBE 20469-3 Pa. $6.95

ANALYSIS OF CHINESE CHARACTERS, C.D. Wilder, J.H. Ingram. 1000 most important characters analyzed according to primitives, phonetics, historical development. Traditional method offers mnemonic aid to beginner, intermediate student of Chinese, Japanese. 365pp.   23045-7 Pa. $4.00

MODERN CHINESE: A BASIC COURSE, Faculty of Peking University. Self study, classroom course in modern Mandarin. Records contain phonetics, vocabulary, sentences, lessons. 249 page book contains all recorded text, translations, grammar, vocabulary, exercises. Best course on market. 3 12" 33⅓ monaural records, book, album.   98832-5 Set $12.50

SLEEPING BEAUTY, illustrated by Arthur Rackham. Perhaps the fullest, most delightful version ever, told by C.S. Evans. Rackham's best work. 49 illustrations. 110pp. 7⅞ x 10¾. 22756-1 Pa. $2.00

THE WONDERFUL WIZARD OF OZ, L. Frank Baum. Facsimile in full color of America's finest children's classic. Introduction by Martin Gardner. 143 illustrations by W.W. Denslow. 267pp. 20691-2 Pa. $2.50

GOOPS AND HOW TO BE THEM, Gelett Burgess. Classic tongue-in-cheek masquerading as etiquette book. 87 verses, 170 cartoons as Goops demonstrate virtues of table manners, neatness, courtesy, more. 88pp. 6½ x 9¼. 22233-0 Pa. $1.50

THE BROWNIES, THEIR BOOK, Palmer Cox. Small as mice, cunning as foxes, exuberant, mischievous, Brownies go to zoo, toy shop, seashore, circus, more. 24 verse adventures. 266 illustrations. 144pp. 6⅝ x 9¼. 21265-3 Pa. $1.75

BILLY WHISKERS: THE AUTOBIOGRAPHY OF A GOAT, Frances Trego Montgomery. Escapades of that rambunctious goat. Favorite from turn of the century America. 24 illustrations. 259pp. 22345-0 Pa. $2.75

THE ROCKET BOOK, Peter Newell. Fritz, janitor's kid, sets off rocket in basement of apartment house; an ingenious hole punched through every page traces course of rocket. 22 duotone drawings, verses. 48pp. 6⅞ x 8⅜. 22044-3 Pa. $1.50

PECK'S BAD BOY AND HIS PA, George W. Peck. Complete double-volume of great American childhood classic. Hennery's ingenious pranks against outraged pomposity of pa and the grocery man. 97 illustrations. Introduction by E.F. Bleiler. 347pp. 20497-9 Pa. $2.50

THE TALE OF PETER RABBIT, Beatrix Potter. The inimitable Peter's terrifying adventure in Mr. McGregor's garden, with all 27 wonderful, full-color Potter illustrations. 55pp. 4¼ x 5½. USO 22827-4 Pa. $1.00

THE TALE OF MRS. TIGGY-WINKLE, Beatrix Potter. Your child will love this story about a very special hedgehog and all 27 wonderful, full-color Potter illustrations. 57pp. 4¼ x 5½. USO 20546-0 Pa. $1.00

THE TALE OF BENJAMIN BUNNY, Beatrix Potter. Peter Rabbit's cousin coaxes him back into Mr. McGregor's garden for a whole new set of adventures. A favorite with children. All 27 full-color illustrations. 59pp. 4¼ x 5½. USO 21102-9 Pa. $1.00

THE MERRY ADVENTURES OF ROBIN HOOD, Howard Pyle. Facsimile of original (1883) edition, finest modern version of English outlaw's adventures. 23 illustrations by Pyle. 296pp. 6½ x 9¼. 22043-5 Pa. $2.75

TWO LITTLE SAVAGES, Ernest Thompson Seton. Adventures of two boys who lived as Indians; explaining Indian ways, woodlore, pioneer methods. 293 illustrations. 286pp. 20985-7 Pa. $3.00

MODERN CHESS STRATEGY, Ludek Pachman. The use of the queen, the active king, exchanges, pawn play, the center, weak squares, etc. Section on rook alone worth price of the book. Stress on the moderns. Often considered the most important book on strategy. 314pp. 20290-9 Pa. $3.00

CHESS STRATEGY, Edward Lasker. One of half-dozen great theoretical works in chess, shows principles of action above and beyond moves. Acclaimed by Capablanca, Keres, etc. 282pp. USO 20528-2 Pa. $2.50

CHESS PRAXIS, THE PRAXIS OF MY SYSTEM, Aron Nimzovich. Founder of hyper-modern chess explains his profound, influential theories that have dominated much of 20th century chess. 109 illustrative games. 369pp. 20296-8 Pa. $3.50

HOW TO PLAY THE CHESS OPENINGS, Eugene Znosko-Borovsky. Clear, profound examinations of just what each opening is intended to do and how opponent can counter. Many sample games, questions and answers. 147pp. 22795-2 Pa. $2.00

THE ART OF CHESS COMBINATION, Eugene Znosko-Borovsky. Modern explanation of principles, varieties, techniques and ideas behind them, illustrated with many examples from great players. 212pp. 20583-5 Pa. $2.00

COMBINATIONS: THE HEART OF CHESS, Irving Chernev. Step-by-step explanation of intricacies of combinative play. 356 combinations by Tarrasch, Botvinnik, Keres, Steinitz, Anderssen, Morphy, Marshall, Capablanca, others, all annotated. 245 pp. 21744-2 Pa. $2.50

HOW TO PLAY CHESS ENDINGS, Eugene Znosko-Borovsky. Thorough instruction manual by fine teacher analyzes each piece individually; many common endgame situations. Examines games by Steinitz, Alekhine, Lasker, others. Emphasis on understanding. 288pp. 21170-3 Pa. $2.75

MORPHY'S GAMES OF CHESS, Philip W. Sergeant. Romantic history, 54 games of greatest player of all time against Anderssen, Bird, Paulsen, Harrwitz; 52 games at odds; 52 blindfold; 100 consultation, informal, other games. Analyses by Anderssen, Steinitz, Morphy himself. 352pp. 20386-7 Pa. $2.75

500 MASTER GAMES OF CHESS, S. Tartakower, J. du Mont. Vast collection of great chess games from 1798-1938, with much material nowhere else readily available. Fully annotated, arranged by opening for easier study. 665pp. 23208-5 Pa. $6.00

THE SOVIET SCHOOL OF CHESS, Alexander Kotov and M. Yudovich. Authoritative work on modern Russian chess. History, conceptual background. 128 fully annotated games (most unavailable elsewhere) by Botvinnik, Keres, Smyslov, Tal, Petrosian, Spassky, more. 390pp. 20026-4 Pa. $3.95

WONDERS AND CURIOSITIES OF CHESS, Irving Chernev. A lifetime's accumulation of such wonders and curiosities as the longest won game, shortest game, chess problem with mate in 1220 moves, and much more unusual material — 356 items in all, over 160 complete games. 146 diagrams. 203pp. 23007-4 Pa. $3.50

THE BEST DR. THORNDYKE DETECTIVE STORIES, R. Austin Freeman. The Case of Oscar Brodski, The Moabite Cipher, and 5 other favorites featuring the great scientific detective, plus his long-believed-lost first adventure — 31 New Inn — reprinted here for the first time. Edited by E.F. Bleiler. USO 20388-3 Pa. $3.00

BEST "THINKING MACHINE" DETECTIVE STORIES, Jacques Futrelle. The Problem of Cell 13 and 11 other stories about Prof. Augustus S.F.X. Van Dusen, including two "lost" stories. First reprinting of several. Edited by E.F. Bleiler. 241pp.
20537-1 Pa. $3.00

UNCLE SILAS, J. Sheridan LeFanu. Victorian Gothic mystery novel, considered by many best of period, even better than Collins or Dickens. Wonderful psychological terror. Introduction by Frederick Shroyer. 436pp.   21715-9 Pa. $4.00

BEST DR. POGGIOLI DETECTIVE STORIES, T.S. Stribling. 15 best stories from EQMM and The Saint offer new adventures in Mexico, Florida, Tennessee hills as Poggioli unravels mysteries and combats Count Jalacki. 217pp. 23227-1 Pa. $3.00

EIGHT DIME NOVELS, selected with an introduction by E.F. Bleiler. Adventures of Old King Brady, Frank James, Nick Carter, Deadwood Dick, Buffalo Bill, The Steam Man, Frank Merriwell, and Horatio Alger — 1877 to 1905. Important, entertaining popular literature in facsimile reprint, with original covers. 190pp. 9 x 12.   22975-0 Pa. $3.50

ALICE'S ADVENTURES UNDER GROUND, Lewis Carroll. Facsimile of ms. Carroll gave Alice Liddell in 1864. Different in many ways from final Alice. Handlettered, illustrated by Carroll. Introduction by Martin Gardner. 128pp. 21482-6 Pa. $1.50

ALICE IN WONDERLAND COLORING BOOK, Lewis Carroll. Pictures by John Tenniel. Large-size versions of the famous illustrations of Alice, Cheshire Cat, Mad Hatter and all the others, waiting for your crayons. Abridged text. 36 illustrations. 64pp. 8¼ x 11.   22853-3 Pa. $1.50

AVENTURES D'ALICE AU PAYS DES MERVEILLES, Lewis Carroll. Buć's translation of "Alice" into French, supervised by Carroll himself. Novel way to learn language. (No English text.) 42 Tenniel illustrations. 196pp.   22836-3 Pa. $2.00

MYTHS AND FOLK TALES OF IRELAND, Jeremiah Curtin. 11 stories that are Irish versions of European fairy tales and 9 stories from the Fenian cycle — 20 tales of legend and magic that comprise an essential work in the history of folklore. 256pp.   22430-9 Pa. $3.00

EAST O' THE SUN AND WEST O' THE MOON, George W. Dasent. Only full edition of favorite, wonderful Norwegian fairytales — Why the Sea is Salt, Boots and the Troll, etc. — with 77 illustrations by Kittelsen & Werenskiöld. 418pp.
22521-6 Pa. $3.50

PERRAULT'S FAIRY TALES, Charles Perrault and Gustave Doré. Original versions of Cinderella, Sleeping Beauty, Little Red Riding Hood, etc. in best translation, with 34 wonderful illustrations by Gustave Doré. 117pp. 8⅛ x 11.   22311-6 Pa. $2.50

CONSTRUCTION OF AMERICAN FURNITURE TREASURES, Lester Margon. 344 detail drawings, complete text on constructing exact reproductions of 38 early American masterpieces: Hepplewhite sideboard, Duncan Phyfe drop-leaf table, mantel clock, gate-leg dining table, Pa. German cupboard, more. 38 plates. 54 photographs. 168pp. 8⅜ x 11¼. 23056-2 Pa. $4.00

JEWELRY MAKING AND DESIGN, Augustus F. Rose, Antonio Cirino. Professional secrets revealed in thorough, practical guide: tools, materials, processes; rings, brooches, chains, cast pieces, enamelling, setting stones, etc. Do not confuse with skimpy introductions: beginner can use, professional can learn from it. Over 200 illustrations. 306pp. 21750-7 Pa. $3.00

METALWORK AND ENAMELLING, Herbert Maryon. Generally conceded best all-around book. Countless trade secrets: materials, tools, soldering, filigree, setting, inlay, niello, repoussé, casting, polishing, etc. For beginner or expert. Author was foremost British expert. 330 illustrations. 335pp. 22702-2 Pa. $3.50

WEAVING WITH FOOT-POWER LOOMS, Edward F. Worst. Setting up a loom, beginning to weave, constructing equipment, using dyes, more, plus over 285 drafts of traditional patterns including Colonial and Swedish weaves. More than 200 other figures. For beginning and advanced. 275pp. 8¾ x 6⅜. 23064-3 Pa. $4.00

WEAVING A NAVAJO BLANKET, Gladys A. Reichard. Foremost anthropologist studied under Navajo women, reveals every step in process from wool, dyeing, spinning, setting up loom, designing, weaving. Much history, symbolism. With this book you could make one yourself. 97 illustrations. 222pp. 22992-0 Pa. $3.00

NATURAL DYES AND HOME DYEING, Rita J. Adrosko. Use natural ingredients: bark, flowers, leaves, lichens, insects etc. Over 135 specific recipes from historical sources for cotton, wool, other fabrics. Genuine premodern handicrafts. 12 illustrations. 160pp. 22688-3 Pa. $2.00

THE HAND DECORATION OF FABRICS, Francis J. Kafka. Outstanding, profusely illustrated guide to stenciling, batik, block printing, tie dyeing, freehand painting, silk screen printing, and novelty decoration. 356 illustrations. 198pp. 6 x 9. 21401-X Pa. $3.00

THOMAS NAST: CARTOONS AND ILLUSTRATIONS, with text by Thomas Nast St. Hill. Father of American political cartooning. Cartoons that destroyed Tweed Ring; inflation, free love, church and state; original Republican elephant and Democratic donkey; Santa Claus; more. 117 illustrations. 146pp. 9 x 12. 22983-1 Pa. $4.00
23067-8 Clothbd. $8.50

FREDERIC REMINGTON: 173 DRAWINGS AND ILLUSTRATIONS. Most famous of the Western artists, most responsible for our myths about the American West in its untamed days. Complete reprinting of Drawings of Frederic Remington (1897), plus other selections. 4 additional drawings in color on covers. 140pp. 9 x 12. 20714-5 Pa. $3.95

EARLY NEW ENGLAND GRAVESTONE RUBBINGS, Edmund V. Gillon, Jr. 43 photographs, 226 rubbings show heavily symbolic, macabre, sometimes humorous primitive American art. Up to early 19th century. 207pp. 8⅜ x 11¼.
21380-3 Pa. $4.00

L.J.M. DAGUERRE: THE HISTORY OF THE DIORAMA AND THE DAGUERREOTYPE, Helmut and Alison Gernsheim. Definitive account. Early history, life and work of Daguerre; discovery of daguerreotype process; diffusion abroad; other early photography. 124 illustrations. 226pp. 6⅙ x 9¼.
22290-X Pa. $4.00

PHOTOGRAPHY AND THE AMERICAN SCENE, Robert Taft. The basic book on American photography as art, recording form, 1839-1889. Development, influence on society, great photographers, types (portraits, war, frontier, etc.), whatever else needed. Inexhaustible. Illustrated with 322 early photos, daguerreotypes, tintypes, stereo slides, etc. 546pp. 6⅛ x 9¼.
21201-7 Pa. $5.00

PHOTOGRAPHIC SKETCHBOOK OF THE CIVIL WAR, Alexander Gardner. Reproduction of 1866 volume with 100 on-the-field photographs: Manassas, Lincoln on battlefield, slave pens, etc. Introduction by E.F. Bleiler. 224pp. 10¾ x 9.
22731-6 Pa. $4.50

THE MOVIES: A PICTURE QUIZ BOOK, Stanley Appelbaum & Hayward Cirker. Match stars with their movies, name actors and actresses, test your movie skill with 241 stills from 236 great movies, 1902-1959. Indexes of performers and films. 128pp. 8⅜ x 9¼.
20222-4 Pa. $2.50

THE TALKIES, Richard Griffith. Anthology of features, articles from Photoplay, 1928-1940, reproduced complete. Stars, famous movies, technical features, fabulous ads, etc.; Garbo, Chaplin, King Kong, Lubitsch, etc. 4 color plates, scores of illustrations. 327pp. 8⅜ x 11¼.
22762-6 Pa. $5.95

THE MOVIE MUSICAL FROM VITAPHONE TO "42ND STREET," edited by Miles Kreuger. Relive the rise of the movie musical as reported in the pages of Photoplay magazine (1926-1933): every movie review, cast list, ad, and record review; every significant feature article, production still, biography, forecast, and gossip story. Profusely illustrated. 367pp. 8⅜ x 11¼.
23154-2 Pa. $6.95

JOHANN SEBASTIAN BACH, Philipp Spitta. Great classic of biography, musical commentary, with hundreds of pieces analyzed. Also good for Bach's contemporaries. 450 musical examples. Total of 1799pp.
EUK 22278-0, 22279-9 Clothbd., Two vol. set $25.00

BEETHOVEN AND HIS NINE SYMPHONIES, Sir George Grove. Thorough history, analysis, commentary on symphonies and some related pieces. For either beginner or advanced student. 436 musical passages. 407pp.
20334-4 Pa. $4.00

MOZART AND HIS PIANO CONCERTOS, Cuthbert Girdlestone. The only full-length study. Detailed analyses of all 21 concertos, sources; 417 musical examples. 509pp.
21271-8 Pa. $4.50

HOUDINI ON MAGIC, Harold Houdini. Edited by Walter Gibson, Morris N. Young. How he escaped; exposés of fake spiritualists; instructions for eye-catching tricks; other fascinating material by and about greatest magician. 155 illustrations. 280pp. 20384-0 Pa. $2.50

HANDBOOK OF THE NUTRITIONAL CONTENTS OF FOOD, U.S. Dept. of Agriculture. Largest, most detailed source of food nutrition information ever prepared. Two mammoth tables: one measuring nutrients in 100 grams of edible portion; the other, in edible portion of 1 pound as purchased. Originally titled Composition of Foods. 190pp. 9 x 12. 21342-0 Pa. $4.00

COMPLETE GUIDE TO HOME CANNING, PRESERVING AND FREEZING, U.S. Dept. of Agriculture. Seven basic manuals with full instructions for jams and jellies; pickles and relishes; canning fruits, vegetables, meat; freezing anything. Really good recipes, exact instructions for optimal results. Save a fortune in food. 156 illustrations. 214pp. 6⅛ x 9¼. 22911-4 Pa. $2.50

THE BREAD TRAY, Louis P. De Gouy. Nearly every bread the cook could buy or make: bread sticks of Italy, fruit breads of Greece, glazed rolls of Vienna, everything from corn pone to croissants. Over 500 recipes altogether. including buns, rolls, muffins, scones, and more. 463pp. 23000-7 Pa. $3.50

CREATIVE HAMBURGER COOKERY, Louis P. De Gouy. 182 unusual recipes for casseroles, meat loaves and hamburgers that turn inexpensive ground meat into memorable main dishes: Arizona chili burgers, burger tamale pie, burger stew, burger corn loaf, burger wine loaf, and more. 120pp. 23001-5 Pa. $1.75

LONG ISLAND SEAFOOD COOKBOOK, J. George Frederick and Jean Joyce. Probably the best American seafood cookbook. Hundreds of recipes. 40 gourmet sauces, 123 recipes using oysters alone! All varieties of fish and seafood amply represented. 324pp. 22677-8 Pa. $3.00

THE EPICUREAN: A COMPLETE TREATISE OF ANALYTICAL AND PRACTICAL STUDIES IN THE CULINARY ART, Charles Ranhofer. Great modern classic. 3,500 recipes from master chef of Delmonico's, turn-of-the-century America's best restaurant. Also explained, many techniques known only to professional chefs. 775 illustrations. 1183pp. 6⅝ x 10. 22680-8 Clothbd. $17.50

THE AMERICAN WINE COOK BOOK, Ted Hatch. Over 700 recipes: old favorites livened up with wine plus many more: Czech fish soup, quince soup, sauce Perigueux, shrimp shortcake, filets Stroganoff, cordon bleu goulash, jambonneau, wine fruit cake, more. 314pp. 22796-0 Pa. $2.50

DELICIOUS VEGETARIAN COOKING, Ivan Baker. Close to 500 delicious and varied recipes: soups, main course dishes (pea, bean, lentil, cheese, vegetable, pasta, and egg dishes), savories, stews, whole-wheat breads and cakes, more. 168pp.
USO 22834-7 Pa. $1.75

THE MAGIC MOVING PICTURE BOOK, Bliss, Sands & Co. The pictures in this book move! Volcanoes erupt, a house burns, a serpentine dancer wiggles her way through a number. By using a specially ruled acetate screen provided, you can obtain these and 15 other startling effects. Originally "The Motograph Moving Picture Book." 32pp. 8¼ x 11. 23224-7 Pa. $1.75

STRING FIGURES AND HOW TO MAKE THEM, Caroline F. Jayne. Fullest, clearest instructions on string figures from around world: Eskimo, Navajo, Lapp, Europe, more. Cats cradle, moving spear, lightning, stars. Introduction by A.C. Haddon. 950 illustrations. 407pp. 20152-X Pa. $3.00

PAPER FOLDING FOR BEGINNERS, William D. Murray and Francis J. Rigney. Clearest book on market for making origami sail boats, roosters, frogs that move legs, cups, bonbon boxes. 40 projects. More than 275 illustrations. Photographs. 94pp. 20713-7 Pa. $1.25

INDIAN SIGN LANGUAGE, William Tomkins. Over 525 signs developed by Sioux, Blackfoot, Cheyenne, Arapahoe and other tribes. Written instructions and diagrams: how to make words, construct sentences. Also 290 pictographs of Sioux and Ojibway tribes. 111pp. 6⅛ x 9¼. 22029-X Pa. $1.50

BOOMERANGS: HOW TO MAKE AND THROW THEM, Bernard S. Mason. Easy to make and throw, dozens of designs: cross-stick, pinwheel, boomabird, tumblestick, Australian curved stick boomerang. Complete throwing instructions. All safe. 99pp. 23028-7 Pa. $1.50

25 KITES THAT FLY, Leslie Hunt. Full, easy to follow instructions for kites made from inexpensive materials. Many novelties. Reeling, raising, designing your own. 70 illustrations. 110pp. 22550-X Pa. $1.25

TRICKS AND GAMES ON THE POOL TABLE, Fred Herrmann. 79 tricks and games, some solitaires, some for 2 or more players, some competitive; mystifying shots and throws, unusual carom, tricks involving cork, coins, a hat, more. 77 figures. 95pp. 21814-7 Pa. $1.25

WOODCRAFT AND CAMPING, Bernard S. Mason. How to make a quick emergency shelter, select woods that will burn immediately, make do with limited supplies, etc. Also making many things out of wood, rawhide, bark, at camp. Formerly titled Woodcraft. 295 illustrations. 580pp. 21951-8 Pa. $4.00

AN INTRODUCTION TO CHESS MOVES AND TACTICS SIMPLY EXPLAINED, Leonard Barden. Informal intermediate introduction: reasons for moves, tactics, openings, traps, positional play, endgame. Isolates patterns. 102pp. USO 21210-6 Pa. $1.35

LASKER'S MANUAL OF CHESS, Dr. Emanuel Lasker. Great world champion offers very thorough coverage of all aspects of chess. Combinations, position play, openings, endgame, aesthetics of chess, philosophy of struggle, much more. Filled with analyzed games. 390pp. 20640-8 Pa. $3.50

DRIED FLOWERS, Sarah Whitlock and Martha Rankin. Concise, clear, practical guide to dehydration, glycerinizing, pressing plant material, and more. Covers use of silica gel. 12 drawings. Originally titled "New Techniques with Dried Flowers." 32pp. 21802-3 Pa. $1.00

ABC OF POULTRY RAISING, J.H. Florea. Poultry expert, editor tells how to raise chickens on home or small business basis. Breeds, feeding, housing, laying, etc. Very concrete, practical. 50 illustrations. 256pp. 23201-8 Pa. $3.00

HOW INDIANS USE WILD PLANTS FOR FOOD, MEDICINE & CRAFTS, Frances Densmore. Smithsonian, Bureau of American Ethnology report presents wealth of material on nearly 200 plants used by Chippewas of Minnesota and Wisconsin. 33 plates plus 122pp. of text. 6⅛ x 9¼. 23019-8 Pa. $2.50

THE HERBAL OR GENERAL HISTORY OF PLANTS, John Gerard. The 1633 edition revised and enlarged by Thomas Johnson. Containing almost 2850 plant descriptions and 2705 superb illustrations, Gerard's Herbal is a monumental work, the book all modern English herbals are derived from, and the one herbal every serious enthusiast should have in its entirety. Original editions are worth perhaps $750. 1678pp. 8½ x 12¼. 23147-X Clothbd. $50.00

A MODERN HERBAL, Margaret Grieve. Much the fullest, most exact, most useful compilation of herbal material. Gigantic alphabetical encyclopedia, from aconite to zedoary, gives botanical information, medical properties, folklore, economic uses, and much else. Indispensable to serious reader. 161 illustrations. 888pp. 6½ x 9¼. USO 22798-7, 22799-5 Pa., Two vol. set $10.00

HOW TO KNOW THE FERNS, Frances T. Parsons. Delightful classic. Identification, fern lore, for Eastern and Central U.S.A. Has introduced thousands to interesting life form. 99 illustrations. 215pp. 20740-4 Pa. $2.50

THE MUSHROOM HANDBOOK, Louis C.C. Krieger. Still the best popular handbook. Full descriptions of 259 species, extremely thorough text, habitats, luminescence, poisons, folklore, etc. 32 color plates; 126 other illustrations. 560pp. 21861-9 Pa. $4.50

HOW TO KNOW THE WILD FRUITS, Maude G. Peterson. Classic guide covers nearly 200 trees, shrubs, smaller plants of the U.S. arranged by color of fruit and then by family. Full text provides names, descriptions, edibility, uses. 80 illustrations. 400pp. 22943-2 Pa. $3.00

COMMON WEEDS OF THE UNITED STATES, U.S. Department of Agriculture. Covers 220 important weeds with illustration, maps, botanical information, plant lore for each. Over 225 illustrations. 463pp. 6⅛ x 9¼. 20504-5 Pa. $4.50

HOW TO KNOW THE WILD FLOWERS, Mrs. William S. Dana. Still best popular book for East and Central USA. Over 500 plants easily identified, with plant lore; arranged according to color and flowering time. 174 plates. 459pp. 20332-8 Pa. $3.50

INCIDENTS OF TRAVEL IN YUCATAN, John L. Stephens. Classic (1843) exploration of jungles of Yucatan, looking for evidences of Maya civilization. Travel adventures, Mexican and Indian culture, etc. Total of 669pp.
20926-1, 20927-X Pa., Two vol. set $5.50

LIVING MY LIFE, Emma Goldman. Candid, no holds barred account by foremost American anarchist: her own life, anarchist movement, famous contemporaries, ideas and their impact. Struggles and confrontations in America, plus deportation to U.S.S.R. Shocking inside account of persecution of anarchists under Lenin. 13 plates. Total of 944pp. 22543-7, 22544-5 Pa., Two vol. set $9.00

AMERICAN INDIANS, George Catlin. Classic account of life among Plains Indians: ceremonies, hunt, warfare, etc. Dover edition reproduces for first time all original paintings. 312 plates. 572pp. of text. 6$\frac{1}{8}$ x 9$\frac{1}{4}$.
22118-0, 22119-9 Pa., Two vol. set $8.00
22140-7, 22144-X Clothbd., Two vol. set $16.00

THE INDIANS' BOOK, Natalie Curtis. Lore, music, narratives, drawings by Indians, collected from cultures of U.S.A. 149 songs in full notation. 45 illustrations. 583pp. 6$\frac{5}{8}$ x 9$\frac{3}{8}$. 21939-9 Pa. $5.00

INDIAN BLANKETS AND THEIR MAKERS, George Wharton James. History, old style wool blankets, changes brought about by traders, symbolism of design and color, a Navajo weaver at work, outline blanket, Kachina blankets, more. Emphasis on Navajo. 130 illustrations, 32 in color. 230pp. 6$\frac{1}{8}$ x 9$\frac{1}{4}$. 22996-3 Pa. $5.00
23068-6 Clothbd. $10.00

AN INTRODUCTION TO THE STUDY OF THE MAYA HIEROGLYPHS, Sylvanus Griswold Morley. Classic study by one of the truly great figures in hieroglyph research. Still the best introduction for the student for reading Maya hieroglyphs. New introduction by J. Eric S. Thompson. 117 illustrations. 284pp. 23108-9 Pa. $4.00

THE ANALECTS OF CONFUCIUS, THE GREAT LEARNING, DOCTRINE OF THE MEAN, Confucius. Edited by James Legge. Full Chinese text, standard English translation on same page, Chinese commentators, editor's annotations; dictionary of characters at rear, plus grammatical comment. Finest edition anywhere of one of world's greatest thinkers. 503pp. 22746-4 Pa. $4.50

THE I CHING (THE BOOK OF CHANGES), translated by James Legge. Complete translation of basic text plus appendices by Confucius, and Chinese commentary of most penetrating divination manual ever prepared. Indispensable to study of early Oriental civilizations, to modern inquiring reader. 448pp.
21062-6 Pa. $3.50

THE EGYPTIAN BOOK OF THE DEAD, E.A. Wallis Budge. Complete reproduction of Ani's papyrus, finest ever found. Full hieroglyphic text, interlinear transliteration, word for word translation, smooth translation. Basic work, for Egyptology, for modern study of psychic matters. Total of 533pp. 6$\frac{1}{2}$ x 9$\frac{1}{4}$.
EBE 21866-X Pa. $4.95

VICTORIAN HOUSES: A TREASURY OF LESSER-KNOWN EXAMPLES, Edmund Gillon and Clay Lancaster. 116 photographs, excellent commentary illustrate distinct characteristics, many borrowings of local Victorian architecture. Octagonal houses, Americanized chalets, grand country estates, small cottages, etc. Rich heritage often overlooked. 116 plates. 11³/₈ x 10. 22966-1 Pa. $4.00

STICKS AND STONES, Lewis Mumford. Great classic of American cultural history; architecture from medieval-inspired earliest forms to 20th century; evolution of structure and style, influence of environment. 21 illustrations. 113pp.
20202-X Pa. $2.00

ON THE LAWS OF JAPANESE PAINTING, Henry P. Bowie. Best substitute for training with genius Oriental master, based on years of study in Kano school. Philosophy, brushes, inks, style, etc. 66 illustrations. 117pp. 6¹/₈ x 9¼. 20030-2 Pa. $4.00

A HANDBOOK OF ANATOMY FOR ART STUDENTS, Arthur Thomson. Virtually exhaustive. Skeletal structure, muscles, heads, special features. Full text, anatomical figures, undraped photos. Male and female. 337 illustrations. 459pp.
21163-0 Pa. $5.00

AN ATLAS OF ANATOMY FOR ARTISTS, Fritz Schider. Finest text, working book. Full text, plus anatomical illustrations; plates by great artists showing anatomy. 593 illustrations. 192pp. 7⁷/₈ x 10¾. 20241-0 Clothbd. $6.95

THE HUMAN FIGURE IN MOTION, Eadweard Muybridge. More than 4500 stopped-action photos, in action series, showing undraped men, women, children jumping, lying down, throwing, sitting, wrestling, carrying, etc. "Unparalleled dictionary for artists," American Artist. Taken by great 19th century photographer. 390pp.
7⁷/₈ x 10⁵/₈. 20204-6 Clothbd. $12.50

AN ATLAS OF ANIMAL ANATOMY FOR ARTISTS, W. Ellenberger et al. Horses, dogs, cats, lions, cattle, deer, etc. Muscles, skeleton, surface features. The basic work. Enlarged edition. 288 illustrations. 151pp. 9³/₈ x 12¼. 20082-5 Pa. $4.00

LETTER FORMS: 110 COMPLETE ALPHABETS, Frederick Lambert. 110 sets of capital letters; 16 lower case alphabets; 70 sets of numbers and other symbols. Edited and expanded by Theodore Menten. 110pp. 8¹/₈ x 11. 22872-X Pa. $2.50

THE METHODS OF CONSTRUCTION OF CELTIC ART, George Bain. Simple geometric techniques for making wonderful Celtic interlacements, spirals, Kells-type initials, animals, humans, etc. Unique for artists, craftsmen. Over 500 illustrations. 160pp. 9 x 12. USO 22923-8 Pa. $4.00

SCULPTURE, PRINCIPLES AND PRACTICE, Louis Slobodkin. Step by step approach to clay, plaster, metals, stone; classical and modern. 253 drawings, photos. 255pp. 8¹/₈ x 11. 22960-2 Pa. $4.50

THE ART OF ETCHING, E.S. Lumsden. Clear, detailed instructions for etching, drypoint, softground, aquatint; from 1st sketch to print. Very detailed, thorough. 200 illustrations. 376pp. 20049-3 Pa. $3.50

CREATIVE LITHOGRAPHY AND HOW TO DO IT, Grant Arnold. Lithography as art form: working directly on stone, transfer of drawings, lithotint, mezzotint, color printing; also metal plates. Detailed, thorough. 27 illustrations. 214pp.
21208-4 Pa. $3.00

DESIGN MOTIFS OF ANCIENT MEXICO, Jorge Enciso. Vigorous, powerful ceramic stamp impressions — Maya, Aztec, Toltec, Olmec. Serpents, gods, priests, dancers, etc. 153pp. 6⅛ x 9¼.
20084-1 Pa. $2.50

AMERICAN INDIAN DESIGN AND DECORATION, Leroy Appleton. Full text, plus more than 700 precise drawings of Inca, Maya, Aztec, Pueblo, Plains, NW Coast basketry, sculpture, painting, pottery, sand paintings, metal, etc. 4 plates in color. 279pp. 8⅜ x 11¼.
22704-9 Pa. $4.50

CHINESE LATTICE DESIGNS, Daniel S. Dye. Incredibly beautiful geometric designs: circles, voluted, simple dissections, etc. Inexhaustible source of ideas, motifs. 1239 illustrations. 469pp. 6⅛ x 9¼.
23096-1 Pa. $5.00

JAPANESE DESIGN MOTIFS, Matsuya Co. Mon, or heraldic designs. Over 4000 typical, beautiful designs: birds, animals, flowers, swords, fans, geometric; all beautifully stylized. 213pp. 11⅜ x 8¼.
22874-6 Pa. $4.95

PERSPECTIVE, Jan Vredeman de Vries. 73 perspective plates from 1604 edition; buildings, townscapes, stairways, fantastic scenes. Remarkable for beauty, surrealistic atmosphere; real eye-catchers. Introduction by Adolf Placzek. 74pp. 11⅜ x 8¼.
20186-4 Pa. $2.75

EARLY AMERICAN DESIGN MOTIFS, Suzanne E. Chapman. 497 motifs, designs, from painting on wood, ceramics, appliqué, glassware, samplers, metal work, etc. Florals, landscapes, birds and animals, geometrics, letters, etc. Inexhaustible. Enlarged edition. 138pp. 8⅜ x 11¼.
22985-8 Pa. $3.50
23084-8 Clothbd. $7.95

VICTORIAN STENCILS FOR DESIGN AND DECORATION, edited by E.V. Gillon, Jr. 113 wonderful ornate Victorian pieces from German sources; florals, geometrics; borders, corner pieces; bird motifs, etc. 64pp. 9⅜ x 12¼.
21995-X Pa. $2.50

ART NOUVEAU: AN ANTHOLOGY OF DESIGN AND ILLUSTRATION FROM THE STUDIO, edited by E.V. Gillon, Jr. Graphic arts: book jackets, posters, engravings, illustrations, decorations; Crane, Beardsley, Bradley and many others. Inexhaustible. 92pp. 8⅛ x 11.
22388-4 Pa. $2.50

ORIGINAL ART DECO DESIGNS, William Rowe. First-rate, highly imaginative modern Art Deco frames, borders, compositions, alphabets, florals, insectals, Wurlitzer-types, etc. Much finest modern Art Deco. 80 plates, 8 in color. 8⅜ x 11¼.
22567-4 Pa. $3.00

HANDBOOK OF DESIGNS AND DEVICES, Clarence P. Hornung. Over 1800 basic geometric designs based on circle, triangle, square, scroll, cross, etc. Largest such collection in existence. 261pp.
20125-2 Pa. $2.50

BUILD YOUR OWN LOW-COST HOME, L.O. Anderson, H.F. Zornig. U.S. Dept. of Agriculture sets of plans, full, detailed, for 11 houses: A-Frame, circular, conventional. Also construction manual. Save hundreds of dollars. 204pp. 11 x 16.
21525-3 Pa. $5.95

HOW TO BUILD A WOOD-FRAME HOUSE, L.O. Anderson. Comprehensive, easy to follow U.S. Government manual: placement, foundations, framing, sheathing, roof, insulation, plaster, finishing — almost everything else. 179 illustrations. 223pp. $7\frac{7}{8}$ x $10\frac{3}{4}$.
22954-8 Pa. $3.50

CONCRETE, MASONRY AND BRICKWORK, U.S. Department of the Army. Practical handbook for the home owner and small builder, manual contains basic principles, techniques, and important background information on construction with concrete, concrete blocks, and brick. 177 figures, 37 tables. 200pp. $6\frac{1}{2}$ x $9\frac{1}{4}$.
23203-4 Pa. $4.00

THE STANDARD BOOK OF QUILT MAKING AND COLLECTING, Marguerite Ickis. Full information, full-sized patterns for making 46 traditional quilts, also 150 other patterns. Quilted cloths, lamé, satin quilts, etc. 483 illustrations. 273pp. $6\frac{7}{8}$ x $9\frac{5}{8}$.
20582-7 Pa. $3.50

101 PATCHWORK PATTERNS, Ruby S. McKim. 101 beautiful, immediately useable patterns, full-size, modern and traditional. Also general information, estimating, quilt lore. 124pp. $7\frac{7}{8}$ x $10\frac{3}{4}$.
20773-0 Pa. $2.50

KNIT YOUR OWN NORWEGIAN SWEATERS, Dale Yarn Company. Complete instructions for 50 authentic sweaters, hats, mittens, gloves, caps, etc. Thoroughly modern designs that command high prices in stores. 24 patterns, 24 color photographs. Nearly 100 charts and other illustrations. 58pp. $8\frac{3}{8}$ x $11\frac{1}{4}$.
23031-7 Pa. $2.50

IRON-ON TRANSFER PATTERNS FOR CREWEL AND EMBROIDERY FROM EARLY AMERICAN SOURCES, edited by Rita Weiss. 75 designs, borders, alphabets, from traditional American sources printed on translucent paper in transfer ink. Reuseable. Instructions. Test patterns. 24pp. $8\frac{1}{4}$ x 11.
23162-3 Pa. $1.50

AMERICAN INDIAN NEEDLEPOINT DESIGNS FOR PILLOWS, BELTS, HANDBAGS AND OTHER PROJECTS, Roslyn Epstein. 37 authentic American Indian designs adapted for modern needlepoint projects. Grid backing makes designs easily transferable to canvas. 48pp. $8\frac{1}{4}$ x 11.
22973-4 Pa. $1.50

CHARTED FOLK DESIGNS FOR CROSS-STITCH EMBROIDERY, Maria Foris & Andreas Foris. 278 charted folk designs, most in 2 colors, from Danube region: florals, fantastic beasts, geometrics, traditional symbols, more. Border and central patterns. 77pp. $8\frac{1}{4}$ x 11.
USO 23191-7 Pa. $2.00

Prices subject to change without notice.
Available at your book dealer or write for free catalogue to Dept. GI, Dover Publications, Inc., 180 Varick St., N.Y., N.Y. 10014. Dover publishes more than 150 books each year on science, elementary and advanced mathematics, biology, music, art, literary history, social sciences and other areas.